POLITICS
ECONOMICS
AND
WELFARE

GIFT

2 4 JAN 2014

POLITICS
ECONOMICS
AND
WELFARE

Planning and Politico-Economic Systems
Resolved into Basic Social Processes

ROBERT A. DAHL
CHARLES E. LINDBLOM

With a new Preface by the authors

The University of Chicago Press
Chicago and London

Robert A. Dahl is Sterling Professor of Political Science at Yale University. Among his many books are *A Preface to Democratic Theory, Who Governs,* and *Polyarchy: Participation and Opposition.*

Charles E. Lindblom is Peletiah Perit Professor of Economics and Political Science at Yale University. Among his books are *The Intelligence of Democracy* and *The Policy-Making Process.*

The University of Chicago Press, Chicago 60637
The University of Chicago Press, Ltd., London

© 1953, 1976 by Robert A. Dahl and Charles E. Lindblom
All rights reserved. Published 1976
Printed in the United States of America

ISBN: 0–226–13428–8 (clothbound); 0–226–13429–6 (paperbound)
Library of Congress Catalog Card Number: 76–8807

CONTENTS

ANALYTICAL TABLE OF CONTENTS

PREFACE 1976

Problems and Incapacities

In the quarter century since *Politics, Economics, and Welfare* was written, the American politico-economic order has displayed its incapacities, even its perversities, more than its merits. It remains both sluggish and feckless in advancing on problems on which it has the advantage of decades of experience in policy making: poverty and maldistribution of income and wealth, racial inequality, health care, public education, inflation and unemployment, and industrial relations, for example. Some observers also claim to see strains of malevolence in it. It is more accurate to say that, more than we used to believe, it too often facilitates rather than constrains the indulgence of man's least worthy motives—in Vietnam, in Watergate, and in corruption in business and government, which the overwhelming evidence suggests is more central than peripheral to the system.

Some of the incapacities and perversities are new: for example, the consequences of new authority that evolving constitutional change has devolved on the presidency. Most, however, are old; they have only been freshly revealed as a consequence of new strains on the system like domestic espionage attendant on the nation's self-chosen role after World War II as an international monitor of communist expansion. Or they are complex combinations of new and old, as in problems posed by large corporations. The specific influences of large private enterprise on government are an old story, but new chapters are written in each decade as the size, functions, and powers of the corporation grow.

Many but not all of this nation's incapacities and perver-

Our thanks to Edward J. Woodhouse for helpful comments on an earlier draft of this Preface.

sities are shared with other nations of the world. The constant reaffirmation of democratic egalitarianism does not, for example, much move the world's polyarchies toward either political or economic or social equality, although Scandinavian experience suggests that under some circumstances the move can be made. In the very home of political democracy, the United Kingdom, so fundamental a resource as public education remains more conspicuously anti-egalitarian than in the United States. And all the polyarchies fumble with inflation and unemployment. The record of polyarchy here and abroad is disturbing.

More ominous than grievous is the possibility that the American system is structurally incapable of coping with a new category of problems, collective rather than distributional. More than some European systems, the American system seems less well adapted to the mobilization of a positive energetic will of the majority—or, for that matter, of any forward moving collectivity—than to what is at best an adjudication of segmental interests and at worst a deference to minority vetoes. The older problems such as industrial relations, income security, or public education were seen as calling for an accomodation of interests, a fairer sharing, an improvement in the position of one group through a negotiated yielding of another. Hence the emphasis on pluralism in American democracy and on bargaining as an instrument for mutual adjustment among them. The new problems, it may turn out, are problems for all of us: their prototypes are energy depletion, environmental degradation, and the gap between the advanced and developing nations.

For these problems something more seems required than a reconciliation of a plurality of interests. A society as a whole, reflecting in its public policies some interests or values shared by a great majority of its citizens, must mobilize intelligence and energy for those common goods whose existence becomes increasingly difficult to deny. But a constitutional structure adapted to a reconciliation of diverse interests may lack mechanisms for articulating common purposes, for mobilizing overwhelming majorities, and for asserting the collectivity's right to act no less than the subcollectivity's right to veto.

These are admittedly evaluative, not scientifically neutral, comments on the American system and its cousins. They speak,

however, for the same egalitarian and liberal aspirations that
were voiced in *Politics, Economics, and Welfare.* We set out
as relevant criteria for appraising the politico-economic techniques analyzed elsewhere in the book the goals of freedom,
rationality, democracy (in the sense of political equality and
the principle of majority rule), "subjective equality," security,
and progress. Writing today we would probably formulate
our criteria somewhat differently, as well as further specify
the more proximate goals to which they point. Yet these goals
still locate valid criteria for judging the performance of American society in the interval since we wrote.

In this introduction we want to mention briefly some of the
shortcomings of American society that bear on the analysis set
out in the book. Our discussion will serve to clarify and also
to qualify what we wrote twenty-five years ago.

The American Polyarchy

Our description of polyarchy as an "untidy and highly
imperfect" approximation to democracy is not, certainly, in the
tradition of yeasty optimism that characterizes so much writing
on that ambiguous subject. Yet some of the conditions and preconditions of polyarchy (described in chapters 10 and 11)
now seem weaker than we believed them to be at the time we
wrote. Developments during the intervening years have also revealed inadequacies attributable not so much to polyarchy generally as to American political institutions.

In chapter 11 we discuss "the breakdown of legislatures"
and remark that "Congressional politicians have not been able
to prevent the creation of enormous domains of control led by
Presidential politicians." What we did not by any means fully
foresee, however, was the development (then in its earlier stages)
of what George Reedy has called the American monarchy and
Arthur Schlesinger, Jr., the imperial presidency. The growth
of the imperial presidency was a steady development, one
cheered on by many people who shared the "ends for social
action," the seven basic values, that we set out in chapter 2.
Often the presidency was seen as the main "democratic" instrument for helping to bring about government policies leading to

greater freedom, democracy, equality, security, and progress. Yet the accumulation of vast political resources in the White House and their manipulation by the president endangered the imperfect solution that polyarchy provides to what in chapter 10 is called the First Problem of Politics—how citizens can keep their rulers from becoming tyrants.

To be sure, some of the factors that helped to make the imperial presidency and Watergate possible were transitory. These include the Vietnam war and the idiosyncratic moral and psychological qualities of Lyndon Johnson and Richard Nixon. But there were also more persistent causes such as the role of the United States as a superpower. These endure even after the weakening of the imperial presidency and the partial re-assertion of Congressional authority that followed Nixon's fall. Although the topic calls for an analysis too extensive for us to make here, we mention two matters of particular concern.

First, the experience of the imperial presidency and Water-gate in its broader meaning argue that one of the preconditions of polyarchy specified in chapter 11 is weaker in the United States than we had supposed. There we emphasize the impor-tance of "social indoctrination and habituation" (today we would probably use the expression "political socialization") in the processes of polyarchy and on the desirability of democracy. Political socialization in democratic and constitutional norms is, as we point out, particularly important for political leaders. Successful political socialization, we suggest, will inhibit cer-tain types of behavior "and even certain 'evil thoughts' " among leaders, such as seriously entertaining the idea of a military sup-pression of Congress. Successful socialization, we note, will also "teach leaders to *expect punishment* if they seriously violate the norms of polyarchy."

Nevertheless recent American presidents (and not only Johnson and Nixon) have seriously violated the norms of poly-archy and democracy, particularly in their free-handed con-duct of foreign and military affairs, and most egregiously during the Vietnam War. And they were not punished for their actions; nor, it seems, did they ever expect to be. President Nixon, it appears, even hoped to avoid punishment for his participation in an ever expanding illegal conspiracy to cover-up violations of laws and the Constitution by his subordinates and close associates.

One can draw only a little solace from the way the norms operated in the Congressional activities that ultimately brought to a near certainty the prospect of Nixon's impeachment, conviction, and removal from office. Along with a large part of the political leadership of the country, Congress had itself been deeply implicated in the expansion of presidential powers and the growth of the imperial presidency. As the events of Watergate unfolded, it was often weak in its responses, reluctant to acknowledge the existence of a crisis, and laggard in imposing legal constraints on the president. Nor did the party system or the voice of opposition leaders offer an alternative to Nixon's leadership during two years of disturbance. If Nixon's bizarre excesses had themselves not finally undone him, his less conspicuous but no less subversive attacks on the constitutional order would apparently not have stirred political leadership to remove or curb him, so feeble appears to have been the institutional response to his transgressions.

The second problem revealed by the experiences of the intervening decades is the difficulty in the American system, crisis aside, of arriving at a relationship between the president and the other political institutions, mainly the Congress, that would satisfy two needs. On the one hand, the president needs to be made responsible and accountable to the public in a genuine and significant way. The chief means for such responsibility and accountability are elections and the Congress. Neither means has worked satisfactorily. At the same time, the political system needs leaders who will sponsor and help to bring about innovation and change in public policies. So far, the American political system has produced no alternative to the presidency as the main source of such leadership. Meeting this need through enlarging the power and influence of the president is, as we have said, one of the important causes of the imperial presidency.

That we have such great difficulty in reconciling these two objectives no doubt says something about inherent conflicts between them. Yet it also suggests to us that the American constitutional and political system is more seriously defective than we thought it was when we were writing.

Although we do not have solutions to propose, Americans are going to have to consider a variety of possibilities: a parliamentary system, including various approximations to it; changes in party organization; and new relations between the president and Congress, for example. We believe that a search for different political and constitutional arrangements ought to have higher priority than it has had on the agenda of academic and public discussion. In particular, political scientists and other analysts need to devote more attention to the major defects in the political system and a search for available solutions. Curiously, professional political scientists have not made that their business, nor did we. At present, our knowledge is so incomplete that even those who understand how poorly the political system functions nonetheless cautiously hold on to present arrangements because the consequences of changes, whether for good or evil, are simply not sufficiently known. We do not suggest scholarly research as a panacea, however. We need to draw on resources of information and intelligence that are widely dispersed to political leaders, journalists, public opinion leaders and many ordinary citizens, as well as to scholars.

The Private American Economy

The American economy has remained much more private and far less public than we earlier supposed that it might become. The excessively private character of the economy has two aspects, one in the realm of attitudes, ideas, and ideology, the other in the realm of practice.

In the realm of attitudes, ideas, and ideology, we Americans have an irrational commitment to private ownership and control of economic enterprises that prevents us from thinking clearly about economic arrangements. This irrational commitment to private ownership and control conflicts with the underlying assumption of this book that a modern economy ought to be thought of and treated as a *social* or *public* economy. We mean by this that the primary justification for the economic order is its achievement of the basic ends for social action described in the second chapter. The adequacy of its performance and alternatives for achieving better performance require social judgments and decisions. These social judgments need to be made effective—translated into public policies—primarily (though not necessarily exclusively) through the processes of polyarchy. Our notion of a good society is one in which the members seek the ends for social action by means of a public economy that is subject to the final say of a democratic government.

In this view, economizing is a set of *social* processes for rational calculation and control. Market mechanisms are, like polyarchy and administrative hierarchies, *sociopolitical processes.* A large economic enterprise, whether publicly or privately owned, is a *political* system. Enterprises and markets are not justified by overriding personal rights to private ownership and control. If they are justified at all, it is only by their performance in achieving social ends. A rational society, then, would choose among various forms of ownership and control of economic enterprises according to how one form or another satisfies the particular social purposes in view. Private ownership and control is but one form among a vast variety of alternatives. There is no reasonable presumption that it is either better or worse than any other form. As a solution, therefore, it should carry with it no special priority.

Government ownership also has no special presumption in its favor. It is here that the perspective of this book differs most from conventional socialist doctrine, which tended to assume that public control of economic enterprises both required and was insured by government ownership. A great deal of additional experience since we wrote confirms our view that ownership of an enterprise by the government, or more vaguely by "society," does not insure public control over the conduct of the enterprise.

In our final chapter, we nonetheless expressed the belief that this doctrinaire faith reflected in conventional socialist doctrine was rapidly declining. At the same time, valid elements in socialist thought were, we thought, becoming rather generally accepted. These valid elements include an understanding of circumstances in which the market system is an inappropriate and deleterious social mechanism, particularly for distributing incomes and handling many community needs; of the significance of control over economic enterprises as an important and proper political issue; and of the inadequacies of competition for insuring public control of economic activity. "Almost everyone has become a socialist," we concluded, "and major socialist criticisms of the economic order have been accepted and acted upon."

We thought therefore that our view of the economy as a social or public activity would gain increasing acceptance among Americans. The task of selecting among the variety of alternatives that we were certain was available and potentially useful would thus become a more rational, social process, less profoundly biased by doctrinaire adherence to one particular form of ownership, whether public or private.

We were wrong. In particular, Americans seem to suffer almost as much today from a doctrinaire bias in favor of private ownership and control of economic enterprises as they did when we wrote. The fact that the dominant form of business enterprise in the United States is the privately owned and controlled corporation is not a product of even a moderately rational public calculation of relative advantages. In fact, no such public inquiry has taken place in the United States.

The reasons why Americans are so addicted to private ownership and control are complex and beyond exploring here. Some of the explanation could probably be found in the ideological transfer that occurred as the country was gradually transformed from a nation of farmers, where private ownership and control of farm enterprises had both a rational social basis in efficiency and democracy and a powerful appeal to immediate interest, to a nation of commerce, banking, and industry. As the transfer progressed, the rational basis vanished while the appeal to immediate interest, though weakened, nonetheless remained. By now, the bias in favor of private ownership and control of economic enterprises is so deeply embedded in the American ideology that many people appear to believe that it is an inherent part of democracy.

This points to the second respect in which the economy is excessively private, that of actual practice. Our belief in the possibility of a non-doctrinaire, pragmatic approach to the question of choice between private and public ownership led us to assume that the comparative advantages of public ownership in many circumstances would lead to an increase in the public sector.[1] Again, we were wrong. This has not occurred. Moreover, the practice of private enterprise continues to give excessive weight to the particularistic interests of managers and investors in economic decisions of great consequence to many others. Consumers and employees, both blue collar and white collar, are only the most obvious of these.

For reasons we develop in the book, the problem of control must be considered as prior to the problem of ownership. As we have already said, government ownership is definitely not a sufficient means to public control. In many cases it is probably not even a necessary means. In some cases, it may be a hindrance. Nonetheless, we are now more inclined to believe that public control of the American economy cannot in fact be achieved without a substantial increase in government ownership. At the very least, there is a need to search for and to introduce new forms of economic enterprise that will contribute more than the existing privately owned and controlled giant corporation to achieving the ends of social action described in the second chapter.

Inequality

Among the ends of social action set out in chapter 2 we emphasize equality in two different but related senses. One is the goal of political equality in the "last say"—among citizens acting as a kind of ultimate court of appeal on the conduct of the government. The other goal, which we called "subjective equality," was our effort to specify a criterion that was less ambiguous than the old utilitarian principle of "the greatest good for the greatest number," and yet would insure consideration in all social decisions to the wants of the larger number as against the wants of a smaller number.[2]

[1] The question of public vs. private ownership is mainly discussed below on pp. 186–193 and 210–218.
[2] Our formulation of the criterion of subjective equality we now think to be unsatisfactory. Since we wrote, a number of analyses have alerted us to problems of fairness in distribution that our criterion would not solve

The inequalities that exist among Americans would look less unacceptable if there were signs of significant progress toward their reduction. What distinguishes a progressive society, after all, is not that it has solved its problems but that it is definitely on the way to solving them. When we wrote, we must surely have believed that the United States was a progressive society. That we believed so was probably not altogether clear even to us; we nowhere said so in the book. But at that time the New Deal was not a remote historical episode. It provided grounds for thinking that reform periods would occur again with some frequency—like Jefferson's revolutions, perhaps, once a generation. During these reform periods, the great structures of American society would be progressively changed to bring about greater equality among Americans. If we held some such assumptions, and we probably did, events have proved us wrong.

We have not had a series of New Deals. To be sure there has been some progress, important legislation has been passed, and many injustices have been reduced. We do not mean to underestimate the historic significance of the decline in racial discrimination that has occurred since we wrote. The changing attitudes and the public actions that have helped to bring this about do reveal a progressive aspect and potentiality to American public life. Though racial discrimination continues to be a massive source of injustice in this country, we expect it to decline steadily in the future. Discrimination against women is also likely to decline. Discrimination based on life-styles, sexual preferences, living arrangements and many other deviations from moral standards also appears to be lessening. There are signs that Americans may be acquiring greater tolerance for diversity.

Yet even if injustices stemming from discrimination were to disappear tomorrow, great inequalities would still exist in the distribution of wealth and income, and therefore in all the opportunities that tend to be affected by income and wealth. Even

---

satisfactorily. We dealt with many of these difficulties in an extended discussion of income (pp. 134ff). Were we writing the book today, however, we might try to link that discussion more closely with a better criterion of distributive justice than our notion of subjective equality provides.

if income, for example, were distributed with no discrimination whatsoever based on race, sex, or other demographic characteristics, enormous disparities would remain. Even more so with wealth. Inequalities in distribution are, of course, not inherently unjust. The differences may be in accordance with an acceptable principle of distributive justice. But in our view the existing distribution in the United States of wealth, income, and many other advantages fails to correspond even in an approximate way with any principle of distributive justice we find acceptable.

Where events have proved us wrong is in supposing, if we did suppose, that reforms would reduce these disparities. These reforms have not occurred. With respect to the distribution of income and wealth, the United States remains pretty much where it was at the time we wrote.

We would also emphasize more strongly today the consequences of maldistribution for political equality. In discussing polyarchy, we present some reasons why it seemed to us "terrifyingly clear that the drive away from equality of control in modern society is extraordinarily powerful" (p. 275). In discussing the distribution of money income, we noted the effects of income inequality on political power. "As everyone knows," we wrote, "money talks in politics; and genuine equality in political power is impossible where income differences create serious inequalities in the power to communicate with other citizens and with members of the control elites" (p. 139).

While our statement is true, it is too narrow. In a discussion on political activity and income equality later in the book, we come closer to the broader point we now want to make. There we wrote that income "heavily influences education and status (particularly in the United States), and through these and its own weight it influences control. . . . Thus a high degree of income equality is prerequisite for a high degree of social equality" (p. 315).

To make the point even more broadly, wealth and income, along with many values that tend to cluster with wealth and income, such as education, status, and access to organizations, all constitute resources that can be used in order to gain influence over other people. Inequalities with respect to these matters are therefore equivalent to inequalities in access to political resources. Inequalities in access to political resources in turn foster inequalities in influence, including influence over the government of the state. More concretely, the present distribution of resources in the United States presents a major obstacle to a satisfactory approximation of the goal of political equality. We cannot move a great deal closer to political equality without moving closer to equality in access to political resources. We cannot move closer to greater equality in access to political resources without greater equality in the distribution of, among other things, wealth and income. And if certain options like voting, free speech, and due process have to be established as "rights" to make democracy work, so also does a fairer share of income and wealth have to become a "right."

Until more Americans accept this view and act on it, the United States will not be the progressive society we wrongly assumed it to be at the time we wrote. Polyarchy may continue to exist at its present level, but democracy will still remain a long way off. To democratize the American polyarchy further will require a redistribution of wealth and income.

It is conceivable that upon reflection a majority of Americans would not really choose to democratize the American polyarchy by reducing inequalities in wealth and income. We cannot know whether this is or is not so until the issue has been explored in public discussion. Possibly the question is slowly moving onto the agenda of American public life. Yet there has never been an adequate public inquiry into the principles of justice that should govern the distribution of wealth and income in the United States.

Pluralism

In setting out our view on the requirements of polyarchy we say: "Polyarchy requires a considerable degree of social pluralism—that is, a diversity of social organizations with a large measure of autonomy with respect to one another" (p. 302). That polyarchy requires a diversity of social organizations not highly controlled by the government of the state, such as political parties, is fairly obvious. Indeed, the existence of relatively autonomous parties might even enter into the definition of polyarchy, though in specifying its characteristics in this book we chose not to do so (p. 277).

During the intervening years since this book first appeared, social pluralism in the sense of autonomous organizational life has gained new advocates in quarters where it had hitherto been attacked; and it has been strongly attacked in quarters where it had hitherto been supported. Although this paradox needs more discussion than we can provide here, it is worth commenting on briefly.

Excessively influenced by the Soviet model and Stalinist ideas, Marxism (at the time we wrote) had largely been transformed into a rigidly antipluralist doctrine. Recently, however, a number of Marxists in Eastern Europe and in some of the Communist parties of Western Europe, particularly the Italian Communist Party, have stressed the desirability and even the necessity of a considerable degree of organizational autonomy, both during the transition to socialism and in a fully socialist society. These views have been stimulated by a renewed concern for democracy after a long period in which Marxist thought was smothered by the antidemocratic theory and practice espoused by Soviet leaders. They are also fostered by experiences in Eastern Europe with the excesses and inefficiencies of highly centralized regimes, and by the rise of Marxist humanism with its concern for autonomy and freedom. As an alternative to authoritarian regimes with centralized command economies, many Marxists now envision a more decentralized socialist society that is also more tolerant of ideological diversity, political conflict, and opposition. Hence the new stress on the desirability of pluralism.

Meanwhile, in the United States and elsewhere pluralism has often come under attack precisely on the ground that it impedes democracy. The debate is often extremely confused. In part, confusion arises over different interpretations of empirical reality: some critics argue that the United States is insufficiently pluralistic, is in fact class dominated; while others argue that it is *too* pluralistic, has no capacity for subordinating minorities to majorities. Confusion also arises because what is represented as democratic pluralist doctrine is often a highly artificial melange of views, many of which no one has actually advanced. Like the portrait of Dorian Gray, this pastiche has acquired a life of its own. Although it would be desirable to have a rigorous statement of the relation of pluralism to democracy and of the main empirical and normative issues involved in the dispute, none exists and we cannot provide one in this brief introduction.

PLURALISM AS AN OBSTACLE TO DEMOCRATIZATION

We may have contributed to the confusion ourselves because in this book the discussion of social pluralism as a *prerequisite* of polyarchy (pp. 302ff) is widely separated from our discussion, very nearly at the end of the book, of the problems generated for democracy by "the growth of gigantic organizations like trade unions, corporations, and farmers' associations" (p. 498). We do not make sufficiently explicit (and were not clear in our own thought) what the two parts of our analysis imply: The degree of social pluralism *necessary* for polyarchy to exist may not be *sufficient* to bring about further democratization.

To put the point in a slightly different way, in order to democratize the government of a large state to the level of contemporary polyarchies, a considerable degree of social pluralism is necessary. This is the aspect of pluralism on which some Marxist humanists have joined liberal thought, emphasizing the dehumanizing and oppressive aspects of highly centralized, hierarchical, bureaucratic socialist systems like that of the Soviet Union. Yet the degree of organizational pluralism that may be sufficient to sustain a polyarchy may *not* be sufficient for democratizing polyarchies still further. It may even present an obstacle to further democratization.

Although we did not achieve clarity of generalization on this point, we did nevertheless sharply criticize the "solution" suggested by an amorphous but influential current of pluralist thought that we called "national bargaining." Today one might be more likely to refer to this elusive body of thought as an example of democratic corporatism. In this view, as we interpreted it, these large organizations are here to stay; they represent people in important ways; they may even be, to quote one writer, "more truly representative than the Congress elected by territorial divisions"; in their bargaining, they form a kind of de facto national parliament; the bargaining process among these giant organized interests, which perhaps ought also to include the government of the state, constitutes a satisfactory process, one even superior to policy-making by territorial bodies like Congress, for arriving at national decisions on economic matters. Better than Congress and political parties, they say, national bargaining satisfies the claims of democracy and the public interest.

We levelled a number of severe objections to this view: National bargaining among organized interests cannot achieve such results as stabilizing the economy, slum clearance, public housing, medical care, and so on. There is no guarantee that bargaining will produce "democratic" decisions in accord with the preferences of the greater number. Much of the inflation of recent years, for example, is the result of bargaining that does not so accord. Hence bargaining is not an alternative to government hierarchy. Nor does it eliminate nongovernmental hierarchies. In fact, it would be effective only to the extent that the bargaining organizations were highly hierarchical. National bargaining would probably therefore encourage the further growth of hierarchy, and often in its worst forms, that is, in private organizations without a code of internal "civil liberties."

It would also have very adverse consequences for political equality. In fact, equality in bargaining power among *organizations* (which some advocates seem to suggest) must necessarily contradict political equality among *individuals*. Even if the organizations themselves were fully democratized, this contradiction would not be resolved. For if an organization with fewer members is to have power in negotiations equal to an organization with larger numbers, as in the U.N. General Assembly, then the principle of political equality among individuals will be violated. If the organizations are not to have equal power in negotiations, then the decisions will not represent the "just balance" among "equal interests" that is so much coveted by the advocates of national bargaining and democratic corporatism.

All these drawbacks are sharply exacerbated by a further factor that we failed to emphasize. In all polyarchies a substantial body of citizens do not participate in or even belong to organizations. They are excluded from the influence over key national decisions that organizations bring to bear. Like other kinds of political participation, participation in organizations is biased by social and economic status. The better-off participate more in organizations and they participate more in politics generally. The worse-off are more likely to be unorganized, and they participate much less or not at all in public life. As a consequence, government decisions reflect and reinforce a structure of inequalities. Because governments respond more to the better-off than to the worse-off, they help to sustain the cycles of political effectiveness and ineffectuality that in turn perpetuate the structure of inequalities.

Whatever the best solution to this problem may be, for Americans, at least, it is not to be found, in our view, in destroying organizational autonomy and replacing autonomy with centralization, command, hierarchy, bureaucracy, and domination by an enlightened elite. The union of a democratic government with a truly public economy is, as this book makes clear, a far more complex and difficult task than was ever envisioned in ideologies created in the nineteenth century. In the twentieth century, no country has yet come close to such a union. One aim of this book is to help generate some of the understanding that might make it possible for Americans to start moving toward that goal.

THE PRIVILEGED PARTICIPATION OF BUSINESS

In our discussion of pluralism we made another error—and it is a continuing error in social science—in regarding businessmen and business groups as playing the same interest-group role as other groups in polyarchal systems, though more powerfully. Businessmen play a distinctive role in polyarchal politics that is qualitatively different from that of any interest group. It is also much more powerful than an interest-group role.

Businessmen—more specifically, corporate leaders—are the main initiators, organizers, and executives in all polyarchal societies, for all these societies throw into the market arena and into the hands of corporate leaders the principal tasks of mobilizing the society's resources for the multifold tasks to which the society's resources can be put. No other group in these societies except government leadership itself carries such a collective responsibility. The function of businessmen is to be "public officials" even if they are not government officials.

Yet businessmen are not ordered by law to perform the many organizational and leadership tasks that are delegated to them. All these societies operate by rules that require that businessmen be induced rather than commanded. It is therefore clear that these societies must provide sufficient benefits or indulgences to businessmen to constitute an inducement for them to perform their assigned tasks.

The consequence of these arrangements—peculiar as they would appear to a man from Mars—is that it becomes a major task of government to design and maintain an inducement system for businessmen, to be solicitous of business interests, and to grant to them, for its value as an incentive, an intimacy of participation in government itself. In all these respects the relation between government and business is unlike the relation between government and any other group in the society.

The implications of this remarkable state of affairs both for public policy on the corporation and for pluralism were not sufficiently explored in our book and have not yet been sufficiently explored. Yet common interpretations that depict the American or any other market-oriented system as a competition among interest groups are seriously in error for their failure to take account of the distinctive privileged position of businessmen in politics. For characterizing many governments of the world, it is necessary to give a prominent place to this component: the distinctive privileged participation of businessmen in government made possible by the routine acknowledgement by government officials of businessmen's special responsibilities and their consequent special claims for indulgences, authority, and other power. Although in addition businessmen play an interest-group role, their distinctive privileged participation in government is something different, more important, and exclusive to them. If we were to lay out a conventional diagram of government, each part located in relation to each other part, we would

have to recognize and place this component—though no one yet
has a name for it—in its relation to the executive, legislature,
parties, and interest groups. It is not subsumed under any of
these; but, like these other components of government, it is an
identifiable and specific process interacting with the others.

CONSENSUS AS AN OBSTACLE TO DEMOCRATIZATION

Perhaps our greatest failing in the discussion of pluralism
was on the relation of consensus to democratic pluralism.
Consensuses of certain kinds among certain participants in politics, we said and still believe, are necessary to polyarchal politics
and in particular to those engaged in political bargaining. But
consensus also constitutes a restriction on the range of alternative policies that will be debated in polyarchal politics. If, compared to hegemonic systems, polyarchies are distinguished by
a competition of ideas, the competition is nevertheless greatly
restricted. We have already noted how disinclined Americans are
to examine possible changes in the role of corporations and of
corporate property. So intolerant of a diversity of opinion are
voters that millions of them disqualified Senator McGovern as
a presidential candidate immediately on hearing his proposal for
a thousand-dollar income base for all families. Examples can be
recited endlessly.

Polyarchal problem solving is impaired not only by the narrow range of public policy discussion but also by the location
of that narrow range. An evident feature of the consensus
prevailing in all the polyarchies is that it endorses attitudes,
values, institutions, and policies of more benefit to the already
favored groups in the society than to the less favored. That is
not surprising; it would be astonishing if an inherited set of
beliefs did not reflect such a bias, and one need not be a Marxist
to appreciate how fundamental the bias is. Its effect, however,
is to cripple to a significant degree the usefulness of polyarchal
and democratic institutions to attain the values we postulated.
The degree of disability is indicated in the continuation of significant political, economic, and social inequality in the United
States by consent of a massive majority that does not yet realize
that long after 1848 it still has "a world to win."

As a research task, the clarification of the subtle relationship between consensus and indoctrinated complacency about existing institutions is especially challenging. In academic political science it is virgin territory. An examination of it will raise questions about the public schools: their sacrifice of political curiosity and creativity to conservative indoctrination, the possibilities for changing their political role, and new institutions or programs for opening minds to opportunities to use rather than be used by politico-economic institutions. It will also raise questions about the mass media: the inappropriateness of a near monopoly of radio and television by commercial broadcasting tied to corporate advertising, the systematic biases thus introduced into mass communications, and possible new uses of the media to enhance the political capacities of citizens.

Incrementalism

Does our distress with the slow pace of advance toward the values we postulated a quarter century ago suggest that incremental policy making, which we expected to carry much of the burden of reform, is far less effective than we thought?[3]

The objections that have been brought against incremental change do not deny that incrementalism is an aid to rationally calculated change. Nor does the objection say that some institutions are impervious to incremental change. In fact, all succumb: in most decades and in most of the polyarchies, incremental change has worked its effects over the distribution of income and wealth, property rights, corporate structure, industrial relations, social security, resource use, energy conservation, and international negotiation. Instead the objection is that incremental change is too slow, pathetically slow, intolerably slow. What has been achieved in redressing the wrongs of inequality, for example, should have been achieved many decades earlier and is still inadequate.

Now it can hardly be questioned that, if one lives in a society that for one reason or another is incapable of more than

---

[3] See especially pages 82 to 85, and our dismissal of "grand alternatives" on page 1.

incremental change, one wastes his time to propose and debate
nonincremental policies. To deal in nonincremental change in
those circumstances is simply to remove oneself from effective
participation in politics, except for those who believe that with-
drawal is itself effective. The objection must therefore be
construed to imply that political systems should be designed so
that they are capable of more than incremental change. But that
we still do not know how to do. All societies are capable of nonincremental change at rare intervals of crisis, but in all of history
we cannot find any societies that can routinely accomodate
nonincremental change. The Soviet Union long ago settled into a
pattern of incremental change. In deliberately fomenting two
major crises, the Great Leap Forward and the Cultural Revolution, Mao tried to hold open possibilities for nonincremental
change in China; but in neither the Leap nor the Revolution did
China succeed in breaking away from incremental policy making. In any society nonincremental change is no more than an
occasional spasm.

Societies change incessantly, but deliberately conceived social change is extraordinarily difficult. If we were writing the
book today, we might give more attention than we did then to
the battery of processes, forces, and institutions that obstruct
reform in the direction of the aspirations we postulated. If societies move forward, they do so not simply because from time
to time reformers mobilize their energies but because from time
to time they manage to outwit, bypass, or dominate the many
energies that are mobilized, often knowingly, against reform.
In the United States more money, energy, and organizational
strength is thrown into obstructing equality than into achieving
it, more into constraining our liberties than into enlarging them,
and more into maintaining the corporate domain as a private
preserve than into making its public acts public. The schools
and the mass media carry messages of reassurance, of pride in
past achievement and hence the status quo, and of hostility to
any fundamental structural reform in economy or polity.

Under these circumstances—and they are the typical circumstances of societies in all ages—it is not obvious how best to
achieve social change in desired directions. Successful change
calls for strategies, wits, and luck. We believe that incremental

policy making is an intelligent adaptation to features of society that make change difficult and slow rather than a cause of that difficulty and slowness.

To opt for incremental change is to believe that a great frequency of small changes will change the society faster than normally impossible large changes, since the pace of change is the product of size of step multiplied by frequency. Yet many people find it deeply satisfying to talk about and advocate large changes with a romantic disregard for their improbability. Taking probabilities into account, incremental policy making will not dramatically overcome the resistance to social change, but it will persevere as relentlessly as water seeps through a leaky dam.

What is required is not the fruitless advocacy of nonincremental reforms (as distinguished from a highly strategic advocacy of it in rare appropriate circumstances) but social inventiveness to increase the frequency with which incremental alterations are made. Granted that the sequences of incremental change proceed too slowly, we believe that the pace can by appropriate reform be speeded—for example, by removal of many of the veto powers widely distributed in the American system. How further to raise the frequency of incremental change is an appropriate major target for research and thoughtful discussion.

Structural Reform

It follows from all we have said that we believe that major structural reforms are required in the American politico-economic system. Only a few years ago, when economists were at the peak of their success in guiding economic policy and when the accomplishments of post World War II social science had seemed to promise a new era in the application of social science to social problems, it was widely believed that by grafting new methods of scientific policymaking and planning onto existing politico-economic institutions, the United States and the other industrialized polyarchies might be able to meet whatever challenges confronted them. We did not share that euphoria and do not now believe that more thoughtful, better

informed, or more scientific problem solving is enough. The
emphasis given to it in the last decade or two has diverted attention from more fundamental requirements. The decision-
making or policymaking institutions themselves are seriously
defective and need to be restructured.

If there is a major role for science, especially social science,
it is in the reconstruction of politico-economic institutions. Yet
that task calls for a great deal more than social science. It calls
for innovative ideas from whomever can produce them, for
constitution building that can only be entrusted to citizens and
political leaders, and for practical judgements the capacity for
which is widely distributed in the society. As we have already
noted, social science is not now well equipped to make a distinctive contribution of its own.

How to achieve structural reform? For all our discontent
with contemporary politico-economic institutions, we are reduced to believing that it is through these very institutions that
society can build better institutions. Is that a reasonable expectation? Perhaps we only reveal here, for all our discontent, the
residual naive optimism of liberalism.[4] Still, social institutions do
change. That is undeniable. And many of them are deliberately
changed, at least very slowly, in the direction of the aspirations
we postulated in this book. We do believe that the pace of controlled change can be accelerated—for example, we have said,
by speeding the sequences of incremental change. With its
indirections, incremental change is a method of "smuggling"
social reform into society. If that fact were more widely understood, there would be more smugglers at work, as well as some
learning of the smuggler's skills. But there are other possibilities

---

[4] The difficulty of using existing unsatisfactory politico-economic
institutions in order to change those very institutions raises again the
venerable question of whether "new men" or new institutions are most
essential for social reform. Given our preoccupation with institutions, we
thought it wise, in the concluding pages of the book, in which we discussed personality formation and the effects on the individual of small-
group life, to acknowledge our respect for approaches to this set of alternatives different from our own. We repeat that acknowledgement here.
Given the subtle interplay between personality and institution, we cannot
be confident that our proclivity to stress large institutional reforms is the
right track.

for accelerating change, many yet to be discovered when social scientists attend more energetically than they have to the task of discovery.

Social scientists, ourselves included, have looked only superficially into processes for controlled social change and have identified them largely with rationalistic attempts to change society. What in fact are, however, the main identifiable instruments of controlled social change? Obviously one is the coercive power of the state as it has been used in the Soviet Union and China. Another, much less well understood, is the "irrational" bias of market systems toward innovation. Market systems have the peculiarity that they permit innovation to be undertaken by persons—normally entrepreneurs—who are permitted to disregard the adverse, sometimes catastrophic, effects of their innovations on others in the society, among them their competitors and their competitor's employees. In recent years a great deal of attention has been drawn to this feature of market systems. It is now better recognized than ever before that some of society's problems, like environmental pollution, are in part attributable to the option that businessmen have to introduce new technologies without regard to wider consequences. But it is still not widely recognized that that same institutional arrangement is a method of systematically strengthening change-making rather than change-retarding forces in the society and that it presumably accounts for some large share of responsibility for high standards of living in the market societies of the world.

In our time and in our society, most of us are now concluding that neither of these change mechanisms is satisfactory. That being so, we have to face up to the fact that existing American political institutions will not solve the problem for us. They carry a contrary bias—against change. The bias was deliberately built into the system at the Constitutional Convention. The inventiveness that went into constitution building at that time needs to be summoned up again to achieve a discrimination that did not occur to the constitutional fathers. A bias against change in the aspirations or general values to be pursued in the system is worth preserving. But the bias against reformulation of proximate goals and against institutional and policy change to attain liberal and egalitarian values is obstructive. That bias needs to be removed. Indeed a contrary "irrational" bias *toward* change is required to offset the powerful forces that operate throughout society to obstruct those changes that approach, but all too slowly, the aspirations still to be prized.

Is it possible to undercut formidable resistance to change without the coerciveness of an authoritarian state or the harsh bias of market innovation? It seems essential that new mechanisms be found, and there is no greater task for social scientists than to join with others in the search.

ROBERT A. DAHL
CHARLES E. LINDBLOM

PREFACE 1953

It is a pity that the term "political economy" can hardly be used today without conjuring up the ghosts of Smith, Ricardo, and the Mills—not to say Thomas Gradgrind and Josiah Bounderby. For the first set of names suggests something respectable but old-fashioned; the second set, something not only old-fashioned but detestable.

Even though modern economies are quite different from the economy so flatteringly depicted by the classical economists and so bitterly by Dickens and Marx, it is a fact as plain as Gradgrind's naïveté or Bounderby's humbug that economic life in the real world today constitutes a *political* economy. The buzzing confusion around us is unmistakably the household noise of a society in which economics is married, if only at common law, to politics. Yet in formal theory today, politics and economics are frequently regarded as distant cousins not quite on speaking terms.

In this book the authors have sought to incorporate certain aspects of politics and economics into a single consistent body of theory. Behind much political and economic theory lies the implicit, sometimes explicit, question: What are the conditions under which numerous individuals can maximize the attainment of their goals through the use of social mechanisms? That question, specifically directed to politico-economic processes, is the focus of this study.

If at first blush it appears that the question turns the inquiry into ethics rather than science, such is nevertheless not the case; what we have done is simply to postulate the goals to be maximized. Hence this is not a treatise on ethics, but, in intention at least, a scientific work in the sense that most of our propositions are meant to be testable by a logical use of empirical evidence. The task of casting politico-economic theory into genuinely testable propositions is, however, a formidable one; and we have no illusions that this volume represents more than a beginning.

The attempt to collaborate on a book of this kind grew out of the discovery about six years ago that each of us was teaching a seminar on "planning" in the Yale Graduate School. Both seminars bore rather similar titles, and, as it turned out, their contents substantially overlapped; yet one presumably was economics, the other political science. For three years thereafter we conducted a joint seminar in which we both participated at every session and on every topic, a process that forced us into a good deal of prior collaboration until we were reasonably sure we understood one another before each seminar began. The seminar led inevitably into a book that kept shifting and reforming as we drafted and re-drafted it.

"Economic planning," we decided, could scarcely be defined sensibly except in very broad terms, namely, as an attempt at rational calculation and control in the use of scarce resources. Yet to make "planning" synonymous with any attempt at rational social action is to make the term more or less superfluous; consequently the word has pretty well dropped out of this book even though the concept it denotes remains the center of our inquiry. Very early it became evident too that no theory could unify politics and economics unless it made explicit the elemental sociological and psychological premises on which both bodies of theory rest. We have therefore drawn—cautiously, we hope—on concepts from these disciplines.

In the past, many social scientists other than economists themselves have been puzzled by the abstract, logical, rigorous, and yet, to the outsider, apparently nonempirical and nonsociological nature of much economic theory. We should like to think that the social processes which the economic theorist has appropriated as the domain of his own guild will now be more accessible to our colleagues in the other social sciences—and hence to their criticisms, insights, hypotheses, and methods.

Initially we had intended to deal in much more precise detail than we have with some specific politico-economic techniques. Our concern with developing a body of theory appropriate to certain aspects of the industrial economies of Western Europe and the United States has, however, drawn us away from this initial purpose. Yet the future of freedom in the West, and certainly in the United States, is inescapably bound up with the future of the four main hierarchical organizations through which so many of our most vital decisions are made—in short, the business corporation, the government bureaucracy, the trade union, and the political party.

We hope in the future to supplement the present volume with a comparative study of these four organizations.

We have been encouraged by the discovery that a wide area of agreement exists on the validity of a great number of propositions about politico-economic affairs. Many of the conflicts between "planners" and antiplanners or socialists and antisocialists prove to be conflicts over goals, but not over the probable specific consequences of utilizing alternative techniques. Many other conflicts flow out of the effort to generalize from specific consequences, on which there is much agreement, to broader consequences for comprehensive goals or values that are not operationally defined. The extent of scientific agreement has therefore been blurred by emphasis on disagreements stemming ultimately from differences in goals and definitions.

Many works appear as "collaborations" but in few can the dialectical process—in the Greek, not the Marxist, sense—have been more heavily relied on. As much as any work by two people can do, each chapter represents the single product of two minds. From a broader perspective the work is the indirect product of countless others; of these, some we know personally and acknowledge elsewhere, some though living, we know only through their writings, while many are decades or centuries dead.

In view of these debts, one would be witless to lay claims to originality. But the framework presented here we have found useful in examining the society in which we live, and perhaps others will also find it useful. Nevertheless, one way to measure the progress of a science of political economy is by the degree to which a book of this kind becomes obsolete.

R. A. D.
C. E. L.

ACKNOWLEDGMENTS

On several scores we are indebted to many persons and institutions for substantial assistance in the project culminating in this book.

We remember gratefully:

For time free from teaching, for travel expenses and for secretarial and editorial help, the Carnegie Corporation, the American Scandinavian Foundation, the John Simon Guggenheim Memorial Foundation, the anonymous donor of the Blanche Elizabeth MacLeish Billings Memorial Award, and Yale University, all of whom have shared the expenses of our research and writing.

For long-continued sympathetic and helpful interest in our work, Professor Edgar S. Furniss, Provost of Yale University, as well as our respective departments at Yale.

For criticism, stimulation, and ideas, our students of both the immediate and less recent past, especially those graduate students with whom in seminar we began to work out the main lines of the project and who in some cases read and criticized earlier drafts of the manuscript. It is easy to pass over one's students in acknowledging one's debts, but our gains from them have been immense.

For clerical and stenographic assistance, a long line of undergraduate assistants made available to us through Bursary Scholarships at Yale: Arnold Lozowick, Ben Walter, Harris Gilbert, Donald Leavenworth, John Eysenbach, Joseph Bow, Morton Freilich, and Walter L. Ross.

For generous and efficient help in the preparation of manuscript, Mrs. Charles P. Larrowe and Mrs. Dahl.

For their time freely given in interviews and for other assistance proffered abroad, a much larger number of people than we can here name. But those hundreds unnamed will doubtless excuse our mentioning a few. For library facilities, office space, and other kindnesses, Nuffield College, Oxford, especially Warden A. Loveday, and D. N. Chester, Fellow of Nuffield. For similar assistance,

Lars-Erik Thunholm of Svenska Handelsbanken in Stockholm. For assistance in arranging interviews and for other kindnesses, Edward van Cleef of The Netherlands Central Planning Bureau at The Hague, Mrs. Kid Kihlbom of Sverige-Amerika Stiftelson, A. Wålstedt in Stockholm, Paul Rykens, Vice-Chairman of Unilever in London, G. Dessus of Electricité de France in Paris, and William Hart, Hemel-Hempstead Development Corporation, England. For help generous almost to the point of folly—for arranging interviews, for providing housing, and for many other contributions to the welfare of Mr. Lindblom and his family when in France, our friend, Miss Anne Joba in Paris.

For their time and trouble taken to read critically part or all of earlier drafts of the manuscript, our many colleagues. The list of their names is itself evidence that the academic community is indeed a community, a group in which no man can stand by himself. Those from whom we have drawn help are: Paul Appleby, Christian Bay, William H. Brown and Mrs. Brown, Claude E. Buxton, Francis W. Coker, Leonard W. Doob, Herbert Feigl, Herman Finer, John Kenneth Galbraith, C. G. Hempel, L. G. Hines, Charles Hyneman, Hans Jenny, Willmoore Kendall, V. O. Key, Klaus Knorr, Robert E. Lane, Harold D. Lasswell, Wayne Leys, Herbert McClosky, John Perry Miller, Max Millikan, Richard Ruggles, Paul Samuelson, Edward Shils, Herbert A. Simon, James Tobin, Robert L. West and Mrs. West, Charles M. Winston, and David McCord Wright.

R. A. D.
C. E. L.

Part I.   INDIVIDUAL GOALS

AND

SOCIAL ACTION

I.

Social Techniques
and
Rational Social Action

I. Introduction

GRAND ALTERNATIVES AND THE "ISMS"

In economic organization and reform, the "great issues" are no longer the great issues, if ever they were. It has become increasingly difficult for thoughtful men to find meaningful alternatives posed in the traditional choices between socialism and capitalism, planning and the free market, regulation and laissez faire, for they find their actual choices neither so simple nor so grand. Not so simple, because economic organization poses knotty problems that can only be solved by painstaking attention to technical details— how else, for example, can inflation be controlled? Nor so grand, because, at least in the Western world, most people neither can nor wish to experiment with the whole pattern of socioeconomic organization to attain goals more easily won. If, for example, taxation will serve the purpose, why "abolish the wages system" to ameliorate income inequality?

Still, the older point of view is not entirely abandoned; it crops up in unexpected places. "The irrational and planless character of society," Erich Fromm writes, "must be replaced by a planned economy. . . ."[1] He does not say, however, what is to be planned, or how, or for what particular purposes; only that "self-realization for the masses of people requires planning."

Even Schumpeter[2] sometimes writes in terms of mythical grand alternatives, introducing, it has appeared to some of his readers, "an anthropomorphic supernatural force, capitalism, which becomes

---

[1] Erich Fromm, *Escape from Freedom*, Rinehart and Co., New York, 1941, p. 272.
[2] Joseph A. Schumpeter, *Capitalism, Socialism and Democracy* (2nd ed.), Harper & Brothers, New York, 1947.

3

the operating force in history."[3] His concept of socialism is in one context sophisticated, in another naïve, because socialism to him is sometimes a product of an accumulation of incremental changes and at other times a system consciously chosen in a particular time and place as an alternative to capitalism. Writing of socialism as planning, he says: "A situation may well emerge in which most people will consider complete planning as the smallest of all possible evils."[4] The starkness of the alternative, the notion of "complete planning" (what can it mean?) are earmarks of a disappearing point of view.

For all their contributions to our understanding of economic organization, Schumpeter, Hayek,[5] Lippmann,[6] Mises,[7] and a host of socialists or planners like Jay,[8] Beckwith,[9] Lorwin,[10] Landauer,[11] Lange,[12] and Mannheim[13] (to say nothing of the older doctrinaire socialists and communists) are to various degrees enmeshed in the now vanishing tradition of the great "isms." The grand alternatives they envision are the ignes fatui of Right and Left alike. Capitalism is now hardly more than a name stretched to cover a large family of economies in which distant cousins, it is true, resemble one another, but no more than do "capitalist" United States and "socialist" Britain. Socialism once stood for equality; but income and inheritance taxation, social security and other techniques of "capitalist" reform have destroyed its distinction. And in the eyes of socialists themselves, public ownership of industry is now simply an implement in

[3] See Walter Eucken, *The Foundations of Economics*, William Hodge and Company, London, 1950, p. 330.

[4] Joseph A. Schumpeter, "The March into Socialism," *American Economic Review*, May, 1950, pp. 446–456.

[5] F. A. Hayek, *The Road to Serfdom*, University of Chicago Press, Chicago, 1944.

[6] Walter Lippmann, *An Inquiry into the Principles of the Good Society*, Little, Brown and Co., Boston, 1937.

[7] Ludwig von Mises, *Human Action*, Yale University Press, New Haven, 1949.

[8] Douglas Jay, *The Socialist Case* (rev. ed.), Faber & Faber, Ltd., London, 1947.

[9] Burnham P. Beckwith, *The Economic Theory of a Socialist Economy*, Stanford University Press, Stanford, 1949.

[10] Lewis L. Lorwin, *Time for Planning; A Social-economic Theory and Program for the Twentieth Century*, Harper & Brothers, New York, 1945.

[11] Karl Landauer, *Theory of National Economic Planning*, University of California Press, Berkeley, 1944.

[12] Oskar R. Lange and Fred M. Taylor, in Benjamin E. Lippincott (ed.), *On the Economic Theory of Socialism*, University of Minnesota Press, Minneapolis, 1938.

[13] Karl Mannheim, *Man and Society in an Age of Reconstruction*, Kegan Paul, Trench, Trubner and Co., London, 1940.

everyone's tool kit for economic reform. Socialism has lost its unique character.

Plan or no plan? Everyone believes in planning in the literal sense of the word; and, for that matter, everyone believes that national governments should execute some plans for economic life. No one favors bad planning. Plan or no plan is no choice at all; the pertinent questions turn on particular techniques: Who shall plan, for what purposes, in what conditions, and by what devices? Free market or regulation? Again, this issue is badly posed. Both institutions are indispensable.

In 1894 Beatrice Webb speculated on how later generations would regard the debate on collectivism. "They will be amazed," she wrote, "that we fought so hard to establish one metaphysical position and to destroy another."[14] Believing that reform posed problems of techniques, not grand alternatives, some of the other Fabians shared Beatrice Webb's view of the then current debate.[15] Although the present generation has not advanced so far beyond Mrs. Webb's that it can yet be amazed at her contemporaries' error, it is at least slowly escaping from the tyranny of the "isms."[16]

Of course great issues remain. Because the whole is sometimes greater than the sum of its parts, another step in a series of reforms may produce more for good or bad than the modest results expected. Reform may pass through breaking points. Even so, further debate on the old alternatives shows no promise of discovering these

[14] Beatrice Webb, *Our Partnership* (edited by Barbara Drake and Margaret I. Cole), Longmans, Green and Co., London, 1948, p. 118.

[15] Francis Williams, "The Program of the British Labour Party; an Historical Survey," *The Journal of Politics*, May, 1950, pp. 189–210, esp. pp. 197–198.

[16] For examples of the newer approach: J. M. Clark, *Guideposts in Time of Change*, Harper & Brothers, New York, 1949; Seba Eldridge and associates, *Development of Collective Enterprise*, University of Kansas Press, Lawrence, 1943; W. Arthur Lewis, *The Principles of Economic Planning*, Allen and Unwin and Dennis Dobson, London, 1949; J. E. Meade, *Planning and the Price Mechanism*, Allen & Unwin, London, 1948; D. W. Chester (ed.), *Lessons of the British War Economy*, Blackwell's, Oxford, 1944; John K. Galbraith, *American Capitalism: The Concept of Countervailing Power*, Houghton Mifflin Co., Boston, 1952; J. M. Clark, *Alternative to Serfdom*, Alfred A. Knopf, New York, 1948; Wilhelm Keilhau, *Principles of Private and Public Planning*, George Allen & Unwin, Ltd., London, 1951; K. R. Popper, *The Open Society and Its Enemies*, G. Routledge & Sons, Ltd., London, 2 vols., 1945; R. H. S. Crossman (ed.), *The New Fabian Essays*, Turnstile Press, London, 1952; and a variety of articles in the journals, such as Marcus J. Fleming, "Production and Price Policies in Public Enterprise," *Economica*, N.S. 17, February, 1950; and C. A. R. Crosland, "Prices and Costs in Nationalized Undertakings," *Oxford Economic Papers*, N.S. 3, January, 1950. See also the current literature on the Schuman Plan.

points, if there are any. Nor does it succeed in turning attention to the countless particular social techniques out of which "systems" are compounded.

SOCIAL TECHNIQUES

In economic life the possibilities for rational social action, for planning, for reform—in short, for solving problems—depend not upon our choice among mythical grand alternatives but largely upon choice among particular social techniques.

THE VARIETY OF POLITICO-ECONOMIC TECHNIQUES. The number of alternative politico-economic techniques is tremendously large. For example, the alternative forms of business enterprise are numerous. One is called private enterprise, but its alternative forms in turn are many. Proprietorship, partnership, and corporation are terms suggesting three kinds of alternative structures significantly different one from the others. Corporations may be relatively simple structures for family ownership or complex bureaucracies with or without owner control. And a corporation operating under a minimum of regulation is different from one subject to securities and exchange regulation; different again from one embedded in a matrix of regulations developed through collective bargaining, from one operating under the ever present threat of antitrust action, or from one subject to rate regulation. The Filbert Corporation, the Ford Motor Company, American Telephone and Telegraph, General Motors, Hart-Schaffner-Marx, Kennecott Copper, and the Pennsylvania Railroad are all corporations; but as techniques for the organization of production they differ from one another in ways quite significant for policy. Whatever the problem, whatever the goal, the number of significantly different alternative techniques will ordinarily be great.

INNOVATION IN POLITICO-ECONOMIC TECHNIQUES. Moreover, the number of alternative techniques is constantly growing by discovery, invention, and innovation. To return to the example of alternative forms of private enterprise, in the United States the Atomic Energy Commission has developed a rather distinctively new form of enterprise, although one similar to the organization of business through contracts in war. Through their contractual relations with the commission, Union Carbon and Carbide, Tennessee

Eastman, General Electric, and other companies are operating under a different structure of cues and incentives from those of the other corporate forms mentioned above. Profit, in the ordinary sense of the term, is gone. So also is independence of investment decisions; price and production polices are subject to negotiation. Yet much of the initiative remains in the hands of the corporations, and their autonomy in a wide variety of decisions is relatively unaffected.

Many people think of invention and innovation in technology, but not in social structure; the bias probably accounts for a frequent failure to take account of the increasing possibilities for rational social reform through the improvement of techniques. We need only list a few inventions and discoveries to observe how they have increased the possibilities of rational social action, even if they often bring new problems in their wakes. The corporation itself was once an innovation; so also were unemployment compensation, food stamps, cost accounting, zoning, Lend-Lease, coöperatives, scientific management, points rationing, slum clearance, government old-age pensions, disability benefits, collective bargaining. Their origins are not so far distant that we cannot visualize a kind of accumulation of competence. Today, the European Payments Union and the Schuman Plan attest the inventiveness of our times.

RATE OF INNOVATION. The rate of increase in techniques is now extremely rapid. Why this is so must be a matter of speculation until the process of invention of social techniques is systematically studied. One hypothesis is that the growth of democracy has made it possible for masses of people to insist that problems be attacked where earlier the absence of any obvious solution to a problem was sufficient to deter any sustained efforts to solve it. Then, too, not until power is made democratic are the frustrations of masses of people necessarily the problems of public policy. Either way, the incentive to think constructively in terms of techniques is now much heightened. Another hypothesis, a corollary of what we have said, is that reform is turning to techniques instead of grand alternatives. A third hypothesis is that in the last few years war and defense have immensely stimulated the search for social as well as technological devices for social control, as is illustrated by the work of the RAND Corporation.

A fourth hypothesis is that the discovery and invention of new social techniques are largely the product of the social sciences, which are themselves relatively new. The particular role of psychology has recently been conspicuous in providing social scientists with a wealth of ideas on how men may be influenced. Lastly, literacy, popular education, and technological revolutions in communication have provided a groundwork for many new patterns of cues and incentives. There are no doubt still other explanations to be found in great shifts in culture such as the decline of traditionalism in Western society.

The process of innovation is both scientific and political. It is not enough that new social techniques be discovered; they must also be put into use. Invention and discovery are only the beginning of a process the next step in which is innovation, a matter of politics. What we are suggesting is that this process taken as a whole is proceeding with astonishing rapidity—it is perhaps the greatest political revolution of our times. Anyone who is not impressed with it can hardly gauge the richness—and dangers—of possible social reform and, failing that, he cannot deal competently with public policy.

Rational and responsible reform may consequently suffer from a serious limitation at the hands of those who fail to grasp the fact that alternatives are many, that new ones can be expected to appear, and that they can be created. A great deal of policy analysis and formulation still rests with those to whom man is man and institutions are institutions and who think of policy as a reshuffling of the same old variables. One of Franklin Roosevelt's great skills as a political leader was his encouragement of new techniques, as illustrated by the National Recovery Administration, the National Labor Relations Board, Lend-Lease, food stamps, and the fifty-destroyer transaction. A contrast was the futile debate during the Second World War over the union shop in American industry, a debate in which many groups refused to consider any new alternatives to the open shop, closed shop, and union shop, although in the War Labor Board the debate finally came to an end with the innovation of the maintenance-of-membership technique. Similarly, one finds in the British debate over broadcasting policy a preoccupation with the British system and American commercial radio as the only two major alternatives; all too seldom attention is given to other alternatives yet to be tried and to still others unknown, yet to be invented. An old saw says that armies are always well prepared to fight the last war. Much of the discussion of social policy suffers from the same disability.

SELECTIVITY IN POLITICO-ECONOMIC TECHNIQUES. The alternative techniques available for a particular problem commonly offer a high degree of selectivity. They permit more precision in choice, more careful adaptation of means to ends, than men sometimes take account of. Consider, for example, the fine gradations in choice of alternative schemes of private enterprise permitted by its multiplicity of forms, existing and conceivable. The refinements in choice permitted by gradations in techniques are not limited to trivial differences among them. They range over a number of continua in which the opposite poles pose such critical alternatives as government power and private power, voluntarism and compulsion, centralization and decentralization, prescription and indoctrination, local determination and national determination.

We can illustrate the array of choices commonly available to policy, each one slightly different from another related to it, and at the same time emphasize once more the large numbers of alternative techniques by diagraming a number of these continua in which the variables are significant and upon which particular techniques suited to some particular problem or goal can be placed. Imagine, for example, the choices open between private ownership and public ownership as polar methods of enterprise organization. Opinions will differ, of course, as to the exact placement of some techniques on such a scale; but despite these differences, the pattern of such a continuum is as in Diagram 1.

The diagram proves nothing; it is only illustrative. Diagram 1 displays something of the variety of techniques possible between an unregulated private enterprise, on the one hand, and a business like the post office run as an ordinary government department, on the other hand. Both to illustrate how "public" ownership and "private" ownership have been stretched in meaning to cover techniques ranging over a long continuum and to show again the invalidity of thinking in terms of comprehensive systems, we have placed the techniques ordinarily associated in the public mind with private enterprise above the line and those commonly associated with socialism below. They overlap; the one set of techniques is not huddled toward one end of the scale, the second set toward the

DIAGRAM I. *A Continuum Showing Some of the Choices Available Between Government Ownership and Private Enterprise*

Government

Private

Below the line: Govt. ownership of part of an industry

Above the line: Joint govt.-private firm

Government						Private
An enterprise operated as an ordinary govt. dept., such as the post office	Public corp. subject to ministerial control	Regulated public utilities	Public corp. with tripartite control	Anti-trust	Subsidized corporation (regulated like those at right)	Corporation subject to misc. corp. regulation, incl. labor and securities	Corporation subject to corporate regulation	A hypothetical small proprietorship subject only to common law

AEC lease and contract
Some types of defense contracts

Worker control Guilds Syndicates

French electricity
French RR

BBC
British RR
TVA
Port of London
Port of N.Y.

Govt. contracts with private producers, as in public housing

Govt. purchases from private sellers, as in British health program and "socialized" medicine

Below the line: techniques popularly described with words such as "nationalized," "socialized," "government owned," and "public enterprise."
Above the line: techniques popularly described with words such as "private enterprise," "private property," and "free enterprise."
On the line: techniques popularly thought to be neither clearly public nor private.

other. Note in particular the placement of "socialized" medicine.

This diagram reveals the foolishness of the debate on nationalization versus private enterprise. It suggests that the Atomic Energy Commission's contractual system may provide more comprehensive public control over enterprises than can be had through the degree of autonomy granted corporations like the nationalized enterprises of Britain or the Port of New York Authority. But whether that is true or not—and we emphasize again that the placement of techniques on such a scale as this must be arbitrary to a degree—for the particular goals sought, the AEC contractual system, like public utility regulation, worker control schemes, subsidies, or securities and exchange regulation, is often better than the formula of nationalization. But each of these techniques offers a slightly different combination of government and private control, and it is therefore possible to choose that particular combination best suited to remedy a particular organizational deficiency.

Note also that choice can range over even more precise gradations than those shown on the diagram, for many of these alternative techniques offer methods of combining public and private power with respect to any one specific kind of entrepreneurial decision which policy might wish to affect. We have also understated the possibilities of precision in choice because readability requires simplification: in most cases we have placed *types* of enterprise on the scale rather than identifying a particular enterprise. There will actually be found a gradation of choice within the type itself.

Diagram 2 illustrates a quite different kind of choice but again displays the fine gradations open to policy makers. In this diagram are arrayed at one extreme various techniques which combine information and education as techniques of control, with compulsive techniques at the other. The diagram illustrates choices among devices for settling labor disputes, which issue is, of course, only one of many possible illustrations.

The separation of techniques above and below the line is more arbitrary than in the previous diagram; we have tried to separate techniques widely considered to be persuasive (above the line) from those widely considered to be coercive (below the line). The overlap will show the invalidity of the distinction as it is often drawn, because some of the techniques widely thought to be persuasive are quite coercive; and it emphasizes again the range of

DIAGRAM 2. *A Continuum Showing Some of the Choices Available Between Compulsion and Information by Government Action, as Illustrated by Techniques for the Settlement of Industrial Disputes*

Information

Compulsion

Above the line:

- Highly organized "voluntary" back-to-work movement supported by local govt., police, businessmen, etc.
- President's back-to-work appeal
- Fact-finding boards with power to recommend settlement
- Fact-finding boards without power to recommend settlement
- "Cooling-off" requirements
- Mediation
- Conciliation
- Informal advice from and consultation with government officials

Below the line:

- Voluntary arbitration
- Compulsory arbitration where no effective means of enforcing the award is at hand
- Compulsory arbitration
- Injunction
- Militia

Above the line: techniques commonly considered as those of "education," "persuasion," and "appeals to reason."
Below the line: techniques commonly considered as those of "power," "coercion," and "orders."

variations to be found within each of the two types of techniques: information and compulsion.

The exact placement of a number of techniques may be disputed; it is a matter of subjective judgment rather than demonstrable fact. But, to repeat, we are trying to prove nothing except the fact of fine gradations in choice, and a change in rank of a number of techniques will not affect the usefulness of the diagram as an illustration. Few people will dispute the general arrangement of the techniques. A Presidential back-to-work appeal, which appears above the line on the extreme left, can be almost as compulsive as an injunction, even if the appeal is coupled with no threat at all. And although compulsory arbitration may be quite compulsive where awards can be enforced, it can also be no more so than a fact-finding board without power to issue a decision. Compulsory arbitration often lacks an effective penalty for disobedience; we have placed it on the scale in two places to indicate the possibility. These subsidiary considerations aside, the important fact is simply that the available techniques offer almost any combination of information and compulsion that might be desired.

Diagram 3 illustrates the gradations possible in what are sometimes called direct and indirect controls over the level of employment and spending. Typically stabilization policy makes heavy use of indirect control, as, for example, in the manipulation of bank reserve requirements or the control of private spending through variations in government expenditure. On the other hand, it is possible to bring business spending decisions under governmental command by nationalization of industry, licensing of investment, and other direct controls over the individual decisions of named persons or enterprises. Again, however, a range of alternatives connects the two extremes by easy gradations. If it is not already obvious, it is worth pointing out that the choice of one technique for one sector of the economy does not ordinarily preclude a wide choice among other techniques in another sector. This fact is apparent from a mere inspection of the techniques scaled in Diagram 3, but the same is true for the techniques on the other scales.

Diagram 4 represents choices between voluntary and compulsory organizations for a variety of purposes, an illustration which should make clear that policy is never restricted to the simple choice between calling upon "government" to perform a given function and leaving its performance, on the other hand, to a "private"

DIAGRAM 3. *A Continuum Showing Some of the Choices Available Between Direct and Indirect Controls, as Illustrated in Techniques to Control the Level of Employment and Spending*

Direct Control

- Nationalization permitting directives on investment
- Variations in public expenditures

- Licensing of private investment

- Anti-trust

- Variations in grants-in-aid to state and local govts.

- Regulation of terms of credit in private transactions, as in installment buying

- Appeals to business on price policy or to unions on wage policies

- Bond sales to consumers

Indirect Control

- Taxes and subsidies
- Manipulation of interest rate and central bank policy
- Secondary effect of public expenditures

DIAGRAM 4. *A Continuum Showing Some of the Choices Available Between Voluntary and Compulsory Organizations*

Voluntary ⟶ **Compulsory**

	Voluntary ←→ Compulsory							
Above the line (governmental)	Advisory councils	Civil service	Contracting members of Agric. Adj. Admin.	NRA code groups / Land-use planning districts	Tax districts	Municipality	An American state	Social security systems	The nation-state
			Guilds and syndicates		Closed-shop union	Class and status groups	Guilds and syndicates		
Below the line (private)	Small private clubs	Political parties / Pressure groups	Professional and business organizations / Unions	Union with maintenance-of-membership rule	Business firm where annuity is lost on separation	Business groups with delegated govt. power: e.g., newsprint users in Great Britain			

Above the line: organizations commonly thought of as governmental.
Below the line: organizations commonly thought of as private.

group. The separation of techniques above and below the line is an incidental reminder that private organizations may be as compulsory as government organizations. The comments on the earlier diagrams should make the meaning of this diagram, as well as of Diagram 5, sufficiently clear without further comment. Diagram 5 is an attempt to show the gradation of choice between procedures closely supervised by central government officials and those possessing a high degree of autonomy. Since government is often widely identified with prescription and private organization with autonomy, a wide range of autonomy-prescription combinations is revealing. The number of these diagrams can be increased indefinitely both by examining other kinds of choices and by examining the same kinds of choices with respect to other problems or goals.

Whether the rapidity of innovation in new techniques of control is or is not the greatest political revolution of our times, techniques and not "isms" are the kernel of rational social action in the Western world. Both socialism and capitalism are dead. The politico-economic systems of the United States and of Britain differ in important respects, to be sure; yet both major parties in both countries are attacking their economic problems with fundamentally the same kinds of techniques. Ideological differences between the parties in each country and between the countries themselves are significant in affecting the choice of techniques; but policy in any case is technique-minded, and it is becoming increasingly difficult in both countries to argue policy in terms of the mythical grand alternatives.

THE AREA OF AGREEMENT ON TECHNIQUES

A curious and encouraging aspect of the debate on economic policy is that ideological differences cannot disguise an emerging agreement on appropriate social techniques. John Jewkes wages furious war on the Left in his *Ordeal by Planning;*[17] but on the particulars of economic policy for Britain he is close to James Meade, a self-described liberal socialist.[18] Both would applaud much of Henry Simons' *A Positive Program for Laissez-Faire,*[19] W. Arthur Lewis' *Principles of Economic Planning,*[20] and Wilhelm Röpke's

[17] John Jewkes, *Ordeal by Planning,* The Macmillan Company, New York, 1948.
[18] James E. Meade, *op. cit.*
[19] Henry C. Simons, *A Positive Program for Laissez-Faire* (Public Policy Pamphlet No. 15), University of Chicago Press, Chicago, 1934.
[20] W. Arthur Lewis, *op. cit.*

DIAGRAM 5. *A Continuum Showing Some of the Choices Available Among Kinds of Public Agencies According to the Degree to Which the Agency's Operations Are Prescribed by a Hierarchical Superior*

Autonomy ←——————————————————————————————————→ **Prescription**

Above the line (British governmental agencies)												
BBC	Coal Board	Local govt.	Bank of England	Organization and Management Division, Treasury	Regulatory commissions	Courts	Reclamation Bureau	Cabinet Secretariat	Budget Bureau	General Acctg. Office	Unemployment compensation	Ministry of Pensions / Stationery Office

Below the line (U.S. governmental agencies)												
Autonomous agencies: e.g., trustees of the New Haven commons	Semi-autonomous agencies such as the Port of New York Authority	Atomic Energy Commission	Supreme Court	TVA — Securities and Exchange Commission			Interstate Commerce Commission					Veterans' Administration

Above the line: British governmental agencies.
Below the line: U.S. governmental agencies.
Placement of British and American agencies is not comparable.

The Social Crisis of Our Time.[21] If conservatives, liberals, socialists, planners, and anti-planners find themselves in growing agreement the closer they press to concrete policy problems, this is a fact of extraordinary significance for the social sciences and for the possibilities of rational politico-economic action.

Still in their infancies, the social sciences are already producing habits of thought, accumulations of knowledge, and theoretical propositions now beginning to command an agreement wholly impossible fifty years ago. To be sure, they do not tell us whether man is rational or not, whether planning can be successful or not, whether governments can wisely administer economic affairs or not. But such questions are badly posed, for we know that man may be both irrational and rational, plans may fail in one circumstance yet succeed in another, governments administer some economic affairs wisely and others not. The social sciences are, however, beginning to identify the critical variables. The substance of the emerging agreement on politico-economic policy is the *prerequisite techniques of rational social action;* this is the achievement of the social sciences.

II. Scope of the Book

THE PREREQUISITES OF RATIONAL SOCIAL ACTION IN THE POLITICO-ECONOMIC AREA

We[22] propose in this book to make the most of this much-to-be-prized emerging agreement by exploring the prerequisites of rational social action in the politico-economic area. We hope to uncover large areas of agreement and, incidentally then, to put an end to sterile controversy over slogans that hide agreement. We do not attempt an evaluation of each of the multitude of specific and detailed techniques we have been discussing; the book is rather an attempt to examine central processes and major techniques so that the basis for choice among more particular techniques is clarified.

At first blush it might appear that an analysis of the prerequisites of rational social action avoids all the interesting questions, because it seems to substitute moralizing for a descriptive science on which predictions could be based. What must a nation do to achieve rational politico-economic organization? This strikes one as

[21] Wilhelm Röpke, *The Social Crisis of Our Time,* William Hodge and Co., London, and University of Chicago Press, Chicago, 1950.
[22] Henceforth meaning the authors, unless otherwise noted.

a less exciting question than: Can a nation achieve rational politico-economic organization? But, depending upon how one looks at these questions, either the second one is unanswerable or both are the same. Whether a nation can achieve rational politico-economic organization depends not only upon the particular economic techniques it employs but upon the political and economic literacy of its citizens, their faiths and attitudes—in fact upon its culture as a whole—as well as upon fortuitous circumstances. Whether a nation can achieve rational social action is therefore beyond anyone's knowledge except when its social processes and techniques can be measured against the prerequisites of rational social action.

If knowledge were adequate, which it is not, it would be possible to pursue the prerequisites of rational social action back to their own prerequisites, and these back to theirs until the prerequisites of rational social action were completely described by prerequisite conditions here and now. Thus, if one requirement for rational social action in politico-economic life is some specified degree of co-ordination in government, which in turn requires a particular relationship between executive and legislature, which in turn requires changes in the present structure of American political parties, which in turn require a two-party system in the South, which in a continued series of turns requires still more specific conditions ending in the requirement that the southern Democrats separate from the Democratic party, one could then predict success or failure in rational social action.

Of course no one can go this far in the statement of prerequisites. No one can either follow any one chain of conditions back to here-and-now or discover the great number of alternative chains, any one of which is a sufficient prerequisite for rationality. But the social sciences have come to a point at which the construction of the chains may be begun, and it will not be the least of the efforts of this book to show where the chains break off, where they interlock, and the location of many missing links.

Because social action is rational or irrational depending upon whether it achieves the ultimate ends toward which it is directed, we shall have to postulate a number of social goals. Beyond that, however, the analysis of prerequisites is a scientific, not a moral, inquiry. It proceeds through the statement of functional or conditional relationships, through description rather than prescription. Descriptive theoretical propositions may cover all imaginable functional relationships pertinent to politico-economic organization; or they may be limited to those descriptive propositions where, in the cause-effect relationship, the effect is desirable because it is either a postulated goal or a means to its achievement. These latter subsequent goals are sometimes called normative descriptive propositions. The prerequisites of rational politico-economic action are stated as normative propositions; but they are arrived at, of course, through descriptive generalizations of other kinds.

Economists will recognize this approach as that of welfare economics, illustrated in Pigou's classic *Economics of Welfare*[23] and in a recently growing literature.[24] We are here undertaking a political economy of welfare, related in aim to the economics of welfare but attempting an integration of economics and political science in the statement of the politico-economic conditions of welfare. We also hope to accomplish some fruitful integration of economic and political theory in the theoretical apparatus employed to arrive at these conditions.

CONCEPT OF PLANNING

In one useful literal meaning of the term, planning is an attempt at rationally calculated action to achieve a goal. The attempt to achieve rational politico-economic action may therefore be described as economic planning whether the attempt employs the market or master mind. But economic planning thus conceived is so different from economic planning as, say, Hayek[25] or Jewkes[26] or Landauer[27] use the term that we shrink from what would otherwise be a convenient shorthand expression. Although we shall consequently use the term only when the risk of misinterpretation is at a minimum, the argument of the book may be thought of as an approach to a new concept of planning.

A good purpose is to be served by reclaiming a useful concept such as planning from the fires of sterile controversy. Whether one

---

[23] Arthur C. Pigou, *Economics of Welfare* (4th ed.), The Macmillan Company, New York, 1938.

[24] For example, Melvin W. Reder, *Studies in the Theory of Welfare Economics*, Columbia University Press, New York, 1947; Paul A. Samuelson, *Foundations of Economic Analysis*, Harvard University Press, Cambridge, 1947; I. M. D. Little, *A Critique of Welfare Economics*, Oxford University Press, New York, 1950; Kenneth J. Arrow, *Social Choice and Individual Values*, John Wiley and Sons, New York, 1951.

[25] F. A. Hayek, *op. cit.*

[26] John Jewkes, *op. cit.*

[27] Karl Landauer, *op. cit.*

likes it or not, words are sometimes the masters of men; and no small part of the barrenness of the controversy over planning is due to man's confusion of the attempt to be rational with the forms the attempts sometimes take simply because the word "planning" has been used to describe both. If the word is rehabilitated, so also is the analysis of the process. The gain is not merely terminological.

THE SEQUENCE OF THE ANALYSIS

The architecture of this book, it is fair to warn the reader, is rather like that of a pyramid or a cone. The early chapters are concerned with assumptions and social processes of great breadth and comprehensiveness that form the foundation for the rest. In moving from one set of chapters to another, the scope narrows. The final chapters, then, deal most specifically with alternative politico-economic techniques.

INDIVIDUAL GOALS AND SOCIAL ACTION. The analysis begins in the immediately following chapter with an examination of goals, ends or values by which social action in the politico-economic area can be appraised. Goals are postulated that will command wide agreement so that the dispute over goals themselves will be minimized in the subsequent analysis of the politico-economic prerequisites for the achievement of these goals.

THE TWIN SOCIAL PROCESSES OF CALCULATION AND CONTROL. To determine the prerequisites of rational politico-economic action, we can by no means jump directly to techniques. Rational social action requires processes for both rational *calculation* and effective *control*. Neither of them is simple. One immediately apparent difficulty in the processes for achieving rational calculation is that men do not wish to be rational in all particular choices and are not necessarily irrational for this feeling. Analysis of rational social action must come to grips immediately with limitations on man's capacity for rational calculation, and his preferences for the irrational and nonrational, as well as with the basic social processes through which he can calculate rationally when he wishes to do so. Only thereafter is it possible to spell out the requirements of rational calculation in economic life.

Similarly we must work slowly down from the general requirements of any system of social control to the more particular requirements of politico-economic controls and to prerequisite techniques. This is a long and difficult road to travel. But sociology, anthropology, and psychology have greatly contributed in recent years to the sophistication of man's knowledge of the basic processes by which men control each other. It is now possible to see that many of the venerable disputes over the possibilities of rational social action, over the possibilities of planning, misconceive the processes of control. Hence, painstaking attention to these processes is immediately rewarding in the controversies it brings to a close. Beyond that, an understanding of the processes of control gives us the beginning of an analytical apparatus for organizing the subsequent analysis.

To begin with these two basic social processes of calculation and control is to begin a long way from prices, markets, corporations, administrative agencies, war production boards, and the other institutions of politico-economic life. But the potentialities both for rational social action to achieve the postulated goals and for blundering into George Orwell's *1984* are rooted in the very elements of social organization common to all social techniques.

THE SOCIAL PROCESS OF ECONOMIZING.   Once the twin processes of calculation and control have been examined, the analysis can be focused on economic activity. For economic activity—the economizing process—is calculation and control with respect to the use of labor and other resources in production. It turns out that the economizing process is distinguished from other calculation-*cum*-control processes because of peculiarities in the kinds of calculations required for economizing.

FOUR CENTRAL SOCIOPOLITICAL PROCESSES.   These peculiarities throw great light on the role of the *price system* as a control and calculation mechanism. This is important because the appropriate role of the price system as a central sociopolitical process becomes a subject for persistent inquiry throughout the remainder of the book. But the circumstances in which the price system is an appropriate process for rational social action in the politico-economic area—in short, for economizing—can be stated only if the alternatives to it are well understood. Consequently the analysis proceeds to an investigation of three other central sociopolitical processes which in different combinations embrace the major possibilities for rational control: *hierarchy, polyarchy,* and *bargaining.*

Processes for calculation and control are in large part processes involving relations of leaders and non-leaders, whether these leaders be government officials or businessmen. Hierarchy is a process in which leaders control non-leaders. One of its most familiar forms is bureaucracy, and everyone recognizes how critical the functioning of bureaucracy is to rational politico-economic action. Polyarchy is a process, sometimes called democracy, in which non-leaders control leaders. The possibilities of economizing are obviously tied up with the effectiveness of this process. Bargaining is a process in which leaders control each other. The American system of checks and balances is a bargaining process; so also is political control through the great pressure groups—business, labor, and agriculture. In a price system all these relations among leaders and non-leaders are found, but in a particular form.

POLITICO-ECONOMIC TECHNIQUES. Examination of the central sociopolitical processes finally makes it possible to turn to an appraisal of the appropriateness in particular circumstances and for particular purposes of the price mechanism as against the other three alternative processes for economizing, as well as to an investigation of the major alternative techniques which combine the four processes. Here, finally, we can come down to such relatively specific questions as, for example, the relative rationality of collective and market choices, the effect of mobilization and war on the appropriate techniques for economizing, and the bearing of ownership of industry on its control.[28]

CHANGING CAPACITIES FOR RATIONAL SOCIAL ACTION

In this book we can state the prerequisites of rational economizing only as we know them at the present time. But the prerequisites change as man's capacities and social techniques change. How fundamentally the possibilities for rationality change in a short time is illustrated in the difficulty most people now have in conceiving of war between, say, Great Britain and the United States or, for that matter, between any two democracies of western Europe. The last British-American war scare was the Venezuela crisis of 1895; since then war as a technique for resolving differences between these two countries has been discarded. The North Atlantic Treaty Organiza-

[28] The Analytical Table of Contents offers a more detailed outline of the analysis from beginning to end. The reader may find it helpful to refer to it from time to time. See also Diagram 6, p. 370 infra.

tion is further evidence of great changes in attitudes and social techniques; a few years ago it would have been impossible. Emerging
new possibilities must therefore not be neglected.

To be sure, new attitudes and techniques do not guarantee rationality; capacities for rationality change markedly both for good
and for bad. One of the most frightening aspects of Orwell's picture of 1984 is permanent war at the periphery of the geographical
areas controlled by the major power combinations; it is not impossible that Korea is the beginning of permanent war. In economic life
changes in the capacity for rationality are less dramatic than in the
field of international relations; yet they are both rapid and large, as
we have already seen. They constitute a potential both for achievement of our social goals and for catastrophe, a potential which is
changing even as we write this book.

2. *Ends and Means*

I. Introduction

WHY DISCUSS VALUES?

This book proposes to describe and analyze different politico-economic techniques, and to appraise them. If we were concerned only with description and analysis, we should have no need to discuss values. But to appraise, one needs criteria. What criteria do we propose?

The things men value are countless. Rational social action, economic planning, and economizing impinge upon an endless variety of these human values. For almost nothing human is alien to politico-economic organization. Yet most readers will probably agree that a small number of key values are peculiarly relevant to an appraisal of alternative techniques—values such as democracy, equality, freedom, and security. They are relevant because they are instrumental to a variety of other values, because they are highly ranked by many of us, and because they are the source of much of the controversy over the desirability of alternative politico-economic techniques. Every reader might construct a slightly different list of relevant values; but the values discussed in this chapter are values that most American and western European readers would also put on their own lists.

SOME INITIAL ASSUMPTIONS

Before the values to be used as criteria can be described, some bits of underbrush need to be cleared away.

In the first place, we do not attempt a demonstration of the ultimate "rightness" of the values we use as criteria. We do indicate a few consequences of acting on these values. But if a reader does not desire these consequences, nothing we say in this book is intended to convince him that he "ought" to subscribe to the values set forth here.

In this chapter our reasons for valuing, say, freedom for other people as well as ourselves are cast in the form of factual statements about the consequences of freedom for our own well-being and that of many others. An intense discussion is raging among contemporary philosophers as to whether "value" statements cast in any other form can have "meaning." Tempting as it is to enter this fierce battle, it is the kind of conflict in which one can only hope to avoid severe maiming by participating in full panoply or remaining a bystander. For present purposes it is more important that there be approximate agreement on the values to be maximized than on their ultimate philosophical explanation, defense, justification, or rationalization. Partly to emphasize our deliberate avoidance of philosophical battle, we shall often use the word "goals" instead of values.

Second, because these goals are to be used as criteria for judging among alternative politico-economic devices, it is important to describe them in operationally useful terms. Typically, philosophical propositions about values are not very useful for policy decisions. As everyone knows who has ever tried to provide operational definitions for the key values so commonly argued about in Western societies, the job is a staggering one. In what follows we have not always succeeded. Here is a frontier area between philosophers and social scientists that so far neither group seems to have mapped out at all adequately.

Third, we have deliberately avoided the language and concepts of natural rights. Readers who accept a natural rights doctrine may, however, find it useful to translate the values discussed in this chapter into their own language.

Fourth, there are some minor but troublesome questions of terminology. Value discussions are typically cast in a framework of "means" and "ends," and at various points in this book we also find it useful to employ conventional means-end terminology. But because most "ends" are themselves means in a lengthy chain of means-and-ends; because an end in one chain of means-ends may be a means in another chain of action; and because a means in one chain may be an end in another, sometimes the language of means-and-ends is slippery and cumbersome. In these cases we shall often find it convenient to distinguish "prime" and "instrumental" goals. A prime goal when attained is a direct source of satisfaction in itself; an instrumental goal, as the name implies, has value only because it facilitates the attainment of one or more prime goals.

No matter what language one employs, however, real life is

too complex for the simplicities of language. Thus in real life many goals that superficially appear to be instrumental are to some extent prime goals too; walking to the postbox to mail a letter is never purely instrumental to the man who enjoys walking. Then, too, many instrumental goals are easily converted into prime goals. The man who has a letter to mail may intend his walk to be purely instrumental, but without regard to his original intentions he may find himself enjoying the fresh air, the sun, the exercise, the activity on the streets. One of the most formidable problems of politics arises because with many people power is so easily converted from a goal that is mostly instrumental to one that provides enormous direct satisfactions, i.e., it is easily converted from an instrumental to a prime goal.

Fifth, although we place a high value on rational calculation in politico-economic affairs, we do not deprecate the need for a rich emotional life with frequent opportunity for uncalculated action, ignore the essential rationality of much unconscious behavior, assume a rationalistic psychology or philosophy, or exaggerate man's capacity for rational action. Rational calculation in social action is such a many-sided problem that the next chapter is entirely given over to an examination of some of its facets.

Sixth, the problem of appraising alternative techniques would be much simpler if a single value criterion were sufficient. But men have a multiplicity of goals. Even the intentionally short list of goals discussed in this chapter, although artificially limited as compared with real life, includes enough goals to create an immensely difficult problem of judgment. For the maximization of one goal frequently conflicts with the maximization of another or even numerous others. Hence, as will be shown later on, rational appraisal is usually a matter of calculating how much one is prepared to sacrifice some attainment of certain goals in order to attain other goals somewhat more fully. For reasons that will appear in later chapters, judgments of this kind are extraordinarily difficult. In some instances in this book, therefore, the application of the criteria to the facts elucidated is less rigorous than would be wished.

In the seventh place, however, the overwhelming bulk of this books consists of factual propositions, inferences from them, and such definitions as may be necessary for precision of language. Most of the book, that is to say, is intended to be empirical social science and not value statements. For in order to judge alternative politico-economic techniques it is first necessary to examine systematically how they operate and the consequences of their operation. Hence anyone who disagrees with the criteria or with the attempt to apply them will nevertheless find in this book a systematic, empirically grounded examination of the main politico-economic devices available to a modern industrial society.

One last point. Not everything can be said at once. This chapter is deliberately restricted to a few main points. The difficulties, the preconditions, the nuances, the complexities—in short, the meaning—of the goals discussed here will be developed only as the book proceeds.

II. Seven Basic Ends for Social Action

The important prime goals of human beings in Western societies include existence or survival, physiological gratifications (through food, sex, sleep, and comfort), love and affection, respect, self-respect, power or control, skill, enlightenment, prestige, aesthetic satisfaction, excitement, novelty, and many others.[1] These are the ultimate criteria by which we would like to test alternative politico-economic devices. But to use criteria of this kind would force one to a level of specificity that would require an encyclopedia of particular techniques.

On the other hand, there are seven goals that govern both the degree to which these prime goals of individuals are attained and the manner of deciding who is to attain his goals when individuals conflict in their goal seeking. For most of the seven, conventional names with extensive historical and emotional associations are at hand; and we shall use these conventional names despite the difficulty of dissociating them from the penumbra created by traditional usage. These seven instrumental goals are freedom, rationality, democracy, subjective equality, security, progress, and appropriate inclusion.

FREEDOM

The question of what one means by "freedom" is surely one of the most controversial in all human history. One man's idea of freedom is often another man's idea of slavery. In addition, almost everywhere the word "freedom" has come to have an entirely fa-

[1] Adapted from a list by Harold D. Lasswell, *Power and Personality*, W. W. Norton and Co., New York, 1948.

vorable meaning. However much people may quarrel over what they mean by freedom, they usually agree that it is entirely good and never bad. Any way we use the term is almost certain to seem arbitrary and wrong-headed to someone.

THE CONDITION OF FREEDOM. However, let us begin the other way around, not with a definition but with a conceivable condition for which a label is needed. The conceivable state of affairs is this: "the absence of obstacles to the realisation of desires."[2] There are, of course, some difficulties in measuring the extent to which this condition exists for any given individual in real life. One test—itself not easy to apply—is the extent to which an individual feels frustrated. The more his desires are blocked, the more frustrated he is likely to feel.

It is useful, too, to distinguish a subjective form of the condition from an objective one. Subjectively one may have a high expectation that his desires will be realized; from his subjective point of view no obstacles exist to block the realization of his desires until his expectations change. However, his expectations might be based on a false appraisal; an observer could therefore conclude that objectively obstacles do exist. It might also be useful to arrange "desires" along a continuum from conscious to unconscious; in any case, unconscious desires surely need to be included.

The condition being described can be maximized by removing obstacles, changing desires, or both. Thus a cripple might achieve his desire to walk by an operation that restored the use of his legs; or he might gradually give up his desire to walk; or like Franklin Roosevelt he might both remove obstacles to his mobility and shift his desires. Particularly since the Renaissance, Western civilization has been preoccupied with removing obstacles to desires; certain Oriental philosophies, on the other hand, are concerned with reducing the pressure of desires. We shall not attempt to determine whether one of these methods is preferable to the other.

It does not seem improper to label the condition we have been describing "freedom," as Bertrand Russell has done; this condition is, then, what we shall mean by freedom.[3]

[2] Bertrand Russell, "Freedom and Government," in Ruth Nanda Anshen (ed.), *Freedom, Its Meaning*, Harcourt, Brace and Co., New York, 1940, p. 251.

[3] This is also Barbara Wootton's definition, in *Freedom Under Planning*, University of North Carolina, Chapel Hill, 1945, pp. 4, 19. It is worth noting that of all the essays in the Ruth Nanda Anshen volume, *op. cit.*, only Russell's contains the same conception as ours—indicating the difficulty of using the word at all.

THREE DEFINITIONS REJECTED.   Perhaps the condition we label
freedom can be made clearer by distinguishing some meanings of
freedom we do *not* intend. First, there is the concept, widely prevalent at various times since the Greeks, that "freedom" consists of
certain more or less definite kinds of behavior that are sometimes
preferred by some people, but not always by all. Goal achievement
outside these bundles is not labeled freedom but something else—in
English, commonly "license."

Describing freedom as a limited bundle of activities has psychological roots in the favorable connotation of the word "freedom." For if freedom can only be good and not bad, then to restrain
the criminal is not to curtail his freedom. But such a definition is
useful only if it is relatively easy to agree on the contents of the
bundle. Yet the contents of the bundle are usually the main point in
the debate. Moreover, it is difficult to hold consistently to such a
definition; almost everyone will admit that he sometimes restrains
the freedom of others—children, for example—because their freedom may be bad for themselves or for other people. But if some
freedom is bad, one can no longer sensibly restrict the word to a
particular bundle of activities regarded as good.

Comparative anthropology also helps one to realize the shortcomings of this definition. For different societies taboo or encourage
quite different kinds of behavior. Yet to say that only they are free
who have the particular bundles of "liberties" defined by, say, nineteenth-century liberalism (or twentieth-century social democracy)
is to reduce the word to a mere equivalent for the goals of nineteenth-century liberalism (or twentieth-century social democracy).
Surely it is not very useful to define freedom in such a way that,
say, a primitive people holding their property in common, and
thereby deprived of the sacred "freedom" of the nineteenth century, is in that respect inevitably less free than our own. If different
individuals are molded by different cultures to feel frustrated by
common ownership in one society and by individual ownership in
another, it seems a sensible use of language to say that individuals in

---

In the same volume, R. M. MacIver criticizes many of the definitions we also ab-
jure but provides none of his own; see pp. 280 ff. Bronislaw Malinowski, although
seeking a scientific definition, denies that certain kinds of goal seeking, such as
"abuse of authority," are "freedom in its sociological sense"; see his *Freedom and
Civilization,* Roy Publishers, New York, 1944, p. 111. Actually, he uses "freedom"
in a normative sense, by definition good, and we cannot but feel that an otherwise excellent book is seriously weakened by a normative intrusion in the guise of
a scientific principle.

the one society achieve freedom through communal ownership
and individuals in the other do not.

A second and somewhat similar conception is based on the
"range" of choices open to the individual. If one individual has but
ten choices open to him and another has a thousand, the second
might be defined as "freer" than the first. But the weakness of such
a definition is obvious once it is reduced to psychological terms.[4]
For what if the first individual feels adequate opportunity to achieve
his goals among the ten choices, whereas the second feels frustrated
because the thousand choices are trivial?

But, it may be said, give one man ten choices, and then give another those ten and a thousand more—surely the latter must be
called freer? Here again: Individual wants vary, and among the
choices open to the second there may still be none that permit him
to approximate his goals.

There is, finally, a definition which except for its subjectivity
is in turn not unlike one by Montesquieu. One decides what is
"free" by first deciding what is "good." One does not feel coerced
in being deprived of the opportunity to act in a way that he feels
is morally bad. Only when one believes an action is morally right
and yet is frustrated in performing it does he lose his freedom.[5]
While this definition is much closer to ours than the others, it
nevertheless seems inadequate on psychological grounds. Frequently
one wishes to perform acts that are prohibited by the conscience
or superego; indeed this is one of the worst frustrations imaginable.
Let the conflict between desire and conscience grow great enough,
and the result is a neurosis. "It is hard to say whether a morbid
conscience is a worse enemy of life than a disease like cancer, but
some comparison of this kind is required to emphasize the shock
produced in the witness when he sees a psychiatric person being
tortured by a conscience."[6]

Hence it seems useful to define freedom as the absence of obstacles to the realization of desires. Subjective freedom is detected
by an absence of frustration; or, if frustrations are present, by the

[4] B. Malinowski, *op. cit.*, pp. 87–88.

[5] Frank H. Knight, *Freedom and Reform*, Harper & Brothers, New York,
1947, pp. 10–13. And cf. Montesquieu, *The Spirit of the Laws* (translated by
Thomas Nugent, revised by J. V. Prichard), D. Appleton and Co., New York,
1900: ". . . In societies directed by laws, liberty can consist only in the sense of
doing what we ought to will, and not being constrained to do what we ought not
to will."

[6] John Dollard and Neal E. Miller, *Personality and Psychotherapy*, McGraw-
Hill Book Co., New York, 1950, p. 141.

individual's expectation that he can make choices that will eliminate his frustrations. Objective freedom is tested by an observer's judgment as to whether an individual, when he is faced with choice situations which the observer expects to arise, will in fact make choices that will attain his desires.[7]

THREE LIMITS ON FREEDOM. Given this definition, it is clear that no one is ever "absolutely free," certainly not in the objective sense. For no one ever attains all his desires. More than that, in all probability no one can be entirely free in any predictable future. Individuals can only be relatively less free or relatively more free; it is this difference in degree that is relevant to appraisal, not the difference between relative and absolute freedom.

One set of limits on freedom is imposed by natural impossibilities, physical, physiological, technological, psychological. If it is a mark of the wise man that he does not wish for the impossible, one is not always wise or sure that what he wants is really impossible. Children, and adults who never outgrow their infantilisms, often want the impossible and thus are inherently and inescapably frustrated.

Second, there are usually conflicts among one's own goals. Thus optimum goal achievement requires one to give up some goals to attain others. Yet this optimum achievement may still leave a residue of frustration. One sees these conflicts daily. A man wants control over others and simultaneously their love and affection; yet he cannot have all he wants of both. At one extreme, some individuals sacrifice love and affection to power, and at the other, some sacrifice power to love and affection. Many attempt to strike a balance somewhere between the extremes. Yet even this balance may leave them moderately frustrated. A completely "adjusted" or "integrated" personality has probably never existed.

A special conflict among goals is imposed by time. One cannot do everything at once. Hence one needs to schedule his goal seeking. And this necessity often leads to bitter frustration.

From a social and political point of view, however, the third

---

[7] To use the absence of frustration or the expectation of frustration as a test for the presence of freedom assumes that frustration is a reciprocal of the realization of desires. It may be, however, that individuals with the same level of frustration may have different levels and intensities of desires, and to the extent that this is the case freedom must be measured both by the level of frustration and the level of satisfaction.

and most important limit on freedom is imposed by the activities of others. John Stuart Mill attempted to work out a formula for freedom that would have limited an individual's goal seeking "only" to the extent that it had adverse consequences for others. But the fact is, in an interdependent society nearly everything one does has *some* consequences for others. The fact of conflicts in goal seeking might be regarded as the fundamental political situation, the basic human condition that everywhere makes it necessary to develop social machinery through which to decide the outcome of such conflicts. Some men, like Hobbes, have argued that conflicts in goal seeking are inherently so great that only overwhelming force in the hands of a sovereign can maintain social peace; even the anarchists, who argue that conflicts are mostly a product of social institutions that can be altered, have tended to admit that the pressure of public opinion and admonition will still be necessary to resolve conflicts in their utopia.

TWO SPURIOUS LIMITS. What has just been said does not mean that there always is a conflict between individual freedom and social organization. It would be difficult to suggest a set of human goals that do not require a vast amount of human coöperation or interaction. Whether one hates or loves people, wishes to extend their freedom or enslave them, wants hierarchy or equality, football games or concentration camps, he cannot succeed in his aims without the coöperation of (or interaction with) others. The democrat, tyrant, liberal, socialist, communist, political boss, businessman, club leader, teacher, conspirator, criminal, the Politburo, the President of the United States, the Pope—all need the coöperation of many other people to achieve their goals. The need for coöperation to achieve goals is a basic fact of human existence.

A great many goals cannot be achieved unless coöperation (or interaction) is relatively stable, persistent, and repetitive. Where coöperation (interaction) among human beings is relatively stable, persistent, and repetitive, this network of interpersonal relations is a social *organization* (or, as it will usually be called in this book, simply an organization). To say that many goals require stable, persistent, and repetitive coöperation or interaction among human beings is therefore to say that some goals require social organizations; it is also to say that freedom requires social organization.

Nor is there always a conflict between individual freedom and social indoctrination. No intelligent person seriously questions the need for social *habituation* or training of "physical" responses; for it is perfectly clear that stable, persistent, and repetitive coöperation among individuals requires habits. Yet the same person who accepts the need for habituation often balks at the need for *social indoctrination* or training of responses in the realm of attitudes, ideas, beliefs, norms, codes, or ethical systems. For a person reared in the liberal democratic tradition is likely to feel that to indoctrinate an individual with a particular set of beliefs is somehow to rob him of his freedom of choice. (Paradoxically, one feels this way only when he himself has been socially indoctrinated with liberal democratic beliefs.)

Admittedly the relation between freedom and social indoctrination is a tricky one. But it is quite false to say that there is always a conflict between them. On the contrary, social organization always requires and always results in social indoctrination (and of course habituation). Hence, freedom requires social indoctrination.

Social organization, as everyone now knows, requires indoctrination because stable, persistent, and repetitive coöperation is impossible unless some of the responses of people who interact are more or less predictable by one another. Life would be a hopeless chaos without this predictability. Even the simplest relations among individuals would become desperately difficult.

To say the same thing in another way, individuals in social organizations must always make some choices among the many different alternatives that are potentially open to a human organism. For stable, persistent, and repetitive relations to exist among individuals, these individuals must make certain responses and avoid others when alternatives are open. Most organizations not merely require certain habitual responses that are often thought of as "physical" habits; they also require responses that are dependent on attitudes, ideas, beliefs, norms, or ethical codes. Hence if individuals are not taught the relevant attitudes, ideas, beliefs, norms, or ethical codes the organization will not achieve the goals of its members or of others whom it is intended to serve. Now to that extent, therefore, the freedom of these individuals is impaired, whereas successful social indoctrination in the appropriate attitudes would expand their freedom.

The case can be seen at its simplest in small primitive groups.

Among the Crow Indians, tribal organization rested upon a process of indoctrination that made possible exceptionally delicate techniques of social control. No one who had committed a serious breach of morality was ever directly punished. Instead, "in the evening, someone might call out to the whole group: 'Did you hear about so-and-so?' Then amid great laughter his transgression would be commented upon in terms of the most scathing ridicule, and this might go on for a long time. The transgressor would be so shamed by the laughter of his fellows that he might even be driven to leave the community and not return until he had in some way redeemed himself."[8]

However, lest the reader think that the phenomenon is confined only to primitive tribes, here are three additional examples. First, democratic government can operate only if (among a variety of other necessary kinds of indoctrination) leaders and non-leaders are indoctrinated with the conviction that officials must leave office when they fail to win a plurality of votes in elections. Second, as Weber and Tawney have shown, a competitive price system as a form of human organization requires indoctrination in attitudes quite different from the ones widely held in the Middle Ages; indeed, as Karl Polanyi has pointed out, for most of man's history and over most of the earth's surface, attitudes incompatible with the competitive price system (or self-regulating market) have been indoctrinated by societies.[9] Third, the operation of the British civil service rests upon a number of processes of social indoctrination that result in unimpeachable honesty, sense of duty, neutrality, and discipline within the service, and exceptionally high status in the society as a whole. The fact that administration, like politics, was originally a prerogative of the aristocracy; that civil service reform took place during the Victorian period; that admission to the civil service was carefully contrived to recruit the honors men of Oxford and Cambridge; that Oxford and Cambridge were aristocratic schools which in turn recruited their students from preparatory schools with the severe and exacting codes typical of many aristocracies—these all helped to engender a process of indoctrination that persists despite the disappearance of some of the historical causes.

[8] Otto Klineberg, *Social Psychology*, Henry Holt and Co., New York, 1940, pp. 192–193.
[9] Karl Polanyi, *The Great Transformation*, Rinehart and Co., New York, 1944.

WHY DESIRE FREEDOM?   A preference for freedom logically should be stated as a preference for the highest possible degree of freedom; i.e., more freedom is preferable to less. There are, of course, innumerable ambiguities even in this qualified statement. For example, should individuals be considered as equals in their claims to more freedom? Does "more freedom" mean that a few individuals should have a great deal more freedom if that decision deprives a great many individuals each of a little freedom? Some of the ambiguities seem all but irremovable.[10] And because there is no entirely satisfactory operational test to measure the degree of freedom possessed by an individual or a group, abstract answers to many questions about freedom would be of very little use in appraising real-life alternatives. Nevertheless, not only in the rest of this chapter but throughout this book we shall try to unravel some of the complexities in the theory and practice of freedom.

But why propose freedom as a goal? Because almost everyone wishes to reduce the obstacles to his desires; by definition almost everyone wants some freedom for himself. But why should one want freedom for others? Some theorists of ruthless egoism, like the obscure anarchist Max Stirner, who based all morality on the individual's search for freedom, assert that freedom consists in the ruthless pursuit of egoistic goals with no consideration for other human beings.[11] Although the case is rarely put so bluntly, there is an underlying similarity in many defenses of "individualism." Yet any such theory is nonsense because it is based, first, upon entirely false psychological assumptions, and second, upon a crude strategic miscalculation.

Most human beings do not even want to ignore the consequences of their actions for everyone else. Without his permission everyone is born into a society of other people on whom he is, at first, inescapably dependent. In his early years almost all his gratifications ultimately require the responses of someone around him. One becomes human in spite of himself. He develops deep emotional needs for the love, affection, and respect of at least some other people; he develops the need also to convey his own love, affection, and respect to others. However distorted, perverted, and

---

[10] The difficulties are illustrated in the essays by the distinguished contributors to the volume edited by Ruth Nanda Anshen, *op. cit.*

[11] See Philip Taft, *Movements for Economic Reform*, Rinehart and Co., New York, 1950, pp. 101–102.

tortured the expression of these needs becomes, few people—except perhaps certain extreme psychotics—ever lose them entirely.

As these needs develop, in quite varying degrees two other responses are acquired. The mechanisms are not well understood, but they prevent most people from striving to be the ruthless egoists of a philosophical abstraction. One is identification; the second is sympathy. Because of identification and sympathy we, at least, want others to enjoy freedom. In the actual or imaginative presence of individuals who are suffering, unhappy, discontented, frustrated in their goal seeking, we, too, feel uneasiness, anxiety, guilt, and a wish that they might achieve their goals. There are distinct limits, to be sure. Hence, we do not trust too much in the identification and sympathy of others to protect our freedoms.

Furthermore, naked egoism is a poor strategic calculation for most people. One's own goal achievement may be impaired in a society that is not organized to provide a large measure of freedom for most of the other members. Absence of freedom means frustration, frustration means discontent and hostility, discontent and hostility may mean recurring violence, instability, irrationality, destructiveness, which in turn may threaten one's own goal achievements. Or alternatively, absence of freedom may mean a kind of barren passivity[12] in social life, a decline in productivity, originality, progress, spontaneity, which will react adversely on our own freedoms.

Admittedly, the data on which people make this strategic calculation are fragmentary; to choose freedom for others is at best a calculated risk; but for all that, one cannot avoid choosing, and the odds seem to us to be on the side of freedom not merely for ourselves but for others in our society as well.

[12] Lippitt and White's well-known experiments with "authoritarian," "democratic," and "laissez faire" boys' groups revealed two kinds of group reaction to "authoritarian" leadership: one was aggression, but the other was such a low level of aggressive activity as to suggest inertness and passivity. See R. Lippitt and Kurt Lewin, "An Experimental Study of the Effect of Democratic and Authoritarian Group Atmospheres," in Lewin, Lippitt, and Escalona, *Studies in Topological and Vector Psychology*, Part I, University of Iowa Studies in Child Welfare, XVI, No. 3, 1940; see also "The Social Climate of Children's Groups," in Roger G. Barker, Jacob S. Kounin, and Herbert F. Wright, *Child Behavior and Development*, McGraw-Hill Book Co., New York, 1943, pp. 485–508. The two experiments by R. Lippitt and by R. Lippitt and R. K. White are referred to by Kurt Lewin in his *Resolving Social Conflicts* (edited by Gertrud Weiss Lewin), Harper & Brothers, New York, 1948; the original report was Kurt Lewin and R. K. White, "Patterns of Aggressive Behavior in Experimentally Created Social Climates," *Journal of Social Psychology*, May, 1939.

Quite clearly, these arguments for the freedom of others cannot be universally persuasive. If one's goals included violence, instability, irrationality, and destructiveness; if one's capacity for identification and sympathy is seriously deformed; if instead one has an overpowering want for power and cruelty—such a person would hardly find persuasive the arguments we have given for wanting freedom for others.

But to people of this kind no arguments for freedom can be persuasive. If they are not persuaded that their own basic human needs and strategic calculations require the freedom of others, then it is unlikely they would be persuaded by the addition of theological or metaphysical considerations seeking to prove that freedom is "good." And if our argument is correct, most readers will not need additional validation of the desirability of freedom. In any case, as we warned at the beginning, we do not propose to push our inquiry on values to an examination of the "ultimate" philosophical grounds, if there are such, on which freedom might be defended as a value.

RATIONALITY

MEANING AND MEASUREMENT OF RATIONALITY. To maximize freedom one must remove obstacles to desires, or adjust desires, or both. These actions frequently require rational calculation and control. This statement seems obvious on its face; and yet, so complex is social reality that the next two chapters must be devoted to exploring the meaning of rational calculation and control in social action.

But first, what do we mean by "rationality"? And how can one test whether one action is more rational than another? The first question is easier to answer than the second. An action is rational to the extent that it is "correctly" designed to maximize goal achievement, given the goal in question and the real world as it exists. Given more than one goal (the usual human situation), an action is rational to the extent that it is correctly designed to maximize *net* goal achievement. When several actions are required to attain goals, rationality requires *coördination*; that is, the actions must be scheduled and dovetailed so that net goal achievement is not diminished by avoidable conflicts among the actions.

If a man is cold and wishes to be warm, it is rational for him to stand a few feet away from a fire. With a unanimity possible on very few questions, almost every adult in the world would agree that it would be irrational for him to jump in the fire or to flee from it. Indeed, assuming one could find out enough about the man's reactions, most people could probably agree on the precise point where it was most rational for him to stand. Yet each individual, wanting a different amount of warmth, might find a slightly different spot more rational for himself.

In such a simple case, it is easy to find satisfactory answers to both our questions. However, although the meaning remains stable and clear enough, the more complex a situation becomes, the more difficult it is to distinguish the more rational action from the less rational. To agree whether one action is more rational than another, observers must agree on the goals involved, their assumptions about reality, and the consequence for goal achievement of certain alternative courses of action given the assumed reality. In the case of the man and the fire, there probably is well-nigh universal understanding of the goal (warmth), the bearing of reality (the fire, the man's body, etc.) on that goal, and the consequences of alternative acts. But data on these three points are often inadequate or difficult to comprehend; hence they are frequently arguable questions.

EFFICIENCY. The more rational action is also the more efficient action. The two terms can be used interchangeably. Stripped of prejudicial inferences, efficiency is the ratio between valued input and valued output. If the desire is to minimize gas consumption and there are no other relevant goals or consequences, a motor that gives twenty miles to the gallon of gas is more efficient than one that gives but fifteen. Just as it is more efficient to use the first motor than the second, by definition it is more rational. An action is rational, as we defined it earlier, to the extent that it is correctly designed to maximize net goal satisfaction, given the goals in question and the real world as it exists. But an action is "correctly" designed to maximize goal satisfaction to the extent that it is efficient, or in other words to the extent that goal satisfaction exceeds goal cost.

Some words of warning about the word "efficiency" are, however, in order. The term has acquired some popular meanings for which there is little sensible defense. Perhaps its widespread use in engineering and business accounts for a popular tendency to define the efficient only in terms of some but not *all* costs and outputs— usually exclusively in terms of those costs and outputs measurable either in physical or in monetary sums. But it is quite clear from what we have said that, if there are *any* valued inputs and outputs— any goal costs and goal satisfactions—that cannot be measured in physical or monetary sums, one simply cannot regard an action measured exclusively by these quantitative symbols as "efficient." If, for example, people place a relatively high value on leisure, leisurely work habits, and workplace conviviality, and a relatively low value on quantitative output, one cannot say that a group of people working according to a leisurely pace and producing a small output is necessarily less efficient than one working at a stiff pace and producing a large output.

ECONOMIZING AS A FORM OF RATIONALITY.   Economizing is rational action in economic life, more particularly in the employment of certain kinds of resources. Alternatively, economizing is the process of arriving at the most efficient employment of these resources to satisfy human desires.[13] It is this form of rationality, of course, that is the central focus of this book.

WHY DESIRE RATIONAL ACTION?   To ask why one values rational action is to demand an almost redundant answer. If one wishes to maximize his freedom or that of others—if, that is to say, he wishes to achieve more of his goals rather than less or wishes others to achieve more of their goals rather than less—then logically he must prefer the more rational, efficient, and economical action to the less rational, efficient, and economical action. For by definition the more rational, efficient, and economical action leads to more net goal achievement.

Perhaps it would be wise to repeat at this point our earlier warning that a commitment to rationality as a goal should not be taken as a commitment to an emotionally thin, desiccated, calculated, and excessively cerebral existence. A satisfying emotional life seems to require opportunity for impulsiveness, spontaneity, the direct expression of "animal spirits" (the human spirit, some might say), risk taking without calculation of the consequences, joy, fun, anger. The most rational act is not necessarily the most carefully calculated one.

[13] Herbert A. Simon, Donald W. Smithburg, and Victor A. Thompson distinguish "efficiency" from rationality substantially as we have just distinguished "economizing," in *Public Administration*, Alfred A. Knopf, New York, 1950, pp. 490 ff.

DEMOCRACY

Because different individuals frequently conflict in their effort to achieve their goals, that is to say, in the attempt to maximize their freedom, a general commitment to freedom is almost meaningless. For the important questions begin to arise when one asks, "Whose freedom?" To say "The freedom of myself and others" takes one only a very little way. For suppose your freedom conflicts with the freedom of someone else? What principles and methods for adjudicating that conflict are you committed to? Democracy is a principle and a method for adjudicating such conflicts.

The democratic goal is twofold. It consists of a condition to be attained and a principle guiding the procedure for attaining it. The condition is political equality, which we define as follows: *Control over governmental decisions is shared so that the preferences of no one citizen are weighted more heavily than the preferences of any other one citizen.* The principle is majority rule, which we define as follows: *Governmental decisions should be controlled by the greater number expressing their preferences in the "last say."*

Democracy is a goal, not an achievement. The main sociopolitical process for approximating (although not achieving) democracy we shall call polyarchy. The characteristics of polyarchy, its prerequisites, and its significance as a device for rational social action on economic matters are discussed in a later chapter. If democracy is one of our goals and if polyarchy is a process for approximating that goal, it follows that we must also value polyarchy as a means. But here we are concerned with the democratic goal itself.

THE CONDITION OF POLITICAL EQUALITY. Before turning to the reasons why one might support this goal, let us make quite certain of its meaning by a few distinctions. Note, to begin with, that we are talking only about control over "governmental" decisions. It does not logically follow that by urging this goal for governments one must also propose it for all other human organizations. In a family with two parents and three small children, in military organizations, in administrative agencies the condition of political equality would often lead to disaster. The fact is, everyone has goals that certain specialized organizations are intended to serve. These goals cannot always be attained by organizations based on political equality. Consequently, in order to attain one's goals, one will forgo political equality within these organizations. Thus, paradoxical as it sometimes seems to the doctrinaire democrat, hierarchical organizations are also necessary for freedom.

Why, then, is political equality significant in *governments*— that is, in organizations that have a sufficient monopoly of control to enforce an orderly settlement of disputes with other organizations in the area?[14] Precisely because whoever controls government usually has the "last word" on a question; whoever controls government can enforce decisions on other organizations in the area. Thus so long as the condition of political equality is approximated, citizens can always decide in what situations and in what organizations they wish to tolerate hierarchy in order to achieve goals that cannot be satisfied by organization on an equalitarian basis. The condition of political equality assigns to the electorate the position of an ultimate court of appeal to decide where else in society the condition of equality may be enforced or forgone.

WHY POLITICAL EQUALITY IS DESIRABLE.   But why should one urge the goal of political equality? Why, in the "court of last appeal," does one want the preferences of no citizen to be weighted more heavily than the preferences of any other citizen? At the very least does not any individual prefer a situation in which *his own* preferences are counted more heavily in governmental decisions? As in the case of freedom, the grounds are the psychological and strategic consequences of political equality.

First, with us, at least, sympathetic identification with other people produces feelings of guilt, anxiety, and distress when we realize that they have significantly less opportunity than we to satisfy their preferences. Presumably many other individuals share this response. Admittedly such feelings are no more an inherent part of "human nature" than are preferences for hierarchy or dictatorship. They are products of an interplay between personality and culture. But they are no less distressing for all that.

A negative support for political equality that supplements the positive feeling of sympathetic identification is the intellectual difficulty of finding any rational basis for concluding that the preferences of some people *should* be counted more heavily in the process

---

[14] All short definitions of government are inherently ambiguous. Throughout this book we use the conventional meaning, according to which the uniformed policeman on the corner is "government" and the night watchman employed by a private concern is not.

of government than the preferences of others. Like sympathetic identification, this intellectual difficulty is culturally inspired. In other times, in other societies, it was "obvious" that some kinds of people should dominate others. But deliberate, self-conscious inquiry into the grounds of authority, aided by modern anthropology, sociology, and psychology, has undermined the persuasiveness of such customary criteria as class, ethnic group, and ethical superiority.

Even in an equalitarian culture, however, by no means everyone feels this sympathetic identification or intellectual compulsion. Yet even in the absence of these feelings a second vital reason for seeking the condition of political equality is a strategic calculation. Like so many important decisions, this one, too, is a calculated risk. Reduced to its boldest terms, our strategy comes to this: we cannot be confident of continued membership in an elite group whose preferences would be counted for more rather than less.

And, as one sees more of the consequences of dictatorship with each passing year, the more plausible this choice becomes; for although almost everyone can imagine inequalitarian utopias of considerable attractiveness, given the social techniques, problems, and human beings of the twentieth century the alternatives are rather narrowly restricted.

The goal of political equality might be justified, too, on theological and metaphysical grounds. But we leave this task to those who find such arguments persuasive and meaningful. Fortunately, those who wish to act in concert to achieve political equality do not need to agree on the reasons why they prefer political equality to its alternatives.

THE PRINCIPLE OF MAJORITY RULE. If political equality is a goal to be striven for, then a means to it is majority rule in the "last say" in governmental decisions. Of course political equality is never attained in the real world, nor does a majority of political equals ever rule even in the complex social process we call polyarchy—the real-world approximation of democracy.[15] Consequently individuals who agree on the goal of political equality often disagree as to the particular political arrangements or even the constitutional setting that will most nearly approximate majority rule given the actual fact of political inequality in the real world. Many arguments that seem

[15] See Chapters 10 and 11, *infra.*

to be disputes over the desirability of political equality and majority rule are really differences over how these democratic goals can be most closely approximated in a given hypothetical or actual situation. This is a very ticklish empirical and theoretical question, particularly in the United States with its peculiar diversities and political traditions, and we defer it to later chapters. But first it is important to know what it is that we wish to approximate.

How can political equals indicate their preferences on government policy? How can they have the "last word" as political equals? One way is by implicit or explicit voting. But in situations other than unanimity, whose votes should prevail? To say that the votes of the greater number should not prevail is to say that political equality is impossible, or that it is undesirable, or both. Political equality may be "impossible" in one of two senses: that it can never be precisely attained, or that it cannot even be closely enough approximated to constitute a relevant human goal. As a later chapter will show, the first appears to be true, the second false. Assuming that political equality is "impossible" in the sense that it can never be precisely attained, but assuming further that political equality can nevertheless be approximated, to deny the principle of majority rule is then to deny that political equality is desirable.

For unless government policy responds to the preferences of the greater number, the preferences of some individuals (the lesser number) must be weighted more heavily than the preferences of some other individuals (the greater number). But to weight preferences in this way is to reject the goal of political equality.

IS MAJORITY RULE REALLY DESIRABLE?   Mere logical inference is not always persuasive. If majority rule is one logical consequence of political equality, do we still prefer that goal as we have stated it? What if our own goals conflict with those of the greater number? Are we willing to take this chance?

To answer is to restate what has already been said. First, sympathetic identification can make one desire others to achieve their goals even when they conflict with certain specific goals of one's own. But in many cases sympathetic identification is weak and desire for specific goals is strong. Here the strategic calculation comes into play. On the whole, even if some rather highly ranked goals were denied one by the greater number, he might still conclude that conflict with the goal seeking of the greater number is less likely than conflict with any smaller number that as a practical matter in the United States is likely to rule.

A commitment to democracy in these terms is, to be sure, always contingent upon what the democracy does. But even those who have grounded democracy on other assumptions than ours have rarely seen fit to argue that one must acquiesce in every democratic decision no matter what consequences a decision might produce. Rousseau called for a right to emigrate. In at least one case, that of the Alien and Sedition Acts, Jefferson flirted with nullification. Should a majority ever unmistakably prefer a governmental policy that clearly violated the fundamental preferences of even the most loyal democrat, he would be faced by a choice of alternatives for which the theory of democracy cannot, by itself, provide an answer. Possible alternatives are revolution and minority rule, passive disobedience, secession, limited confederation, emigration, concealment, passive acquiescence, shift in goals, cynicism, hope for future change—or what not.

But the vital point is this: Our observations (however impressionistic these must be) of the goals sought by large numbers of people in the United States suggest that our goals and those of the greater number are not likely to be in such fundamental conflict as to force us to seek an alternative to the goal of political equality and the derivative goal of majority rule. To be sure, because we choose among probabilities and not among certainties, it is possible that goals such as ours might be better achieved by a non-democratic government. But we see little evidence that this is the case.

Democracy is a calculated risk. Yet its operation and precondition require the growth of institutions, the acquisition of deeply rooted habits, stability over time. Men cannot change governmental institutions as they shift gears in an automobile. Hence even a contingent commitment to democracy implies a commitment to all the durable and not easily altered social processes that help to approximate it: traditions, social indoctrination in the value of democracy, a widely accepted prescribed and operating constitution, deeply rooted rights and duties. A decision to support democracy is contingent, but it is not something to be put on and off like a garment.

SUBJECTIVE EQUALITY

In searching for goals useful as criteria for appraising alternative politico-economic techniques, so far we have set forth three—

freedom, rationality, and democracy—on which a great many intelligent citizens of western societies could no doubt quickly agree. But what of equality "in general"? Is this also an appropriate criterion for judging the consequences of alternative techniques?

WHAT IT IS.   Although there is no *necessary* connection between the argument for political equality and the goal of general equality, our own preference for political equality is based upon a psychological want and a strategic calculation that may well be applicable to general equality. But unfortunately, general equality is almost impossible to define. For example, one might want to call the following the condition of objective equality. *All objects of preference are distributed on an equal basis to all individuals.* But this would be an irrational rule for maximizing each individual's goal achievement. For not all individuals have the same preferences. If people were left to their own devices, they would no doubt prefer to redistribute the objects so that each would tend to get those he wanted most and lose those he wanted least.

The heart of the matter is whether one wants individuals (adults) to have equal freedom so far as is humanly possible. A commitment to freedom has little meaning until this question is answered; for does one mean the freedom of one to exploit many, or the equal freedom of all, or some alternative different from either of these?

The goal postulated here and called the condition of subjective equality is unavoidably ambiguous, but perhaps it is best stated in this way: *The condition of subjective equality exists wherever, in any specific situation in which more people rather than less can have the opportunity to achieve their goals, the decision is for the greater number rather than for any lesser number.*

Some of the inevitable ambiguities of this goal will become clearer in later chapters. Yet even if the application of this principle to specific circumstances is one of the most formidable challenges to man's wit and social techniques that he could set for himself, its meaning is clear enough to serve as a general guide, a "set" of mind, a controlling attitude. It is clear that subjective equality is incompatible with wide differences not merely in wealth and income but in education, housing, medical care, control, respect, status, and dignity. Admittedly there are numerous technical difficulties in securing a more equalitarian distribution of items like these; but a genuine commitment to subjective equality as a goal is a constant challenge to the imagination, resourcefulness, knowledge, and drive needed to overcome the barriers.

THE CRITERIA OF WELFARE ECONOMICS. Economists may ask why we do not postulate the criteria used in welfare economics as guides to distribution of values. One common criterion is the "maximization of want satisfaction," according to which an optimum is achieved when no further shifting around of the distribution of values will benefit anyone more that it harms someone else. This criterion is not satisfactory for our purposes for at least two reasons: First, it formally defines a kind of optimum without throwing any light on what the important values are. Second, even if one can compare A's gain with B's loss, it does not follow that a gain for A is worth achieving only if it is greater than B's loss. Whether it is worth achieving depends upon who A is, what the values are, and what the previous distribution of values was. In some cases it is desirable that A and B have equal claims on values, but not always.

A second criterion has been developed in an attempt to avoid the necessity for interpersonal comparisons of frustrations, satisfactions, intensities of feeling, or utilities. Roughly, an optimum is defined as a condition in which no one can be benefited without harming someone. In other words, if no one is harmed by a change in the distribution of values, and someone is benefited, the change is desirable. The defect of this criterion is not that it is useless (both criteria are extremely useful for particular purposes) but that it can be applied only in a limited number of cases, because most gains are in fact offset by losses to someone.[16]

WHY SEEK SUBJECTIVE EQUALITY? As with democracy, so the struggle for subjective equality is a risk one takes on the evidence that he will achieve a variety of his goals more fully in a society of equals than in a society of unequals. For one thing, sympathetic identification may lead to deep feelings of distress, anxiety, and guilt if those with whom one identifies are notably more frustrated in their goal seeking than he is himself, particularly if one knows he could help to remove some of the obstacles to their goal seeking.

[16] For a discussion of these criteria, see I. M. D. Little, *A Critique of Welfare Economics*, Oxford University Press, New York, 1950.

As we have already said, however, the way in which one identifies with others is evidently a product of learning; many people do
not feel much sense of identification with depressed individuals or
groups. Indeed, it is a good hypothesis that in highly inegalitarian,
class- or caste-ridden societies, the mechanism of identification actually protects inequalities. For individuals in one class learn to identify among themselves but not with individuals in another class; this
class identification limits the guilt felt by an upper class toward an
inferior and the envy felt by an inferior class toward upper classes.

A second and perhaps more substantial reason for wanting
subjective equality is a strategic calculation. One cannot be at all
sure that he would be among the elite to whom the advantages of
inequality would accrue; or even if he could, the resulting frustrations and tensions in the society might soon lead to a pervasive insecurity, instability, hostility, and revenge seeking that would deprive one of far more than would a general condition of equality.
To be sure, one can imagine a hierarchical society with a high degree of agreement and mutual respect. But given the social techniques available in modern American society and the demands and
expectations of American citizens, this seems highly unlikely. Again,
the practical alternatives are more narrowly limited than the range
suggested by an uncritical survey of historical or utopian alternatives.

LIMITS TO SUBJECTIVE EQUALITY.   Nevertheless one must recognize limits to the goal. For one thing, there are inherent limits imposed by the difficulty of defining very clearly what subjective
equality would be. Given individual differences, capacities, and
preferences plus the play of accident and luck, the problem of describing a condition of subjective equality with any precision is, as
we have just shown and as we shall show again later, all but impossible.

But in addition to these inherent limits there is the plain fact
that complete attainment of the condition of subjective equality
may conflict with a number of other goals. At some point, therefore, the margin of more equality is less preferable than heightened
achievement of other goals. For example, one might well prefer
more things distributed somewhat unequally to significantly fewer
distributed equally. This preference would not necessarily be irrational even if one were near the bottom of the heap.

Then, too, a minimum level of agreement, as will be shown later, is a prerequisite for polyarchy; polyarchy is a prerequisite for approximating the democratic goal. If rapid achievement of subjective equality threatens agreement, at some point it may prove desirable to put the brakes on equality rather than annihilate social agreement. Moreover, social techniques are often crude and frequently replete with undesirable and unanticipated consequences. Yet more sensitive techniques may conflict with subjective equality. Thus if subjective equality could be completely achieved only by destroying the price system and substituting some cruder and less sensitive method of allocating resources—as seems likely—the advantages of retaining the price system far outweigh any possible gains from the attempt to establish subjective equality by rather crude social techniques whose consequences cannot be entirely anticipated.

SECURITY

It is sometimes said that security is at war with freedom. But given any useful definition of the two terms, this assertion cannot be true. For when is an individual secure? Here again it is helpful to distinguish a subjective and an objective condition. Subjectively, one is secure to the extent that he has a high or confident expectation that he will continue to have opportunities to achieve his goals. To an observer, one is objectively secure if, in the observer's view, one's confident expectation is based on a correct view of reality. To the extent that one feels fear and anxiety, he is insecure. No one is, of course, ever entirely secure.

Are freedom and security at war then? Obviously not. On the contrary, if we have properly defined security, then security and freedom are much the same thing; security is merely an aspect of freedom. A free individual is secure, and a secure individual is free. For if one cannot achieve his goals, he is neither free nor secure; and if one can achieve his goals, he is both free and secure.

Is there no difference between freedom and security? The difference is one of emphasis only. To speak of security is to emphasize that one is or expects to be free *over time*. But since this emphasis is already implicit in our definition of freedom, it is correct to say that security is merely an aspect or mode of freedom. It is a useful word to employ in discussing the likelihood that the freedoms of some individual or group will persist over some period of time.

Because security, as a mode of freedom, depends upon an interplay between desires and obstacles, one must never forget that both sides of the equation are equally important. In keeping with its emphasis on achieving freedom by removing external obstacles, Western civilization has been preoccupied with environmental threats to security of a somewhat impersonal sort; these, the obvious and easiest obstacles to deal with, have been the focus of government policies—workmen's compensation, old-age pensions, unemployment insurance, health insurance, police systems, sanitation, armaments, etc. Recently there has been increasing realization that to remove impersonal obstacles does not provide security if basic human desires for affection, respect, self-respect, variety, and solidarity are frustrated. This has been most forcefully dramatized by the frustrations of the aged. But the phenomenon of pseudo security appears in a great variety of forms, particularly in the United States. For example, because respect, self-respect, status, and control are so heavily dependent on income, in a somewhat inegalitarian society like that in the United States pursuing the chimera of higher wages in behalf of more "security" is an endless drive for pseudo security.

No one, we said, is ever entirely secure. Death is inevitable. And although men have invented a number of devices for reducing their anxieties over the prospect of inevitable death—mostly by denying it—a residue of anxiety is perhaps inherent in the existential fact, as Fromm has called it, that life as we know it terminates in death. Then, too, there is chance, accident, the fortuitous. There are natural disaster, disease, and events in their social environment men cannot master.

But more important for our purposes than these inherent limits is the fact that security, too, may conflict with other goals. Or perhaps a more accurate way of stating the conflict is to say that the desire to be secure about some goals may conflict with the desire to be secure about others. In such situations one must adjust margins, leaving an inevitable residue of insecurity.

Then, too, probably most people do not really want "absolute" security, if such a state is imaginable; "optimum" security would probably still leave an area of challenge, risk, doubt, danger, hazard, and anxiety. Men are not lotus-eaters.

And short-run security may conflict with long-run security; therefore one must choose. But the more one places his bets on short-run security, the more his anxieties about the future may increase. And the more one defers goal achievement into the inscrutable long-run future, the more one may increase his anxieties as to whether the goals will in fact ever be achieved.

Finally, subjective security is often at war, not with freedom, but with objective security. A certain minimum level of subjective insecurity may be necessary to induce individuals and groups to take precautions against the future. Certainly the history of polyarchies in international politics suggests that great security feelings in the present tend to bring about policies that promise tremendous insecurity for the future.

PROGRESS

Americans in particular have always placed a high value on "progress"—although what they mean by that magic word is not always clear. Yet behind the ambiguities of the word lies one clear and sense-making goal. One progresses to the extent that his opportunities for net goal achievement increase. Hence, like security, progress is a mode of freedom; for progress is an increase of freedom.

Progress, then, is always relative to some conception of goal achievement. To a medievalist like Hilaire Belloc every major development since the Renaissance was a hideous retrogression because it narrowed men's opportunities for achieving goals valued by Belloc; to a nineteenth-century optimist the same developments represented progress. To one who places a high value on physical output and a low value on communal life, the modern city represents progress; to one with the opposite preferences, "conurbation" is a step toward a barbarization as ugly as the word itself. However, if one specifies the goals against which progress is to be measured, the relativity of progress presents no special problems of application.

APPROPRIATE INCLUSION

In setting forth goals to serve as criteria for appraising different politico-economic techniques, we have so far deliberately begged one vital question. We have advocated the goal of freedom for ourselves "and others," but we have not defined what "others" we had in mind. We have made a case for political and subjective equality "with others." What others? We want security for "others" as well as ourselves; progress for others. Who are these others? The whole human race? People who agree with us? Americans? Members of the Western "democracies"?

Many statements of goals are intended as universals for the entire human species at all times and all places. Our aim is more modest. We say merely that these are goals we wish to achieve in conjunction with those who also want these or complementary goals. Whether the "others" include a small group or the whole human race therefore becomes a pragmatic question that can be satisfactorily decided only for each goal and each situation. Because one finds it inconvenient to reopen the question every time he makes a decision, as a practical necessity one must adopt certain persistent working assumptions about the "others"; but these always remain open to modification.

Let us put the point this way. The problem of inclusiveness is a problem of adjusting margins. What are the likely consequences for the goal in question if we include this group or exclude that one? In any case, how likely is any particular line of exclusion-inclusion? Are there some convenient cultural, institutional, historical grounds of exclusion and inclusion?

The democratic goal raises the question of inclusion in its most practical form. For it would be one thing to want "everyone" to live in a democracy; but it would be quite another to want "everyone" to live in the *same* democracy.

For the purposes of this volume, the United States is the territorial nation-state within which we wish to maximize democracy. But the boundaries of the United States provide no fixed and eternal basis of inclusion-exclusion. The most that can be said is that the United States offers a sufficiently practical organization to furnish us with the conceptual basis necessary to a discussion of techniques for achieving the goals we have discussed.

For however loudly the super-patriots may insist on the territorial nation-state as an almost divinely approved design for inclusion and exclusion, it seems clear that exclusion-inclusion on the basis of the territorial nation-state, or on any other basis, is entirely a pragmatic question. If as a practical matter one needs to operate with more or less stable assumptions about the answers, nonetheless any answer must be tentative. For the answer would vary with the particular goals involved and their bearing on other goals, the availability of social techniques to achieve the goals, ease of identification, historical and geographical factors, and many other circumstances.

One quite practical consideration that limits any abstract principle of inclusion-exclusion is the "organizational load." At some point the diversity of organizations based upon specialized constituencies places an overwhelming burden on the process of decision making. There are, then, clear advantages in reducing the number of organizations by providing a simpler, if more arbitrary, basis of inclusion. This is undoubtedly one reason why, quite aside from questions of agreement or irrational loyalties, the territorial nation-state will have to remain as a vital subunit or organization—just as the states, despite all the prophets of doom, have remained in the American federal system.

American history serves as a convenient illustration of the way in which one might wish to vary the unit of inclusion-exclusion under different historical circumstances. What should the group be among which "the greater number" should have the last word? It is by no means inconsistent to argue that the goals set forth in this chapter would have been best achieved in 1800 if the group with the last word were fellow citizens of one's state, in which case a limited confederacy with other states would be the most one might wish to enter; in 1950 if the group were fellow citizens of all the United States, in which case one would prefer a unitary state to a confederacy or a federal state; and in 19xx if the group were fellow citizens of an Atlantic Union.

Lest it appear that a bigger unit of organization is always preferable to a smaller one (surely, like its converse, one of the great fallacies of our age), it is important to remember that the argument cuts both ways. Within a territorial nation-state like the United States there exist many small units within which a great many specific goals can be more efficiently achieved than within an organization comprising the whole American electorate. Operation of a grade school is an obvious example. There are a vast variety of such cases; and, indeed, it seems highly desirable even to stimulate the existence of small units of self-government and participation at the expense of some loss of control over substantive issues by the larger units. It would be well to keep this warning in mind throughout this book, which is concentrated so heavily on rational social action at the nation-state level. Such a focus should not be taken to mean that the values of small group life are trivial, for on the contrary they are enormous; but it would take us too far afield to consider the prerequisites for developing a healthy and vigorous small group life.

Moreover, one should also remember that taking the United States as a convenient unit of inclusion for maximizing democracy does not mean that the freedom, subjective equality, and progress of individuals outside of the United States is of no concern to us. The fact is that the "others" whose freedom we wish to maximize is bound to be somewhat ambiguous and may vary from one context to another. Finally, in so far as the United States is a focus of this book, the examination and appraisal of politico-economic techniques is concerned with their usefulness not merely for our domestic economy but for international trade as well.

III. Basic Means of Social Action

The remainder of this book is an examination of the social processes through which the seven values just discussed can be maximized whenever scarce resources are significantly involved. It follows that the social processes we are about to examine are also valued by us as means.

Obviously, social processes that facilitate *rational calculation* are indispensable means to the ends not merely of rationality but of freedom, democracy, subjective equality, security, and progress. So too are social processes that facilitate *control;* one must control others to remove obstacles to one's own desires, and one must be controlled by others to remove obstacles to theirs.

Calculation and control in economic life, which we call economizing, are dependent upon four crucial social processes. These are the *price system*, control by leaders (*hierarchy*), control over leaders (*polyarchy*), and control among leaders (*bargaining*). Clearly, then, if one wishes to approximate the seven ends of social action discussed in this chapter one must also value these means, or at least certain ways of using these means. All of these means will be discussed in the chapters that follow.

Part II. TWO BASIC KINDS

OF

SOCIAL PROCESSES

3.

Some Social Processes for Rational Calculation

I. Introduction

There are two basic prerequisites to rational social action by an individual or group. The actor must make rational calculations about the ways in which the attainment of his goals can be maximized in the real world. And the actor must be able to control others whose responses are needed to bring about the desired state of affairs. The first problem, calculation, is discussed in this chapter; the second problem, control, in the next.

BASIC PROBLEMS OF RATIONAL CALCULATION

Some of the difficulties and prospects of rational calculation are suggested by the following case. In 1939 Congressmen had to vote (or avoid voting) on a highly complicated bill that finally became the Reclamation Project Act of 1939. Among other things, the act laid down standards to guide the Secretary of the Interior in deciding the rates to be charged for electric power generated and sold at irrigation dams.[1] The problem of these rates is an abstruse one, and it is unlikely that many Congressmen understood then, or understand now, all the relevant consequences of their choices. Or even if they understood the consequences, they had to appraise them mainly for their bearing on future elections. Only a few Congressmen who had been present during the hearings on the bill before the House Committee on Irrigation and Reclamations knew anything of the issues involved.

Roughly speaking, the government could fix power prices to cover one or more of the following costs:

[1] 53 Stat. 1187, Sections 9 (a) and 9 (c). This case was originally called to our attention in Paul Appleby, *Policy and Administration*, University of Alabama Press, University, Alabama, 1949, pp. 126 ff. The authors are indebted to Mr. Arnold Lozowick for a detailed study of the politico-economic aspects of the case.

1. The annual operation, maintenance, and replacement allowances of the whole irrigation project.
2. The repayment, over a period of years, of the government's investment in power facilities, built as a part of the irrigation project.
3. The repayment, either in whole or in part, over a period of years, of the government's investment in irrigation facilities. Government policy has been to set the price of power on many reclamation projects high enough to pay off some of the irrigation costs. Established policy thus provided that water users were to be subsidized at the expense of power users.
4. Interest charges on the power investment. (Statutory policy dating back to 1906 has determined that water users do not pay interest on the investment in the *irrigation* facilities; theoretically power prices might be set to cover an interest charge on irrigation facilities but such a policy has never been seriously urged.)

That power prices would be set to cover the first three items was generally accepted, in so far as anyone understood the issue at all. Only the last item was controversial. But in their hearings members of the House committee scarcely went into the fourth item. From later discussions in Congress one gets the clear impression that few if any Congressmen had ever separated the problem into the four components set forth above. Nor did the government bureaucracies do it for them. As a result, when the act was passed its instructions to the Secretary of the Interior on power pricing were highly ambiguous.

Later on, as a result of a squabble between two competitive bureaucracies in the Interior Department, the Solicitor was required to rule as to the meaning of the section. Members of the Power Division of Interior contended that interest charges on the power investment should not be included in power costs. If interest were included, then power prices at reclamation projects would have to be too high; but if interest were not included, then taxpayers in the rest of the country would subsidize power consumers near reclamation projects in the West. In a flatly "political" decision, the Solicitor ruled, in effect, that interest charges on the power investment need not be included.[2]

[2] Both this decision and a supplemental one are reprinted in Hearings on the Interior Department Appropriation Bill for 1948, House Appropriations Committee, February 19, 1947, 80th Congress, 1st Session, pp. 9–24. The Solicitor accepted neither the view of the Power Division, that interest charges on power need not be included, nor the then view of the Reclamation Bureau, that they should be included. He rejected both, and came out with a third formula that had

In so far as Congress had any discernible intention at all, the ruling was counter to what was intended. Yet the ruling has never been upset by Congressional action; many Congressmen do not seem to understand what has actually taken place; to this day the alternatives have never been systematically examined. And one gathers that because indirect subsidies to power users at government reclamation projects have now begun, few Congressmen from reclamation areas will vote against them in the future.

Even this condensed and necessarily oversimplified account points to certain basic problems of rational calculation. Four of these are:

Information—e.g., how could the committee, and much less the whole Congress, go about acquiring the facts it needed for a competent decision?

Communication—e.g., are executive memoranda, committee hearings, and Congressional debates adequate techniques for communicating information on a technical problem of rate fixing?

The number of variables—e.g., how many readers can hold in their minds the four costs that might be covered, the possible combinations, and the probable consequences of including or excluding each?

The complexity of the relations among the variables—e.g., do the power costs bear some more or less fixed proportion to the other costs or do they vary widely from one dam to another?

As everyone knows, there are severe limits to man's capacity for overcoming these difficulties. One important limit is set by man's capacities as a thinking animal, for his abilities are meager in comparison with the problems he can create. Another is set by the level of knowledge that exists in a given field at a given time. Nevertheless a number of social techniques, the heritage of civilized man, have proved to be of enormous utility as aids to rational social action.

MAN AS A THINKING ANIMAL

Every literate person is aware today of the dramatically altered conception of man's capacities for rational calculation flowing from the discoveries and events since Freud first reported his and Breuer's

---

precisely the same results as the elimination of the interest charges on power. One can understand why Congressmen were badly confused about the whole affair. And not only Congressmen!

findings on hysteria in 1893—an event, paradoxically, that itself marked a high point in rational calculation. In recent decades a widespread and often faddish interest in psychiatry, psychoanalysis, psychology, and anthropology combined with the phenomena of totalitarianism, genocide, concentration camps, and war have led some people to despair of man as a species. Others regard the evidence as sufficient proof that any discussion about rational calculation is useless. Before examining the confusions underlying this latter position, it may be well to set down soberly some of the obvious limitations to man's capacity for rational action.

First, there is the plain fact that, like Winnie-the-Pooh, he is an animal of very little brain. The number of alternatives man would need to consider in order to act rationally is very often far beyond his limited mental capacity. Little more than six thousand years ago men were mostly simple hunters, herdsmen, or crop raisers. Compared with the previous million years, the animal man reached a high and complex stage of social development when he became a herdsman and joined with others to follow and eventually tame and breed the reindeer and other beasts. It took man another two thousand years before he learned how to hitch a wagon to his animals, almost another millennium before he mounted and rode horseback. There seems to be no evidence that the brain of man has changed in six thousand years.

Freud and his successors have made explicit many additional impediments that may or may not be inherent, but in any event are widely prevalent. Roughly, this is their picture of man: He is autistic; he distorts reality to suit inner needs and then makes his distorted picture of reality the premise of his actions. He is compulsive. He projects his own motives and reality views on others; represses powerful and urgent wants deep into the unconscious for fear of penalties from conscience or the responses of others, only to have his repressed wants unrecognizably displaced on other goals; acquires and displays exaggerated fears; colors the world with emotional tones of forgotten childhood; expresses hatreds and resentments coming from long-buried events; rationalizes all his actions; and throws a veil of hypocrisy and dishonesty not only over his outer behavior in order to deceive others but even over his innermost wishes in order to deceive himself. This is a harsh, grotesque picture, a caricature, but let it stand as a warning not to romanticize man's capacity for rational social action.

A special kind of handicap, furthermore, impedes rational calculation; it is difficult to use such foresight as feeble brain and personality might otherwise permit because often one cannot judge between present goal achievement and future—partly because one cannot always know what he wants until he has tested the goal; concrete experience often is the only adequate test. Then, too, future rewards and punishments are heavily discounted as compared with present; in acquiring habits, for example, the longer a reward or punishment is delayed after a response, the less likely is the response to be learned. A response that leads to an immediate but moderate reduction in tensions can thus become habitual even though it produces a severe increase of tensions much later.[3]

Rational calculation is a burden, too. And there is a stubborn paradox in the fact that many important prime goals cannot be achieved by conscious calculation· for these goals calculation must be unconscious. The consciously calculated action is often the enemy of the rational, goal-maximizing action, particularly in many intimate relationships where the goals of love, affection, respect, and spontaneity are prized. This paradox has led many sensitive writers to deprecate rational calculation; in his *Notes from Underground*, Dostoevski's protagonist revolts against "reason" in words that will find an echo in many a heart:

. . . Reason is nothing but reason and satisfies only the rational side of man's nature, while will is a manifestation of the whole life, that is, of the whole human life including reason and all the impulses. And although our life, in this manifestation of it, is often worthless, yet it is life and not simply extracting square roots.
. . . Granted that man does nothing but seek that mathematical certainty, he traverses oceans, sacrifices his life in the quest, but to succeed, really to find it, he dreads, I assure you. He feels that when he has found it there will be nothing for him to look for. . . . He loves the process of attaining, but does not quite like to have attained, and that, of course, is very absurd. In fact, man is a comical creature; there seems to be a kind of jest in it all!

Man's limited mental capacity, lack of emotional integration, inhibited foresight, and need for uncalculated actions—all this we take for granted. But to accept these premises is not to adopt certain irrelevant conclusions sometimes inferred from them: (1) That

[3] John Dollard and Neal E. Miller, *Personality and Psychotherapy*, McGraw-Hill Book Co., New York, 1950, pp. 187–188.

to postulate rationality as a goal (among others) is to exaggerate man's capacity for rational calculation. This proposition is no more valid than to say that to postulate freedom as a goal (among others) is to deny man's capacity for unfreedom and to exaggerate his capacity for freedom. To postulate rationality as a goal is merely to suppose that some increment of rationality or freedom, however slight, is desirable and possible. (2) That to postulate rationality as a goal is to adopt an eighteenth-century view of man, an outdated psychology, or various philosophical positions known as rationalism. There is no logical connection between the goal of rationality and any of these views. (3) That to emphasize the importance of rational calculation is to exaggerate the usefulness of conscious thought. In part this objection stems from a confusion of *rational* calculation with *conscious* calculation, a confusion stemming from certain almost ineradicable verbal obstacles. As we have already said, unconscious or impulsive actions can be highly rational or efficient because many goals can be attained in no other way.

In some cases, as with love, affection, and spontaneity, goals cannot be obtained except by an emotional experience that is violated by conscious calculation. In other cases the variables are so many, or the relations among them are so subtle and complex, or the communication of information is so dependent on cues which only the unconscious will pick up, that intuitive judgment is more rational than conscious calculation. An attempt explicitly to list and weigh all the factors affecting a decision simply "jams" the intuitive process (about which little is known) and produces a less rational judgment.[4]

One valid point, however, ought not to be overlooked. Subsidiary irrationalities are sometimes inevitable by-products of rational goal achievement. It will be shown in a moment that a social code is a necessary aid to rational calculation, yet a social code is almost certain to contain some commitments to irrational action. But completely to liberate men from a social code is only to plunge them into a morass of indecision and create a perfect environment for mass irrationality.

[4] In a series of experiments at Massachusetts Institute of Technology Alex Bavelas has shown that if an individual who must choose among an array of alternatives is given relevant and correct information about the alternatives, beyond a certain point additional information results in less rational choices. The results have not, however, been published.

CONSEQUENCES OF LIMITED KNOWLEDGE

Every literate person could list many kinds of decisions where so little is now known that calculations cannot be rational. In some instances a purely random action probably has about as much chance of success as a calculated one. Over against this one could list many types of action where calculation can be highly rational. Compare, for example, the calculations of an engineering firm on the probable savings to be derived from a new machine with the calculations of social scientists on the consequences for human personalities of increased mechanization. The profile of human knowledge is a ragged one.

These sharp differences in the level of knowledge suggest three conclusions about rational calculation.

First, repetitive events enhance opportunities for rational calculation. Among other things, this fact leads to the *paradox of specialization*. When one specializes he focuses his attention on certain categories of repetitive events; by decreasing the number of variables at the focus of attention, specialization enables one to increase his capacity for rational calculation about these particular categories. This increased capacity for rational calculation enables men to undertake social actions hitherto impossible. But these social actions have unforeseen consequences—unforeseen in part because men can become specialists only by ignoring some of the variables. Hence a calculation that is rational in the short run or with respect to certain limited goals may prove to be irrational in the long run or with respect to different goals.

The fact that repetitive events facilitate rational calculation also explains why history as a discipline is so often of little value in prediction. "History" never repeats itself; vast knowledge about one unique constellation of events is not necessarily of much help in predicting the outcome of another unique constellation of events.

This is, incidentally, one reason why governmental action must often take place at a lower level of rational calculation than, say, business and industrial actions. The important policy choices made by governments are usually made in relatively non-repetitive situations, in which correct forecasting is difficult or impossible. Assuming equal capacities for rational action, policy makers in government typically face much more difficult poblems than policy makers in business.

Second, to decide whether an attempt at rational calculation is worth the candle itself requires rational calculation. The cost and probability of obtaining the needed knowledge must be compared with the importance of the goals involved. If highly ranked goals are involved, even a slight increase in the rationality of calculations may outweigh a heavy investment required to impove calculations. If trivial goals are involved, then a great increase in the rationality of calculations may not be worth even a small cost.

Third, waste and error are inherent costs of the attempt to make rational calculations. Many important decisions are necessarily calculated risks and therefore entail the possibility of waste and error. Thus, during the Second World War Manhattan Engineer District spent more than $300 million in hastily constructing two major plants for the separation of U-235 from normal uranium. Both plants later proved to be too uneconomical relative to the gaseous diffusion process and were finally shut down or dismantled. A Congressional investigating committee nevertheless concluded that "the large investment which both plants represent was eminently justified in terms of wartime emergency and the state of knowledge existing at the time construction began."[5]

II. Some Aids to Rational Calculation

Despite man's limits as a thinking animal, in the short space of six thousand years he has nevertheless enormously raised the level of knowledge in one sphere of life after another. And despite the fact that at any given moment knowledge is uneven, limited, and dispersed, man has nevertheless created a civilization beyond the capacity of his ancestors even to imagine. He has created this civilization and keeps it going by using an extensive variety of social processes that facilitate rational calculation. The core of civilization is simply the accumulation of these aids. Education is the act of transmitting them.

Recall the four problems brought out by the decision on electric power pricing at Reclamation Bureau dams: information, communication, the number of variables, and the complexity of the interrelations among the variables. In considering aids to rational calculation, it is convenient to distinguish those primarily significant

[5] U.S. Congress, Investigation into the United States Atomic Energy Commission: Report of the Joint Committee on Atomic Energy (81st Congress, 1st Session, Senate Report No. 1169), October 13, 1949, p. 10.

for both information and communication, those that cope with the great number and complex relations of variables, and those that deal in a comprehensive way with all four problems. There are many processes. In what follows we merely touch upon a few that are particularly significant for rational calculation in social action:

Processes for information and communication
  1. Discussion
  2. Codification

Processes to reduce the number and complexity of variables
  1. Quantification in comparable values
  2. Sampling
  3. Delegation

Comprehensive processes
  1. Science
  2. Incrementalism
  3. Calculated risk
  4. Utopianism

PROCESSES FOR INFORMATION AND COMMUNICATION

DISCUSSION. Discussion is perhaps the oldest and most universal process for facilitating rational calculation in social action. It is found in tribal council, Greek deme, Curia Regis, Constitutional Convention, New England town meeting, Politburo, cabinet, peace conference, collective bargaining session, family discussion, neighborhood group, and argument in the general store.

Discussion is a kind of social introspection and partial rehearsal of experiences. Just as introspection and testing by experience are vital private aids to the individual in discovering what he prefers, so discussion is an important social technique for arriving at an understanding of one's preferences. Discussion permits a rapid display of alternative proposals, in the course of which the responses of different people are usually exhibited and examined. This examination helps one to clarify his own preferences, both because the experience of others, particularly other like-minded people, may be a relevant pretesting for oneself and because one cannot always know what his preferences are until he can forecast the reponses of others. Discussion also makes possible a quick exchange of factual information and examination and verification of means-end relations. Discussion may, of course, take place in writing, as many famous discussions have taken place; but then participation is bound to be restricted, cumbersome, and time-consuming.

Voting is nearly always preceded by discussion. This is a well-nigh universal association, found not merely in the theory and practice of modern polyarchies but in primitive tribes as well. Indeed, discussion is itself frequently a form of implicit voting. Voting and discussion are commonly found together because voting is typically used where the participants want a more or less accurate indication of voters' preferences. That discussion usually precedes voting thus indicates that its utility as an aid to rational social choice has been widely recognized. Conversely, when leaders do not really wish an accurate indication of voters' preferences but need the ritual of voting as an aid in propaganda or in helping to establish legitimacy, as in the plebiscites and elections of totalitarian countries, they attempt to limit or eliminate discussion.

Discussion is also widely used in making market choices, although in this case it consists mostly of highly informal and often somewhat accidental exchanges among a few people, as when housewives talk about makes of washing machines and their husbands of automobiles. In no Western society has discussion about market choices been so carefully organized, institutionalized, and protected by law and custom as has discussion about voting choices. Nevertheless, discussion of market choices is so ubiquitous that business leaders who wish to distort the consumers' choices by unilateral propaganda are perhaps no less vulnerable to discussion than are political leaders.

Yet discussion has some serious drawbacks as an aid to rational calculation. Although it is time-saving among a few, it is time-consuming among many. And discussion by itself cannot generate answers to complex factual questions if the participants do not posses the factual knowledge. Probably the House Committee on Irrigation and Reclamation could have discussed the pricing problem among themselves endlessly without arriving at a very rational solution. In such cases arrangements must be made for introducing scientific or sub-scientific findings into the discussion.

CODIFICATION. Codification is the reduction and unification to more or less self-consistent principles (from the point of view of those who accept the code as valid) of hitherto disorderly and unsystematized propositions. It is convenient to distinguish between the codification of knowledge about fact and the codification of social norms, or a social code.

Of great advantage to nineteenth-century policy makers was the extent to which the factual assumptions of liberalism had been codified through the writings of Locke, Adam Smith, and Jeremy Bentham in Great Britain, and in the United States by people like Washington, Jefferson, the authors of the *Federalist* papers, and the fifty-five men at the Constitutional Convention of 1787. In budgetary policy, parliamentary debates guided by men like Peel, Gladstone, Parnell, Cobden, Goschen, and Harcourt produced a codification of budgetary theory that governed virtually every Chancellor of the Exchequer from Peel to Snowden.[6] It is true, of course, that bad theory may be codified along with good. Yet there is no escape from the need for codifying, for without a code the world would be a meaningless jumble.

The need for codifying observations about fact is reasonably clear; less obvious, perhaps, is the need for a social code, a body of indoctrinated and partly unconscious norms. For at first blush it seems paradoxical that an indoctrinated and only partly conscious social code should in any way assist in the process of rational social action; indeed, it seems to have been a widely held view in the eighteenth century that the more fully social codes were undermined, the more choices would be "open" to people, and the freer they would be. Some of this bias is reflected by many modern liberals.

Yet without unconscious predispositions to govern a very large area of his life, the individual would be thrown into unbearable uncertainty and confusion. Instead of fostering freedom, the absence of a social code creates a thralldom of fear and anxiety that becomes insupportable. One cannot turn every choice into an endless philosophical appraisal without verging on madness; and even if one could, one can regress only so far in definition and analysis without coming to a dead stop against unanalyzable, indoctrinated preference. Social mechanisms would also break down; for nearly all major social processes require some kind of indoctrinated social code if they are to operate efficiently, particularly during moments of crisis.

Like the factual codes, the social codes of nineteenth-century Christianity and liberalism have also been substantially undermined

[6] D. H. MacGregor, *Public Aspects of Finance,* Oxford University Press, New York, 1939, pp. 10 ff.

in the twentieth century, and so far no widely shared social code of equal self-consistency has taken their place. In the United States, grade school and high school continue to indoctrinate in the older social codes; family, peers, and other social organizations often indoctrinate in rival codes; the conflict, resulting in confusion, uncertainty, anxiety, opportunism, and flight to leadership has often been noted. Yet it is possible that the second half of the twentieth century may witness the emergence of a social code as unified as that of the nineteenth; certainly in economic affairs, as we hope to show, the areas of agreement are widening.

PROCESSES FOR REDUCING THE NUMBER AND COMPLEXITY OF VARIABLES

QUANTIFICATION IN COMPARABLE VALUES. The central obstacle to rational calculation is the difficulty of weighing the relevant alternatives and deciding which is most valuable. One common reason for this difficulty is the great number of variables involved; often a person finds himself unable even to hold all the variables in his mind in order to compare them. Given three conditions, this difficulty can be greatly reduced in social action: if the net value of the different alternatives can be more or less accurately expressed in quantities, if the quantities are in comparable units of value, and if some process exists by which values expressed in quantities are actually affixed to different alternatives. Given these three conditions it would be a relatively simple matter to rank the different alternatives according to their net value—the excess of gain to one's goals over cost to one's goals—and choose the alternative of highest value.

In effect, Bentham argued that the value of all goals can be quantified in terms of pleasure, that pleasure provides the common unit, and that a process could be established for affixing values on different alternatives; these assumptions were the essence of his hedonistic calculism. But in fact for a great variety of human actions, one or more of these conditions is lacking; the reasons for this will be examined in a moment, when we consider the limitations of science as a comprehensive aid to rational calculation.

There is, however, one situation where these conditions are often approximated: in the complex social process that constitutes a price system. The operation, advantages, deficiencies, and preconditions of the price system are discussed in later chapters; meanwhile, let no one suppose that a price system *always* facilitates rational calculation. For a major problem of rational calculation in politico-economic affairs is the attempt to decide just when and in what respects a price system is an aid to rational calculation and when and in what respects it is not.

SAMPLING. Because quantification in comparable values is frequently impossible, men must resort to other devices for coping with large numbers of complex variables. One method is sampling. "Sample" is used here in the ordinary dictionary sense of the term as "a part shown to prove the quality of the whole; a representative part; a specimen." Without sampling, people could operate only at a very low level of rational calculation; with the aid of it, they can often participate intelligently in extremely complicated social choices.

Examine, for example, a large corporation or a government agency. In a few rare situations, a superior really does know as much as his subordinate about the subordinate's job. But the growth and the advantages of specialization make this condition unlikely. The AEC commissioners and the general manager can scarcely be expected to know as much about building and operating reactors as the head of the reactor division; if they did, they would probably get a new chief for the reactor division. How, then, can they judge whether he is doing what they want him to do? If they were only concerned with extremes, their task would be easier. For example, if all the reactors blew up after the head of the reactor division assured them this could not happen, it would not take much knowledge to decide to fire him. But rational action is rarely a problem of choosing among such extremes; it is a problem of adjusting margins—of deciding, for example, whether General Electric is a somewhat less effective contractor than Union Carbide, and if so, why, and what can be done to improve its operation.

In practice, when the superior cannot know as much as his subordinate about the subordinate's task, there are a variety of things he can do to try to keep his subordinate responsive. Most executives evidently test the reliability of their subordinates by a kind of sampling process. If a subordinate makes errors in those areas his boss does not know about, the executive can extrapolate this into the unknown areas—and get a new subordinate. Congressional committees, for example, have spent an inordinate amount of time examining the administration of the three contractor-operated AEC communities. Here is something with which they are familiar; where they regard their own judgment as about as good as that of anyone in the commission; and where they believe they can get some idea as to the efficiency of the operation as a whole. Every important executive in a large organization must follow somewhat the same procedure.

Where direct sampling is impossible, the executive may have to obtain the verdict of others who are presumed to know as much as the subordinate, i.e., indirect sampling. The Atomic Energy Commission makes use of a number of advisory committees; for example, a General Advisory Committee of outstanding scientists is consulted on important policy questions such as the decision to proceed with the hydrogen bomb. Most complicated operations require elaborate processes by means of which experts check on experts for the benefit of a superior who is not expert in the particular matter; auditing and accounting are common samples. The possibilities of collusion are minimized in various ways: separate organizations, different lines of advancement, professional codes.

Superiors can also take into account professional status, or reputation among colleagues and competitors, or the record of apparent successes and failures in the past. The main operating contractors of the AEC have been Du Pont, Union Carbide and Carbon, and General Electric; the high reputation of these companies, their record of previous achievements were undoubtedly prime factors in the commission's decision to take them on as contractors.

Sampling is also used in voting—often badly no doubt. Few citizens have enough knowledge of the issues and the candidates' personalities to choose without sampling. In small towns where everyone is well known to everyone else, rational sampling is obviously much less difficult than in city, state, and national elections. In one recent sample poll of eight thousand adults, respondents were asked to indicate the national Senators whose actions they approved and disapproved of most. Asked for their reasons for approving, much the largest number said they liked his personal characteristics: interestingly enough, 41 percent of the politically very active so replied as compared with 25 percent of the politically very inactive. In giving their reasons for disapproval, 34 percent of the politically very active said they did not like his personal characteristics, compared with 28 percent of the politically very inactive.[7] Of course these people gave other reasons, too, including the Senator's program or stand on issues.

The fact that voters sample, in part, on the basis of impalpable personal characteristics is often taken as a sign that the voting process among large groups of people is bound to be irrational, but this does not necessarily follow. Because representatives must exercise a large measure of discretion in the modern world, rational delegation is facilitated if the delegate has preferences similar to those of his superior, in this case the voter. To take personal characteristics heavily into account in voting is thus not so irrational as it seems, particularly where it is supplemented, as the evidence indicates it is, by considerations of the candidate's stand on general issues.

DELEGATION TO LEADERS. Sampling is usually necessary whenever one delegates to someone else the opportunity to make choices in his behalf. By delegating some of his choices to others, an individual can decrease the number of variables he has to deal with. In many social organizations individuals delegate choices to leaders.[8] Leaders in turn frequently delegate choices to non-leaders. To be sure, coercive delegates may inhibit rational calculation, and leaders frequently become coercive; for this reason some people underestimate the role of leadership in rational social choice. In many situations optimum rationality would be impossible without leaders to whom choices can be delegated. For non-leaders may lack the knowledge, and be quite aware of it; or they may not have the time to concentrate on some kinds of choices—leadership is, after all, a form of specialization; or they may not wish to bear the burden of making decisions on certain issues. In some cases individuals do not know what they want and yet are reasonably sure they do not want what they now have; for example, where people wish to change their aesthetic or intellectual standards because they are dissatisfied with those they have, they may delegate choices to leaders for a

---

[7] Julian L. Woodward and Elmo Roper, "Political Activity of American Citizens," *American Political Science Review*, December, 1950, pp. 872–885; see Tables VIII and IX, pp. 881–882. For unexplained reasons a much higher percentage of Republicans than Democrats gave personal characteristics for their choices.

[8] As used here, "leaders" are those who have significantly greater control over decisions than other members of a group. The problem of definition is a ticklish one, however; some of the difficulties are discussed *infra*, Chapter 8.

period of time. Thus, in Great Britain, a main purpose of the BBC is education; unlike American radio, BBC does not seek to schedule its program simply to meet current popular taste. Yet large parliamentary majorities have steadfastly refused to make the BBC more responsive to popular taste, for there seems to be widespread agreement among the politically active that a function of BBC, unlike that of American radio, is to change the aesthetic and intellectual level of its listeners, not solely to cater to it.

Economists have traditionally ignored the role of leadership in rational calculation because they have either adopted the Benthamite view that no one can know his own wants better than the individual himself or decided that, whatever the case, economists could not go behind the individual choice to examine its rationality without getting into a mare's nest. Yet the example of the BBC indicates a possibility that, given some goals, delegation and leadership may be much more rational than market choice.

Some people (Frank Knight, for example) have attempted to infer that economic planning is bound to be irrational because planning requires delegation of power to leaders and "completely rational delegation of power is a self-contradiction."[9] In this passage, Professor Knight is concerned with centralized hierarchical planning. But that consideration to one side, it is difficult to know what significant conclusions one can draw from his statement. If he merely means that no one is ever capable of making completely rational calculations, then this is hardly enlightening; such a conclusion would also apply to market choices, as Knight would be the first to admit. If, however, Professor Knight insists that optimum rationality in a given situation can never call for delegation, then he is plainly wrong. For every alternative to delegation may actually lead to much greater irrationality. As a practical mechanism the price system could not function without it, nor could any business firm, research agency, university, or government bureau.

Professor Knight attempts to reinforce his point by arguing that "to choose a doctor rationally, the individual would have to know all medical science, and in addition know how much of this is available through each of the possible selections, their respective competence, and also their trustworthiness. He is comparatively helpless. . . ."[10] It is true that many of man's problems arise because

[9] Frank H. Knight, "The Planful Act," in *Freedom and Reform*, Harper & Brothers, New York, 1947, p. 339.
[10] *Ibid.*, p. 358.

he is not omniscient. But obviously one should not avoid the care of a physician simply because one takes a calculated risk in choosing a doctor. The difficulties of choosing a doctor in fact arise when one doctor chooses another for treating himself, when a university department recommends an appointment, a corporation promotes an executive, or a housewife buys a week's groceries. In all of these cases, optimum rationality requires delegation and sampling. To say that delegation and sampling always carry an element of risk is only to say that man is not God.

DELEGATION TO EXPERTS. Leaders are, of course, more or less expert in leadership. Conversely, with respect to some participants in an organization, experts are usually leaders precisely because their expertness helps them to acquire significantly greater control over decisions than other participants exert. But let us focus for the moment on the expert as "one who has special skill or knowledge in a subject" other than leadership.

Delegation to experts has become an indispensable aid to rational calculation in modern life. In business, government, education, military affairs, communications—indeed, in almost all organizations—leaders and non-leaders decrease the number of variables they must deal with by delegating some choices to individuals who have "special skill or knowledge in a subject." The choices delegated to experts range from determining what set of facts is correct to choosing the goals to be maximized. How to delegate to experts choice of factual assumptions without granting them an unwanted choice among the very goals to be maximized is, however, a staggering problem. In this sense, delegation to experts is both an indispensable aid and an unremitting threat to rational calculation.

If prescribed superiors are to make rational calculations, the relationship between them and experts must be such that the superiors can specify goals and the experts will indicate the relative costs and gains of the various alternative means for maximizing the achievement of these preferences. For example, the House Committee on Irrigation and Reclamation might have employed some engineers, accountants, and economists to sort out the various alternatives for pricing electric power at reclamation dams and to estimate what each alternative would probably involve in costs to taxpayers, indirect subsidies to power and water consumers, effects on agricultural growth and production, population, and the like.

Applying their own schedule of preferences, committee members could then choose among these alternatives.

But committee members could be led into irrational decisions in two ways: if for the preferences of his superior the expert surreptitiously substituted a different set to be maximized; or, alternatively, if on a question in which the committee member was less competent he substituted his judgment for the expert analysis of the relative costs and gains of alternative techniques. Yet to keep these types of judgment separate is difficult. The superior may not be able to articulate his preferences to the expert, and will find it even more difficult to articulate the points at which one preference should give way to another. In government advisory commissions, for example, top leaders usually specify goals so vaguely that the experts can and must load the policy proposals with their own private preferences.

Experts have their own axes to grind, and it is easy for them to rationalize (e.g., as being in "the public interest") the substitution of their own goals for those of their superiors. One suspects, for example, that the House Committee on Irrigation and Reclamation could have obtained little help from the Department of the Interior in examining alternative power prices. For the Reclamation Bureau and Solicitor's Office would have been strongly tempted to load the data to suit their own policy preferences. But even experts employed directly by the committee might have done the same; no technical field is more marked by moral fervor than reclamation and conservation. Then, too, whether or not the lay superior is more competent than the alleged expert to decide a particular factual question is itself frequently unclear in the real world. In 1944 some western governors and the Bureau of Reclamation in the upper Missouri Valley disagreed vociferously and publicly with army engineers over the question of whether a deepening of the Missouri River channel from six to nine feet from Sioux City to St. Louis would or would not significantly reduce the water available to upstream farmers.[11]

Sometimes these differences simply indicate a stubborn unwillingness on the part of the layman to recognize his own limits. Sometimes they reflect a well-grounded suspicion of self-appointed "experts." But there is a more profound source of difficulty: there

[11] Cf. the article on the Missouri Basin by Robert W. Glasgow, in the New York *Herald Tribune*, August 22, 1949, p. 2.

is no satisfactory and easily accessible body of knowledge for determining the kinds of questions on which a lay judgment is likely to be superior to an expert judgment in a particular case. Almost everyone who is not an expert in a field quickly sees the proverbial limitations of the expert: that his superior knowledge of certain specialized kinds of repetitive events does not usually fit well with the conditions of real life. For in real-life decisions many different kinds of events are relevant to a rational judgment; yet each kind of event may be the bailiwick of a different specialty—or none at all. Successful administrators—tested by their capacity for maximizing the goals of the organization—know that the judgment of experts must be overruled at many points, not because the experts' body of factual propositions is wrong, but because it does not apply closely enough to real life. "In an emergency the able but unimaginative expert is a public danger," said Lloyd George, who had no hesitancy in overruling the experts in the War Office. "On the one hand their thorough knowledge of the details of the business, and their high reputation, give them an authority which it is difficult for the amateur to set aside. While in a situation for which there is no precedent experience often entangles the expert."[12]

Experts or specialists must be coördinated in a multi-goal, multi-fact universe. At present, policy makers in business and government tend to be specialists in the art of coördination; in this sense, the coördination of experts is itself a task for experts. But as experts in coördination, most policy makers possess little articulated or formal theory, and such theory as they might articulate would probably prove to be naïve. Yet experience seems to show that this pragmatic and untheoretical mind is typically more successful at coördination than is the theoretical. One reason evidently is that the variables with which the policy maker must deal in a complex situation are too numerous and too impalpable to be articulated and reduced to relevant theory. When the theorist attempts to make policy judgments as he would theoretical judgments, he simply becomes a naïve policy maker. What the practical man means by his contrast between impractical theory and practical common sense is really a contrast between good (but intuitive) theory and bad (but explicit) theory. The fact is, the successful policy maker operates with good theory that is inexplicit, inarticulate, and mostly

---

[12] Quoted in K. B. Smellie, *A Hundred Years of English Government*, Duckworth, London, 1937, p. 286.

unconscious; he draws heavily on intuition or on experience stored away in memory, fragmentary, disorderly. The theorist who fails at policy making operates with a bad theory, and it is bad partly because he has tried to keep it explicit, articulate, conscious, and orderly.[13]

DELEGATION TO MACHINES. Many theoreticians resent this untidy subordination of articulate theory to inarticulate. If the number of variables on which judgments are based exceed the capacity of the human mind to juggle simultaneously, then somehow technical arrangements must be made for reinforcing man's limited capacities. Techniques regarded by some people as of great potential importance are mathematics and electronic calculators. Crudely stated, if there are too many variables for the human mind to handle at once in policy judgments, the problem is to reduce the variables to mathematical equations that can be fed into electronic calculators for a solution. Thereby, it might be suggested, an entirely new level of rationality in policy decisions would be possible, a leap forward roughly equivalent to the invention of language, writing, printing, or mathematics itself.

It is not really open to doubt that mathematics and electronic calculators can be of enormous aid in a number of specialized situations where quantification in comparable values is possible. The air force, for example, has been pushing the development of electronic calculators for use in calculating detailed requirements in aircraft supplies and personnel for various strategic objectives. Calculations that in the past would have taken thousands of people many months, or as a practical matter could never have been made at all, can now be made in a few minutes. Thus the possibility of examining the costs of alternatives of gigantic scope with a rapidity far beyond any practical achievement in the past is now dawning.

Yet it would be easy to exaggerate what mathematics and electronic calculators are capable of. For as a substitute for decisions by human beings through social organizations the electronic computer suffers from several basic limitations. First, computers are of use only if what is wanted can be specified in numbers. But in a great many cases preferences cannot even be articulated, let alone articulated with some kind of price tag on them. This is one reason why

---

[13] Cf. the experiments of Alex Bavelas cited in footnote 4. The expert is more likely to feel the need for an excess of information, detail, explicit listing of data, etc., than is the experienced administrator.

delegation to other people is such an important mechanism for scheduling goals. If the delegate is crudely representative, he can often make choices that other participants will find satisfactory even if these other participants could never articulate their goals; in such cases no machine could ever substitute for delegation.

Second, no one ever wants simply a given quantity of something; one has numerous preferences and his choice of quantities of any one item depends on how much he has to give up in alternative items. Yet in most cases it would be intellectually impossible to hold all the alternatives in his head in order to indicate how much of one item he would forgo in order to achieve slightly more of another. Often, too, he does not know how much he wants to forgo until he is experiencing the situation. Nor can we simply turn to another calculating machine; it is, after all, the preferences of human beings that are important.

Third, much factual knowledge even about consequences is inarticulate; like the knowledge of successful administrators it is based on personal or group experience and remains uncodified. Knowledge of consequences is necessary if costs and benefits are to be calculated; yet experts do not always possess this knowledge, and "practical" people are unable to articulate it. In these cases, the machine could never indicate costs accurately; indeed, its cumulative error might be enormous.

It may be replied to this last point that in principle such knowledge is obtainable. Yet even if this is the case, the knowledge is not available now and may not be for decades and centuries. Moreover, if in principle knowledge of consequences is obtainable, it is unlikely that the obstacles in the way of articulating and coding preferences can ever be fully overcome. Indeed, the amount of harassment, questioning, and interviewing required would be intolerable.

Fourth and finally, assuming all the previous problems away, could mathematics and machine calculation substitute everywhere for policy makers and thereby eliminate the irrationalities of policy makers? Pretty clearly not. For this could be the case only if human beings were themselves machines without any goals of their own to maximize—obviously a contradiction in terms. Someone must control those who run the calculations and machines. Someone must control these controllers, etc. At every point there would be opportunities for attempting to feed into the calculator one's own preferences. Doubtless, pressure groups would organize for just such a purpose. Could such distortion and deception be checked by machine calculation? Even assuming such a technical possibility, at some point someone would have to decide what set of results to adopt and the punishments to be administered in case of a refusal of subordinates or outvoted minorities to comply.

It would be all but inhuman, then, if struggle for control over the computers did not become a central issue of social existence. One can even fancy that the struggle would involve such complex and esoteric issues as to take place only among small rival elites bent on exploiting a passive and stupefied mass—until finally the hitherto helpless mass acquired leaders, staged a revolt, and smashed all the machines: the Luddites of the brave new world. In the last analysis, neither mathematics nor electronic computers, even in principle, can exorcise the hard facts of power.

We have dwelt at such length on the limits of mathematical equations and electronic computers only to indicate that the problem of an excessive number of variables in social actions is certain to be a persistent one. Perhaps most people accept this point without argument. But if any should seek to retain a utopian hope that the solution can be made much simpler if only it is first made more complex, analysis of the limits of mathematics and computers may help to dispel these lingering doubts.

COMPREHENSIVE PROCESSES FOR RATIONAL CALCU-LATION

Now consider some rather comprehensive processes for dealing with the difficulties of rational calculation.

SCIENCE. Scientists deal with the problem of information by systematic observation; with the problem of communication by developing a precise and logical language usually including the language of mathematics; with the problems of an excessive number of and complex relations among variables by specialization, controlled by experiment, quantification, rigorous and systematic analysis, and exclusion of phenomena not amenable to these methods. At one extreme these methods may result in a precise, verified, harmonious system of "laws" and at another in failure to decrease the sea of human ignorance by a single drop. Most of what is produced by these methods lies somewhere between the two extremes.

These methods have become of prime importance to rational social action. To an extent that only the most fanciful of our ancestors believed possible a few centuries ago, rational calculation in one area of social action after another, from medicine to erosion control, has been facilitated by the application of the methods of science. Between Disraeli or Lincoln's day and our own, the art of government, for example, has been transformed. One important development is the expert or quasi-expert commission. In Great Britain, as Herman Finer points out, the royal commission of inquiry, beginning with that of 1832 on the administration of towns, is "an apparatus of exploration . . . invented for the social field, as mightily influential in its sphere as the invention of the microscope had been in physics and medicine."[14] In the United States, commissions appointed by the Chief Executive or by President and Congress jointly have become a standard practice.

The growth of research as a tool of policy makers has also constituted a minor revolution; in 1918 it was still possible for the Haldane Committee in Britain to recommend a central Department of Research, a proposal that at the time seemed to exaggerate the role of research and by now seems like a quaint misunderstanding of its importance to every department, branch, and bureau of government. Since World War II, a new development has taken place with the extensive use of contracts for research to universities, research institutions, and even specialized contractors such as RAND for the air forces and Operations Research for the army, organizations that have acquired outstanding scholars for research on policy problems of high secrecy. Bureaucracy itself is a method for bringing scientific judgments to bear on policy decisions; the growth of bureaucracy in modern government is itself partly an index of the increased capacity of government to make use of expert knowledge.

Just as early democratic theorists neglected the problem of scientific knowledge in government policy, so economists neglected the question in market choices. It was plausible to assume that consumers and entrepreneurs were competent enough to make rather rational choices in the market. Scientific methods for assisting the consumer have lagged considerably behind developments in government. Organizations such as Consumers Research reach a rel-

[14] Herman Finer, *Theory and Practice of Modern Government*, Henry Holt and Co., New York, 1949, p. 47; cf. also pp. 447–449.

atively small group of members; and in making large and relatively non-repetitive purchases of complicated objects such as houses, furniture, or securities, consumers have few aids.

Some large business organizations, on the other hand, have paralleled government, or even outpaced it, in employing scientific methods for aiding in policy choices. Market research is one development. The growth of business bureaucracies is another. Possibly a more recent one is operations research in business; this is an attempt to separate out the variables in the decisions of a given firm that can be stated quantitatively and reduce them to orderly formulas so that the alternatives are clarified; no one should pretend that the elements of hunch and experience are eliminated, only that their role may be somewhat reduced.[15]

Yet some difficult problems of using scientific methods remain. For one thing, thinking as to the use of scientific methods has lagged behind need, and practice has lagged behind thought. It is only slowly coming to be recognized that prerequisites for rational calculation have fundamentally changed in the past century. To take one example, legislative bodies have been handicapped because of their unwillingness or inability to make use of expert knowledge; the House Committee on Irrigation and Reclamation that dealt with the problem of pricing power at western reclamation dams evidently employed no qualified economist, or even a high-grade accountant, and it found difficulty in using expert knowledge in the executive branch. Not until the Reorganization Act of 1946 did Congress permit its standing committees each to employ four professional aides. Even so, some committees have failed to take advantage of this proviso, and those that have do not always understand how to use their professional help or that of government agencies.

Nor is it enough simply to hire experts. One neglected aspect of the problem is communication. Often laymen and experts cannot communicate with one another except through intermediaries who can translate the preferences of the layman in terms useful to the expert, and can translate expert findings about techniques into terms understandable to laymen. Educational institutions have done little to narrow the gap; undergraduates are turned out as laymen, and graduate students as specialists, but almost nowhere is there a serious concern with turning out "translators." Professional groups have done little or nothing; they usually disapprove of "populariza-

---

[15] Herbert Solow, "Operations Research," *Fortune*, April, 1951, pp. 105 ff.

tion" but provide no alternative to the hasty or inaccurate popularizer.

Although literacy in economic theory may be rising, there are significant failures here as elsewhere. Here, too, not much has been done to train competent translators. Thus probably only a tiny handful of Congressmen or newspaper editors, governors, or radio commentators have any worth-while grasp of post-Keynesian economic theory. Then, too, economic theory has tended to postulate a highly restricted set of goals and reality situations within which maximizing takes place; this is often analytically useful and necessary, but if conclusions based on th. arbitrary world were translated and accepted, policy makers would often be less rather than more able to make intelligent policy decisions.

These difficulties are remediable. But some are not. At various places in this chapter we have by inference indicated certain limits to the applicability of rigorous scientific methods to social action. It may be useful to summarize these limits here. One set of difficulties has to do with the characteristics of certain variables in social action, the other with information and communication.

Man, as we have said, has many goals. They cannot all be attained simultaneously, and the attainment of some conflicts with the attainment of others. Hence to maximize his total goal achievement an individual must constantly trade some achievement of one goal for more achievement of another; that is to say, he must maximize at the margin. Moreover, as one goal is approached, its urgency declines; in the language of some psychologists, its drive value diminishes; in the language of the economist, goals are subject to diminishing marginal utility. Taking these two facts together—that to make rational calculations one must maximize at the margin, and that goals are subject to diminishing marginal utility—it follows that margins are constantly fluctuating. For all these reasons, it is usually impossible to quantify the value of alternative courses of action in comparable units. For there cannot be any fixed, quantifiable unit of measure.

For these reasons, too, the problem of information and communication is intensified. In the absence of quantities, qualitative and inexact language must be used to describe policy alternatives. How otherwise, for example, can one calculate the gains and losses of a given program of income equalization and each of the relevant alternatives? Even assuming one can know most of the consequences of each, how many units of dignity and respect are worth, for example, x units of gross national product?

Moreover, information and communication are handicapped because in many instances men cannot know whether they prefer one alternative to another until they have experienced them both. Yet often the choice of one alternative excludes the other.

These are apparently irremovable obstacles. Compared with them the absence of factual information about some of the consequences that are in principle predictable is an obstacle that can be removed with the growth of scientific knowledge. Yet as a practical matter even this obstacle is, at present, a gigantic one. In innumerable cases what is in principle predictable is, today, in fact unpredictable. In principle the impact of various taxes on business investment is predictable; and in time policy makers may actually be able to predict these impacts with high precision. But they cannot do so now.

For all these reasons, rigorous scientific methods, although extremely important to rational calculation in social policy, are severely limited. They are a supplement to, but not a substitute for, additional comprehensive aids to rational calculation.

INCREMENTALISM.   One such additional aid is incrementalism.[16] Incrementalism is a method of social action that takes existing reality as one alternative and compares the probable gains and losses of closely related alternatives by making relatively small adjustments in existing reality, or making larger adjustments about whose consequences approximately as much is known as about the consequences of existing reality, or both. Where small increments will clearly not achieve desired goals, the consequences of large increments are not fully known, and existing reality is clearly undesirable, incrementalism may have to give way to a calculated risk. Thus scientific methods, incrementalism, and calculated risks are on a continuum of policy methods.

Why is emphasis on alternatives closely related to existing reality an aid to rational calculation? First, the consequences of alternatives that bear a remote relation to existing reality are generally more difficult to predict.

Second, as we have reiterated many times, people cannot ac-

[16] Incrementalism has much in common with what Karl Popper calls "piecemeal social engineering." Karl Popper, *The Open Society and Its Enemies,* G. Routledge & Sons, Ltd., London, 1945, Vol. I, pp. 139–144.

curately foresee their own wants. Even assuming a perfect forecast of events, men cannot rationally choose among alternatives drastically different from present reality; only after they have tested the alternatives by choosing and then experiencing could they know whether they really wanted them. To be sure, they can exclude many unwanted alternatives without actually testing them. Most people do not need to live in a concentration camp, have an accident, get sick, become unemployed, or be disgraced in order to find out they would not like it. But it is much more difficult to know which of the remaining alternatives is preferable when the obviously undesirable alternatives are excluded. Incrementalism is a process of constantly testing one's preferences by experience.

Third, because an individual has many goals, some of which conflict with one another, rational action as we have shown requires a delicate and changing compromise among goals and a constant attention to the points where a marginal adjustment will bring about a gain in goal attainment. This is incrementalism in individual action, and the logic applies equally to social action.

Fourth, incrementalism is an aid to verifying the results of one's choices. This is in keeping with the principle of isolating a single variable. Results after one has acted can be compared with conditions before the change, and the relation of the particular choice to the particular changes is more easily determined.

Fifth, incrementalism helps to insure control. Incremental change gives prescribed superiors an opportunity to issue rather detailed instructions or to check in detail the actions of their subordinates. As a general matter, the larger the increments of change, the more difficult it is for prescribed superiors to check on their subordinates or even to give instructions that are any more than a blank check.

Sixth, incrementalism is reversible. When mistakes are made, they can more easily be repaired.

Seventh, incrementalism permits both the survival and the continual alteration of the operating organization. The attempt to secure abrupt change by prescription usually fails because the operating organization, with its own codes and norms, resists sudden, large-scale change. To achieve large-scale change, the norms and codes of the operating organization must somehow be destroyed. But the outcome of the effort to destroy these norms and codes is usually quite unpredictable, first because one cannot foresee the consequences of the hierarchical control system used to destroy them, and second because one cannot be at all sure what norms will take the place of those already existing. Revolutionaries have invariably underestimated the persistence of operating codes and norms, their own capacity for replacing the old with new ones to their liking, and the probability of Thermidor following hard on the heels of Terror.

Eighth, for all these reasons, incrementalism is an aid to the rationality of the electorate and therefore to polyarchy. Indeed, it is the system of change practiced in all the durable polyarchies of the West.

Incrementalism should not be confused with a simple commitment to the idea that gradual change is always preferable to rapid change. The greater the degree of scientific knowledge available about a given instrumental goal, and provided people are reasonably confident about their preferences, the larger is the increment of change that can be rationally made.

Nor should incrementalism be confused with what is sometimes called "experimentalism" in social change; for "experimentalism" may be either incremental or not. Actually, in societies where a high degree of subjective equality is a goal, "experimentalism" is, in one limited sense, automatically ruled out; for in such societies, to "experiment" with people is forbidden.

But perhaps this is only a verbal question, depending on whether one means deliberate and conscious experimentation with people or *post hoc* examination of events in a more or less scientific fashion. In the second sense, there need to be no conflict between incrementalism and "experimentalism"; for the data given by on-going events may always be taken as an "experiment." In the United States, the forty-eight individual states are not deliberately used for "experimenting" with alternative solutions to social problems; but different solutions are in fact often produced, and this body of comparative experience can sometimes be used to arrive at an appraisal of alternatives without any conscious and deliberate "experimentation." Nor is there much conscious and deliberate experimentation with a variety of forms for organizing industrial operations; but *in fact* a variety of forms are created, some of which persist and expand and some of which die out as business leaders learn by observation the relative advantages and disadvantages of one form or the other.

A prerequisite for rational incrementalism in social actions is, of course, a considerable degree of agreement on basic goals. For in this case because differences among participants can be narrowed down and isolated, and because agreement exists on basic objectives, the task becomes one of finding rather specific techniques to rather specific goals. This prior agreement, too, will show up in the programs and policies of competing political leaders and particularly in the platforms or policies of political parties; the familiar complaint that competing parties are like Tweedledum and Tweedledee need reflect no more than that, as in the United States, a widespread agreement exists on basic issues. In this case citizens are in a position to distinguish and choose political leaders on the basis of relatively minor differences rather than major ones, and rational incremental change is facilitated.

CALCULATED RISKS. Incrementalism is not always satisfactory. On the continuum of policy methods, extension of the Homestead Acts to Alaska was incremental. But the first Homestead Acts were something of a calculated risk. Existing reality was clearly undesirable to policy makers, but no one could forecast with much certainty about the consequences of homesteading western lands. Yet, on balance, the risk seemed to policy makers to entail no consequences worse than those of existing reality.

Calculated risks are often necessary because scientific methods have not yet produced tested knowledge about the probable consequences of large incremental changes, small changes will clearly not achieve desired goals, and existing reality is highly undesirable. If the Weimar Republic was salvageable at all, probably it could have been saved only by leaders and non-leaders willing to move much more rapidly toward social reform than German democrats recognized; certainly in 1933 in the United States some rather abrupt changes had to be made.

In such situations, the calculated risk is the most rational action one can undertake—for all alternatives, including the alternative of simply continuing existing policies, are calculated risks. Conservative objections to reform are often reducible to the idea that when the future is unknown (as it usually is) it is wiser to "do nothing." But it is impossible to "do nothing"; doing nothing is equivalent to continuing existing policies; yet in many situations, to continue existing policies is a greater risk than to discard them in favor of an alternative calculated risk. The conservative is merely one who prefers to take risks without calculating them.

UTOPIANISM. If men must often take calculated risks in social action, a commitment to rational calculation nevertheless implies that the calculated risk should always be frankly recognized as a decision the results of which are in part, often in large part, indeterminate. In this respect incrementalism and the calculated risk are fundamentally at odds with holistic or utopian reform, which as Popper has eloquently demonstrated is the antithesis of rational calculation. For where the incremental approach leads to the conclusion, not that large-scale changes should never be made, but that the larger they are the more indeterminate is the outcome, the utopian is convinced that his particular set of large-scale changes will have an outcome that may be pretty much predicted. Holistic or utopian planners object to the idea of "patching up an old system." The metaphor is, of course, a prejudicial one. Patching up an old system is the most rational way to change it, for the patch constitutes about as big a change as one can comprehend at a time. The ultimate result of "patching" is a transformation of the social system. Capitalism was only a series of patches on feudalism.

Within limits, all change tends to be incremental in nature; the codes and norms of the operating social organizations defy attempts at abrupt transformation into a brave new world that exists only in blueprints of the utopian engineers. Utopians not only reject this as a social fact; they also reject the idea that incrementalism can be more rational than holistic reform. Utopianism occurs in many unsuspected places; for example, although, beginning in 1930, the Army and Navy Munitions Board developed an industrial mobilization plan for use in event of war, when war finally came the plan was never used.[17] The plan was not utopian because it was unused; but it was unused because it was utopian. And it was utopian in supposing that the outcome of a large-scale change like the outbreak of war and mobilization was predictable enough to be significantly influenced by advance blueprints.

Much writing on economic planning takes holistic premises for granted, without ever making them explicit. There is a common intellectual syndrome consisting of an interest in large-scale reform

[17] Herbert A. Simon, Donald W. Smithburg, and Victor A. Thompson, *Public Administration*, Alfred A. Knopf, New York, 1950, pp. 448–449.

and a preoccupation with "planning." One of the most perceptive planners, who sometimes seems to accept holistic premises, is Lewis Mumford. For example, he has written that in order to plan we need a new kind of intellectual process. ". . . We have still to develop what Patrick Geddes used sometimes to call the art of simultaneous thinking: the ability to deal with a multitude of related phenomena at the same time, and of composing, in a single picture both the qualitative and the quantitative attributes of these phenomena."[18] Yet except for very small segments of activity, is it really possible to perform such intellectual feats? If anyone attempted to draw up a comprehensive plan for all of society, would not the plan be wildly irrational simply because no one can really deal with "a multitude of related phenomena at the same time"? And is it true, as Mumford later suggests, that the inability to think in this fashion is a cultural heritage of laissez-faire individualism? Is it not rather a result of man's inherently limited brain faced with modern complexity?

Against such a view, holistic planners sometimes argue that to act rationally people need a rather complete model portraying rather precisely the kind of society they wish to achieve; in a word, they need a utopia. The difficulty is, however, that hardly anyone can have any except the crudest approximation of the kind of society he would prefer to his existing one. To create a blueprint of such a society is merely to foster an illusion of certainty in a world of uncertainty. Thus holists solve the problem of rational calculation by postulating it out of existence. In effect they say that when people know precisely what they want and the most efficient way to get it, it is irrational for them not to choose this most efficient means.

But this, of course, is only a tautology; and like many tautologies it is not very useful. For the key problem arises because people do not often know precisely what they want in advance; and even when they do, the most efficient way to realize their wants in politico-economic matters is usually somewhat indeterminate. People discover what they want by living; wants grow and change with experience.

Sometimes holistic planners justify the need for utopias by arguing that one must be "for" something, not merely against exist-

[18] Lewis Mumford, in a Foreword to Findlay Mackenzie (ed.), *Planned Society, Yesterday, Today, Tomorrow*, Prentice-Hall, New York, 1937, p. vii.

ing defects. Often one hears it said that a weakness of liberalism is that it is only against current evils, but stands for nothing. But this, too, is a dangerous fallacy. To contend only against known evils is perhaps the highest degree of rational calculation men can perform. To be sure, logically one cannot oppose known evils without presupposing that there is a better alternative. But one need not know the details of the alternative; one can arrive at the details by incremental adjustments away from existing evils. It is easier to decide that concentration camps are an evil to be avoided than to know which of all the alternatives to concentration camps is the most perfect.

Have utopias no value, then, as aids to rational calculation? To say this would be to go too far.[19] As models, utopias stimulate the imagination. They indicate directions in which alternatives to existing reality might be looked for. Democracy, as we have defined it, is undoubtedly a utopia; taken together, the goals set forth in Chapter 2 are a brief outline of a utopian society.

Utopias also help one to focus on long-run goals; unaided by the imaginative impact of utopias, incrementalism might easily degenerate into petty change, fear of the future, a placid tolerance of existing distress, and an irrational unwillingness to take calculated risks.

More than that, utopias have a psychological function as aids to motivation. Because of their motivating power they can be highly dangerous; caught up in the spirit of a utopia, one can easily forget all the difficulties of rational calculation discussed in this chapter and the great utility of pedestrian aids to rational calculation of the kind set forth here. Yet if all these warnings can be remembered, then utopias are important as a goad to action, a goal to inspire the dedication, devotion, and energies of the faithful. Social movements that have powerfully influenced men's lives—usually through the catalysis of a small and dedicated elite—have invariably had their utopias. Would Christianity, or democracy, or laissez-faire capitalism, or socialism, or alas, communism, Nazism, and the corporate state have had their power over men's minds, energies, and emotions without their utopias?

The danger is not that man has utopias. It is his use of utopias to blind himself to the art and science of rational calculation.

[19] Cf. Raymond Ruyer, *L'Utopie et les utopies*, Presses Universitaires de France, Paris, 1950, chaps. 1–3.

III. Mechanisms for Scheduling Goals

Aids to calculation of the kind just discussed are obviously of enormous importance both to rational individual action and to rational social action. Without them, effective planning in politico-economic affairs would be impossible. But these aids, and others like them, are not sufficient. Most choices relevant to politico-economic affairs require the responses of other individuals to be effective. That is, not only must an individual make up his mind about alternatives, but in a loose sense a group must make up "its" mind. When the choices of individuals require the responses of others to be effective, there are a limited number of basic ways by means of which alternatives can be cast up, a selection made, and the selected goal or goals scheduled for action. Four such mechanisms in politico-economic affairs are voting, market choice, delegation, and autonomous social choice.[20] We have referred to the first three at various points in this chapter; although the fourth is of relatively slight importance in politico-economic actions, the others require further discussion.

VOTING

Where voting is used, goals are scheduled by counting the expressed preferences of participants according to some agreed basis. The agreed basis for tabulating preferences may range from individual equality, as in democracy, to extensive inequality, as in the old Prussian system of three-class suffrage, under which the Krupp family alone was able to elect the whole representation of Essen.[21] The greater the inequality, the more voting becomes like delegation. Similarly, the proportion of favorable votes required for a decision may extend from unanimity to a small minority; the requirement of unanimity gives minorities a veto power—as is roughly the case with the Senate filibuster—and is a negative form of minority rule, of which the positive form is simply to grant the minority special power. Here again, the smaller the minority capable of vetoing or making a decision, the closer voting verges on delegation.

[20] An overlapping but somewhat different classification will be found in Kenneth J. Arrow, *Social Choice and Individual Values*, John Wiley and Sons, New York, 1951, pp. 1 ff., and in Frank Knight, "Human Nature and World Democracy," in *Freedom and Reform*, Harper & Brothers, New York, 1947, pp. 308–310.

[21] Herman Finer, *op. cit.*, p. 229.

Voting may be either explicit, as in elections, or implicit, as in a meeting of the Society of Friends. Implicit voting verges on autonomous social choice.

As a mechanism for scheduling goals, voting is well-nigh universal; it is prevalent in widely differing cultures and in many different time periods. In this sense it is a mechanism that "comes naturally" to man, a mechanism so obvious and usually so easily legitimized that it is discovered and rediscovered again and again.

MARKET CHOICE

Where market choices are made, goals are scheduled through a process of exchanging objects of preference; each party to the transaction exchanges an object for another of at least equivalent value to him. The goals scheduled by market choices are expressed in relative prices and may be reduced to statements such as "When you give me six pieces of carved ivory I will give you one magic cure" or "When you give me eighty-two cents I will give you a dozen eggs." Like voting, market choices are a well-nigh universal form of scheduling goals and may be found in societies as diverse as the United States, the USSR, European feudalism, and primitive tribes. Of course the extent to which market choices are used to schedule goals varies greatly; as compared with the American or west European economies, the USSR, European feudalism, and primitive tribes significantly restrict the use of market choices for scheduling goals. But it would probably be impossible to find a society that did not make some use of market choices.

DELEGATION

Where goals are scheduled by delegation, one individual or group chooses the goals and others participate only by acquiescing in the choice. Delegation, too, is universal. But it is useful to distinguish types of delegation along a continuum running from legitimate to coercive. When delegation is legitimate, the delegate makes the choice of goals and the other participants acquiesce in his choice with feelings that they "ought" to acquiesce: goals chosen by the delegates are or come to be the goals of all participants. The delegate may possess legitimacy because of *charisma;* or because he is representative, for example, in a group of like-minded people where one is chosen by lot to make choices for the rest; or—a special case of representativeness—because the group is bound by a body of norms which the delegate bespeaks when he makes his choices.

When delegation is coercive, the delegate makes the choice, but other participants acquiesce in the choice because they expect certain rewards and deprivations for compliance, although compliance lacks the approval of the conscience. Therefore acquiescence produces feelings of frustration, anxiety, and constraint. An extreme form of coercive delegation is totalitarian leadership, applied against recalcitrant minorities.

AUTONOMOUS SOCIAL CHOICE

When there is no delegation, voting, or market choice, goals are sometimes scheduled by autonomous social choice. In this case, each individual adjusts his goals autonomously until a schedule is arrived at, as when a group of people start out with a number of alternative paths across a field and finally accept as customary a single given path. Autonomous social choice is a highly important social mechanism, but it has limited relevance as a mechanism for scheduling goals in the process of economizing in a modern industrial society.

One word about delegation. Among themselves delegates and nondelegates alike may use the mechanisms of voting, market choice, and autonomous social choice for scheduling goals. Any group of people who cannot arrive at a schedule of goals by any of these three methods may find it necessary to resort to delegation. But delegates in turn may be unable to arrive at a schedule of goals by any of these three methods, and they in turn may resort to delegation. This progression may continue until choice is finally delegated to a single individual, who will not need to employ voting, market choice, or autonomous social choice, for he can choose as an individual; yet his individual choice is in fact a social choice if it is acquiesced in by the other participants.

A basic issue in the literature of politico-economic organization is the relative rationality of voting, market choices, and delegation in scheduling goals. A curious professional bias colors much of the discussion. Economists tend to deprecate the rationality of voting and delegation as compared with market choices, and non-economists tend to deprecate the rationality of market choices as compared with voting and delegation.

Much of this book is, in effect, an examination and appraisal of these mechanisms. But because they are only devices for scheduling goals, to be effective they must be a part of a social process that also includes control; this, the companion process to rational calculation, is the subject of the next chapter.

4.

Some Social
Processes
for Control

Calculation is only one of two major components of rational social action. The other is control, the subject of this chapter. All economies, such as those of the United States, Great Britain, and the USSR, are combinations of various elemental techniques of control. Differences between the economy of one country and that of another—say, the United States and the Soviet Union—cannot be explained, as is often assumed, by saying that each relies on a different technique of control. For the elementary techniques of control are present in all complex economies. The difference lies in the combination. Just as the same three or four chemical elements may produce quite different compounds depending on the quantities of each that are used, so too different combinations of four basic control techniques will produce economies as different (and as similar) as those of the United States and the USSR. Indeed, it will be shown that the basic methods of control tend to be combined into certain typical constellations of politico-economic techniques and the economies of different countries are really different combinations of these politico-economic techniques.

I. Some Characteristics of Control

CONTROL REDUCIBLE TO DIRECT CONTROL

A quick check with one's own experience will corroborate four important aspects of control. First, large units of indirect control such as a corporation, a trade union, or the stock market, usually consist of many small units of direct control. To say that the corporation president controls the responses of the plant foreman is a useful abstraction, meaning that the responses of the plant foreman are functionally dependent on the acts of the corporation president. But even in an enterprise of a few hundred people, the corporation president usually finds it necessary to control the plant foreman through an intermediate chain of other individuals. This intermediate chain is necessary because the number of people that any one person can act on *directly* is usually small, although of course the number varies with different individuals, different situations, and different tasks. Hence because generals, corporation presidents, bureau chiefs, party leaders, and other executives all find it impossible to exercise direct control over more than a handful of the participants in their organizations, they must work through chains of direct control if they are to control these people at all.

Consequently, the elemental techniques of control examined in this chapter are techniques of *direct* control; in the last analysis chains of control in every economic order, political society, or other human organization are reducible to links of direct control. So that this will not be forgotten, hereafter in this chapter we capitalize Control whenever we mean *direct* control. In this sense, Control is always a direct relationship between two or more human beings. In loose language, A Controls the responses of B if A's acts cause B to respond in a definite way. To put it in stricter but more cumbersome language: *B is Controlled by A to the extent that B's responses are dependent on A's acts in an immediate and direct functional relationship.*

CONTROLLERS AND SUPERIORS NOT IDENTICAL

Second, the controller (the one who Controls) and the subordinate (the one who is Controlled) are not always identical with the prescribed or even the usual superior and subordinate. Often the nominal subordinate Controls his nominal superior; indeed, this is probably inevitable in any complex organization. The nominal subordinate has a thousand opportunities to exert Control over his superior; the superior must rely on the judgment of his nominal subordinate in certain decisions, or the superior deliberately grants discretion to the nominal subordinate and accepts his decisions as binding, or the subordinate negotiates with another employer in order to induce his superior to grant him a raise. Nor is it only a matter of a nominal subordinate's Controlling his superior. Sometimes X, the nominal subordinate of A, is the actual subordinate of B.

PRESCRIBED AND OPERATING ORGANIZATIONS. This discrepancy between nominal and actual superior or subordinate is one instance of a common phenomenon that may be called the discrepancy between prescribed and operating organizations. A *prescription* is any implied or explicit instruction that a particular act or set of acts ought to be performed. When one or more individuals instruct some people to engage in certain stable, persistent, and repetitive relationships, their instructions can be said to constitute a prescribed organization or (since technically the instructions do not constitute an organization at all) a prescribed charter for an organization.[1] There can be as many prescribed organizations, therefore, as there are prescribers.

Any observable, actual, real-life behavior we call *operating* behavior when we wish to distinguish it from prescribed behavior. Thus one can distinguish prescribed and operating charters, norms, codes, goals, and organizations.

For a great variety of reasons, relationships in operating organizations are rarely identical with those set forth in prescription. Four common reasons are:

1. Prescriptions can rarely anticipate all possible situations that will arise. Hence new relationships grow up that, for a time, are not found in any set of prescriptions and may never be incorporated into the official prescriptions of superiors.

2. Prescriptions may conflict; the operating organization cannot fit them all. In the Hawthorne works studied by Roethlisberger and Dickson, the organization prescribed by top officials conflicted with what actually developed and came to be implicitly prescribed by workers.

3. To be effective, prescriptions may require techniques of control that are in fact lacking for any one of a vast number of reasons, including such possibilities as these: there are technical difficulties such as communication; control is held by others who em-

---

[1] F. J. Roethlisberger and W. J. Dickson called this the "formal" organization, in *Management and the Worker*, Harvard University Press, Cambridge, 1939, p. 558. Others have sometimes spoken of the "formal" organization, although there is by no means consistency in the usage of that term. Chester Barnard, for example, appears to use "formal organization" in a different sense in *The Functions of the Executive*, Harvard University Press, Cambridge, 1938, p. 4; and see Herbert A. Simon, *Administrative Behavior*, The Macmillan Company, New York, 1947, pp. 147–149. Because of these ambiguities, we have chosen what we think is the more descriptive term, "prescribed."

ploy it to nullify the prescriptions in question; social indoctrination and habituation have failed to cultivate the necessary responses; etc., etc.

4. Prescriptions may be intended for propaganda, morale, public relations, psychological warfare, deceit, etc., rather than as a genuine organizational charter.

CONTROL IS OFTEN NOT INTENDED

Third, much control is unintended. The boss who comes to work in a grumpy mood may not intend to induce his secretary to treat him gently; yet the responses of a good secretary are as definitely Controlled as if the boss had deliberately asked her to smooth the way a little more than usual that day. Consumers who buy a commodity may not intend to control the activities of producers; but often they do so more effectively than if they had commanded producers to behave in some particular way. Writers on planning have usually neglected unintended control on the false assumption that it is in some way the negation of rational social action.

CONTROL ON CONTINUUM WITH AUTONOMY

Fourth, Controlled behavior may best be thought of as lying at one end of a continuum of which the other end is autonomous behavior. Autonomy is the absence of immediate and direct Control. An individual's responses are autonomous or uncontrolled to the extent that no other people can bring about these responses in a definite way. More precisely: *With respect to A, B's responses are autonomous to the extent that they are not dependent on the acts of A in an immediate and direct functional relationship.*

Thus responses may be autonomous with respect to some people but Controlled by others; or responses may be entirely autonomous in the sense that no other people can bring them about. In either case, however, autonomous action can be an important part of coördinated effort to bring about some desired state of affairs. For the question is whether the autonomous actions are predictable by those who seek coördination. Many autonomous actions are determined mostly by an apparently unique combination of events in which the individual finds himself at some given moment. Because such actions cannot be predicted, they cannot be scheduled. But autonomous responses are often habitual and repetitive, and hence predictable to individuals who cannot Control the responses.

Such responses can be scheduled as a part of the coördinated actions of several people. Thus because German artillery units were usually quite methodical in their interdicting fire on a road junction outside their observation, after first timing the enemy artillery fire to discover the safe intervals Allied troops could often move their vehicles safely.

II. Control Through the Subjective Field

To Control people one must produce responses in them. To produce responses in others, usually one must act on their subjective "field" of awareness, that is, each individual's own special conscious and unconscious awareness of the universe made up of the self and its relations with other objects, resources and capacities, feelings of reward and deprivation, symbols and expectations.[2] One may, of course, act on some elements in an individual's field to influence other elements.

OTHER METHODS

There are ways of producing responses in other people, to be sure, that do not involve acting on their psychological "field." But these ways are not very important in social behavior, and assuredly not in rational social action. For example, you can physically manipulate other people as you might any inanimate object, a stick, a stone, a stream, a machine. The terms "force" and "violence" are sometimes used as if they were equivalents of physical manipulation. Actually what one usually means when he says that force or violence is an important method of controlling others is this: Some people control others by making them fearful of severe punishment if they do not obey. Even when torture is used to produce pain which in turn induces confession, the action is ultimately successful only because it acts on the psychological field of the victim.[3]

[2] The term "field" as used here is meant only as we have defined it, and should not be taken as an attempt to approximate its meaning in physics, in the sociology of Karl Mannheim, or in the psychological theories of Kurt Lewin. This caution applies to all the terms used in this chapter. Wherever possible we have deliberately restricted ourselves to elementary assumptions common to most or all psychological theories. Although our language is eclectic, no one should read into our terms the specific definitions of the psychologists with whom some of the terms are commonly associated.

[3] Another possibility is to act directly on a person's psychophysical capacities by surgery, drugs, and the like. Soviet techniques for extracting confession, by depriving an individual of sleep and keeping him on a starvation diet, might also

In politico-economic action Control to all intents and purposes means action on psychological fields. Admittedly, as with so many useful distinctions, physical manipulation, manipulation of psychophysical capacities, and action on psychological fields all lie along a continuum; but the differences in real life are gross enough so that hereafter Control may safely be taken to require action on the psychological field.

WAYS OF ACTING ON A PERSON'S FIELD

How one can penetrate the field in order to produce a response is a matter of some controversy and ambiguity among contemporary psychologists. Nevertheless, one must make assumptions; and it is probably best if they are made explicit.

There appear to be several possible ways of acting on an individual's field. One is to *change his resources and capacities* for rewarding or penalizing others, and in this way altering his expectations, and hence his responses. When a politician is put in or out of office, his resources for influencing public policy are significantly altered. In economic life one can change an individual's behavior by increasing or decreasing his money.

But the principle system for altering a person's field and so Controlling his responses is to influence his *expectations of rewards and deprivations*, or, as these will be variously called in this book, his incentives, or his gratifications, gains, satisfactions, or goal achievement, and his punishments, losses, penalties, costs, or dissatisfactions. One's incentives may be altered by teaching him that a given stimulus (or signal, communication, cue, or item of information) will be followed by certain rewards or deprivations, and that a particular response will avoid the deprivation or win the reward. The signals or communications that induce actions may or may not constitute rewards or deprivations by themselves.

Specifically, then, one can Control another person's field by acting on his information, signals, communications, cues, or symbols and thereby affecting his expectations about rewards or deprivations; or one can act on the rewards and deprivations that actually

be put in this category. Although this method, and possibly the development of some of the newer drugs, may vastly enhance the possibilities of direct psychophysical manipulation, for the purposes of this book these methods may be ignored.

operate on the subordinate, thereby affecting his expectations; or one can act on both.[4]

III. Four Basic Control Techniques

For our purposes it is convenient to distinguish four techniques of Controlling others by acting on their fields to produce a response. First, one may act on another's field without intending to do so; we call this spontaneous field Control. If one reads that the price of a particular stock is rising, the information may directly stimulate a pleasurable feeling of well-being in one who owns the stock; to one who does not own the stock, the information may provide no such gratification. But in both cases the reader might take the information as a cue to buy more of the stock in the expectation of future rewards.

Second, one may deliberately manipulate another's field by command. Third, one may deliberately manipulate another's field by means other than command. These three relationships, it is evident, are all unilateral; symbolically they are A $\longrightarrow$ B relationships. But many relationships are reciprocal, that is, two or more people manipulate the fields of one another; symbolically the reciprocal relationship may be expressed as A $\longleftrightarrow$ B or A $\longleftrightarrow$ B,

$$\text{A} \searrow \swarrow \text{C}$$

etc.[5]

SPONTANEOUS FIELD CONTROL

THREE PARADOXES. Spontaneous Control of another person's field is perhaps the most paradoxical of all the Control techniques. First paradox: it is a basic Control technique in all social organizations, yet many people do not even think of it as a form of Control.

[4] It may also be possible, as some eminent psychologists believe, to influence behavior by manipulating the objects or symbols in the individual's environment, even if the individual's expectations of rewards and deprivations are in no way affected. However, we have not found it necessary to make use of this assumption and in the rest of the book it is ignored.

[5] The following is a schematic summary of the relation of the four Control techniques:

Unilateral	Multilateral
Spontaneous field Control	= Spontaneous field Control
Manipulated field Control ⎫	= Reciprocity
Command ⎭	

Second paradox: it is sometimes the most tyrannical Control to which a person is ever subjected in his entire lifetime, yet to anarchists the society of perfect freedom operates entirely with spontaneous field Controls. Third paradox: because it is unintended rather than deliberate Control, it can be pictured as the antithesis of planning, yet it is one of the most important techniques of Control and therefore of rational social action.

What is this paradoxical Control technique? It works this way: Often when you act, as unintended by-products of your behavior you produce signals about rewards or deprivations or even the rewards and deprivations themselves; these signals, rewards, and deprivations influence another person's expectations of rewards and deprivations. He responds in an attempt to avoid the threatened deprivations or secure the expected gratifications; yet you did not deliberately seek to produce his response. Thus his response is functionally dependent on your original act; unintentionally you Control his response. This is spontaneous field Control.[6]

This technique of Control is strategically important to rational social action in economic affairs because, as we shall see later, it is fundamental to the operation of a price system. Other Control techniques also operate in a price system, but spontaneous field Control plays a crucial part.

BOTH TYRANNICAL AND FREE.   One can now understand the three paradoxes of spontaneous field Control. It is sometimes tyrannical because it is so hard to escape: among family, neighbors, colleagues, employees, superiors, acquaintances—wherever one goes a network of spontaneous field Controls envelops him. Moreover, many of the gratifications and deprivations it dispenses are of exceptional importance to the human organism: love and hate, affection and hostility, friendship and enmity, respect and contempt, sometimes money and power. Because these incentives are so intense, one will strive mightily to avoid the deprivations and gain the gratifications; but often one must choose between a heavily penalized response and an alternative that may be only slightly less penalizing to

---

[6] Use of the word "spontaneous" does not mean that the actions of the controller are uncaused. The controller's actions may themselves be produced by the Control of others. Even if autonomous, presumably they are caused by interaction with nonhuman objects in the environment, or by built-in personality factors, etc. Neither the term "spontaneous" nor the term "autonomous" is intended to imply that any human action is uncaused.

him. This is "tyranny," i.e., a severe deprivation of one's freedom by others.

By contrast, anarchists, looking for a voluntary system of social order, could mistakenly identify spontaneous field Control as a noncoercive substitute for state-enforced commands because they did not always see either that it was Control or that it could be tyrannical. They did not always see it was Control because, like the secret ink described in our boyhood detective novels, it is invisible by the usual tests: there are no commands, no articulated directives, no evident statutes or laws, no specified judicial systems, no prisons for violators. Yet their anarchist society could be as coercive as the "social" tyrannies of Main Street, which would also pass these inadequate tests.

WHY "PLANNERS" DISCOUNT IT.   One can also see why writers on planning have often been hostile to spontaneous field Controls. For one thing, spontaneous field Controls seem relatively unpredictable and erratic. If you substitute commands for spontaneous field Controls, the planner implies, order will prevail over chaos. Then again, to socialist and even to many nonsocialist planners, spontaneous field Controls seem identical with a private, competitive economy or laissez-faire capitalism; laissez-faire capitalism they think is evil; therefore spontaneous field Controls are evil. Those who hold to this view deny that spontaneous field Controls are Controls at all, hence they see that the worker or consumer is controlled by command and manipulation but are blind to spontaneous field Controls over the entrepreneur. Consequently, just as the neoclassical economists exaggerated the role spontaneous field Controls could play in a market economy, so planners have often romanticized the possibilities of command and manipulation of field as substitutes for spontaneous field Controls.

WHY IT DOES NOT SEEM TO BE CONTROL.   Why does spontaneous field Control often not seem to be Control? Observers may simply fail, like the anarchists, to "see" Control operating because there are no commands, explicit laws, specialized enforcement agents, judges, or recognized means of punishment. Controllers may fail to see it because they do not intend the Controlled action and hence their attention is focused elsewhere. Even those who are Controlled may not "feel" the Control for these reasons. Moreover, any

Controls create an atmosphere of permissiveness if the deprivations are slight, if they emphasize rewards rather than deprivations, or if they create a variety of rewards and deprivations among which one may choose in performing the desired response. In principle, command can also operate this way, but usually it does not, for reasons that will become clear in a moment. Hence both spontaneous and manipulated field Controls often give the Controlled individual a feeling that he is performing an autonomous action.

WHY IT IS UBIQUITOUS. Why is spontaneous field Control so commonplace and universal? There are a great variety of reasons for its ubiquity. Some but not all of these also explain the universality of the other forms of Control. The main reasons are:[7]

1. The cues, gratifications, and deprivations are inevitably created by basic human relationships in fundamental human organizations, such as family, kin group, neighborhood, work place, market, friendship group, religious association.

2. It is also a universal control technique because many of the gratifications and deprivations through which it operates are deepseated wants and avoidances of the human organism: love, affection, respect, solidarity, friendship, for example. To achieve these rewards, often the subordinate literally wants to be Controlled. For example, many people avidly long to make responses that will earn them love and avoid hate.

3. It is universal because many vital goals can be achieved only by spontaneous field Control. Although its symbols, rewards, and penalties can be and often are manipulated deliberately, there appears to be a certain degree of psychological incompatibility between deliberate manipulation and some of the important gratifications. If one constantly attempts deliberately to manipulate his loves, hates, affections, friendships, and respect in order to Control others, the value of his love, friendship, and respect tends to depreciate: Control thereupon declines. An element of spontaneity seems to be necessary to valued love, friendship, and respect relations.

Parenthetically, and as corroborative evidence of this last point, one common criticism Americans make of their own culture is the widespread tendency to "prostitute" or "corrupt" these highly valued gratifications through deliberate manipulation in advertising,

[7] Spontaneous field Control in a price system is a special case. All the reasons given here do not necessarily apply to it.

speeches, business "friendships," corporate recruitment and promotion policies, the false joviality and conviviality of the Rotary Club, etc. The result is a serious depreciation in the value of the act; i.e., it ceases to stimulate intense gratification, or even much of a sense of deprivation when it is lost.

4. It is universal because it is quickly learned. Because, as we have just seen, the human organism in most cultures is powerfully motivated to earn the rewards and avoid the deprivations frequently employed in spontaneous field Control, the required responses tend to be learned quickly. Children, for example, speedily learn to respond appropriately to such things as facial expressions, intonations, pitch and volume of voice, choice of words, physical stance.

5. It is universal because spontaneous field Control can be unusually sensitive; compared with it the other techniques are crude and imprecise. In roles where sensitive responses are needed, or the appropriate response requires adjustment to relatively small changes in social stimuli, rewards, and penalties, spontaneous field Control may be necessary. To civilize or socialize a child is in great part to teach him to submit readily to spontaneous field Controls. Jane Austen's novels indicate that the elaborate courtesy of the eighteenth-century gentry in England was mainly a matter of spontaneous field Control. In contemporary society, too, many roles require the individual to subordinate himself to spontaneous field Controls: orators, lawyers, teachers, hostesses, secretaries, and even parents must learn to make sensitive and minutely adjusted responses to by-product stimuli, rewards, and penalties of others.

6. It is universal because it is simple, economical, and easily created. Deliberate calculation and deliberate control of relevant consequences are often felt to be added costs. At the very least, they require additional effort from people. People tend to indulge in deliberate calculation and control, therefore, only when failures to do so appear to be penalizing. To the extent that spontaneous field Control is a way of avoiding deliberate calculation and control, the creation of specialized machinery for enforcement, and specialized organs deliberately devoted to coördinating social activity, it has a kind of *prima-facie* case in its favor.

7. It is ubiquitous because, as we saw, it can be "permissive." Though as we have seen it need not necessarily do so, it may permit a sense of "free choice." To many people in many cultures this feeling is desired in itself. In addition, the existence of this state of

mind may help make for enthusiasm and initiative, qualities also often regarded as desirable.

8. Finally, spontaneous field Control can often be employed, and perhaps usually is, in a bilateral or multilateral relationship. If it begins as a unilateral relationship, often it is easily converted into a bilateral one. Consequently, people may be able to Control one another without damaging subjective equality. Although subjective equality is not a universally demanded goal, in any societal organization where subjective equality is highly valued, spontaneous field Controls will be widely used in bilateral and multilateral relationships. Even in a highly oligarchical societal organization there would be some demand for subjective equality among the oligarchs, and among the subordinates.

MANIPULATED FIELD CONTROL

Very often a spontaneous field Control is potentially a manipulated field Control. The young child's cries bring the mother to its crib. At first the Control is spontaneous. But soon the child learns that a cry will be followed by mother's attention; then it cries whenever it wants attention. The child now operates a manipulated field Control. Or again: for years consumers buy in the market with no intention of controlling prices. Then a period of inflation alerts them to the rising cost of living; they stage buyers' strikes in an attempt to bring down prices. Now they operate manipulated field Controls. Another example: oligopolists control each other through manipulated field Controls. Or still again: at one time in the United States the rate of interest was little more than a price paid for the use of capital; it was fixed by multilateral spontaneous field Controls. Only on rare occasions was it deliberately manipulated, as when Biddle and the Second Bank of the United States created a crisis in a vain attempt to frighten Jackson and the Bank's enemies. Today, the Federal Reserve Board relies heavily on the rate of interest to manipulate the fields of bankers, businessmen, and consumers.

WHAT IT IS. A manipulated field Control, then, is deliberate action on another person's field (by means other than command) in order to secure a definite response, by manipulating signals about rewards and deprivations, or by manipulating rewards and deprivations themselves, or both. Thus the subordinate's expectations about rewards and deprivations are affected; and he responds so as to secure the expected rewards or avoid the expected deprivations.

WHY IT IS UBIQUITOUS.   Deliberate manipulation of another's field by acting on information, rewards, and deprivations appears to be as universal, widespread, and comprehensive as spontaneous field Control, and for many of the same reasons:

1. The cues, gratifications, and deprivations of ordinary day-to-day life can be used in this way.

2. Highly ranked gratifications and deprivations can be manipulated to *some* extent. Affection, love, respect, sympathy, hostility, encouragement, friendship, and status are to some extent manipulated as gratifications and deprivations in a wide variety of human groups. But perhaps two instrumental goals, power and income, are most easily manipulated for purposes of Control. Both can be manipulated in relatively fine gradations; they can be used to establish chains of control for large numbers of people; and, because in many societies they are instrumental to a wide variety of prime and other instrumental goals, they are highly effective as rewards and penalties.

3. Because of the importance of the goals used as gratifications and deprivations, the required responses tend to be quickly learned.

4. The Control can be used in a rather sensitive way.

5. Manipulation through cues, gratifications, and deprivations can—though it need not—stimulate feelings of "free choice" and evoke enthusiasm and initiative.

DIFFERENCES.   Yet these similarities do not mean that the differences between spontaneous and manipulated field Controls are not often very great. In one respect they are significantly different. It is difficult for one person or a small group of people to coördinate the activities of large numbers of people through spontaneous field Controls or chains of such Controls; leaders are unlikely to generate the appropriate rewards, penalties, and communications simply as by-products of their own behavior. A social organization operating mostly through spontaneous field Controls would necessarily either be very small or highly dispersed and decentralized. By contrast, deliberate manipulation of expectations through information, rewards, and deprivations opens up possibilities for centralized control by the few over the many. In every large, centralized organization manipulated field Controls must play a highly significant role.

COMMAND

The two Control techniques we have described so far are universal, widespread, comprehensive; probably they are components in almost all Control relationships found in the real world. As compared with these, command is an important but marginal system. For the number of actions Controlled by command seems to be relatively small in most human organizations.[8]

WHAT IT IS. What does one mean by a command? Is there a difference, as popular language implies, between being "asked" to do something and being "commanded" to do it? Although command is not always used in any single sense, a distinct shade of meaning is usually associated with the word: to give a command is to threaten someone with deprivations if he does not obey. And this is the way in which we use the term in isolating command as a third major technique of Control that needs special attention. To put it precisely: *To command is to Control the response of a subordinate exclusively by virtue of a penalty prescribed by the Controller for nonperformance of an implied or stipulated directive, so that the subordinate expects that his failure to respond as directed will result in the initiation of penalties by his superior.*[9]

COMMAND IS MARGINAL. Like the anarchists, many people confuse law with command and command with Control; they see the great number of acts stipulated by law in a modern society and conclude that command is everywhere. But laws are merely in the *form* of commands; they *appear* to be commands because on their face they do no more than prescribe penalties for nonperformance of certain directives stated in the body of the law. Yet as modern stu-

---

[8] In different language, this has been pointed out by other observers. Cf. *The Sociology of Georg Simmel* (translated, edited, and with introduction by Kurt H. Wolff), Free Press, Glencoe, Ill., 1950, pp. 182–183; Charles Merriam, *Political Power, Its Composition and Incidence*, McGraw-Hill Book Co., New York, 1934, pp. 22 ff.

[9] Command in this sense appears to be rather similar to what Harold Lasswell and Abraham Kaplan mean by power. "Power is . . . the process of affecting policies of others with the help of (actual or threatened) severe deprivations for non-conformity with the policies intended." See their *Power and Society*, Yale University Press, New Haven, 1950, p. 76.

dents of the sociology of law point out, the form of the law does not explain why most people obey the law; it only explains why a relatively small number of people obey it. To explain why most people obey laws one needs to examine a complex body of rewards and deprivations through spontaneous and manipulated field Controls that are not invoked by courts but by family, friends, teachers, neighbors, acquaintances, colleagues, superiors, nominal subordinates, and so on. Hence the common paradox of the sociologists: "If a law is not supported by the mores of the community, it is ineffectual; if it is, the law is unnecessary." The paradox is false, of course, because although it is marginal, command can be catalytic. But the paradox correctly suggests the limited role of command in law enforcement.[10]

WHY COMMAND IS MARGINAL. Why is command usually restricted to a relatively small number of acts? For one thing, command usually requires prior training in order to teach the signals, the correct responses, and the appropriate penalties for failure to perform the response. To train people efficiently it is usually necessary to reward them. Hence to establish a command system and keep it going with new recruits often requires one or more of the other Control techniques.

Moreover, for a variety of reasons the fact that pure command imposes deprivations and offers no rewards seriously restricts its utility as a Control technique:

1. Nominal subordinates have no incentive to obey the command if they can devise a way to escape the penalties. (If there is any incentive other than fear of penalties, then a pure Command technique no longer exists.) Hence a considerable amount of ingenuity and energy will tend to be diverted into avoiding commands and escaping the penalties. The failure of prohibition in the United States is a case in point.

2. Command in the limited sense used here is difficult to legitimize. For if an individual is rewarded by his conscience for obeying

[10] The USSR may offer an exception to what we have said about the marginal character of command. Unfortunately, the information necessary to a sound judgment is inadequate. The Soviet Union probably gives a more prominent role to control through command than any other society has ever done. Yet in the three great control hierarchies—party, secret police, and administrative bureaucracy—rewards are manipulated in the form of power, status, and income. Soviet citizens are also manipulated by propaganda—in part, no doubt, to render them more amenable to command.

an order, in the strict sense an element of manipulation of field has been blended with the command Control. It is true, however, that one may intellectually accept the necessity of command as part of a total network of Controls and accept the command as legitimate even if obedience to the particular command is motivated by no expectations of rewards.

3. Because command is difficult to legitimize, it requires specialized machinery for detection, enforcement, and meting out punishment. Specialized machinery is costly.

4. Although the evidence is not entirely clear, it appears that in a pure command situation there is little incentive to industry, enthusiasm, loyalty, innovations, creativity, drive. Dictatorships, military organizations, and other hierarchical systems therefore employ other Control techniques in order to produce responses of this kind. Even slavery is rarely a *pure* command system; yet slavery has usually proved less productive than "free" labor.

5. Because command only imposes deprivations, it is inherently frustrating. Yet relations between controllers and subordinates are certain to be strained if the controller has nothing to offer his subordinates except deprivations. Such a relationship obviously endangers the minimum agreement necessary for organizational stability. A pure command society—one entirely ridden by fear—would seriously threaten social stability.

6. For all these reasons, therefore, superiors themselves find it unprofitable and inefficient to rely exclusively on command. The institution of a system of rewards is an obvious method of minimizing the disadvantages of command. Even totalitarian leaders find it efficient to introduce rewards, e.g., Stakhanovism.

Then, too, many of the most highly ranked goals cannot be obtained by command. As has already been shown, love, affection, respect, friendship, dignity, and solidarity require manipulated field Controls at the very least, and often spontaneous field Controls. Hence thousands of day-to-day relationships are immune to command. Command can only destroy such relationships; it can never achieve them.

Finally, command is possible only under conditions of social organization that prevent subordinates from fleeing the reach of the superior. "The conditions in which many primitive peoples live, afford one safeguard against any form of oppression, and that is the possibility of a group or even an individual separating from the com-

munity and forming a settlement of their own."[11] Under these conditions penalties for disobedience must be administered with extreme care and hence command is curtailed.[12] Even in contemporary
societies, the more "voluntary" a group—that is, the more easily a
member can withdraw and achieve his goals in an alternative group
—the less reason any member has for obeying a command, and
therefore the more limited the capacity of leaders to achieve Control
through command. As will be shown in a later chapter, this social
fact is of extraordinary importance as a condition for polyarchy.

RECIPROCITY

In the real world Control is rarely unilateral.[13] As we have already pointed out, spontaneous Control of another's field is quite
commonly employed by two or more people in a bilateral or multilateral relationship. Yet even in hierarchical organizations there are
many situations in which people can employ command or manipulated field Controls, or both, against one another. Such a bilateral or
multilateral relationship, in which two or more people are Controlling one another through command or manipulation of fields or
both, we shall call reciprocity.

Given goals such as subjective equality, democracy, and freedom, reciprocity is a Control technique of vital importance. If
Control of human beings by human beings cannot be eliminated,
reciprocity is an alternative to anarchy. And if great inequalities in
control are undesirable, reciprocity is an alternative to tyranny.

IV. Control and Coördination

These four fundamental techniques of Control—spontaneous field Control, manipulated field Control, command, and reci-

[11] Gunnar Landtman, *The Origin of the Inequality of the Social Classes*, Uni-
versity of Chicago, Chicago, 1938, p. 320. Cf. also Richard Thurnwald, *Werden,
Wandel, und Gestaltung von Staat und Kultur im Lichte der Volkerforschung*, in
Die Menschliche Gesellschaft, Vierter Band, Walter de Gruyter & Co., Berlin and
Leipzig, 1935, pp. 86 ff.

[12] "Among the Kiwai Papuans . . . there is no one to hinder malcontents from
going away. . . . If among the Kayans of Borneo, some portion of a tribe are
dissatisfied with the conduct of their chief, they leave their former village. . . .
Among the Punans, also, in case of disagreement, one or more of the members of
the band may refuse to accept the judgment of the leader and of the majority; he
or they will withdraw from the community. . . ." Gunnar Landtman, *op. cit.*,
p. 320.

[13] Cf. *The Sociology of Georg Simmel*, p. 185, and Herbert Goldhamer and
Edward A. Shils, "Types of Power and Status," *The American Journal of
Sociology*, September, 1939, p. 178.

procity—are the building blocks from which all social systems are constructed.

LIMITS ON DIRECT CONTROL

Yet these Control techniques are not always sufficient to bring about a desired state of affairs. For one thing, the physical universe can be manipulated only within limits. Although these limits are widening rapidly, as everyone knows they are still narrow. In the face of a widespread drought throughout Asia no Controls could prevent mass starvation.

The social universe is also refractory. As with the physical universe, the limits within which the social universe can be controlled are widening but still narrow. Totalitarian leaders relying heavily on command and centralized manipulation of field are frequently just as much thwarted by human personalities and social organization as polyarchal societies relying heavily on reciprocity. Then, too, there is the eternal dilemma of means and ends. For just as a totalitarian commitment to unilateral control as a means rules out a number of important ends that can be maximized only through reciprocity and spontaneous field systems, so too a democratic commitment to ends allowable only by reciprocity and spontaneous field systems rules out some of the means of control available to totalitarians. Moreover, in every society important areas of individual autonomy are never effectively breached by direct controls. Hence the limits on control, like the limits on rational calculation, are so great that only marginal changes can sensibly be expected from attempts at rational social action, whether in totalitarian or in polyarchal societies.

METHODS OF ROUNDABOUT CONTROL

Nevertheless, even when a desired state of affairs cannot be brought about in the first instance by Control or a chain of control over particular acts, what is desired can sometimes be brought about by indirection.

1. AFFECTING PERSONALITY. Where particular desired acts cannot now be produced, Control can be used in the first instance to *affect personalities*, so that later either an individual's responses produce the desired results or Controls may then be employed that would be unworkable with his present personality. Thus polyarchal societies are possible only because, in the first instance, Controls are

used to indoctrinate and habituate individuals in the kinds of responses subsequently needed to operate polyarchy.

2. AFFECTING ROLES. Control can be used in the first instance to *affect roles*. When a person is faced with a particular agenda (schedule of things-to-be-done) or a class of agendas, he may act in a particular way; if his responses when faced with a particular agenda or class of agendas are more or less habitual and repetitive, then these responses may be said to make up his role.[14] A prosecuting attorney has a role different from that of a defense lawyer. A judge's role is not that of an attorney. Depending upon whether the agenda calls for prosecuting an alleged criminal, defending him, or insuring him a fair trial, the same man tends to make quite different responses.

Control is necessary in the first instance to indoctrinate an individual so that he will later play his role in some desired way. An individual must be taught the kinds of autonomous responses he should make and the kinds of Controls he should accept in the roles he is expected to play in life. In the United States many people are taught responses appropriate to the businessman's role with their first newspaper route, magazine sales, church bazaar, or household chore. Many of these responses subsequently become autonomous. The individual learns, for example, that in his business role he should not apply the precepts of Christian charity stressed in a number of his nonbusiness roles. He is taught to play a variety of apparently conflicting roles by compartmentalizing each of them. Thus responses he would find abhorrent or idiotic in one role seem just and sensible in another.

3. AFFECTING AGENDAS. Control may also be used in the first instance to achieve a subsequent desired result by *affecting the agenda*. This is a matter of affecting the kind of decision that must be made and perhaps changing the people who need to make the decision. For example, some of the aids to rational calculation also make possible changes in an agenda. Thus, to delegate some decisions to others or to quantify the value of alternatives in comparable units can also change the agenda and permit Control where it was difficult or impossible before.

[14] See Talcott Parsons and Edward A. Shils, *Toward a General Theory of Action*, Harvard University Press, Cambridge, 1951, p. 23. Parsons and Shils emphasize the expectations of self and others, rather than the repetitive responses as the distinguishing characteristic of role. We have found the present concept more convenient for our purposes.

To change the agenda is one of the most dramatic and far-reaching methods of government economic planning in war and mobilization. During mobilization and war when raw materials, machinery, and consumer goods are no longer allocated through the price system but by government priorities and direct allotments, the agendas of businessmen and government leaders are profoundly altered. Businessmen and government leaders face a vast new agenda of complex decisions that hitherto were made by no one individual or committee. Government leaders in particular are required to make centralized decisions of staggering complexity, allocating steel, copper, aluminum, and dozens of other materials in a tremendous variety of raw, semifinished, and finished states to the manufacture of an even greater number of semifinished and finished products.

The decisions to be made are of such magnitude that no one individual or committee could possibly make them all; hence, after the agenda is initially changed by substituting government priorities and allocations for the price system, individuals and committees in top policy-making positions continue to change their own agendas by decentralization. The central administrative problem facing leaders in a war economy is to discover the minimum agenda for themselves that is compatible with the need for centralized decision and the maximum agenda compatible with their own capacities. The continual reorganization of war agencies is a long experiment with the agenda.[15]

V. Some Conditions for Effective Control

Often the conditions that make for effective Control are absent. What are some of the most important conditions?

CONSISTENCY BETWEEN CONTROLLER'S AND SUBORDINATE'S GOALS

First, the goals of the would-be controller must be consistent with at least some of the goals of the individual he hopes to Con-

---

[15] There is no clear dichotomy dividing Control over particular acts in order to achieve the immediate coöperation of others from Control over particular acts that in the first instance affect personality, roles, or agenda, because (a) there is always some time lag between the action of a Controller and the responses of a subordinate, (b) the desired response from the subordinate is usually preceded by some intervening responses, and (c) it is not always easy to decide whether a response is unique or repetitive.

trol. It is as easy to exaggerate the pliability of human personalities as to underestimate it. In recent years Marxism, Leninism, behaviorism, advertising, early propaganda studies, and the dissemination of anthropological knowledge about diverse cultures all have fostered the erroneous conclusion that human beings can be made in almost any mold; and further that in cases where immediate Control is limited, one merely needs to Control the rearing of the next generation.

But men are not infinitely pliable.[16] In every society some people stubbornly persist in seeking goals that conflict with their would-be controllers. Primitive societies, though relatively homogeneous as compared with our own, have to cope with deviants; and they handle their deviants in a variety of ways, at one extreme accepting them as magicians or medicine men and at the other extreme subjecting them to torture, exile, or execution. In any society deviants present something of a problem. If controllers deal vigorously with them this action often creates goal conflicts with still other people. Yet if the recalcitrants are permitted to go their way, they may influence others.

ADEQUATE REWARDS AND PENALTIES

Second, controllers need an adequate system of rewards and penalties. Yet it is often impossible for would-be controllers to create such a system even where there are no ineradicable conflicts in goals. For they may lack knowledge and resources. We have already stressed the role of rewards and penalties in Control, and it seems superfluous to do more at this point than emphasize it again as a formally necessary condition.

INTERNALIZED REWARDS AND PENALTIES

FUNCTION OF THE CONSCIENCE. Not all the rewards and deprivations to which a person responds are external. The source of

[16] For example, "Though every biological fact is given a social meaning, the stuff provided by heredity is not infinitely plastic." Clyde Kluckhohn and Henry A. Murray, "A Conception of Personality," in Kluckhohn and Murray (eds.), *Personality in Nature, Society and Culture*, Alfred A. Knopf, New York, 1949, p. 107. And see Clark L. Hull, *Principles of Behavior*, Appleton-Century-Crofts, New York, 1943, pp. 59–60; Otto Klineberg, *Social Psychology*, Henry Holt and Co., New York, 1940, pp. 160–162; George P. Murdock, "The Common Denominator of Cultures," in Ralph Linton (ed.), *The Science of Man in the World Crisis*, Columbia University Press, New York, 1945, pp. 127–129; Gardner Murphy, *Personality*, Harper & Brothers, New York, 1947, pp. 127–129, 620, et seq.; Edward Chace Tolman, "Motivation, Learning, and Adjustment," *Proceedings*, American Philosophical Society, vol. 84, 1941, pp. 543–550.

many rewards and deprivations is internal, in the sense that these rewards and deprivations are inflicted by the self on the self in such forms as shame, pride, self-respect, anxiety, or self-approval. Such internalized rewards and deprivations constitute the individual's conscience (or superego). Because these rewards and deprivations are internalized, once they are built into the individual they are not easily manipulated.

Hence great social effort is invested in building into people some particular type of conscience. A heavy investment in training the superegos of people in a social organization often pays rich dividends because of two vital functions carried on by the conscience.

AS SURROGATE CONTROL. First, the conscience is useful as a surrogate control; this fact makes it possible for superiors to repose enough confidence in subordinates to grant them discretion. For example, the Atomic Energy Commission in effect has at its disposal a vast amount of "patronage" in the form of contract awards to private corporations for the design, construction, and operation of its facilities. The Joint Congressional Committee, the Budget Bureau, and the White House might have created an extensive supervisory system to insure that contracts were fairly awarded; but such a system would be cumbersome and costly to administer. So far, extensive external supervision over contract awards has been avoided; in effect, confidence in the consciences of the commissioners and their employees permits Congress and the President to grant a large measure of discretion to the commission.

It is not too much to say that the operations of many organizations—industrial, commercial, governmental, religious, educational —would initially come to a halt if superiors could place no reliance on the consciences of subordinates. To function at all, these organizations would have to be made much more centralized and hierarchical; the gains of decentralization and discretion would largely be lost.

AS SOURCE OF LEGITIMACY. A closely related function of the conscience is to help establish legitimacy. Control is legitimate to the extent that it is approved or regarded as "right."[17] The test of

[17] The concept of legitimacy has been strangely neglected in American political science. Herbert A. Simon, Donald W. Smithburg, and Victor A. Thompson

"rightness" may be rather conscious, articulated, logically struc-
tured norms (such as a theory of the appropriate role of judicial review in a democratic order). Or the test may be the less conscious,
more incoherent norms with less logical structure and abstract
theory, the "feeling" of what is right and wrong in a given instance.
The second is more inaccessible to manipulation than the first; it is
more nearly the domain of the conscience. Because it is more inaccessible, controllers are often unable to achieve many of the responses they seek.

Because legitimacy is tested subjectively, what is legitimate
Control to a controller may be illegitimate to a subordinate; what is
legitimate to one subordinate may not be legitimate to another.
Partly because of this complexity, partly because of the multiple
superiors of modern pluralistic societies, and partly because of the
breakdown of consistent belief systems,[18] clear-cut legitimacy is
probably much rarer in modern Western societies than in the past
or in many primitive societies. Thus Control, like so many other
social phenomena, tends to be ranged between the pure polar types
of legitimacy and illegitimacy. A decade after Pearl Harbor Americans were still sharply divided over the legitimacy of Roosevelt's
Control over foreign policy decisions during the year preceding the
Japanese attack.

Legitimacy is not indispensable to all Control. Nevertheless
lack of legitimacy imposes heavy costs on the controllers. For legitimacy facilitates the operation of organizations requiring enthusiasm,
loyalty, discretion, decentralization, and careful judgment. It is
difficult to imagine how the atomic bomb could have been designed,
developed, and constructed in the time it was if every participant
of the Manhattan Engineer District had regarded General Groves'
Control as entirely illegitimate.

APPROPRIATE IDENTIFICATION

The way in which one identifies himself with others is often
crucial in determining how, and indeed whether, he can be induced

have recently helped to restore it, in *Public Administration*, Alfred A. Knopf,
New York, 1950.
   [18] Karl Mannheim, *Diagnosis of Our Time*, Kegan Paul, Trench, Trubner &
Co., London, 1943, pp. 17 ff.; Alexander H. Leighton, *The Governing of Men*,
Princeton University Press, Princeton, 1946, pp. 322–325; Sebastian de Grazia, *The
Political Community*, University of Chicago Press, Chicago, 1948, *passim.*

to respond in a way desired by someone else.[19] Yet, because it is internalized, like the conscience, it is not easy to manipulate.

One's planes of identification may facilitate or frustrate Control. The small child exerts Control over the parent partly because it is so easy for the parent to identify with the child. The docility of white-collar workers in business organizations no doubt partly stems from their tendency to identify themselves with their superiors. But in recent years urban workers have evidently identified themselves more and more with one another; the plane of identification with business leaders has snapped.[20] Workers are therefore more responsive to working-class leaders, less responsive to business leaders.

One important consequence of altering a role is often to alter one's identifications, the "self" at the focus of attention and striving. In his various roles as son, friend, father, husband, neighbor, club member, retail purchaser, business executive, and voter, the individual may have rather different identifications. Controls one submits to as father he would find intolerable as business executive, and vice versa. His identifications in the act of buying a lamb roast, a set of matched irons, a car, or a house may be rather different from one another, and even more different from his identifications in the act of voting in a polling booth, a town meeting, or a legislative body.

Thus identification can impose stubborn restraints on Control; and often controllers can do little more than accept the identifications of their subordinates as given, and alter their own Controls accordingly.

COMMUNICATIONS

Finally, Control requires effective transmission of cues, signals, stimuli, or information. In the interwar years the competitive price system was looked on with a certain disdain by many reformers and

[19] In political science the most extensive use of the concept of identification is in the various works of Harold Lasswell. With respect to the subject at hand, however, cf. Herbert A. Simon, *op. cit.*, chap. 10. The term "identification" has been used in various ways, but the most suitable for our purposes is the one by Simon: "A person identifies himself with a group when in making a decision he evaluates the several alternatives of choice in terms of their consequences for the specified group." *Ibid.*, p. 205.

[20] This is strongly indicated by a comparison of Lynd's two studies of Middletown. See Robert S. Lynd, *Middletown*, Harcourt, Brace and Co., New York, 1929, and *Middletown in Transition*, Harcourt, Brace and Co., New York, 1937.

planners. Experience with hierarchical coördination of national economies during wartime and in postwar reconstruction in some countries—particularly in Great Britain—has stripped some of the glamour from hierarchy, however, and has restored a little to the price system. One important reason for this change in mood is the realization that hierarchical coördination of a national economy imposes such a staggering burden on communications that the dilemma of central coördination vs. decentralized discretion is never satisfactorily resolved. By comparison the ease of coördination through the price system in some circumstances seems rather more attractive to many "national planners" than it did during the interwar years when they were still unfamiliar with this problem of hierarchical coördination.

Sometimes one important reason for changing an agenda is to make possible a different system for transmitting information. Thus to change the agenda from hierarchical allocations of raw materials in wartime to allocations through a competitive price system is to work a profound change in the system of communications.

These, then, are some of the critical prerequisites of Control. Once stated, they seem rather formal and obvious. But sometimes it is easier to forget the obvious than the obscure.

VI. Freedom, Equality, Rationality, and Control

FREEDOM AND CONTROL

There is no necessary blood feud between freedom and control. On the contrary, freedom requires control. As we have shown in a previous chapter, freedom often requires social organization. Yet every social organization is a system of controls. It follows that freedom must often require some system of controls.

One may reach the same conclusion by another route. Most of us have highly valued goals we cannot achieve unless we are able regularly to secure the responses of others; regularly to secure the response of others is to Control them; hence our own freedom requires each of us to Control some others in certain respects. Conversely, some of our goals like friendship and love cannot be achieved unless we allow others to Control us in some respects.[21]

[21] Confusion over the relationship between freedom, control, and autonomy is sometimes compounded by a failure to distinguish the freedom of (1) the subordinate, (2) the controller, and (3) others affected by the actions of the subordinate or controller.

Sometimes freedom is confused with autonomy—the absence of Control. But if what we have just said is true, freedom cannot be identical with autonomy. (Possibly the controversy over "free will" vs. "determinism" might be more meaningful if cast in terms that carefully distinguished autonomy, Control, and freedom.) To be sure, autonomous actions may sometimes be necessary to one's freedom because occasionally one's goals cannot be attained except by autonomous action. Many aesthetic satisfactions are of this kind. But whenever one's own goals require the responses of others, to rely on autonomous action is to frustrate one's own freedom.

What, then, is the bearing on freedom of the four techniques of Control discussed earlier in this chapter?

FREEDOM AND SPONTANEOUS FIELD CONTROL. As has already been shown, spontaneous field Controls are among the most tyrannical most of us ever know. Because such important gratifications and deprivations as love and hate or respect and contempt are dispensed through spontaneous field Controls, possibly no other system of control can be so frustrating, so oppressive. Literature and real life are both full of the tyrannies of the family, the neighbors, the small town, the office, one's colleagues, relatives, even friends operating through spontaneous field Controls. It is doubtful whether even command can wreak the harm of some spontaneous field Controls; for spontaneous field Controls can, and often do, provoke overwhelming frustration, anxiety, despair, hatred; permanently wreck personalities; and create the sufferings of neurotics and psychotics. In the last analysis, probably far more people are in mental institutions and prisons because of spontaneous field Controls than because of command.

The very fact that spontaneous field Control is unintentional is often the source of its tyrannies. Controllers do not even know they are responsible for the misery of their victims. The checks imposed by sympathetic identification may therefore be missing or come too late. Yet, unlike command, spontaneous field Controls need not frustrate the goals of the subordinate. Unlike command, and like certain forms of manipulated field Controls, some forms of spontaneous field Controls are compatible with the freedom both of controller and of subordinate. No doubt it is because spontaneous field Controls *can* in some circumstances lead to the mutual freedom of subordinates and controllers that Controls of this kind are so often implicitly identified with freedom; a possible condition of freedom is wrongly taken as a sufficient condition.

MANIPULATED FIELD CONTROL. Much the same can be said of manipulated field Controls. There is no one-for-one relation between manipulated field Controls and freedom. Whether they increase or decrease freedom depends upon the situation, the specific kind of manipulated field Controls used in that situation, and whose freedom is under consideration.

But the ways in which one can manipulate the field of another have significantly different consequences for freedom. Two sets of alternatives are particularly important: (1) whether one manipulates symbols of reality in order to clarify or to confuse individuals' understanding of reality and (2) whether one manipulates the field of an individual with rewards or with deprivations. Let us examine both of these sets of alternatives from the standpoint of the individual controlled.

1. Manipulating symbols of reality in order to control others may be done in two ways (these are really ends of a continuum), which have usually been valued quite differently in the Greco-Roman culture and its derivatives. The effort to manipulate symbols in order to clarify the subordinate's understanding of reality—i.e., to provide him with expectations that will prove to be correct when he acts in accordance with them—has usually been highly valued by the norms of Western societies. Parents, teachers, political leaders, and others are expected to rely heavily on this method of manipulated field Control. But one may also manipulate symbols of reality in order to transmit false expectations, as is often done in propaganda, advertising, and political campaigns. Although widely practiced, and in recent generations developed to a high art, this type of manipulated field Control conflicts violently with certain persistent norms of Western culture.

Men like Jefferson have urged widespread education, dissemination of correct information, discussion, freedom of speech, and freedom of press all as necessary instruments to individual freedom. Their assumption has been that these institutions are necessary if people are to obtain a correct understanding of reality. The better individuals comprehend reality, they further assume, the more efficiently they can attain their goals. The more efficiently people can attain their goals, the more liberated they are. Hence in the liberal democratic view there is a direct connection between one's freedom and his understanding of reality.

Even if early liberal democrats like Jefferson and Paine employed an excessively rationalistic psychology, modern psychology lends strength to their basic assumption. Because ignorance of reality is an important source of frustrating actions, ignorance does diminish freedom. Perhaps the most enslaved people in any society are the neurotics; and the neurotic is in one sense a person who has learned a false view of the reality around him.

To be sure, if reality itself is frustrating, then merely to understand it will not make one free. The child living in a disreputable slum with embittered, quarreling parents will not be liberated simply by being made to understand his immediate environment and the world beyond. In social life, sometimes an individual is less frustrated if he does *not* know what his fellows think of his actions.

Yet despite these difficulties, the liberal democratic view is basically sound. For if reality is frustrating, the need is not merely to understand it but to change it. And if reality is frustrating, there is a powerful motivation for changing it. To understand reality, then, is to increase the chances for changing it in desired ways. To understand reality even when it is frustrating is often a necessary condition for an increase of freedom.

An unbridgeable gulf divides the case of the liberal democrat from the case of Dostoevski's Grand Inquisitor. Reality is often inherently so frustrating (runs the attack on the liberal case) that people can survive only with myths. To manipulate symbols in order to confuse reality is better for mankind than to increase their understanding, it is said, because understanding will only multiply their despair. Only a very short step divides the Grand Inquisitor from Lenin's "Truth is a bourgeois virtue."

The liberal democratic case rests on the premise that, even if ignorance may decrease frustration in the short run, in the long run ignorance will significantly increase frustration by reducing one's capacity for dealing effectively with reality. And if it be said that the deceptions are only to be temporary, the liberal democrat will reply that controllers who can impose "temporary" deceptions are almost certain to be in a position of control from which they can convert temporary deceptions into permanent ones.

The liberal democratic case is, then, an argument for scientific investigation, freedom of inquiry, and a belief that truth is open-ended.

2. As for the second set of alternatives, manipulated field Controls that employ rewards clearly grant more freedom to the Controlled individual than command can ever do; for command is inherently frustrating to the subordinate. But even without commanding an individual, one can manipulate the field of a subordinate by affecting the deprivations that actually operate on him. This is not to command him, because the individual does not have the expectation that the controller will initiate certain prescribed penalties for his failure to obey some specific directive of the controller.

Whether manipulation of operating penalties is more or less frustrating than command, it is impossible to generalize. Because command is a more ostensible, direct, person-to-person relationship, perhaps it can offend status, self-respect, and dignity of individuals more than does manipulation of operating penalties. Manipulation of field seems to be more suitable for creating "permissive" situations, i.e., situations in which a particular response is attained although the individual can choose among a variety of rewards and penalties. On the other hand, manipulation of operating penalties can create frustration and despair merely because the subordinate cannot always clearly identify and attack the controller (even if only secretly). Thus the question must be left unsettled. This fact in itself has some significance, because sometimes it is assumed that to act on operating penalties must inevitably lead to greater freedom than to command.

COMMAND.   In appraising command it is particularly vital to distinguish the freedom of subordinate, of controller, and of third parties. For if the freedom of the subordinate were the only concern, then command would rarely be used. For command is a method of Control by threats of deprivation; it directly and necessarily reduces the immediate freedom of the subordinate. The other control techniques *can* be used in such a way as to increase the immediate freedom both of controllers and of subordinates. Command never can directly increase the freedom of the subordinate; the freedom of the controller is always attained at the immediate expense of the subordinate. For the subordinate can never earn any immediate rewards for what he does; he can only escape deprivations. Hence, in a pure command situation the subordinate does not seek goals rewarding to himself; he can only seek goals rewarding to the controller.

Yet if the freedom of the subordinate is always infringed by command, the freedom of the controller or of third parties sometimes requires it. Take the suppression of crime. Not, of course, that impulses to criminality are mainly controlled by command. As we have already indicated, command in the form of law, prescribed penalties, police, courts, and prisons is a marginal factor in controlling criminality. Yet few of us would dispense with command; for we do want to use it against the marginal human beings who can be inhibited from criminality only by the expectation of judicial penalties, or by imprisonment and the actual limitation of the criminal's resources for committing crimes.

RECIPROCITY. Unlike command, reciprocity need not inherently limit the freedom of any participant. But wherever there is less than complete agreement on goals among all the participants in a reciprocal arrangement someone's freedom is bound to be restrained. Hence reciprocity is mainly important to freedom as a system for arriving at decisions as to whose freedom will be permitted or curtailed, and by how much, in cases of conflict.

CONCLUSION. Thus even a short examination of the relationships between freedom and the four control techniques shows that no one of them is more indispensable to freedom than the others and no one of them is inherently more productive of freedom than the others. This is, we think, an important conclusion. For there is a tendency to assume that one type of Control is intrinsically superior to the others; or that from goals like political equality and freedom one can logically establish the superiority of, say, reciprocity over command. This, as has been shown, is false.

The most one can say—and this too is important— is that command always infringes the freedom of subordinates and the other techniques need not. A society concerned with maximizing freedom must therefore be inventive in discovering effective alternatives to command. But it must be equally inventive in discovering effective alternatives when the other control techniques infringe upon freedom.

And in all situations where democracy is a dominant goal, reciprocal Controls are necessary among the participants. Command and manipulated field Controls are unilateral. The Control relationship they make possible is inherently an unequal one; the subordinate is not the political equal of the controller. Hence reciprocal Controls are the only tolerable ones among political equals *qua* political equals. Not only reciprocity but maximum reciprocity is required. Any deviation from maximum reciprocity means political inequality.

SUBJECTIVE EQUALITY

Like political equality, subjective equality is not always a goal to be maximized. This difficult and admittedly ambiguous goal, it will be recalled, was stated this way: *Wherever in any specific situation in which more people rather than less can have the opportunity to achieve their goals, the decision is for the greater number rather than for any lesser number.* Thus a relationship of subjective equality requires in general that rewards and deprivations be distributed more or less equally

COMMAND. If one considers only the relationship between controller and subordinate, clearly pure command inherently violates subjective equality. For pure command, remember, can inflict only deprivations on the subordinate, whereas the controller is usually in a position to reward himself through the actions of his subordinate. Hence command increases the opportunity for the controller to attain his goals at the expense of the subordinate's opportunities. The subordinate must do the bidding of the controller or suffer punishment; the subordinate's own goals—aside from his desire to escape punishment—are neglected. For to the extent that the subordinate gains anything by the action, other than an escape from punishment initiated by the controller, he is rewarded; and if he is rewarded, something more than a pure command relationship must exist.

MANIPULATED AND SPONTANEOUS FIELD CONTROLS. Unlike the case with political equality, manipulated and spontaneous field Controls may or may not violate subjective equality. Any unilateral Control does create the possibility, of course, that the subordinate may suffer at the expense of the controller. But neither manipulated nor spontaneous field Controls *need* to produce this result. For the controller can use these Controls to grant rewards to the subordinate. Hence, the subordinate can maximize some of his goals within such a relationship.

RECIPROCITY. As a practical matter, however, some element of reciprocity is the best guarantee that Controls will be used to reward the individuals controlled. Any unilateral relationship is potentially exploitative. The crucial guarantee that rewards and deprivations will be distributed on something like an equal basis is the fact of mutual Control. Alike in intimate personal relationships such as love and friendship and in the more impersonal relationships of work place, store, town hall, and federal office building, what makes for subjective equality is the fact that each participant exercises some Control over the other.

So far we have been concerned only with the subjective equality of the individual Controlled. As was seen in the case of freedom, however, one cannot appraise the utility of a Control technique only from that standpoint; for one must also consider the controller and any third parties who may be affected. Then too, one's appraisal is likely to vary with one's concern over the outcome of a specific decision.

In many cases involving the action of other people one has little concern with the outcome of a specific decision; yet one might have a strong preference that the outcome, whatever it might be, should not significantly violate subjective equality among the participants. In such cases it is logical merely to rule out any relationship that will significantly violate subjective equality.

In practice, a tremendous variety of social relationships is disposed of in this way. No particular outcome is demanded by third parties. But the relationship is regulated so that A can Control B only if B expects to gain by it; any relationship where A can Control B only at B's expense is ruled out by various laws and regulations. Indeed, laissez-faire liberalism was hardly more than an application of this idea to all or nearly all economic relationships. And the changes from laissez faire to the modern highly regulatory state are a result not so much of an abandonment of the rule as of a growing belief that the rule could not be realistically applied to many situations. For laissez faire actually permitted much more unilateral control by entrepreneurs over workers and consumers than the theory recognized. The modern regulatory state is an attempt, then, not to arrive at specific decisions by government action, but to rule out relationships that significantly violate subjective equality.

RATIONALITY AND CONTROL

To achieve a variety of goals as complex as those of Chapter 2, a more or less rational society, it should now be clear, would need to use all four Control techniques in a formidable array of different combinations and permutations. To describe all the combinations needed would take not a book but an encyclopedia of many volumes. Even if all the needed combinations were known, and certainly they are not, even to list them would doubtless take as many pages as there are in this book. In the rest of this volume we content ourselves with describing some of the major combinations most relevant to problems of government economic planning.

Before turning to these, however, it may be worth while to indicate in summary form the necessary relationships between the four Control techniques and the goal-scheduling devices discussed in the previous chapter. For the way in which a group of people schedules goals is dependent on its choice of Control techniques; and conversely, the Control techniques a group employs are dependent on its choice of goal-scheduling devices:

1. To schedule goals through:

Voting or implicit voting	requires	Reciprocity
Market choices or other spontaneous choices	requires	Spontaneous field Control
Delegation	requires	Command and/or manipulated field Control

2. Conversely, Control by:

Reciprocity	requires	Voting or implicit voting
Spontaneous field Control	requires	Market choices or other spontaneous choices
Command and/or manipulated field Control	requires	Delegation

A look at these relationships reinforces our previous conclusion. Because goals like those of Chapter 2 require all of the scheduling devices listed above, it follows that they also require all of the Control techniques. Conversely, because goals like those of Chapter 2 require all of the Control techniques, it follows that they also require all of the scheduling devices.

One final warning: Even when one knows the goals he wants to achieve, it is often difficult to decide intelligently which Control technique, or which combination of Control techniques, to employ. There are two main reasons for this difficulty. First, rarely can anyone know all the relevant consequences of using one Control tech-

nique rather than another. Indeed, there is one vital set of consequences about which relatively little is known, and these are the
long-run consequences for the personalities of the people involved.[22]
Hence choosing one technique or combination is to some extent
groping in the dark. Second, one technique can often be converted
into another, thus interjecting an indeterminate element in the decision, for not only must one calculate the probable consequences of
one technique as against another in a given situation; one must also
try to calculate both the likelihood that one technique will be converted into another and the probable consequences of such a
change. In the past, laissez-faire liberals sometimes ignored this
point. Under the benevolent jurisdiction of Say's Law, which ruled
out mass unemployment and the consequent exploitation of labor,
they often failed to see that in depression the entrepreneur was able
to Control his employees by command with little reciprocal restraint. Labor was not in fact mobile; nor did a worker always have
alternative employment; and in the worst circumstances, he rented
a company house and went into debt at a company store. Hence, an
unscrupulous employer possessed a large element of Control; he
could direct the workers to accept certain working conditions on
penalty of severe, unilateral deprivations if the workers refused.
Thus an ostensible system of reciprocal Controls was converted
into a command system.

One must always reckon with this possibility. One crucial test
of governmental techniques, for example, is supplied not by normal
operations but by crisis. For in crisis and its aftermath a society discovers the forms into which its governmental techniques can be
converted.

[22] Some relevant questions are raised but few are answered in our final chapter.

Part III

SOCIAL PROCESSES

FOR

ECONOMIZING

5.

Social Processes for Economizing

I. The Six Processes

Given the values postulated in Chapter 2, what processes are necessary to rational calculation and control in economic life? Or, alternatively, what processes are required for economizing? There are many ways to describe economizing, but six familiar processes can be identified:

1. DISTRIBUTION OF CLAIMS ON RESOURCES. The first is a process of calculation and control for achieving a preferred distribution of claims on labor and other resources. Not all of everyone's goals can be satisfied in economic life. Economizing, therefore, requires a process for determining whose goals shall have priority and to what extent. Shall all members of the community have equal claims on labor and other resources, or some more than others? How much more? Shall all enjoy some minimum claim on resources or shall some be wholly deprived? The process for allotment of claims may be the threat of force in the hands of an elite, custom, discussion, or voting. In a money economy, claims largely take the form of money income.

2. STABILIZATION. The second is a process of calculation and control for reconciling total claims with total resources to be claimed. Stabilization requires that resources be neither under- nor over-allocated. The consequence of the first is unemployment; the consequence of the second is that some claims cannot be made effective. To describe stability is easy; to achieve it is not. From the 1930's until quite recently, economic instability so overshadowed other economic problems that the stabilization process came to be thought of as the largest part of economizing. The experience of the 1930's is enough to demonstrate that instability can waste resources more alarmingly than can imperfections in any of the other econo-

mizing processes. Between 1933 and 1937, unemployment in the United States was never below seven million, and it reached fourteen million. Between 1929 and 1933 national income fell by almost one-half. These are familiar figures; but they are worth some emphasis if only because, as socialists have for a long time correctly argued, techniques of economic organization incapable of restricting fluctuations in income and employment to a much narrower range and to shorter duration will be considered intolerable regardless of their efficacy for other aspects of economizing.

3. CHOICE.   The third is a process of calculation and control by which those persons who have claims may choose among alternatives and signal the responses desired. In modern economies the communication of preferences from claim holders to the management of business enterprises requires an elaborate mechanism. Given the values postulated, the process must accommodate occupational choices—such as between different jobs or between work and leisure—and other producer preferences, as well as consumer choices among alternative goods and services.

4. ALLOCATION.   The fourth is a process of calculation and control for inducing responses to choice. A reward and penalty system is required to induce workers and resource owners to put their productive capacities to the uses called for.

5. RESOURCE DEVELOPMENT.   The fifth process is spawned by the fourth. It is a process of calculation and control for increasing the quantity of resources. One method is to allocate some resources to the production of more resources. But development may also be accomplished by discovery and invention. In Europe, Africa, Asia, and South America, economic policy is today in large part given over to increasing production by the development of natural and capital resources. Postwar reconstruction and the development of backward areas have imposed a burden on governments to raise production by the immediate expedient of large-scale investment. In these circumstances, attention to refinements of the choice and allocation processes is easily overshadowed, although particular choices and allocations remain important.

6. HIGH RESOURCE OUTPUT.   The sixth is a process of calculation and control for achieving high output from resources in their allocations. Resource output depends, of course, upon the allocation of resources. Workers who do not have capital equipment allocated to them cannot produce much. But many other factors affect resource output—among others, the intelligence, skill, industry, pre-

cision, and speed with which management and employees in an organization discharge their duties.

II. The Requirements of "Good" Economizing

Given the values postulated, what is a desirable, preferred, or ideal distribution of claims, pattern of choice, allocation of resources, rate of resource development, and level of resource output? The stabilization process poses no such question, since stability was easily defined. For the other processes, however, criteria are not immediately apparent. We shall suggest some criteria for each process, beginning with resource development.

REQUIREMENTS FOR RESOURCE DEVELOPMENT

Extrapolating past trends, real gross national product in the United States can be expected to rise on an average of about 3.5 percent each year or, in other words, to double every twenty years.[1] For the future, the actual rate of growth will, of course, depend upon a variety of influences that make extrapolation somewhat dangerous. But it appears that with the prospect of less waste of resources through instability than previously, the increase can easily rise significantly above an average of 3.5 percent.

What is a desirable rate of resource development? "The more, the better" is not a correct answer because a maximum rate of development is at war with other goals no less important. Existing resources cannot always be used to produce both consumer goods and new productive capacity; resource development is therefore often at the cost of present consumption. Moreover, British experience in recent years has shown that ambitious plans for resource development encourage overcommitment of resources and consequent instability. Britain has also experienced conflict between resource development and income redistribution, for both make demands upon the government's budget. Even the choice and allocation processes may suffer from too rapid resource development. If development is encouraged by granting enterprises a larger degree of autonomy than they would otherwise have, as is sometimes proposed,[2] the gain is sometimes at the cost of consumer control over choice and allocation.

[1] Simon S. Kuznets, *Uses of National Income in Peace and War*, National Bureau of Economic Research, Occasional Paper No. 6, New York, 1942.
[2] Kenneth E. Boulding, "In Defense of Monopoly," *Quarterly Journal of Economics*, vol. 59, 1945, pp. 524–542.

On the other hand, resource development sometimes facilitates other processes. It runs hand in hand with processes for achieving high resources output, as illustrated by techniques for improving technical practices and production organization within business enterprises. And resource development through education and occupational training is indistinguishable from processes for high resource output. It will also be seen shortly that a major reason for more equality of income is that it permits greater investment in human productive capacity than is otherwise possible; hence, processes for resource development and the distribution of claims sometimes supplement each other.

The proper rate of development is therefore a matter of subjective preference. Presumably many people will quickly agree that the rate should be pushed very far whenever it is possible to do so without serious conflict with other objectives. Discovery and invention are most promising in this respect because they make development possible with a relatively small drain on resources for other purposes. So far, too, as development can be had through equalizing educational opportunities, a rapid rate is desirable. Beyond that, opinions may differ. Conflicts between distribution of claims or stabilization, on one hand, and resource development, on the other, pose difficult problems of choice which can only be resolved *ad hoc*. So also do conflicts between the choice and allocation processes and resource development.

In several economies resource development offers the possibility of raising standards of living by one-third in ten or fifteen years.[3] Such gains as these are well worth the sacrifice of some incremental gains in other social processes. The benefits of resource development are worth stressing, for economic theory has slighted them in its preoccupation with the choice and allocation processes. Only in the last few years has the theory of economic development come to the center of the stage.

REQUIREMENTS FOR RESOURCE OUTPUT

A recent book on taxes and incentives has this to say about desirable resource output: "Insofar as existing tax schedules cause executive personnel to refuse to assume the maximum responsibilities

[3] Since 1850 output per man-hour in the United States is estimated to have increased 18 percent per decade. See J. Frederic Dewhurst and associates, *America's Needs and Resources*, The Twentieth Century Fund, New York, 1947, pp. 22–25.

they are capable of carrying, or cause them to put forth less than their best efforts in their present tasks, they must be adjudged socially and economically undesirable."[4] Most emphatically, however, ideal output is not maximum output. The statement is true only if one cares nothing for the distribution of real income, nothing for leisure, nothing for peace of mind, nothing for the individual's freedom to set his own pace—only, in short, if output is the one and only social goal.

Given the values postulated earlier, production deserves no general priority over better income distribution or many other social goals, especially intangibles such as justice, fair play, and an equitable distribution of status, prestige, and control. Where, for example, workers do not attain maximum output in their jobs, the loss is not equivalent to the enterprise's lost product. From the loss of product must be subtracted a variety of benefits. Admittedly, these values are not always gained when production is lost; but for Western economies generally the gains of leisure alone are large.

Increased resource output will not be achieved primarily by inducing people to work harder. If this were the only method available, one could not be at all confident that still higher output was desirable. Increased output can be pursued through better technical practices in industry, industrial relations, and training. These possibilities—and there are many more—are enough to indicate that higher resource output is possible without the hardships either of more stringent discipline or of exhausting work schedules. Hence, increased resource output can often be had at very low cost.

But because, like resource development, high resource output is not always costless, the optimum rate is therefore again a matter of subjective preference. Most people will agree that processes for raising resource output should fully exploit the possibilities of achieving both higher output and equality in educational opportunity at the same time. They will also wish to exploit possibilities of raising productivity by methods that do not increase the tension or other burdens of work. Beyond such truisms, the proper level is a matter for *ad hoc* consideration.

As in the case of resource development, the potential gains from higher resource output have sometimes been neglected by economists in their preoccupation with choice and allocation. The

[4] Lewis H. Kimmel, *Taxes and Economic Incentives*, The Brookings Institution, Washington, 1950, pp. 104–105.

study of critical factors in resource output (aside from allocation itself as a factor) has been left largely to students of industrial relations and managerial practices.[5] Their estimates of what might be gained without offsetting disadvantages range from 25 percent to 50 percent.[6] These are crude and somewhat ambiguous estimates, but they suggest that processes for attaining high resource output hold great promise.

COMPLICATIONS IN THE DISTRIBUTION, CHOICE, AND ALLOCATION PROCESSES

For the distribution of claims and for the choice and allocation processes, it is possible to go much further in describing a desirable or preferred position than is the case for resource development and output. To be sure, a desirable distribution of claims is a matter of subjective preference, as is the case with resource development and output. Nevertheless, one's subjective preference will depend upon how one resolves a number of particular issues to be discussed. And for choice and allocation, it is possible to spell out more or less objective criteria for optima. We shall consider distribution first.

III. Requirements for the Distribution of Claims

Economizing begins with scarce resources and ends with goods, services, leisure, and other values in the hands of consumers. It is efficient only if the right goods, services, and other values get into the right hands. Whether they do or not, in modern industrialized economies, depends in large part upon the distribution of claims in the form of *money* income. But the distribution of *real* income and leisure depends only in part upon the distribution of money income because real income also depends upon the pattern of consumers' choices and the way in which holders of resources respond. Hence, although we judge the distribution of money income by its effects on the distribution of real income and leisure, other influences on real income distribution cannot be neglected.

---

[5] Cf., for example, Chester Barnard, *The Functions of the Executive,* Harvard University Press, Cambridge, 1938; Fritz J. Roethlisberger and W. J. Dickson, *Management and the Worker,* Harvard University Press, Cambridge, 1939; Fritz J. Roethlisberger, *Management and Morale,* Harvard University Press, Cambridge, 1941; Burleigh B. Gardner, *Human Relations in Industry,* Richard D. Irwin, Inc., Chicago, 1945.

[6] R. P. Lynton, *Incentives and Management in British Industry,* Routledge and Kegan Paul, Ltd., London, 1949, p. 65.

Can an optimum be described? A large number of variables and limited knowledge about them combine to make description impossible. Notwithstanding, we believe that some patterns of distribution can be shown to be less desirable than others; and it is possible to indicate the direction that incremental adjustments in distribution probably should take. With the present distribution of money and real income as a starting point, will a movement toward more or toward less equality better approximate the postulated goals?

In the United States the market distribution of money income is quite unequal. In 1948, for example, the average family income before taxes was roughly $4000, the median below $3500. But while almost one-third of these incomes were less than $2000, an almost equal number were above $5000. And if the national money income were divided into two parts, slightly more than half would go to 80 percent of the population and slightly less than half would go to the richest 20 percent. The top 5 percent of the population had as much income to divide up among themselves as the bottom 40 percent.[7]

But taxation and transfer payments achieve a shift toward equality. As everyone knows, income taxation alone sharply reduces very high incomes; income tax rates for 1951, for example, took roughly one-fourth of a $20,000 income of a childless couple. For the range of income in which the great bulk of families are found, however, the equalization effects of taxation are small. In the United States, some taxes are regressive; but, considering the progressive income tax alone, even its effects on equalization are narrowly limited. Here is the percentage distribution of money incomes by spending units, before and after federal income taxes.[8]

Income Groups	Before Taxes	After Taxes
Under $1,000	14	15
$1,000–$1,999	19	21
$2,000–$2,999	21	23
$3,000–$3,999	19	18
$4,000–$4,999	11	11
$5,000–$7,499	11	8
$7,500–$9,999	2	2
$10,000 and over	3	2

[7] U.S. President, *The Economic Report of the President Transmitted to the Congress January, 1950*, U.S. Government Printing Office, Washington, 1950.

[8] U.S. President, *The Economic Report of the President Transmitted to the Congress January, 1951*, U.S. Government Printing Office, Washington, 1951, Table B-1, p. 226.

The transfer of income through social security and other welfare expenditures is not easily estimated, because much of this expenditure is supported by taxes on those who receive the payments and services. For the United States, the net transfer achieved by taxes and transfer payments and services is probably not in any case more than 10 percent of the national income. In the absence of adequate calculations for the United States, the best evidence for this statement is the elaborate calculations of redistribution in Great Britain in 1937, which show that taxation and public expenditure probably transferred from the rich to the poor 5 to 6 percent of the national income.[9] If this amount appears inconsequential, another way of putting it is that working-class incomes were increased in Britain by 8 to 14 percent by redistributive finance.[10] American and British redistribution is now more substantial than before the war; but 1937 was marked by unusually high transfer payments for the prewar period. In any case, the 10 percent estimate for the United States is almost certain to be high; the correct figure may easily be less than 5 percent. The transfer in Sweden has been estimated at 10 percent.[11]

EQUALITY AND INEQUALITY

SOME UNACCEPTABLE CRITERIA. A common doctrine justifying movement toward inequality is that individuals have a "right" to take out of the community income what they have put into it; income shares should equal individual "contributions" to society. But for two reasons the doctrine is unacceptable. First, although its advocates appeal to the need for incentives, the doctrine does not clarify the relation between size of differential and strength of incentive. That is to say, this doctrine is often asserted to justify distributive patterns that will maintain desirable incentives, but whether the patterns do maintain incentives is not investigated. "Contribution" theories might easily produce such inequality as to demoralize a population rather than develop desirable incentives.

Second, advocates of this doctrine sometimes do not justify it by reference to incentives but simply declare that people "deserve" to be rewarded according to what they do. Or they assert that it is

[9] Tibor Barna, *Redistribution of Incomes Through Public Finance in 1937*, Oxford University Press, New York, 1945, p. 233.
[10] *Ibid.*, p. 232.
[11] Erik Lindahl, "Swedish Experiences in Economic Planning," *American Economic Review*, Papers and Proceedings, May, 1950, p. 12.

"natural" or "obvious," or that "this is the way things should be."
In this kind of statement, fact and moral judgment are confused.
There is no obvious ethical justification for the position, and we
find no merit in rewards other than those which perform particular
functions, such as providing incentives to desired activity. Granted
that a *quid pro quo* in distributive shares seems to find sanction in
deeply ingrained feelings of fairness in many minds, we can only
recognize this as a sociological fact, not a guide to policy. In large
part, advocacy of this doctrine is explained by the strong hold of
the doctrine of natural rights.

On the other side of the fence are various equalitarian criteria.
If natural rights doctrines are used to rationalize an interest in preserving existing inequalities of income, certain dogmatic equalitarian
doctrines are also seized upon to rationalize complete equality. No
man deserves more than any other man, some equalitarians declare.
It seems "obvious" or "natural" to them that, in the absence of any
special circumstances, A and B should be given the same rewards
and opportunities. This is merely another version of natural rights.

An analogy between political equality and income equality is
sometimes incorrectly developed into a justification of the latter.
The argument is sometimes strikingly presented through the contrast between strict equality of voting in ideal democratic life and
extreme inequality in the casting of dollar votes in the market. If it
is indefensible to grant more than one vote to any one person, how
can A be justified in possessing 100,000 dollar votes if B has only
1000? But the case for political equality is for political equality in
the "last say" only. For many reasons, special voting rights or other
unequal controls are given to particular persons or groups. None
of this is inconsistent with political equality if there remains equality in determining the circumstances in which such special arrangements can be made and terminated.

It has sometimes been suggested that formal economic theory
provides a value-free objective argument for complete equality of
income.[12] The argument runs something like this: In order to maximize the satisfaction of wants, it is necessary to put income into the
hands of those to whom the utility of additional income is highest.
Generally the utility of additional income is highest for those with
the least income. Hence, redistribution from high to low income

[12] See Abba P. Lerner, *The Economics of Control*, The Macmillan Company,
New York, 1944. For a similar example, see Howard R. Bowen, *Toward Social
Economy*, Rinehart and Co., New York, 1948, chap. 19.

recipients will maximize want satisfaction. Hence, equality is called for.

The most serious of several flaws in the argument is that its conclusion is hidden in its initial assumption. What does it mean to maximize want satisfaction? It means that "no part of the consumption goods or the income of the society shall go to any individual but the one who can obtain the greatest satisfaction from its consumption."[13] Now this is clearly a prescription for the distribution of shares and, as such, is a statement of value and not of fact or definition. No doubt it seems perfectly clear to some people that it is desirable to maximize satisfaction. But an *obiter dictum* that income should be distributed in order to take care of the greater wants instead of the smaller is a value judgment, not an objective, scientific proposition.

Rejecting these arguments for inequality and equality, we believe that incremental shifts in income distribution toward more equality are desirable on three grounds: for subjective equality, for political equality and stability, and as an investment in resources.

SUBJECTIVE EQUALITY. It is not necessary to labor the connection between more equalization of income and the goal of subjective equality postulated in Chapter 2. Equal opportunity to attain goals is inconsistent with the degree of income inequality prevailing in the United States and other economies of the Western world. Many of the most common goals of individuals are consumption goals; clearly if equality of opportunity to achieve consumption goals were an absolute, equal income distribution would be required. And aside from consumption goals, opportunities to move freely in society, to participate in government and civic activities, to be educated, to possess status and respect, and to find congenial employment are all dependent upon one's income. If there is any disagreement on the desirability of more income equality on the grounds of subjective equality, it must go back to the goal of subjective equality itself, for the closeness of the relationship between subjective equality and income distribution is hardly debatable.

Because goals conflict with one another, subjective equality gives little clue as to how far equalization should be pushed and no clue at all concerning other goals with which equalization might clash. These problems we shall have to consider; for the moment,

[13] Abba P. Lerner, *op. cit.,* p. 25.

however, the bearing of subjective equality on income can be simply stated and the complications deferred.

POLITICAL EQUALITY AND STABILITY. Although this second reason for incremental movements toward equality is subordinate to the first, it cannot lightly be passed over. Indeed, it requires more spelling out than the first reason. Disparities in income are often a source of tension in society, and this in turn is a source of political instability through a breakdown of agreement.

Because political instability has many roots, agreement may decline for many other reasons; and, on the other hand, disparities in income may breed only a kind of tension having little political consequence. Generalizations on the relationship between inequality and political instability are consequently hazardous. But although the postwar instability of French and Italian politics has many causes, it is in part an illustration of the consequences of an unsatisfactory distribution of income. In these and other examples the dependence of agreement and political stability upon some degree of income equalization seems reasonably clear.

Income inequalities in the United States do not appear great enough to threaten stability. Yet they may be sufficient to explain, say, the impossibility of administering a successful anti-inflation program through price and wage controls. Most people wish to minimize inflation, but agreement on what needs to be done founders on each group's desire to improve its income. Earlier, the intolerable income position of the aged in the United States nurtured not only the Townsend Plan but "ham and eggs" and a dozen other panaceas. If these schemes were no threat to agreement, they were no doubt a blight on rational calculation.

Where tensions threaten consensus or calculation, the danger is never absent that the ensuing political instability will threaten the very survival of polyarchy, for the desirability of free speech, freely competing political parties or free elections may no longer command agreement. This is one of the more serious aspects of political instability in France and Italy, for example, and was presumably one aspect of Longism in the United States in the 1930's.

Income inequality, however, threatens equality in political power more directly than through its effect on agreement. Political equality is not guaranteed by formal rules such as "one man, one vote." As everyone knows, money talks in politics; and genuine equality in political power is impossible where income differences create serious inequalities in the power to communicate with other citizens and with members of the control elites, although these failures in communication have other roots as well. Inequality obstructs the achievement of democracy.

Today the greatest threat to agreement, stability, and democratic government is at a level where it sometimes goes unrecognized. Communism seeks to win the world away from the agreement so far formed on the desirability of democracy, and its tactics have already shattered the stability of one country after another. It has fed upon discontent with inequality of all kinds. Because the problem is enormously complicated, it would be foolish to hope to rid the world of this threat solely by more equality of income. Yet it would be equally foolish to ignore the contribution that a better distribution of income within both advanced and backward economies might make to an agreement on the value of democracy.

INVESTMENT IN HUMAN CAPACITIES.   Another way of looking at the distribution of claims is to consider distribution as an investment process. For any economy, the major resource is man himself; and his claims to food, medical care, education, and other values are a measure of the care with which his productive capacities are stimulated and exploited. The United States has carried public education, scholarships, and technical training very far; even so, the existing distribution of income is inconsistent with as full a utilization of human resources as could reasonably be desired. There are still more untrained than trained able minds, just as there are many man-hours of production lost because low income means poorer health.

How much manpower is wasted? The President's Commission on Higher Education reports that the waste is large. The effects of income level on education are, of course, often not only direct but also indirect, for example in influencing the level of aspiration. On the basis of a follow-up study of boys in the sixth grade, in 1926, in Pennsylvania schools, it would appear that out of a given number of boys with the same intelligence quotients four times as many boys from the highest occupational income groups will go to college as from the lowest occupational income groups. From another study, for every high-school graduate who was in the upper 10 percent of his class and subsequently entered college, another graduate of equal rank did not. For students from the upper one-third of their high-school classes, two do not enter college for every one who does.[14] These studies are limited, but they show that only a minority of the able young minds in this country are given college training.

They are confirmed by other studies showing that while almost all children of the high-income families finish high school and while 70 to 90 percent of them go to college (the percentages vary, of course, depending upon the particular high-income group chosen), among the lowest-income groups only a third finish high school and only 1 to 5 percent go to college.[15] The difference in opportunity is clear; the educational differences are much too large to be attributable to differences in capacity correlated with income.

Educational deficiencies attributable in large part to income distribution show up even in expenditures on elementary education. In the United States in 1940, annual teachers' salaries in public elementary and secondary schools ranged from an average of $559 in Mississippi to an average of $2604 in New York. Current expenditures per pupil ranged from an average of $31 in Mississippi to an average of $157 in New York.[16]

Similar inequalities appear in physical fitness. Chronic illness is three times as prevalent among the poor as among the well-to-do, and disability destroys three times as many work days for the very low income groups as for those at upper income levels.[17]

If for the last hundred years Western economies had invested less in capital equipment and more in human capacities, they might have developed their productive capacity even more rapidly.[18] Whether this conjecture is true or not, the waste of manpower due to income inequality is enormous.

[14] President's Commission on Higher Education, *Higher Education for Democracy*, U.S. Government Printing Office, Washington, 1947, Vol. II, pp. 13–15.
[15] Testimony of John L. Thurstone, U.S. Congress, Joint Committee on the Economic Report, *Hearings*, Subcommittee on Low-Income Families, December 12–20, 1950, U.S. Government Printing Office, Washington, 1950, pp. 4–5. For additional evidence, see U.S. Congress, Joint Committee on the Economic Report, *Low-Income Families and Economic Stability*, Materials on the Problem of Low-Income Families Assembled by the Staff of the Subcommittee on Low-Income Families (81st Congress, 2nd Session), U.S. Government Printing Office, Washington, 1950 (Senate Document No. 231), pp. 16–19.
[16] J. Frederic Dewhurst and associates, *America's Needs and Resources*, The Twentieth Century Fund, New York, 1947, pp. 310–311.
[17] *Ibid.*, p. 249.
[18] H. D. Henderson, *Supply and Demand*, Harcourt, Brace and Co., New York, 1922, p. 131.

THE DIMENSIONS OF A DISTRIBUTION PATTERN

Beyond a general endorsement of "more equality, but not too much," it is impossible to deal intelligently with distribution without making more specific the particular goals which more income equalization might attain. Equality and inequality are only crude terms. What particular pattern of income distribution should be sought and for what reasons?

Consider the statement: "Some people do not have enough income." In part, such a statement simply recognizes that, resources being limited and hence national income never as large as would be wished, there is simply not enough income to satisfy our goals regardless of its pattern of distribution. But, so far as it refers to an inadequacy in distribution it has many possible meanings.

It may mean that some individuals or families do not have enough real income, even considering both what they buy with their money income and free community services available to them. It may also mean that they do not have enough disposable cash income after taxes. Or it may mean that they do not have enough of some particular service or commodity, such as housing or education, which is thought to be critical. And sometimes it means that some people suffer from the stigma attached to their low earnings, quite aside from their standard of living. These propositions only begin to identify the many problems subsumed under the heading of maldistribution of income; it is apparent that an attempt even to list all the problems would run into difficulties.

We can, however, simplify the incredibly complex problem of equitable distribution by classifying the principal variables affecting the choice of a preferred distribution.

First, maldistribution is a problem both of *size* of shares and also of *direction and speed of change in* size of shares. That is to say, an income share may frustrate an individual, not only because it is small, but because it may decline rapidly even if still large, or because it fails to continue to grow, even if already large.

Second, what is divided up may be any of the following:

1. Money or real income.
2. Income excluding or including leisure.
3. Income before taxes, subsidies, and free government services; or income after taxes, subsidies, and free government services; or income after taxes, subsidies, free government services, interpersonal gifts, and charity.

4. Particular goods and services, the consumption of which is important to the community.
5. Current income or income over a long period, such as a family cycle.
6. Earned income (from wages and salaries) or unearned (interest and dividends).
7. Inherited or noninherited income.
8. Current income or accumulated wealth.[19]
9. Income at the start of life (i.e., income as a resource for the subsequent development of income earning capacity) or income as an end product in adult life.

Third, standards may reflect the community's concern with the welfare of an isolated individual, at one extreme, or the group's survival as a group, at the other. The distribution of income may therefore be held to constitute a problem by reason of its failure to meet any one or more of the commonly used standards:

1. Physical subsistence and bodily health.
2. Need, however defined.
3. Simple equality.
4. Some other socially acceptable minimum standards of consumption for the individual.
5. Minimum consumption of certain named goods and services.
6. Personal integrity where (through inequalities in consumption and education or through differences in social mobility, opportunity, or habits of thought and behavior) maldistribution is thought to degrade personality and character.
7. Political stability and polyarchy where maldistribution is thought to produce acute social tensions.
8. Social harmony, and mutual solidarity, respect, and identification where (through differences in consumption, education, social mobility, opportunity, or habits of thought and behavior) maldistribution is thought to create class difference and produce a failure of communication between classes.

Fourth, the nature of the problem of maldistribution depends

---

[19] Despite the inadequacy of statistical estimates, the distribution of wealth is known to be more unequal in the United States than the distribution of income. A study of liquid asset holdings throws some light on the pattern. In the United States, in 1945, roughly 20 percent of the spending units with the most liquid assets owned 77 percent of the total amount of liquid assets; the lower 20 percent owned practically none. See Bureau of Agricultural Economics, *National Survey of Liquid Asset Holdings, Spending and Saving*, U.S. Government Printing Office, Washington, 1946, Part I, p. 7.

upon whose income is inadequate. This suggests that particular problems of maldistribution arise in connection with:

1. The income of individuals.
2. The income of families.
3. The income of children.
4. The income of particular individuals for whom the community may feel a special responsibility, such as widowed mothers.
5. The income of major economic groups taken as groups, as illustrated in a concern felt in some quarters for the abstraction called "farm income."
6. Income of special groups who for a variety of reasons may as groups suffer particular deprivation, as illustrated by the concern for the inadequacy of medical care in rural areas.

Fifth, since income and wealth serve a variety of purposes for the individual, the problem varies according to what purpose is thought to be badly served by a maldistribution of income. The purposes or income objectives include at least the following:

1. Consumption.
2. Status, both where income is a source of status itself and where income makes it possible for the individual to acquire status through particular uses of his income.
3. Security.
4. Control.
5. The further development of earning capacity.
6. Cultural and social opportunities.
7. Leisure time.
8. Self-respect.

SOME CONCLUSIONS

PRIORITIES IN DISTRIBUTION. Which of these many aspects of the distribution process is most important? The answer depends on one's values; but a great amount of light is thrown on the answer by an identification of the low-income groups in the United States.

In 1948, one-third of nonfarm families received less than $2000 per year. These low-income families show rather specific characteristics. Families headed by persons over sixty-four years of age account for one-fourth of the low-income families. Almost as many low-income families are headed by women. And in over half of these families headed by women the family heads are not employed.

Clearly broken homes are a major low-income problem. Of the low-income families whose heads are not over sixty-four, roughly one out of five is nonwhite. Three-fifths of the low-income family heads have had only an elementary-school education or less. A smaller but still sizable group are the disabled. Between a half and a third of the low-income families are without employment at least part of the year. Finally, one-third of the low-income families are headed by unskilled or only slightly skilled workers.[20] Hence, low income can be largely tied to old age, broken homes, color, education, and occupation; and reforms in distribution should be largely directed toward these groups.

Moreover, for fairly obvious reasons, inequality at the start of life—inequalities in the opportunities for children to develop themselves and their earning capacities as they mature—constitutes a relatively more urgent problem than many of the others. Inequalities in wealth can also be singled out as an urgent problem. They beget inequalities in income. In addition, because property income is commonly thought of as unearned, inequalities arising from the earnings of property probably produce greater tensions than do inequalities from wages and salaries. Moreover, inequality in property is often a source of undesirable differences in status, social mobility, and social class even apart from those differences originating in income inequality.

PHYSICAL OR SOCIAL NEEDS. In the United States the major social evils are probably due less to inequality in consumption, leisure time, or security than to inequality in status, cultural and social opportunities, and control. Here we run into intangibles and can proceed only with caution. But it is not unreasonable to suggest that lower-income groups are injured not so much by their diets or homes as by their limited opportunities for creative and imaginative activity, responsible participation, public recognition, prestige, personal achievement, and the like. Satisfying opportunities for the development of personality require more than a full stomach, adequate dress, and a home. Unfortunately, these important intangibles are not easily controlled. Physical subsistence has been a relatively concrete goal to pursue; one can choose among alternative techniques. But how to pursue the elimination of class conflict, or the

[20] Testimony of Dewey Anderson, U.S. Congress, Joint Committee on the Economic Report, *Hearings*, Subcommittee on Low-Income Families, December 12–20, 1950, U.S. Government Printing Office, Washington, 1950, pp. 492–498.

development of the best in human personality, is largely guess-work.[21]

In Great Britain, the United States, Scandinavia, and some other Western economies, public policy has already come closer to an optimum than might at first appear, even if the gap between goal and accomplishment remains large. Aside from the possibility of large-scale destruction of productive capacity in war, physical subsistence is no longer an issue in income distribution. And public policy establishes minimum standards for critically important goods and services like health and education. In 1950, in Great Britain, government expenditures (aside from contributions paid in to national insurance by beneficiaries) on social security, education, housing, family allowances, health, and food subsidies totaled £1303 million.[22] Welfare expenditures are about 18 percent of British national income; they are about 5 percent of national income in the United States.

Hence, although much remains to be done, the more easily defined problems of nutrition, health, housing, and education are slowly diminishing in importance relative to problems of status, prestige, control, participation, and creative activity. And to the extent that problems of nutrition, health, and education remain, they increasingly intertwine with the intangibles. Almost no one in the United States, for example, lacks income sufficient for dental care. Yet large numbers of people are convinced they cannot afford it. The explanation is, of course, that social standards and pressures compel them to turn their expenditures in other directions. Dental and medical care, even nutrition, can more easily be neglected for long periods than kinds of consumption that are the price of social acceptance. Everyone must dress to meet minimum social standards, regardless of his health.

Several studies of minimum diets show how wide the gap is between the requirements of physical survival and minimum social standards. Nothing is more essential to physical survival than food; yet even "minimum" food budgets run way beyond the requirements of survival. In 1944, at a time when social workers and home

[21] For some conflicting views on the cultural consequences of income equalization, see R. H. Tawney, *Equality*, George Allen & Unwin, Ltd., London, 1931, and Bertrand de Jouvenal, *The Ethics of Redistribution*, The University Press, Cambridge, England, 1951.

[22] Barbara Lewis and R.H.B. Condie, "The British Social Security Program," *The Journal of Politics*, May, 1950, p. 342.

economists estimated minimum food budgets per person to be not less than $135 and in most calculations higher, $60 worth of wheat flour, evaporated milk, cabbage, spinach, dried navy beans, pancake flour and pork liver would meet a year's nutritional needs for one individual.[23] The $60 diet lacks palatability and variety; a year's consumption of it would satisfy only a few of the pleasures that individuals take from eating. And this is precisely the point: income requirements are set by other than biological needs.

The implications of this fact run a little further than might at first be supposed. For, if social standards largely determine minimum income needs and if social standards are largely set by those members of the community who can afford to set them, the possibilities of solving income problems simply by increasing the size of the national income are much reduced. Increasing the size of the national income bids fair to raise the social standards that people must meet.[24] Only to a limited extent, therefore, can many of the income goals listed above be met by a larger national income without further equalization.

COMPLICATIONS OF DISTRIBUTION. Finally, it is clear that no simple goal can control the distribution of income. Instead, particular adjustments in particular income flows are needed to meet particular problems. Many different kinds of problems are intertwined; and, conversely, there are many different and somewhat contradictory goals. One might therefore question, for example, tax measures designed to make income shares generally more equal, not only because such general measures may fail to meet the most urgent of the particular problems just identified but also because the term "generally more equal" has no specific meaning. No one can "solve" the problem of the best distribution of income. Because there are many problems, not one, the search for solutions to each will require much attention. The determination of social goals with respect to income distribution becomes as difficult a task as can be imagined.

Reforms designed to attack any one of the problems isolated can be expected to aggravate some one or more of the other problems. For example, attempts to provide an equal start in life or to

[23] George J. Stigler, "The Cost of Subsistence," *Journal of Farm Economics*, May, 1945, pp. 303–314.
[24] For an impressive illustration see Jay Taylor, "Going Broke on $10,000 a Year," *Harper's*, July, 1952, pp. 60–65.

remedy inequalities in the distribution of income among children can, in their effects on family solidarity, produce quite unpredictable results for family incomes and for intra-family distribution.

It is also clear that the technique of distribution is often as important to the goal as the shift in income itself. We cannot policy-wise decide first on the distribution of shares we wish to achieve and then choose the technique. A given pattern of shares is sometimes desirable only if it can be achieved by a particular technique. For example, distribution through charity may be desired where no other distribution would be tolerated. Or distribution through taxation may be desired where distribution through charity would be thought demoralizing. Still further, where techniques can alter earning capacity, it will be possible to approach equality more closely without damaging incentives than where taxes or subsidies are used to redistribute income.

OBSTACLES TO EQUALIZATION

We are still without an adequate answer to the question: Just how far toward equality does a desirable distribution of claims go? In a poor society, like India, income equalization pushed very far would be catastrophic, for leadership in politics, the arts, science, and most other aspects of social organization can hardly develop in such a society unless it is in a favored income position. Even Gandhi required a favored income position. In wealthier societies, although complete equalization would be attended by some of the same difficulties, national wealth makes it possible to move incrementally toward equalization without them. Still, there may be a limit. Similarly, to the extent that equalization turns rivalry for preferred income position into rivalry for power, the consequences of equalization may be adverse. Or equalization may destroy desirable cultural diversity.

It is because no one knows very precisely what the effects of income equalization might be that we cannot defend more than incremental alterations in the distribution of income, the results of which can be observed and used as a guide to subsequent policy. Given present limitations on man's knowledge, an incremental attitude toward distribution goals is much sounder than attempts to predict the consequences of great alterations in distribution for leadership, power, cultural diversity, and other aspects of social organization. Hence, again, no one can define a preferred or optimum distribution of claims; one can only specify desirable directions.

There is, however, one major limitation on equalization so widely discussed—in fact, so greatly feared—that no discussion of income goals is complete without mention of it. This is the incentive question. How far can equalization go without undermining desirable incentives? This question requires a careful answer. It is subordinate to the larger question of a preferred or optimum distribution of claims, yet its complexities require extended discussion.

LIMITED KNOWLEDGE OF INCENTIVES. Incentives, or rewards and penalties, pose an impossibly large subject. Fortunately, "the incentive problem" in income distribution pertains to a limited number of specific incentives. The problem arises from the use of differential money rewards to induce certain responses critical to production.[25] But the amount of useful systematic, verified knowledge on the relation of income to incentives is small.[26] The freedom with which confirmed opinion is expressed on the relationships is out of proportion to knowledge.

Deficiencies in knowledge are specific. Only short-run effects can be observed, and even these only with difficulty. Yet in the long run an adjustment of expectations may take place so that a given reward or penalty produces quite different responses than earlier. In addition, empirical information usually describes how some people respond to changes in distribution; how representative their responses are is not known. Moreover, no one has yet attempted a systematic examination of available empirical data for evidence on the degree to which advantageous changes in incentives

[25] In describing the requirements of effective economizing in this chapter, we have been trying to avoid confusing the requirements themselves with particular techniques through which the requirements can be met, for the latter are to be discussed in later chapters. In the case of income distribution, however, the technique of differential money rewards for controlling production bears so closely upon the limits to which equalization can be pushed that we cannot hold to the distinction between requirement and technique.

[26] For a sample of the literature see the following authors, each of whom recognizes the limitations of knowledge on the subject: Dennis H. Robertson, *Economic Fragments*, P. S. King & Son, Ltd., London, 1931, chap. I, pp. 1–22; J. M. Clark, "Economics and Modern Psychology," *Journal of Political Economy*, February, 1918, pp. 146 ff.; Klaus E. Knorr, "Welfare-State Measures and the Free Market in International Trade," *American Economic Review*, Papers and Proceedings, May, 1951, pp. 431–444; R. H. Tawney, *op. cit.*; J. J. Spengler, "Sociological Presuppositions in Economic Theory," *Southern Economic Journal*, October, 1940, pp. 142 ff.; R. P. Lynton, *op. cit.*; Thomas H. Sanders, *Effects of Taxation on Executives*, Division of Research, Graduate School of Business, Harvard University Press, Cambridge, 1951; Lewis H. Kimmel, *op. cit.*

offset adverse effects. Finally, most studies of incentives cannot disentangle the effects of a particular pattern of income distribution from either (1) the sometimes quite distinctively different effects of a particular tax or other technique used to achieve the distribution or (2) the effects of a transitory process of adjustment to a new pattern of distribution.[27] The core of these difficulties is that man acts in a field in which income differentials are only one element. He is influenced by other controls, as well as by role and personality.

SOME GENERAL COMMENTS ON INCENTIVES. How necessary are existing differentials? From the scanty evidence available for Western economies, it is quite as difficult to show that smaller differentials threaten incentive as to show that they would stimulate incentive. A common expectation that substantially reduced differentials will impair incentives is not demonstrably more rational than a conviction that the size of existing differentials is a barrier to production. This proposition can best be supported by examining each of several incentives in turn. But let us first take account of some frequent general misconceptions about income differentials.

1. Money rewards are often confused with differential money rewards. In fact, however, money rewards may be necessary when differential rewards are not. Moreover, because differences in income and differences in status, prestige, and control tend to be correlated, the possibilities of harnessing status, prestige, and control incentives without money differentials, as with dollar-a-year men, are easily underestimated.

2. Furthermore, money income is both reward and resource. Reduction of differentials to raise the money incomes of low-income groups will increase their resources, in turn often heightening their incentives. For the effectiveness of money rewards in controlling behavior depends upon both their size and their attainability, and an increase in an individual's resources puts otherwise impossible rewards within his reach. The effectiveness of a reward is reduced, the longer the reward is delayed,[28] and its effectiveness is wholly lost if the reward is thought to be unobtainable. At an

---

[27] For an illustration, see Lewis H. Kimmel, *op. cit.* He recognizes all these defects in his study.

[28] John Dollard and Neal E. Miller, *Personality and Psychotherapy*, McGraw-Hill Book Co., New York, 1950, pp. 187–188.

extreme, apathy is a probable product of great inequality in incomes.

3. Even where rewards are obtainable, it does not follow that the more rewards, the better for effective incentive. For when too many of the rewards of life are contingent upon performance and too few granted outright, insecurity and despair may be more common reactions than the responses which the rewards are designed to call forth. A classic example is work restriction growing out of fear of unemployment.[29] Larger shares of money income as a right, coupled with smaller differentials for variations in performance, may encourage employees to respond less hesitatingly to money incentives.

4. Where income differentials are clearly needed for incentives, evidence is still lacking on whether the most effective reward is one's rank on the income ladder or the size of the differential. Income differentials before taxes are generally thought to possess incentive effects, even if taxes subsequently remove much of the difference in size of income. Note how often a man's status in the economy is described by his salary. Clearly this suggests possibilities for reconciling incentives with relatively small differentials in disposable money income. Just as a corporate executive is motivated to increase corporate earnings even if he does not share in them, so also is he motivated to win the prestige of a high salary even if he cannot spend much of it.

5. The clearest evidence of responses dependent upon differentials is in the use of special money rewards to induce overtime work; in many circumstances extra effort can be had only by a premium rate of pay. Unfortunately, the use of differentials for any one individual to induce extra effort is occasionally confused with the use of differentials between, say, doctors and manual laborers to induce men to become doctors. The two situations are quite different, and the need for interpersonal differentials in the second is much less easily established than the need for an intrapersonal differential in the first.

6. This raises the question of the work-leisure choice. Despite a not uncommon belief that high income for work is necessary to dispose the individual toward work and against leisure, high pay

[29] R. P. Lynton, *op. cit.*, pp. 65 ff., 75 f.; Klaus Knorr, *op. cit.*, p. 441; E. Mayo, *The Human Problems of an Industrial Civilization*, The Macmillan Company, New York, 1933.

for work may dispose an individual toward leisure. No doubt high pay makes work attractive; but the consequent high income makes leisure also attractive. Whether, therefore, large income differentials turn the work-leisure choice in one direction or the other will depend, among other things, on preferences of the individual for purchasable goods and leisure at the margin. The state of knowledge does not permit generalizing on these marginal preferences, although they would appear to be different for different income groups; but clearly, marginal preferences are not such that more equality necessarily means less work.[30] Moreover, reduction of inequality, say, through restriction of inheritance can actually increase the strength of money income incentives to work for those who would otherwise, because of their wealth, be less sensitive to them.

In summarizing interviews with executives, a recent study of the effects of taxation on executives illustrates this point:

> The cases in which the evidence showed executives to be working harder were at least equal in number to those indicating less effort, and the former were more definitely recognizable as a tax influence. There seems to be something in taxes analogous to the influence of the rate of interest on the amount of savings. Just as there are some determined souls who save more when the interest rate is reduced, in order to reach a desired goal of income from savings, so the same types of men are apt to work harder when taxes are increased, in order to have an income after taxes which is adequate to support the standard of living, and furnish the protections to their families, which they had set themselves as an objective.[31]

7. Because high resource output is required for economizing, but maximum resource output is not, income equalization that reduces work and increases leisure may be either desirable or undesirable. In some circumstances, however, redistributive taxation for income equalization appears necessarily to cause an undesirable bias toward leisure. A payment may be offered for services that are not forthcoming because the supplier prefers leisure to the payment, minus taxes. Consumers of the services prefer the service to the money they are offering, and the supplier prefers the payment to leisure if he does not have to pay the tax. Although everyone concerned would be better off if the money could be exchanged for

---

[30] Lewis H. Kimmel, *op. cit.*, p. 99.
[31] Thomas H. Sanders, *op. cit.*, pp. 20–21.

the service, the transaction will not take place because of the re-distributive tax. But this is an adverse incentive effect only on the assumption that the supplier's work-leisure choices are not already biased toward work. This is not an unreasonable assumption; yet it ought not to be forgotten that work-leisure preferences are heavily influenced by rivalry and emulation, which themselves are to a degree a product of existing inequality. Their effect may be to create an irrational disposition toward work at the margin.

8. The need for differentials is sometimes exaggerated because adverse effects of taxation on incentives are confused with adverse effects of equalization. Income tax rates in both the United States and Great Britain have stirred fears that more equalization threatens incentives. But high taxes are attributable to a variety of governmental expenditures of which equalizing expenditures are only a part. Whether higher taxes threaten incentives or not is debatable; but, granting for the sake of argument that they do, the only conclusion one can draw is that more equalization will be possible when, say, the tax burden for military expenditures is reduced. Because only 5 percent of government expenditures in the United States is for welfare (education, health, social security, and so forth), it is clear that taxes for these purposes can be increased greatly if other expenditures decline.

Moreover, taxation has adverse effects on incentives quite aside from the amount of income it transfers. Consequently, there are many possibilities for resolving conflicts of incentives and taxation in such a way as to make both high taxation and income redistribution less troublesome; business taxation is especially afflicted with unnecessary obstacles to desirable incentives.[32] One of the major contributions that tax reform can make to some kinds of incentives is, of course, in reducing taxes on margins; that is, in avoiding reduction of money rewards for responses at the margin.

9. Finally, the need for large differentials may be exaggerated because, as differentials are reduced, deterioration in incentives is more quickly observed than improvement. If informal work restrictions among factory workers were reduced by reduction of differentials which increased low incomes, the cause of the consequent increase in output would be difficult to establish. Similarly, it is not easy to find concrete examples of new energies unleashed by

[32] For suggestions, see Ralph S. Brown, Jr., "Techniques for Influencing Private Investment," in Max F. Millikan (ed.), *Income Stabilization for a Developing Democracy*, Yale University Press, New Haven, 1953.

the higher hopes and better training which income equalization may permit. On the other hand, it is easy to find examples of deterioration of incentives; for people react quickly and obviously to redistribution through tax increases.

THE INCENTIVE TO BE DILIGENT. Let us now examine particular incentives classified somewhat arbitrarily to focus on important incentive problems. One is the incentive to work diligently. It can hardly be doubted that skill, industry, and discipline in work are the product of countless variables in a person's field and of role and personality; work habits differ from culture to culture. British and American workers and managers, for example, display different attitudes toward work, supervision, craftsmanship, and speed of operation that cannot be explained by differential money rewards. And within any one culture differential money rewards are of limited importance in transforming a less industrious workman into a more industrious one.

Evidence shows the limited success of incentive wage schemes. For roughly three-fourths of all employees, both in the United States and Great Britain, payment is by time, not piece. The majority of workers "have a material incentive to come to work. Once at the workplace, however, it is literally immaterial to them whether they produce more or less."[33] And, as for the role of incentive wages for the minority, one observer has said of the system: "Generally speaking, it is successful whenever it helps to foster good industrial relations; on the other hand, good industrial relations are a prerequisite to its successful working."[34]

A recent study supports the same opinion of managerial incentives to diligence. "The evidence of the interviews tends to show that the extent to which business executives have reduced their work and effort, as a result of taxes, has frequently been much exaggerated. . . . A great many reasons have been cited to show why effort has been sustained in spite of taxation. They cover the whole area of nonfinancial incentives to work, as well as the compulsions of administrative organization and disciplines."[35]

THE INCENTIVE TO SAVE. Considering the incentive to save broadly, and taking account of the capacity to save as well as the

[33] R. P. Lynton, op. cit., pp. 84 ff.
[34] F. Zweig, Productivity and Trade Unions, Blackwell's, Oxford, 1951, p. 53.
[35] Thomas H. Sanders, op. cit., p. 12. For a similar study and a similar result, see Lewis H. Kimmel, op. cit.

inducement to do so, this incentive is probably more dependent upon income differentials than is the incentive to diligence. Motives for saving may be increased or decreased by reducing differentials, but the traditional and essentially correct argument is that the capacity of the well-to-do to save will be much reduced by reduction of differentials which reduce high incomes. The very poor live beyond their incomes; on the middle class and the well-to-do Western societies lean heavily for savings. In 1949 the lowest fifth of income units spent 150 percent of their incomes; the upper fifth saved 16 percent.[36]

Yet this argument does not mean that any reduction of differentials that reduces the incentive or capacity to save thwarts capital growth. Although dependence of savings on income differentials is sometimes stated simply, the relation between differentials and savings is in fact quite complex. In the first place, individual consumers cannot save in the sense in which economists find it convenient to use the term. They can "not spend" by putting funds into bank accounts, annuities, stocks and bonds; but whether "not spending" accomplishes an actual saving of national income—a withholding from consumption of a segment of real income for use in future production—depends upon whether the "not spending" of consumers is offset by a category of business spending, that is, by business investment. If "not spending" is matched by business investment, actual saving takes place, because savings and investment are merely two ways of looking at the same process of capital accumulation. If "not spending" is not matched by investment, income and employment decline, and there is neither new saving nor new investment—simply an outright reduction in spending. Given the critical role of investment, savings are therefore more likely to determine whether prices rise or fall than to determine the rate of capital accumulation.

The consequence, then, of the "not spending" of the well-to-do may sometimes be disastrous; it depends upon incentives to invest, which we shall consider below. But, clearly, one source of incentive to invest is consumer spending, and, while "not spending" may make funds available to businessmen, consumer spending is what makes it profitable for them to put the funds into business activity. Hence, the question of what differentials in income shares will provide the appropriate volume of spending and "not spend-

[36] U.S. President, *The Economic Report of the President Transmitted to the Congress January, 1951*, p. 225.

ing" is delicate; it is not simply a matter of "the larger, the better."

Of course, resource development may be encouraged in a variety of other ways than by the saving-investment process. Invention and discovery increase productive capacity even without increase in the quantity of investment. As they wear out, old machines and techniques can be replaced with more productive ones. And equalization, we have already said, is a method of developing human productive resources.

Nor is individual or family "not spending" the only possible source of funds for capital development. In the United States a substantial proportion of total savings is accomplished by corporations; internal saving, in the form of undistributed profits and depreciation allowances, far exceeds the volume of funds secured through capital markets.[37] This could be developed through tax and other legislation into an even more important source of funds consistent with substantial equalization of income. Another alternative is some kind of governmental responsibility for savings through, for example, compulsory savings from each individual collected along with income taxes.

THE INCENTIVE TO INNOVATE. Lack of factual data requires that we dispose of the incentive to innovate with brevity. Some individuals are content to do their work according to instructions they never question; others cannot put their hands on a machine or on material without speculating on how the work might be done better. No systematic knowledge is available to explain the difference between the two, except that temperament, intelligence, identifications, and skills are more critical than money rewards. Where innovating becomes a routine job, as in a research laboratory, its incentives are the incentives to be diligent.

Business innovation is of several different overlapping types. First, innovation may take the form of new investment; this we shall turn to presently. Second, it may be primarily directed to cost reduction. Cost reduction is a major managerial responsibility in market enterprises; the incentives favorable to it are the incentives to diligence: to good quality of work, speed, and accuracy in decision making. These, which were discussed above, are largely the product of personality, indoctrination, and influences on one's field other than money rewards and penalties. Third, innovation may be

[37] See Lewis H. Kimmel, *op. cit.,* pp. 87–88.

thought of as imaginative, creative action. But this cannot easily be controlled by money rewards and penalties; it is the product of role and personality.

THE INCENTIVE TO INVEST. The incentive to invest refers to inducements to expand spending on payroll, equipment, materials, and plant. It is the incentive to undertake new business. Now the traditional motive for undertaking new business is profits. From this it is easy to conclude that the more profits, the more business undertaken; and in turn it has been inferred that a reduction of income differentials will reduce the incentive. The reasoning is oversimplified if only because it neglects the influence on the attractiveness of business expenditure of such factors as consumer spending, the availability of competent employees, the political stability of the society, and the buoyancy and optimism bred by cultural factors, all of which are themselves greatly influenced by the distribution of income.

Beyond these complications are those attributable to the changing character of the profit motive. In modern corporate business, every participant, right up through top management, is typically a wage or salaried employee; and, although management may own stock in the company, its earnings come predominantly from salaries.[38] Consequently, managerial incentives are not primarily the receipt of profits immediately shared by members of top management, and the profit motive becomes complex. Businessmen become indoctrinated or otherwise motivated to act as though they were immediately gaining or losing by a share of profits or losses. Salary adjustments may facilitate the motivation, but they are not adequate in themselves.[39]

The rewards of business investment are varied.[40] Sometimes it appears that a record of high corporate earnings is its own reward; sometimes the reward is promotion, reputation among business colleagues, prestige in the society, power, or wealth. Some businessmen are more driven to expansion than to wealth; others more to wealth or to a quiet life than to expansion or power. Given the variety of motives and differences among businessmen, it is impossible to draw

[38] Robert A. Gordon, *Business Leadership in the Large Corporation*, The Brookings Institution, Washington, 1945, chaps. 12 and 13.
[39] We return to the profit motive in later chapters.
[40] Thomas H. Sanders, *op. cit.*, pp. 21-26.

any meaningful conclusion on the dependence of the investment incentive on existing differentials.

A great pool of unexploited managerial talents is to be found in any Western society. In the United States, for example, inequalities in education and imperfections in recruitment close the doors to large numbers of potentially capable executives. Of these many are disposed to pursue money gains; others are disposed to particular non-monetary rewards, such as power and prestige; still others are willing to play the managerial game for whatever stakes are to be won. A plausible hypothesis is that the last two groups, without the first, are sufficiently large to carry on business activity as vigorously as might be wished. To put the hypothesis conservatively: Given time for recruitment of new generations of management—such time as is provided by the gradualness with which more equalization must be attempted in any case—and given improved recruitment, an adequate supply of vigorous, imaginative management can be had through much smaller differentials in money income than those now prevailing.

Of Great Britain an economist has written: "The future of the supply of first-class business management in this country depends perhaps less on the future level of business salaries and profits than on the extent to which we choose to divert systematically into business channels our notable supplies of the temperament which finds its meat and drink in the making of momentous decisions. . . ."[41] In either Britain or the United States the evidence that there is a great pool of unexploited managerial talent is not conclusive but is nevertheless persuasive.

It has already been shown that only a minority—even if now a large one—of able young minds in the United States are given a college education. Because recruitment of management is increasingly from college graduates, the majority of able minds are increasingly cut off from access to management positions. Moreover, opportunity to enter the ranks of business leadership is still much influenced by the ancestry, though probably less so than twenty years ago, when Taussig and Joslyn found that 60 percent of American business leaders were the sons of businessmen.[42] Occupa-

---

[41] D. H. Robertson, *op. cit.*, p. 19.

[42] F. W. Taussig and C. S. Joslyn, *American Business Leaders,* The Macmillan Company, New York, 1932, p. 122. Cf. C. A. Anderson, J. C. Brown and M. J. Bowman, "Intelligence and Occupational Mobility," *Journal of Political Economy*, June, 1952, pp. 218–239.

tional mobility is much impaired in the United States both by education and by social barriers to communication among able young men and existing business leadership.

To be sure, it might be argued that a higher proportion of sons of businessmen can, in fact, make better business leaders than sons of members of any other occupational group. Considering, however, the small size of the businessmen group in the population, Taussig's 60 percent figure is not explainable by correlation between occupation and intelligence of children;[43] and it is unlikely that businessmen impart to their children any other characteristic abilities of business leadership, the distribution of which in the population is sufficient to explain the 60 percent figure.

THE INCENTIVE TO ALLOCATE.   The incentive to allocate one's own labor among various employments and the incentive to allocate one's own capital, land, or other resources are both included in the incentive to allocate.

A first crude allocation of labor is accomplished largely by the accident of birth. Family circumstances dispose most young people both to an area and to an occupational level. Occupational preferences considered without regard to money refine the choice to a degree. More precise allocation is then accomplished by vacancies and wage differentials. But existing wage differentials may be necessary only because of barriers to mobility that can be removed. Entrance to the skills and the professions—to the best jobs generally—is at present restricted in a number of ways, ranging from limited access to medical schools to municipal licensing of electricians, and always including inequality in educational opportunity arising from income inequality.

With these restrictions significantly reduced, the need for differentials would be reduced. If certain occupations could not be filled, it would be those in which the work was undesirable or the status low. Hence, differentials needed for occupational mobility would be reversed. Today's low-paid jobs would be highly paid. For geographical mobility, money differentials for incentives are more obviously required; money differentials appear to be essential to move a bricklayer, an engineer, or a lawyer from one employee to another, from one part of a metropolitan area to another, or from

[43] Douglas Fryer, "Occupational-Intelligence Standards," in Bruce V. Moore and George W. Hartmann (eds.), *Readings in Industrial Psychology*, D. Appleton-Century Co., New York, 1931.

one part of the nation to another. Non-monetary incentives appear to be of limited use as inducements for this kind of movement, unless a promotion is involved.

Yet geographical mobility rarely need be more than marginal, and marginal movements often take place for reasons quite unconnected with income differentials. For numerous reasons, including dissatisfaction with their jobs, employees become separated from their employers and cast about for new positions. Similarly, families move from city to city for climate and health, because of dissatisfaction with the pattern of their lives in a vague searching for opportunities, or to be united with friends and relatives. Thus in many circumstances the mere offer of a position is enough to recruit labor. That is to say, members of a constantly changing, floating segment of the labor supply will be brought to rest where positions are available, without the inducement of money differentials.

To be sure, some circumstances call for movements of workers beyond those which can be accomplished by the inevitable marginal mobility of the labor supply. For these movements, special inducements even beyond existing differentials are often required, as when pledges of housing and transportation were required to recruit workers during the Second World War. It appears that existing income differentials sometimes fall between two stools. They are either unnecessarily large, on the one hand, or inadequate, on the other; they do not in either case serve efficiently to induce desired allocations.[44] Furthermore, income equalization can contribute to geographical mobility by making it financially possible for wage earners to move.

For non-labor resources, existing differentials are more important. Unlike differentials to induce occupational mobility, they do not commonly represent inducements to overcome restricted entry into an employment. Still, generalization is difficult. Reduction of income differentials could have either of two opposite effects. It might cause capital owners to allocate more carefully than before in order to take advantage of every possible gain. Contrariwise, it might cause them to attach little importance to finding the most profitable of several alternative allocations. Perhaps the most nearly demonstrable adverse effect of reducing differentials is the possi-

[44] On money incentives, vacancies, and other factors in mobility, see Lloyd G. Reynolds and Joseph Shister, *Job Horizons*, Harper & Brothers, New York, 1949, esp. pp. 84–88.

bility of turning investment toward the safest of ventures, because equalization does not permit large rewards to be paid for running risks. There is some evidence that present tax rates in the United States have this effect.[45]

INCREMENTALISM IN DISTRIBUTION. Like all discussions of incentives, the present one is inconclusive. Yet what has been said about incentives is enough to show that incentive problems do not invalidate the case for adjustments in the direction of equal income shares. The preservation of desirable incentives is not the obvious obstacle to more equalization that it is sometimes made out to be. On the other hand, the present state of knowledge of incentives constitutes one more reason, in addition to those given earlier, for believing that an optimum or ideal distribution cannot be defined. It confirms the necessity for proceeding by incremental adjustments so that the consequences of one step can be examined before another is taken.

Moreover, incentives and responses are constantly changing autonomously; changes in distribution therefore constitute an alteration of a continuously changing field. What rewards and penalties will be most effective in inducing desired responses will consequently depend upon circumstances only to a degree subject to the control of public policy. The suggestion is that a cafeteria of rewards and penalties is a more certain method of inducing responses than reliance on one or two incentives; and this is, of course, one of the great virtues of the money incentive—it is a claim check through which one may claim any of countless numbers of rewards.

IV. Requirements for Choice and Allocation

In turning now to the choice and allocation processes, we shall find the ground firmer under our feet.

But first a caution about the importance of choice and allocation. The choice and allocation processes have traditionally been bound together in theoretical economics. Until stabilization theory displaced it, the theory of choice and allocation was the dominant part of economics; to some economists choice and allocation were the central economic processes. The consequent narrowness of economic theory at the time was often attributed by critics to the

[45] Lewis H. Kimmel, *op. cit.*, pp. 92–94.

classical tradition originating more than in any other one person in
Adam Smith. Curiously, Smith was more concerned with the distribution of claims, high resource output, and resource development
than were his twentieth-century successors; despite the limitations
of the classical economists, it is not true that they are responsible
for the preoccupation of pre-Keynesian economics with choice and
allocation. Nor was Marshall so narrowly occupied with these
processes as to explain the relative neglect of the other economizing
mechanisms in late Marshallian economics.

How, then, did the economizing process come to be viewed so
largely in terms of choice and allocation mechanisms? One answer
is that scarcity, choice, and allocation are the distinguishing problems of economic calculation, as we have already seen. Thus skill
in dealing with calculation problems involving scarcity, choice of
ends, estimate of costs, and the assignment of resources to their
most productive uses became the distinctive skill of the economist;
he became a specialist in supply and demand, relative prices, utility,
and marginalism. When he left these problems he could display few
particular insights or competences in which he obviously excelled.
On the distribution of claims, he might feel less capable than a
philosopher; on resource development, less informed than a his-
torian; on high resource output, less well qualified than a sociologist
or engineer.

In addition, the choice-allocation processes lent themselves to
the construction of models in which the conditions of attaining a
maximum of some quantity could be examined. A large branch of
economic theory could then be deduced; and, conversely, those
lines of investigation which sought an immediate empirical or statistical basis for theoretical generalization ran into almost impossible
difficulties, as they did also in the other social sciences. Hence,
economists tended to follow not the line of least resistance but
the only line in which the resistance could be overcome at all. The
exceptions were few and were largely concentrated in monetary
theory. By the time the prospects for non-deductive empirically
grounded theory were significantly improved, the mold was set.

The meeting of the Austrian school of theory and the classical
tradition in the nineteenth century was fateful. For a number of
reasons, and partly because their work was not so immediately
motivated by the social problems of their time and place, the Aus-
trians developed in the nineteenth century a body of economic

theory which sprang almost exclusively from the abstract problems of calculation. Both the tools they developed and the elegance of their results appear to have impressed the English and American economists with the pleasures and rewards to be had from cultivating the fields of choice and allocation. Once economists constructed abstract, logically satisfying, and intricate analytical apparatus, it may also have been that the study of economics appealed to those young people in the universities who, wanting to study society, could find no satisfaction in the amorphous body of knowledge possessed by the other social sciences. Choosing to become economists because of the lure of the refinements of its methodology, they may have been reluctant to grapple with those economic processes which could not be mastered with the tools of choice and allocation theory.

We may also wonder whether a preoccupation with choice-allocation theory did not permit economists to avoid some embarrassing problems. In choice-allocation theory, their prescriptions were always on the side of the angels, for they were doing nothing more for the benefit of policy makers than spelling out the implications of rationality. The Law of Comparative Advantage, for example, simply described how rational men acted, from which it was not a dangerous jump to a prescription that men should so act. Even where their prescription that man be rational ran afoul of sectional interests, the economists, though usually then disregarded, were conceded to have kept their virtue. How different this situation might have been had economists felt the same enthusiasm for defining an optimum distribution of income as for an optimum allocation of resources, if they had pushed with vigor the equalitarian notions that some of them believed their cursory explorations in ideal or preferred distribution forced upon them.

Morally, politically, and intellectually, the economist was spared by his concentration on the choice-allocation processes. It is interesting to see how he attempted to find a place for the other processes under the choice-allocation rubric in order to extend his field without losing its advantages. Resource development was easily incorporated as a problem in choice between present and deferred consumption or in allocation of resources between consumption and producer goods. This explanation was good as far as it went, but it left outside of the main body of economic theory, except for such efforts as Schumpeter's *Theory of Economic De-*

velopment,[46] an adequate account of development processes which would consider important variables that could not be fitted into choice-allocation theory. Similarly, economics tended to imply, although hesitantly because it was known to be a half-truth, that high resource output depended primarily on correct allocation of resources and the incentives to efficiency of the competitive process.

CHOICE AND COST

The requirements of rational choice and allocation can be spelled out rather simply and systematically; we begin with processes for choice.

ECONOMIC CALCULATION. What kind of problem in calculation does the chooser face? Typically, any one of several means can be employed to achieve a given desired end. Often too, however, a given means can be employed to achieve any one or more of a variety of desired ends. Where the latter is possible—where one means can be put to a number of desired uses—the given means is sometimes inadequate for the simultaneous achievement of all the desired ends for which it can be used. The means is sufficient at any one time to achieve two or three of a dozen possible goals, but no more. In this circumstance the use of a means to serve some desired ends requires that the achievement of other ends be forgone. The core of the choice problem then becomes the calculation of which ends are worth sacrificing, and to what degree, in order to make possible the attainment of others. In short, the core is the calculation of costs—of what must be forgone to achieve a goal.

This is the problem of calculation that distinguishes the economizing process. Multiplicity of possible desired ends for given means, inadequacy of the means to attain all desired ends, and a consequent necessity for sacrificing one end to another—these three are the calculation problems of the economizing process.[47]

Rational choice, therefore, calls for a more complicated process than merely ranking preferences for commodities, services, leisure, and other values to be had from the employment of scarce resources and then choosing from the high end of the list. If the costs—the forgone alternatives—are great for values high on his list, a chooser

---

[46] Joseph A. Schumpeter, *The Theory of Economic Development*, Harvard University Press, Cambridge, 1936.

[47] Probably all decisions and activities involve at least some means which are inadequate relative to the uses to which they might be put; hence, all calculation has an economic aspect.

will choose lower-ranking values. On almost anyone's preference scale, a new home will rank higher than a package of cigarettes, yet people choose to consume more packages of cigarettes than new homes. Nor can a central authority simply choose the top items on a priority table without regard to cost. For central authority and individual consumer alike, scarcity of resources stands in the way.

For rational choice every chooser must rank his preferences not for alternative goods but for alternative combinations. The choice open to him is not between a house and a cigarette but between (1) a house plus what a small balance of unexhausted claims can obtain for him and (2) cigarettes plus what a large balance of unexhausted claims can obtain. Formally and logically this poses a problem of maximization. Which of all the combinations to be acquired from given claims is preferred to all others?

But ordinarily an individual chooser cannot grasp the problem put this way, nor can a central authority. The number of different commodities and services available in a Western economy runs into the millions—even into the billions, depending upon the method of classification—and alternative combinations or packages of them are for all practical purposes countless. Expediency, therefore, ordinarily compels each chooser to compare alternative combinations by comparing different marginal alterations he can make in his combination. He compares, even if only implicitly, particular possible additions to a combination with particular possible subtractions from it that would be required to permit the additions. He chooses not by comparing many combinations but by comparing an increment with a decrement, that is, a marginal gain with a marginal loss. In short, he compares a marginal value received with a marginal cost. Choice is rationally calculated by a chooser when no possible new increment is preferable to what must be forgone to achieve it— that is, when marginal value to be had is not greater (or less) than marginal cost.

MARGINAL COST. Let us be clear about the kind of cost information that is prerequisite to rational choice. The relevant cost is the alternative forgone by an individual when he makes a choice, not among alternative combinations, nor among once-and-for-all supplies of cigarettes, automobiles, or housing, but among incremental additions to and subtractions from his package. The relevant cost of a choice to a chooser is the alternative the sacrifice of which is immediately contingent upon the particular alternative he chooses and which he can escape if he does not make the choice. This is marginal cost.[48]

FURTHER COMPLICATIONS IN COST CALCULATIONS. A further prerequisite to rational choice is that cost calculations take account of the fact that costs vary according to the pattern of choice for the economy as a whole. The costs of achieving any goal depend upon what kinds of resources can be used for its achievement, and this in turn depends upon what other demands are made upon these resources by people with claims. As other demands change, costs change. Cost calculations must therefore take account of changing relative scarcities of different resources. Costs cannot ordinarily be stated simply in terms of weights, volumes, or energy units if rational calculation is to be achieved.

The demands made upon resources are not merely those of individuals as consumers. Most individuals are also producers; and their preferences, say, for one kind of work over another are also relevant to calculations of alternative goals forgone in attempts to achieve any one goal. Hence a calculation of cost must take account of the ways in which occupational and other preferences of individuals as producers affect the relative scarcities of resources. Again, this is the case whether individuals choose directly for themselves or turn choice over to a central authority.

A MANAGEABLE AGENDA. Calculating costs, weighting them to take account of relative scarcities, and effecting choice next requires some method of simplifying the number of variables with which any one chooser must cope. Two major methods are available for creating manageable agendas. One is *delegation:* breaking unmanageable decisions into smaller, more manageable decisions to be made by different persons. The other is *quantification:* finding a common denominator for a multitude of variables so that many can be handled as one. In particular, a quantification of costs is desirable. Later chapters will consider alternative techniques for delegation and quantification. Obviously a price system is one, but there are others.

ALLOCATION

Any one product can be produced in alternative ways, and any one resource can be employed in alternative ways. Assuming that

[48] Marginal calculations are methods of approximating a maximum. In subsequent chapters we shall consider circumstances in which they fail to do so.

choices are made among various products and services, which resources shall be used for which products?[49] The correctness of an allocation of particular resources to particular products depends upon preferences. A process is required for rationing out scarce resources to their most preferred employments, taking into account preferences of individuals both as consumers and as producers.

MARGINAL CALCULATION. Roughly speaking, rational resource allocation is achieved when no marginal units of any resource can advantageously be moved to another use, that is to say, when any given kind of resource is equally "useful," "productive," or "valuable" at the margin in all the alternative allocations to which it is assigned. As with choice, alternative patterns as a whole ordinarily need not be compared; all that needs to be asked is whether a marginal adjustment can be found that improves an existing pattern.

But what is the test of the usefulness, productivity, or value of a resource? It is the resource's capacity for satisfying the choices of those with claims. That is, a resource's worth in a particular use depends both upon the degree of preference which choosers have for the commodity or service and upon the physical productivity of the resource. These two determine its marginal value product. If, then, the distribution of claims is in some sense optimal and if choice is rationally calculated, the condition of correct resource allocation is that the marginal value product of any resource is equal in all its employment.[50]

The conclusion can be restated to show its relationship to the condition of correct choice. If a resource is withdrawn from one marginal use and applied to another, the marginal value product in the former use is the cost of employing the resource in the latter, because it is the forgone alternative. Hence, it can be said that allocation is correct when the marginal cost of using a resource is equal to the marginal value received from its use. For choice and

[49] But, because choice depends on cost and cost on the total of demands on resources, the allocation of resources to different demands intertwines the choice and allocation processes. Yet, for simplicity, we discuss allocation and choice as though they can be separated.

[50] In later chapters it will be necessary to take account of qualifications to this generalization. One complication in achieving correct resource allocation is that every different allocation of resources is a different distribution of real income. Yet an allocation can be defended as correct only on the assumption that the distribution of income is in some sense ideal. These complications, however, can be passed over at this point.

allocation alike, the condition of an optimum is that value received and forgone be equal at the margin.

The allocation process is not limited to the assignment of basic resources, such as natural resources and labor to the production of consumer goods and services. Many intermediate goods such as equipment and raw material must be assigned to production of consumer goods and, conversely, many resources must be assigned to the production of intermediate goods. For these two kinds of assignments, the condition of correct allocation is, again, that marginal cost and marginal value received be equal. For allocations to the production of intermediate goods, the values to be received are represented by the marginal value product of these goods when they are in turn used to produce consumer goods either directly or through the production of other intermediate goods.

A MANAGEABLE AGENDA. Again, the complexity of the problem is staggering. Both for calculation and for control, simplification through quantification and delegation is required. Again, as in the case of choice, quantification of costs is especially helpful.

V. Techniques for Economizing

The conditions of a preferred distribution of claims, correct choice and allocation, stability, high resource output, and resource development have now been carried to a point where alternative processes for satisfying the conditions can be examined. The immediately following group of eight chapters examines four central sociopolitical processes: price system, hierarchy, polyarchy, and bargaining. Out of these processes emerge all the particular techniques of politico-economic organization, which the then following group of chapters will subsequently examine.

Part IV.   FOUR CENTRAL
SOCIO-
POLITICAL
PROCESSES

6.

I. Leaders and Non-Leaders

Of crucial importance to the economizing process, as well as to many other social processes, are the relations between leaders and non-leaders. They are also critical to the way one evaluates society. Many of the goals of Chapter 1 require certain relationships and exclude others.

Yet in no complex society, even a totalitarian one, is there any single exclusively prevailing relationship. Some relationships predominate in totalitarian societies and others in constitutional democracies; but specific instances of certain basic kinds of relationship can be found in both.

One could classify the United States, for example, as a hierarchical society, that is, one in which leaders exercise a very high degree of unilateral control over non-leaders. Observers like Gaetano Mosca, Roberto Michels, and Vilfredo Pareto in Europe and James Burnham in the United States have emphasized the importance of this relationship even in societies that are thought of as democratic. From quite another point of view, Marxists and particularly Leninists and Stalinists have also emphasized this feature of Western "bourgeois democracies."

An observer could also classify the United States as a democratic society, that is, one in which non-leaders exercise a high degree of control over leaders. Because the role of leadership in "democracies" has never been fully assimilated to the classical theory of democratic rule, in this book we call societies of this kind polyarchies. But it is clear that observers who emphasize the "democratic" quality of American society, from De Tocqueville and Bryce to contemporary political scientists like D. W. Brogan and Herman Finer, all are emphasizing the high degree of control that non-leaders exercise over leaders.

One could also classify the United States essentially as a bargaining society, that is, one in which important decisions are made primarily by negotiations among leaders, who in turn may have a variety of relationships with their followers. John R. Commons, for example, evidently regarded this as a central feature of American society.[1] It is implicit in certain analyses of American politics—for example, David Truman's *The Governmental Process*.[2] In a deliberately more restricted view of the phenomenon, J. K. Galbraith has recently made this conception the center of his theory of "countervailing power" in the American economy.[3]

One could even classify the United States as essentially a market society, that is, one in which important decisions are made primarily by business leaders controlled largely through a price system. Admittedly, the growth of the welfare state has made this view of the United States less plausible than it would have been a generation ago; still, hasty European observers sometimes accept it. And few observers would contest the proposition that such a description is a good first approximation to an important segment of American society.

One could make a persuasive case for each of these classifications only because the United States, like most European countries, is all four at once. Indeed, it is not too much to say that the first three patterns exist to some extent in all societies; the fourth is probably somewhat less universal.

Each one of these four sociopolitical processes is necessary to economizing. Any complex society intelligently bent on using its resources efficiently must, unavoidably, make some use of all four of them. Any society that attempts to exclude any one of them altogether is bound to be the poorer. And any ideology or party program that concentrates on one or two of the four processes to the exclusion of the others is bound to be an ideology or program which, if applied in practice, would inevitably lead to a seriously impoverished economy. We set this view forth categorically at this point because the rest of this book will, we think, establish it beyond quibble for anyone who doubts it at the outset.

[1] John R. Commons, *The Economics of Collective Action*, The Macmillan Company, New York, 1950.
[2] David Truman, *The Governmental Process*, Alfred A. Knopf, New York, 1951.
[3] John K. Galbraith, *American Capitalism: The Concept of Countervailing Power*, Houghton Mifflin Co., Boston, 1952.

We shall discuss each of these four sociopolitical processes in order eventually to determine the circumstances in which each is appropriate for economizing. Because, of the four, the price system is most highly specialized to the economizing function, we begin with it; in explaining how its differentiated mechanisms facilitate calculation and control in economizing, we shall further clarify the economizing process itself. Subsequently, the significance of characteristics of hierarchy, polyarchy, and bargaining for the economizing process will be clarified.

II. The Price System as a Process for Rational Calculation and Control

AS A PROCESS FOR RATIONAL CALCULATION

In the preceding chapter it was explained that the peculiarities of calculation marking the economizing process—limited means and multiplicity of ends—make it essential that calculation be simplified. The most promising methods for reducing the number of different variables with which any one person must deal in economizing are quantification and delegation. It is immediately apparent that a price system accomplishes both. First, in a price system an enormous number of different values are represented by prices which serve as a common denominator of values. Second, a price system dispenses with a central authority and delegates decisions to a large number of persons whose decisions are coördinated without even a supervisory central agency.

In a price system, rational consumer choice is facilitated by a numerical representation of alternative values; similarly, occupational choice is facilitated by a numerical representation of what can be gained in each of several alternative employments. For leadership, rational calculation is immensely simplified too. Instead of grappling with a complex production plan involving thousands of kinds of resources and millions of commodities and services, each leader simply needs to decide whether to buy or sell a relatively narrow range of resources, materials, or consumer goods whose values are quantitatively comparable. The function of leadership in a price system is, in fact, so much reduced in complexity that businessmen are sometimes not even recognized to be major leaders in a basic sociopolitical process.

Comprehensive quantification of values through prices and extreme decentralization through delegation, then, are two marks of a price system. But for rational calculation it is not enough that values be stated in prices; it is also required that all prices represent alternative values forgone at the margin—marginal costs. They must not simply be arbitrary numbers. Our concept of a price system is that prices do represent marginal costs, though not perfectly.

If they are to do so, two conditions must be met. First, the prices each entrepreneur pays for materials and factors of production shall represent their marginal costs, that is to say, their marginal values in alternative uses. Second, each entrepreneur shall be required to govern price-production policy so that his selling prices are roughly equal to his marginal outlays for materials and factors of production.

How are these two conditions met in a price system? If there are many wage earners and capital owners offering their services and resources to entrepreneurs, the possibility that any one of them can compel the entrepreneur to pay a price higher than the resource's value in another use (to another entrepreneur) is remote.[4] Similarly, if there are many consumers bidding for goods and services, the possibility that any one consumer can long compel the entrepreneur to sell at prices below marginal cost is remote.[5] The major difficulty in meeting the two conditions arises from the possibility that the entrepreneur will be able to sell at prices higher than marginal cost or buy labor or other resources at prices lower than their alternative values at the margin. To prevent him from doing this, specific controls over the entrepreneur are necessary. Some of the possible controls go under the name "competition," but competition is only one method of control in a price system. We shall examine the various controls shortly; here it is sufficient simply to make the point that a price system requires specific controls over the entrepreneur which facilitate correct cost calculation by restraining him from raising his selling prices above marginal cost or reducing his buying prices below marginal cost of resources, materials, and equipment.

Finally, in a price system, prices must vary to clear the market. That is to say, prices must vary so that there are no buyers willing to buy at the prevailing price who cannot find sellers, and no sellers

[4] The obvious exception is unionism and collective bargaining, which is a special case to be taken up in Chapter 17.

[5] In a private enterprise price system, the entrepreneur is also free to close down his business rather than run indefinitely a loss.

willing to sell at the prevailing price who cannot find buyers. This requirement of a price system serves a particular purpose. Only when the condition is met does a price represent the bids of all alternative buyers and sellers, hence represent all alternatives forgone.

It is possible to specify other characteristics of a price system as a mechanism for rational calculation either by moving to the more refined description employed in formal economic theory or by moving in the direction of its legal foundations. But its distinguishing characteristics are already well enough defined for present purposes, except for a few to be specified in the description of a price system as a process of control.

AS A PROCESS FOR CONTROL

The price system is a process of control over leaders by non-leaders, control over non-leaders by leaders, and control over leaders by other leaders. It is thus a highly specialized mechanism for harnessing to the economizing process patterns of control discussed in subsequent chapters.

It facilitates control by leaders over non-leaders in two ways. First, it is a mechanism by which leaders can, through payment of wages, rents, interest, and other money rewards, induce workers and other holders of resources to submit to hierarchical controls within the enterprise. That is to say, it is the control mechanism (operating through manipulation of field) through which groups of participants in the productive process are brought together under a common control and discipline without which "efficient" production is impossible. Second, it is a mechanism through which leaders control consumers so that they do not attempt to consume more production than is available. This is accomplished through spontaneous and manipulated controls over the distribution of money income and over prices of consumer goods and services.

How the price system accomplishes control by non-leaders over leaders is not so obvious, although the elements of the process are clear. Control by non-leaders begins with consumer and occupational free choice.[6] Consumers control the businessman because they pay him only for producing what they wish. Holders of resources, including labor, control the businessman because they can

---

[6] We use the traditional terms "consumer free choice" and "occupational free choice" in a technical sense to describe market choices. Whether they are "really" free or not is not germane here.

threaten to offer their productive services to another businessman.[7]

If control is to be effective, consumers and resource holders must correctly understand the alternatives open to them; hence effective control requires all the conditions of rational calculation that have just been identified. Two conditions in particular are critical: price must vary to clear the market, and marginal costs and price must be equal. If these two conditions are met, it is clear that businessmen are not refusing to respond to the signals received through consumer and occupational free choices. For if prices have cleared the market, it is clear that businessmen have not left willing buyers or sellers unsatisfied. And if marginal cost and price are equal, it is clear that, say, an increase in consumer demand has effected a response in production and has not simply permitted the businessman to sell the same quantity as before but at a higher price.

No one will deny that in Western economies prices do in fact vary to clear the market, except for temporary disequilibria or for goods subject to price control or rationing. But, again, it is not obvious that marginal cost and price are even roughly equal. Hence, the particular control processes which restrain the businessman from selling too high or buying too low are crucial in a price system. These particular control processes deserve the most careful attention because they are the core of the price system. They are essential to both rational calculation and control.

Before we turn to these controls, let us take note of the controls by leaders over other leaders characteristic of a price system. In a price system neither consumers nor resource holders appear in every transaction. A large number of transactions are between entrepreneurs alone. In a price system it is necessary that entrepreneurs control each other in these transactions in such a way as to facilitate control over businessmen by consumers and resource holders, that is to say, to facilitate control of the leaders by the non-leaders. If entrepreneurial transactions violate neither the condition that prices clear the market nor the condition that price and marginal cost be equal, they will facilitate the desired control. Again, however, just how entrepreneurial transactions can be restrained from violating these conditions depends upon the critical processes

----

[7] For simplicity, we use the term "occupational free choice" to refer to choices of all resource holders with respect to the "occupation" or employment of their resources.

for controlling the entrepreneur which we have already mentioned and which remain to be explained.

RECAPITULATION

A price system is, then, a highly differentiated sociopolitical process for controlling the relations between leaders and non-leaders in the economizing process. It simplifies the economizing process primarily by quantification through prices and delegation through decentralization. Its more particular characteristics are free consumer and occupational choices, specific controls to compel entrepreneurs to respond to the consumer and occupational choices expressed, and an elaborate mechanism of manipulated field control through which leaders can organize production by bringing resource holders under hierarchical controls within each enterprise. Both to achieve correct cost calculations and to control the entrepreneur, it is necessary in a price system that prices vary to clear the market and that prices equal marginal costs. The processes most difficult to understand—at the same time the processes most critical to the effectiveness of the price system—are those through which the entrepreneur is controlled in such a way that he neither sells at prices above marginal cost nor buys at prices below the marginal cost (alternative value at the margin) of resources, materials, and productive services. To these processes we now turn.

III. Control over the Businessman

In much economic theory the businessman as a leader never comes into focus. In the theory of perfect competition he withers away, like the state in pure communism. To be sure, the theory of monopolistic competition pictures him as an active leader deeply involved in sales strategy. But even this picture of him hardly suggests that, when he molds consumer tastes, introduces new lines, fights off rivals, and wins the support of consumers, he is a brother of the polyarchical leader who molds political preferences, experiments with appeals to voters, fights off his rivals, and somehow wins the support of the electorate.

No general agreement prevails on how the businessman is controlled in the price system. Competition, some friends of the price system allege, is the effective method by which consumers control businessmen. But if competition is not dead, others will reply, it is surely dying; monopoly has taken its place. A recent contribution to the debate finds a process of control in the countervailing power of large buyers and sellers, suggesting that a range of alternative controls beyond competition may be found.[8] Disagreement on how price system controls function may, however, be due more to inattention than to confirmed difference of opinion. In any case, methodical examination of price system controls uncovers a pattern that reduces the area of dispute.

The price system is characterized by one primary and a number of supplementary controls through which the businessman may be restrained. Like all controls, they function imperfectly. At their best they are inadequate for stabilization and control of income distribution, and in ordinary circumstances they are deficient on many other counts. Yet they lay powerful restraints on entrepreneurial policy.

THE PRIMARY CONTROL

The most universal price system control over the businessman in all Western societies is one achieved by spontaneous alteration of field. Because it is spontaneous, it is relentless; its cues and incentives call for no fallible enforcement agency. As a seller, the businessman is spontaneously controlled by the possibility open to his customers to spend their funds on other products rather than meet his high prices.[9] As a buyer, he is spontaneously controlled by the possibility that his suppliers will turn to other buyers rather than accept his low price. This primary spontaneous control is not dependent upon rivalry among many firms in any one industry;[10] and it controls businessmen of all kinds, whether small proprietors, corporate executives, managers of coöperatives, or directors of public corporations

[8] John K. Galbraith, op. cit.

[9] To be sure, a buyer may deliberately control the entrepreneur by manipulating his field with a threat to buy the product of another industry rather than submit to what he considers excessively high prices. But this is rarer than the common control achieved over every entrepreneur as a by-product of the consumer's ability to turn away from any one product to any of the many other products that incessantly compete for his dollar.

[10] As the ensuing discussion shows, the distinction between substitution between industries and substitution between firms in the same industry is useful to a discussion of control even if an attempt to describe the difference precisely runs into great difficulties in defining an industry and compels the subordination of the industry-firm distinction to distinctions based on differences in elasticity of demand.

and other government business enterprises. All buyers and sellers face the threat of substitution.

Although familiar to economists, this control often escapes attention, for, as a control over sellers, its universality is not obvious. Some illustrations reveal its scope. When the price of coffee rose substantially in the fall of 1949 because of rumors of a crop failure in Brazil, sales of tea grew; in many sections of the United States, tea sales increased 50 percent.[11] Another example is the refusal of the American Viscose Company to increase its price on rayon yarn to follow the lead of Du Pont in 1949; a vice-president explained that the company feared both the substitution of wool and cotton by its customers and the substitution of wool and cotton products by the customers of the mills weaving rayon products.[12]

If a single firm sells aluminum, its management will find some of its customers turning quickly to steel rather than pay a high price for aluminum. For passenger coaches for the railroads can be made from either; so can many kitchen utensils. If the price of automobiles is too high, consumers will buy fewer automobiles and perhaps spend more of their money on their homes, on railroad tickets, on amusements, or on books. If the price of clothing is too high, consumers will make clothing last longer. If there were only one firm selling springs for mattresses, its control over price would be limited because mattresses can be made with sponge rubber, felt, horsehair, and still other materials.

To control a seller, not all buyers need to turn to substitutes; there must only be substantial loss of sales at the margin. Just how tightly the businessman will be controlled depends upon the extent to which his total receipts fall off with high prices and the relation of his costs of production to output. If a high price puts the buyer in a position where he still spends more on a commodity while buying less of it, the primary control is, of course, ineffective.

KINDS OF SUBSTITUTION. What are the major categories of substitutes to which buyers may turn?

1. A product of another industry superficially different but enough alike to be interchangeable for some uses. Glass and metal are different products in everyday terminology; but for some purposes they are practically identical. Copper wire and steel wire

[11] Alfred R. Oxenfeldt, *Industrial Pricing and Market Practices*, Prentice-Hall, New York, 1951, p. 371.
[12] *Ibid.*

come from different industries but are excellent substitutes for each other in many uses. Other examples are coal and oil, metal and wood, ice and electric refrigerators, the cinema and the night club, railroads and motor transport. Substitutes may be more distantly related than these—for example, gasoline and urban transportation for a car owner, newspapers and radios, fishing tackle and cigars, automobiles and apartments, clothing and furniture.

2. Personal services. If the price of a washing machine is too high, some consumers will send their laundry out. Buyers may shift from a nursery school to a nursemaid or a baby sitter, from ready-made clothing to a dressmaker or tailor, from ready-made kitchen cabinets to a carpenter, and even from a new car to a mechanic for the old one. In industry, machine-labor substitution is, of course, common.

3. Home production. As a limit on prices, substitution of home production for finished goods and services is common. Shaving and home haircuts are substitutes for a barber's services. Sewing, baking, and cleaning are substitutes for clothing, bakery products, or a housemaid's services. Many men do their own painting and carpentry rather than pay the wage rates of these skilled trades, and many women find substitutes in their own labor for vacuum cleaners, kitchen mixers, hair dryers, dishwashers, and the like.

4. Commodities from abroad. Restrictions on international trade often limit the possibilities of this kind of substitution. But it nevertheless remains important, even in a relatively self-contained economy like that of the United States.

5. Second-hand products. This embraces a larger number of possibilities for substitution than immediately appears. The outstanding example is the second-hand automobile market in the United States, which offers a great supply of automobiles as substitutes for new cars. Other examples are second-hand household appliances, houses, furniture, and factory equipment. The principal substitution of used products for new products goes on almost unnoticed, as when an automobile owner decides to make his old auto do for a few more years rather than buy a new one or when a businessman decides to stretch the life of old equipment rather than pay a high price for new. This process of substitution between new and presently held goods is a major limit on price manipulation in the case of all durable goods. Both rising standards of living and mechanization slowly increase the proportion of durable goods in Western economies.

6. Generalized substitution. In many cases a consumer substitutes an alternative satisfaction which bears no particular relationship to the commodity he turns away from. For example, a high price on television sets will cause some consumers to substitute clothing. Clothing is a substitute for television because, for satisfactions achieved per dollar of expenditure, they believe clothing to be a more attractive expenditure. A high price on electric power will not necessarily induce consumers to buy candles. But they may use electricity sparingly and substitute expenditures on a large number of other commodities. Within limits, all products substitute for all other products.

These various possibilities of substitution control the businessman in his sales to consumers and other businessmen alike. The penalty of substitution can be imposed by any buyer, and once imposed it controls a chain of sellers. For example, if the customer will not pay the retailer's price, the retailer will not pay the wholesaler's price and the wholesaler will not pay the manufacturer's price. Each member of the chain is penalized by the spontaneous control of the consumer.

GROWING STRENGTH OF PRIMARY CONTROL. For at least three reasons the primary control over businessmen as sellers is growing in effectiveness. First, the laboratory constantly turns out a stream of new products and techniques. The plastics industry, for example, produces a flood of substitutes for older products that insistently eats away at islands of power over price. Because the laboratories have learned how to give one product many of the characteristics of another product, wood, rubber, plastics, steel, copper, aluminum, and glass are closer rivals than ever before. Second, as the standard of living rises, the proportion of the consumer's budget spent on what are called necessities, where substitution is difficult, declines. To take an extreme case, it is easier to substitute port for champagne, or a book for a movie, than to find a substitute for potatoes. Third, urbanization and improved transportation decrease the consumer's dependence on any one source of supply. Most people can buy foodstuffs and household goods, for example, from any one of a number of shops, and retailers in turn can typically draw on several alternative sources for their stocks.

Because the primary control is always supported by several supplementary controls, the question never arises as to whether it is adequate by itself. Even given agreed standards, judgment must do duty for proof, and wide differences of opinion are to be expected. Let us not, however, rule out the possibility that the primary control alone might be as effective as hierarchical controls alone in the absence of a price system.

SUPPLEMENTARY CONTROLS

Although in all markets the businessman will be controlled to a degree by substitution among various products and by alternative offers of other businessmen to resource owners and labor, markets differ from one another in their *supplementary* controls over the businessman. To describe the alternative supplementary controls, it is helpful to imagine price mechanisms of different kinds, each distinguished by an exclusive reliance on one or another of the supplementary controls actually to be found in the market. In the real world most price systems combine all the alternative supplementary controls, though in different ways.

Price system control can be made effective in a wide variety of circumstances, can be altered as market or corporate structures alter, can simultaneously focus a number of specific controls on any one entrepreneur, and does not rest solely on the conditions postulated in the theories of pure or perfect competition.

SPONTANEOUS PRICE MECHANISM. The most common supplementary control requires many firms in each industry. Control is then exerted because buyers and sellers can turn to other entrepreneurs in the same industry. No one intends to control the entrepreneur in this way; he is controlled as an epiphenomenon of the acts of both buyers and suppliers of materials and resources. Both this and the primary control operate spontaneously through the possibilities of substitution. The effect of having many firms in the same industry is to make substitution of any one firm for another much easier for buyer and seller alike, for the same product is available from many firms and there are more firms to sell to. Given enough firms in each industry, this supplementary control requires no enforcement and hence never lapses by virtue of the negligence of an enforcement agency, because enforcement is spontaneous.

In all Western economies, including those like the British that are sometimes called socialist, this is the supplementary control most heavily relied upon. A price mechanism employing this spontaneous supplementary control through rivalry among firms in the same industry is commonly called competitive. Everyone is familiar with it under that name; but, as will be seen shortly, it is only one of several controls that can be so described.

BARGAINING PRICE MECHANISM. A second kind of supplementary control is reciprocity or bargaining. A buyer controls an entrepreneur from whom he buys or a seller controls one to whom he sells by the deliberate exercise of command or manipulation of field. Hence, the policies followed by the entrepreneur emerge from their reciprocal attempts to control each other. What techniques may be used by a buyer or seller to control a businessman? Two rather different possibilities appear, and neither requires large numbers of firms in each industry.

COMPETITIVE BARGAINING PRICE MECHANISM. The first case is that the buyer or seller—it will usually be a buyer in this case—controls the entrepreneur by the threat or fact of substitution. An automobile manufacturer bargains with a steel corporation over the price of steel with an implicit or explicit threat to produce steel himself if he is not satisfied with the price. Sometimes it is enough to threaten to look about actively for another supplier, perhaps to finance the expansion of a competing steel company at present unable to supply him.

NONCOMPETITIVE BARGAINING PRICE MECHANISM. The second case is that the buyer or seller—it will usually be a seller in this case—controls the entrepreneur not by substitution but through power over price he enjoys because price system controls over him are weak. Very roughly, the distinction between the two kinds of bargaining is this: In the first case, A controls B by reducing the monopoly power of B; in the second, he controls B by increasing his own monopoly power. Trade unions and milk producers cooperatives, for example, use the second kind of control.

The first type of bargaining is competitive in the sense that it uses the threat or fact of substitution to achieve control. It bears a family resemblance both to the primary control and to spontaneous supplementary control, both of which also operate through substitution. It is, however, a deliberate, nonspontaneous competitive control.

The effectiveness of this type of bargaining rests on its double incentive to find a substitute. In the spontaneous supplementary control, the possibilities of substitution depend upon the number of competing entrepreneurs, any one of whom is motivated to compete with others because of gains of selling at a profit (the gains not necessarily being restricted to the profits themselves). In the manipulated competition of bargaining, an additional incentive is the gain accruing to an entrepreneur because he will buy from himself. A competitive bargainer can look forward to the ordinary rewards of entrepreneurship as well as savings to himself as a buyer if he opens, say, a new parts plant rather than pay a high price to other entrepreneurs for the components of the product he has been manufacturing. His threat cannot, therefore, be taken lightly.

Competitive bargaining is also effective because it can force entry. In the theory of competition, ease of entry into an industry is critical to the success of competition. A common deficiency in spontaneous supplementary control is that potential competitors can neither raise the funds for nor risk the losses of forcing their way into an industry. Obstacles to entry include both the heavy capitalization required, as for steel, and the tactics of the firms already in the industry, as in the classic case of the National Cash Register Company in the United States. But clearly the large mail-order houses or the automobile, steel, chemical, and electrical products firms are excellently equipped to force entry into industries from which they buy and to which they sell. They possess financial resources, an operating organization, and an established reputation.

Of all the alternative supplementary controls, the least reliable is that dependent upon noncompetitive bargaining. True, the price-production policies of an enterprise not otherwise subject to an effective supplementary control can often be controlled by another enterprise with monopoly power as a buyer. Similarly, a powerful buyer can be controlled by a powerful seller. But there are dangers. First, buyer and seller can often come to an agreement at the expense of the ultimate consumer. Second, a crude process of setting one monopoly against another offers no reasonable assurance that the one will not then overpower the other.

In this second case, the remedy may be an increase in the power of the weaker partner. One can well imagine a cumulation of power on both sides in a hopeless pursuit of some kind of equality in their control over each other. Certainly this kind of supplementary control tends toward no stable equilibrium of control. The power of the adversaries can grow to the point where it seriously compromises consumer control through the market system. This kind of bargaining price system may easily grow into a bargaining system outside the price mechanism and free from its controls.

These weaknesses of a noncompetitive bargaining price mechanism are revealed in the development of collective bargaining in Western economies. Control by entrepreneurs over employees is arbitrary in varying degrees. Because employees can agree on practices to weaken competition among themselves, the union wins some control over wages. Here, then, is a clear case of an attempt to control a buyer by setting a strong seller against him. But some entrepreneurs prefer to coöperate with the union rather than fight it, specifically to trade wage and other concessions to the employees for security against strikes and other benefits for the employer. The benefits to both parties can be at the expense of consumers, who pay the bill through higher prices. Union controls can also become as unresponsive as the previous employer controls if the many elements in bargaining power are so composed in a particular market as to produce a preponderance of union power rather than a kind of equilibrium.[13] In such cases, bargaining fails as a control.

A final problem in noncompetitive bargaining price mechanisms is that they easily slip over into hierarchy; and, again, collective bargaining is a case in point. So much is at stake in the decisions of great bargaining groups in labor-management relations that government cannot keep its hands off; wage policy comes increasingly to be hierarchically controlled by government, as recent experience in Western economies will testify. Whether hierarchical control of wages is or is not desirable, the point is that a noncompetitive bargaining price mechanism is unstable; it easily undergoes a transformation into a different system.

Despite these shortcomings, however, noncompetitive bargaining is an important form of control in some markets and plays at least a subordinate role in almost every transaction between entrepreneurs. For, since the other controls are never perfect, almost every entrepreneur exerts some control over price. Hence, in almost every transaction between businessmen they both control each other to a degree. Bargaining of this kind is least developed in agricultural products; it is most developed in the construction industry

[13] See, for example, Charles E. Lindblom, *Unions and Capitalism*, Yale University Press, New Haven, 1949, chap. 9; Lloyd G. Reynolds, *Labor Economics and Labor Relations*, Prentice-Hall, New York, 1949, chaps. 8, 18.

and in pricing of specialized tools and equipment for industry, as well as in the labor market. Even in retailing it is not absent.

HIERARCHICAL PRICE MECHANISMS.   Still another type of supplementary control over the entrepreneur is government hierarchy. Governments can, for example, require that entrepreneurs' costs at the margin approximate price. Public utility regulation, antitrust and minimum wage legislation, agricultural price supports, and nationalization of firms or industries are possible devices of hierarchical control. Governments may also exert supplementary hierarchical control by manipulating markets, through buying and selling a commodity in order to control its price. We refer to hierarchical control in its most common form as a *mandatory price mechanism*, and to hierarchical control through market manipulation as a *manipulated market price mechanism*.

Of the two types of hierarchical price mechanisms, market manipulation is less important than the mandatory type for fairly obvious reasons. To be sure, a centrally directed hierarchy might control enterprise policy by buying or selling on the market large enough quantities of a commodity to control price. But ordinarily a government must actually produce a commodity in order to have a supply of it available for manipulating the market. In any case the government must formulate in advance a price policy which its manipulations are to achieve. For both reasons, it is commonly easier for the government to set prices directly by prescription or veto or by prescribing the price policy of its own enterprises.

Where government control does not supplement a price mechanism but displaces it by centrally determined production goals, spontaneous and mandatory controls over price clash. The black market is a symptom. Manipulation of the market may then be more effective than mandatory controls. But where mandatory controls are used as a supplementary control in a price system, they give effect to consumer choices. Hence, conflict between spontaneous and mandatory controls is minimized in a price system. Both may be used.

GOVERNMENT   OWNERSHIP   IN   A   MANDATORY   PRICE MECHANISM.   Given the traditional debate over public and private ownership of industry, it is worth while digressing briefly on the mandatory price system in the form of public ownership for the light thrown by this controversy on the functions appropriate to mandatory price system controls.

Although to many socialists public ownership of business is intended to set the price system aside in favor of hierarchy, public ownership is intended by other socialists to substitute a mandatory price mechanism for a spontaneous or bargaining price mechanism.[14] For three major reasons the latter have not uncommonly exaggerated the advantages of a mandatory price mechanism.

First, they have expected great consequences to follow from the elimination of private property in enterprises. The decline of public ownership as a central socialist faith betrays their more recent realization that the bundle of rules called private property constitutes a system of control largely indispensable for the achievement of their own goals. British socialists, for example, find that they do not want a wholesale substitution of new cues and incentives for those of property in, say, British railroads. Because instead they wish to make incremental adjustments in cues and incentives, they have put the managers of the railroads, as well as the managers of other nationalized industries, in positions where they are instructed, within broad limits, to carry on very much as though they were private owners of the industry.[15]

Second, the now vanishing socialist belief in the general superiority of the mandatory price system has often represented an uncritical attitude toward the efficacy of *prescription* as a control mechanism. Prescription without adequate rewards and penalties does not achieve control; but, on the whole, socialists have bypassed the problem of adequate rewards and penalties for publicly owned enterprises. They have also underestimated the efficacy of indoctrination as against prescription. It has been persuasively argued, for example, that government prescriptions to the management of the Bank of England after nationalization accomplished less precise, less flexible, less subtle control over the Bank than had been accomplished before nationalization through years of indoctrination of private managers of the Bank with respect to their public responsibilities, particularly their obligation to consult with and re-

[14] For summaries of reasons given for recent nationalizations in Britain and France, see Ben Lewis, *British Planning and Nationalization*, The Twentieth Century Fund, New York, 1952, pp. 43–45; and P. Aubry, "The Nationalization of Public Utilities and Basic Industries in France," Ambassade de France, Service de L'Information, Series IV, French Opinion, No. 26, March, 1949.

[15] D. N. Chester, *The Nationalized Industries: A Statutory Analysis*, Institute of Public Administration, London, 1948.

spond to the advice of the Treasury.[16] Clearly, many of the difficulties the French have met in their nationalization ventures are traceable to conflict between prescription and indoctrination.[17]

Third, where socialists have faced up to the necessity for supplementing mandatory prescriptions with adequate incentives, they have often fallen back on the argument that incentives of status, prestige, public service, and the like are powerful. Granted that they are indeed powerful, these incentives are not easily harnessed to the particular kinds of prescriptions needed in a mandatory price mechanism. They may be sufficient to induce men to work hard, imaginatively, and creatively; but they are not demonstrably adequate for inducing the particular responses required of businessmen in a price mechanism. Somehow, if a price mechanism is to work at all, businessmen must be induced to respond to particular price and inventory cues through which buyers and sellers signal their desires to businessmen. An intricate incentive system is required for the intricacies of the choice and allocation processes. Just how businessmen are to be induced to respond to their prescriptions in a mandatory price system is a large and relatively unexamined issue.[18]

Although many socialists fell into these errors, some of their principal reasons for espousing the mandatory price mechanism were often more valid than the reasons used by their opponents to justify the spontaneous price mechanism. A price mechanism doomed to recurrent large-scale depression and capable of breakdowns like that of the 1930's, where in the United States roughly one-third of the gainfully employed lost their jobs, can be defended no more easily than the mandatory price mechanism, which the socialists believed could end depressions. In recent years, of course, socialist and nonsocialist have been drawn together in their conviction that depression is better attacked with weapons other than na-

[16] Roy Harrod, *Are These Hardships Necessary?* Hart-Davis, London, 1947, Appendix.

[17] P. Aubry, *op. cit.*

[18] It is sometimes said that economic theory has demonstrated the workability of a price system based on public ownership. Again, all that economic theory has shown at most is that prescriptions can be formulated that, if followed, would accomplish a subordination of production to consumer and occupational free choice. Theory has demonstrated that these prescriptions (see, for example, "the Rule" in A. P. Lerner, *The Economics of Control*, The Macmillan Company, New York, 1944) signal the same responses as the cues of a spontaneous price mechanism; but theory has not attacked the question of whether adequate incentives can be constructed to make the signals effective for control. It is this limitation in the theoretical prescriptions that makes it possible, though somewhat misleading, to say, as has been said, that economic theory has shown a socialist price system to be economically, but not politically, workable.

tionalization and that the spontaneous and bargaining price mechanisms need not forever go through the wringer of depression. Hence, socialist and nonsocialist alike look upon the mandatory price mechanism as one of several possible price mechanisms, its appropriateness dependent upon particular circumstances in an industry.

This non-doctrinaire attitude toward public ownership is most firmly established in Scandinavia. As a Norwegian economist put it: "Even among those who believe most in the benefits of government control, nationalization is regarded as only one means alongside many others by which the government may increase welfare under certain conditions and circumstances, and this measure is not to be applied in any field of the economy until careful investigations have proved that it may be expected to lead to desirable results."[19]

This being so, it is not possible to go far at all in suggesting the circumstances in which public ownership is suitable, but a few suggestions can be made. One possibility is that public ownership may be necessary in order to legitimize control. This is an intangible, but one so important that we shall return to it in a later chapter.[20] A second possibility is that public ownership can simplify the problem of control where many circumstances converge to make hierarchical regulation of an industry necessary on many points. Where a miscellany of regulations go so far as to leave little scope for nongovernmental management to act, a double set of controllers can be reduced to one by public ownership. Third, the risks of investment may sometimes preclude private ownership. This eventuality is, however, less probable than appears at first glance, for many techniques are available for hierarchical assumption of the risks of private enterprises. Even the enormous risks of atomic energy production in the United States have not prevented the Atomic Energy Commission from using private enterprise for production; and most observers would probably agree that the AEC contract program is superior to nationalization of these industries as a form of control.[21]

Fourth, it is conceivable that subtle changes occur in the personality and role of the private entrepreneur with the result that he becomes insufficiently responsive to market controls. Schumpeter,

[19] Petter Jakob Bjerve, "Government Economic Planning and Control," in Henning Friis (ed.), *Scandinavia Between East and West*, Cornell University Press, Ithaca, 1950, p. 52.

[20] See Chapter 17.

[21] But see the criticisms of James R. Newman, "The Atomic Energy Industry: An Experiment in Hybridization," 60 *Yale Law Journal* 1263, (December, 1951).

190 POLITICS, ECONOMICS, AND WELFARE

for example, has pointed out possible consequences for the entrepreneurial role of such factors as changing political leadership in America, the bureaucratization of business, and changing identification of the businessman with his family.[22] Actually, the factors undermining the entrepreneurial vigor of private businessmen in Schumpeter's analysis would largely affect entrepreneurship in any kind of price mechanism; consequently, they are possible criteria for choice between price system and hierarchy more than for choice between alternative price mechanisms.

More important, the response of businessmen to price system cues and incentives is a product of so many factors in the businessman's field that prediction is impossible (at least in the present state of knowledge). Even where one can be confident that a large number of factors are reducing the effectiveness of controls over private entrepreneurs, other factors are always strengthening these controls; and the effect of both kinds of factors may be reversed several times in a few decades. If, to Schumpeter, the bureaucratization of innovation promised the decline of private enterprise, its bureaucratization in Union Carbon and Carbide, General Electric, and Tennessee Eastman in the atomic energy program holds out enormous promise for private enterprise.

As already suggested, where a choice is to be made between private and public ownership, an intelligent choice requires a painstaking examination of the strengths and weaknesses of both kinds of control in a particular industry or firm. Fom this it follows that the relative merits of private and public ownership for the future will depend upon the development of market structures (with their consequences for spontaneous and bargaining controls over private enterprise) and the development of hierarchical controls. If market structures become less favorable to private enterprise, and developments, say, in party discipline or in the recruitment and indoctrination of civil servants are favorable, it is not at all inconceivable that the public ownership movement, now at low tide, will rise again.

For the present, although the scope of mandatory price mechanism controls is broad, that of public enterprise is narrow. Aside from public enterprises, the major hierarchical controls over price are achieved through public utility regulation, antitrust and minimum wage legislation, farm price supports, government participation in collective bargaining, resale price maintenance legislation,

[22] Joseph A. Schumpeter, *Capitalism, Socialism and Democracy* (2nd ed.), Harper & Brothers, New York, 1947, Part II.

and legislation controlling price discrimination and government sponsorship of marketing agreements. Every business is subject, therefore, to the hierarchical supplementary control, although it is the dominant supplementary control in only a small minority of business. Government sales of its own services and commodities to consumers accounts for only 5 percent of consumer income.[23] The public utilities, including transportation and communication, account for only about 8 percent of all employment,[24] although the high capital-labor ratio in many public utilities means that these industries are a larger element in the economy than the number of employed indicates.

AUTONOMOUS PRICE MECHANISM. A final possibility is that autonomous action supplements the primary control in such a way as makes supplementary control over the businessman unnecessary. Where the entrepreneur both buys from and sells to himself, his autonomous decisions require no control. In consumers' coöperatives actively controlled by member-customers, the persons who decide price-production policy and those who buy the products are one and the same. Another example is purchases by a corporation from a subsidiary at prices prescribed by the parent company. Producers' coöperatives—a fruit growers' exchange, for example—illustrate the possibilities of restraining an entrepreneur from depressing the price at which he buys, for the individuals who control buying policies and those who sell to the coöperative are the same. Still another example is an enterprise that sells to its own distributive organization. But all these are examples of either buyer or seller control, but not both. A pure type may be imagined in which a business is owned by its customers, who also own all the immediate sources of supply to the company and provide it with its labor, but this must be rare indeed. But companies vertically integrated under one management are close to such a pure type.

Neither producer nor consumer coöperatives are a large part of the American economy. In the United States, consumer coöperatives do about 2 percent of total retail business, and producer coöperatives are largely limited to marketing organizations in agriculture—dairy coöperatives, for example—that are part of government control schemes. In Scandinavian economies their role is, of course, larger. Roughly 40 percent of Danish, more than a quarter of Nor-

[23] Alfred R. Oxenfeldt, *op. cit.,* p. 388.
[24] *Ibid.,* p. 398.

wegian, and nearly half of Swedish families belong to consumers' coöperatives. Consumer coöperatives account for about 10 percent of retail business in Denmark and Sweden. Producer coöperatives are even more important in their fields. In Denmark they process over 90 percent of all milk and almost 90 percent of all hogs. In Sweden almost every farmer is a member of a producer coöperative; producer coöperatives account for 95 percent of all milk, 96 percent of all butter, and 87 percent of all cheese. Only in Norway are producer coöperatives weak.[25]

Consumer coöperation is the one great reform movement that recognizes the merits of the price system. This recognition is both its weakness and its strength. On the one hand, the movement is sometimes narrow in asserting the adequacy of the price system sans monopoly, as though problems of income distribution, insecurity, and inequality of income and status would fade away with the disappearance of monopoly. On the other hand, the movement has been able to pass from aspiration to realization, even in the United States, because in proposing to improve the price system it has made use of a coördinating mechanism at hand (instead of in blueprint), only imperfectly developed, and hence easily improved upon.

Beyond coöperatives, the scope of an autonomous price mechanism is partly hidden from view by vertical integration. When enterprises trading with each other in a productive chain are combined, transactions that once appeared on the market take place within the integrated enterprise. Where differences of interests once made it desirable for the management of one of the enterprises to control price to the disadvantage of another, unified control now eliminates this possibility. Individuals in one part of the enterprise may still pursue policies opposed to those of other individuals in it; but a common central management of the integrated firm takes the place of what were formerly different individuals, some buying and some selling. The problem of control over these buyers and sellers is minimized within the disappearance of their inter-enterprise transactions.

Ownership of an enterprise by either supplier or consumer, but not both, sometimes obstructs rather than facilitates control. For example, through farmer ownership of milk-processing plants and elimination of competitors among farmers as sellers, dairy coöperatives can make entrepreneurial policy responsive to the sup-

[25] Henning Friis (ed.), *op. cit.*, pp. 203, 208–210, 214; Gunnar Hecksher, "Pluralist Democracy," *Social Research,* December, 1948, p. 433.

pliers of milk but unresponsive to milk consumers. Buyer control can also be at the expense of suppliers, as in a consumers' coöperative. Moreover, although autonomy avoids the necessity for external control over the enterprise, an elaborate polyarchy may be needed within the enterprise to safeguard effective consumer or supplier control of leadership. Thus a large consumer coöperative structure, as in Sweden, becomes a kind of polyarchal price mechanism.

THE VARIETY OF PRICE SYSTEM CONTROLS

What has already been said should be enough to show that the price system is a more comprehensive control system than that ordinarily embraced in the word "competition." Price system controls, moreover, make use of spontaneous control, manipulation of field, command, and reciprocity. Hence the eggs are not all in one basket. The variety of price system controls is worth emphasis as an antidote to the view fashionable in some circles that the price system is a utopian concept. But this begins to run ahead of our story. We shall have more to say about the price system in the next chapter. Here let us recapitulate with an outline of the various controls over the businessman that we have identified.

Kind of Price Mechanism	Its Distinguishing Supplementary Control[26]	The Control Common to All Price Mechanisms
1. Spontaneous Price Mechanism	Spontaneous: Intra-industry substitution	
2. Bargaining Price Mechanisms	Manipulation of field by bargainers	
a. Competitive Bargaining Price Mechanism	a. Manipulation through substitution	
b. Noncompetitive Bargaining Price Mechanism	b. Manipulation by other methods	Primary control achieved through
3. Hierarchical Price Mechanisms	Command and manipulation of field by government	spontaneous interproduct substitution
a. Mandatory Price Mechanism	a. Heavy reliance on prescription	
b. Manipulated Price Mechanism	b. Heavy reliance on manipulation of field	
4. Autonomous Price Mechanism	Autonomous behavior: No supplementary control required	

[26] Of all the supplementary controls distinguished in this chapter, Galbraith includes three in his countervailing power: competitive and noncompetitive bargaining and mandatory control. See John K. Galbraith, *op. cit.*

7.

The Price System: Control of and by Leaders (Continued)

The barest outlines of the price system having been sketched out, as a control it will be better understood if we pursue its description further. First, the place of competition and monopoly in the price system should be clarified. Second, the controls abstractly described in the preceding chapter should be seen in their everyday garbs—as they appear in business practices. Third, the price system under government ownership of industry merits further examination. And finally, we wish to clarify the importance of role and personality in price system controls.

I. Competition and Monopoly

If one could begin an analysis of price system controls with a tabula rasa, it might be desirable to dispense with the concept of competition and use only specific terms for the primary and each of the supplementary controls. The fact is, however, that in most minds the effectiveness of price system controls appears to be bound up with two kinds of processes, one called competition, the other monopoly. We cannot avoid facing up to these two concepts, for no picture of price system controls is very convincing if these two central figures are left out. Differences of opinion on the scope of competition and monopoly are many, some representing more problems in terminology, others not. Is competition dead or alive? Is monopoly a flaw in competition or an alternative to it?

COMPETITIVE CONTROLS AND THE CONCEPT OF MONOPOLY

THE TWO SPONTANEOUS COMPETITIVE CONTROLS. Competitive controls include spontaneous primary control, spontaneous supplementary control, and competitive bargaining. The first two are more often identified with competition than is the third. Because they control in what appears to be an absence of control, they have never been well understood except by economists and others who have discerned in action uncoördinated by any central hierarchy a systematic pattern of control. It was Adam Smith's great contribution to social science that he perceived the pattern and saw its significance.

One of the fashions of our times, common to many sociologists, educators, political scientists, historians, and even some economists, is that of smiling with condescending tolerance whenever the name of Adam Smith is mentioned. His great book was quite descriptively entitled *An Inquiry into the Nature and Causes of the Wealth of Nations*, but he is somehow fixed in many minds as having written an exposition of how to ride the economic bicycle backwards without hands. Actually, of course, Smith's work was a great progressive force in his day. And his "invisible hand" better characterizes his idea of control than "hands off" or laissez faire.

Since his time his "invisible hand," as well as his "economic man," has been subjected to much gentle scoffing. There is something quaint about the terms, and it is difficult to speak them without seeming naïve. Yet with a language less appropriate to our times than his, Smith grasped a concept quite as appropriate to our times as to his. He perceived the potentialities of socioeconomic coördination largely by means of spontaneous competitive controls. This represents an intellectual accomplishment of such magnitude that not even the now outmoded social philosophy and psychology which Smith and his school confused with it can detract from its significance for the whole of social science.

No one can ever precisely say where a new idea comes from and how it comes to take hold of so many minds that it becomes a force in the world. But it is not too far wrong to say that the *Wealth of Nations* set into motion a line of thought only now bearing its full fruit. We can say that Adam Smith "discovered" the concept of spontaneous field control in political economy. He and the classical school which derived from him awakened the world to the possibilities of spontaneous field control; and it is Smith again, dressed in modern terminological clothing, who has been awakening the doctrinaire planners to the virtues of spontaneous control in the price system.

To be sure, Smith never generalized from spontaneous field control to the idea of field structure in general, nor from "competitive" price system to price system in general. But those who today wish to generalize Smith's crude concept of a price system to make of it a concept identifying a fundamental type of social coördination are merely acknowledging again—or at last—the power today as in 1776 of the "invisible hand." A central concept in the recent economic literature on planning is the price system; a principal debate, on its role, merits, limitations.[1] Smith was a revolutionary in the best sense of the word. Modern revolutionaries—in the same sense of the word—are taking up not very far from where he and his school left the discussion of how to organize economic life.

Many a good idea has gone down the drain to be lost for a hundred years because it had somehow become dissolved in a mixture of dubious metaphysics or psychology which had to be thrown out. Thus much of what Adam Smith said about spontaneous controls in a price system has had to be reclaimed from the waste products of human thought. Then, too, in the high period of classical economics the claims made for the price system were exaggerated to absurdity by persons who apparently believed that spontaneous field controls—though they did not call them that—could almost completely supplant hierarchical organization if only given the chance. Finally, much as Smith accomplished, neither he nor his followers made much of the possibilities of competitive control through bargaining and the potentialities for price system organization through noncompetitive supplementary controls.

THE MEANING OF MONOPOLY.   Of the three competitive controls, the first gives us an immediate clue as to the meaning of monopoly. At an extreme, monopoly means one firm only in each industry. By this definition, a monopoly-ridden price system is one in which the businessman is controlled by the spontaneous primary control alone. Now the primary control is itself powerful. Although not a satisfactory alternative because better alternatives are available, it is not demonstrably less effective than the controls of a centrally directed economy without a price system. Hence, a monopoly-dominated economy is not an uncontrolled economy or an economy permitting unlimited discretion to its entrepreneurs. And it is, in fact, a kind of competitive price system.

[1] Cf. the works cited in Chapter 1.

Monopoly defined more broadly takes several forms: single-seller monopoly, duopoly, oligopoly, as well as their counterparts when the monopolist is a buyer, a monopsonist. But by any of these connotations monopoly commonly refers to defects in the supplementary spontaneous control over the entrepreneur and not to an absence of the primary spontaneous control, which is itself competitive. For the most part, the term "monopoly" is used as though it were at one extreme of—or described a range of—positions on a continuum. When it is so used, it refers to an extreme on a scale ranging from the primary competitive control alone (monopoly) to the primary and spontaneous supplementary control taken together (competition).

Monopoly has still other meanings. Supplementary competitive control may be made effective through bargaining; and hierarchy, autonomy, or noncompetitive bargaining may prevail in the absence of spontaneous competition. "Monopoly" is often applied to these controls as well. Hence, if it is simply stated that a firm is a monopoly, this may mean either that it is controlled only by the primary spontaneous control or that it is also controlled by one or more supplementary controls other than the spontaneous. Thus "monopoly" may refer to organization (1) through the primary control alone, (2) through the primary control when supplemented by competitive bargaining, or (3) through the primary control supplemented by noncompetitive bargaining, hierarchy, or autonomy. In the first two of these cases, monopoly is a kind of competitive control; in the third, it is a mixture of competitive with noncompetitive controls. Clearly, it is the anthithesis neither of competition nor of effective control.

BIG BUSINESS AND GROUP CONTROLS

It should now be clear that big business is not necessarily an enemy of effective price system control or even of competitive control. For, even if many competing firms in an industry give way to a few giants, they may be controlled through a combination of the primary control, which is competitive, and any of the noncompetitive supplementary mechanisms. Perhaps more often they will be controlled through a combination of the primary control and competitive bargaining.[2]

[2] The argument that big business is free from competitive control also falls into the error of confusing absolute size of enterprise with its size relative to its market. A number of recent studies agree that, despite impressive observable evi-

Aside from the growth of big business, the greatest apparent threat to competitive control is group control over price by businessmen: price leadership, market sharing, standard costs, and other formal and informal devices for price agreement. Mandatory controls such as antitrust have often been imposed on businessmen to frustrate their own group controls; but, as everyone knows, mandatory controls cannot wholly stamp out agreement among buyers or among sellers.

The formal conditions of pure competition prohibit group control over price. In the real world, however, price changes must be initiated somewhere by particular individuals; and devices for group control may be useful for scheduling price movements called for by the rewards and penalties of competitive controls. In the model of pure competition, the economist has not had to concern himself with what would be interesting to a sociologist inspecting prices. The sociologist might ask who leads in setting the price and who follows, how the price is set, and when. He would reject the terminology sometimes used in economic theory that says prices are set by no one, that they "get" set without anyone's setting them. But the economist too knows that the invisible hand works through the hands of buyers and sellers. It is incorrect to infer from his words "automatic" and "impersonal" that individuals appear as purposive and deliberate decision makers only where competition breaks down. Group controls over prices often appear, simply because some specific institutional arrangement is necessary to change prices.[3]

In the absence of some method of group control, coördination is threatened for a variety of reasons. Where it is difficult to estimate the effects of a change in price upon total receipts and total costs,

---

dence that businesses in the United States are larger than fifty years ago, the proportion of production concentrated in the hands of a few dominant firms has remained almost unchanged. If it has increased or decreased, it is, as one observer put it, "at the pace of a glacial drift," not measurable by present statistical techniques. See M. A. Adelman, "The Measurement of Industrial Concentration," *Review of Economics and Statistics*, November, 1951, pp. 269–296; see also Warren G. Nutter, *The Extent of Enterprise Monopoly in the United States, 1899–1939*, University of Chicago Press, Chicago, 1951. Such studies as these do not, of course, prove that industry is not highly concentrated—they specifically assert that it is—but they undermine both the easy but mistaken identification of size with concentration and the not uncommon opinion that the growth of big business necessarily means that the economy is less competitive than it was fifty or more years ago.

[3] Cf. Alfred R. Oxenfeldt, *Industrial Pricing and Market Practices*, Prentice-Hall, New York, 1951, chap. 3.

competitive pressures are more likely to spread a downward error than an upward error. Prices may be driven to an unworkably low level. Small firms, unstandardized products, or poor accounting may account for the difficulty of accurate cost and receipts estimates. Or for various reasons an industry may tend toward overcapacity with consequent destructive competition. The possibilities of malcoördination are many.[4]

Unfortunately, the useful functions performed by group controls are often cited to justify a great variety of restrictive practices. Good judgment requires discrimination, but discrimination is difficult in the present state of knowledge of industrial price policies and of tests by which policies may be judged. Our point is not that group controls are inevitably helpful to effective competitive control; it is that they are not inevitably harmful to it.

Both in big business and in group controls over price, noneconomists sometimes believe they see a system of organization alternative to competition. They see, for example, industries dominated by a few large business units, each highly mechanized and displaying an elaborate, tightly knit hierarchical system of control over every aspect of its work from the general accounting office down to the disposition of chewing gum wrappers left on the grounds. They contrast this with the tattered appearance of industries composed of many firms, their managers fighting each other, some firms barely surviving, others in bankruptcy. It seems clear to them that competition is not order but disorder. Order is hierarchy, they believe; hierarchy is to be found in big business and in combinations; hence, big business and combinations are the instruments of economic order.

The major premise is apparently no less appealing for being incorrect. In being identified with disorder, competition is suffering the same abuse as anarchy, which is perhaps the ideal spon-

[4] For discussion see Edward S. Mason, "Monopoly in Law and Economics," in American Economic Association's *Readings in the Social Control of Industry*, The Blakiston Co., Philadelphia, 1942, pp. 25–48; Edgar M. Hoover, "Price and Production Policies of Large Scale Enterprises," *American Economic Review*, Supplement 1939, pp. 102 ff.; William Fellner, *Competition Among the Few*, Alfred A. Knopf, New York, 1949; P. W. S. Andrews, *Manufacturing Business*, Macmillan and Co., London, 1949; C. D. Hyson and F. H. Sanderson, "Monopolistic Discrimination in the Cranberry Industry," *Quarterly Journal of Economics*, May, 1945, pp. 330–369; Carroll R. Daugherty, Melvin G. de Chazeau, and S. S. Stratton, *The Economics of the Iron and Steel Industry*, McGraw-Hill Book Co., New York, 1937, pp. 546–567; Clarence D. Long, Jr., "Newsprint: Costs and Competition," *Harvard Business Review*, vol. 18, 1939–1940, pp. 372 ff; J. A. Guthrie, *The Newsprint Paper Industry*, Harvard University Press, Cambridge, 1941.

taneous field system. Anarchy has come to mean confusion; but it has another meaning: a system of spontaneous coördination. Just as it is easy to slip from the concept of anarchy as order without hierarchy to the idea of no order at all, so it is easy to slip from competition as order without hierarchy to competition as no order at all.

Moreover, order is not the same as the absence of change. Competition is often identified with disorder—hence, by some doubtful logic, monopoly with order—because competition means losses as well as profits and because it calls for a never ending procession of bankruptcy. But preferences change; so also do technology and resources. If an economy is to economize, the first requirement is adaptability. An economic *order* provides for the systematic elimination of the obsolete and inefficient, as well as for constant experimentation. The test of genuine experimentation is that much of it fails.

MONOPOLISTIC COMPETITION

Many firms avoid price competition and seek to expand through product differentiation. Is this procedure evidence of a significant failure of competitive control? For some products, product differentiation offers the consumer more desirable alternatives from which to choose than would otherwise be possible. To be sure, one requirement of pure competition is not met where product differentiation proceeds apace—namely, the requirement that there be many sellers of a standardized product. But the deficiency is often minor.[5] Indeed, it may be no deficiency at all, where the differentiated products continue to substitute closely with each other.

In some quarters the theory of monopolistic competition has had the effect of underestimating the role of competitive control. The publications of Chamberlin and Robinson in 1933 accomplished—or were part of, depending on one's view—a revolution in economic theory.[6] The interest of economists in monopoly was stimulated by their pleasure in new conceptual tools. It conse-

---

[5] Even on a purely theoretical plane, the significance of product differentiation as a departure from competitive conditions may often be minor. Alfred Nicols, "Rehabilitation of Pure Competition," *Quarterly Journal of Economics,* November, 1947, pp. 31–63.

[6] Edward H. Chamberlin, *The Theory of Monopolistic Competition,* Harvard University Press, Cambridge, 1933; Joan Robinson, *The Economics of Imperfect Competition,* Macmillan and Co., London, 1933.

quently became easy to mistake a heightened interest in monopoly among economists for more monopoly in the economy. Then, too, the new theory focused attention on more concrete institutions in the market than had the theory of pure competition: economists began to classify market structures and to seek rough correlations between structure and price policy. This approach could hardly fail to emphasize the discretionary elements in price determination and hence, again, to confuse the economists' increasing awareness of monopoly with increasing monopoly itself.

The new theoretical developments made it increasingly clear that the older theories both of competition and of monopoly covered extreme or limiting cases. But they generalized the theory of monopoly to cover the in-between cases which embrace all real-world markets, giving a superficial impression that a more or less competitive economy was suddenly discovered to be more or less monopolistic. What had changed, of course, was only the economist's concepts and language, and his understanding of the economy.

"Monopolistic competition" can be read simply as impure competition—that is, competition that fails to correspond in every detail with the hypothetical ideal of the theory of pure competition. Thus conceived, it is the competition of any real-world economy. But instead "monopolistic competition" sometimes is read as "monopoly," where monopoly is then taken to be the antithesis of competition. Hence monopolistic competition theory sometimes comes to be thought of as the theory of something quite different from and opposed to the theory of competition. But monopolistic competition is equivalent to monopoly only if monopoly is defined to cover even minor departures from the analytical ideal. And, as we have seen, monopoly is in any case a form of competition and not its antithesis.

The new theories seemed convincing evidence of monopoly because they seemed to describe actual market operations and relationships more exactly than did the older theory of competition. But in fact the new theories were describing in a practical way the imperfections in the economy, not its underlying coördinating framework. In this sense the new theories were even more abstract than the old, though appearances were to the contrary, because one could understand their significance only by assuming they related to a system of economic coördination itself not explained by the theories.[7]

All this is not to say that the new insights permitted by the new theories were misinterpreted or badly used. Among some economists the theory of perfect competition had created a predisposition to overestimate the role of competition as a control and this the new theories overcame. But in so doing the new theories gave rise in some quarters to misconceptions as to what, in the real world outside theory, had changed when theory changed. An illustration is to be found in a summary of the development of the theory of monopoly in the 1930's and 1940's in the *Survey of Contemporary Economics*, published by the American Economic Association:

At a more sophisticated level, the new work did strike a blow at the concept of inherent order in capitalist behavior. . . . Under some circumstances, this might have been revolutionary. No idea is more deeply rooted in non-socialist economics than that of a rule of competition where the controlling *tendency* is for resources to be employed by firms and distributed between industries in such manner that they are combined with maximum efficiency into products that give maximum satisfaction. . . . But the doctrine was only completely vulnerable at one point and that was where monopoly entered—the defenders and attackers entirely agreed that monopoly (*cum* oligopoly) was deeply subversive of the competitive model. And, since oligopoly was stubbornly resistant to incorporation in a new system, at least by the old methods, it destroyed without leaving anything in its place.[8]

Only if it is clear that "monopoly" subverts the competitive model and not the real-world competitive system, that it resists incorporation into a new system of theory and not into an economic system, and finally that it "destroyed" theory but not economies are the propositions valid. But neither the author of the statement nor the men to whom he refers in his further comments keep clear the distinction between theory and reality, for he continues:

One or two scholars have seen the development in the foregoing light. The late Heinrich von Stackelberg . . . who dealt extensively

[7] These comments follow in part William H. Nicholls, "Social Biases and Recent Theories of Competition," *Quarterly Journal of Economics,* November, 1943, pp. 1–26.
[8] John K. Galbraith, "Monopoly and the Concentration of Economic Power," in Howard S. Ellis (ed.), *Survey of Contemporary Economics,* published for the Amercan Economic Association by The Blakiston Co., Philadelphia, 1949, p. 109.

with the problem of oligopoly seems as a result of his analysis to have abandoned all hope for an economic order except as provided by the State. . . . Professor Eduard Heiman has also expressed alarm at the implications of the theory. He suggests that "it is time to recognize that the concept of a system of monopoly is self-contradictory and the very negation of everything economics stands for."[9]

If, before the development of the theory of monopolistic competition, the concept of pure competition led economists to over-estimate the precision of competitive controls, it was troublesome to the non-economist because of the apparent discrepancy between theory and the observable facts of economic life. Not understanding the limits of the economist's conceptual apparatus, a large number of social scientists threw the apparatus away and settled down in a conviction that monopoly was everywhere powerful, competition everywhere weak. This is the kind of mistake they were in no danger of making in their own fields because they did not always have the precise model-building apparatus of the economist.

UNSETTLED ISSUES

Because competition embraces three controls over the businessman (primary and two supplementary), and because monopoly is either a form of competition or a combination of competitive with noncompetitive controls, and because neither big business, group controls, nor monopolistic competition is necessarily anti-competitive, we conclude that competitive controls are both pervasive and effective. Such a conclusion is incapable of formal proof, and a more precise appraisal of the strength of competitive controls awaits the further development of theoretical apparatus for that purpose. Our primary purpose in this chapter, however, is to describe the various market mechanisms which are prerequisite to control over the businessman as a leader. Since in so doing we have been able to show, first, that the primary control is universal and, second, that many supplementary controls are available, the traditional questions on competition and monopoly become subsidiary. Indeed, for some years now economists have been reformulating their inquiries into market controls in order to by-pass the ambiguities of the monopoly competition issue.[10]

[9] *Ibid.*, pp. 109–110.
[10] For example, Edward S. Mason, *op. cit.*, pp. 46–47.

II. Business Practices and the Prerequisites of Control

The price system is a curious institution. To some people it appears to be an impressive combination of very powerful controls; to others it is hardly more than an analytical model found in economic theory rather than in the real world. This state of affairs is symptomatic of the difficulty of understanding spontaneous controls, on which the price system leans so heavily. But there is another explanation of the discrepancy in views. To achieve precision, economists often describe a price system by identifying the conditions of a perfect or pure type; they do not adequately describe the characteristics by which it can be identified in actual economic life. Their procedure is not necessarily defective, but it leaves a gap.

This section of the chapter seeks to bridge this gap between the prerequisites of effective price system controls and the kind of practices to be observed everywhere in business. It is addressed primarily to those who cannot reconcile their impressions of business practices with our description of price system controls. Some business practices cannot be reconciled with effective control, but many can.

THE MARGINAL COST PROBLEM

The major issue posed by observed business policies is this: Effective price system controls would compel businessmen to govern price-production policy so that marginal cost and price are equal. But businessmen in fact appear to govern their policies by various practices bearing no relation to the marginal principle.

THE MEASUREMENT OF MARGINAL COSTS. Let us first ask with what precision marginal costs should be calculated. A basic difficulty is that costs should measure alternative values forgone in the economy, yet these cannot be measured accurately in many circumstances. Although the market registers alternative values in the prices of inputs used by a firm at the time of purchase, once the equipment or raw material is taken off the market and brought into the firm, a continuing objective measure of its alternative uses does not exist. Hence real-world marginal calculations look quite different from the marginal calculations in theory.

A catalogue of some of the most troublesome problems of measurement of cost begins with the fact that *there are many marginal costs to choose from.* Marginal costs depend on how near-sighted one is. The marginal cost of increasing production by one thousand units per day for one month is ordinarily less than the marginal cost of an equal but permanent increase in production, because production may be temporarily increased without incurring new costs that would be necessary for continued large production. Moreover, the costs properly considered incremental or marginal vary from day to day as contracts come up for renewal. In contemplation of a new contract, the cost to be contracted for becomes the marginal cost of the output for which it is to be incurred. But once the contract is signed, the cost becomes fixed and no longer marginal except in contemplation of the contract. Which of many possible marginal costs is most relevant to price depends on the period ahead for which a price is to be set and production scheduled. For these reasons, any real-world marginal calculations will contain arbitrary elements.

There is also the problem of marginal costs for peak loads and other large changes in output. In the case of industries like electricity with regularly recurring peak loads at high costs, shall the peak costs be allocated to the peak period or distributed over all output? The strict logic of marginalism is on one side in this question, the many advantages of convenience and price stability on the other. This is a problem actually broader than that of the peak, since cost may fluctuate for many reasons.

Fluctuating prices make planning of purchases by both consumers and businessmen difficult; and, since the virtue of the marginal principle is that it is an aid to rationality, nothing is gained by pushing it to the point where it makes rational choice quite difficult. In addition, fluctuating prices sometimes complicate both the method of payment and cost accounting within the firm. Finally, if prices rise sharply as costs rise, they reduce the real incomes of those who must buy at the high price. For temporary changes in costs and prices, these income shifts may be capricious and undesirable. For all these reasons, a loose application of marginalism is frequently desirable.

Where firms produce many different commodities, the allocation of costs to each kind of production is necessarily rough. The United States Steel Corporation sells some fifty thousand different variations in quantity and quality of fifty basic commodities. International Harvester stocks 250,000 separate parts for servicing agricultural implements. "Ideally," costs should be precisely calculated for each. But it is a question of whether the game is worth the candle, and for cases such as these no one can dispute the answer.

Strictly applied, marginalism also requires charging to each consumer for each of his purchases the expenses of making the sale to him. It costs more to sell to a customer who dallies over his purchases than to someone who knows what he wants. Imagine, however, the confusion of consumers watching prices rise minute by minute as they weigh their choice. All these problems raise questions of the value of precision. Marginalism pushed to its strict logic denies that precision itself has extraordinarily high marginal costs.

A second group of difficulties in the measurement of cost and demand are those which arise from *the impossibility of getting statistical equivalents to theoretical concepts*. Suppose, for example, that a firm resolves all the questions posed, by the adoption of certain rules of thumb governing the time periods, the classes of commodities, and the groups of customers for whom separate marginal costs are to be calculated. Could it then proceed with its calculations? The answer is, of course, that prices for input cannot always be known in advance, nor can output per worker, nor maintenance expenses, nor a number of other variables. For that matter, even if there is no uncertainty about the future, the present is difficult enough, for many errors are possible in working down from aggregate costs to costs per unit of output.

A final problem illustrative of difficulties in calculation of marginal cost arises where a firm's unit costs decline as output expands so that, were production expanded until marginal cost was equal to price, price would not cover total costs. The application of the marginal cost rule here requires the enterprise to run at a loss. If it runs at a loss, the deficit becomes a cost to taxpayers or to whoever covers the loss. In such a case the marginal rule is defective, since it does not necessarily facilitate rational choice and may require those who do not consume a good to forgo alternatives because others have chosen to consume it.

Marginal cost calculations, it should not be forgotten, are useful so far as they facilitate rational choice and allocation. As a general rule, the more precisely marginal costs can be calculated, the more rational the choice and allocation. But we have already seen that it is not always rational to pursue marginal calculation to the point of estimating the costs of delivering a commodity into the hands of a particular customer, and we are now simply saying that, for other reasons, it is not always rational to pursue marginalism to a calculation of the costs of increments of output from a given plant. At best, a businessman can typically calculate marginal costs only for blocks of additional production; he cannot calculate them for an increase in production from one thousand units per week to one thousand and one. Hence, all marginal cost calculations will fall short of being precise, and a variety of considerations, such as we have been discussing, will indicate how far precision should be pursued.

In the last case discussed, operating at a loss to satisfy the marginal cost rule may be objectionable for the reasons already given. In addition, it loses one of the virtues of the price system, namely, that if cues do not produce the desired response, consequent penalties are ordinarily quick and certain in the form of losses. Where the marginal cost criterion prohibits the use of losses as penalties, it is necessary to pay subsidies to the firms. In consequence, uncertainty and subjectivity are introduced into rewards and penalties for an occasional gain that may not be worth the sacrifice.

BUSINESS PRACTICES ON MARGINAL COSTS. Many business routines that appear to depart from marginalism in price-output decisions are in fact accommodations to the complexities in marginal cost calculation just listed. Because the number of variables with which policy must deal, the number of relationships among the variables, and the complications of the time periods involved make routines or formulas necessary,[11] these practices are not the *prima-facie* evidence of departures from marginal cost that they are sometimes taken to be.

What routines are used? A study of British manufacturing business concludes:

(1) that the price which a business will normally quote for a particular product will equal the estimated average direct costs of production plus a costing-margin . . . ; (2) that the costing-margin will normally tend to cover the costs of the indirect factors of production and provide a

[11] Joe S. Bain, "Price and Production Policies," in Howard S. Ellis (ed.), *op. cit.*, p. 153.

normal level of profit looking at industry as a whole, and may reflect any general permanent changes in the prices of indirect factors or production, but will remain constant, given the organization of the individual business, whatever the level of its output; (3) that, given the prices of the direct factors of production, price will tend to remain unchanged whatever the level of output; (4) that, at that price, the business will have a more or less clearly defined market and will sell the amount which its customers demand from it, its sales thus equaling its limited share of the market. . . .[12]

This description of price-output routines is roughly confirmed by other investigators both for Britain and for the United States.[13] An American study comes to these conclusions:

It is clear from a number of recent studies of large firms producing for sale (rather than to specification) that, for the firms studied, the economist's long run cost function more nearly approximates the costs that are taken into account in pricing than does the short run cost function. The standard cost calculations of General Motors and International Harvester are unit costs which, at standard volume of output (with respect to which the plant and equipment were presumably designed) and in the absence of changes in wage rates, material costs or factor efficiencies, may be expected to recapture the plant investment within its conservatively anticipated lifetime. This is one version of the full cost principle of Hall and Hitch, and it would seem to be in fairly wide use among business firms in this country as well as in England.[14]

If average costs per unit are fairly stable over a wide range of output, then price policy based on variable costs plus a markup is not significantly different from marginal cost pricing except at high outputs where average and marginal costs diverge. Even then, if businessmen follow a practice of using a higher markup at high outputs, the discrepancy between average cost pricing and marginal

[12] P. W. S. Andrews, *op. cit.*, pp. 184 f.

[13] R. L. Hall and C. J. Hitch, "Price Theory and Business Behavior," *Oxford Economic Papers*, No. 2, May, 1939, pp. 12–45. Some of these studies have been criticized for exaggerating deviations from marginalism. (R. F. Kahn, "Oxford Studies in the Price Mechanism," *Economic Journal*, March, 1952, pp. 119–130.)

[14] Conference on Price Research, National Bureau of Economic Research, *Cost Behavior and Price Policy*, NBER, New York, 1943, p. 286. This same study also observes that outright marginal cost calculations are not infrequent, as illustrated by a firm following a full-cost pricing routine and trying to rid itself of those products which show low profits in favor of those which show high. "The process of selection and rejection here followed may well lead to a fair approximation of the maximum profit position aimed at in an estimation of marginal costs and revenue." (*Ibid.*, pp. 284–285.)

cost pricing is minor. Whether average costs are in fact stable over a wide range of output, and whether businessmen generally use a higher markup for high outputs, however, is disputable.

Customary routines are also sometimes an intelligent approximation to marginalism in the face of uncertainty. Where sellers know neither their marginal costs nor revenues for the period ahead for which a price-output decision must be made, the possibility that cost-price relationships may be worse than expected must be anticipated. For this reason the seller will not try to equal any given present marginal cost to present price but will on the other hand make certain that his price is sufficient to cover all his costs. Such an explanation makes full-cost pricing a kind of least-risk marginal calculation.[15] Break-even-point pricing and markup pricing have also been interpreted as methods of approximating a long-run marginal cost rule by elevating "an intrinsically minor feature of a long-run optimum position to a guiding rule."[16] Attempts have also been made to reconcile common routines and long-run marginalism by clarification of language and concept between businessmen and economists.[17]

Does this kind of evidence permit any conclusions to be drawn? The answer is that between these policies and a reasonable use of the marginal rule neither a serious discrepancy nor a reconciliation is demonstrable.[18] Clearly, however, no unbridgeable gap separates business practices from the requirements of effective market control. To be sure, some practices of the kind under discussion frustrate the approximation to marginalism necessary to effective price system control. But the most that can be expected of any one of the central sociopolitical processes—whether hierarchy, polyarchy, or bargaining—is that it is effective in many situations, though not universally. It is because of this, of course, that all four of the central sociopolitical processes are necessary.

It ought not to be forgotten that the business firm is a major instrument for disturbing as well as establishing equilibrium. It is

[15] William Fellner, *op. cit.*, chap. 5.

[16] Martin Bronfenbrenner, "Imperfect Competition on a Long-Run Basis," *The Journal of Business of the University of Chicago*, April, 1950, pp. 81–93.

[17] P. Wiles, "Empirical Research and Marginal Analysis," *Economic Journal*, September, 1950, pp. 515–530.

[18] See W. J. Eiteman, *Price Determination—Business Practice Versus Economic Theory*, University of Michigan School of Business Administration, Ann Arbor, 1949; P. Wiles, *op. cit.*; R. F. Kahn, *op. cit.*, pp. 119–130; R. A. Lester, "Shortcomings of Marginal Analysis for Wage-Employment Problems," *American Economic Review*, March, 1946, pp. 63–82.

one of the most successful social instruments for innovation that
has yet been devised. Businessmen do not simply produce; they also
experiment, innovate, invent, and plan. To make the most out of
the business firm as an instrument for progress, and to encourage
its adaptability, loose control over its responses to immediate consumers may be desirable to a degree. It may function most vigorously if some looseness in control permits elements of security in
its personnel, capital equipment, and income.

Moreover, its decision makers must not be called upon to concentrate all their time and attention, both of which are scarce, on
accounting and price-output policy. "Correct" costing and pricing
can be a full-time occupation for top management. But because
time and attention are scarce resources, the use of simplified approximations to correctness may be quite desirable, especially since
conventions and rules of thumb become the basis for effective hierarchical control within the firm. They can serve as rules, widely
understood by the various levels of the hierarchy, objective enough
so that violations can be fairly definitely identified and corrected.

III. Further Observations on Public Ownership

Now that some of the real-world complications of marginalism have been examined, it is possible to carry the earlier appraisal of the mandatory price system with government ownership
further.

THE ALLEGED SIMPLICITY OF A MANDATORY PRICE MECHANISM

At one extreme of the argument on the workability of a mandatory price mechanism, of which Von Mises is representative,[19] it
is argued that rational calculation in a mandatory price system is
impossible because, in the absence of many competing buyers and
sellers, prices cannot be made to reflect costs correctly or to govern
production on a cost-price calculus. Many economists at the opposite extreme, including Oskar Lange and Abba P. Lerner,[20] argue

[19] Mises' original article appeared in German under the title, "Die Wirtschafts-
rechnung im sozialistischen Gemeinwesen," 47 *Archiv f. Sozpolitik* 86 (1920); this
article was translated into English and appears as "Economic Calculation in the
Socialist Commonwealth" in F. A. von Hayek (ed.), *Collectivist Economic Planning*, G. Routledge & Sons, Ltd., London, 1935, pp. 87–130.

[20] Oskar R. Lange in Oskar R. Lange and Fred M. Taylor, *On the Economic
Theory of Socialism*, University of Minnesota Press, Minneapolis, 1938; Abba P.
Lerner, *The Economics of Control*, The Macmillan Company, New York, 1944.

that a socialist price system can indeed be operated in the real world on the basis of no more than a few simple and quantitative instructions to sellers: primarily instructions to govern their outputs by adjustments of production that bring marginal cost equal to price. As in many disputes, truth seems to lie somewhere between.

Consider the latter extreme. Lange suggested that it would be possible to operate a decentralized socialist economy through the use of two kinds of agencies with a simple hierarchical prescription for each. Price-setting agencies would set prices on commodities under their jurisdiction according to the prescription that price must be varied to clear the market. Enterprises would operate on the prescription that production should be varied in order to bring marginal costs equal to price. These two hierarchical prescriptions, it was argued, would provide sufficient coördination for the firms in the economy and would make more detailed controls unnecessary except for new investment. Rules like these, it was said, were simple, hence easily enforceable; objective, hence unambiguous; quantitative, hence their results measurable. For these reasons, discretion would be minimized and responsiveness maximized.[21]

As an analytical model in economic theory, this picture of a socialist price system is valid; the consensus of economists is that Von Mises was wrong in not granting at least this much. Indeed, the socialist model is only a companion piece to the model of a perfectly competitive price system. But to use the socialist model to describe a possible real-world economic system is to commit the same error as that committed by those who identify perfect competition with a real-world system.

COMPLICATIONS IN THE MODEL

Consider the difficulties just described in calculating marginal costs. Marginal costs vary according to the time period ahead for which they are calculated. They fluctuate from day to day depending upon what cost commitments come up for renewal, as in rent contracts. On many operations marginal costs cannot be calculated except at more expense than the calculation is worth. Finally, ignorance and uncertainty make estimates and guesses necessary. For these and other reasons mentioned, routines for cost calculation and cost-price policy are necessary; and in some circumstances average cost calculations must be taken as the closest practicable approxima-

[21] Oskar R. Lange, *op. cit.*

tion to the marginal principle. Hence to instruct producers to increase or decrease their rates of production until marginal costs are
brought equal to price is not to give them an unambiguous, objective, easily enforceable rule, deviations from which can be quickly
spotted and corrected.

Furthermore, to allow prices to rise and fall to clear the market
is sometimes a source of instability and diseconomy. Moreover,
sharp price increases for some commodities may effect an unwanted
reduction in the real incomes of low-income families. And in circumstances where the marginal rule is at odds with the solvency of
the enterprise, it may be wise to modify the marginal rule to avoid
subsidies and to maintain the autonomy of the enterprise.

Hence many qualifications have to be made to adapt such simple price system rules as Lange's or Lerner's to the complexities of
the real world. Perhaps freer exchange of information among enterprises in a socialist economy would necessitate fewer modifications
of simple marginalism to take account of ignorance and uncertainty;
perhaps, too, it is easier to lay down workable rules to government-
owned enterprises than to private enterprises always straining for
monopoly controls over price. Nevertheless, in the absence of competition between firms, a hierarchy would be necessary to spell out
supplementary rules to limit discretion; the complexity of workable
rules might turn out to be greater for a socialist price system than
for a competitive price system.

No simple procedure, then, is available by which a socialist
price system can easily and simply decentralize, objectify, simplify,
and quantify, as Lange and Lerner have argued. Nevertheless, a
workable socialist price mechanism is possible in some sectors of
the economy in the same sense that a spontaneous price system is.
And in its sectors a workable socialist price system, like a spontaneous price system in its sectors, can provide a rough, imperfect, but
nevertheless essential set of techniques for simplification, objectifi-
cation, quantification, and decentralization. Prescriptions need not
set forth the policies of the enterprise in all possible circumstances,
as they would have to do in the absence of a price system; they need
only prescribe general patterns of response to market cues. To the
extent that a socialist price mechanism fails in simplicity and precision, its failures are much the same as those of competition.

A fair inference from the present state of the controversy over the possibility of a socialist price system would run something like this: A workable but quite imperfect socialist price mechanism is possible for some sectors of the economy; how far it can be extended is as much a matter of controversy as with all other types of economic coördination. A workable socialist price system will presumably possess most of the strengths and weaknesses of a spontaneous price system; both are price systems and both employ spontaneous field structures as their primary controls. But the socialist price system has certain distinctive characteristics and problems of its own. For example, it cannot, as some of its more extreme advocates have hoped, virtually eliminate discretionary entrepreneurial power and the consequent dangers of irresponsiveness. Whether mandatory or spontaneous, a price system is essentially a pattern of organization in which decisions are made according to certain rules; although these rules may narrow the range of discretion, they can never even come close to eliminating it. What particular rules should be followed—that is, what particular price-output policies should be administered—remains as much a subject for further inquiry as the proper price policies for spontaneous and bargaining price mechanisms.

CRITERIA FOR WORKABLE MANDATORY PRICE MECHANISMS

Hence the relevant question is no longer the workability of a socialist price mechanism but its particular merits, shortcomings, and prerequisites. But the possibilities of a mandatory price system, it should be remembered, are not limited to nationalized enterprises. Short of government ownership, the combination of hierarchy with price system can be and is used to remedy deficiencies in the price system. Governments actually do use rules that might be developed to regulate price-output relationships in privately owned industries in order to maintain the price system at a higher level of performance than would otherwise be possible. This is roughly what is attempted in public utility regulation, and it is quite possible that the technique can be extended more widely into the regulation of monopoly.

Public utility regulation, industrial price policies, monopoly, and socialist price systems have in the past been studied largely as different subjects by different groups of economists not in close touch with one another in their writing. A book like Lerner's *Economics of Control*,[22] for example, evidently drew almost nothing from a study of industrial price policies and public utility regulation. On the other hand, most works on utility regulation (there are some notable exceptions) have been little influenced by studies either of pricing problems under socialism or of actual industrial price policies. Likewise, the theoretical fields of industrial price policies and monopoly only recently have begun to merge; both the achievement and the failure of their integration is displayed in the essays on these two subjects in the *Survey of Contemporary Economics*.[23] Most surprising of all is the hiatus between those economists who have been trying desperately to find criteria for workable competition and those who have been trying to find workable rules for hierarchical price mechanisms. For central to all these studies is the search for workable criteria for price-production policies in price systems.

The possibilities of progress on this problem are much increased by recent tendencies for those studies to use the same language and ask the same questions. The most recent discussions of socialist pricing, for example, are quite removed from the utopianism of the writers of some years ago, as the studies of such economists as Little, Lewis, Crosland, Meade, and Fleming will show.[24] Some of these economists are finding that the difference between the practical rules of the public utility engineers and the theoretical rules of the economists is smaller than the difference in language customarily used to discuss them. And where the two are significantly different, the engineers can sometimes teach the economists rather than vice versa.[25]

THE FEASIBILITY OF MANDATORY PRICE MECHANISMS

BENEFITS TO LEADERSHIP. One may doubt, of course, whether government leaders and subordinates will ever wish to concern

---

[22] *Op. cit.*

[23] See Joe S. Bain, "Price and Production Policies," and John K. Galbraith, "Monopoly and the Concentration of Economic Power," both in Howard S. Ellis (ed.), *op. cit.*, pp. 129–173 and 99–128.

[24] See, for example, I. M. D. Little, *A Critique of Welfare Economics*, Oxford University Press, New York, 1950; W. Arthur Lewis, *Overhead Costs: Some Essays in Economic Analysis*, Allen and Unwin, London, 1949; C. A. R. Crosland, "Prices and Costs in Nationalized Undertakings," *Oxford Economic Papers*, N.S. no. 3, January, 1950; J. E. Meade, *Planning and the Price Mechanism*, Allen and Unwin, London, 1948; J. Marcus Fleming, "Production and Price Policies in Public Enterprise," *Economica*, N.S. vol. 17, February, 1950.

[25] W. Arthur Lewis, *op. cit.*, p. 14 n.

themselves with the niceties of correct prescriptions for mandatory price mechanisms when they are faced with regulating either private or nationalized industries. At first glance, direct hierarchical control without reference to a price system would seem to be easier. But government officials derive many advantages for price system rules; hence, even to politicians they are not merely a dull, technical, apolitical matter.

In the first place, politicians and administrators often want rules to which they can represent themselves as bound in order to get safely out of the cross fire of warring interest groups. Second, legislative and executive politicians often wish to avoid direct responsibility for regulation by passing the immediate responsibility on to professional administrators. But, because failures are held against the elected officials, they cannot give these administrators a free hand; therefore they fasten definite obligations upon administrators by rules. If they must have rules, price system rules are useful. For they must permit great adaptability in the enterprise and at the same time tie regulations fairly closely to a principle whose enforcement save politicians a great amount of trouble, namely, that every enterprise must stand on its own feet by covering its costs. Third, mandatory price system rules are also relatively easy to lay on as supplements to the price system rules of a spontaneous price mechanism, with which they are in no severe conflict.

DECENTRALIZATION. Finally, the use of mandatory price mechanisms is an alternative—perhaps the only feasible one—to an excess of centralization that threatens to grow out of recent attempts to extend government hierarchical controls over business enterprise. The British Coal Board now operates the largest centrally controlled business in the world; and, like other nationalized industries, it has been heavily criticized for overcentralization even by British socialists. G. D. H. Cole's statement of the problem of centralization is concrete, vigorous, and not obviously oversimplified. Writing on British socialist reform since the last war, he says:

. . . Democratic Socialism, when it is able to win power, greatly improves the material conditions and security of the bottom third of the people, but has failed, so far, to stimulate the will to serve without which these achievements are bound to remain precarious. . . .

The question, then, for British Socialists is . . . how to get a new impulse behind their attempt to advance towards Socialism in their own way. I think they are failing in this because they have not understood that there are only two methods of shaking men out of their lethargy and of creating the necessary leadership. One is the centralized, authoritarian way of building up a strongly disciplined party which makes itself the sole source of power and confers great subordinate power on its agents at every level, so that they drive on the people in the exercise of their own enjoyment of authority. This was the Nazi way; and it is also the Communist way. The only alternative is to diffuse power, to fling power and responsibility into many hands, to rely on the people throwing up their own leaders in the groups to which they belong—and then to give these leaders the fullest encouragement to use their own initiative and to lead the rest of the people by example and influence, and not by the exercise of authority delegated from the center. . . .[26]

. . . The National Board system is unsatisfactory because it generates no enthusiasm anywhere. A bad cross between bureaucracy and big business, it gives the worker no sense that the responsibility for high output at low cost now rests on him. It gives the consumer no sense of participation; it makes him feel that he is more than ever up against a vast, uncontrollable monopolistic machine. I can see all the reasons that made the Public Corporation seem to its sponsors a sound compromise: what they forgot was that socialization depends for its efficiency on the release of new springs of energy among the people— on making them feel that the show is theirs to make or mar.[27]

Cole's insistence on a decentralized socialism once seemed academic. He appeared to be dealing with hypothetical problems that would be faced, if at all, by some vague society in the distant future. But the growth of government controls over economic life in Britain and elsewhere in the Western world has abruptly converted Cole's dilemma of socialism into a dilemma here and now.

Perhaps the picture is not so black as Cole paints it. Perhaps neither workers, consumers, nor citizens in general want the participation Cole seeks for them. Perhaps participation should not be urged on people if they do not want it. But if the problem is anything like Cole believes it to be and if the solution to it is decentralization, the eternal question must again be posed: How are the decentralized units to be coördinated if not through a mandatory price mechanism? A price mechanism does not leave the en-

[26] G. D. H. Cole, "Shall Socialism Fail?" *The New Statesman and Nation,* May 5, 1951, pp. 496 ff.
[27] *Ibid.,* p. 524.

terprise uncontrolled. And in substituting the spontaneous controls of consumers for highly centralized direction, in some situations it offers the maximum possibilities for flinging (to use Cole's words) "power and responsibility into many hands."

Nationalized enterprises are nationalized partly because of a desire to substitute some degree of collective control for market control and consumer free choice. Hence, to organize nationalized enterprises solely through a mandatory price mechanism would frustrate some of the aims of nationalization: in pure form a mandatory price mechanism would prohibit the collective non-market control that nationalization is designed to achieve. Nationalization, like regulation, must therefore seek a compromise between market control through the price system and collective control through bargaining or hierarchy. One of the virtues of the mandatory price mechanism is that it can help to limit collective control to the particular decisions over which collective control is primarily desired; the residual controls can be left to the market.

For example, nationalization permits the British Transport Commission to issue, as it does, a set of hierarchical prescriptions stating what classes of commodities and shipments shall use road transport and what classes shall use rail. Yet nationalization does not compel the authority to take this particular burden on itself. Instead, prices on various kinds of services could be set to represent roughly their relative costs; consumers of the services would then make the choice between rail or road transport. Appropriate rate adjustments to reflect relative scarcities of various kinds of services can avoid either over- or under-utilization of any class of service.[28]

The doctrine of decentralized socialism, of decentralizing the great number of governmental controls now exercised over economic life in the United States and western Europe, is more radical than the socialism and reform now advocated by the major democratic parties of the Left. That the price system has very radical potentialities for undermining a hierarchy-ridden society has always been hinted at in its family resemblance to anarchy.

Indeed, a hierarchical price system can decentralize by coordinating the economic activity not only of individual enterprises but of different geographical areas, as in international trade. Thus

[28] W. Arthur Lewis, *op. cit.*, pp. 32–43.

the system offers the possibility of decentralizing decisions not only to the business firm or industry as a "local" unit but also to a region as a "local" unit.

At present it seems preposterous even to mention the possibility of operating, say, the British economy with the help of a price mechanism integrating perhaps ten little economic systems within the larger economy, each of which might itself be internally coördinated with the help of a price system. Nevertheless, the suggestion indicates the radical decentralizing reforms possible with the help of hierarchical price system. And no one can tell when new conditions may make such an idea worth discussing—if only to reject it. Centralization may well become such a frightening problem that it will some day be profitable to debate the advisability of making five or ten Swedish economies out of the British economy and a score or two of them out of the American.

IV. Agenda, Role, and Personality in the Price System

PRICE SYSTEM AGENDAS

Non-economists sometimes find it difficult to understand the price system as a control process because economists have tended to be preoccupied with changing the agenda as a method of control to the exclusion of role and personality, even to the neglect of control over particular acts. It will be remembered that control can be accomplished through any of these channels. While non-economists commonly expect that a description of a control process will run largely in terms of contols over particular acts or over role and personality, these elementary elements of control often drop out of the economist's picture of the price system.

In the simplest terms, a price system is a highly differentiated social mechanism for breaking decision making into manageable units and for organizing decisions and acts in ways quite specifically different from the form they otherwise would take. It is a method, thus, of establishing a different agenda from that prevailing, say, in a centrally controlled economy. A discussion of the price system is largely concerned with working out the consequences for human behavior of a peculiar agenda different from that to be found in other sectors of social organization. It has, therefore, been possible

for economics to make great headway in "explaining" the economizing process in a price system by going no further than observing
the distinctive forms of decision making and actions imposed upon
the participants in the economic process by the peculiarities of price
system agendas.

THE NEGLECT OF ROLE AND PERSONALITY

To appreciate the extent to which preoccupation with the
agenda may foreclose other lines of inquiry into role and personality
it need only be considered how inadequately informed economists
and non-economists alike are on control processes in economic life
where the influence of the agenda is not a sufficient explanation of
behavior. For example, the peculiarities of the price system agenda
go a long way to explain entrepreneurial policy; yet most business
enterprises are bureaucracies in which many members face not the
cues, rewards, and penalties of the market but instead those prescribed by their superiors in the hierarchy. For these people—and
they may be in important positions of control in the enterprise—we
cannot understand behavior solely by reference to a price system
agenda; role and personality are critical.

The importance of role and personality to price system coordination is illustrated in differences between many New England
enterprises and their counterparts elsewhere in the United States. In
recent years, innovations in textiles have created profitable markets
for products of synthetic fibers blended with natural fibers. Price
system cues have called for the expansion of production; yet, with
a few significant exceptions, market signals have not induced New
England manufacturers to respond as manufacturers elsewhere have
responded.

The Committee on the New England Economy of the Council
of Economic Advisers attributes the difference in response in large
part to differences in role and personality. "The regions that are
entering the industrial arena now start with a fresh approach, with
young and aggressive managements, with a labor force uninhibited
by traditional methods, with the most modern plants, and with
prospects and locations geared to a $250–$300 billion national economy."[29] On the other hand, in New England, the problem is re-

[29] Council of Economic Advisors, Committee on the New England Economy,
The New England Economy, A Report to the President, U.S. Government Printing
Office, Washington, July, 1951.

peatedly one of "getting new ideas across," of "inflexibility of thought and action."[30]

An adequate picture of the economizing process in a price system requires that we perceive both how action may be influenced by the kind of agendas people face and how it may be influenced by role, personality, and controls over particular acts in any given agenda..

ROLE AND PERSONALITY REQUIREMENTS OF A PRICE SYSTEM

THE MEANS-ENDS VIEW. We can begin by inquiring into the kind of roles that must be played by persons facing price system agendas and asking further whether any particular kind of personality is required.[31] R. H. Tawney and Max Weber, among others, have observed that the kind of individual suited to and to some extent created by a market economy is different from medieval man in personality characteristics important for the viability of a price system.[32] At least three differences are identifiable: one, in attitudes toward the authority of tradition as against the force of rationality; a second in the attractiveness of the rewards of social solidarity, stability, ritual, companionship, sociability, and security of status as against rewards purchasable with money; and a third in a view of work as creative activity, itself a primary goal, as against an instrumental view of work.

In each of these three respects, "modern" man is distinguished by his means-ends view.[33] If rational calculation in the eyes of the "market" man is more compelling than tradition, it is partly because he thinks of his behavior as an adaptation of means to ends. If

[30] Ibid.

[31] We do not believe that a personality type should be valued solely as an instrument for economizing. Still, we do want to understand personality as an instrument. But see Chapter 18.

[32] See, for example, R. H. Tawney, Religion and the Rise of Capitalism, Harcourt, Brace and Co., New York, 1926, and Max Weber, The Protestant Ethic and the Spirit of Capitalism (translated by Talcott Parsons), Charles Scribner's Sons, New York, 1930.

[33] Of course, "modern" man is not easily defined or identified. Role and personality characteristics of wage earners in underdeveloped areas are such as to make price system cues and incentives very weak (see Wilbert E. Moore, Industrialization and Labor, Cornell University Press, Ithaca, 1951, chap. 7). If these individuals are not "modern" men, what of the British coal miners, whose failure to respond to price system cues and rewards as other British workers do has become a major difficulty in the coal industry?

he finds money relatively more rewarding than, say, the pleasures of neighborhood or the securities of status, it is again partly because he finds in money a means to the achievement of a wide variety of objectives. And if work is more instrumental than primary as a goal, it is again partly because he sharply distinguishes work as a means where his forebears treated work itself as an end.

Because speculation must largely take the place of systematic observation in defining the personality required in a price system, we aim at very limited objectives at this point in the analysis. However, it is worth observing that one cannot define the choice-allocation processes, or economizing, or rationality itself except by distinguishing sharply between means and ends, even where one recognizes that any given end is probably also a means or vice versa.

The price system is only one of the mechanisms by which individuals economize. But it may be even more dependent than hierarchy or bargaining upon means-end calculating man. For one thing, it requires quantitative calculation; and, although one may take it for granted that all men can calculate quantitatively, one cannot safely assume that all personality types are willing to do so or can do it well. It also settles on every individual participant's shoulders a burden of decision making that he could easily delegate to a few leaders in hierarchy or bargaining; hence, it requires personalities willing to bear such burdens. Perhaps more important, it requires a personality type capable of playing a surprisingly large number of different roles, in each of which the ends are somewhat different from those in each of the others.

RAPID ROLE CHANGING. The large number of roles which individuals in a price system are called upon to play requires that they look upon role-playing itself as a means, and this approach requires a complication of the means-ends view more essential than in any other mechanism for economizing. Specialization of function in a price system, the character of the functions specialized, and occupational mobility all call for a personality capable of shifting even a dozen times a day from one role to another.

In any society, to be sure, any one person may be called upon to develop certain fairly standardized responses as a family member, another set as a friend or neighbor, still another as a citizen. But these roles do not differ greatly in their characteristic values and attitudes; all require identification with a group and indoctrination with values such as honesty, loyalty, obedience, and fair play which are necessary to the functioning of any group.

In a price system, however, one individual may play the roles of employer, employee, salesman, fair competitor, and public servant in addition to the others already mentioned. The employer role in an effective price system calls for a combination of identification of employer with employees and a simultaneous willingness to regard the employees as machines; without this combination employers could not be expected to motivate their employees (by identification with them) and at the same time cut off their wages and force their reallocation or retirement when, owing to changes in consumer preferences of employee disability or old age, their usefulness to the employer is at an end. As a "fair competitor" the same individual is required to accept a group code which condemns as "chiseling" the attitude toward other businessmen he shows to his employees. "Live and let live" is a more binding prescription for "fair competitors" than for employers. In a different market milieu the same competitor may be excused from obligations to his competitors and may with good conscience exploit his advantages over them with a minimum of inhibition. Yet he may also be asked by political leaders or his business colleagues, say, in a time of an acute shortage of supply, to act the role of the business statesman, to consider himself a public servant and his power over scarce supplies as a public trust. And in any case his role as a salesman often calls upon him to run through a series of sub-roles to ingratiate himself with each customer.

That the price system requires a personality capable of stepping quickly and easily from any one role to others quite different may be read to imply that the price system requires the destruction of personality—that is, the destruction of stable goals and attitudes. Such an inference is at least premature at this stage of the analysis and in any case much more difficult to justify than the more cautious conclusion that the price system requires changing roles. It may, of course, also be true that a role-changing personality is not so much required for a price system as for the exploitation of opportunities for personal gain in a price system. The distinction is a subtle one but may be false; as will be confirmed in later chapters, the kind of role-changing personality just described is probably indeed a prerequisite of any real-world price system. Observers of the price system often fail to understand its dependence on active role-playing, largely because formal economic theory tends to cast each participant in the single role of a vending machine.

THE SELF-INTEREST ROLE.   One of the most demanding role requirements in a price system we have not mentioned with the others because it deserves a very special emphasis. This is the "self-interest" role. Now, of course, all motivated conduct is self-interested. But in price system agendas individuals are often required to play a role to which the term "self-interest" was once commonly applied to distinguish it from a role marked by broader identifications, sometimes called altruistic. To take an extreme example, the succesful operation of a price system requires under some circumstances that leaders foreclose mortgages even if they "hate to do it." Or businessmen are required to act on "sound business principles" reflecting a particular interpretation of self-interest, even if they must arbitrarily disregard a number of relevant personal goals or values in so acting.[34]

One way to state the distinction between the "self-interest" important to one's role in the price system and self-interest as more ordinarily conceived is to say that the former is narrow, the latter broad, the former concerned with one's interest in money and market gains, the other with the values of friendship, solidarity, neighborhood, and self-respect. One of the difficulties of maintaining a price system is that the "self-interest" role is one that individuals do not play in their noneconomic activities and do not find entirely congenial when they must assume it in the market.

Why does a price system require the narrow "self-interest" role if it is not congenial? The answer is that the controls of the price system operate largely through money rewards and penalties. If too many other values influence behavior, controls are weakened. Money rewards and penalties can be manipulated where many of the others cannot. If self-interest narrowly conceived is a vice, it is a case of private vices becoming public virtues, as Mandeville observed in his *Fable of the Bees*.

THE BUSINESS STATESMAN ROLE.   The necessity of a narrow self-interest role is becoming increasingly clear in light of the tend-

[34] On the self-interest role, see, "The Motivation of Economic Activities," in Talcott Parsons, *Essays in Sociological Theory Pure and Applied*, Free Press, Glencoe, Ill., 1949.

ency for many businessmen in recent years to wish to play the "business statesman" role. Two kinds of morality are shaping the role of businessmen. One teaches the businessman to be "fair." The other teaches him to be competitive. The one morality calls for the industrial statesman, the public servant, the compromiser of the interest of public, employees, and stockholder; the other calls for "old-fashioned" profit seeking, for the pursuit of narrowly defined self-interest.

In a large number of cases the possibilities of price system control over the businessman hinge on his concern for money gains and losses for his enterprise, because these can be manipulated by consumers, and on his indifference to many other values that cannot be so manipulated. The industrial statesman is often a businessman whose values permit him to escape control. If he acts in the "public interest," as he claims, it may only be because he has been free to define it as he wishes.

This criticism of the business statesman role should not be pushed too far. First, we find it difficult to conceive of the possibility that the management of a large firm would act without regard to an indoctrinated concern for some values other than money gains and rewards, just as we find it difficult to imagine a civil servant controlled without reliance on the inhibitions which similar indoctrination produces in him. In both cases, the indoctrination creates a role for the businessman and civil servant to play, and playing the role implements control on two counts: it leads men to accept particular controls that they would otherwise resist, and it changes the kinds of decisions that they make when their actions are autonomous. Illustrations are dangerous because business decisions are the product of many factors; but relatively successful securities and exchange regulation, for example, is possible only because businessmen accept certain values other than profit and loss.

Second, and paradoxically, a public-servant role is required to create a synthetic "self-interest" role. Corporate managers must play a role in which they behave as though corporate profits and losses are personal gains and losses. Through salary adjustments, bonuses, promotions, and demotions, the two kinds of gains and losses can, of course, be made to coincide to a high degree. But salaried businessmen, in contrast to profit-taking owner-operators, are to some degree insulated from the rewards and deprivations of the market. And top management, which itself is commonly salaried in the large corporations, can, if it wishes, pay salaries and bonuses and award promotions to itself with very little regard for the profits and losses of the corporate enterprise, thus insulating itself remarkably from market incentives.[35]

Hence, a role must be indoctrinated, an identification between businessman and corporation must take place, so that price and inventory movements, profits and losses—the whole mechanism of price system control over production—become in fact controls over responses of the particular people who make corporate policy regardless of personal money gain or loss. Without it, market cues, rewards, and penalties are very weak by the time they reach any person in a corporation capable of making the signaled and desired response.

IRRATIONALITY. Still another requirement for role and personality is that the businessman be irrational to a degree. That is, he must develop dispositions to by-pass rational *ad hoc* calculations to some extent. Both his public-servant role and his identification with the corporation require him to develop habitual responses which are different from those he would show if he rationally calculated his decision, and which may even be at odds with the responses consistent with his long-term success as a businessman. If this point appears to be so obvious as to deserve no mention because it is true of everyone, it should be noted that, as a statement of a prerequisite for a price system, it complicates a common assumption in economic theory that rationality is a condition of an optimum.

THE DISPOSITION TO GAMBLE. Finally, it has often been said that the price system economy cannot survive if businessmen are not disposed to gamble—to face the uncertainties of economic life with perhaps more confidence than could be expected of other groups in the population. We do not actually know to what degree, if at all, businessmen's behavior is dependent upon peculiarities of personality such as this argument suggests. But we can be fairly sure that, if an unusual disposition to take chances is required at all, the requirement varies according to the pattern of supplementary controls discussed in this chapter. A supplementary control over the entrepreneur which is exercised through private property and rivalry

[35] Robert A. Gordon, *Business Leadership in the Large Corporation*, The Brookings Institution, Washington, 1945, chap. 5.

among firms in an industry, for example, would appear to place a higher premium on a risk-taking personality than a supplementary control made effective through governmental assumption of risk of loss of assets and hierarchical direction of price-production policy.

V. Limitations of the Price System

We have been describing in this chapter one of four central sociopolitical processes for economizing. What it can accomplish has been made clear; its greatest limitation is that a price system is a highly specialized process and adaptable to a much narrower range of problems than is the case for the other processes. This and other limitations will be spelled out in later chapters. We turn now to the other three central sociopolitical processes which can be harnessed to economizing. Thereafter we shall be able to appraise their relative strengths and weaknesses. Each is indispensable in its place; the task is to determine the circumstances in which each is inappropriate.

8.

Hierarchy:
Control
by Leaders

I. Leaders and Hierarchies

Hierarchy is a familiar, widespread, and important social process for economizing. In this chapter and the next we shall examine some of its basic characteristics as a social process in order to understand its bearing on economizing; but our analysis of it as a process for economizing will not be completed until the end of the book.

Roughly, a hierarchical process of organization is one in which leaders exercise a very high degree of unilateral control over non-leaders. But this definition is only a first approximation; as usual there are some thorny problems of labeling precisely what it is that we wish to isolate and discuss.

HIERARCHY NOT PURE UNILATERAL CONTROL

In the first place, few if any organizations, as we emphasized in a preceding chapter, exhibit purely unilateral control relationships. Subordinates are rarely without some controls over their superiors. Purely unilateral control is too uncommon in economizing even to be a very useful abstract model for analysis. Therefore, despite the difficulties it creates for precise labeling of particular organizations or processes, we use the term "hierarchy" to refer to a "very high degree" but not a pure case of unilateral control. Two pragmatic but not precise tests can be used to distinguish a hierarchical organization: Non-leaders cannot peacefully displace leaders after explicit or implicit voting; and leaders substantially decide when, in what conditions, and with whom consultation takes place. The first helps to distinguish hierarchy from polyarchy, the second, to distinguish it from bargaining.

WHO IS A LEADER?

Second, it has proved difficult for sociologists and political scientists to find a useful operational definition for distinguishing "leaders."[1] A good first approximation is to say that if individuals in a group were ranked according to the "extent" of their control over one another, the leader or leaders would be those with "significantly" greater control. If no one had "significantly" greater control, in that group there would be no leaders. Thus one could locate control relationships along a continuum of equal control—disparate control. Leaders are those with disparate control. The difficulty, of course, is with the concepts "extent" of control and "significantly" greater control.

EXTENT OF CONTROL. Political scientists and sociologists have developed no agreed methods for measuring the "extent" of control. Lasswell and Kaplan in their exceptionally precise and inventive systematic study[2] suggest a distinction between the *weight* of influence or "the degree to which policies are affected"; the *domain* of influence or "the persons whose policies are affected"; and the *scope* of influence or "the values implicated in the policies."

Even these careful distinctions, however, by no means provide an unambiguous method for determining whether A has "more" control than B over, say, C, D, or Z. For A may control a few responses of decisive importance to a few highly ranked goals of B, C, D, and Z; and B may control many responses of moderate importance to a great many low-ranked goals of A, C, D, and Z. Under these conditions, evidently one cannot properly speak of *a* leader among A, B, C, D, and Z; one can only speak of A's leadership in one kind of situation and B's leadership in another. What is more, it would be dangerous to try to decide whether in his position as leader A has "more" control than B in his position as leader. For there seems to be no satisfactory common denominator to which different forms of control can always be reduced in order to rank them.

To be precise one should therefore avoid comparisons between

---

[1] An excellent and exhaustive discussion of this definitional problem is contained in Alvin W. Gouldner (ed.), *Studies in Leadership: Leadership and Democratic Action*, Harper & Brothers, New York, 1950, "Introduction," pp. 3–49. We have not, however, followed Gouldner's definitional suggestions.

[2] Harold D. Lasswell and Abraham Kaplan, *Power and Society: A Framework for Political Inquiry*, Yale University Press, New Haven, 1950, pp. 73–77.

the "extent" of control by leaders in different situations where the forms of control are not strictly comparable—where, for example, the different controls are not all reducible either to the sheer number of people affected, or to the number of responses, or to the number of goals affected, or (and this is undoubtedly the critical problem) to the number of goals weighted by their rank or importance. So far as possible we do avoid such comparisons in this book. But a useful analysis of alternative social techniques would be impossible without some such comparisons. In these cases, then, we shall try to make clear by the context specifically what we mean by "more" control in one situation than another. For the most part, the differences in the "extent" of control we wish to talk about are gross enough so that, by themselves, difficulties in precision will not upset the substantive argument.

SIGNIFICANTLY GREATER CONTROL.   The concept "significantly" must be used in the same pragmatic and approximate way. In examining the possibility of absolute and complete equality of control, the control of a dynamic, persuasive member in a Quaker meeting is "significantly" greater than that of a passive, inarticulate, and unpopular member. On the other hand, in deciding whether a typical Quaker meeting is democratic, polyarchal, or hierarchical, we should be inclined to say that the differences in control in Quaker meetings are not "significantly" great. Typically, Quaker meetings come about as close to political equality as it is humanly possible to do; consequently one can call these organizations "democratic."

HIERARCHY IS ON A CONTINUUM

At best, therefore, in both theoretical model and real world the concept of a hierarchical process is bound to include a variety of subtypes differing from one another in ways that are quite significant for some purposes. Thus one could construct a continuum or several continua that tried to take some of the main variables into account, such as the type of actions controlled, the degree to which control is concentrated in the top leadership or dispersed military-fashion down a chain of control, the discrepancy between prescribed and operating controls, the extent and kinds of countering reciprocal controls, etc. Although such a classification would be too complex for our purposes, the reader might well keep the possibility in mind as a guard against some of the inevitable oversimplifications that we must employ in these chapters. The word "hierarchy" cuts a big swath through the field of social processes.

LEADERS AND THE INITIATION OF ACTIONS

One aspect of leadership that is sometimes confusing is the role of leaders in initiating the actions taken by the group. Among two or three individuals, no doubt the leader is commonly the one who most frequently initiates the actions taken by the group. But the larger the group the less likely is the leader to initiate actions *directly*. As one writer has said: "It is *not*, therefore, the individual who first develops an idea or makes a suggestion . . . who is necessarily a leader, in the sense proposed. The leader would be, rather, that individual who is able by his support or espousement of the proposal to legitimate it. He transforms it into something to which group members are obliged to orient themselves."[3]

In a large organization the greater number of decisions are initiated by individuals or groups other than top leadership. For the most part, the leaders veto, endorse, modify, postpone, and pigeon-hole actions or proposed actions initiated by others.[4] Nevertheless—and this is vital—the leader is in a strategic position to initiate actions when he feels they are needed; and as Chester Barnard has written, "The occasions of decision on the initiative of the executive are the most important test of his capacity. Out of his understanding of the situation . . . it is to be determined whether something needs to be done or corrected."[5] Moreover the leaders can initiate and modify actions that will affect the whole structure and process for initiating actions within the organization.

Hence the *strategic opportunity* of the leader to initiate actions when he wishes to do so is one of his most important characteristics, not only in a hierarchy but in polyarchy and bargaining as well.

II. Hierarchy and the Democratic Creed

One of the most striking features of Western society today is the vital and ubiquitous role of hierarchical processes. This might not be striking at all if the fact did not run flatly counter to some of the ideology, and much of the ethos, of democracy. Such a

[3] Gouldner, *op. cit.*, p. 19. The reader should bear in mind that we do not follow Gouldner's own specific definition of leadership, p. 17.

[4] Cf. Chester I. Barnard, *The Functions of the Executive*, Harvard University Press, Cambridge, 1945, pp. 190 ff.

[5] *Ibid.*, p. 191.

conflict between ideals and reality is particularly evident in the United States. Though perhaps wrong in detail, Jefferson was right in principle in insisting that equality of power required an agrarian society. He correctly foresaw that an urban society would lean heavily on hierarchy. Because Americans accepted his conclusions but not his sociological premises, we in this country have had to embrace two unreconciled ideologies, one for public declamation, the other for private use. The one is radically egalitarian and if pursued would demand a revolutionary transformation in the whole structure of our present society; the other is radically hierarchical and its pursuit has in fact led to a revolutionary transformation of the whole agrarian structure of society that prevailed before the Civil War.

Modern America stands in blunt contrast to the pre-Civil War agrarian society within which radical democracy became the accepted creed. Wherever one turns today he finds people participating in and acutely dependent upon powerful hierarchical processes often operating in organizations gigantic in size and scope. Corporations, trade unions, government agencies, party organizations, political machines, lobby groups, professional associations, specialized organizations speaking for veterans, farmers, or businessmen, some churches, many large universities—through all these, hierarchical relationships play in the lives of ordinary people a decisive part that Jefferson in 1800 or Jackson in 1830 would have said was irreconcilable with democracy and hardly distinguishable from tyranny. Some of the organizations have a greater membership than many of the states and cities of Jefferson's day; some possess assets and liabilities greater than those of the federal government of that time; many manipulate rewards and deprivations more powerful and comprehensive in their effects than those of any unit of government in 1800. Jackson fought the Second Bank of the United States because of a profound conviction that large private organizations through which a few exercised control over the many were intolerable in a democratic order. But the Bank was puny beside the giant hierarchies of modern American life.

The transformation in the distribution of control from that time until this has been revolutionary. Differences in control then, as now, were significant; but roughly speaking, they reflected differences in personal resources of various kinds: birth, wealth, income, status, personality, intelligence, geography, luck. And the importance of these personal resources as a means for controlling other people was limited because the United States was overwhelmingly a country of small farmers and an open frontier. Slavery, of course, was an institution that was never successfully assimilated to the idea of an agrarian society of free and equal citizens.

Although differences in control today continue to reflect differences in personal resources, they are vastly magnified by hierarchical social processes. Whatever the differences in personal resources, people at the top of these processes—and particularly those genuinely skilled in running organizations in which hierarchical processes are found—are enormously more powerful than those below. Even if there were "equal opportunity for all to get to the top," the harsh fact is that those who get to the top would still be enormously more powerful than those below. Competitive recruitment does not necessarily weaken the hierarchical character of society; indeed, by invoking the superficially "democratic" principle of equality (of opportunity, not control!), competitive recruitment may actually stabilize the hierarchical character of society by giving it legitimacy.

Perhaps the most notable aspect of this revolution is the way in which Americans now accept its results. After some skirmishes (the Populists were among the last tattered remnant of the agrarian forces to deny legitimacy to the new order), most Americans seem to have accepted the fact of hierarchy without quite being aware of it. By now, Americans have been pretty well "broken" to hierarchy; and social indoctrination increasingly facilitates the role Americans must play in hierarchical organizations.

The individual's experience with three kinds of hierarchical organizations above all others seems to have accomplished this indoctrination. The business corporation was the first, the pioneer, the advance guard of the revolution. From the Civil War on, more and more Americans accustomed themselves to working for, investing in, or consuming the products of large, hierarchical corporations. Next was the military. Two wars, even before Korea, habituated an extraordinarily large percentage of the adult male population, many of them during their most formative years, to a stricter hierarchy than they had ever known. Many service men profoundly disliked the hierarchical element in the military; but very few seem to have openly questioned the basic rationality of

hierarchical control in military organizations. The Civil War practice of officer election, for example, is every bit as dead as the
agrarian democracy that made it seem so logical. The third is government agencies. The spectacular growth of federal, state, and
local government hierarchies helped to indoctrinate millions of
citizens dependent on them as employees or clients.

The advantages of hierarchical organizations in business, military life, government, and elsewhere seem so obvious and their conflict with equal control so blatant that liberal democratic theory and
social practice tend to be unreconciled. In practice, laissez-faire
liberalism produced giant business hierarchies whose existence in
turn stimulated other "private" and governmental hierarchies. But
in its theory, laissez-faire liberalism ignored these hierarchical organizations by a polite convention that they were little more than
voluntary associations composed of freely contracting participants.
This legerdemain simultaneously excluded hierarchical control from
the books and fostered it in real life.

Modern welfare-state liberals have made a pass at reconciliation
by insisting that business hierarchies should be offset by trade union
and government hierarchies. But they cannot deny that bargaining
among leaders of giant hierarchies scarcely fulfills the promise of
the traditional democratic creed; at the same time, they are reluctant
to give up that creed. On this point, democratic socialists are hardly
distinguishable from welfare liberals. They know now that socialization somewhat alters the techniques for controlling hierarchies;
but it does not exorcise the fact of hierarchy.

Two questions arise, then. First, given the goals of Chapter 2,
what are the gains and what are the costs of hierarchy? Second,
under what conditions do the gains outweigh the costs? In short,
when and how should a society pursuing the goals of Chapter 2
make use of hierarchy? The first question is the subject of the remainder of this chapter. The second question is a complex one and
is in fact one way of posing the subject of most of this book.

III. Bureaucracy: Its Distinguishing Characteristics

Bureaucracy is the ubiquitous modern organization within
which hierarchical processes are most commonly encountered;
bureaucracy is also one of the most widely used and portentous

social instruments for economizing found in contemporary societies. Most of the gains and costs of hierarchy can be discovered by an examination of bureaucratic organizations.

The term "bureaucracy" itself is, of course, ambiguous. By bureaucracy many people mean an organization marked by certain characteristics widely held to be undesirable, chiefly internal red tape, "passing the buck," excessive inflexibility, impersonality, and overcentralization. On the other hand, an increasing number of sociologists, political scientists, and writers on administration mean by bureaucracy an organization marked by certain structural features that cannot be readily called either desirable or undesirable *per se*.

Actually, both groups seem to be concerned, for the most part, with the same type of hierarchical process; for, as will be seen in this chapter, organizations with the structural characteristics that distinguish "bureaucracies" to sociologists and political scientists tend also to produce the characteristics (red tape, passing the buck, inflexibility, impersonality, and overcentralization) that so many people object to in what they regard as bureaucracies.

To begin with, then, let us distinguish the important structural features of what we propose to call a "bureaucratic" organization. Max Weber was one of the first to try to set forth these characteristics. Unfortunately, however, his "pure type" was a mélange of features not rigorously related to the conditions that brought them about.[6] Nevertheless, most of the writers since Weber who have attempted to describe what they mean by "bureaucracy" are indebted to him.[7] By now considerable agreement exists on the fol-

[6] Weber's analysis in *The Theory of Social and Economic Organization* (translated by A. M. Henderson and Talcott Parsons and edited by Talcott Parsons), Oxford University Press, New York, 1947, has now been brought together in an ingenious *Reader in Bureaucracy*, by Robert K. Merton, Ailsa P. Gray, Barbara Hockey, and Hanan C. Selvin (eds.), Free Press, Glencoe, Ill., 1952, Cf. there also the criticisms of Carl J. Friedrich, "Some Observations on Weber's Analysis of Bureaucracy," pp. 27 ff.

[7] Cf., for example, Robert Dubin's excellent "Technical Characteristics of a Bureaucracy," in Robert Dubin (ed.), *Human Relations in Administration, The Sociology of Organization, with Readings and Cases*, Prentice-Hall, New York, 1951, pp. 156 ff. Also Carl J. Friedrich, *Constitutional Government and Democracy, Theory and Practice in Europe and America* (rev. ed.), Ginn and Co., Boston, 1950, pp. 44–57. See Herman Finer, *Theory and Practice of Modern Government* (rev. ed.), Henry Holt and Co., New York, 1949, for an excellent discussion of both structural features and the characteristics commonly criticized in government civil service; he confines "bureaucracy" to the latter, chap. 28. Cf. also S. E. Finer, *A Primer of Public Administration*, Frederick Muller, Ltd., London, 1950, pp. 34–36.

lowing structural features as critical in distinguishing a "bureaucracy" from other organizations.

CONSCIOUS ADAPTATION OF MEANS TO ENDS.   The prescribed charter of a bureaucracy represents, to a very high degree, a conscious and deliberate attempt to adapt the structure and personnel of the organization to the most efficient achievement of goals prescribed by the top leaders in, or outside, the bureaucracy. The operating charter tends, of course, to depart from prescription, sometimes quite extensively. Yet it is fair to say that the charter prescribed by top leaders, and supposedly reflecting a rational adaptation of means to ends, significantly influences not only the operating organization but the whole ethos of bureaucracies. More than most organizations, the structure of bureaucracies is molded by the deliberate striving of controllers for what they conceive to be a "rational" and "efficient" adaptation of means to ends. This is not to deny, however, that an observer may judge a bureaucracy as highly inefficient and irrational, either because he disagrees with the ends maximized by the bureaucracy, or because he concludes that the ends are not really being efficiently maximized by the organization, or both.

HIERARCHIES.   Bureaucracies are marked by a more or less lengthy chain of controllers and subordinates; control is echeloned so that each controller is himself a subordinate of another controller. In this sense, bureaucracies are "pyramidal," for a relatively small number of people at the top are enabled by the chain of control to control (more or less) a relatively large number of people below them. Superiors can usually reduce the number of control links when they wish to control subordinates, and can increase them when they wish to limit or delay control over themselves by their nominal subordinates.

PRESCRIBED AND LIMITED DISCRETION.   In bureaucracies the discretion of each subordinate and controller is usually prescribed and limited. That is, the range of alternatives each individual and unit can properly consider in making official choices is more or less explicitly defined and limited by a set of prescriptions.

SPECIALIZATION OF SKILL AND FUNCTION.   These limitations on the discretion of subordinates and controllers tend to be arranged so as to produce a high degree of specialization of skill and function within the organization. Of course this characteristic is not peculiar to bureaucracies but it is too significant an element to be ignored.

SEPARATION OF OWNERSHIP. As individuals, members of the bureaucracy do not own the tools and instruments with which they work. Property rights are vested in the bureaucracy as a whole, or more commonly in some prescribed organization to which, by legal fiction, the bureaucracy pertains.

In describing bureaucracy by these five characteristics, we arrive at a neutral concept of bureaucracy. It does not seek to prove by definition that bureaucracy is either desirable or undesirable. Moreover, the concept applies to a wide variety of modern organizations—not merely to most government agencies and military units but equally to most large businesses and in varying degrees to aspects of the trade union movement, churches (notably, of course, the Roman Catholic Church), pressure groups and propaganda organizations like the National Association of Manufacturers, chambers of commerce, museums, libraries, consumer coöperatives, educational institutions, charitable organizations, hospitals.

IV. The Dynamics of Bureaucracy: The Objective Gains

The number of bureaucracies is rapidly increasing. In organizations where one might least expect it, from small colleges to beach clubs, bureaucracy shows a strong tendency to appear. In stark contrast to the world of Thomas Jefferson and Andrew Jackson, the world of the modern American rushes headlong toward bureaucratization. Why do organizations develop in which these five characteristics appear as a cluster?

We suggest five reasons. Two reasons stem from the magnitude of the task: (1) the need for a relatively small number of people to coördinate the actions of relatively large numbers of people and (2) the need to make complex decisions beyond the competence of any one person to make. Another reason is (3) the advantages of the division of labor. In these three instances, the "need" or "advantage" is a cause of bureaucracy, of course, only to the extent that those who influence the decision to institute a bureaucracy subjectively believe in the need or advantage. But two other reasons are predominantly psychological or subjective in character: (4) the desire for status and control as ends and (5) a cultural bias in favor of deliberate, conscious efforts at an apparently rational adaptation of means to ends. These are not necessarily the only reasons, but they are probably most significant to an analysis of bureaucracy as an economizing device.

COÖRDINATING LARGE NUMBERS OF PEOPLE

A bureaucratic organization is one important way by which a relatively small number of people can coördinate the activities of a relatively large number of people.

So long as members of a group can all maintain direct, face-to-face contact with one another, members can coördinate their diverse activities without bureaucracy. In small groups, many actions can be coördinated through reciprocity, spontaneous controls, and simple hierarchies; that is to say, there is no pressing need for elaborate hierarchies, prescribed and limited discretion, a high degree of specialization, separation of ownership, and not even much conscious effort at setting up a "rational" organization. Discussion, consultation, elections, the authority of leaders, common habits, traditions, and shared norms may be sufficient to insure that the actions of each member contribute to goals widely shared in the group —contribute enough, at least, so that the group feels no strong pressure to alter its organization. In small groups the allocation of labor to different tasks, to hunting, preparing food, tilling the fields, providing for future needs, fighting the enemy, enforcing justice, caring for the helpless, the ill, and the aged, training and indoctrinating the young—all can be adequately handled without bureaucracy.

Where decisions can no longer be arrived at by face-to-face contacts among all members of the group, the problem of coördination (allocating labor, for example) becomes more complicated. Even so, bureaucracy is not necessarily required. There are several alternatives to hierarchy-bureaucracy.

COÖRDINATION THROUGH A FREE CONFEDERACY. A number of small groups operating without bureaucracies might form a "free confederacy" in order to coördinate their activities and yet avoid bureaucratization. The theoretical conception of coördination in a non-bureaucratized but large-scale society shows up in oddly diverse places—for example, in Rousseau and in Marx (*The Civil War in France*), as well as in Jefferson, at least by implication. For by implication some such conception as this must have been behind Jefferson's elusive ideal of a highly decentralized federalism with the locus of control in states and local communities.

But of course a "free confederacy" of this kind is a standing invitation to secession. It is logical to proceed to the view of the Virginia and Kentucky Resolutions, drafted by Jefferson and Madison, that actions of the central government held by one member state to violate the basic bargain—the constitution—should not be enforceable in that state. This view leads with inexorable logic to the position taken by South Carolina in 1832 in the Nullification Ordinance and from there to the South Carolina declaration of secession in 1860. Indeed, as Lincoln pointed out in his first inaugural address, the same logic must be applied within the states to other subgroups, and within each subgroup to the individuals, until one reaches the (to Lincoln) *reductio ad absurdum* that each individual may in turn secede if he dislikes the bargain arrived at in his group.

Nevertheless, in so far as a society operating exclusively in this fashion could exist, the effort to coördinate the activities of a large number of people would not (by itself) create a need for hierarchy-bureaucracy.

COÖRDINATION THROUGH RECIPROCITY AND SPONTANEOUS CONTROLS. To some extent actions of a large number of people can be coördinated through reciprocal and spontaneous controls without hierarchy-bureaucracy, *provided* that the people have the same or similar norms and conceptions of reality. No doubt if all traffic police were eliminated tomorrow, for a very long time most drivers all over the United States would continue to drive on the right-hand side of the road. In fact, if it were not for the coördination achieved among large numbers of drivers by spontaneous and manipulated field controls acting on similar norms and reality views about safety and convenience, traffic control even by a numerous police force would soon break down. Still, the "provided" is vital. Let there be only one driver out of a hundred who does not believe in driving on the right, or who insists against all social disapproval that a speed of sixty miles an hour down a crowded street is quite safe, and the remaining ninety-nine will clamor for a bureaucratic organization in the shape of a police force.

COÖRDINATION THROUGH A PRICE SYSTEM. The diverse activities of large numbers of people can also be coördinated in some cases through a price system. Although it is an oversimplification to think of an economy operating with the price system as lacking in bureaucracy (large business organizations are, after all, bureaucracies), the price system provides an alternative to making a wide range of decisions through bureaucracy. The decisions of each of a number of competing furniture manufacturers to increase production of dining-room tables are not controlled by hierarchy-bureaucracy. Thus when direct allocations replace the "free" market in wartime, everyone is aware that the organization for allocating resources has fundamentally changed; a bureaucratic organization displaces a nonbureaucratic one.

WHEN COÖRDINATION REQUIRES BUREAUCRACY. Because confederacy is often impossible, individuals are usually not unanimous in their norms and reality views, and the price system is highly specialized to limited uses only,[8] bureaucracy is often the indispensable means by which a small number of individuals can coördinate the actions of a large number. The cluster of characteristics that distinguish bureaucracy emerge as inevitable elements in the alternative that now remains open. If the individuals at the top of the bureaucracy can coördinate their activities (and one reason for "one-man control" is to reduce the problem of coördination at the top), they can then coördinate the activities of numerous other people through hierarchical arrangements that vest superiors with critical unilateral controls over subordinates: i.e., by a "more or less lengthy chain" of echeloned control lines. Because the alternatives to bureaucracy depend in large part on spontaneous field controls, when these controls fail coördination requires a "conscious and deliberate attempt" to adapt organizational means to the ends of the top leaders. Because spontaneous field controls are inadequate, the individual's discretion must be "more or less explicitly defined and limited by a set of prescriptions" that will coördinate the actions of one individual with those of another. Add together these three requirements of coördination and the outlines of what we have called bureaucracy begin to emerge. But why does coördination in these circumstances require that individuals be separated from their tools

[8] We shall, of course, subsequently ask what these limited uses are; see Chapters 14, 15, 16.

and instruments? Why must ownership be vested in the bureaucracy itself? The answer is that ownership is control, and control cannot be prescribed down through a chain of control relationships if subordinates can control their tools. For if they can, every attempt at unilateral control is turned into bargaining.

COMPLEXITY

Organizations with bureaucratic characteristics may also be produced by the need to make decisions in situations where the number of variables or the amount of information required is so great that no one person can expect to make a competent decision. Hence a bureaucracy is an aid to rational calculation.

To take an extreme example, suppose a group of people want to make an atom bomb, and none of them knows how. The obvious first step is for one or more of them to "upgrade" their competence by training and specialization. Still, the limits of the human brain are so narrow that any one of them, even if he is a Nobel physicist or a brilliant engineer, is unlikely ever to assimilate and comprehend enough correct information about all the variables. Hence the obvious next step is to decrease the complexity of the decision any one person has to make, i.e., to reduce the number of variables any one person has to deal with in making decisions, by changing his agenda.

REDUCING COMPLEXITY THROUGH THE PRICE SYSTEM. To change an agenda in order to reduce the number of variables any one person has to deal with, again two courses of action may be explored. One, it was shown in an earlier chapter,[9] is to try to *quantify the variables* in order to reduce them to some common denominator of costs and benefits. One important way to quantify variables and reduce them to a common denominator of costs and benefits, it has also been shown, is by means of market choices in a price system.[10] But this solution is not always technically possible. Before one could put price tags on the costs and benefits of the gaseous diffusion process for extracting U-235 and compare them with the costs and benefits of the electromagnetic method, one would first have to invent, design, and construct these two methods; during these stages, price tags are relevant but they do not help solve technical problems of engineering and physics. And even where a price system is tech-

[9] Chapter 3.
[10] Chapter 5.

nically possible, for a number of reasons explained later in this book,[11] it is not always a satisfactory way to allocate resources.

REDUCING COMPLEXITY THROUGH DELEGATION. Where market choices in a price system are technically impossible or not desired, a second way to change the agenda is to *decentralize by delegation*. That is, the decision can be split up by allocating different parts of it to different people, in this way reducing the number of variables with which any one mind has to deal. One common way of splitting up a decision is to divide it up by subject matter; another (the distinction is only a pragmatic one) is to divide it up according to the extent of control exercised by each. A third is to combine both methods in the familiar pattern of large organization so that a pyramid of specialized individuals and units is created.[12] This is, of course, the way in which the atom bomb has been invented and produced, and the way in which business and government agencies simplify their agendas.

CONSEQUENCES OF DELEGATION. For several reasons this way of changing the agenda in order to simplify the decisions each person faces tends to produce the cluster of characteristics that distinguish bureaucracy. Delegation of different subject matters to different people is, of course, a form of specialization. Moreover, extensive delegation of varying "amounts" of control to different people—also a form of specialization—produces a hierarchical chain of control. Delegation of different subject matters and "amounts" of control is accomplished by prescribing what each individual can do. In an organization of specialists, each person must also be limited or the basic goal of decreasing the number of variables each person takes into account—which is the reason for this type of organization in the first place—will be violated.

Separation of ownership and skill is a logical concomitant; there is no reason to suppose that the basis on which decisions must be split up will conform with the accidents of individual ownership of tools and equipment. Moreover, a variety of organizations may have to be experimented with as new problems arise; indeed, in a complex operation in which new techniques are being developed,

[11] Chapters 14, 15, 16.
[12] Cf. Herbert Simon's distinction between functional status and hierarchical status, in Herbert A. Simon, Donald W. Smithburg, and Victor A. Thompson, *Public Administration*, Alfred A. Knopf, New York, 1950, p. 191.

reorganization must be almost continuous. Hence individual owner-ship of tools and equipment would be a major obstacle to a rational organization. Finally, all this adds up to the need for a more or less conscious and deliberate attempt to adapt organizational means to ends. In order to simplify decisions, top controllers have every incentive to work out an organizational charter deliberately de-signed, in their view, to attain this goal.

DIVISION OF LABOR

The third gain from bureaucracy is division of labor. That division of labor leads to efficiency in many situations is too well known to be reargued. But, as in the case of size, division of labor may or may not require a bureaucratic organization. The main al-ternatives are, again, much the same. Division of labor can often be secured in a small face-to-face group through reciprocity, sponta-neous field controls, and simple hierarchies; and in a large group through a "free confederacy," or similar norms and conceptions of reality, or a price system.

Two comments on these alternatives are necessary beyond what has already been said about them. First, even small groups that could otherwise operate without bureaucracy may have to become bureaucratized if they wish to achieve a high degree of division of labor. That is to say, other things being equal, the greater the divi-sion of labor, the less can face-to-face contacts among ordinary members, or leaders and non-leaders, take the place of an extension of hierarchy. Second, of all the alternatives to bureaucratic coördi-nation of highly specialized workers, the price system is easily the most important, as Adam Smith pointed out long ago.

When conditions are lacking for these alternatives, however, why does division of labor tend to produce the particular cluster of characteristics that distinguish a bureaucratic organization? Divi-sion of labor is, of course, specialization of skill and function. To obtain specialization of skill and function under these conditions, the discretion of workers must be prescribed; it must also be limited, lest the advantages of specialization be lost. Because the specialized skills desired do not coincide with the ownership of tools and in-struments, it would be foolish to require members to own their own tools.

Concern with the maximum gain from division of labor readily stimulates a more or less rational, carefully calculated attempt to adapt organization means to ends. And because the number of specialized subordinates any one person can control directly is limited, and yet the whole gain from specialization depends upon coördination, a chain of control must be set up consisting of numerous links of controllers and subordinates.

V. The Dynamics of Bureaucracy: Subjective Factors

From what has been said so far it is clear that bureaucratic organization is a highly rational and efficient solution to problems that arise in certain situations. Although observers might disagree about the conditions of a specific situation, given preconditions of the kind that have just been set forth, probably most observers would agree that the bureaucratic solution is a rational one. But there are certain other situations in which bureaucracy may arise when its rationality as a form of ogranization is much more open to doubt.

DESIRE FOR STATUS AND CONTROL AS ENDS

One additional reason for the bureaucratization of social organizations is to provide status and control for the people in the organization, particularly those in the top echelons.[13]

That bureaucracy can be a source of control for those to whom control is a prime goal of some importance needs no laboring. But the existence of a prescribed hierarchy also tends to convey status, even if status is not always coördinate with position in the hierarchy. Hence one of the aspects of bureaucracies that constantly amuses observers (at least observers from outside *that* bureaucracy) is the importance of status symbols within bureaucracies: whom one may call by his first name; how big one's office is, the kind of desk, the amount of secretarial staff, telephones, interoffice communication systems, rugs, etc. In the OPA, "One person suddenly raised to the rank of division director was so anxious to get the rug distinction that he took the first one he saw lying in the hall and put it in his office. It was too large, and so he cut it in half, later to discover that

---

[13] Chester Barnard lists six "pathological aspects of status" in his article "Functions of Status Systems," in William F. Whyte (ed.), *Industry and Society*, McGraw-Hill Book Co., New York, 1946, chap. 4. Simon, Smithburg, and Thompson, *op. cit.*, pp. 207–209, have drawn upon Barnard's suggestions for a luminous discussion of four aspects. And cf. generally the discussion on "The Structure of Authority and Status," *ibid.*, chap. 9.

he had cut in half the rug being saved for the OPA Assistant Administrator."[14] But government bureaucracies are no different from any others. "Recently, for example, a large midwestern corporation almost lost one of its most valuable V.P.'s. In a shift of offices, inadvertently he was given a metal desk instead of the mahogany variety common to his bracket. Why? He pondered and fretted, and began reading hurts, omens, and hidden meanings in every casual conversation. Eventually the matter came out in the open, for the V.P. could go on no longer; he was on the brink of a complete nervous breakdown."[15]

It is altogether possible that the peculiar predisposition of Americans for bureaucratizing social organizations is in part explicable as a desire for formalized status. In the absence of a monarchal court and a hereditary aristocracy as a source of formalized status, Americans have invariably turned to other sources. In the post-Civil War period, money was a widely although by no means universally accepted source of status. In recent decades, however, money seems to have declined in significance as a source of status in the United States, at least among some groups, whereas power and influence, or control, have increased. Thus Charles E. Wilson as director of war mobilization had considerably higher status than Charles E. Wilson as head of General Electric.

But Americans are also pragmatic about organization. Hence to acquire status, their organizations must have a "rational" appearance. That is to say, there must be some apparent justification for the hierarchical chain of control that is simultaneously a vital source of status and a basic distinguishing characteristic of bureaucracy. This need for a justification requires an imitation of the conditions that provide a rational basis for hierarchy. Hence "empire building" takes place in order to increase the number of people who need to be coördinated; or simple problems must be made to seem extraordinarily complex; or economies must be made to appear from extreme division of labor.

The organization produced as a rationalized (rather than a rational) result of these imitation conditions must in turn be an imitation of those organizations that genuinely face the real conditions rather than the imitation ones. The need to imitate not merely the

[14] See the amusing account of status symbols in OPA in Victor A. Thompson, *The Regulatory Process in OPA Rationing*, King's Crown Press, New York, 1951, chap. 10; quoted in Simon, Smithburg, and Thompson, *op. cit.*, pp. 205–207.
[15] "Problem for the Front Office," *Fortune*, May, 1951, p. 81.

conditions but also the precise characteristics of "rational" bureaucracy furnishes further reason for specialization, for detailed prescriptions defining what subordinates can and cannot do, for separating ownership and skill so that control and status may be more easily manipulated, and for drawing up elaborate tables of organizations—i.e., for creating an organization in the image of bureaucracy.

It is altogether possible, then, that the powerful pressure toward the bureaucratization of social life in the United States and elsewhere can be reduced only if, among other things, alternative sources of status are provided in the society.

A RATIONALISTIC BIAS

Finally, each of the preceding four conditions itself presupposes a cultural bias in favor of deliberate, conscious, and apparently rational adaptation of means to ends. One reason for the speed with which the bureaucratization of social life proceeds is that to the modern mind no other way of looking at organization seems sensible. For example, a close correlation exists between the pragmatic attitude of Americans toward organization and their propensity for bureaucratizing social relationships. For bureaucracy is above all a triumph for the deliberate, calculated, conscious attempt to adapt means to ends in the most rational manner.

People who were to invest all their organizational life with mystery, ritual, and unshakeable tradition would develop an approximation to bureaucracy only by accident; certainly there would be no dynamic drive toward it. Likewise people who thought of all organizational life primarily as a source of joy, spontaneity, friendship, respect, and other prime goals, and only secondarily as a source of instrumental goals, would be little inclined toward bureaucracy. Finally, people who had no awareness at all of organization, who did not "see" it, would be unlikely to develop bureaucracies.

Although each of these attitudes could no doubt be found in varying degrees in modern society, none of them is really characteristic of the modern Western outlook—or, for that matter, of the official ideology in ruling elites in the USSR and most of the Orient. One could almost define the "modern" attitude toward organization as a rejection of the three attitudes mentioned above; which is to say, the "modern" mind is predisposed toward solving an array of organizational problems through bureaucracy.

Even on its own terms, however—that is, in terms of rational adaptation of means to ends—there is, of course, one vital weakness in this point of view: the tendency to forget that coördination can come about through reciprocity and through spontaneous field controls. The second of these is more often ignored than the first, for it is easy to forget that coördination can be a by-product rather than a conscious, deliberately organized achievement. Fortunately for people with the kinds of goals postulated in Chapter 2, these alternatives are not mutually exclusive, as many planners and anti-planners often seem to assume. But here we are running ahead of ourselves.

9.

*Hierarchy: Control
by
Leaders* (Continued)

It is easy to see, then, why bureaucracy flourishes in the conditions of modern life, why leaders in business, government, trade unions, churches, hospitals, universities, and elsewhere turn so readily to it, and why citizens, customers, workers, church members, patients, teachers, and others not only tolerate it but frequently demand it. For it provides a framework within which hierarchy can be a process of control highly advantageous to great numbers of people.

Yet bureaucracy imposes costs, too. It is the purpose of this chapter to examine some of these costs. For in appraising the usefulness of hierarchy specifically as a process for economizing, as we shall do in a more detailed way in later chapters, these costs must be kept constantly in mind.

The costs of bureaucracy we discuss in this chapter are inherent tendencies in the sense that they are produced both by the circumstances that call forth bureaucracy and by the characteristic form it takes. Although the subject of widespread criticism, some of these costs seem to us relatively minor in their probable long-run effects on social structure, personalities, and the goals of Chapter 2; certain others loom up of far more importance. Admittedly this distinction between minor and major costs represents a valuation that not everyone will share, but taken tentatively it is a convenient method of classifying two sets of costs.

I. The Minor Costs

The minor costs are internal red tape, "passing the buck" or reluctance of individuals in the bureaucracy to make decisions, rigidity and inflexibility, impersonality, and overcentralization.[1]

[1] Most of these have been subject to heated criticism. Cf. Ludwig von Mises, *Bureaucracy*, Yale University Press, New Haven, 1944; John H. Crider, *The Bu-*

RED TAPE

The proliferation of rules and regulations prescribing the conduct of decision making—which is presumably what one means by
red tape—is inherent in bureaucracy.[2] If discretion is to be limited
and prescribed, rules and regulations are necessary. Specialization,
too, requires rules and regulations, for the area of the specialized
individuals and groups must be defined lest they overstep their
proper jurisdiction and make for trouble. Foremen cannot be permitted to decide questions that ought to go to the personnel director, nor can the personnel director make decisions that require the
concurrence of the general manager or the board of directors. Hierarchy must be roughly defined by rules and regulations to distinguish what the subordinate and what the superior must do. Thus
rules and regulations are the mortar that hold large and complex
organizations together. But for all that they are costs.

Moreover, red tape can easily grow beyond what is necessary
for rational calculation and control. For example, one of the conditions that makes for irrational or imitation bureaucracy—the striving for status and control—also expresses itself in a fatuous cultivation of rules and regulations. Then, too, some of the distinguishing
characteristics of bureaucracy predispose it to a pathological development. The prescriptions that necessarily limit one's discretion are
at the focus of attention. Because hierarchy makes for difficulties in
communication, subordinates easily lose sight of the major goals of
the top leaders. And specialization has a double effect: it develops
a concern for protecting and defining one's special role and it even
creates specialists whose main job is the creation of rules and regulations. For all these reasons, the rules tend to become so highly
valued that the bureaucratic official finds it rewarding to spin out

reaucrat, J. B. Lippincott Co., Philadelphia, 1944; Lawrence Sullivan, *The Dead
Hand of Bureaucracy*, The Bobbs-Merrill Co., Indianapolis, 1940; James M. Beck,
Our Wonderland of Bureaucracy, The Macmillan Company, New York, 1932. It is
significant regarding the writing on this subject that all the above are polemics,
and three out of four contain no definition of "bureaucracy" or "bureaucrat." For
more balanced analysis of the aspects of bureaucracy commonly regarded as objectionable, see the selections in Part 6, "The Bureaucrat," and Part 7, "Social
Pathologies of Bureaucracy," in Robert K. Merton, Ailsa P. Gray, Barbara Hockey,
Hanan C. Selvin (eds.), *Reader in Bureaucracy*, Free Press, Glencoe, Ill., 1952, pp.
363 ff.
    [2] Cf. Charles Hyneman, *Bureaucracy in a Democracy*, Harper & Brothers,
New York, 1950, chap. 24, and Alvin W. Gouldner, "Red Tape as a Social Problem," in Robert K. Merton et al., *op. cit.*, pp. 410 ff.

new ones or rigorously apply the old ones at the expense of clients and superiors.[3]

The proliferation of rules and regulations is, then, another instance in which excessive pursuit of consicous and articulate calculations can actually impede rational social action. Habits, folkways, and unarticulated understandings can often make for more rational social action than do attempts to formalize the underlying rules, for organizations, like human minds, sometimes seem to develop the capacity for dealing with many problems too complex to cope with by conscious and deliberate prescriptions.

PASSING THE BUCK

Reluctance to render a decision combined with an effort to push the decision on to someone else—what Americans call "passing the buck"—is also inherent in bureaucratic structures. Specialization helps the specialist to make competent decisions within his domain of enterprise, but it also means that he may be incompetent outside it. What appears to an outsider to be a weak-kneed refusal to come to the point may actually be a healthy limitation of the specialist's power. Hierarchy operates in the same direction, for one of the major purposes of hierarchy is to *prevent* subordinates from making decisions they ought not to make. In a complex organization, coordination would be impossible if the members did not know when to "pass the buck."

But again, in its pathological stage, "passing the buck" may go beyond what is necessary for efficient coördination or rational decision making and actually obstruct the goals of superiors and clients. Hierarchy and specialization can have debilitating effects on the capacity for making decisions. Significantly, in their report recommending the establishment of a competitive civil service in England in 1853, Northcote and Trevelyan urged that members be recruited directly into the top layers of the governmental bureaucracy so as to avoid the tedious training in petty decisions that well might ruin the capacities of the ablest young men out of Oxford and Cambridge.[4] This principle was adopted and undoubtedly has helped to limit, although it has not eliminated, the pathological development

[3] Cf. Robert K. Merton, *Social Theory and Social Structure*, Free Press, Glencoe, Ill., 1949, pp. 155–156.

[4] For a discussion of the report by Northcote and Trevelyan, see Herman Finer, *Theory and Practice of Modern Government*, Henry Holt and Co., New York, 1949, pp. 763–765.

of an incapacity for making decisions in the British civil service.

Poets and writers throughout the world have testified eloquently to the existence of this pathological condition in government bureaucracies. A minor incident in Gogol's famous story, *The Cloak*, turns on the promotion of the protagonist, a government copyist for many years, to a position where in his copying he must make minor decisions about changes in spelling, punctuation, and syntax. He proves quite unable to bear the new burden! Nor is "passing the buck" restricted to governmental bureaucracies; nearly everyone has had some equally infuriating experiences with the bureaucracies of business and industry.[5]

As the incident in Gogol's story suggests, bureaucracies not only may recruit personalities predisposed to avoiding risks but may also have profound long-run effects on personality structure. Unfortunately, empirical knowledge in this area is at present too skimpy for generalization. It has been suggested that the bureaucratization of social organizations may vastly reduce the role of the adventurous, risk-taking, nonconformist personality and indeed drastically decrease opportunities for intellectual, aesthetic, and even physical risk and adventure to a point where life is drab, gray, and colorless. This is a possibility that should never be lost sight of, but we do not have enough evidence to decide how likely it is.

INFLEXIBILITY

Excessive rigidity or inflexibility is an incapacity for making changes rapidly enough to maximize the goals for which an organization is ostensibly set up. In most human organizations, bureaucratic and nonbureaucratic, there are some forces making for stability. Because learning new responses represents a psychological cost to the individual, new responses must be heavily rewarded or the old ones heavily penalized or both. And because organizational changes frequently involve serious loss of status, control, income, and other values for some people in the organization, the losers will fight the change. For both reasons, superiors who wish to change an

---

[5] Marshall E. Dimock and Howard K. Hyde, "Bureaucratic Problems in Business Organizations," in Robert Dubin (ed.), *Human Relations in Administration, The Sociology of Organization*, Prentice-Hall, New York, 1951, pp. 168–171, esp. p. 170. This is a selection from their Temporary National Economic Committee Monograph No. 11, *Bureaucracy and Trusteeship in Large Corporations*, U.S. Government Printing Office, Washington, 1940.

organization must be heavily armed with and ready to use rewards and deprivations against subordinates. Yet superiors frequently lack such heavy rewards and deprivations or they identify too much with their subordinates to treat them ruthlessly.

Bureaucracies are probably no more predisposed to inflexibility than many other organizations. Perhaps what often makes them seem so is the obvious contrast between their stability and the pretension to rational adaptation of organizational means to ends—a contrast less striking where there is no pretension to organizational rationality. Indeed, a certain measure of inflexibility in a bureaucratic organization is not only inevitable but quite healthy. The complicated charter of an organization is not easily learned; retraining is therefore a cost to be avoided if possible. Moreover, an understanding of the prescribed and operating charters helps one to understand his own function; these charters furnish the employer with a sense of purpose and so permit self-respect. Frequent changes in the charters are bound to raise doubts about the purposes of the organization and one's role in it; therefore morale declines, as it does in a number of government agencies in wartime. Then, too, changes involve shifts in status, and rapid changes prevent clear-cut status from emerging. For this reason, too, repeated changes in the organizational structure, as in war agencies, may seriously damage the morale of some members.

Although bureaucracies may be no more inflexible than many other organizations, and although a certain measure of inflexibility is an inevitable cost of bureaucracy as a device for rational calculation and control, there are also some special factors in bureaucracies that predispose them to excessive inflexibility: (1) Because specialists are not always easy to replace, they are in a strong bargaining position; hence they can resist change. (2) Rules and regulations, the mortar of organizations, can often be turned against the ruthless superior. (3) Those at the top of the hierarchy are themselves frequently not insulated from the rewards of stability. (4) Superiors who become habituated to operating with rules and regulations may lose the necessary ruthlessness. (5) Hierarchy and the resulting status system make for problems in communication between echelons; hence subordinates may be unable to convince superiors of the justification for change, just as superiors may be unable to justify it in understandable terms to subordinates.

IMPERSONALITY

No doubt bureaucracies do make for impersonality in relationships both within the bureaucracy and with clients outside it. A bias in favor of a deliberate adaptation of organizational means to ends requires that human relationships be viewed as instrumental means to the prescribed goals of the organization, not as sources of direct prime goal achievement. Joy, love, friendship, pity, and affection must all be curbed—unless they happen to foster the prescribed goals of the organization. The fact of mere numbers also helps to make for impersonality; because no one can hope to know everyone else in the organization, some impersonality is inevitable even if it is covered up by superficial friendliness. Size and specialization, moreover, can increase daily contacts to a point where any except impersonal relationships would place a staggering load on one's emotional resources; impersonality is a psychological necessity. Hierarchy requires impersonality, too. If one must maintain unilateral controls, he dare not permit himself to develop close personal ties with his subordinates, for to do so automatically strengthens reciprocity. Thus junior officers in the army who permit themselves to develop an affection for their subordinates sometimes find it difficult to send them on dangerous missions.

When do the costs of impersonality offset the gains? This is so much a question of value that no two observers are likely to agree. If bureaucratic organizations are necessary, then impersonality is also necessary. If the impersonality of modern bureaucracies is regarded as excessive, the only workable alternative is not to personalize bureaucratic relationships but to reduce the role of bureaucracies in modern life.

EXCESSIVE CENTRALIZATION

The common dilemma of decentralized discretion versus centralized coördination is at the heart of bureaucratic organizations. When large numbers of specialists must be coördinated in the absence of a free confederacy, common norms and reality views, or a price system, then the top leaders are regularly faced with the choice of making decisions themselves or delegating to subordinates. If they delegate to subordinates, coördination may decline; if they do not, top leadership may be overloaded. Very often the difference between an organizational genius and a commonplace leader is, no doubt, little more than an acute insight about where to draw the line.

But organizational geniuses are few and bureaucratic organizations are many. The temptation to centralize is evidently more overpowering than the rewards expected from decentralization. Ruthless and successful struggles to rise to top leadership in an organization through reliance on one's own judgment probably do not predispose one to great confidence in the judgment of those who have not made the grade. Conversely, some individuals rise to the top after years as subordinates and cannot throw off their habitual concern for details that are now petty. And from the highest peak one cannot help noting how much more there is to the world than the pygmies in the valleys and on the hills below can possibly see. Evidently, too, some people feel a threat to their status if subordinates begin to make important decisions.

Finally, top leaders in a bureaucratic organization are not necessarily free agents. They in turn are subject to external controls. Focusing responsibility for the success of the organization directly on top leaders generates a temptation to make all the important decisions at the top in order to prevent subordinates from making the wrong ones. Thus the Hickenlooper investigations of the Atomic Energy Commission in 1949 accelerated a process of centralization within the commission that some employees believed would deprive it of the advantages secured from a deliberate policy of decentralization hitherto developed under the forceful leadership of David Lilienthal.[6]

Probably no entirely satisfactory solutions to the dilemma of centralization versus decentralization exist. Certainly there are no obvious ones. For this reason bureaucratic organizations sometimes fluctuate unstably from one pole to the other, for the present evils of the one are vivid and painful while the gains from a move in the other direction are obvious and attractive. In later chapters we shall see this dilemma in hierarchical politico-economic techniques.

II. The Major Costs

If these were the only special costs of the bureaucratic form, the potential net gain from bureaucracy as a device for economizing would be enormously greater than it is. Now, however, we

[6] Robert A. Dahl and Ralph S. Brown, Jr., *Domestic Control of Atomic Energy*, Social Science Research Council, Pamphlet 8, New York, 1951, p. 56.

must turn to some additional special costs that are almost always un-measurable, impalpable, controversial, but quite possibly very great. These are (1) failures in economizing, (2) the creation of inequality, and (3) difficulties of control by superiors and clients.

FAILURES IN ECONOMIZING

The charge is often made that bureaucracies are wasteful of manpower, materials, and money. But in part this is to identify bureaucracy solely with government. If one takes the internal money costs as a criterion—that is, the cost actually charged in money terms to the accounts of the organization—the members of business bureaucracies have somewhat greater incentives to reduce costs than do members of government bureaucracies.[7] Not, of course, that members of either are much influenced directly by the "profit motive" if that is precisely defined, for they do not own the tools and equipment with which they work and hence, strictly speaking, never receive profits.

Nevertheless, as we have seen, some of the top leaders in business bureaucracies do stand to gain from increased profits, through a variety of ways in which profits and losses for the enterprise are made effective as gains and losses for individuals; and with a few exceptions this is not the case in government bureaucracies. In business, profits may lead to promotion, bonus, or salary increase. They are a sign of success and therefore assume status in the business community, if not always elsewhere. Then, too, the ethos of business enterprise leads to somewhat different indoctrination; businessmen are indoctrinated by a business culture to make profits. Not only are profits instrumental to status, power, and income, but they permit more immediate satisfactions like self-respect and self-approval; to make a profit is an achievement in itself.

These differences in the motivation of superiors result in important influences on subordinate members of the business bureaucracy. Promotion, future, security, increase in wages and salaries, status in the firm, affection or respect of one's superiors: all these in some measure hinge upon one's capacity for helping the superiors of the business bureaucracy to attain their goals.

Then, too—although the point is easily exaggerated—the simplicity of the goals of business superiors enables them to set up cost-

[7] A point we return to in more detail in Chapter 16.

accounting systems and other measuring devices that help to gauge the contribution of the members of the business with an appearance of precision that is much more difficult in multi-purpose government bureaucracies. For these reasons and for others to be examined in later chapters, throughout the organization there is a stronger stimulus to internal economizing; it becomes a matter for organization, procedure, indoctrination, and attention in a way that it usually does not in a government bureaucracy. Symbolic of the difference is the fact that in England double-entry bookkeeping was used for several centuries among business firms before it was adopted by government, after 1830.

Now assuming that the distinction between business and government bureaucracies is a sound one, it does not establish, as is so often mistakenly assumed, that bureaucracy *per se* tends to internal wastefulness. It merely establishes the fact that government bureaucracies do not keep internal costs down as well as do business bureaucracies. If it means that bureaucracy in government is wasteful, it also means that bureaucracy in business is not. Both are bureaucracies.

Moreover, even differences between government and business bureaucracies in their capacity to keep down internal costs would prove nothing about either the *external* costs of bureaucracy or the relative external costs of government and business bureaucracies, i.e., costs to society that are not actually charged in money terms to the organization itself. In a wide variety of situations the internal economies of business bureaucracies are more than offset by the external costs they create, and the internal wastes of government bureaucracies are more than offset by the external social gains. These possibilities are analyzed in some detail in later chapters. Meanwhile two points about the utility of bureaucracy as a device for economizing are worth reëmphasis. First, the relevant choice is often not between bureaucracy and an alternative to bureaucracy but between government and business bureaucracy. Second, it is always difficult and often impossible to measure the internal diseconomies and external gains and costs of bureaucracy.

INEQUALITY

Internally hierarchies typically produce inequality of control, status, and income. Therefore they endanger both subjective equality and political equality.

SUBJECTIVE INEQUALITY. In a society of hierarchical organizations leaders can shift rewards to themselves and deprivations to non-leaders. Hence extensive hierarchy is likely also to produce great inequalities in dignity, respect, opportunity, education, housing, recreation, leisure, security, etc. Equal freedom for everyone is therefore most unlikely, for differences in control, status, and income enable leaders to achieve their goals more easily than non-leaders. Although both consequences are seen at their fullest in the Soviet system, no Western society escapes them, no matter whether it is called "socialist," "capitalist," or "mixed welfare state."

POLITICAL INEQUALITY. The goal of political equality, it will be recalled, does not require equally shared control in all situations, but only in some forum where the last word may be had. However, political equality "in the last say" can suffer in a highly hierarchical society. For it is one thing to make a logical distinction between political equality and general equality of control; but it is quite another to enforce that distinction in real life. The plain fact is, of course, that a leader at the top of a modern hierarchy—corporations, trade unions, government agencies, political parties—tends inevitably to exert more control over government policy than does any one of his subordinates.

The hierarchical leader is more than simply a spokesman for all or a majority of the people in his organization counted as equals; that is, his own preferences count for significantly more than those of any one of his subordinates. In influencing nominations, campaign contributions, voting turnout, voters' attitudes, opinion leaders, legislation, the White House, and administrative action, the hierarchical leader is not a mere adding machine automatically running up totals on preferences among alternative policies, counting each member in the organization, including himself, as the equal of every other. On the contrary, his is the hand that runs the adding machine; and when he comes to the point where he must add in the weight of his own individual preferences with those of all the others in his organization he may decide to count his own preferences, not as equal, but as worth ten or a hundred or a thousand times more than the preferences of everyone else in the organization.

Of course, the conditions of polyarchy examined in the next chapter do impose real limits on the entent to which hierarchical leaders can minimize political equality. John L. Lewis was not, after all, able to deliver the vote of coal miners to Wendell Willkie in the 1940 campaign. But can anyone doubt that the private, individual preferences of John L. Lewis count for far more in making government policy than the preferences of any other one person in the United Mine Workers? Or that the private, individual preferences of the president or chairman of the board of any large corporation count for far more than the preferences of any one of his stock holders or workers (unless they, too, happen to be leaders of other organizations)? To restate a point made earlier, people like Jefferson and Rousseau were in principle right in arguing that full political equality is impossible in a society with large hierarchical organizations.

Thus, although polyarchy and hierarchy check and balance each other, and although polyarchy actually requires hierarchy, as we shall see later, hierarchies impose limits on the extent to which political equality is attainable.

DIFFICULTIES OF CONTROL

What has just been said suggests a third and closely related cost: Any nominal superiors "outside" the hierarchy may have great difficulty in controlling it whether they are citizens in a polyarchy or not. Many hierarchies are nominally subordinate and some are actually subordinate to other people: for example, to leaders of a higher echelon, who have nominal or operating control over several hierarchies; or even to non-leaders acting collectively through elections or marked choices.

The main relationships in which the problem of control over hierarchies arises are between citizens and various governmental hierarchies, politicians and government bureaucracies, workers and trade union leaders, workers and business leaders, trade union leaders and business leaders, consumers and business leaders, consumers and government hierarchies, and stockholders and business hierarchies.

In order for those "outside" the hierarchy to exercise significant control over it in any of these relationships, one or more of four techniques must be employed. Polyarchy, again is one. A super-hierarchy[8] is another. But control over the hierarchy may also be achieved through bargaining or a price system. Only if the con-

---

[8] That is, a controlling hierarchy superimposed on the subordinate hierarchy which is to be controlled.

ditions for none of these are present is external control over the hierarchy impossible.

Such is the case with the last relationship listed above—between stockholders and business hierarchies. For there the conditions necessary for effective competition among leaders for the support of non-leaders do not exist (the conditions are examined in the next chapter); hence polyarchy is impossible. On the whole, too, conditions are unfavorable for separate stockholders' protective organizations; therefore bargaining is impossible. Nor can stockholders do much to affect company policies through the price system. And for all these reasons, a super-hierarchy would merely diminish stockholder control still further. Hence one of the facts of business life is that the rank and file of stockholders have relatively little control over corporate hierarchies.[9]

In *The Managerial Revolution*[10] James Burnham argued in effect that, just as stockholders are unable to exert effective control over business leaders, so the conditions are absent for effective control over all other important "managerial" hierarchies. It followed, he thought, that a managerial ruling class was bound to emerge. There appear to be two fundamental errors in Burnham's argument. First, Burnham seriously underestimated the viability and achievements of polyarchy,[11] bargaining, and price systems as methods of control, as we hope to show in subsequent chapters. Second, for this reason he exaggerated the potential control of the technicians, his "managers," as compared with other hierarchical leaders such as politicians.

Nevertheless, Burnham's exaggerated argument, like that of Gaetano Mosca in *The Ruling Class*,[12] has a sound core of truth. In a society dependent upon a widespread use of hierarchical organizations, even where some external control is possible through polyarchy, bargaining, or price system, important limits are set by the nature of hierarchy. Three basic conditions of control, it will be

[9] William Z. Ripley, *Main Street and Wall Street*, Little, Brown and Co., Boston, 1927; Adolf A. Berle and Gardiner C. Means, *The Modern Corporation and Private Property*, The Macmillan Company, New York, 1934.

[10] James Burnham, *The Managerial Revolution*, The John Day Co., New York, 1941.

[11] At that time Burnham seems to have misunderstood polyarchy; subsequently, in *The Machiavellians, Defenders of Freedom*, The John Day Co., New York, 1943, he seems to have revised his earlier views.

[12] Gaetano Mosca, *The Ruling Class*, McGraw-Hill Book Co., New York, 1939.

recalled from an earlier chapter, are (1) adequate rewards and deprivations, (2) appropriate identifications, and (3) adequate communication between controllers and controlled.[13] In the group of relationships mentioned above (if the relation between stockholders and business hierarchies is disregarded) these conditions of control are attenuated. Let us consider each in turn.

INADEQUATE REWARDS AND DEPRIVATIONS. Because hierarchies give leaders increased control, status, income, and opportunity to achieve other goals, it is difficult for non-leaders through collective action, as in polyarchy and price systems, to set up an adequate structure of rewards and deprivations. On the contrary many highly important rewards and deprivations are manipulated by the leaders themselves through their hierarchies, not merely to maintain control within the hierarchy but to prevent effective control by outsiders. Money, propaganda, threats to withdraw their skills, hiring and firing, promotions and demotions in status and control—all tend to weaken control by non-leaders through polyarchy and market choices.

Hence effective external control over one hierarchy often requires an equally powerful offsetting hierarchy that can mobilize sufficient rewards and deprivations to bargain with its opposite number, as trade unions have learned to do; this is also the reason that much of the nominally unilateral control over hierarchies—as in the relation between the President and his cabinet officers and bureau chiefs—turns out upon examination to be bargaining.

Super-hierarchies may, of course, accumulate sufficient rewards and deprivations to exercise effective control over all the sub-hierarchies. One of the constant ideals set forth in American theories about public administration is the ideal chief executive (president, governor, mayor, or city manager), a single man at the pinnacle of a super-hierarchy who possesses sufficient rewards and penalties to enforce his unilateral control over the administrative agencies. Unfortunately, however, if chief executives can accumulate such a powerful array of rewards and deprivations, then these may also be employed against polyarchal controls.[14] Hence control of the major hierarchies of modern society exclusively by

[13] Cf. Chapter 4.
[14] Cf. Chapter 12.

super-hierarchies seems to be possible, if at all, only in totalitarian regimes; and in fact even there the element of bargaining is not unimportant.

Despite all this, it would be folly to conclude with Burnham that the rewards and deprivations at the disposal of non-leaders are insignificant in Western societies. Polyarchy, bargaining, market choices, and various combinations of these do in fact serve to hold leaders in check to a quite remarkable degree; but here again subsequent chapters are required to carry us further.

FAULTY IDENTIFICATION. That identifications frequently impose obstacles to external control is most easily seen in relations between government political leaders and government bureaucracies; but the nature of the problem in government bureaucracies indicates that the difficulty is really more widespread.

In two ways the civil servant's identifications limit his responsiveness.[15] First, he is a professional, part of an educated corps of managers and specialists with a goodly measure of group esprit and common identification. Because civil servants share similar problems, identification helps to develop mutual sympathy and understanding. One problem they share in common is the constant threat posed to their status, power, and security by political superiors in the executive and legislature. Second, the civil servant is also a part of a particular organization with which he strongly identifies himself. Powerful organizational loyalties flourish. To curtail the organization's funds, reduce its personnel, cut down its prescribed power, make it more vulnerable to attack—these are attacks on the civil servant's *own* sense of status, power, and security. Consequently he will be much less responsive to efforts by his political superiors to curtail the organization than to expand it.[16]

FAILURES OF COMMUNICATION. Inadequate communication is also a frequent obstacle to effective control. Because the hierarchy originates much of the information its nominal superiors require in order to act intelligently, and because the superiors are usually less expert on any particular subject than some of their nominal subordinates, it is often possible for the hierarchy to manipulate com-

[15] Cf. Herbert A. Simon, Donald W. Smithburg, and Victor A. Thompson, *Public Administration*, Alfred A. Knopf, New York, 1950, pp. 532–535.

[16] Cf. Chester Barnard, "Functions of Status Systems," in William F. Whyte (ed.), *Industry and Society*, McGraw-Hill Book Co., New York, 1946, pp. 159–160.

munications in order to control their nominal superiors. This is a familiar charge against foreign offices all over the world, and no doubt one with some validity. But it applies equally to many other relationships. Stockholders depend on their corporate hierarchies to keep them informed; in the United States manipulation of information in this relationship was notorious before the Securities Exchange Act was passed. And even that act has done little to insure that stockholders can uncover the mistakes and inadequacies of corporate management. Workers and trade union leaders in turn need information about company costs and earnings in order to determine strike and wage policies; yet they find it difficult to obtain anything more than business leaders wish them to know. Even voters are partly dependent on politicians to keep them informed about what the politicians and their policies have done, are doing, and will do.

In these situations the saving element is the existence of a plurality of competing and conflicting hierarchies that provide alternative sources of information to those who need to make decisions. Even dictatorships evidently must provide for alternative systems of communication, lest the nominal leaders become the captives of their staffs. The same principle is followed in polyarchies whenever external control over some hierarchy is strongly desired; in polyarchies, however, the arrangements must obviously be somewhat different from dictatorship because the control needed is that of non-leaders over leaders. But the principle is the same.

III. Prerequisites to the Rational Use of Hierarchy

Hierarchy generates great benefits and great costs. Although it is indispensable to modern civilization, if improperly employed it may snuff out the central core of Western values. How then can hierarchy, particularly in the specific organizational setting of bureaucracy, be used for rational calculation and control in economic life in order to maximize the values of Chapter 2? The rest of this chapter is hardly more than a preliminary sketch of some general answers to that question. The question is, indeed, a central and persistent question of this whole book. Most of the remaining chapters touch upon it, some generally, some quite specifically. As the book continues to unfold, then, the outlines of an approach to the answer will, we hope, become progressively clearer.

ACCEPTANCE OF HIERARCHY

The first requirement for the rational use of hierarchy is acceptance of it. For within the confines of a large-scale industrial society there is no escape from hierarchy and its problems. No modern industrial society can approximate the values of Chapter 2 without four types of organization in which the hierarchical component is bound to be strong: large-scale enterprises, specific government agencies, the military, and the central hierarchy of government itself. Most people would also agree on the need for a fifth basic hierarchy: trade unions.

Neither "socialist" Britain nor "capitalist" United States escapes these hierarchical prerequisites. Nor, certainly, does "communist" Russia. If, in contrast to the USSR, polyarchy, bargaining, and price systems in Britain and the United States soften the harsh outlines of hierarchy, Britain and the United States are hardly distinguishable in the extent of their reliance on hierarchy.

Neither socialism nor any other grand alternative open to an industrial society offers an escape from hierarchy. In countries like Great Britain, New Zealand, and Sweden, socialist welfare policies have reduced the differences in status, control, and freedom produced primarily by differences in income, but not those produced by one's location in a control hierarchy. Moreover, socialization of industry has not reduced and of course cannot reduce the scope of hierarchy. For the dynamic factors that give rise to it—the need for coördinating large numbers of people, complexity, and the division of labor—all remain; if anything, by reducing the scope of the price system as a method of coördination, of resolving complex decisions, and of insuring division of labor, socialists in pursuing nationalization have increased the amount of hierarchy required.

SOME FALSE PREREQUISITES

Attempts to minimize one cost of hierarchy very frequently increase another. Many solutions to the problem of hierarchy are superficial cures because they do little more than displace one costly consequence with a different one. By their emphasis on one cost and their neglect of others, such "solutions" nevertheless enjoy a certain persuasiveness. A common example is the customary attack on government bureaucracies by those spokesmen for business hierarchies who carefully emphasize the costs of government bureaucracies and ignore those of business.

If one examines each of the major costs discussed above, it is easy to see why the attempt to minimize one cost of hierarchy may often increase another. For example, one way to cope with the problem of internal economy might be to replace government bureaucracies by competitive business bureaucracies; but of course any such solution ignores the external social costs that competitive business bureaucracies create or are unable to take into account, for which the government bureaucracy is established in the first place. Or one may insist on stricter rules; many politicians and publicists appear to believe that internal wastes in government can be cured by carefully drawn rules and regulations. Yet one common result of their efforts is mainly to increase the amount of red tape in government operations out of all proportion to any possible savings. If government suffers more from red tape than does business, in large part the reason is that governments are required by public opinion to enforce much more detailed controls over "public" expenditures than businessmen are over "private" expenditures.[17]

Alternatively, one way to meet the problem of external costs is to replace business hierarchies with government bureaucracy; but in this case internal costs will probably rise. Or the business hierarchy may be regulated; but such regulation requires an additional government hierarchy. Or some of the affected persons may be provided with organizations through which they can bargain, as in the case of workers. But then the parties to the bargain may simply shift the external costs to other unrepresented groups, such as consumers; moreover, the problem of coördination may then become a serious one, as it has in the case of employers and trade unions.

The problem of securing external control over a hierarchy is beset with an equally nettlesome alternative. Most socialists and many latter-day liberals have assumed that government hierarchies are more easily controlled than business hierarchies; hence the way to economic democracy is, oddly enough, via government hierarchies. But it does not follow even in a more or less healthy polyarchy that nationalization will maximize outside control over the

---

[17] E.g., in an exchange between a vice-president of General Electric Company and a Congressman, the corporation executive freely admitted that General Electric did not attempt to work out cost breakdowns on detailed items demanded by Congressmen as a customary part of their budget hearings. Cf. the testimony of Vice-President Winne and the queries of Congressman Hinshaw, in Joint Committee on Atomic Energy, *Investigation into the United States Atomic Energy Project, Hearings* (81st Congress, 1st Session), May 26–July 11, 1949 (22 vols.), pp. 521–523.

hierarchical organization. In Great Britain the power of a coal miner, coal consumer, or ordinary citizen vis-à-vis the coal "bosses" does not seem to have changed much with nationalization, as many socialists like G. D. H. Cole have been the first to point out. What often happens in such cases is that a rather different control system, with somewhat different techniques, leaders, and goals, replaces the old control system. Because the two are not strictly comparable, it is frequently difficult to say whether the new is more or less hierarchical than the old. But the experience so far with nationalization and other forms of bureaucracy is enough to permit one to conclude that displacement of business hierarchies by government does not, by itself, notably decrease the hierarchical component.

Another way to deal with the problem of external controls is to increase the opportunities for bargaining. Much of the New Deal, for example, consisted of measures to increase the bargaining strength of various groups who were unable to exert much control over powerful hierarchies. But often, as we shall see later, even this method requires an enormous expansion of new hierarchies, governmental and nongovernmental, over which external control is far from easy.

Finally, many critics of American government policy point out, quite rightly, that because coördination among the diverse government hierarchies, political and administrative, is poor, more coördination is needed. But an increase in coördination may require more hierarchy, not less—particularly in the executive branch and in the political parties. Indeed, those who criticize the government for its lack of coördination often oppose every effort to strengthen either the hierarchical component or the polyarchical at the expense of bargaining in order to secure better coördination. We shall have more to say about this problem in a later chapter.[18]

Conversely, there are those who, ever since Marx, have been critical of the "anarchy of production" under capitalism. Their major premise, usually implicit rather than explicit, is that a shift of control to government hierarchies will necessarily increase coördination and eliminate the "anarchy of production"; yet, as is becoming increasingly clear from chapter to chapter, this simple premise is replete with false assumptions. One cannot assume that more government hierarchy is always a cure for failures of coördination among nongovernmental hierarchies.

One could go on through other problems of hierarchy to show

[18] Chapters 12 and 13.

that in many cases attacks on one cost of hierarchy generate others. The point of all this is not to prove that the costs of hierarchy cannot be reduced; for it does not follow from what we have said that the cure is always worse than the disease. The point is, rather, that one should be suspicious of easy cures for the problems of hierarchy, for in all probability the proposal in question will push hierarchy into place in one spot only to have it break out of place somewhere else.

MARGINAL GAINS

Nevertheless marginal gains are possible; and a commitment to incrementalism means that, where marginal gains are possible, they should be seized. That an attempt to decrease some costs may frequently lead to increases in other costs is no argument for not acting to decrease the costs of hierarchy. Only if the decreases were always balanced or exceeded by the increases would it be irrational to act. But there is no evidence that this is so. All that we have argued so far is that one should have relatively modest expectations about the returns from any proposal for dealing with hierarchy. Modest expectations may be insufficient to satisfy the utopian or holistic planner. But they are quite enough for anyone committed to the incrementalist view.

Indeed, if our first point above is true, then only a proposal to do away with industrial society in certain quite specific ways is likely to promise a vast, comprehensive, revolutionary reduction in hierarchy. Aside from the fact that not many people seriously propose to do away with industrialization, any such proposal inherently contains so many unpredictable elements that no one can be sure what the outcome would be. On incrementalist grounds or even as a calculated risk, this alternative must be rejected until and unless further technological and social changes make the outcome more predictable.

But on the same grounds, every potential gain ought to be seized, however slight it may be. For example, increased consultation and other forms of reciprocity between leaders and non-leaders in large enterprises (which we discuss in Chapter 17) may not produce the kind of revolutionary transformation in control relations that comprehensive reformers desire. But incrementalists will not sniff at the small gains they make possible. We shall suggest other possibilities in later chapters.

A whole range of devices is necessary to cover different situations. There is no single, simple formula to cover them all. A society committed to a simple formula is bound to have more trouble with its hierarchies than a society with a variety of tools in its kit. To take a single example, the American atomic energy operation represents an ingenious attempt to combine the advantages of government ownership of plant and final control over policy with the advantages of operation by experienced private corporations. Nationalization (in the British sense), regulation, and free enterprise were all rejected in favor of the contract method. The contract method has its problems and its critics.[19] Yet it marks a notable step forward in the development of politico-economic techniques for avoiding some of the drawbacks both of straight government operation and of pure free enterprise without at the same time leading to the cumbersome quasi-judicial procedures of the regulatory commission.

USE OF PRICE SYSTEMS

Some form of price system is indispensable if hierarchy is to be held within desirable limits in industrial societies. Price mechanisms, including the hierarchical price mechanism, are, as we showed in Chapters 6 and 7, astonishing decentralizers. Without them, the burden on the central government becomes so staggering that only a weakening of controls by citizens and the legislative body, such as takes place in wartime, makes it possible for the executive to discharge its incredible task of coördination. Some observers of British government over the past several decades of depression, war, and postwar emergency seriously raise the question whether the central government can go on indefinitely under the strain of centralized decisions. A permanent Secretary of the Board of Trade has written: ". . . I fear greatly for the central machine of government. It seems to me very doubtful whether it can for long stand a continuance of present pressures. And I most seriously think that people should begin thinking now of the sort of measures, and pretty radical ones, that would lighten the load." [20] As compared with a hierarchical economy the price system is one such "radical" method of simplifying and lightening the agenda of policy makers.

[19] Some of the problems are discussed in Robert A. Dahl and Ralph S. Brown, Jr., *op. cit.* The most extensive criticism of the device is to be found in James R. Newman, "The Atomic Energy Industry: An Experiment in Hybridization," 60 *Yale Law Journal* 1263 (December, 1951).

[20] See *Public Administration*, vol. 26, 1948, p. 91; quoted in D. N. Chester, *Central and Local Government, Financial and Administrative Relations*, Macmillan and Co., London, 1951, p. 326. For Chester's own sober views, see *ibid.*, pp. 327 ff.

UNIFIED POLITICAL CONTROLS

In the United States at least, political controls over governmental and some nongovernmental hierarchies need to be unified. This assertion is paradoxical at first blush, for it is tantamount to saying that hierarchy can be kept within tolerable limits only by more hierarchy. Yet this is exactly what we do mean to say. Political leadership is not sufficiently unified to enable the spokesmen for the "majority" to control effectively the policies of powerful hierarchies like government agencies, corporations, and trade unions. Earlier we said that polyarchal controls help to limit hierarchy. But in the United States polyarchal controls are weakened because government leaders are incapable of unified, coördinated, cohesive action against many of the powerful hierarchies of American life. Hence the actual control over hierarchy is considerably less than the control we believe to be potential.[21]

DECENTRALIZATION TO SMALL GROUPS

There appear to be some largely unexploited possibilities for decreasing the need for hierarchy by decentralizing decisions to small groups. To be sure, many fans of the small group are utopian. But their utopianism should not divert us from the hard core of truth in their argument: that in some situations one alternative to hierarchy is small-group decisions made through spontaneous field systems and reciprocity.[22]

Small-group life develops around a number of important focal points where people are in frequent contact: the place where people live—the home, school, neighborhood, town, and among intermediate groups the city, state, and region; the place where people work; the groups in which people meet to help set standards or make demands about work—professional groups, trade unions, guilds; the gatherings of people who meet to exchange goods, services, and money—market groups of various kinds, including retail stores and consumer coöps; ethnic and racial identification; the process of friendship. The last, of course, cuts across all the others; it is one of the vital functions of small groups that cannot be carried on by large ones.

Public policy can inhibit or stimulate the life of one or another of these small groups in two significant ways. First, the autonomy of

[21] Cf. Chapters 12 and 13.
[22] Cf. Chapter 18.

this or that type of small group may be either inhibited or stimulated by public policy. Second, to some extent the frequency of contact or "interaction" is influenced by public policies. Why is frequency of contact important? Because the following two propositions appear to be roughly true: (1) To the extent that their goals are potentially compatible, the more frequently people interact with one another the greater is their liking for one another.[23] (2) To the extent that people who regularly interact in the course of some activity like one another, they will engage in additional joint activities, and these additional activities may further strengthen the sentiments of liking.[24] Thus, solidarity will grow up.

In the past, important public policies have been made without much knowledge of or regard for distant but significant effects conducted through such innocent human materials as liking and disliking. Probably not many people specifically wanted to destroy the functioning of a small New England community like "Hilltown." Yet industrialization and giantism severely limited Hilltown's autonomy and all but wiped it out as a focal point of human interaction. Town government and town meeting remained, but the power of the town declined. Militia training and management of church affairs disappeared. The town's control of highways, schools, and relief was greatly reduced. Hilltown no longer even sent its own representative to the state legislature, for it had become part of a larger electoral district. So much for autonomy. Meanwhile the number of activities that Hilltowners carried on together decreased. People scattered outward in the morning, to return at night; even at night they did not see much of other Hilltowners, for they went out of town for their movies, restaurants, dances. Farming gave way to factory work. Farm bees vanished. The general stores lost money as people shopped elsewhere. Social life was impoverished; informal visiting declined, parties diminished, and some people saw almost nobody outside of business. Hilltown is no longer much of a social organization; it is a spot on a map, a piece of ground with houses on it where people are sheltered, eat, sleep, defecate, copulate; these basic physiological functions are carried on in Hilltown, but it is not a valued source of prime goal satisfactions like friendship, solidarity, and respect, nor is it vital in social indoctrination, or social control, or responsiveness, or rational solutions to the problems of

[23] Drawn from George C. Homans, *The Human Group*, Harcourt, Brace and Co., New York, 1950, pp. 111–113, 115–118, 242–243, 244–247, where the necessary qualifications may also be found.
[24] *Ibid.*, p. 118.

Hilltowners. It is not even marked by much agreement or disagreement; the mood among Hilltowners is one of indifference to one another. It has no solidarity. If Hilltowners retain some emotional content to their lives, that fact does not show up in Hilltown.[25]

Over the past century a great complex of social decisions has killed off thousands and thousands of Hilltowns in the United States. Yet as a nation we can scarcely afford to kill off all these groups simply out of indifference or ignorance. In many ways the geographical group holds the greatest promise of all small groups and yet has been most ravaged by modern industrialization and urbanism. For the "neighborhood" of from one to five thousand people is a potential source of a tremendous number of amenities and prime goal satisfactions that are now neglected; the impoverishment of life since the Middle Ages by the destruction of the geographical group as a functioning unit is incalculable; it is difficult to say whether the great benefits of industralization have offset the enormous losses in prime goal satisfactions like respect, affection, friendship, and solidarity generated by the disruption of small, cohesive geographical groups with considerable autonomy. Lewis Mumford argues with an impressive analysis that we have been the losers; nor need one romanticize or approve of the other features of the medieval life to conclude that in the organization of our towns and cities all the great efforts of modern industrialism have created barren wasteland out of richness, beauty, and human warmth.[26] Perhaps as good a test as any is the unwillingness or incapacity of people in large cities to reproduce themselves, not only in the United States but elsewhere.[27] Modern cities are literally death traps.

Nor is it only a question of prime goals. Because the neighborhood is where children grow, it is the only small group that directly encompasses both children and adults—indeed, the entire family. In the neighborhood peer groups the character of young people is formed—for good or ill. As Doc, a corner-boy leader, told W. F. Whyte: "Fellows around here don't know what to do except within the radius of about three hundred yards. That's the truth, Bill. They come home from work, hang on the corner, go up to eat, back on the corner, up to a show, and they come back to hang on the corner. If they're not on the corner, it's likely the boys there will know

[25] *Ibid.*, pp. 359–361, 365–366.
[26] Lewis Mumford, *The Culture of Cities*, Harcourt, Brace and Co., New York, 1938.
[27] Cf. for example, Baker Brownell, *The Human Community, Its Philosophy and Practice for a Time of Crisis*, Harper & Brothers, New York, 1950, p. 11.

where you can find them. Most of them stick to one corner. It's only rarely that a fellow will change his corner."[28]

It is for these reasons that people distressed by the decline in group autonomy associated with modern society, like Mary Parker Follette and Baker Brownell, place such an importance on the neighborhood or the small town.[29] Even cities can develop neighborhoods with a higher degree of autonomy, conscious planning, integration, and social control.[30] Some assistance can come from the giant units of government—the cities, states, and the federal government; in the two-year period ending November, 1951, for example, the Federal Housing and Home Finance Agency had lent communities $25 million for planning local public works projects.[31] Yet the main solution cannot lie with government aid, which should be a result but cannot be a cause. Here is one case in which change requires *demands* from the "grass roots"—however inappropriate that metaphor may be to describe the barren wastelands of the modern city. Neighborhoods cannot be imposed on people; they can only be developed by the people in them. This development requires techniques like the study group, which seems to have worked with considerable success in a number of small Montana towns during an experiment conducted in that state under the supervision of Baker Brownell. On a large scale, one may contrast deadening results of "planning from above" in one of the new towns in England, Stevenage, and the results of "planning from below" in the new town of Peterlee in the Durham area—where, for example, a survey of the local inhabitants was carried out by miners' wives under the direction of a sociologist. One is bureaucratic and hierarchical; the other is based on a high degree of reciprocity.[32] In this case as in others it would be futile to look for a kind of spontaneous mass movement

[28] William Foote Whyte, *Street Corner Society*, University of Chicago Press, Chicago, 1943, p. 256.
[29] Mary Parker Follett, *The New State, Group Organization the Solution of Popular Government*, Longmans, Green and Co., New York, 1918, and Baker Brownell, *op. cit.*
[30] Cf. The Netherlands, Institute for Social Research of the Netherlands' People, Commission on the Distribution of Population, *The Distribution of Population in the Netherlands*, First Report, Part IA, The Hague, 1948, English summary, pp. 87–95.
[31] The New York *Times*, November 4, 1951, Section I, p. 49.
[32] From Robert Bruce Black, "Brave New Britain: The British Town and Country Planning System," unpublished Ph.D. dissertation, Harvard University, Department of Political Economy and Government, 1950; Harold Orlans, *Utopia, Ltd., The Story of the English New Town of Stevenage*, Yale University Press, New Haven, 1953.

of the kind romanticized by Rosa Luxemburg and many other revolutionaries; the revolution necessary to convert cities into integrated neighborhoods requires leaders and organization. But the point is, the leaders must live and work in thousands and thousands of potential neighborhoods in the cities of the United States.

Specific policies or programs can only be the product of far more detailed analyses than can be given in this book. For the development of small-group autonomy, solidarity, and health requires an infinity of policies and programs. First things first. What is of first priority is to reverse the bias of modern times, weaken the influence of the cult of the colossal, and undertake the search for practical means to a vigorous small group.

WAR AND HIERARCHY

These, then, are the broad outlines of an approach that is explored in subsequent chapters. But it is only fair to point out that one remaining factor may largely nullify any significant efforts to decrease the scope of hierarchy in the United States or any other Western country. War certainly—and semi-mobilization possibly—will reduce the scope of the price system, because, for reasons to be explained later, with a high degree of mobilization it is to some extent necessary to substitute centralized for price system allocations. Moreover, war requires such a high degree of coördination of the activities of a nation to the dominant purpose of security or victory that decentralization of decisions to small and somewhat autonomous groups becomes hazardous. Under these conditions, the development of more unified controls in the hands of political leaders—which is stimulated by the needs of mobilization and conducting a war—is likely to go hand in hand with a general weakening in the conditions necessary for polyarchal controls over leaders. The best forecast for a long mobilization is an increase in hierarchy, not a decrease.

10.

Polyarchy:
Control
of Leaders

I. Introduction

POLYARCHY AND THE FIRST PROBLEM OF POLITICS

From about the time of the American Revolution until the First World War the prevailing mood of partisans of democracy was one of unlimited confidence. The "iron law" of oligarchy was intellectually repealed, and political equality was looked upon as certain to prevail in an inevitable victory of democracy over tyranny. Marx and Engels were as much in the grip of this tradition as Lincoln and Gladstone.

There were important critics of this view, yet their impact was slight. But since the First World War, and more notably since the Second, a great tidal shift in attitude by Western intellectuals reflects a new awareness of the strength of tendencies to inequality. Contrast the intellectual mood of today with that of a half-century ago—let us say during the period of the great Liberal reforms in England after the 1906 elections. To be sure there were some, like Dicey, who professed to see in the advance of the welfare state—or socialism, as he called it—a genuine threat to liberty. But it is no great exaggeration to say that the Fabians more nearly reflected the predominant intellectual mood of the day. Shaw, the Webbs, H. G. Wells were the intellectual advance guard; and the great Liberal politicians and administrators, like Balfour, Lloyd George, the young Churchill, and Haldane, were—we can now see—not far behind. The central tenets of that Liberal-Labor creed were two. A larger measure of welfare, security, and equality could and should be extended to the masses by means of government power—an extension which would strengthen, not weaken, the advance to democracy. Only reactionaries and a few anarchists really doubted the validity of this creed. In the United States this intellectual mood and the political forces upholding it were not dominant for another generation, and in France the intellectual and political power of the Popular Front coincided roughly with the reform period of the New Deal in the United States.

It may now be justly charged against those intellectuals that they played down, or even missed, what may well be called the First Problem of Politics. This is the antique and yet ever recurring problem of how citizens can keep their rulers from becoming tyrants. As one looks through the writings of the Fabians and their counterparts in the United States and France, one finds curiously little concern with that problem. Perhaps they believed that it was virtually solved.

The belief that the First Problem of Politics is still unsolved and that those earlier optimists who believed otherwise were quite fundamentally wrong seems to mark off our time from one so shortly past. For now it has become possible to believe that *1984*, if a caricature, is at least a caricature of a quite possible future and, indeed, for much of the earth's surface a quite visible present. One has only to compare the inverted utopias written today with those of the past to realize the void between us and our predecessors; take Orwell's *1984*, or the *Animal Farm*, or Koestler's *The Age of Longing* and compare these with, say, Bellamy's *Looking Backward*.

A few years ago, it was still possible for E. F. M. Durbin to write: "It is . . . important to realize that a growth in the economic power of the State need not compromise our political liberty since it rests in the hands of a democratically elected Parliament, and the guarantee of our freedom remains where it always did, in the *political* constitution and practice of our society."[1] It is not so much that Durbin's statement is wrong; what strikes us today is the inadequacy of the syllogism.

What has brought about this change of mood? One can, of course, hardly underestimate the force of a few anarchists and critics like Orwell or ex-communists like Koestler. *1984* and *Darkness at Noon* have been profoundly influential political tracts. Bertrand de Jouvenal's *Power*[2] has persuasively (if, as we believe, inaccurately) argued the thesis that the whole history of man is one of

---

[1] E. F. M. Durbin, *Problems of Economic Planning*, Routledge and Kegan Paul, Ltd., London, 1949, p. 60. It is only fair to say that Durbin had assayed the political problem much more comprehensively in his *Politics of Democratic Socialism*, G. Routledge and Sons, Ltd., London, 1940.

[2] Bertrand de Jouvenal, *On Power*, New York, The Viking Press, 1949.

the continued growth in control by government. Still, what has happened to generate and give plausibility to views of this kind? Five things, mainly.

First, in the USSR what at one time evidently seemed to many intellectuals a vast step toward social justice, equality, and a new democracy eventuated in rank injustice; incredible inequality of control, status, security, and income; and an arbitrary tyranny of a scope and power probably never before experienced by mankind.

Second, the growth and expansion of dictatorship, not merely in the Soviet Union but in Germany, Italy, Spain, Portugal, Argentina, and its defeat of polyarchy in some of these countries, no longer permits us to believe that democracy is somehow the normal or inevitable condition of men, and tyranny abnormal. Even a left-wing democratic socialist like R. H. S. Crossman now finds it necessary to conclude that:

> Slavery of the acquiescent majority to the ruthless few is the hereditary state of mankind. It is not power itself, but the legitimation of the lust for power, which corrupts absolutely. So, the rulers of the free society must be rendered impotent to indulge their natural instincts by an elaborate system of social indoctrination. The Western tradition has fashioned a breed of political eunuchs, parliamentarians whose aim is no longer to destroy their opponents but to defeat them in argument, no longer to enslave the masses but to serve them responsibly. Democracy of this kind is as unnatural as a well-kept flower bed: totalitarianism as natural as the jungle of weeds and suckers which overrun our garden when we leave it untended for a single season.[3]

No antidemocratic intellectual, neither Pareto, nor Mosca, nor Michels ever put the case more strongly than this representative of English democratic socialism!

Third, the temptations of control in modern society are enormous. Frank Knight once wrote that the probability that the people in control would be individuals who would dislike the possession and exercise of control is on a level with the probability that an extremely tender-hearted person would get the job of whipping master on a slave plantation. In every society there are potential tyrants, and positions of control tend to attract the potential tyrants.

Fourth, the rise of secret police, torture, and the concentration camp as normal instruments of rulership over much of the world

[3] R. H. S. Crossman, "Know Thine Enemy," *The New Statesman and Nation,* April 21, 1951, p. 453.

calls attention to fundamental changes in social technique. In attempting to discover the sociological basis of majority rule, one sociologist has written: "What, finally, is the ultimate ground for the power which the majority exercises? The answer is so deceptively simple as to discourage ready acceptance. It rests in the elemental fact . . . that the majority is stronger than the minority or, in Simmel's words, 'das die Vielen mächtiger sind als die Wenigen.' . . . Given the same organization, the larger number can always control the smaller, can command its services, and secure its compliance."[4] But this statement is no longer valid. Because relatively simple firearms gave supremacy to foot soldiers between the American Revolution and, perhaps, the First World War, it was roughly true during this short historical period that the greater number could, on a showdown, defeat the lesser number; and even if this fact alone could not explain the existence of majority rule, it became evident that majority rule was finally enforceable by the expectation of physical force and severe punishment.[5] But it is no longer true that the majority can bring every minority to heel by the threat of force and punishment. On the contrary, as the history of the past generation has so vividly illustrated, it is now quite possible for small minorities to subjugate large majorities, and to maintain them indefinitely in subjection.[6]

Fifth, from a rare, abnormal, and even extinguishable event war has come to appear as a recurring probability that can only be avoided, in our lifetime at least, by a permanent mobilization of manpower and resources such as, in the immediate past, took place only during periods of war.

In sum, it is now terrifyingly clear that the drive away from equality of control in modern society is extraordinarily powerful. Despite this drive, however, in some societies the democratic goal is still roughly and crudely approximated, in the sense that nonleaders exercise a relatively high degree of control over leaders. The constellation of social processes that makes this possible we call polyarchy. Polyarchy, not democracy, is the actual solution to the

[4] Arnold Bierstadt, "The Sociology of Minorities," *American Sociological Review*, December, 1948, pp. 709–710.

[5] S. B. McKinley, *Democracy and Military Power*, Vanguard Press, New York, 1934.

[6] Karl Mannheim, *Diagnosis of Our Time*, Kegan Paul, Trench, Trubner and Co., Ltd., London, 1943, pp. 2–3; also, Karl Mannheim, *Man and Society in an Age of Reconstruction*, Kegan Paul, Trench, Trubner and Co., Ltd., London, 1940, p. 48.

First Problem of Politics. Like most actual solutions to difficult problems it is untidy and highly imperfect.

DEMOCRACY, POLYARCHY, AND DICTATORSHIP

In order to identify an organization by one of its important components, one can speak of a polyarchal organization, a polyarchal government, or, where the conditions of a society facilitate the operation of a polyarchal government, a polyarchal society, Because of the importance of the "last say" and the importance of government to the "last say," polyarchy in government is, of course, a prerequisite for an approximation of the democratic goal; and it is with polyarchal governments that this chapter is concerned. But all governments, in the broad sense, that are usually called "democratic" are in fact mixtures of hierarchy (particularly in administration), bargaining (particularly in legislation), and polyarchy (particularly in relations between elected leaders and ordinary citizens). Hence in this chapter we are really describing the *polyarchal component* in those governments where it plays a prevailing part; nevertheless, because it is useful and customary to distinguish governments by their prevailing element, it is convenient to refer to some governments as polyarchal governments.

Now if governments were placed on a continuum running from full achievement of democracy to an exclusively unilateral dictatorship, no real-world instance would fit either end of the continuum. Polyarchy and modern dictatorships would both fall a good deal short of the extremes. And they would be closer together than ardent democrats would find comforting.

Yet the difference in positions on the continuum is of crucial significance. The difference is spelled out in a variety of specific consequences—for example, the difference between concentration camps and ordinary prisons, or between 10,000,000 or more prisoners in the USSR and 162,000 in the United States.

POLYARCHY AND ECONOMIZING

But what has polyarchy to do with economizing? In the first place, polyarchy is itself a process for economizing. The American federal budget, for example, has become a decisive influence on stability, size and distribution of incomes, investment, and innovation not only in the United States but all over the world. Secondly, polyarchy is one of the major processes for shaping and changing the methods of economizing in the rest of society; thus the shift from laissez faire to welfare state was brought about largely through polyarchal processes. Thirdly, polyarchy is a means for controlling hierarchy, and hierarchy is an important economizing process. Thus the question of the gains and losses of substituting hierarchy for price system is, in Western polyarchal societies, really a question of substituting economizing decisions made through polyarchy-cum-hierarchy for economizing decisions made through a price system.

The question "Is planning compatible with democracy?" our readers will recognize by now is virtually without meaning. But behind the ill-phrased query lies a proper concern with the probable effects of various techniques for economizing on the conditions necessary to polyarchy. Pretty clearly, to understand these effects is a task of a large part of this book.

To perform that task we must isolate as carefully as possible the necessary conditions for polyarchy. If these can be isolated, the effects of the politico economic techniques analyzed in earlier and later chapters can be estimated with more precision. Hence the function of this chapter is primarily to isolate these conditions and in the course of so doing to relate them to some of the common arguments about "economic planning" in a democracy.

II. Characteristics and Conditions of Polyarchy

CHARACTERISTICS

So far the term "polyarchy" has not been given much operational significance. It is very easy to say that the USSR is not polyarchy and the United States, Great Britain, Canada, New Zealand, Australia, France, Norway, Sweden, Denmark, Mexico, and Israel (to take some important representative examples) are. For it is correct to say that in these latter countries non-leaders exercise a high degree of control over governmental leaders, and in the USSR they do not. But to make "a high degree of control" meaningful some additional criteria are needed. The most important ones are these:

1. Most adults in the organization have the opportunity to vote in elections with no significant rewards and penalties directly attached either to the act of voting or to the choice among candidates.

2. In elections the vote of each member has about the same weight.

3. Non-elected officials are subordinate to elected leaders in making organization policy. That is, when they so wish, elected leaders can have the last word on policy with non-elected officials.

4. Elected leaders in turn are subordinate to non-leaders, in the sense that those in office will be displaced by alternative leaders in a peaceful and relatively prompt manner whenever a greater number of voters cast their votes for alternative leaders than for those in office.

5. Adults in the organization have available to them several alternative sources of information, including some that are not under significant unilateral control by government leaders. "Available" in this context means only that members who wish to do so can utilize these sources without incurring penalties initiated by government leaders or their subordinates.

6. Members of the organization who accept these rules have an opportunity, either directly or through delegates, to offer rival policies and candidates without severe penalties for their doing so.

One could debate many of the terms in each of these criteria. Political theorists do so endlessly.[7] How many adults is "most"? What are "severe" penalties? How equally weighted must votes be to have "about the same weight"? For example, does the federal system in the United States permit this country to qualify fully as a polyarchy? How soon is "relatively prompt"? Just how subordinate must non-elected officials be? No doubt further operational criteria could be set up for each of these short-hand symbols, but the important quarrels over the application of the criteria will arise over factual disputes, not over definitional questions. If the authors' view of the facts—a view shared by most noncommunist antifascists—is correct, then clearly the Soviet Union and Spain lack all the characteristics of polyarchy; so do most large American corporations; and many trade unions and some boss-ridden municipalities lack several important ones.

Each of the criteria can therefore be expressed in terms of a continuum. For example, because the voters of Nevada elect the same number of Senators as all the voters of New York State, the

---

[7] The extraordinary difficulty of handling terms related to democracy and polyarchy is vividly illustrated in "Analytical Survey of Agreements and Disagreements," by Arne Naess and Stein Rokkan, based on the replies of 100 scholars to a UNESCO questionnaire on the meaning of democracy, in Richard McKeon (ed.), *Democracy in a World of Tensions: A Symposium Prepared by UNESCO,* University of Chicago Press, Chicago, 1951, pp. 447 ff.

American national government meets the second criterion of polyarchy less fully than does, say, Great Britain. Moreover, a process
is polyarchal only with respect to a given membership. Before
women were permitted to vote in France, French national government was a polyarchy for men only. In the United States, the South
as a whole has never been a polyarchy for Negroes or indeed even
for many poor whites. But for registered Democrats in the South
the party primary is a polyarchal process.

POLYARCHY IN SMALL GROUPS

What processes are prerequisite to organizations with the characteristics listed above?

TWO CONFLICTING TENDENCIES.   An examination of small
groups will help in answering the question.[8] In small groups, where
dicisions can be made through face-to-face relations, it is relatively
easy to see two distinct and partly counterbalancing tendencies at
work. First, there is for several reasons a visible tendency away from
equality of control to inequality of control. Roberto Michels, generalizing from rather larger groups, the European socialist parties,
tagged this tendency the "iron law of oligarchy." Indeed, the tendency is so plainly visible that observers like Michels failed to pay
much attention to a counteracting second tendency away from
purely unilateral control which we might call the "counteracting
law of reciprocity."

The basic reasons for this second tendency have already been
examined in our chapter on control, where it was explained why no
organizations ever operate exclusively through the unilateral use
of command, and manipulation of field, but invariably create at
least some relations of reciprocity. We shall not repeat that discussion here; but it is worth emphasizing again that Michels—and

[8] For example, William Foote Whyte, *Street Corner Society*, University of
Chicago Press, Chicago, 1943; George C. Homans, *The Human Group*, Harcourt,
Brace and Co., New York, 1950; Gunnar Landtman, *The Origin of the Inequality
of the Social Classes*, University of Chicago Press, Chicago, 1938; Alexander H.
Leighton, *The Governing of Men*, Princeton University Press, Princeton, 1946;
Richard Thurnwald, *Die Menschliche Gesellschaft*, Vierter Band, *Werden, Wandel, und Gestaltung von Staat und Kultur im Lichte Der Völkerforschung*,
Walter de Gruyter and Co., Berlin and Leipzig, 1935, pp. 14 ff., 86 ff. Cf. also the
insightful hypotheses of Alexander Rüstow. *Ortsbestimmung der Gegenwart, Eine
universalgeschichtliche Kulturkritik*, Erster Band, *Ursprung der Herrschaft*, Eugen
Rentch Verlag, Erlenbach-Zurich, 1950, Parts I and II, on the transition from
small-group life to the larger, class-structured society in the development of civilization.

other observers, like Mosca, who fix upon the theory of a ruling class—have selected out one set of tendencies and substantially ignored another.

One must admit, however, that in small groups as well as in large there is wide variation in the extent to which one tendency or the other prevails. If the first tendency prevailed exclusively, every organization would be a pure unilateral dictatorship; if the second, a pure democracy. A polyarchy is a special combination of both, in which the tendency to reciprocity sufficiently counteracts the tendency to unilateral control so that the characteristics cited earlier in this section can exist.

Hence two further questions present themselves. First, what are the principle conditions in small groups that create the tendency away from equality of control? Second, what are the conditions in small groups necessary to strengthen the tendency toward reciprocity sufficiently so that an organization has the characteristics of polyarchy?

CONDITIONS FOR TENDENCIES TOWARD INEQUALITY.   As for the first question, in any given situation individuals cannot exert equal control unless they are all equal in relevant knowledge, skills, opportunities, and activity or unless inequalities in these four items accidentally cancel out one another. Of course people rarely are equal in all four respects and it is quite fortuitous if inequalities cancel out. Even if one turns to extremely simple primitive societies where an extraordinary degree of social and political equality sometimes prevails, one finds differences in knowledge, skill, opportunities, and activities creating differences in control. And if one takes slightly more complex societies, the differences are magnified. Even in the simplest societies, there are differences in physique, ability, and personality. There are good warriors and poor warriors; some men are eloquent, some are not. There are men—and women. There are persons "suffering from physical or mental disability, idlers who are good for nothing, widowers who have not married again and therefore have no one to help them in their work, braggarts who bore the others, etc.—all these are 'down a little bit.'"[9] Out of all this, some men gain increased status and control; typically they constitute the council of elders. A man who gains status and control because of his prowess, eloquence, successes, or judgment

[9] Landtman, *op. cit.*, pp. 8–9.

is often automatically coöpted into the council of elders, as among the Kiwai Papuans or the Ashantis; as his status and control decline, he drops out of the council.[10] Thus even in the highly egalitarian societies characteristic of many primitive folk differences in personality, goals, and abilities lead to inequalities of political knowledge, skill, and activity; these in turn lead to inequalities of control.

In the simpler primitive societies like the Kiwai Papuans the consequences of these differences are greatly vitiated by a number of conditions. Except between the sexes, division of labor is slight. There is little disparity in the distribution of property. Every man does the same work and no one employs servants. Joint ownership is common. The supply of fertile land is unlimited. Prestige is acquired by sharing, not monopolizing, the results of hunting and fishing. Status is not easily inherited, because it rests not on birth but upon personal prowess or ability. Oppression is difficult because malcontents can and do hive off and form new communities of their own.[11]

But in more complicated small societies the differences in personality, goals, and abilities that lead to differences in political knowledge, skill, and interest inevitably lead to a disparity in political opportunities. With increased division of labor the opportunities and profitability of exploitation and inequality are—as compared with the simpler primitive societies—increased. For example, among hunters and fishers the requirements of a nomadic existence render slavery rather unproductive; out of eighty-three hunting and fishing tribes examined by one student, in sixty-five there were no slaves. On the other hand, among agricultural tribes slavery tends to be productive and therefore more widely used.[12] Division of labor also introduces differences in status and opportunities. Occupations that require a special aptitude and training or, as with the warrior, admired qualities like courage and stoicism tend to give extra status to the craft. Other work is despised, and those who perform it sink to the bottom of the social scale; oddly enough, butchers, musicians, and blacksmiths are generally despised among uncivilized and semi-civilized people. Differences such as these help to create hereditary status and opportunities. Increased wealth due to the division of labor also makes it possible for those with the greater control and

[10] *Ibid.*, pp. 310–311.
[11] *Ibid.*, pp. 5–8, 319–320.
[12] H. J. Nieboer, *Slavery as an Industrial System*, M. Nijhoff, The Hague, 1900, pp. 267, 295; quoted in Landtman, *op. cit.*, pp. 230–231.

status to reward themselves—or to be rewarded by the tribe out of gratitude and respect. Then, too, the sons of influential elders are better trained for leadership and more readily accepted by the tribe. And priesthoods develop, surrounded by an aura of mystery and power in propitiating the local gods.[13]

It is difficult to imagine any way in which any small society is likely to be organized that will not lead to *some* differential political opportunities because of accidents of birth, some inherited or acquired wealth or status, education, experience, and even propinquity or accidental accessibility to techniques of control. Add to these the inherent differences in personality, goals, and abilities that lead to differences in political knowledge, skill, and interest. It follows that complete equality of control is highly improbable under any conditions likely to exist among human beings.

No doubt we have labored the point unduly. Most people would accept it without quibble. But the point is worth laboring if it helps one to remember that to maintain the conditions even of polyarchy is a constant battle. Equality of control is an unstable equilibrium. Differences in knowledge, skill, opportunity and activity create inequalities of control; these in turn tend to generate further differences, which create further inequalities. Hence the struggle to maintain a polyarchal organization is never won; indeed, it is always on the verge of being lost.

TWO KEY CONDITIONS FOR TENDENCIES TO RECIPROCITY. But if the battle is never won, neither is it always lost. Polyarchal organizations do survive in small groups and in large. What are the conditions in small groups that counteract the tendencies toward inequality of control and strengthen reciprocity?

One solution is somehow to maintain an extremely simple society in which extraordinarily powerful social indoctrination imposes a widely shared desire for uniformity and a relentless taboo against differences in control. That such a society can exist is suggested by Ruth Benedict's well-known description of the Zuñi Indians of the American Southwest.[14]

This is not, however, the central solution typical of Western societies; moreover, it is evidently so out of reach of modern nation-states that it will be ignored in the discussion that follows. Not

[13] Landtman, *op. cit., passim.*
[14] Ruth Benedict, *Patterns of Culture,* Houghton Mifflin Co., Boston, 1934.

that the Zuñi and Occidental approaches are mutually exclusive, for some indoctrination against certain kinds of inequalities of control is a prerequisite to polyarchy, as will be shown in a moment. But the overall solution is quite different.

The other alternative, then, is to maintain two key conditions. First, leaders must win their control by competing with one another for the support of non-leaders. Political competition may take either blunt or subtle forms, and one must not look for the complex paraphernalia of political campaigns in every polyarchal organization. Second, non-leaders must have an opportunity to switch their support away from the incumbent leaders to their rivals.

Given these two conditions, leaders will be highly responsive to the preferences of non-leaders or lose their control. To put it differently, these two conditions help to establish reciprocal and to weaken unilateral controls.[15]

Moreover, the presence of these conditions means that two or more hierarchical organizations can actually contribute to the operation of a polyarchal organization. Political parties, as Michels observed, tend to be oligarchical—or as we would say, hierarchical. But two or more political parties competing with one another for the votes of citizens can make a polyarchy.

The presence of these two conditions forces a balance between the "iron law" of oligarchy and the counteracting "law" of reciprocity. Take the street-corner gangs studied by Whyte, for example. These were so strongly hierarchical that it would be stretching the term to call them polyarchies. Nevertheless, because the two key conditions were to some extent present, a notable element of reciprocity appeared in the relations between the leader of a gang and his followers. The leader was distinctly limited in what he could do; if he failed to satisfy the preferences of his members he lost his control over them. A corner-boy leader often lost his position, for example, because his boys discovered he was pocketing the money given to the club by some politician.[16] Or if the

---

[15] For somewhat different discussions of the role of political competition (and in large groups), see Joseph A. Schumpeter, *Capitalism, Socialism and Democracy* (2nd ed.), Harper & Brothers, New York, 1947, and James Burnham, *The Machiavellians*, The John Day Co., New York, 1943. Schumpeter argued that political competition guaranteed only a choice among leaders, not among policies. Thus in his view the significance of political competition for translating citizen preferences into public policy was negligible. This assumption is false unless one can show that choice among rival leaders is completely divorced from preferences as to policy. Schumpeter did not show this, nor in our view could he.

[16] William Foote Whyte, *op. cit.*, pp. 217–218.

corner-boy leader himself went into politics and, after mobilizing his friends behind him, dropped out of the contest to support another politician, "his followers feel that he has 'sold out,' and it is difficult for him to continue as a political figure of any prominence. He may be able to retain some personal following if he is able to do favors for the boys, but he will no longer have a chance to win an election."[17] The limits of leadership are also indicated by the willingness of the corner boys to sell their vote to the politician—and then vote as they pleased. As the supporter of one candidate, Fiumara, said to the boys: "Don't be chumps. Take their dough. You can use it, but then go in and vote for Fiumara."[18] And the leader must remain a member of the group; if he moves up in the hierarchy, his direct influence on the group declines, and some other leader takes over. If the old leader wishes to retain indirect influence over the group he must maintain cordial relations with the new leaders.[19]

Under these conditions, then, the leader must be responsive to his followers. He cannot "deliver" their support to any and every goal he happens to prefer. His power is restricted by intangible but effective limits.

But the "iron law" of oligarchy is not repealed; it is only weakened. This is the other facet of polyarchy. For if polyarchy is distinguished from hierarchy by the high degree of control non-leaders have over leaders, it is distinguished from democracy by the fact that leaders by no means share equal control over policy with non-leaders. Even the fact that an organization is small and intimate is no guarantee that it is egalitarian. Within limits, Doc, one of the Cornerville leaders, could always get his gang to do what he wanted: to bowl, or go to the settlement house for meetings, or build a camp, or support him in politics. Yet he was highly skillful —at times downright brilliant—in calculating how far he could change their initial preferences and how far he had to give in to them.

It is now possible to see more clearly the true bearing of voluntary organizations on freedom. It is much more difficult for leaders to tyrannize over members of their organizations if these members can withdraw and join another organization with substantially equivalent benefits. In this situation the tyrannical leader will be-

[17] *Ibid.*, p. 209.
[18] *Ibid.*, p. 244.
[19] *Ibid.*, p. 214.

come a leader without a following. Thus there is a core of sound common sense in the liberal preference for voluntary organizations as against the corporatist preference for compulsory ones. For a compulsory organization significantly limits the ease with which members can rid themselves of an unpopular leader.

POLYARCHAL GOVERNMENTS

How does it happen that a number of nation-states of the modern world manage to "solve" the First Problem of Politics? How are polyarchal governments maintained?

Our examination of the conditions of polyarchy in small groups gives a clue. For the same two key conditions that counteract inequality exist in societies with polyarchal governments. First, despite the rise of dictatorships elsewhere, in these countries there appears to be no significant diminution in competition among politicians for citizen support. On the contrary, in the United States, for example, competition by political leaders for citizen support is probably as strong as it has ever been. Second, citizens still have an opportunity to switch their support away from leaders in office to their rivals. Hence if political leaders are not highly responsive to non-leaders, they lose their control.

As we shall see in a moment, the responsiveness of leaders in polyarchies is a good deal more complicated than a simple function of their expectation of votes in the next election. But, given the preconditions to be examined below, there can be no doubt that this expectation keeps them highly responsive, sometimes astonishingly so. The fear that a bloc of voters will support the opposition in the next election if not given at least some of what it wants; the desire to forestall criticism; the realization that a legislative alliance might crumble if a leader chooses one policy rather than another; the willingness to listen to pressure groups; the abruptness with which some obscure matter suddenly becomes high policy because a group here or there is making a row over it; the sensitivity to charges and the need for countercharges—all are clearly evident in the behavior of polyarchal leaders and all are testimony to the need such leaders feel to respond to ordinary citizens and subleaders. As one British writer has put it:

The people of this country control their government not by the way they voted "last time" but by the way they may vote "next time."

Moreover the electorate is an extraordinarily sensitive umpire. The vast mass of voters are convinced Labor or Conservative supporters roughly equal in numbers. It is the "floating vote" which by swinging its support turns one government out and installs its rivals. Now this is only some 3 or 4 percent of the total electorate, i.e., some 2000 voters in the average constituency. Furthermore, no government knows quite who these people are! It may be the "housewife," the cyclists or the motorists. Every minority complaint must be wet-nursed. Consequently every decision of the Cabinet is a calculated risk.[20]

Many antidemocratic critics dislike polyarchy precisely because of this feature; and many others who appear to believe in the democratic goal are decidedly unhappy because "politics" (meaning competitive politics) plays such a significant part in governmental decisions. But one cannot have it both ways. Competitive politics may displease the fastidious but polyarchy could not survive without it.

So long as the two key conditions can exist, polyarchy can exist. But why do the key conditions exist? The two key conditions of polyarchy obviously do not exist in a vacuum, nor are they simply accidental. On the contrary, they in turn are dependent on still other conditions. It is to these preconditions that we now turn.

[20] S. E. Finer, *A Primer of Public Administration*, Frederick Muller, Ltd., London, 1950, p. 32.

II.

*Polyarchy: Control
of
Leaders* (Continued)

What, then, are the preconditions of polyarchy and how do these bear on the major problems of rational social action in economic affairs? That is the problem of this chapter.

I. The Preconditions of Polyarchy

SOCIAL INDOCTRINATION

Polyarchy requires social indoctrination and habituation in the process of polyarchy and the desirability of democracy. In a letter to F. A. Hayek, commenting on *Road to Serfdom* which Hayek had recently published and suggesting that he had perhaps slightly confused "the moral and material issues," Keynes wrote: "Dangerous acts can be done safely in a community which thinks and feels rightly, which would be the way to hell if they were executed by those who think and feel wrongly."[1] In this fashion Keynes underscored the need for social indoctrination if polyarchy is to be maintained.

If one examines the operation of polyarchy and imaginatively penetrates the obvious appearances of free speech, the operation of the press, parties, elections, and defeated governments voluntarily abdicating office, at last one discovers an underlying factor on which this entire structure depends. It is the consciences, norms, and habits of the people in the society, leaders and non-leaders alike. For it is these that define what uses of control are legitimate and what are illegitimate; what behavior is acceptable and what is not. And if these definitions, commands, permissions, and approvals prescribed by the norms, habits, and consciences of the people are not appropriate to polyarchy, then no written constitutions, no guaran-

[1] Roy F. Harrod, *Life of John Maynard Keynes*, Harcourt, Brace and Co., New York, 1951, p. 437.

tees, no prescribed codes, no laws will achieve it. To be sure, constitutional symbols and prescriptions are helpful. But if political leaders and non-leaders alike were not indoctrinated to believe deeply, for example, that it is profoundly immoral for a defeated government to attempt to stay in office, then no constitutional prohibition against their staying would be workable. Indeed, to endure through periods of crisis, decade after decade, from one generation to the next, the norms and habits must be built into the very depths of the unconscious so that the temptations to avoid fundamental requirements hardly rise into question. A nation that begins seriously to discuss whether there will ever be another election is not likely to have one.

How the appropriate consciences, norms, and habits have developed in some societies is a complex and little understood matter of history. Three observations may be made, however. First, the appropriate consciences, norms, and habits have been widely developed in some countries but evidently not in others. Second, their development in the past has been largely unconscious, unintentional, unplanned. Third, what in the past was unconscious, unintentional, and unplanned can to some extent now be done consciously, intentionally, and planfully; and to some extent it is. This last point we shall take up again in a later chapter.

Whatever the reasons, in some societies behavior conducive to reciprocal control tends to be rewarded; and at least some kinds of behavior conducive to unilateral control tend to be penalized. In thousands of ways, some crude, some subtle, some deliberate, some unconscious, the behavior and the conscience of youth are shaped into a mold that, on the whole, condemns behavior that seems to violate the pattern of polyarchal control in government. The individual is indoctrinated with myths, belief systems—the miranda and credenda of power, Merriam calls them—and admiration for and legitimation of a certain structure of control.

A society employs many techniques: hero worship (what immense political consequences inhere in the fact that a nation venerates the mythical qualities of a Lincoln or Jefferson, or a Gladstone and a Burke, rather than those of, say, a Bismarck and a Frederick the Great!); history; story; ceremonials; parades; oratory; music. In modern times, the public-school system, particularly in the United States, has become a powerful vehicle of social indoctrination in the myths necessary to polyarchy. The theater, movies, books, magazines, newspapers pour upon the individual a steady stream of admonition serving to distinguish acceptable from unacceptable political behavior. In the ubiquitous voluntary clubs characteristic of the United States youth and adults learn what political behavior is taboo, what is approved and rewarded. In these ways individuals are indoctrinated with an unreasoned inner conviction of the fitness and rightness—in a word, the legitimacy—of polyarchal systems.[2]

INDOCTRINATION OF LEADERS. Political leaders are products of this process. The process may sometimes be inadequate. But in three ways it tends to turn the aspirations of leaders away from unilateral control to reciprocity. First, *it inhibits certain types of behavior*, and even certain "evil thoughts." It is unlikely that any recent American President even in his moments of bitterest struggle with Congress has ever given an instant's conscious thought to, say, military suppression of the Congress. In England Professor Laski may have contemplated the possibility that a Labor victory might require the suppression of the Tories, but it seems unlikely that any party leader on either side is ever permitted by his conscience to contemplate this prospect with equanimity. And this circumstance is what makes suppression unnecessary.

To be sure, thwarted and inhibited impulses are usually not killed off; rationalizations are vital in canalizing the use of control in acceptable ways. For the indoctrination process also works in this second way: *it permits certain approved substitute behavior*. The President whose unconscious wish might be to shoot all Congressmen is left free to slay them over the microphone, or by manipulating patronage.

And in the third place, social indoctrination teaches political leaders to *expect punishment* if they seriously violate the norms of polyarchy. This punishment may be either in the form of defeat in their attempt to "misuse" control, or, if they are successful, in the form of hatred, contempt, and loathing. Would any normal prod-

---

[2] That polyarchy—or indeed any stable structure of control—must rest upon successful social indoctrination is now hardly contested. See, for example, Charles E. Merriam, *Systematic Politics*, University of Chicago Press, Chicago, 1945, p. 195; also, Charles E. Merriam, *Political Power, Its Composition and Incidence*, McGraw-Hill Book Co., New York, 1934; R. M. MacIver, *The Web of Government*, The Macmillan Company, New York, 1947, pp. 4–5, 175; Bertrand de Jouvenal, *On Power*, The Viking Press, New York, 1949, pp. 194–195; Alexander Leighton, *The Governing of Men*, Princeton University Press, Princeton, 1946, pp. 288–290.

uct of the process of indoctrination in the United States relish the thought of being known as "the President who destroyed American democracy"?

INDOCTRINATION OF LEADERS IS NOT ENOUGH. Nevertheless, for several reasons it would be folly to rely exclusively upon the training, habits, and expectations of the top leaders in office. In the first place, social indoctrination inculcates inconsistent goals; it does not produce a wholly unified belief system, integrated, at peace with itself, and unreservedly endorsing polyarchy.[3] In the United States the Lincoln myth teaches us to venerate him not only because of his rejection of the temptations of power but also because of his willingness to assume almost dictatorial control to maintain a mystical entity called "the Union." On the whole, too, American political myths give approval to strong leaders who flout the Congress in the name of "the people."

But even more important are some of the norms indoctrinated, not to maintain polyarchy, but to maintain "capitalism." The two bodies of norms are sometimes inconsistent; which state of affairs perhaps helps to explain the passivity of many citizens toward a political boss who runs his political machine quite frankly as a moneymaking business enterprise. The beliefs of polyarchy necessarily must emphasize the virtues of certain constitutional means; but some of the beliefs of capitalism emphasize the virtues of certain results—whatever the means. "Contemporary American culture," it has been observed, "appears to approximate the polar type in which great emphasis upon certain success-goals occurs without equivalent emphasis upon institutional means."[4] Thus some political leaders may be more indoctrinated with that aspect of American capitalist beliefs which emphasizes success at any price, and less with the American democratic beliefs.

Furthermore, even if the myths were not internally inconsistent, not every one is indoctrinated with the same norms and habits. Probably every society has its deviants. In primitive societies the social deviants are probably fewer, more easily identified by the members, more easily controlled by social subordination, special roles, ostracism, or death. There may be what Kardiner calls a

---

[3] Sebastian de Grazia, *The Political Community*, University of Chicago Press, Chicago, 1948.

[4] Robert K. Merton, *Social Theory and Social Structure*, Free Press, Glencoe, Ill., 1949, p. 129.

"basic" personality type in these communities, and although deviations exist within the basic type, there may be relatively few who display a fundamentally different personality type. But whatever may be true of primitive tribes, in a large and diverse society like the United States, it is unlikely that a basic or normal personality type is predominant.[5] Thus social deviants are less easy to identify and to control. Some observers have proposed that political candidates undergo psychological testing to control this matter; but this does not seem to be a solution likely to be adopted in the immediate future.

Moreover, most of us are social deviants at times, and all of us perhaps are potentially so, given the appropriate circumstances. The transformation of a leader's goals and preferences through the alchemy of power is so commonplace that, even if it remains something of an enigma how and why power does corrupt, one can scarcely contest the fact that with some people it does. Presumably what happens, in these cases, is that the leader in power learns new behavior, new habits, new wants, new rewards.

Thus Robespierre first comes to the National Assembly with the most humane postulates of Rousseau as his code; a man of powerful moral conscience and unimpeachable democratic convictions, he stands firmly against all flights the Assembly would make toward dictatorship. But between the beginning of the Revolution and Thermidor, the village lawyer whose integrity and self-restraint are there rewarded by the approval of self and others is gradually transformed by a new situation where unilateral control is ever more rewarding, and the threat of a decline in control creates more and more inner tensions and anxieties. So first he opposes, then he tolerates, and at last he supports the Terror.[6]

Finally, polyarchies must from time to time face crises that require something close to dictatorship. The capacity of a polyarchy to survive is tested less by its action in normal periods than by what happens in these crises. Britain, Norway, and the United

[5] We leave open here the question of whether there is a specific "democratic personality," as Karl Mannheim and others have argued; cf. Karl Mannheim, *Freedom, Power and Democratic Planning*, Oxford University Press, New York, 1950. That there is a personality predisposed to antidemocratic views and activities now seems well established. Cf. especially T. W. Adorno, Else Frenkel-Brunswik, Daniel J. Levinson, and Sanford R. Nevitt, *The Authoritarian Personality*, Harper & Brothers, New York, 1950, and Leo Lowenthal and Norbert Guterman, *Prophets of Deceit*, Harper & Brothers, New York, 1949.

[6] Hilaire Belloc, *Robespierre*, Charles Scribner's Sons, New York, 1902.

States, for example, have survived them substantially intact; Weimar Germany was unable to do so. Crises require vigorous leaders; opportunities increase for dictatorial types to rise into control; the rewards of unilateral control increase; even the best democrat is surrounded with temptations and rationalizations for increasing and maintaining his unilateral controls.

INDOCTRINATION OF NON-LEADERS NECESSARY. For all these reasons no polyarchy is likely to endure if it relies exclusively on the habits and ingrained self-restraint of its top leaders. Non-leaders and subordinate leaders must also be indoctrinated. For if the men around a potential tyrant refuse to coöperate, tyranny becomes impossible.

In sum, the process of social indoctrination and habituation need not and indeed in a large and complex society probably cannot prevent every potential tyrant from getting into a position of control; what it can and must do is to indoctrinate a sufficient number among the political leaders, the military, the administrators, the police, and the great mass of ordinary citizens[7] so that the potential tyrant cannot secure the coöperation he needs. Against the ambition of those who are not potential tyrants, the interplay between inhibitions, substitutions, and expectations of failure will be enough. Against the ambitions of those who are potential tyrants, the final guardian of polyarchy is the norms and habits of those who are not.

INDOCTRINATION AND THE GROWTH OF HIERARCHY IN THE ECONOMY. Many of the classic controversies over the proper functions of price system, collective choice, and government action have assumed a close connection between social indoctrination in democratic norms and the constellation of economizing devices used in the society. Actually the relation appears to be an indeterminate one, and most generalizations are bound to be overhasty.

One common allegation is that the extension of government hierarchies in economizing will undermine the habits, norms, and consciences necessary to polyarchy. Thus Frank Knight once wrote:

[7] Here as elsewhere in this book we do not use the term "ordinary" citizens with any pejorative implications. The authors of this book are ordinary citizens and so are most of the people they know.

It seems to me certain: (a) that the governing personnel in a so-cialistic state would be in a position to perpetuate themselves in power if they wished to do so; (b) that they would be compelled to assume permanence of tenure and freedom from the necessity of seeking frequent re-election, as a condition of administering the economic life of a modern nation, even if they did not wish to do so; and (c) that they would wish to do so—that we cannot reasonably imagine political power on the scale involved falling into the hands of persons of whom this would not be true.[8]

Generalizations such as these, however, seem to be derived al-most entirely from a priori reasoning and the rather irrelevant ex-perience of nations that were never deeply indoctrinated in demo-cratic beliefs. The bulk of the evidence appears to indicate that in Western polyarchal societies it is not the extension of government hierarchy that limits the political process but the political process that limits the extension of government hierarchy.

That is to say, whenever attempts at planning through hier-archy begin to seem oppressive to enough people, in countries with strong traditions of polyarchy citizens employ the political process to call a halt, and even to throw out the politicians in office. In the American elections of 1946, enough voters were evidently frustrated by wartime and postwar controls to break the sixteen-year succession of Democratic electoral victories. In New Zealand, elections in 1949 banished a Labor government that had been in office for fourteen years; in 1951 the voters again returned a non-Labor government. In Australia, elections in 1949 dismissed a Labor government that had held office for ten years, and denied them office once more in 1951. In 1950, a British election reduced the Labor party's majority in the House of Commons almost to the vanishing point; and a year later Labor lost its parliamentary ma-jority.

The signs of oppression, of breakdown in polyarchy are hard to find. Have opposition and criticism been weakened in Norway, Sweden, Denmark, and Holland by government hierarchies? In all these countries the government's electoral majority is usually quite slim. Hence the activities of these governments do not have to seem oppressive to a very large percentage of the electorate to cause a shift to the opposition party, and defeat the party in office. The Re-

[8] Frank H. Knight, *Freedom and Reform*, Harper & Brothers, New York, 1947, p. 139 n.

publican landslide in the American Presidential election of 1952 scarcely supports the proposition that the hierarchical controls of the welfare state inevitably destroy the capacity of citizens to displace their leaders.

Can it be argued that in the United States and other countries the politically active are being seduced by hierarchy to a point where the major parties must pledge further hierarchical extensions of government into economic life? If this were the case, then of course merely to vote one party out of office would not represent a check to hierarchy, and the process might continue until polyarchy is undermined. That this is a possibility implicit in modern industrial society can hardly be gainsaid. But in so far as this is true, it is worth recalling our point that the grand alternative "isms" do not seem to contain a solution. One would need to search for solutions outside the setting of a complex industrial society—and yet, as we have argued, no one can predict the consequences of a shift to a new society drastically different from existing reality.

In any case, however, the proposition is as difficult to establish as it is to disprove. What is the evidence that the extension of hierarchy is seducing citizens into acceptance of norms and habits inconsistent with polyarchy? It is not self-evident that in showing a preference for hierarchy citizens are acting irrationally even where democratic goals are involved, or that a majority of the politically active no longer wish to stop the extension of hierarchy even when its extension interferes with polyarchy. For as we have already shown, hierarchy is a highly rational process for social action and under certain conditions it can be controlled. Hence through the stumbling incrementalism of polyarchy a new and relatively more rational balance of hierarchy within polyarchy may be evolving. No one can say with confidence whether this is the case, but most of this book is devoted to showing both the broad lines along which it might develop and its preconditions.

BASIC AGREEMENT

Polyarchy also requires agreement on those basic issues and those methods that facilitate peaceful competition and the opportunity for non-leaders to switch their support to rival leaders. If citizens do not agree that polyarchy is desirable, polyarchy cannot *continue* to operate. If citizens of a country do not agree in wanting polyarchy, they cannot be made to have it by hierarchy. To be sure, the example of Turkey suggests that citizens can sometimes be induced by hierarchy to agree to *want* polyarchy; but until it is wanted it cannot function. If an overwhelming majority of active voters in the United States should genuinely agree in preferring dictatorship to polyarchy, there would be no way to maintain polyarchy and at the same time prevent an overwhelming majority from voting dictatorial leaders into Congress and the White House.

AGREEMENT ON WHAT?   Agreement is necessary both on basic processes and on basic policies. Social indoctrination is of course vital in order to create this agreement on basic processes and basic policies.

As to basic processes, agreement must create what Mosca called a "high level of juridical defense" for electoral competition. It must produce widely held norms, enforceable through operating legal codes, covering at least four points without which electoral competition would be a farce. First, there must be agreement that political leaders can legitimately acquire office only by winning a plurality of votes following an election campaign, and that they must peaceably leave office when they have lost an election. This norm is so deeply ingrained in members of polyarchal societies that it is easy to lose sight of the enormous importance of this system of automatically conferring legitimacy by a ritual of adding up scratches on pieces of paper put into boxes by ordinary citizens. Modern dictatorships reveal a keen sense of this legitimizing process in their fantastic efforts to enact the ritual without giving it the operational consequences it has in polyarchies.

Second, there must be agreement that most adults have a legal right to participate in elections without expectation of rewards or penalties administered for the mere act of voting or choice of candidate. In the United States for a generation after the Constitutional Convention, limitations on suffrage made government the prerogative more nearly of a propertied oligarchy than of "most adults." Yet here the tradition was substantially settled, despite the fulminations first of the Federalists and then of the Whigs, by the time Jackson left the White House. At least it has never seriously been challenged since, except of course in the South where white oligarchy—although declining—still prevails. Even in the North, bribery, petty patronage, and vote frauds are common enough in elections to indicate that if the norm of universal adult suffrage is substantially unchallenged, the norm guaranteeing the opportunity to participate in elections without expectations of rewards or penalties administered for the mere act of voting is not yet completely established. But the norm is settled enough to create a scandal and public furor if any *national* official attempts to violate it.

Third, there must be agreement that rival politicians should have a legally enforceable opportunity to organize themselves compactly for the purpose of winning votes, which is to say, an opportunity for political parties. In both England and the United States the legitimacy of political parties seems to have been publicly accepted about the same time—somewhere between 1800 and 1832. Since that time, parties have become both legitimized and institutionalized, and suppression of any party accepting the norms we have been discussing would be tantamount to revolution.

Fourth, there must be agreement that citizens should have the legally enforceable opportunity to criticize the government. This guarantee is probably important, less because it permits the great mass of people to bring criticism directly to bear on their government than because it permits small, attentive groups—what one observer has called attentive elites[9]—to bring their more or less instructed and skillful criticism to bear on government. As with most other aspects of modern life, even public criticism is a specialized occupation; exposure and criticism of what the government is doing falls to reporters, editors, columnists, pressure-group bureaucracies, Congressional committees, Presidential commissions, party organs, specialized citizen groups, and the like. Even the attentive elites are often highly specialized; a bill to lower barriers to wool imports will not activate the same attentive elites as one to lower barriers to immigration.

Sometimes it is assumed that agreement on these norms, which define the basic methods of polyarchy, is enough. This assumption is probably valid, but it conceals a further prerequisite: that there be agreement on basic policy. Unfortunately it is difficult to say what "agreement on basic policy" must include. But the more violently people disagree about basic policy, the less likely it is that they will continue to accept the basic methods of polyarchy. If a minority comes to believe that the policies of a majority will forever destroy their opportunity to attain their most important goals, their agreement on the methods of polyarchy is certain to be strained.

"All, too, will bear in mind this sacred principle," Jefferson

[9] Gabriel A. Almond, *The American People and Foreign Policy*, Harcourt, Brace and Co., New York, 1950.

said in his first inaugural, "that though *the will of the majority is in all cases to prevail,* that will, to be rightful, must be reasonable." (Our italics.) Yet if it is "unreasonable" to a large minority, "the will of the majority" is unlikely to prevail. For certainly there is some point beyond which even the most convinced democrat is unlikely to abide by the policies of polyarchal leaders, even if he concedes that the leaders speak for a majority.

Before the Civil War, when the politically active in the South became convinced that a northern majority would ultimately destroy slavery if it had its way, Calhoun developed in the doctrine of concurrent majorities the view that no important national governmental policy should be adopted without the concurrence of all the important sectional minorities. His was a rather abstract formulation of the proposition that no polyarchy can survive if the policies of the majority so greatly provoke some large minority that it comes to prefer violent opposition to peaceful acquiescence. When that doctrine was rejected, Civil War was inevitable. One does not need to accept either the constitutional theory or the specific application of the doctrine proposed by Calhoun to agree that, as a statement of social fact and a prediction, Calhoun's view was essentially correct.

The more highly ranked one's preferences for polyarchy, presumably the further one will go in accepting repugnant policies. But only if one has *no* goals higher than polyarchy would he always prefer the success of polyarchy to its destruction. Such people are probably rare; at the very least, they are unlikely to be such an overwhelming majority in any country that the methods of polyarchy can long continue despite wide differences in views on truly crucial issues.

WHO MUST AGREE? Who must agree sufficiently on basic methods and basic policies so that political competition and citizen choice among rival leaders is a tolerable system for making decisions? All leaders? All governmental leaders? Some non-leaders? All citizens?

Pretty clearly the answer is that at any given time only the politically active need to agree. Agreement by the politically passive at any given moment is unnecessary. This is, of course, only slightly more than a tautology. To strengthen, support, or undermine polyarchy, a person must take some politically relevant action. If his response to a policy or a procedure he dislikes is always merely to ignore it or kick his dog, his disagreement will have no effect on the methods of polyarchy.

Like most simple answers, this one conceals some vital qualifications, including the facts that a "high" level of political activity is itself a precondition for polyarchy and that individuals presently inactive may subsequently become politically active. But for the moment we postpone a discussion of these points and let stand the rather formalistic and not very illuminating statement that a precondition for polyarchy is agreement among the politically active and the potentially active.

HOW MUCH AGREEMENT?   How much agreement among the politically active and potentially active on basic methods and policies is necessary to maintain political competition and the opportunity of citizens to switch their support to rival leaders? Unfortunately there is no really satisfactory way to answer this question. At least two complex variables are involved—the number of people holding disagreeing views and the intensity with which they hold these views. The difficulties of measuring opinion and the lack of useful historical data mean that any answer is certain to be circular or based on inadequate evidence.

By definition the American Civil War indicated insufficient agreement. France's history of civil wars, revolutions, and coups indicate that the bare minimum of agreement has often been lacking, and the Fourth Republic has come perilously close to insufficient agreement. The Weimar Republic foundered for lack of agreement, and so did the democratic revolution in Russia in 1917. The stability of Great Britain has been taken to indicate relatively great agreement; the peacefulness of social change in New Zealand (at least until recently) is often cited also as an instance of high agreement. Since the Civil War, agreement in the United States has evidently been sufficient for polyarchy; but some observers believe that agreement here is rather lower than in some of the other English-speaking polyarchies.

What are the operational criteria for determining whether sufficient agreement exists on methods and policies among the politically active and potentially active? Some indexes are useful. For example:

  1. Homogeneity of views on formal constitutional theory. Thus in Great Britain agreement on constitutional theory—how basic

political institutions work and how they ought to work—seems, at least to many American observers, to be considerably greater than in the United States. Both countries enjoy much higher agreement than France, where the political spectrum runs from preferences for dictatorship, through approval of monarchy, to demands for a Presidential system, to a strengthening of the cabinet, to a desire for legislative supremacy.

2. The proportion of political prisoners in the total population, the amount of violence in political affairs, the extent to which command is used in enforcing government policy. However, cultural differences make this index somewhat unreliable.

3. Diversity in the proposals and implicit goals of the major parties.

4. The stability or discontinuity of government policy with changing administrations.

These are no more than impressionistic but common sense tests. Applied against the decade preceding the American Civil War, they seem to be validated. Wide discrepancies did develop in formal constitutional theory, political violence did seem to increase (Bloody Kansas, Sumner's brutal beating, John Brown), disagreement over the question of slavery in western territories visibly mounted, and government policy shifted abruptly (Dred Scott, the Compromise of 1850, the compromise of 1854, Lincoln's policy on the western territories). Conversely applied to recent British experience, not excluding the 1945 elections which followed six years of war mobilization and coalition government, the tests confirm common impressions of high homogeneity—but only, perhaps, because these are the indexes most observers have used to arrive at that impression in the first place.

This is a largely unexplored area, and there are serious difficulties in exploring it. Nevertheless, in discussing certain problems of rational social action it will be necessary to make some assumptions about the state of agreement and the effect of it on polyarchy. The best we can do in such cases is to make our assumptions as explicit as possible.

RATIONAL SOCIAL ACTION AND "OVERRIDING PURPOSE." At this point it may be desirable to lay the ghost of an old proposition about "planning." It is frequently said that a government or a society cannot "plan" unless it has some "overriding purpose" to which all others are subordinated. Hence, it is said, "democratic" societies can "plan" in war but not in peace. For only in war can enough individuals agree on a single "overriding purpose." Peacetime planning would therefore require dictatorship to enforce agreement. By now we need scarcely remind our readers that this statement, like so many others on the subject of planning, has almost no meaning. Rational social action does not require a single overriding purpose; on the contrary, it usually requires a carefully thought-out adjustment of potentially or actually conflicting actions aimed at a variety of purposes. It is probably not even true that economizing entirely through government hierarchies requires a single overriding purpose. In any case, economizing through various kinds of price system evidently does not, and this is as much a part of rational social action as economizing through government hierarchies.

RATIONAL SOCIAL ACTION AND STABLE POLICIES.   An argument to be taken somewhat more seriously is the charge that government policies in polyarchies must inherently be too unstable to make much rational action possible, at least through government and in economic affairs. Political competition and the resulting alternation of parties in polyarchies means, it is argued, that policies will be unstable. Hence future policy will always be so indeterminate that government planning is all but useless.

This argument rests upon two misconceptions. First, it is not true that to be effective government economic planning always requires forecasts for a longer period than the intervals between elections. Even if it were true that parties with substantially different policies alternate in office every four or five years, much economic planning could be accomplished in the intervals. Indeed, on many subjects forecasts of much longer than a year are highly unreliable. Too many additional factors besides elections can be so indeterminate as to make long-range calculations irrational on a variety of important questions such as balance of payments, international trade, the number of unemployed, amount of savings, investment, new construction, and the like.

Second, it is not even true that in polyarchies the alternation of parties leads to great instability of policy. On the contrary; once enacted, many basic policies are highly stable. The idea that party alternation leads to instability of basic policy is mostly a myth constructed by imagining what polyarchies might be like rather than by observing what they actually are. In Great Britain the overwhelming bulk of the Labor party's reforms were accepted by the Conservatives when they came into power. In New Zealand and Australia the defeat of labor governments was not followed by abrupt shifts in policy. In the United States the changes of the New Deal and Fair Deal, like those of Wilson's New Freedom, have come to be substantially accepted by both parties.

Moreover, it is not even true that frequent party alternation is a necessary feature of polyarchies; in the United States, for example, there has tended to be a "normal" majority party and a "normal" minority party; the former is usually in office most of the time until there is a tidal shift in voting habits. Jeffersonian Democracy, Jacksonian Democracy, McKinley Republicanism, and Roosevelt Democracy are all examples of this tendency.

This tendency of policies once enacted to persevere is no accident in polyarchies. It is related to the process itself. For if there is sufficient agreement on processes and policies to operate polyarchy, there is likely to be enough agreement to make for considerable stability in policy. Conversely, if alternating parties really do adopt widely different policies, agreement is so weak that polyarchy itself is endangered. For so long as the great bulk of politically active and potentially active citizens more or less agree on basic policies, political competition (most vividly in a two-party system) will drive the major parties toward the center. Neither party can win if its program is very much different from that of the other. Hence a high degree of continuity will result; there may be breaks in the continuity, if the center of public opinion shifts abruptly or if there are cumulative changes which, for some reason, neither party exploits; but these take place rather infrequently.

If, on the other hand, the great bulk of politically active citizens are so sharply divided that political competition drives the major parties toward the extremes rather than toward the center, then polyarchy itself is in danger. Roughly, this is what happened in the United States in the decade before the Civil War. In this situation, long-range planning (for example, how to settle the western territories) is futile; the basic policies of one administration will be undone by the next. But this is not a necessary result of polyarchy; indeed, it is a prelude to disaster.

It is true, however, that sometimes basic policies are enacted over which the "center" is sharply divided and likely to be so for a

302   POLITICS, ECONOMICS, AND WELFARE

considerable period, even in polyarchies where on most other issues
the "center" is more or less agreed. In such cases basic policy is
bound to be unstable, and planning beyond the next election is
futile. The nationalization of steel may have been such a case in
Great Britain, although it may also have been nothing more than a
case of Conservative miscalculation about the amount of popular
opposition to steel nationalization. Or perhaps it was not a basic issue; if steel is not to remain nationalized it is to be comprehensively
regulated in any case. Whatever the circumstance, the *most* politically active were so sharply divided that neither a Labor nor a
Conservative government could plan realistically for the future.

SOCIAL PLURALISM

*Polyarchy requires a considerable degree of social pluralism—
that is, a diversity of social organizations with a large measure of
autonomy with respect to one another.* Here again one immediately
runs into frustrating problems of measurement. No one can say with
much precision how much social pluralism there needs to be, how
many social organizations per capita, how autonomous they must
be. But the general principle is clear. Social pluralism exists in a
society to the extent that there exist a number of different organizations through which control is exerted and over which no unified
body of leaders exerts control.

A very high degree of social pluralism does not necessarily
mean a very low state of agreement; this is a possible consequence
but not an inevitable one. Social pluralism is probably greater in
the United States than in France, but agreement is also higher. In
the United States a more uniform social indoctrination sufficiently
permeates diverse groups so that they can exist with a large measure
of agreement on basic method and policy; in France conflicting
political norms are indoctrinated in a smaller number of diverse
groups and the result is a low state of agreement.

The United States between 1820 and 1850 was an extreme case
of social pluralism combined with a relatively high state of agreement. Political alliances represented shifting combinations of leaders
responsive to a wide diversity of social organizations: large southern
slaveholders, small slaveholders, small southern farmers without
slaves, western grain growers, farmers of the Ohio Valley, financiers, debtors, importers and exporters, eastern merchants, east coast
manufacturers, artisans in eastern cities, Congregationalists, Bap-

tists, Methodists, Episcopalians—to name a few. Diversity was so great that these groups were even internally pluralistic.[10] Political skill consisted of facilitating combinations among those groups big enough to win at the polls, or at least powerful enough to prevent any serious threat to their goals. This high degree of social pluralism did not produce civil war. On the contrary, the Civil War came about when, after 1850, there was a temporary and limited consolidation of these groups into several large alliances between which there was much more serious disagreement than there had been before.

WHY PLURALISM IS NECESSARY. Reasoning from what they conceived to be the experience of very small, face-to-face organizations, many people have been blinded to the importance of social pluralism in large societies. Early democratic ideologues like Rousseau were downright hostile to social pluralism; and no doubt this is one of the reasons political parties and caucuses initially seemed reprehensible to many observers. From thinking about small face-to-face organizations, Rousseau could regard the individual himself as the unit; he could plausibly argue that subgroup loyalties were unnecessary as a protection against the community and undesirable as a threat to agreement. Hence the idea of a society composed of "factions" is the very opposite of most utopias.[11] That Rousseau, like most utopians, had precious little empirical information to go on permitted him to slur over the powerful subgroup loyalties operating even in most small organizations—for example, the strength of "family" loyalties in small egalitarian tribes.[12]

Why is some degree of social pluralism a necessary condition for polyarchy, at least in the modern nation-state? Whatever the case may be in small organizations, in large areas some degree of social pluralism is necessary to polyarchy, for in at least five ways it limits the capacity of officeholders to extend their control over ordinary citizens.

First, social pluralism means the existence of social organiza-

[10] See Frederick J. Turner, *The United States 1830–1850*, Henry Holt and Co., New York, 1935.

[11] "Il n'y a guère de dissidents dans les sociétés utopiennes. Pas ou peu d'opposition, de partis qui se combattent." Raymond Ruyer, *L'Utopie et les utopies*, Presses Universitaires de France, Paris, 1950, p. 44.

[12] Cf. Richard Thurnwald, *Werden, Wandel und Gestaltung von Staat und Kultur*, in *Die Menschliche Gesellschaft*, Vierter Band, Walter de Gruyter and Co., Berlin and Leipzig, 1945, pp. 14 et seq.

tions, organizational loyalties, organizational leaders; in union there is strength. A lone citizen speaking only for himself can often be intimidated by officials; but a spokesman for a body of citizens is less easily cowed. If the official has sanctions, so does the organization leader: publicity, votes, and even the threat of resistance. And besides there is a kind of psychological multiplier effect to organization membership; the knowledge that one is not alone often helps reinforce one's courage and determination. (Refugees from totalitarian rule report that one of the most unnerving features of totalitarian society is the feeling of loneliness in the individual who may secretly be opposed to the regime.) Then, too, organization leaders are likely to have more status than ordinary citizens; they are more likely to move easily in official circles, to command the respect and deference of officials.

Second, social pluralism facilitates competition by insuring the existence of rival leaders with differing loyalties and support. Thus the possibility that officeholders will become uncontrollable is reduced; for officeholders are only one group of leaders, or, more likely, themselves consist of many competing leaders. To wipe out other leaders, revolutionaries must first possess the loyalty and support of more people than they are likely to win over in a pluralistic society; diversified organizational loyalties inhibit this kind of loyalty.

Third, social pluralism facilitates the rise of political leaders whose main skill is negotiating settlements among conflicting social organizations. Thus the whole cast of the political elites is modified by pluralism; the fanatic, the Messianic type, the leader whose aim is to consolidate the supremacy of some small group tend to trip themselves up on the barrier of groups and group loyalties. The Federalists, concerned with maintaining the domination of eastern financial and commercial interests, were unable to compete with the Jeffersonian alliance; they died out as a party. All important American politicians have been excellent negotiators of group alliances, from Jefferson and Jackson to Roosevelt and Truman. Nor is it any different in England: Peel, Disraeli, Gladstone, Asquith, Lloyd George, Baldwin, Churchill, Attlee all show to a marked degree the capacity to ride herd on an unwieldy political alliance. Much of the energy of political elites is expended simply in the effort to hold the alliance together. Incautious moves to extend one's control may bring about defections to the other side.

Fourth, social pluralism increases the probability that one is simultaneously a member of more than one social organization; hence action by a leader against what seems to be an enemy organization may in fact strike against his own alliance. In Jackson's day this phenomenon existed in almost laboratory purity. One might be a resident of the Ohio Valley and therefore tied to the South by the need to keep open the Mississippi, but increasingly tied to the Northeast by railroads and canals. Of Connecticut stock, he might have married a girl whose parents came out of Virginia and Tennessee. A Congregationalist, he may have had little sympathy with the popishness of southern Episcopalianism. A grain grower, he lobbied for railways and canals to transport his products to the East. His children may have moved west—or gone east for their education. Thus during this period, until slavery in the western territories became a fundamentally divisive issue after 1850, the diversity of memberships characteristic of any particular individual made it necessary for political leaders to proceed cautiously in a spirit of moderation and compromise. Purists may find the results distressingly untidy; but one result was to force American political leaders to perfect the art of working out not merely an agreement among members of their own alliance but also an agreement with the opposition. Henry Clay and Stephen Douglas are only extreme examples of the political craft as it must be practiced in a pluralistic society.

Fifth, social pluralism has some important consequences for information and communication. It increases the probability that alternative sources of information not under direct government control will be technically available to citizens. It is true, of course, that many citizens expose themselves to information that confirms their own norms and those of the group.[13] But as we said earlier, effective criticism of policy or political leaders is a somewhat specialized function; and those who specialize in criticism and communication *can* make use of alternative sources of information.

Communication of politically relevant information in a large and heterogeneous polyarchy like the United States is an exceedingly complex matter, and any simplified description of it is likely to be wrong. One aspect of the process, however, is undoubtedly the way in which group leaders in a pluralistic society act as a focus of

[13] Many studies of communication have confirmed this fact; cf., for example, Paul Lazarsfeld, Bernard Berelson, and Hazel Gaudet, *The People's Choice*, Duell, Sloan and Pearce, New York, 1944.

information, criticism, and communication. The group leader is the sensitive point of contact: with members of his own group, with other leaders at his own level, with higher leaders. A variety of leaders sensitive to the desires of non-leaders in their group, the limits of their own control, the coöperativeness of allied group leaders, and the responsiveness of more powerful leaders bring their specialized influence to bear on other leaders in behalf of group goals, and at the same time restrain their own group within the bounds set by the leaders' frequently more realistic calculations of what is possible. Hence, a great deal of politically relevant communication is of a specialized kind, moving up, down, and across a complex chain of leaders.

In these ways social pluralism develops a complex distribution of control. It does not eliminate hierarchical organizations but it makes polyarchal government possible. Ordinary citizens control their immediate leaders and are controlled by them. These leaders in turn control other leaders and are controlled by them. Hence a society of reciprocal relationships exists to control government policy. A national political alliance is therefore a vast and slightly shaky enterprise, not a monolith but a pile of billiard balls held together with a poor grade of paste.

SOCIAL PLURALISM AND MASS DEMOCRACY.   Many critics of mass democracy, like Ortega y Gasset, Wilhelm Röpke, and Bertrand de Jouvenal, have argued that "mass democracy" carries in itself the seeds of its own destruction because the creed of mass democracy leads inevitably to the destruction of social pluralism and so, by leaving the individual citizen helpless before the powerful official, paves the way for tyranny. The argument is usually coupled with criticism of the "leveling tendencies" of government control over economic life (in "mass democracies," at any rate); for, the argument goes, this must lead to a destruction of the autonomy of social groups and hence to the overwhelming supremacy of government officials who oppress the people in the name of the people. Indeed, De Jouvenal argues that absolutist political leaders inevitably exploit the aims of egalitarianism in order to destroy the intervening layers of group leaders and so enable absolutism to triumph. The two Horrible Examples, of course, are the Bolsheviks and the Jacobins, who, by destroying all preëxisting powerful social organizations in order to achieve an ideal equality, instead produced the

Terror, Thermidor, and Napoleon because there was no longer any leadership to stand up against those who controlled the government.

If it were true that the wide expansion of political equality, the sensitivity of leaders to the desires of ordinary citizens, and a widespread concern for subjective equality meant a destruction of social pluralism, then undoubtedly "mass democracy" would destroy itself. But is social pluralism really being destroyed in contemporary welfare states? There is little evidence that this is the case. Perhaps the fear of "mass democracy" is peculiarly European; for the United States has been a mass democracy since Jackson's day—in the sense that political leaders compete for the support of all strata of the population and therefore attempt to satisfy "mass" tastes, desires, and preferences. To Americans, then, "mass democracy" is simply the "democracy" they have known for a century and a quarter.

Moreover, an examination of the polyarchal societies in which welfare states have developed does not confirm the decline in social pluralism. Swedish society, for example, is highly pluralistic, and the important social groups such as employers' federations, trade unions, and coöperatives have actually become legitimized.[14] The New Deal and the Fair Deal in the United States have evidently vastly strengthened social pluralism by fostering and helping to convey legitimacy to great labor and farm organizations. Probably the number of politically relevant social organizations has multiplied greatly since Jackson's time, including the Farm Bureau Federation, Grange, Farmers' Union, American Federation of Labor, Congress of Industrial Organizations, National Association of Manufacturers, Chamber of Commerce, American Medical Association, American Bar Association, National Association of Real Estate Boards, American Legion, Veterans of Foreign Wars, National Rivers and Harbors Congress, the regions, the states, the cities and towns, and thousands of other social organizations.

Indeed, as we shall see in later chapters, social pluralism is so great in the United States that, combined with the constitutional structure, the extent of bargaining among diverse social groups in making government policy is a dominant feature of our political system.

Finally, to some extent the very conception of modern "mass

[14] Gunnar Heckscher, "Pluralist Democracy, The Swedish Experience," *Social Research*, December, 1948, pp. 418–461.

society" as lacking in groups appears to stem from an excessively hasty view of the superficial appearances of modern urban life. Systematic studies do not bear out the assertion that small groups have dissolved in the caldron of the great society. Whyte found, for example, that a slum district like Cornerville—which to the casual middle-class observer from outside might look entirely unorganized, structureless and amorphous—actually "has a complex and well-established organization of its own. . . . In every group there was a hierarchical structure of social relations binding the individuals to one another. . . ."[15] There is no evidence that people who grow up in slums are more lonely and unorganized than people who grow up in small towns. Certainly the Corner boys were not. If anything, as Homans points out, "many slums marked by high rates of crime . . . are over-organized rather than underorganized."[16] Perhaps observers like Röpke and Ortega y Gasset have mistaken social conflict for social disorganization or *anomie*.

SOCIAL AND CONSTITUTIONAL SEPARATION OF POWERS. Social pluralism, then, is a form of "social separation of powers." Like most American writers, a European like Röpke concerned with "mass democracy" not only stresses the importance of social pluralism but also lauds the "wisdom of the fathers of the American Constitution" who "clearly foresaw the danger of democratic tyranny by the majority" and so introduced "the American Constitution with its complicated system of 'checks and balances' "; Röpke regards this as "an excellent example of how, with some intelligence, one can avoid jumping from the frying pan into the fire."[17] But it follows from what we have said about social pluralism that (1) if *social* checks and balances do not exist, then prescribed constitutional checks and balances are hardly sufficient to prevent tyranny by political leaders (whether in the name of the majority or minority does not matter); and (2) if *social* checks and balances do exist, then prescribed constitutional checks may not be so desirable a means to polyarchy as Röpke seems to think. Since the end of the eighteenth century, Great Britain has managed to get along without them. And by any test known to us, it would be impossible for any-

[15] W. F. Whyte, *Street Corner Society*, University of Chicago Press, Chicago, 1943, p. viii.

[16] George C. Homans, *The Human Group*, Harcourt, Brace and Co., New York, 1950, pp. 336–337.

[17] Wilhelm Röpke, *The Social Crisis of Our Time*, University of Chicago Press, Chicago, 1950, p. 97.

one to show that polyarchy works better in the United States than
in Great Britain.

SOCIAL PLURALISM AND BARGAINING. From what we have
said it is clear that a considerable measure of bargaining is an inherent aspect of polyarchy. For the resolution of group conflict and the
search for agreement is largely carried on by bargaining. Because of
the importance of bargaining not only to polyarchy but as a general
social process it is discussed in the following two chapters.

POLITICAL ACTIVITY

Polyarchy also requires a relatively high degree of political
activity. That is, enough people must participate in the governmental process so that political leaders compete for the support of
a large and more or less representative cross section of the population.

Admittedly this is a rather imprecise formulation; in what follows we shall attempt to refine it a little. But one cannot be very
precise. Both the United States and New Zealand are polyarchies.
Yet in the United States on the average about 60 percent of the national electorate participate in elections, whereas in New Zealand
more than 80 percent regularly participate and sometimes more
than 90 percent do so. In practice, moreover, even in one country
the extent of political activity varies enormously from one policy-
making situation to another, from complete apathy to widespread
activity. Then, too, political "activity" is itself a difficult kind of
behavior to measure. The number of variables is large, including
the number of people involved, the intensity with which they pursue their goals, the type of activity they indulge in, the political
position and location of those who are active, their status, degree of
control over others, and so on.

THE LOW LEVEL OF POLITICAL ACTIVITY. It would be very
useful, although extremely difficult, to develop even a highly oversimplified classification and tabulation of policy decisions in the
United States according to the extent of political activity involved.
Such an oversimplified classification would have to show the approximate percentage of the electorate that was "active" on a given
issue and a crude distribution of their expressed preferences, with
similar categories for elected government leaders, non-elected gov-

ernment leaders, and other leaders. No one has ever prepared one, and the task is too gigantic for us to have done ourselves. Without having done it, we nevertheless think it all but certain that one conclusion would emerge from any such effort. In a very large number of important governmental decisions only a small minority of the electorate expresses or apparently even possesses any definite preferences at all among the alternatives in dispute. And it is equally safe to say that very little specific national policy is ever a product of an expressed preference for a specific alternative by an overwhelming majority of the electorate.

If, for example, the number of people who significantly influenced the decision to go ahead with the hydrogen bomb were assembled in one place, it would hardly fill a conference room.[18] To take some other recent decisions, how many people indicated their preferences in a politically relevant way when governmental leaders: decided to contract with large corporations for operating the atomic energy installations?[19] legislated against imports of European cheese and other agricultural products?[20] refused for the umpteenth time to approve the St. Lawrence Seaway project?[21] passed legislation setting up the Council of Economic Advisors?[22] agreed on the Pick-Sloan plan for the Missouri Valley?[23] Each of these decisions was the product of a tiny minority.

How many people ever bring pressure to bear on their representatives in Congress to act one way or another? In a national sample examined by Julian Woodward and Elmo Roper, only 13 percent said they had written or talked at least once in the past year to a Congressman or other public official to let him know what the respondent wanted done about a public issue, and only 7 percent had done so two or more times. Only 11 percent had worked for the election of a political candidate in the last four years, and only 7

[18] Robert A. Dahl and Ralph S. Brown, Jr., *Domestic Control of Atomic Energy*, Social Science Research Council Pamphlet 8, New York, 1951.
[19] *Ibid.*
[20] See Hans Landsberg, "The Role of Cheese in Our Foreign Policy," *The Reporter*, May 27, 1952, pp. 32–34. See also E. E. Schattschneider, *Politics, Pressures, and the Tariff*, Prentice-Hall, New York, 1935.
[21] The legislative history and background have been discussed by Jack B. Schmetterer, "St. Lawrence Seaway Project: A Study of Pressure Groups," senior essay submitted to the Political Science Department of Yale University, 1952.
[22] Stephen Bailey, *Congress Makes a Law*, Columbia University Press, New York, 1950.
[23] See U.S. Commission on Organization of the Executive Branch of the Government, Task Force Report on *Natural Resources* (Appendix L), U.S. Government Printing Office, Washington, January, 1949, pp. 107–148.

percent had contributed money to a party or a candidate in the last four years.[24]

AMBIGUOUS AND CONFLICTING PREFERENCES. Moreover, human beings have many sorts of preferences. For example, it would be instructive to locate preferences along six continua like these:

influenced by informed knowledge of consequences	reflecting ignorance of consequences
high in rank[25]	low in rank
intense[25]	apathetic
stable	transitory
broad (multi-goal)	narrow (single-goal)
influenced by identifications with many people ("altruistic")	influenced by identifications with few people ("selfish")

Obviously many combinations are possible and probably many different combinations of preferences influence policy in polyarchies. But one conclusion is reasonably sure. It is inevitable in a large polyarchy that many important policy decisions reflect preferences lo-

[24] Julian L. Woodward and Elmo Roper, "Political Activity of American Citizens," *American Political Science Review,* December, 1950, Table II, p. 874. An earlier poll taken by Gallup (see American Institute of Public Opinion Poll, September 24, 1949) showed the following: To the question, "Have you ever written or wired your Congressman or Senator in Washington?" the response was:

By Occupation	Yes	No	By Education	Yes	No
Prof. and business	33%	67%	College	39%	61%
White collar	20	80	High school	21	79
Farmers	17	83	Grammar school	11	89
Manual workers	12	88			

[25] These are not necessarily identical pairs. One may rank polyarchy as more important than profit derived from the sale of blue cheese, and in a clear case of conflict one would choose polyarchy over profits. But so long as these do not conflict, one may feel intensely about the profits of the blue cheese industry and apathetic about polyarchy.

cated on the right end of most or all of these possible continua. And undoubtedly, too, policy that reflects one set of preferences of an individual may conflict with another set. He may approve of policies that accord with preferences that are relatively low in rank, intense, and transitory but conflict with some of his own highly ranked preferences that are stable but happen not to be activated and hence are preferences about which he is, at the moment, apathetic.

In practice, then, the democratic goal that governmental decisions should accord with the preferences of the greater number of adults in the society is extraordinarily difficult to approximate, and rarely, if ever, is it closely approximated. For the greater number of people often do not have definite preferences on a given issue; or when they do, often they do not act on them; or their preferences are often so ambiguous and conflicting that one set of "preferences of the greater number" violates another set of "preferences of the greater number" which for some reason were not acted on.

THE LEVEL OF ACTIVITY REQUIRED.   This discrepancy between polyarchy and democracy arouses anxieties among those who wish to approximate democracy more closely, and rightly so. Keeping this fact in mind, let us suggest some general lines of approach to the question of the level of political activity required as a precondition for polyarchy.

A considerable measure of political inactivity is not *by itself* a sign that the democratic goal is not being roughly approximated by a polyarchy. For example, if voting drops off after the introduction of a city-manager system, the reason *may* be that the city manager is so responsive to the greater number that he is solving many of the problems which, because they had hitherto gone unsolved, had stirred up political action. (But conversely it may also be that many citizens now feel that political leadership is out of their orbit of control, and, although frustrated, they simply give up the effort to control their leaders.)

The question, then, is not so much whether citizens are active but whether they have the opportunity to exert control through activity when they wish to do so. To take a purely abstract and unreal situation, if every citizen *could* vote for rival leaders in every election and *would* do so if existing leaders dissatisfied him, and if existing leaders knew this to be so, then a high degree of political inactivity might only mean that existing leaders were in fact powerfully controlled by citizens in a variety of subtle ways: through a basic agreement on values and techniques, through information communicated by a small number of group leaders or representative citizens, and through leaders' expectations of defeat if they failed to choose policies preferred by a majority of citizens.

The opportunity to exert control through elections and other forms of political activity, however, is never equally distributed. Voting studies and opinion polls indicate that higher-income people tend to be more politically active than lower-income people, and the better educated more than the poorly educated.[26] Moreover, because campaigns are exceedingly costly, the wealthier a person is, the more strategic his position for bringing pressure to bear on politicians; hence even if in elections the wealthy few cannot always defeat the many with low incomes, a single wealthy man can make his preferences count for considerably more in making government policy than a single poor man.

Therefore the problem is not so much one of insuring that every citizen is politically active on every issue as it is one of insuring that all citizens have approximately equal opportunity to act, using "opportunity" in a realistic rather than legalistic sense. If all citizens have an approximately equal opportunity to act, there is a high probability that those who do act will be roughly representative of those who do not. In this case a polyarchy would possess in effect two stages of indirect representation: through the prescribed

[26] In the Woodward and Roper study, *op. cit.*, it was shown that only 12 percent of the persons of the "D" or low economic level are politically active as against 69 percent of the "A's" or highest economic level; 36 percent of the "A's" were "very active" as against 3 percent of the "D's"; 34 percent of executives and 31 percent of professional people were "very active" as compared with 11 percent for farmers, 6 percent for laboring people, and 5 percent for Negroes; 24 percent of the college educated were "very active" as against 5 percent of those with only grade-school education. See Table IV, p. 877. The following table based on Warner and Lunt's study of "Yankee City" is also highly revealing (see William Lloyd Warner and Paul S. Lunt, *The Social Life of a Modern Community* [Yankee City Series, vol. 1], Yale University Press, New Haven, 1941, pp. 88, 369–372):

	Upper		Middle		Lower	
	Upper-Upper	Lower-Upper	Upper-Middle	Lower-Middle	Upper-Lower	Lower-Lower
% of total population	1.44	1.56	10.22	28.12	32.00	25.22
% of total voters	1.25	1.61	14.11	34.34	34.19	14.49
Offices in city government	2.30	3.70	19.10	34.50	35.30	5.10
(1) high control	6.10	8.20	34.70	36.70	14.30	0
(2) mediate control	0	3.20	25.00	46.80	25.00	0
(3) subordinates	0	0	1.80	25.50	61.80	10.90

elections to public office and, below these, through the operating official "elections" for members of the politically active. Probably something like this procedure does happen in polyarchies.

Equal opportunity to act is not, however, a product merely of legal rights. It is a product of a variety of factors that make for differences in understanding the key points in the political process, access to them, methods of exploiting this access, optimism and buoyancy about the prospect of success, and willingness to act.[27] Some of these factors probably cannot be rationally influenced given the present state of knowledge and techniques. Three that to some extent can are income, wealth, and education. A fourth that may become important as knowledge increases is personality. Each of these is discussed at various points in this book, and we shall say something more about income and political activity in a moment.

Nevertheless, many policy decisions cannot actually reflect any specific preferences of the greater number. About the most that can be said for polyarchy is that, if the opportunities for political action are kept open to a representative section of the adult population, specific policies will rarely violate highly ranked, intense, stable, and relatively broad preferences of the greater number for a longer period than about the interval between elections. That is, a very great deal of government policy is bound to reflect the specific preferences of small minorities rather than majorities. But so long as the opportunity for political action is kept open to the greater number, such policies will be determined within broad and often vague limits set by widely shared norms and the expectations of policy makers that they will activate the greater number against them whenever, in placating minorities, they exceed the boundaries set by the highly ranked, intense, and stable preferences of the greater number.

This is to put the matter negatively. Stated positively, politicians compete for office, search out issues, capitalize on current frustrations, and initiate criticism, debate, legislation, and administrative action in order to give their constituents what they seem to want. The politician maintains a sensitive listening post; a small rustle among his constituents often makes a big noise in his office. Communication is difficult and some preferences are more easily activated than others; but it is to the advantage of the political leader to

    [27] David Truman, *The Governmental Process*, Alfred A. Knopf, New York, 1951, has made "access" the center of his explanation of differences of control in making government policy.

discover and support what a majority of his politically active constituents want and can achieve through governmental action. No other group of individuals is so completely dedicated to that task.

POLITICAL ACTIVITY AND INCOME EQUALITY. As noted, political activity and control are closely correlated with income, education, and status.[28] They are probably also dependent on other variables—personality and intelligence factors—about which little is known.[29] These little-known variables may in turn affect income, education, and through them status. Certainly there is little reason to suppose that approximate income equality would produce approximately equal political activity and control.

Nevertheless, as was shown in an earlier chapter, income is a a crucial factor. It heavily influences education and status (particularly in the United States), and through these and its own weight it influences control. When it is remembered that a campaign for a Congressional seat can easily cost $15,000–25,000 and a Senatorial campaign can cost half a million dollars or more, it is not difficult to see why "money talks."[30] Thus a high degree of income equality is a prerequisite for a high degree of political equality.

CIRCULATION

Polyarchy also requires that the principal limit on entrance into a position of political leadership must be the inability to win elections. Recruitment, that is to say, must not be significantly limited by the unilateral control of existing political leaders. In modern times Vilfredo Pareto and Gaetano Mosca have emphasized the importance of the "circulation of elites"—although they were professedly describing not simply political elites in polyarchies but all stable ruling classes. Circulation means that the political elites constantly renew themselves by recruiting new members from in-

[28] Cf. Woodward and Roper, *op. cit.*, Table IV, p. 877; see footnote 45, *supra.*
[29] Cf. David Riesman and Nathan Glazer, "Criteria for Public Apathy," in Alvin W. Gouldner (ed.), *Studies in Leadership: Leadership and Democratic Action*, Harper & Brothers, New York, 1950, pp. 505–559.
[30] In 1949 "*The New York Times* estimated that if the previous year was any guide, the two Senatorial candidates [in New York State] and their supporting organizations would spend more than $1 million in the election effort. There is no way of estimating exactly how much was spent to re-elect Herbert Lehman as United States Senator in 1950. His own organization . . . spent $170,805." Stephen K. Bailey and Howard D. Samuel, *Congress at Work*, Henry Holt and Co., New York, 1952, p. 23. On the costs of a Congressman's campaign, see *ibid.*, pp. 42–59; and cf. V. O. Key, Jr., *Southern Politics in State and Nation*, Alfred A. Knopf, New York, 1949, pp. 467–468.

316 POLITICS, ECONOMICS, AND WELFARE

dividuals and groups not hitherto included. The preceding four conditions and the one that follows do, as a by-product, stimulate circulation.

Although relatively easy circulation into the political elites is probably a necessary condition for polyarchy, it is far from being a sufficient condition. Modern dictatorships, in both Germany and Russia, have also relied heavily on circulation; so one cannot say that circulation is peculiarly a requirement of polyarchy. But it does accomplish three purposes vital to polyarchy. (1) It inhibits those outside the leader group from seeking to control government by revolutionary means. (2) It secures the representation of hitherto unrepresented preferences. (3) And it facilitates the social indoctrination of political leaders.

A look at English and American history will illustrate these points. With perhaps one or two exceptions, such as the Puritan Revolution, what strikes one in both countries is the fact that, on the one hand, circulation was always sufficiently easy so that the political leaders usually included all other important leader groups, and, on the other, circulation was gradual rather than abrupt. The first point meant that no great discrepancies were ever permitted to develop between those who had control outside government but not control in government; hence there was little ground for revolution. The second meant that political leadership was never swamped by newcomers; hence the old leaders could indoctrinate the newcomers gradually with the doctrines appropriate to their tasks.

Students of English political mores have commonly noted that the British aristocracy has been renewing itself for centuries.[31] It is less commonly remembered that the American experience was somewhat similar, although the transition to polyarchy, when it came, was a little more abrupt—yet infinitely less abrupt than in France, where the Jacobins attempted, and of course failed, to accomplish in three years what in this country required almost two centuries and in England almost three. For a century and a half before the American Revolution a relatively small group, an aristocracy in all but name, had struggled in each of the colonies to wrest increasing control from the royal governor—save in Rhode Island and Connecticut where this battle was won by charters that permitted an elected governor. The franchise was narrow and lim-

[31] Eg., Roy Lewis and Angus Maude, *The English Middle Classes*, Alfred A. Knopf, New York, 1950; K. B. Smellie, *A Hundred Years of English Government*, Duckworth, London, 1937.

ited to property holders. But it enabled the political elites to learn the arts of self-government: how to manage assemblies, how to fight powerful executives and bureaucracies, how to split if need be into factions without wrecking the spirit of compromise, how to carry on government by discussion and negotiation. By 1776 a century and a half of colonial struggle had reduced most of the royal governors to frustrated impotence; the local legislatures had learned to use the power of the purse just as the House of Commons learned it.

Political leaders trained in these local legislatures dominated the Constitutional Convention in 1787. Later in the states of the new republic the franchise was initially limited to the small minority whose leaders had dominated the convention; and the first generation of leaders under the new Constitution were drawn from the old, experienced leadership. By Jackson's time, the various states had mostly eliminated the barriers to universal white manhood suffrage, although here and there, as in Virginia, the struggle for widening the franchise went on. Nevertheless the break was not abrupt. The new leaders only gradually replaced the old. The transition to universal manhood suffrage was on the whole relatively painless.

Thus all the functions of circulation were accomplished: Despite some close calls—as evidenced by the Virginia and Kentucky Resolutions, the Alien and Sedition Acts, the conspiracy of the Federalists, and the Hartford Convention—revolution was unnecessary, because no important leaders remained unrepresented among the political leadership; the unrepresented got their spokesmen like Jackson and Benton; and the older leaders helped to indoctrinate the new ones in the arts of self-government.

One cannot reduce the matter to a quantitative proposition but the general rule is clear: Circulation must be rapid enough to prevent the exclusion of any people with significant control outside government; it must be gradual enough so that the existing leadership is not swamped and therefore incapable of transmitting the habits of polyarchal control.

In modern times, universal suffrage means that entry through wealth and birth become less important than before, and political skill becomes more important. No one can be excluded from political leadership because he lacks wealth and family provided he has enough skill to garner votes. Indeed, even where entry into political leadership comes via administration, management, or communication, the advantages of wealth and birth tend to give way to those of skill. Thus in a society where recruitment into political leadership is primarily on the basis of skill, the existence of widespread public schooling automatically facilitates rapid circulation and makes a stoppage in circulation virtually impossible. The problem in the United States is, perhaps, not whether there is sufficient circulation but whether there is so much circulation that new leaders are inadequately indoctrinated in the habits of polyarchal control.

OTHER PRECONDITIONS OF POLYARCHY

A prerequisite to many of the preceding conditions is a society with a considerable degree of psychological security, limited disparity of wealth and income, and perhaps widespread education. Many democratic theorists—Rousseau and Jefferson among others —have explicitly or implicitly emphasized these as conditions for democracy. Surely they are necessary to polyarchy.

However, these are not conditions that can be easily converted into satisfactory operational criteria and we propose to say little more about them. It is clear, however, that psychological insecurity is likely to produce responses that undermine the conditions set forth earlier—to increase the bitterness and hostility of campaigns, stimulate violence at one extreme and apathy at another, generate irrational resentments and hatreds for opponents and their leaders, create longings for decisive dictatorial leaders unhampered by reciprocal restraints, disrupt agreement on basic policy and methods, and in general destroy the complacent acceptance of political competition among rival leaders that is so crucial to polyarchy.

Differences in wealth generate differences in control outside government and therefore in it; advantages in wealth buy advantages of education, status, knowledge, information, propaganda, and organization, and hence advantages of control. The advantages of control outside government not merely prevent the attainment of the democratic goal of equally shared control in government; they may even go so far as to prevent the process of polyarchy from operating. Hardly anyone today denies this fact, even conservative American Republicans. The real operational question is the extent of the differentials in wealth compatible with polyarchy. And on this point no one can really provide an answer. In the past such differences have been quite great in the United States; yet polyarchy survived.

It has long been assumed that widespread literacy is a precondition for polyarchy because it is difficult for the illiterate to understand the processes of polyarchy, exert control over leaders who can manipulate propaganda, and grasp the significance of the alternative leaders or policies presented to them. The experiment of universal suffrage in India casts some doubt on the thesis, at least as the experiment has worked so far. At the other pole, probably many rather small groups dealing with simple and familiar problems could operate polyarchy even if the group consisted mostly of illiterates. But doubtless few of our readers will quarrel with the proposition that widespread illiteracy and ignorance immeasurably increase the probabilities that polyarchy will fail to survive in any modern, complex, industralized society.

INTERDEPENDENCE OF THE PRECONDITIONS

These six conditions, in sum, seem to be necessary to polyarchy. Operating together, they form a kind of organic whole, if we may use that phrase without suggesting anything metaphysical or mystical about the "organism." We mean only that they are interdependent, like parts of the body. They interact on one another. In discussing them separately for analytical purposes we have been looking at them as a medical student studies the human anatomy by dissection; he does not forget that to dissect the severed arm of a cadaver will not tell him all he needs to know about the healthy arm of a living man. Social indoctrination facilitates political circulation, maintenance and toleration of social pluralism, agreement, and political activity. Agreement facilitates social indoctrination and toleration of social pluralism. Political activity facilitates circulation and may facilitate social pluralism, agreement, and social indoctrination. And so it goes. It would be a wasted metaphysical effort to ask which comes first or which is a preresquisite to the others. All are interdependent; all are vital to the process of polyarchy.

II. A Special Problem: The Breakdown of Legislatures

It is now possible to see why the effect on polyarchy of any particular economic policy or trend of policies is so difficult to discern with confidence. Most of the preconditions of polyarchy are hard to measure; they have not been measured over time and are not being measured now; hence one can only hazard a guess as to the consequences of an economizing technique or policy on these preconditions. Then, too, sometimes one can know some of the effects but not all. Moreover, a particular technique or even an entire set of government policies may strengthen one precondition and weaken another—increase political activity, for example, and decrease basic agreement. Hence in this area of discussion with dogmatic predictions made in strident tones, modesty and suspended judgment are perhaps the wisest course of the social scientist.

It should be clear, however, that most of the difficulties of using polyarchy as an economizing device are difficulties inherent in polyarchy itself. Economizing decisions made through polyarchal processes are neither more or less irrational, undemocratic, influenced by the politically active, or likely to undermine the conditions of polyarchy than a host of other polyarchal decisions—on war, foreign policy, and civil liberties, for example.

One special problem worth emphasis, however, arises because of the sheer number and complexity of decisions political leaders must make as collective choice and hierarchical controls replace a price system. The danger point here is the breakdown in control over policy by popular legislatures. To be sure, the legislature is only one of the instruments of control necessary in polyarchies. But like Voltaire's Deity, if polyarchies did not have one they would have to invent it. It is difficult to imagine how politicians and government bureaucracies could be controlled by citizens without some group of elected politicians performing the functions common to legislatures of supervision, criticism, opposition, and participation in the making of policy.

Yet almost everywhere legislative politicians appear to have passed the zenith of their powers; they are everywhere being displaced by executive politicians. The growth of government action has required decisions that in sheer number, detail, prerequisite knowledge, and dispatch cannot be made by legislatures; thus great discretion passes to executive politicians. Even the decisions still made by legislatures, like the question of pricing power at reclamation dams, impose an extraordinary burden and often presuppose an excessive measure of time, knowledge, and energy on the part of legislators.

The action of legislative politicians has been the example par excellence of coördination by bargaining; yet in many nations, to discharge their burden of work, accomplish the program on which they were elected, and deal with the great number of emergencies, legislative politicians have more and more subjected themselves to hierarchical controls through rules, practices, and organizations that strengthen the power of party leaders. This is particularly the case in Britain and New Zealand; in neither country does the ordinary member expect to accomplish many *fundamental* changes in the government's program by anything he may say on the floor. The real opportunities for ordinary members to influence party leaders are now largely confined to the party caucus.[32] The legislature serves as a kind of continuing embodiment of the election returns; it guarantees that executive politicians will roughly adhere to their campaign programs or, in dealing with emergencies and new demands, will not stray excessively from basic pubic attitudes as reflected by legislative politicians. But the role of legislative politicians in deliberately shaping the great bulk of the decisions made by executive politicians is exceedingly attenuated. They are umpires, who sometimes rule the ball out of bounds; but they do not carry the ball themselves or, except by enforcing the basic rules, determine the strategy.

In the United States, legislative politicians probably maintain much more individual control, particularly in the Senate, than anywhere else in the world. The Senate is perhaps the only major legislative organ of a large nation-state which operates chiefly by reciprocity. Yet Congressional politicians have not been able to prevent the creation of enormous domains of control led by Presidential politicians. With its present organization Congress has more than it can do; further extension of government hierarchy can only mean a diminution of Congressional control over the economic confederacy, if by "Congressional" we mean control that reflects the preferences of a majority of both houses. On the other hand, because Congressional politicians are too heavily burdened to keep tab on government policies, and improperly organized to act in coördination with executive politicians, individual Congressional politicians may be expected to play important individual roles as parts of one group or another in the economic confederations. This opportunity is the natural lot of the committee chairmen, who will share control in a group that exerts influence over railroads, or electric power, or

---

[32] For example, cf. Leslie Lipson, *The Politics of Equality*, University of Chicago Press, Chicago, 1948, p. 319.

flood control, or shipbuilding, or communications, or fuels, or atomic energy, or many other "states" in the confederation.

POSSIBLE REFORMS

One major limit to effective reorganization of the American Congress to meet its modern tasks is the extent to which bargaining is built into the American political system—a point we shall take up in the following chapters. Certain reforms, however, are marginally important and perhaps possible. First, the growth of unified parties might help to curtail the individual and often irresponsible power of individual Congressmen and at the same time increase the weight of a Congressional majority, which would then have, as it does not now have, the opportunity to carry through a consistent program. But it is only fair to point out that unified parties would probably also increase the hierarchical and decrease the bargaining character of the party system as it now operates in Congress. Second, some steps could be taken to relieve Congressional politicians of details that consume their time, energy, and abilities to such an extent that they have little left for the big issues. The simple adoption of an electric recorder for roll calls and votes, one observer calculates, would have saved the 78th Congress as much as two calendar months.[33] A good deal of minor legislation could be handled adequately by administrative officials; if it is a question of losing control over minor legislation or major policy, there is hardly any doubt where the choice should lie. The device of permitting decisions by executive politicians and their subordinates, with an opportunity to review or vote the action in Congress, is a procedure that, on the basis both of extensive British experience and of our own limited practice, should be considerably extended.

Yet when all these and other limited gains are made, Congress, like the House of Commons and the French Assembly, will still be heavily overloaded. To argue that the problems of the legislature can be solved by shifting its burdens to the executive is merely to contend that popular control over governmental decisions is no longer possible and that under these circumstances decisions by a professional bureaucracy are preferable to decisions by politicians. Probably the problem of the modern legislature cannot be solved. But it can be reduced by changing and simplifying the agenda of

[33] George B. Galloway, *Congress at the Crossroads*, Thomas Y. Crowell Co., New York, 1946, p. 80.

legislators. One way to simplify the agenda of economic decisions, we have seen, is a price system. And from the narrow perspective of democratic values this pragmatic advantage of a price system is, alone, a sufficient reason for retaining it as a major component in the economic order of a modern industrial society.

12.

Bargaining:
Control
Among Leaders

Bargaining is a form of reciprocal control among leaders. It takes place among leaders when all of certain conditions are met; what these conditions are will be seen shortly. Bargaining exists in all societies. In general, the extent to which it takes place is inversely related to the amount of hierarchy and the extent of initial agreement. Even in modern totalitarian societies, however, some bargaining takes place. During the Second World War, for example, German policy toward Russia was subject to a constant tug-of-war among four main groups, one including Himmler, Bormann, and Hitler himself, another around Alfred Rosenberg, a third around Goebbels, and a fourth of professional soldiers and diplomats.[1]

And in polyarchal societies with a high degree of agreement some bargaining takes place for reasons that were examined in the last chapter; it was shown there that social pluralism makes bargaining necessary and basic agreement makes it possible. Thus in countries like Great Britain, New Zealand, and Sweden, where a rather wide area of values and understandings appears to be covered in the basic agreements, bargaining nevertheless takes place. In the United States social pluralism is probably greater than in these three countries, and the area of basic agreement is probably narrower; as a result bargaining, a vital feature in all polyarchies, is a predominant one in the American polyarchy.

I. Bargaining and Economizing

Some types of bargaining have conventionally been regarded as a part of "economic" life—collective bargaining, for

[1] George Fischer, "Der Fall Wlassow," *Der Monat*, June, 1951, pp. 263 ff.; esp. pp. 265–267. Jules Monnerot has persuasively argued that the domination of the Politburo depends on its skill in maintaining a bargaining relation among the three main hierarchies—the party, the secret police, and the nonparty "technician." By

example; in a later chapter we examine the conditions and consequences of bargaining in the form of rather specific politico-economic techniques.[2] But the kind of bargaining we direct attention
to in this and the next chapter is governmental or "political" bargaining, not only because this kind of bargaining is indispensable to
polyarchy, but also because "political" bargaining is itself frequently a politico-economic process by which decisions about scarce
resources are arrived at. Finally, and this is perhaps most important
of all, its extent and characteristics in government significantly influence decisions about all other politico-economic devices. Indeed,
as we shall see in the next chapter, perhaps the most fateful limit on
American capacity for rational social action in economic affairs is
the enormous extent to which bargaining shapes all our governmental decisions.

II. Political Bargaining in Polyarchy

It would be desirable to know a good deal about the function of bargaining in all polyarchies. But because of significant differences in the processes of political bargaining in different nations
a monumental study would be required before one could safely
generalize. Our description of the process is drawn chiefly from
American experience.

THE BARGAINERS

In this country the principal participants in the process of bargaining over national governmental policy fall into these categories:
1. Leaders of national, state, and local party organizations, including politicians in the executive branch and Congress.
2. Congressional committee chairmen.
3. Leaders of government bureaucracies, including bureau chiefs,
   department heads, the President, and other politicians.
4. Leaders of nongovernmental, nonparty organizations organized
   primarily for purposes other than bargaining with government
   leaders, including leaders in trade unions, business firms, religious
   organizations, professional associations, and the like.

---

throwing its support to any two of these hierarchies, Monnerot argues, the Politburo can always control the third. Jules Monnerot, "Mécanisme politique de
l'absolutisme," *Preuves* (Cahiers Mensuels du Congrès pour la Liberté de la Culture), July, 1951, pp. 1 ff.
  [2] Chapter 17.

5. Leaders of nonparty organizations organized primarily to bargain with government leaders, i.e., special-purpose pressure groups, including organizations such as the National Association of Real Estate Boards, veterans' organizations, the Farm Bureau Federation.
6. Opinion leaders working in communications, particularly mass communications, including publicists, newspaper editors, reporters, columnists, radio broadcasters, etc.
7. Individuals of special prestige, status, or control, including men like Bernard Baruch, Herbert Hoover, General MacArthur, etc.

These are not mutually exclusive groups, nor are they sharply defined, nor is the list an exhaustive one. But it is safe to say that most government policy is strongly influenced by bargaining among individuals in one or more of these categories. It is impossible to estimate how many people all the categories include; but pretty clearly the total is a relatively small percentage of the American people.

A vast amount of bargaining takes place among individuals in these categories while policy choices are being made. In nominations, drafting party platforms, campaigns, legislation, administration, caucuses, conventions, Congressional committee hearings, the floor, offices, and hallways of Congress, White House meetings, interdepartmental committees, formal and informal meetings of cabinet officers, departments, independent regulatory commissions, and courts of law—everywhere in government, leaders find it necessary, desirable, and possible to bargain with other leaders before policy choices can be made and enforced. The lines of control prescribed by law, constitution, executive order, and organization charts are crisscrossed by a tangled skein of bargaining relations, some ephemeral, some in change, some relatively stable.

WHY BARGAINING TAKES PLACE

SOCIAL PLURALISM. If leaders agreed on everything they would have no need to bargain; if on nothing, they could not bargain. Leaders bargain because they disagree and expect that further agreement is possible and will be profitable—and the profit sought may accrue not merely to the individual self but to the group, an alliance of groups, a region, a nation, unborn generations, "the public interest." Hence bargaining takes place because it is necessary, possible, and thought to be profitable.

Social pluralism, as we have said, makes some bargaining necessary in all polyarchies. For if groups working through a common government retain some degree of autonomy with respect to one another—and this is what social pluralism means—they can arrive at governmental decisions only through bargaining. Moreover, groups engaged in national bargaining—political parties, government bureaucracies, pressure groups, legislative chambers—are themselves composed of groups, and these in turn break down still further. Hence bargaining is found at all levels in polyarchy, not merely among top leaders, but between top leaders and subordinates up and down a lengthy chain of reciprocal control.

It is worth dwelling on this subsidiary point a moment. Most of the leaders in the categories just mentioned are leaders by sufferance. Although the hierarchical component is great in parties, government agencies, nongovernmental hierarchies, pressure groups, and communications, these organizations are also, in varying degrees, marked by internal bargaining and even in some cases by polyarchy. The fact that most of these organizations are voluntary, or partly voluntary, means that leaders cannot push their unilateral control too far; if they do, they will lose their following. Hence the governmental process is not merely a matter of having these top leaders strike a bargain. They must bargain in turn with sub-leaders, who have their sub-leaders to bargain with, and so on down to the last echelon of activity.

It would be as easy to exaggerate this feature as to minimize it, and one must not forget that there is a great variation from one organization to another. But probably as good a simplified concept as any for picturing the governmental process from citizen to top policy makers is to think of it as a chain of leaders, each dependent on the support and acquiescence of followers below and leaders above.

In his description of Cornerville gangs, Whyte indicates a pattern that is specifically applicable to urban politics in a predominantly Italo-American working-class neighborhood; because these people are near the bottom of the social scale, the hierarchy is longer and more pronounced than for a middle-class neighborhood, but, softened in its outlines and expanded to a larger arena, the description suggests a typical pattern of national politics.

According to Cornerville people society is made up of big people and little people—with intermediaries serving to bridge the gaps between them. The masses of Cornerville people are little people. They cannot approach the big people directly but must have an intermediary to intercede for them. They gain this intercession by establishing connections with the intermediary, by performing services for him, and thus making him obligated to them. The intermediary performs the same functions for the big man. The interactions of big shots, intermediaries, and little guys build up a hierarchy of personal relations based upon a system of reciprocal obligations.

Corner gangs such as the Nortons and the cliques of the Cornerville Social and Athletic Club fit in at the bottom of the hierarchy, although certain social distinctions are made between them. Corner-boy leaders like Doc, Don Romano, and Carlo Tedesco served as intermediaries, representing the interests of their followers to the higher ups. Chick and his college boys ranked above the corner boys, but they stood at the bottom of another hierarchy, which was controlled from outside the district. There are, of course, wide differences in rank between big shots. Viewed from the street corner of Shelby Street, Tony Cataldo was a big shot, and the relations of the corner-boy followers to him were regulated by their leaders. On the other hand, he served as an intermediary, dealing with big shots for the corner boys and trying to control the corner boys for the big shots. T. S., the racket boss, and George Ravello, the state senator, were the biggest men in Cornerville. T. S. handled those below him through his immediate subordinates. While Ravello refused to allow any formal distinctions to come between himself and the corner boys, the man on the bottom fared better when he approached the politician through an intermediary who had a connection than when he tried to bridge the gap alone.[3]

Social pluralism goes a long way, therefore, to explain the existence of bargaining. But it does not, by itself, explain the extent of bargaining in, say, the United States. For if autonomous groups were not interdependent, or if they were fully in agreement at the outset, they would scarcely need to bargain.

SOCIAL PLURALISM PLUS INTERDEPENDENCE. The more the actions of one group are thought to be capable of adversely or beneficially affecting another, the more the second group is likely to protect itself by attempting to control the first. In the United States, as in other polyarchies, social pluralism has been accompanied by increasing interdependence. Hence the interdependent groups must bargain with one another for protection and advantage.

[3] William Foote Whyte, *Street Corner Society*, University of Chicago Press, Chicago, 1943, pp. 271–272. It should be remembered that the "boys" are actually men in their twenties.

SOCIAL PLURALISM PLUS INTERDEPENDENCE PLUS INITIAL DISAGREEMENT AND POTENTIAL AGREEMENT. But groups with enough autonomy to enforce bargaining and enough interdependence to profit by it are still not stimulated to bargain *unless* they initially disagree and yet expect that increased agreement is possible. Social pluralism need not inevitably stimulate initial disagreements but evidently it tends to; for group life helps to create some identifications, norms, and reality views that are shared in each group but not in all, and these can easily come into conflict. As everyone knows, in the United States different individuals identify with a great diversity of different groups with differing norms and identifications, and this is undoubtedly one of the reasons for the proliferation of bargaining in this country.

The existence of group loyalties creates side effects that also increase bargaining. For example, leaders in one organization cannot necessarily exert much control over non-leaders in another. This is an obvious point, but often overlooked by individuals who think of the leaders in a community as falling mainly in the middle and upper classes.[4] In the low-income area examined by Whyte, for example, a man could get ahead either as a Republican or as a Democrat. But if he became a Republican, he lost his influence in Cornerville; if he remained a Democrat he could keep his influence in Cornerville, but he was barred from the opportunities for status and control he could gain as a Republican.

Then, too, many individuals belong to several groups, and when these conflict they feel the "cross pressures" of conflicting group loyalties. One way to escape these cross pressures is by political apathy—a flight from the conflict.[5] Another, however, is to reduce the conflict by compromise through bargaining.[6] Moreover, the social indoctrination we spoke of as a prerequisite to polyarchy helps establish widely accepted norms cutting across many groups.

[4] Evidently a common failing of foreign affairs organizations that ostensibly aim their educational efforts at the "American people" but concentrate on middle- and upper-class people, who may not even be leaders in their own groups, let alone the bulk of the population. Cf. Bernard Cohen, "Private Organizations and Public Education in World Affairs," Ph.D dissertation in the Yale University library, unpublished.

[5] Paul Lazarsfeld, Bernard Berelson, and Hazel Gaudet, *The People's Choice*, Duell, Sloan and Pearce, New York, 1944.

[6] It is quite possible that the relatively high degree of political apathy that is believed to exist in the United States—measured, for example, by election turnouts —is directly related to the relatively high degree of bargaining that takes place. They may be two reactions to the same conditions, namely, social pluralism-interdependence-group conflict.

Hence bargaining is both possible and profitable. It is our hypothesis that cleavages in identification and loyalty are sharper in the United States than in Great Britain, and more numerous but less sharp than in France. But it is difficult to test a comparison of this kind, and we are content to offer the proposition merely as a hypothesis. In any case the attitudes of Americans toward governmental policies are shaped by a wide variety of identifications and loyalties.[7]

CONFLICTING IDENTIFICATIONS

A listing of some of the major types of groups that give rise to loyalties and identifications most relevant to political choices in the United States is itself impressive evidence of the need for bargaining:

1. Family or kinship groups. An aggregation of kinship groups often provides the hard core of the machine vote. Moreover, children are strongly influenced by the indoctrination of their parents. West wrote of Plainville, "A man is born into his political party just as he is born into probable future membership in the church of his parents."[8]

2. People who make their living in similar ways. This is the economic interest that Madison in his famous *Federalist Paper No. 10* insisted was the ground of all politics. The role in American political history of slaveholders, grain growers, artisans, commercial interests, land speculators, railroad entrepreneurs, financiers, and numerous other groups is most easily, if not always completely, explained on this basis.[9]

3. People of similar aggregate wealth or income. Public opinion polls and election studies confirm the obvious: differences in

[7] The group basis of politics was first emphasized in this country in a book that has been strangely neglected until recently, namely, Arthur F. Bentley, *The Process of Government*, University of Chicago Press, Chicago, 1908. The most systematic recent statement is David B. Truman, *The Governmental Process*, Alfred A. Knopf, New York, 1951. Cf. also Earl Latham, *The Group Basis of Politics: A Study in Basing-Point Legislation*, Cornell University Press, Ithaca, 1952.

[8] James West, *Plainville U.S.A.*, Columbia University Press, New York, 1945, p. 85.

[9] Frederick Jackson Turner, *The United States 1830–1850*, Henry Holt and Co., New York, 1935; Arthur M. Schlesinger, Jr., *The Age of Jackson*, Little, Brown and Co., Boston, 1945; Comer Vann Woodward, *Reunion and Reaction, the Compromise of 1877 and the End of Reconstruction*, Little, Brown and Co., Boston, 1951; E. E. Schattschneider, *Politics, Pressures and the Tariff*, Prentice-Hall, New York, 1935; Richard Centers, *The Psychology of the Social Classes*, Princeton University Press, Princeton, 1949.

wealth and income are reflected by differences in political attitudes.[10]

4. People of similar social status. Warner and his associates have
found a sixfold set of status groups in a settled eastern community and five in the West. Individuals with similar social status
tend to agree politically.[11]

5. People who believe they belong to the same class. Although class
is not very sharply distinguished from groups based on social
status, aggregate wealth or income, and ways of making a living,
Richard Centers in his study of a nation-wide sample found that
people did identify themselves with a "class," and differences in
class identifications were correlated with differences in political
attitudes. Fifty-one percent of his sample said they belonged to
the working class; 43 percent put themselves in the middle class.
Occupation helps one to identify his class; for example, nearly
three-quarters of all business, professional, and white collar
workers identified themselves with the middle or upper classes,
whereas 79 percent of all manual workers identified themselves
with the working and lower classes.[12] But aside from occupation,
nearly half the sample believed that the most important thing to
know about a person from the standpoint of membership in a
class was the way the person "believes and feels about certain
things."[13] Nor can it be said that class consciousness is merely a
roundabout method of identification by occupation or wealth.
For people of the same occupational grouping may identify
themselves with different "classes"—that is to say, put different
class labels on themselves; when they do, they also tend to have
different political attitudes. For example, those who regard themselves as members of the working class tend to be somewhat

[10] For example, Sam Lubell, *The Future of American Politics*, Harper &
Brothers, New York, 1952, p. 51. Lazarsfeld, Berelson, and Gaudet, *op. cit.* And
answers to the following polling questions: Do you think the interests of employers
and employees are, by their very nature, opposed, or are they basically the same?
(See *Fortune*, "The Fortune Survey XXVII," February, 1940.) Do you think the
government should provide for all people who have no other means of obtaining
a living? (See *Fortune*, "The Fortune Survey XXVIII," March, 1940.) The President proposes a 28% (about one-fourth) reduction in Federal grants for relief.
Do you approve or disapprove of this cut? (See American Institute of Public
Opinion poll, February 18, 1940.) The list could be extended indefinitely.

[11] See W. Lloyd Warner, Marchia Meeker, and Kenneth Eells, *Social Class in
America*, Science Research Associates, Inc., Chicago, 1949.

[12] See Richard Centers, *op. cit.*, p. 85.

[13] *Ibid.*, pp. 90–91.

more "radical" than members of the same occupational group who regard themselves as middle class.[14]

6. People of the same religious faith.[15]
7. People who belong to a similar racial or ethnic group.[16]
8. People who live or have lived in the same geographical area. "Regionalism" as a phenomenon has been vastly exaggerated in American politics. There are and have been no homogeneous regions in this country. The South, which is often cited as the most homogeneous area of the nation, has actually been constantly beset by deep internecine quarrels dating back to colonial times.[17] Explanations of political loyalties in terms of regionalism are better read in terms of economic class, social status, wealth, or occupation. Ties with one's locality, on the other hand, appear to be quite strong and probably exert some influence on political attitudes. West writes: "Plainvillers belong to a 'region' of four or five neighboring counties, to 'this quarter of the state,' to 'this state,' to 'this section of the United States,' and to the nation. Yet only feeble sentiments attach to all of these larger areas, except the state and the nation. . . . None of these sentiments compares in intensity or complexity with the feeling for Woodland County and for Plainville. A still smaller geographical unit to which people are attached by residence and sentiment is the neighborhood."[18]
9. Finally, there are some identifications that can be explained as arising out of a common historical experience that is kept alive by myth, folk story, tradition. Mountain Republicans in the South, concentrated mostly on the hills from which Virginia, North Carolina, and Tennessee fan out, are Republicans today mostly because of a long historical experience that includes a century and a half of conflict with the wealthier landowners in the flatlands, hostility to the Confederacy in the Civil War, and the Reconstruction experience. Their political and social goals probably come closer to those of the New Deal and Fair Deal

[14] *Ibid.*, pp. 126–127. Unfortunately, Centers' data about occupational groups leaves something to be desired.

[15] Cf. Lazarsfeld, Berelson, and Gaudet, *op. cit.*, and Lubell, *op. cit.*

[16] Cf. William F. Whyte, *op. cit.*, p. 230; Sam Lubell, *op. cit.*; V. O. Key, Jr., *Southern Politics in State and Nation*, Alfred A. Knopf, New York, 1949.

[17] V. O. Key, Jr., *op. cit., passim.*

[18] James West, *op. cit.*, p. 56.

than to those of the people who dominate the Republican party. But they cannot identify themselves as Democrats.[19]

In sum, because different individuals identify with different groups, a compromise arrived at by bargaining is *necessary* to a successful election alliance. Because individuals in different groups may also share membership in another group, compromise by bargaining is *stimulated*. Because individuals in different groups share some common values, bargaining is *possible*. And because different issues activate different combinations of groups, compromise by bargaining is *continuous*.

III. The Politician as Key Bargainer

Despite a curious unwillingness on the part of Americans to respect the politician—a reluctance that no doubt arises in part from the very role that is thrust upon him—the politician is a key figure in American life as he must be in any polyarchy. For the politician is, above all, the man whose career depends upon successful negotiation of bargains. To win office he must negotiate electoral alliances. To satisfy his electoral alliance he must negotiate alliances with other legislators and with administrators, for his control depends upon negotiation. Most of his time is consumed in bargaining. This is the skill he cultivates; it is the skill that distinguishes the master-politician from the political failure. And if the politician frequently neglects the substantive issues of policy in order to maintain, restore, or strengthen his alliances, this is a part of the price a bargaining society must pay to maintain a modicum of social peace.

The politician is as much the human embodiment of a bargaining society as any single role-player can be. The role spreads from government to business, to trade unions, to universities, and to other organizations where bargaining takes place. Originally identified as an individual who concentrates much of his time and energy in getting into governmental office, the word is now commonly used to include any person in any organization whose main skill is his ability to control by negotiating alliances. This is the political skill, or better, the politician's skill.

Because he is a bargainer, a negotiator, the politician does not often give orders. He can rarely employ unilateral controls. Even as a chief executive or a cabinet official he soon discovers that his

[19] V. O. Key, Jr., *op. cit.*, p. 285.

control depends on his skill in bargaining. It may be, therefore, that the politician's role tends to be filled by a range of personality types rather different from the range one finds in positions where unilateral control is more pronounced. Not much is known on this subject; it is our impression, however, that American politicians, as leaders whose control depends upon successful bargaining, tend to have attitudes toward the control process substantially different from those of other American leaders, like those in business and administration, whose control depends upon a successful use of hierarchy. Probably the role both attracts and shapes the men who play it.

In any case the role calls for actions such as compromise, renunciation, face-saving of oneself, which are morally ambiguous or even downright immoral to people with morally rigorous standards. Yet without the work of the politician a bargaining society would fly into its myriad separate warring parts—and the pieces would be put together, no doubt, by the strong hierarchical leader who would reduce the need for politicians by destroying the autonomy of social organizations. Because some bargaining is inherent in polyarchy, and because the politician fulfills the bargaining role, the politician, the negotiator of alliances, is an inherent part of polyarchy.

In another day and another country, George Bernard Shaw, remembering his own personal experiences in politics and observing insightfully what the politician's role must be, was stimulated to wrath when a labor candidate named Joseph Burgess refused to compromise on some issue—thus rejecting the politician's role—and thereby lost a seat in Parliament:

When I think of my own unfortunate character, smirched with compromise, rotted with opportunism, mildewed by expediency . . . dragged through the mud of borough council and Battersea elections, stretched out of shape with wire-pulling, putrified by permeation, worn out by 25 years pushing to gain an inch here, or straining to stem a backrush, I do think Joe might have put up with just a speck or two on those white robes of his for the sake of the millions of poor devils who cannot afford any character at all because they have no friend in Parliament. Oh, these moral dandies, these spiritual toffs, these superior persons. Who is Joe anyhow that he should not risk his soul occasionally like the rest of us?[20]

[20] Hesketh Pearson, *G.B.S.*, Harper & Brothers, New York, 1942, p. 156, quoted in Stephen K. Bailey and Howard D. Samuel, *Congress at Work*, Henry Holt and Co., New York, 1952, p. 5.

THE ADDITIONAL CONSTITUTIONAL FACTOR IN AMERICAN BARGAINING

Some amount of bargaining—let us emphasize it again—is necessary, possible, and thought by the participants themselves to be profitable in polyarchies. Bargaining is made necessary, possible, and profitable by social pluralism-interdependence-disagreement against a background of basic agreement. Both social pluralism, with its tendencies to disagreement, and basic agreement are necessary to polyarchy. But if these exist, is anything gained or lost by superimposing on this system of social checks and balances a complex network of governmental checks and balances? That is the central constitutional question of the United States, and it goes to the heart of the problem of rational social action through American governmental machinery.

Roughly two alternatives are open to a polyarchal society. Relying on social pluralism, it may minimize prescribed checks and balances in its constitutional arrangements. This does not mean that operating checks and balances will not exist. On the contrary, in manifold ways leaders will find their control checked by the need to win a plurality of votes in elections and in the legislature; hence the need to form alliances, and hence the need to bargain with other leaders. Moreover, although governmental leaders may be relieved of prescribed constitutional checks among different governmental branches, organizational necessities stimulate innumerable internal controls that foster bargaining. At a minimum, policy making needs to be specialized in a bureaucracy, an executive, and a legislative body; and even these institutions must develop additional internal checks, such as legislative committees, specialized staff offices for the executive, and administrative departments.

The second main alternative is the American solution, which superimposes additional checks and balances upon the inherent social, organizational, and polyarchal checks that must in any case already exist in a polyarchy.

In the United States the structure of government prescribed by the Constitution, court decisions, and traditions vastly increases the amount of bargaining that must take place before policies can be made. Federalism; the composition and procedures of the Senate; the bicameral legislature; the separation of President and Congress, and the checks and balances between them; differences in their constituencies; fixed and overlapping terms of Representatives, Senators, and the President; constitutional restraints on legislative authority; judicial review; the amending process; a decentralized party system; and the devolution of power to committee chairmen in Congress whose position is automatically derived from seniority— all these provide a variety of narrow defiles where a skillful and aggressive group may fatally mine the path of any group of threatening leaders.[21] The necessity for constant bargaining is thus built into the very structure of American government.

THE FUNDAMENTAL CONSEQUENCE

The strategic consequence of this arrangement, as the Constitutional Convention evidently intended, has been that *no unified, cohesive, acknowledged, and legitimate representative-leaders of the "national majority" exist in the United States.* Often the President claims to represent one national majority, and Congress (or a majority of both houses) another. The convention did its work so well that even when a Congressional majority is nominally of the same party as the President, ordinarily they do not speak with the same voice. In a previous chapter we said that on a great many policy questions the "preferences of the greater number" or "the majority" is a fiction. But even if there were a national majority in the United States, it could not rule unless it were so overwhelmingly large as to include within its massive range the diverse "majorities" for which different elements in the bureaucracy, the President, and Congressmen all claim to speak.

THE CONSEQUENCES SPELLED OUT

This fundamental consequence has many facets. The most important are worth spelling out.

BLOCKED LEADERSHIP. *Policy proposals of one set of unified leaders can usually be blocked by other leaders.* To be sure, in every polyarchy there are, as we said in a previous chapter, strategic minorities with unusual control resulting from differences in wealth, education, status, access, or election significance. But in the United

[21] J. Allen Smith emphasized this feature of the American Constitution, and the resulting control it gave to minorities, in his pioneering work, *The Spirit of American Government*, The Macmillan Company, New York, 1907. Cf. also David Truman, *op. cit.*, pp. 322–325, 353–354. For a painstaking examination of the features of American government that foster and limit majority rule, see Arthur Holcombe, *Our More Perfect Union*, Harvard University Press, Cambridge, 1950.

States their opportunities are compounded by the many additional points at which action can be checked. For example, although they are a minority within a minority of the South, which is itself distinctly a minority of the nation, southern Senators have successfully resisted every effort by rival leaders to enact fair employment practices legislation—even after such legislation was demanded in the 1948 electoral platform of the Democratic party and the Dixiecrats who opposed it won only a million votes to President Truman's twenty-four million and Governor Dewey's twenty-two million! Other outstanding examples of effective blocking of one set of leaders by another are actions by the House Rules Committee in stopping legislation supported by the President or even a House majority,[22] the Senate filibuster, legislative "riders" (despite the rules) on important legislation or appropriation bills which the President dare not veto, the difficulty the President has in controlling the Corps of Engineers,[23] and the difficulty Congress has in controlling the Reclamation Bureau.

MINORITY CONTROL. It follows as an inevitable consequence of the first point that *many strategically placed leaders who represent minorities are in a position to insist on their demands through bargaining*. Usually these entrenched leaders cannot be dislodged through the operation of polyarchal controls; indeed, given the machinery and traditions of American government, their position is earned by polyarchal processes. Nor can any other set of leaders exert hierarchal control over them. Hence bargaining is the only alternative to accepting their veto. If any set of leaders wishes to enact positive policy (inaction is itself, of course, a policy), they must accommodate themselves to every group with a veto over their policy proposals.

[22] See Representative Irving M. Engel, "The Seven Conservatives Who Bottleneck Our Laws," *The Reporter*, August 5, 1952, pp. 17–18. Earl Latham, *op. cit.*, criticizes the view that minorities in this country can actually exercise a "veto" against national legislation. Cf. at p. 35, footnote 37, his criticisms of John Fischer, "Unwritten Rules of American Politics," *Harper's Magazine*, November, 1948. Latham argues that "the assumption that there is a minority veto must show that minorities can always exercise it . . . and that no minority is without it." Neither, he says, is true. The proposition is not open to Latham's objections when stated cautiously, however; namely, on many issues of government policy, delegates of a lesser number can prevent or weaken policies they believe damaging to them or their clients, although these policies are desired and sought by delegates of a larger number. It is in this realistic sense that we use the term "veto" here.

[23] See "The King's River Project in the Basin of the Great Central Valley," in Harold Stein (ed.), *Public Administration and Policy Development*, A Case Book, Harcourt, Brace and Co. New York, 1952, pp. 533–572.

WIDESPREAD ACCEPTANCE. *Conversely government policy therefore requires widespread acceptance among the politically active.* In a preceding chapter we saw that some measure of agreement on policy among the politically active was a precondition for polyarchy. Admittedly the prerequisite amount is difficult to measure. But it seems highly probable that the extent of acceptance, if not agreement, among the politically active on any given issue required in the United States is notably higher than in Great Britain. And in so far as this is the case, it happens because there are many more positions in our political system from which a minority can veto policy. Hence their acquiescence must be obtained by bargaining.

Many Americans regard this situation as highly desirable. John C. Calhoun sought to convert it into an even more explicit constitutional theory and practice than already exists. Later, the experience of the Civil War evidently strengthened the conviction that no large minority should ever be pushed very far. Then, too, in a laissez-faire age one could plausibly maintain that positive government action was always a danger; hence widespread agreement reflecting the preferences of more than a mere majority of the electorate, or of the politically active, was desirable as a bar to oppressive government policy.

Logically this position was always somewhat weak, for to justify giving a minority a veto is to assert, in effect, that the majority either cannot or should not control government policy. Either assertion is to deny the goal of political equality. Yet given the American milieu, theorists and ideologues have unsuccessfully tried to join the doctrine of minority veto with the goal of political equality.

What might have been persuasive in a laissez-faire age becomes less obviously so in the contemporary world. For government *inaction* is as much a choice of policy as government action. It is difficult to show that the power of a well-placed minority to block government sponsorship of low-cost housing, medical care, or redistribution of incomes is somehow less oppressive than the power of a majority to obtain these things.

Other advantages of minority veto can be alleged. It is sometimes argued that the need for widespread acceptance among the politically active turns the legislative process into a powerful instrument of civic education. When a policy proposal has undergone two sets of committee hearings, debates in two houses, one or more formal statements from the President and a cabinet officer or two, a White House press conference, and numerous attacks, supporting speeches, and rebuttals by opinion leaders and pressure groups, it may be argued that the attentive public is almost certain to be as thoroughly educated about the bill as is possible in a polyarchy.

It might be argued, too, that the great advantage of requiring widespread agreement is the stability such agreement lends to any government policy once it is enacted. In an earlier chapter we pointed out that in healthy polyarchies the precondition of agreement itself makes for rather stable policies. In the United States, stability is further strengthened because the opportunity of numerous minorities to veto policy forces policy makers to secure their acquiescence in advance.

There is great merit in both these arguments. But the very condition that brings about these results also qualifies the arguments in several important ways that we are now to examine.

IRRATIONAL AGREEMENT.   *The need for widespread acceptance among the politically active often produces irrational agreement through logrolling.* Logrolling is a means of getting the acquiescence of every leader who has enough control to block or weaken your policy proposal, by trading your consent to the proposal of another leader for his consent to your proposal. In this case it is quite possible for everyone to get his specific policy accepted; yet the sum total of these specific policies may be quite unsuitable to a majority.

The very process of logrolling obscures the general consequences of the final deal to the majority. For each party is so intent on his specific proposal that the final deal is analyzed almost exclusively in terms of its effects on one's specific proposal. Indeed, usually no machinery even exists to analyze the general consequences. This is the case, for example, with appropriations for the "civil functions" of the army, the annual pork barrel of rivers and harbors improvements. In none of the hearings is there much interest in or analysis of the general consequence of the program for economic stability, government expenditures, and taxes.

For generations tariff policy was arrived at exclusively by logrolling. The question was never posed whether a majority of the politically active really preferred ever-rising tariffs to tariff reductions; the question was whether a specific active minority believed it stood to gain or lose by a tariff increase. Because the gains on tariff reductions are widespread, general, and for any specific tariff slight, and the gains from tariff increases are very significant for small, active groups, tariffs inevitably went up as long as the question was posed in specific bargaining terms in Congress. For it seemed to each party to the bargain that it stood to gain more than it lost.

Although it would be both an oversimplification and false to say that an alteration in the way the question was posed explains the entire change in American tariff policy, it is true that a decision to defeat or renew the Reciprocal Trade Agreements Act (which delegates *specific* adjustments to the executive) forces Congress to consider the general consequences of American tariff policy. Specific bargains over tariffs are not, of course, entirely excluded; bargaining is too important an element in American policy making to lead to so radical a conclusion. Logrolling still shows up in amendments to the trade agreements acts or, more commonly, as amendments or riders on other important legislation. Still, specific bargains are no longer, as they once were, the *whole* process of making tariff policy.

It should not be supposed, incidentally, that merely to shift a part of policy making from Congress to the executive and the bureaucracies will always eliminate or even reduce bargaining. It may only shift the locus of the bargaining process.

CONTROL BY THE ORGANIZED.   *The prevalence of bargaining results in public policies shaped to fit the demands of those who are highly organized.* The policy process tends to reflect the goals of the highly organized because organizations provide leaders with the negotiable rewards and deprivations that make control over other leaders possible. The highly organized, in turn, tend to be those individuals who identify themselves easily with one another; conversely, those who do not identify tend not to be organized.

Paradoxically, political support for the economizing process presupposes an identification that in practice turns out to be one of the weakest in our society: the consumer. The classical and neo-classical economists developed a body of theory that projected onto the whole economy the goals of a rational consumer. The concept of rational economic behavior, whether through the price system or through government action, is an answer to the question: What is the most rational (economical) way to use resources, assuming consumption to be the prime goal of economic activity? Yet the action of consuming goods and services is patently one that does not lead easily to mutual identification in our society. Because consumers' identifications are weak, their organizations are weak or nonexistent. Even in countries like England and Sweden with strong consumer coöperative movements, the consumer organizations have considerably less influence on public policy than do producer organizations.

It is roughly true, as everyone knows, that the same group of people tend to push their goals as producers and let their goals as consumers slide. Because politics reflects the goals of the organized, the goals people have as producers are reflected in public policy, not the goals they might or should have in order to be rational consumers. Thus assuming the values of the economizing process, much public policy is bound to be irrational, whether it is enacted in the name of McKinley capitalism, free enterprise, the Fair Deal, economic planning, socialism, or the Middle Way.

To a large extent, this may be the case in any polyarchy; the experience of Britain, France, and Sweden, for example, is not notably different from that of the United States. For all three countries the "producers" are more highly organized than the consumers, although in Sweden the influence of producers is somewhat tempered by the consumer coöperative movement.

FAILURE TO CONTROL BUREAUCRACY. *It follows, too, that there is little unified control over government bureaucracies by elected leaders.* "Responsible government," an English writer said, "may require that any detail of administration may be made the occasion of a political battle, yet the stability of democracy depends on the development of a political sagacity that will not butcher an administration to make a party holiday."[24] Control of government bureaucracies by political superiors requires a fine balance: too detailed direction of politicians destroys the area of discretionary judgment indispensable if rational decisions are to be made about complex technical questions; yet too little direction means a weakening of polyarchy. Unhappily the American political process is admirably designed to achieve both results at the same time.

To say that there is no dominant group of politicians unified

[24] K. B. Smellie, *A Hundred Years of English Government*, Duckworth, London, 1950, p. 57.

enough to coördinate government policy is equivalent to saying that there is no dominant group of politicians unified enough to control all the bureaucratic agencies. Even the most casual study of the relations between government bureaucracies and their prescribed political superiors shows this to be the case. Each bureaucratic agency is a part of a special network of control relations consisting of its clients, who often can be stimulated to lobby in behalf of the agency when its control, status, or security is threatened; its bureaucratic allies; its bureaucratic rivals; its links with Congressional politicians, usually in the legislative committee with jurisdiction over its activities, or in the appropriations subcommittee handling its budget; its links with Presidential politicians and their subordinates—cabinet officers, White House aides, Budget Bureau officials.

Some agencies like the Budget Bureau are "Presidential agencies" in the sense that they are responsive mostly to Presidential politicians; others are clearly "Congressional agencies"; others are partly captured by individuals or organizations outside the government; still others lean one way or another but manage to retain considerable autonomy with respect to all outside controls. Very few agencies ever face a unified group of elected political leaders determined and able to exercise control over the agency in order to achieve some agreed-upon goals.

Government bureaucracy, then, more nearly resembles the arena of international politics than a group of disciplined subordinates responsive to the control of common superiors. Indeed, the control of politicians over bureaucratic agencies is not altogether unlike that of the United Nations Security Council over the nation-states of the world. And the results are not dissimilar. First, control is weak, because numerous opportunities are provided the bureaucracies to divide and conquer their prescribed superiors. Second, conflict among politicians as to who shall exercise control over the bureaucracies is intense, bitter, and often destructive. Thus the "fine balance" we spoke of earlier is rarely achieved. For if the first result means that polyarchy is attenuated, the second means that the competence of the bureaucratic agencies is often impaired by conflicts between competing groups of politicians.

Bureaucratic leaders are participants in a bargaining process. If their status, power, or security is threatened by Presidential politicians, they stimulate an alliance with Congressional politicians.

Conversely, if menaced by Congressional politicians, they look to the Presidential politicians for allies. In either case they may also induce their clients to use their influence to "save" the agency from the threats of one group of politicians or another. Naturally allies cannot be had for nothing; bureaucratic leaders bargain with suitable rewards: loyalty, information, remission of penalties, projects, or a host of other alternatives. As a result the ties with one group of politicians often become so strong that prescribed superiors in another group are unable to exert effective control.

Thus the Corps of Engineers from 1940 to 1944 flatly refused to abide by the President's explicit order that the King's River project in California be carried out by the Reclamation Bureau; confident of support from the House Committee on Flood Control, the Corps deliberately violated the President's instructions and flagrantly lobbied for its own jurisdiction over the project [25] Conversely, the Budget Bureau's loyalty to the President is so well known that most Congressional politicians now take the alliance for granted and assume they can do little to control Budget's policies.[26] Sometimes, too, if political superiors threaten to agree on a program that would endanger the control, status, or security of an agency, the agency may combine with its worst enemy to defeat the attack; when in 1944 the President advocated a Missouri Valley Authority to unify the work carried on by a half-dozen different federal agencies, the Corps of Engineers and the Reclamation Bureau promptly produced the Pick-Sloan Plan, which allocated spheres of influence in the Missouri Valley and guaranteed the continued dominance of both agencies in the area.

Typically, although by no means always, conflicts over control take place between a group of Presidential politicians and a group of Congressional politicians, each of which also tries to recruit allies from among other politicians, Congressional and Presidential, among the various bureaucratic agencies, and among pressure groups that might be activated. In such a conflict, the competence of an agency may suffer. For example, an agency pursuing policies supported by Presidential politicians and opposed by strategically placed Congressional politicians may find its program mercilessly slashed in the appropriations committees, or be sub-

[25] See "The King's River Project in the Basin of the Great Central Valley," in Harold Stein (ed.), *op. cit.*

[26] Herbert A. Simon, Donald W. Smithburg, and Victor A. Thompson, *Public Administration*, Alfred A. Knopf, New York, 1950, p. 447.

jected to detailed legislation prescribing what it must or must not do, or suffer in numerous investigations that destroy morale, impair recruitment, and consume much valuable time. Again and again, bureaucratic agencies in Washington are caught squarely in the middle of a policy dispute between Presidential and Congressional politicians; it is not uncommon to "butcher an administration to make a party holiday," as the State Department has learned.

SIGNIFICANCE OF THESE CONSEQUENCES FOR RATIONAL SOCIAL ACTION

From all the foregoing, it follows that coördination of government policies will vary greatly according to the scope of bargaining in government. *In American national government, bargaining is the strategic limit on rational social action and therefore on rational politico-economic action to a degree not to be found in Great Britain, Canada, New Zealand, Scandinavia, and probably some other Western governments.*

At best, in any country of great size and complexity, government policy is bound to contain many inconsistencies. First, the limits on rational calculation are great; the aids discussed in Chapter 3 are helpful but not magical. Second, in any sociopolitical system some bargaining exists, and bargaining creates an opportunity for inconsistent compromise policies to emerge. German policy vis-à-vis the Russians in the Second World War, we indicated, was an example of bargaining; a certain inconsistency did indeed result. Hence, fundamental limits both to calculation and to control make it highly improbable that all the policies of any government will converge to maximize the goal achievement of those for whose benefit the policies are intended.

Yet the American governmental process, marked as it is by a high degree of bargaining, still further increases the likelihood of situations in which one set of policies cancels out another.[27]

For example, one aim of Marshall Plan aid to Europe was to increase production and dollar earnings of European countries. Therefore, one set of officials encouraged Europeans to develop exports to the United States. This country helped form the International Trade Organization and stimulated acceptance by western Europe of the General Agreement on Tariff and Trade which this government also signed. Some tariff reductions resulted. Yet

[27] *Ibid.,* pp. 435–436; and David Truman, *op. cit.,* pp. 275, 437–438.

. . . after five years of promises by the Administration, Congress still has not passed any customs simplification law. The United States has not joined the I.T.O. Unilaterally and in violation of the General Agreement on Tariffs and Trade, the United States slapped quotas on imports of cheese, milk products and casein, thus at one blow crippling the major dollar-earning industries in Italy, Denmark, the Netherlands, Norway and New Zealand. Since mid-1950 the axe has fallen on fur-felt hat bodies, almonds and cheese. In the form of hearings under the so-called "escape clause" in the American reciprocal trade law . . . the axe is now hanging over motorcycles, bicycles, wines, pottery, "blue cheese," tobacco, pipes and wood screws.[28]

One does not need to decide which set of policies is preferable in order to conclude that they are inconsistent.

It is instructive to compare the American policy process with the British. Whether Congress and the President are more truly "representative" of the majority in this country than cabinet and Commons are in Britain or whether it is the other way round are questions that cannot be verified by any operational tests. But this much can be said. Unlike the United States, in Great Britain a more or less unified, cohesive, acknowledged, and legitimate set of representative-leaders of the "national majority" does exist.[29] The "national majority" may well be a fiction; but for most practical purposes the cabinet is accepted *as if* it were the legitimate representative of the "national majority." Hence, the governmental policy is so organized that in so far as the cabinet itself can be co-ordinated, governmental policy can be coördinated, and against a unified cabinet there is slight opportunity for minority leaders to obstruct cabinet policy, exercise a veto, or compel bargains that seriously conflict with important cabinet policies.

In Britain most bargaining over policy takes place among an essentially unified group of leaders of a single party operating within a very broad context of agreement; in the United States between diverse and conflicting leaders of numerous political alliances operating within a narrow context of ageement.

One can scarcely exaggerate the importance of this point. It means among other things that the experience of Britain or, say, Sewden is limited in its relevancy to the American scene. It means

[28] New York *Times*, Sunday, April 27, 1952, Section 4, p. 8.

[29] It should be pointed out that the differences cannot be explained solely by reference to governmental characteristics. Social structural factors are also important.

that government economic policy in this country is certain to be more chaotic, incoherent, and contradictory than in Britain or Sweden. It means that, whatever might be the difficulties of coordination in government planning as practiced in Britain or Sweden, with the same programs in the United States the difficulties of coördination would be many times greater.

In Great Britain a cabinet typically comes into office with all the constitutional discretion it requires to carry out a coördinated program—or at least what its members think is a coördinated program. The cabinet knows that it can get whatever legislation it needs to carry out its proposals; if it insists, amendments and alterations will be slight; if it cannot get what it believes is basic to the success of its program, it will resign. The last step, however, has become rare in this century. Except for a few cabinets that have tried to govern without a party majority behind them, like the Labor governments of 1924 and 1929, no government in more than half a century has left office before the expiration of its full term or its own decision to call an election. Since the Parliament Act of 1911, no government with a majority in the Commons has had to worry much about the powers of the House of Lords; since the recent Labor party reforms even the Lords' power to delay ordinary legislation for more than one session has been eliminated.

Behind the cabinet, then, stands a party majority that may be counted on to support the program on which the party was elected, as interpreted for the most part by the cabinet. At the apex is the Prime Minister and a small inner cabinet of varying size. Beneath this group are the other ministers, subordinate to the leadership and coördinated by the cabinet secretariat, the standing committees, and the recent innovation of "grouped ministries."[30] At the next layer are, on the administrative side, a disciplined civil service coordinated in numerous ways by the Treasury and, on the parliamentary side, the parliamentary party with the whips and the caucus to keep it in line. Thus although the system requires some bargaining, it is marked by a clear hierarchy of controllers possessing ample control over subordinates.

It would be absurd to say that the system presents no difficulties of coördination. Important parts of the bureaucracy tend to fly off on conflicting missions. Thus despite grave coal shortages

[30] S. E. Finer, *A Primer of Public Administration*, Frederick Muller, Ltd., London, 1950, p. 37. Cf. also pp. 46–49 for further details of the system.

extending over a number of years, the nationalized power industry was not persuaded until 1951 to terminate an advertising campaign that increased sales of electrical equipment to consumers and thereby increased the consumption of coal for producing electric power. Or again, despite the coal shortage the Ministry of Town and Country Planning continued to approve new housing developments that relied on the highly inefficient open grate for heat. Indeed, that ministry furnished an example of uncoördinated policy very typical of the United States. Its policies frequently were by-passed and contradicted by the Board of Trade's Location of Industry program, by the control over local government exercised by the Ministry of Health, and by the Treasury; the net result was a jungle of frustration and conflict that would have seemed familiar to any American civil servant.[31]

Some ex-cabinet ministers have gone so far as to say, as has Leopold Amery, that "the one thing that is hardly ever discussed is general policy. . . . There are only departmental policies. . . . The whole system is one of mutual friction and delay with at best some partial measures of mutual adjustment between unrelated policies. It is quite incompatible with any coherent planning of policy as a whole or with the effective execution of such a policy."[32]

Despite these qualifications, the differences between the two systems are striking. For example, in 1951 a cabinet reshuffle combined the job of town and country planning, supervision of local government, and location of industry—an attempt, through hierarchical arrangements, to overcome the difficulty just mentioned. Or again, when the Conservatives came into office in 1951, the Prime Minister appointed three "Overlords," each of which was to help coördinate several departments; an additional "Overlord" was appointed to act as "an additional eyes and ears and brain" for Mr. Churchill. Thus the hierarchical component was intended to be further strengthened.[33] There were later criticisms of the arrangement.[34] But the point is clear. The cabinet is itself a relatively unified body of policy makers; and, within a powerful system of polyarchal controls, it possesses a very considerable amount of hierarchical con-

[31] Robert Bruce Black, "Brave New Britain: The British Town and Country Planning System," unpublished Ph.D. dissertation, Harvard University, 1950, pp. 137–138.
[32] Leopold Amery, *Thoughts on the Constitution,* Oxford University Press, New York, 1947, p. 87; quoted in S. E. Finer, *op. cit.,* p. 51.
[33] *The Economist,* December 1, 1951, p. 1307.
[34] *Ibid.,* May 3, 1952, pp. 277–278, and May 10, 1952, pp. 353 ff.

trol over all other policy makers. The hierarchical controls are tempered by bargaining but rarely nullified.

Within the limits of human capacity and party unity, the opportunities for coördination are great. The Labor cabinet came into office in 1945 knowing that it could enact its program; that Commons would not substantially alter that program or introduce contradictions and inconsistencies not already there; that it had five years during which it could work; that it could plan out a legislative timetable covering all the major pieces of legislation required over the five-year period; that it could create, shift, adjust, or abolish any administrative agency it felt necessary; that its ministers would stick by the program—or get out; that administrative officials would not set up special pipe lines to the House of Commons to by-pass, frustrate, and elude the cabinet; that the opposition would have opportunity to debate the program and embarrass the cabinet whenever it could—but not to frustrate the policies; that in five years an election would be held in which the electorate could either reëlect Labor or elevate the opposition to office with all the foregoing discretion and equal opportunities to prove that it could do a more acceptable job of running the country.

It is altogether doubtful, then, that Americans could operate a system of centralized government controls over the economy with even the relative success the British have achieved in recent years. Americans are forced to operate with a much larger cushion for errors stemming from inconsistent and contradictory policies. So far, through two world wars, two periods of reconversion, a major depression, and a cold war, our resources have evidently been sufficient to offset losses resulting from breakdowns in coördination, and we have missed outright disaster. But if the survival of this country should ever come to depend upon squeezing the utmost from our resources, and hence on reducing conflicting policies to a minimum, the stark alternatives would be failure—or a drastic change in the policy process.

13.

Bargaining: Control Among Leaders (Continued)

I. Prerequisites to Rational Social Action in the United States

Given the consequences of bargaining just described, what are the prerequisites of increasing the capacity of Americans for rational social action through their national government? Or is the predominant role of bargaining in national politics inherent as long as the United States remains a polyarchy? No one can give confident answers to these questions. (Partly for this reason, there seems to be little disposition on the part of influential Americans to make significant alterations in the policy process.) Certainly the adoption of a parliamentary system along British lines, or some version of it, may be ruled out, not only because no one knows enough to predict how it would work in the United States, but also because support for the idea is almost nonexistent. Although incremental change provides better opportunity for rational calculation than comprehensive alterations like substitution of the British system, there is little evidence even of a desire for incremental change, at least in a direction that would increase opportunities for rational calculation and yet maintain or strengthen polyarchal controls.

Nevertheless, certain alternatives are worth examining.

BUREAUCRATIC COÖRDINATION

One common proposal for dealing with the malcoördination of bargaining is to turn much of the job of coördinating policy over to government bureaucracies. Particularly among students of public administration one finds often a tendency to idealize the rationality and responsiveness of government bureaucracies; alongside this idealized portrait of bureaucracy real-life politicians cut a very sorry figure. And because no unified political group can legitimately claim title as representative-leaders of the national majority, it has even been argued that government bureaucracies are the true representatives of majority preferences or of that more elusive abstraction "the public interest."

It is quite true, of course, that when elected political leaders are more or less agreed on a policy, decisions on sub-policy may often be shifted to the bureaucracies. And when elected political leaders are not agreed, sometimes government bureaucracies can seize the opportunity to make the decision. But if political leadership is not agreed, then to shift a decision on major policy to the bureaucracies is typically only to shift the locus of bargaining. If this is not the case, it can only mean that bureaucracies either are not controlled by political leaders or are somehow insulated from all but one segment of them. To advocate the first is to argue that an autonomous hierarchy is preferable to polyarchy; to advocate the second is to beg two important questions: whether such insulation from all but one set of leaders is either possible or desirable.

Thus the idea that a re-creation of something like the National Resources Planning Board would make coördinated planning possible in this country is false. The fact is that the NRPB, as should have been expected, was inherently unable to achieve coördinated planning. To be sure, it had slight legal authority, but this explanation for its failure hardly goes to the root of its difficulties. These stemmed from the fact that it had no magic substance to dissolve the American political process and create a new one more congenial to coördination. It did a commendable amount of preplanning: making studies, writing reports, holding conferences. But what little actual planning it accomplished depended upon its ability to secure coördination among the warring regiments in Washington and elsewhere; this ability, in turn, depended upon the support it got from politicians. The NRPB could therefore do no more than the authority of the President enabled it to do; and, because it lacked support from politicians centered in Congress and in other parts of the executive branch, in practice it could accomplish very much less than could the President himself. Congress's scuttling of NRPB in 1943 did not mean the end of coördinated planning in the United States; for coördinated planning had never existed. Ironically, for a few years thereafter more coördinated planning existed than ever before because the exigencies of war made it possible for WPB and the Byrnes office to do what the NRPB could never do.

The Bureau of the Budget and the Council of Economic Advisors suffer from the same inherent handicap as would the national economic council that has been repeatedly proposed. As marginal contributions they are no doubt useful. But no one should suppose that by administrative fiat they can possibly overcome the fundamental lack of coördination inherent in the American political process; and to any person who believes polyarchy is desirable, the solution should be a repugnant one even if it were possible.

PRESIDENTIAL COÖRDINATION

If control by elected politicians is requisite to polyarchy, and if elected politicians cannot agree on policy, then one solution is to strengthen the hierarchical controls of one more or less unified group over other leaders. In this way, as in Great Britain, hierarchical controls would significantly limit the amount of bargaining that must take place.

In essence this is the solution of those who would "strengthen the Presidency." The President possesses more hierarchical controls than any other single figure in the government; indeed, he is often described somewhat romantically and certainly ambiguously as the "most powerful democratic executive in the world." Yet like everyone else in the American policy process, the President must bargain constantly—with Congressional leaders, individual Congressmen, his department heads, bureau chiefs, and leaders of nongovernmental organizations. One common proposal is to increase the President's hierarchical controls in one or both of two ways.

PRESIDENT AS GENERAL MANAGER. One variant is to give the President more hierarchical control over the government bureaucracies. This was the central position of both the President's Committee on Administrative Management in 1937 and the Hoover Commission in 1948. Yet there are two fatal defects in this theory. First, at base it amounts to little more than saying that the problem could be solved by solving the problem. If Presidential politicians could be given "sufficient" power over the bureaucracies, the bureaucracies would be responsive to Presidential politicians—a neat tautology. The problem is the "if." The fact is, the basic policy process created by the prescribed and accepted constitutional structure itself makes the "if" utopian. For so long as Congressional politicians conflict with Presidential politicians each group is bound to use control over the bureaucracies as one of its weapons. Given the facts of American politics, there is no escaping the conclusion.

Proponents of the "President as general manager" theory evidently have unconsciously postulated a relation between executive politicians and legislative politicians that prevails only in a two-party parliamentary system as in Great Britain. No serious conflict between executive and legislative politicians can long persist there; for conflict automatically generates a chain of events that sooner or later ends with a set of executive politicians who have the confidence of a disciplined majority of the legislative politicians. Consequently the bureaucracies are never simply pawns in a conflict; conflict over policy takes place instead between the opposition and the cabinet with its disciplined majority in the House of Commons.

To put it oversimply, so long as the cabinet retains the confidence of a disciplined majority, members of that majority have no need to strike at the cabinet's power by controlling administrative "details." They can permit the fullest measure of cabinet control over the government bureaucracies because they believe the basic policy goals of the cabinet are substantially identical with their own. Yet this is precisely the reverse of the typical situation in American national politics. Presidential politicians rarely if ever do have the confidence of a disciplined majority of both houses of Congress. It is inevitable, then, that some Congressional politicians will employ every control available to them to secure *their* goals.

Even if, somehow, the President's *prescribed* hierarchical controls over government bureaucracies could be vastly increased beyond what he has at present, it is questionable whether the President's *operating* hierarchical controls can be increased nearly as much as the proponents of this solution suppose. The idea that the President himself has the time, the energy, or the knowledge to exert control over his prescribed bureaucratic subordinates is a myth that would scarcely demand serious examination if so many serious proposals did not assume it. Nor do we get any further by employing the *mystique* of "the Presidency" or "the institutionalization of the Presidency," for this is merely to substitute an ambiguous phrase for a problem. In the end, the "institutionalization" consists of Presidential politicians and their subordinates, of varying loyalties and goals—only one of whom, a most harassed man, happens to be elected. There is little evidence that this one elected official can effectively control the Presidential politicians and "overhead units" that speak in his name.[1] Hence (and this is the second defect in the theory) this solution would merely mean that control over the bureaucracies would shift from elected politicians—in so far as they now exert control—to non-elected leaders in the bureaucracies themselves and in nongovernmental organizations.

PRESIDENT AS PARTY LEADER. The second variant runs aground on the same shoals. Under this proposal, the President's hierarchical controls as "party leader" would be strengthened; how this change would be brought about varies with the proposal. Yet, somehow, the President's own program would become the program around which all members of his party in Congress, and of course in the executive branch, would unite. At least one party, the party in office, would thus be unified; then perhaps even the opposition party would be forced to match this solidarity in order to be effective. In this fashion bargaining would be reduced, and many of the features of the governmental process mentioned in Part III of the last chapter would be eliminated. This proposal must be distinguished from the "party government" idea, which we shall come to in a moment, for it is really not so much party government as Presidential rule under the external forms of party government.

The difficulties with this proposal are, again, that Congressmen of the President's party have little incentive for exchanging their bargaining controls over the President and the bureaucracy for complete acquiescence in whatever he proposes. In the second place, if Congressmen should accept this odd exchange it would in fact mean a shift of operating control not merely to the President but, for the reasons cited above, to non-elected officials. And in the third place, it would simply shift the locus of such bargaining as now takes place in Congress to the executive branch.

PARTY GOVERNMENT

A third proposal is "party government." This does at least go to the heart of the problem. Roughly, this solution is to graft on the American government system a general approximation of the British party system. It has many versions. Charles Hyneman, for example, proposes a party council of Presidential and Congressional

[1] Herbert A. Simon, Donald W. Smithburg, and Victor A. Thompson, *Public Administration*, Alfred A. Knopf, New York, 1950, pp. 536–540, effectively torpedo this myth. And cf. Charles Hyneman, *Bureaucracy in a Democracy*, Harper & Brothers, New York, 1950.

politicians. The President would coöpt into this council any member of his party in Congress or the executive branch whose bargaining controls were so great that the program of the council could not be passed or administered without his agreement. The "party" program would not be simply the President's *diktat*. As under the previous proposal it would be the product of bargaining and compromise *in the council*. The council would, of course, find it necessary to eliminate seniority in selecting Congressional committee members and chairmen; instead, these would be party members who actively prosecuted the "party" program. The party caucus would be strengthened as a means for communication, maintaining party unity, and insuring that the council was sufficiently representative of the various sections of the party.[2]

Hence, it might be argued, a set of unified, cohesive, acknowledged, and ultimately legitimate representative-leaders of the "national majority" would develop. Policy proposals by this set of leaders could not be easily blocked, for once the bargaining was concluded in the party council, party leaders would wield very considerable strength against all opponents. The bargaining power of strategically placed minorities would be reduced. A "national majority" could carry out its program without having to mobilize much more than a majority of the politically active on its side. Logrolling would be reduced. Coördinated policy would be possible, or at least as much as is possible in any system of polyarchal government. Party leaders could bring unified control to bear over bureaucratic leaders. And to some extent even the demands of the highly organized would have to be tempered, for the national political party is, above all, the one great organization available to the otherwise unorganized.

IS PARTY GOVERNMENT POSSIBLE? It must be admitted at the outset that political scientists are far from agreeing on the practicality of this proposal. Aside from complicated value conflicts over the desirability of party government in the United States, no one can ever say with confidence that it is even possible. Briefly, party government may be impossible because political leaders would not

[2] Charles Hyneman, *op. cit.*; see also E. E. Schattschneider, *Party Government*, Farrar and Rinehart, New York, 1942; and his *Struggle for Party Government*, University of Maryland Department of Government and Politics, College Park, 1948; and—with less emphasis on party—E. S. Corwin, *The President: Office and Powers*, 3rd ed., New York University Press, New York, 1948.

gain from it, because the diversity of social organizations and goals in the United States makes a unified program impossible (the party council might need to coöpt all party members in Congress!), or because the constitutional structure of checks and balances would make it unworkable. As to the last, Hyneman points out that the geographical basis of the Senate is an obvious obstacle and may need to be eliminated. Separate elections and overlapping terms for Senators, Congressmen, and the President may also raise serious difficulties in obtaining a single "mandate" from the "majority."

It would take us too far afield to examine all these problems, particularly the constitutional ones.[3] The obvious question is why, if the proposal would achieve all it purports to, has it not already been adopted? The answer can be put this way. All the proposals we have been examining run aground on the fact that the politically active seem to prefer that the additional governmental checks of the American system be superimposed on the checks already imposed by the social pluralism-interdependence-disagreement-agreement inherent in polyarchy. In a country where social pluralism and disagreement are great relative to the amount of basic agreement, almost every social group can make a rational calculation that its advantage lies in keeping open the opportunity to block action and insist on bargaining, along the lines sketched out earlier. Hence only if basic agreement increases on enough issues among enough groups will there be support among the politically active for overriding some of the present governmental checks by party government.

Is basic agreement increasing or likely to increase in the United States? It would take us too far afield to seek a comprehensive answer, but one facet of a possible answer is significant: an increasing number of people in a wide assortment of social groups seem to agree that the costs of an uncoördinated economy are very great

[3] For some representative views and data, cf. American Political Science Association, Committee on Political Parties, *Toward a More Responsible Two-Party System*, Rinehart and Co., New York, 1950; Julius Turner, "Responsible Parties: A Dissent from the Floor," *American Political Science Review*, March, 1951, pp. 143–152; Austin Ranney, "Toward a More Responsible Two-Party System: A Commentary," *American Political Science Review*, June, 1951, pp. 488–499; Pendleton Herring, *The Politics of Democracy*, W. W. Norton and Co., New York, 1940; George L. Grassmuck, *Sectional Biases in Congress on Foreign Policy*, Johns Hopkins Press, Baltimore, 1951; Thomas K. Finletter, *Can Representative Government Do the Job?* Harcourt, Brace and Co., New York, 1945; Alexander Heard, *A Two-Party South?* University of North Carolina Press, Chapel Hill, 1952; Julius Turner, *Party and Constituency: Pressures on Congress*, Johns Hopkins Press, Baltimore, 1951.

and that the national government must play a central role in coordinating at least some kinds of economic activities. If enough
people among the politically active come to agree on this one end,
then they must ultimately agree on party government as a means.

Inability to moderate inflation and unemployment, for example, is a serious liability to any party nominally in power, for the
party's nominal control combined with its actual impotence can
lead to serious electoral repercussions. The pathetically short triumph of nominal Republican control over Congress was probably
terminated so abruptly in 1948 in part, at least, because the Republican majority in Congress showed neither predisposition nor capacity for halting the postwar inflation. Thus a party that cannot
coördinate the economy may lose elections, and a heterogeneous
party without unity cannot coördinate the economy. In such a case,
it will be to the plain advantage of many politicians to unite behind
a common program.

CONSEQUENCES OF STRATIFICATION. Even so, the difficulty
of securing any coherent and coördinated set of policies will continue to be great if there are such marked diversities of attitude from
one constituency to another that a nominal "majority" in favor of
vigorous efforts, say, to halt inflation still contains widely different
views as to how this is to be done. The most important development
here is the stratification of American society brought on by industrialization, urbanism, and the bureaucratization of social organizations.[4] For political predispositions are strongly shaped by occupational and status group identifications and the similarity of activities,
habits, and communication media.

For example, on the proper role of the government in economic
life, "whereas nine-tenths of large business owners and managers
and over three-fourths of professional and small businessmen cling
to the traditional belief that the role of government should be limited to the insuring of good opportunities for the individual's pursuit
of his own economic destiny, only about three-tenths of semi-skilled
and unskilled workers profess such a conviction."[5] From a battery
of questions—which it must be confessed are not altogether satis-

[4] Sam Lubell, *The Future of American Politics*, Harper & Brothers, New
York, 1952.
[5] Richard Centers, *The Psychology of the Social Classes*, Princeton University
Press, Princeton, 1949, pp. 60–64.

factory ones—Richard Centers has constructed a pattern of "ultra-conservatism," "conservatism," "indeterminate" (which Centers has decided are "liberals"), "radical" and "ultra-radical." As might be expected, the responses of the people in Centers' nation-wide sample varied significantly with their occupational, economic, or control position. For example, "whereas almost nine-tenths—87 percent— of large business owners and managers are either conservative or ultra-conservative in political and economic orientation, only about one-fifth—21 percent—of semi-skilled manual workers are so oriented."[6] These differences were, of course, reflected in their voting; 75 percent of the Republican vote among his sample in the 1944 Presidential election came from conservatives and ultra-conservatives.[7]

It is possible that the basic core of the New Deal and Fair Deal alliance—urban workers, the new middle class of white-collar workers, urban political machines, and an important share of farmers and farm laborers—will become sufficiently homogeneous to permit the development of a more unified party—a solution, to be sure, that depends upon the effects of southern and midwestern industrialization for a truly stable alliance.

LOCAL IDENTIFICATION. It is sometimes said that unified party government cannot be achieved unless local identifications are broken down. Yet, to destroy local identifications in order to leave the individual with no loyalties except to the Leviathan nation-state is hardly a solution to be wished for by anyone except a totalitarian. Need a loss of local identification be an inevitable prerequisite for unified parties capable of coördinating the economy? This is a difficult question to answer. We think the dilemma is false, but the evidence is by no means conclusive.

At first blush, British experience over the past decade or so seems to confirm the truth of the dilemma posed by the question. Unified parties, a unitary rather than a federal constitution, parliamentary supremacy in constitutional theory and cabinet supremacy in fact: all these permit a relatively high degree of coördination of national policy in Britain as compared with the United States. Yet it seems to be a fact that increased efforts to coördinate economic

[6] *Ibid.*, p. 56. Cf. also pp. 59, 109–114.
[7] *Ibid.*, p. 48. Cf. also Table 5, p. 46.

policy have gone hand in hand with a decline in energy, autonomy, activity, and enthusiasm in local government.[8] Other small and intermediate groups appear to have suffered an equal decline in autonomy; hierarchical planning in war and peace has significantly restricted the opportunities for group autonomy.

Despite all this it would be premature to argue that the fault somehow lies with unified parties and a political process that facilitates coördination of national policy. For this would be to overlook one crucial fact: no English government in the past several generations has been interested enough in small-group autonomy to employ its undoubted capacities for coördinating national policy in order to stimulate the autonomous life of small groups. To find an explanation for the alleged decline in the vigor of local government in England one must look not to party organization but to the party programs and the series of crises that have helped to shape public policy in England as elsewhere since 1914; for avowed party goals and recurring emergencies have reduced the goal of small-group autonomy to a matter of low priority. Unemployment, the dole, rearmament, war mobilization, national health, social security, nationalization, redistribution of incomes, stability, international trade, the dollar shortage: these have been the concerns of government in England as elsewhere. It is no wonder that small-group autonomy has declined.

Thus the English experience is inconclusive. No one can say what the situation would be like today if party programs and the opportunities of the British situation had brought into power a government that genuinely wished to strengthen small-group autonomy. Would town and country planning, for example, be as centralized as it is today?

Moreover, the argument is founded on still another misconception: that the American political process has in fact facilitated small-group autonomy, particularly in local communities. There is no doubt that the American political process does allow small groups to protest effectively when their goals are threatened. So-called "local interests" are often powerful in national decisions. Yet because "local interests" are influential in national decisions, it does

---

[8] Cf. Samuel Edward Finer, *A Primer of Public Administration*, Frederick Muller, Ltd., London, 1950. "By the end of the Second World War the local authorities were considered less as councils in their own right than as mere local instruments of departmental policy" (p. 103). And *The Economist*, July 21, 1951, p. 141, argues that there has been a real decline in the vigor of local government since World War II.

not follow that American politics really fosters local autonomy. There is little evidence to indicate that American local government, for example, is any more vigorous and flourishing than British local government; according to many observers it is the other way around. Then, too, national policy about local units can be co-ordinated no better than any other kind of national policy; hence local units of government are subject to improvised and conflicting policies that do not necessarily favor strong local autonomy. Even if an administration came into office anxious to stimulate local autonomy, one finds difficulty in imagining how it could actually carry through any coherent program to that end. Moreover, as we shall see in a moment, the American political process stimulates centralized emergency coördination; and just as the national "co-ordinator" may take over other sectors of national policy because coördinated decisions could not otherwise be made, so too he may take over many local functions because as a nation we have been unable to work out any system of coördination via the political process. The history of work relief furnishes an instructive example.[9] From 1933 to 1935 under FERA, work relief was administered by states and localities on a grant-in-aid basis; a remarkable amount of local autonomy existed. Yet nothing in the American political process prevented this system from being replaced by the more centralized WPA in 1935.

And in any case what are these "local interests" to which politicians are so responsive? There is a tendency in some quarters to envision the Congressman as a real "delegate" of a "local majority." But he is no such thing. Only a tiny minority of the local population has any direct contact with Congressmen. Few people even know their Congressman's name.[10] Between elections, for most purposes the local constituency of the Congressional politician is made up of tiny but influential minorities of wealth, status, and power. For most people the only act of participation in national policy decisions they ever perform is to cast a ballot every two or four years. But a number of tiny and well-organized pressure groups

[9] Edward Ainsworth Williams, *Federal Aid for Relief*, Columbia University Press, New York, 1939. And Arthur W. MacMahon, John D. Millet, and Gladys Ogden, *The Administration of Federal Work Relief*, Public Administration Service, Chicago, 1941.
[10] In 1946, 8 percent of one New York constituency knew who their Congressman was; by dint of regular radio speeches and extraordinarily hard work, over two years Representative Jacob Javits managed to build this up to the unusual figure of 33 percent. New York *Herald Tribune*, September 22, 1948, p. 16.

wield great influence between elections by dint of strategic political activity ranging from conversations with the local boss and visits to Washington, to campaign contributions and well-subsidized propaganda. Leaders of these minorities constitute much of the "field" of the Congressman; he and they are part of a small group with many of the usual characteristics of small groups, including indoctrination, social control, status, friendship, solidarity, responsiveness, reciprocity. Obviously more unified parties could not repeal "the iron law of oligarchy"; but they could strengthen the role of the real majority in local communities whose only participation in the national decisions is their choice between two broad alternatives at election time. Under the present political process this election-time choice is largely nullified by the political efficiency of the small minorities who manage to wield their influence between elections.

Finally, the political process as it now operates penalizes politicians who develop local programs and rewards those who operate by personal favors. There is much to be said for the urban political machine as a device for humanizing political relationships in giant cities like Chicago, New York, Boston, and Philadelphia; but political machines are organized to grant personal favors, not to develop community programs.[11] Unified parties would not automatically become programmatic; but they would make programmatic parties possible.

What we have said about local autonomy applies to small groups in general. Simply because pressure groups are powerful in determining national policy in the United States, one cannot infer that small-group autonomy is fostered among the great majority of people who are, when national decisions are made, largely passive bystanders. Indeed, the autonomy of the passive, unorganized, and powerless is often the sacrificial victim of the active, organized, and powerful minorities. "States righters" want autonomy for local elites of wealth, power, and status in order to destroy opportunities for autonomous group action by those who are now unorganized and powerless.

A predisposition for better coördination of national policy is not incompatible with a desire for strengthening small-group autonomy; indeed, there is no reason the two should not go together. If

---

[11] Whyte points this out as a characteristic of Cornerville; see William Foote Whyte, *Street Corner Society*, University of Chicago Press, Chicago, 1943, p. 252.

enough voters had strong preferences about local autonomy, then unified and competing parties would strive to develop programs for strengthening local autonomy. It would be politically suicidal for them to do otherwise. Thus in Great Britain the desirability of central government assistance in town and country planning was so widely accepted that it never even became a party issue; members of both parties agreed on it.[12] In the last analysis, then, if the politically active want small-group autonomy, that goal will be fostered by unified parties; if the politically active do not want it, no party system will preserve it.

In view of what we have said about local identifications and in view of the considerations previously discussed, the solution of party government appears to be the most congenial to the kinds of goals set forth in Chapter 2; and it may be possible. Until it arrives, however, economic policy will either have to be made in the bargaining milieu we have already described, or somehow that bargaining milieu will have to be by-passed. Proposals for bureaucratic coördination and a "strong" President are really of the latter kind. In actual fact neither has gained much acceptance as a substitute for bargaining. There remains one alternative that is less a proposal than a recurring response. This is the device of the temporary administrative "strong man."

EMERGENCY COÖRDINATION[13]

What happens to the bargaining process in times of crisis when high-ranking goals of all major groups are seriously endangered and quick action is required, as in the depths of a depression, during mobilization, or on the outbreak of war? At such moments the bargaining process is much too costly in time and other resources. For a time, indeed, even demands for bargaining decline as basic agreements are activated; strategic minorities partly abdicate their blocking role in order to unite in support of a program presumably dedicated to the achievement of more widely shared goals.

This situation facilitates a "temporary" change in the governmental process. Hierarchical controls are significantly increased.

---

[12] Robert Bruce Black, "Brave New Britain: the British Town and Country Planning System," unpublished Ph.D. dissertation, Harvard University, Department of Political Economy and Government, 1950, pp. 51–52.

[13] For a study of the political problems of emergency coördination, an examination of some alternatives, and a proposal, see Herman Miles Somers, *Presidential Agency*, Harvard University Press, Cambridge, 1950, esp. Introduction and chap. 7.

Obstreperous minority leaders who insist on bargaining "have their heads knocked together" and speedy solutions result.

The President is the main instrument of unified action in our political system; hence his prescribed hierarchical controls are enlarged in times of crisis. But the President is one individual, and he must delegate. Having delegated, he has neither the time, the energy, nor the knowledge to exercise much supervision over all his nominal subordinates. Increasingly during the Second World War, for example, Roosevelt delegated the control of the war economy to others, so that he might concentrate on military and foreign policy decisions. Or again, in 1951 a decision was made to cope with mobilization by building a war economy atop our civilian economy rather than by converting the existing economy to war production. "The big decision to build two economies instead of converting one was made, primarily, by Charles E. Wilson when he took the job of defense mobilizer. . . . This great policy decision was never debated in Congress or presented to the American people."[14]

A large measure of autonomy for top policy makers is thus inevitable in times of crisis. As an English writer has said, during the First World War the parliamentary constitution had to go into cold storage for the duration.[15] Or as Lincoln said, "Was it possible to lose the nation and yet preserve the Constitution?" Still, the question is not whether there shall be extensive autonomy, but how much and located with what individuals?

EMERGENCY   COÖRDINATION   BY   GREAT   TECHNICIANS. Three general alternatives suggest themselves. First, a high degree of hierarchical control may be granted to supposedly successful managers or technicians who have not been active participants in the process of governmental bargaining, who are not politicians, and who are cut off, so far as this is possible, from the normal bargaining process. One thinks of Bernard Baruch in the First World War, General Johnson and the NRA, William Knudsen and Donald Nelson in OPM, Charles Wilson in WPB (and, after the outbreak of the Korean war, Director of Economic Stabilization), Ferdinand

[14] Robert Dean, "Our Permanent War Economy," *The New Leader*, January 7, 1952, p. 2. It is true, of course, that the decision might have been taken in expectation of subsequent political responses that would have confirmed the decision.
[15] K. B. Smellie, *A Hundred Years of English Government*, Duckworth, London, 1950, p. 178.

Eberstadt in the War Department, Leon Henderson in OPA, James Forrestal in the Department of Defense, and General Marshall in the State Department. Their initial prestige, the mood of crisis, the President's support, all contribute to a partial relief from the normal bargaining process.

But bargaining is not entirely eliminated. Its locus is shifted to the emergency agencies under the super-managers and super-technicians. Their hierarchical controls vary directly, and the extent of bargaining varies inversely, with the mood of crisis, the President's support, and their own prestige.[16] At times their hierarchical control drastically declines and the need for bargaining spreads until the typical patterning of bargaining politics begins to reappear. At this point, if not, indeed, much earlier, the super-technicians are likely to find themselves incompetent in the one skill that now becomes paramount, the politician's skill.[17]

EMERGENCY COÖRDINATION BY POLITICIANS. Hence a second alternative is for the President to appoint politicians who have, in effect, a blank check to use as much hierarchical control as they can manage to win for themselves during the crisis. Thus during the Second World War, the year 1943 saw the technicians give way to politicians. James F. Byrnes left the Supreme Court and became "assistant president" with extraordinary influence in mediating disputes and coördinating policy. Prentiss Brown, a former Senator, became Price Administrator. Marvin Jones, a former Congressman, was appointed Food Administrator. Fred Vinson, a former Congressman who had been appointed by Roosevelt to the Court of Appeals, became Director of Economic Stabilization.[18] Meanwhile the Truman Committee in the Senate had become a major force in making policy and breaking administrators.

The difficulty with this alternative as a governmental solution for relatively normal times is that either it leaves the bargaining process unaltered, which represents no gain, or, as with Byrnes, bargaining is significantly displaced by hierarchical controls, which raises some serious problems both for the President and for polyarchy. As for the President, if any other political leader can significantly displace bargaining with hierarchical controls, he must

---

[16] H. M. Somers, op. cit., chap. 1.

[17] For example, cf. Somers' appraisal of Donald Nelson's personality and skills, ibid., note 61, pp. 38–39.

[18] Sam Lubell, op cit., p. 18.

possess skill, status, rewards, and deprivations that enable him to threaten the supremacy of the President himself. As for polyarchy, what guarantee is there that the policies of these officials will operate roughly within the preferences of the greater number?

To say that these officials are responsive to President, Congress, pressure groups, and future elections is to beg the question. For if, as we have argued, strategic minorities can compel bargaining, what reason has one for supposing that the policies of these officials will not reflect the demands of strategic minorities—for example, of well-placed committee chairmen in Congress? And if the control of strategic minorities is to be eliminated, how is this significant change to be brought about? Here again, as with "strengthening the President" or "administrative coördination" there is a danger that circular logic may avoid the central problem, namely, the *process* through which the need, desire, and opportunity for bargaining are all to be decreased.

EMERGENCY COÖRDINATION BY UNIFIED POLITICAL LEADERSHIP. Hence we return to an earlier proposition. Administrative arrangements are no substitute for unified political leadership. Indeed, the previous "solution" is workable only in so far as emergency conditions activate underlying agreement and increase the basic unity of political leaders. If political leaders with diverse and conflicting goals can insist on bargaining, then no administrative arrangement in a polyarchal system can, by itself, significantly decrease the intensity of bargaining and its consequences for policy. In such a situation policy makers can avoid bargaining only by avoiding control by elected officials; and if they can avoid such controls, polyarchy is weakened.

The most appropriate prerequisite to coördination is, then, the party council. Placed in that setting and modified accordingly, the emergency alternatives just mentioned hold no greater dangers for polyarchy than crisis and the need for delegation must always hold. For in that case basic policy would be supervised by a unified body of leaders, elected by a "national majority," concerned with maintaining the confidence of that "majority" through future elections, sensitive to opposition criticism, yet possessed of sufficient control to coördinate policy without ceaseless bargaining and compromise with strategic minorities.

However, lest we be accused of having adopted a circular argument ourselves, we hasten to point out that this solution, like the others, presupposes a reduction in bargaining—presumably along the lines indicated earlier in connection with our discussion of party government. And as we said then, although, given the goals of Chapter 2, it may be a desirable solution and even a possible one, until it arrives policy must necessarily be made in a bargaining milieu—except, perhaps, in moments of great crisis when bargaining is temporarily reduced by the displacement and abdication of some of the normal claimants.

Part V.   POLITICO-
ECONOMIC
TECHNIQUES

14.
Price System, Hierarchy,
and Polyarchy
for Choice and Allocation

I. Introduction

All modern industrialized economies combine, though in different ways, the four central sociopolitical processes: price system, hierarchy, polyarchy, and bargaining. Each of these processes has been examined at some length, and some conclusions have already been drawn concerning their suitability for economizing. The present group of chapters now descends to a lower level of generality; where the preceding chapters analyzed the general strengths and weaknesses of these processes, the present chapters will focus more sharply on hierarchical, polyarchal, and bargaining politico-economic techniques. And analysis of the price system will be carried further now that it can be compared with three alternative processes. (Diagram 6, p. 370, summarizes the main outline of the analysis to this point.)

THE ALTERNATIVES

This and the following two chapters will appraise one set of alternatives: hierarchical and polyarchal techniques, on the one hand, and price system techniques, on the other. For both hierarchy and polyarchy are methods for central direction of economic life, whereas the price system is a method of extreme decentralization. This and the following chapter are limited to the choice and allocation processes; a subsequent chapter discusses price system, hierarchy, and polyarchy with respect to other aspects of economizing. Thereafter we shall appraise bargaining. Its techniques are numerous; they include collective bargaining, worker control schemes, and informal bargaining among leaders of business, labor, and agriculture.

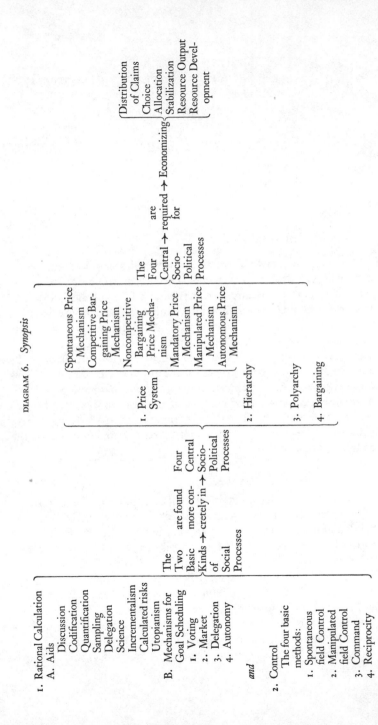

DIAGRAM 6. *Synopsis*

1. Rational Calculation
   A. Aids
      Discussion
      Codification
      Quantification
      Sampling
      Delegation
      Science
      Incrementalism
      Calculated risks
      Utopianism
   B. Mechanisms for Goal Scheduling
      1. Voting
      2. Market
      3. Delegation
      4. Autonomy

and

2. Control
   The four basic methods:
      1. Spontaneous field Control
      2. Manipulated field Control
      3. Command
      4. Reciprocity

The Two Basic Kinds → are found more con- → of Social Processes → cretely in

Four Central Socio-Political Processes

1. Price System
   Spontaneous Price Mechanism
   Competitive Bargaining Price Mechanism
   Noncompetitive Bargaining Price Mechanism
   Mandatory Price Mechanism
   Manipulated Price Mechanism
   Autonomous Price Mechanism

2. Hierarchy

3. Polyarchy

4. Bargaining

The Four Central Socio-Political Processes → are required for → Economizing

   Distribution of Claims
   Choice
   Allocation
   Stabilization
   Resource Output
   Resource Development

THE COMMON ELEMENTS

But no matter what combination of politico-economic techniques is most appropriate to the achievement of our postulated goals, any economy maximizing such goals will probably rest on certain common techniques and institutions. Economizing will be carried out in large part through business enterprises. Whether public or private, centrally controlled through hierarchy or subordinated to the market, enterprises will probably continue to operate as more or less identifiable and somewhat autonomous units. Large-scale war aside, they will recruit manpower through price system techniques, and free occupational choice will not be seriously curtailed. In large businesses management will be a salaried group; and within each large enterprise internal hierarchical controls will be dominant. Whether public or private, most businesses will sell to consumers on a market, although an increasing number may produce for sale or delivery to government agencies. Thus consumer free choice will presumably remain dominant as a technique for *distributing* goods and services, even if hierarchical direction of production undermines consumer free choice as a technique for *directing* production.

These relatively stable characteristics of politico-economic organization are of the greatest importance in appraising the relative merits of alternative politico-economic techniques. In the first place, they suggest that alternative techniques may not differ in performance so much as might be inferred from the stress in this chapter on their differences. Secondly, because of these similarities, critical influences on the performance of different techniques may be obscured.

Consider the fact that any large enterprise, whether coördinated by a central hierarchy, by bargaining, or by a price mechanism, must be internally organized as a hierarchy. The way hierarchy operates within various enterprises may be more significant for the efficiency with which management uses its resources or for its capacity to innovate than are differences among enterprises in external controls. This statement does not mean, of course, that external controls are not worth debating; they may in fact be the only variable that can be controlled. But it does mean that no one should expect too much from a change in external controls.

On the other hand, differences in forms of control—the difference, say, between a spontaneous and a bargaining price mechanism

—may give rise in subtle and little understood ways to differences in the incentives and roles of management or employees generally. It is not easy to identify the independent and dependent variables in a situation where a core of common techniques of economic organization is overlaid in each enterprise with differing supplementary controls. Similarly, hierarchy, polyarchy, and price system offer alternative agendas; but facing each of these agendas is a businessman who, whether private citizen or civil servant, will act as he does only partly because of the peculiarities of his particular agenda and the immediate controls imposed upon him. The most significant variables affecting his behavior may be unknown at present.

Analysis of central controls and price system is therefore not easily accomplished. Issues become extremely complex. We shall proceed, however, through a series of steps, four in this chapter, three in the next.

II. Shortcomings of Hierarchical and Polyarchal Politico-Economic Techniques

We can take a first step toward an understanding of the appropriate functions for price system and central controls by a brief survey of the shortcomings of central politico-economic techniques. The general deficiencies of hierarchical and polyarchial controls have been explained in earlier chapters; it is especially worth recalling that hierarchy suffers from red tape, "passing the buck," timidity, inflexibility, impersonality, and overcentralization, even though these features of hierarchy have healthy as well as pathological aspects. We now wish, however, to push on to an examination of technical defects in hierarchy and polyarchy which are particularly important to economizing.

For choice and allocation, the particular shortcomings of polyarchy and hierarchy stem not from deficiencies of differentiated structures for choice, costing, and allocation, as we shall see is the case with the price system, but from the absence of sufficiently differentiated structures for these purposes.

To people who have little knowledge of the operations of large hierarchies, hierarchy appears orderly. It appears to have logic and symmetry; the possibility of controlling even the most complex social action appears to be logically contained in the pyramid of responsibility upward and the chains of control downward. In actual fact, however, limitations on the span of control and the absence of suitable specialized mechanisms create a never ending search for an appropriate pattern of organization. Large hierarchical organizations are so complex that simply to describe them is almost impossibly difficult.[1] The consequent instability of hierarchies is illustrated by the frequency of reorganization of United States wartime controls. Not until the war was almost over did a basic pattern of hierarchical control last for as long as nine months. Major reorganization took place twice in 1940, four times in 1941, five times in 1942, four times in 1943, and twice in 1944.[2]

PROBLEMS OF CALCULATION

INADEQUATE COST INFORMATION. Many of the difficulties of central control arise directly from the fact that choices and allocations are made without adequate cost information. In neither hierarchy nor polyarchy is it possible to quantify marginal costs. Inevitably, of course, choices and allocations will be made by persons who weigh the alternative course of action in some way or other. Hence no decision is taken if it is not believed to be worth its cost—that is, if in the mind of the decision maker it is not a better decision than any possible alternative. But what is needed is as precise an estimate as possible of the desirability at the margin of any proposed choice as against the desirability at the margin of the forgone alternatives. This is what hierarchy and polyarchy lack.

Where the decision maker is contemplating, say, a number of possible production schedules for different commodities, he needs to know not simply the physical quantities of resources used up in each line of production but these physical quantities weighted to take account of the fact that because some resources are relatively more scarce than others they must be allocated more sparingly. Only when quantities are so weighted can he know what alternative production he forgoes by proceeding with the production of any one commodity. Moreover, where central controls attempt to organize economic life on the basis of the values postulated in Chapter 2, they must take into account among alternative values not only the prefer-

---

[1] See how difficult it is simply to comprehend the intricate patterns of wartime hierarchical controls; for example, in David Novick, Melven Anshen, and W. C. Truppner, *Wartime Production Controls*, Columbia University Press, New York, 1949.
[2] Luther Gulick, *Administrative Reflections from World War II*, University of Alabama, University, Alabama, 1948, p. 28.

ences of people as consumers but their preferences for one kind of production or work rather than another. Hence, correct calculation must count these preferences in costs. Again, this process is beyond the capacity of hierarchy and polyarchy.

Where decision makers wish to take account of their own preferences alone, the problem of representing them systematically so that they can weight their cost calculations is still difficult: there remains in any case the old problem of apples and horses, which cannot be added. A common denominator is required to arrive at comparable estimates of input requirements for different commodities and services.

The obvious way to meet these difficulties is to use a numbers system, assigning numbers to each resource or factor of production and weighting each assignment of numbers according to preferences and scarcities. The preferences of consumers and producers can be tested by their behavior on a market. But this proposal solves the problems of central control by instituting a price system. Again it is clear that hierarchy and polyarchy are without specialized institutional mechanisms for calculating costs.

This shortcoming of hierarchy has plagued many economies. In the German Nazi economy, for example, a price freeze was ordered in 1936. Both for hierarchical planners and for individual business enterprises thereafter, changes in costs—that is, changes in actual scarcities—could not be reflected in prices. "Public works and investment for armaments brought about big discrepancies between the centrally planned needs and earlier demand curves. . . . No improvement in the methods of calculation could get around this fact. The prices which the firms reckoned with in their books failed as an expression of scarcities, and so lost their controlling function."[3] To be sure, production continued; the central authorities made choices and allocations. But they had no guidelines to choice such as are provided in a price system. The same is true for much of wartime production planning of the Western economies during the Second World War. War compels the abandonment of the price system, in part; but, having done so, it leaves central authorities without adequate cost information.

The inadequacy of cost calculations in hierarchy can be quite specifically illustrated for a particular commodity. In Germany,

[3] Walter Eucken, "On the Theory of the Centrally Administered Economy; An Analysis of the German Experiment," *Economica*, May, 1948, p. 91.

copper beechwood was long used only for fuel and charcoal but gradually came to have many important uses. If soaked in tar, it was excellent for railway ties. Artificial drying and steaming opened up many possible uses for furniture. It became valuable for plywood and was finally found to be a basic material for the production of cellulose. For the central authorities in the 1930's, its allocation presented no small problem. As a prerequisite to rational allocation, they needed to know what it would cost in alternatives forgone to assign beechwood to any one particular use. In terms of alternatives, what was beechwood worth? This information they did not have, for, although beechwood had a price, it had been frozen since 1932 and was consequently no longer a useful measure of cost.[4]

For the United States the inadequacy of cost calculations in hierarchy is best illustrated in wartime production planning. It is obscured, however, for two reasons. First, the United States entered the war with a great supply of unemployed resources that could be allocated to war production. Consequently, the war never compelled policy makers to give the attention to costs—to forgone alternatives—that would otherwise have been necessary. Second, there is no way to measure the discrepancy between accurate cost estimates and the implicit and subjective cost estimates necessarily used in wartime controls. Then, too, studies of the wartime economy have not investigated the adequacy of wartime cost information. In some studies prices are assumed to have represented costs during the war, despite their gross inaccuracies for wartime cost measurements; and in many other studies, political and administrative problems have been allowed to overshadow this critical element in hierarchical economizing.[5]

[4] *Ibid.,* pp. 91–92.

[5] Preoccupied as they were with immediate political and administrative problems, many wartime administrators were often somewhat less sensitive to cost problems. Not calculating in terms of costs, yet nevertheless caught up by the urgency of the allocation problem, some of them came through the war with little comprehension of how differently they would have had to confront the allocation problem if military requirements had pressed much harder on available resources. Somers' account of manpower allocation confirms this conclusion: "Manpower is the ultimate limiting resource of an economy. Our nation was rich in this vital resource. During the defense and early war periods, the labor force was expanded by several millions . . . ; unprecedented migration was providing manpower . . . , and job simplification and training programs helped to meet the enormous demands both for production and the armed forces. . . . Until the summer of 1943, the manpower problems were largely of a 'spot' character, confined to specific issues. . . . These 'bottlenecks,' however, were extremely serious. . . . Unfortunately, the over-all situation, being generally favorable, tended to temper the appearance of emergency. . . . As a result, spot improvisation and indirect measures became the pattern. . . .

Nevertheless, errors in costing cannot be concealed. Even at the level of statistical estimation of resource requirements for various kinds of output, calculations were seriously deficient. "When reports on actual performance against calculated programs were not made from an auditable record of individual actions, the statistical estimates of performance actually varied by as much as 100 percent from the action taken as ultimately developed through records of account."[6] In the official War Production Board history, the difficulties of calculating costs are revealed in the board's difficulties in estimating military requirements and their relation to resources available, without which estimates costs cannot be known. "Claimant agencies," it is reported, "sometimes tended to exaggerate their needs to improve their bargaining position and sometimes understated needs in recognition of unavoidable limitations in the supply of resources. Consequently, it was almost impossible at any time to judge whether or not *real* requirements, as distinguished from *stated* requirements, were being satisfied." Moreover, "there was no adequate wartime governmental machinery for the basic adjustment of military requirements to the supply of resources."[7]

Difficulties of inadequate cost calculation are illustrated in manpower control in World War II.[8] Should jobs be brought to workers, or should workers be brought to jobs? There were severe limits on the degree to which workers could be induced to move; on the other hand, it was difficult to control procurement so as to throw contracts into labor surplus areas. Whatever the guise in which this problem was posed to administrators, it was in fact a problem in costs. In terms of alternatives forgone, is it more costly to move workers to equipment or equipment to workers? In a price system, the decision is simplified because the costs of both alternatives are

By 1944 . . . manpower became the major 'bottleneck' in war production. But, by this time, the sense of urgency and fear over the military outcome of the war had diminished. . . ." H. M. Somers, *Presidential Agency*, Harvard University Press, Cambridge, 1950, pp. 138–139.

[6] David Novick, Melven Anshen, and W. C. Truppner, *op. cit.*, p. 368. We do not use this and other examples of deficiencies in hierarchical controls during World War II to show that hierarchical controls were a mistake during the war. There was no alternative; just as, given the values postulated in Chapter 2, there is often no alternative to the price system in other particular circumstances, despite the many deficiencies of the price system. All we wish to do here is recognize the limitations of hierarchy for what they are (just as subsequently we shall examine the limitations of the price system).

[7] U.S. Civilian Production Administration, *Industrial Mobilization for War*, U.S. Government Printing Office, Washington, 1947, Vol. I, pp. 982–983.

[8] H. M. Somers, *op. cit.*, p. 142.

quantified in price; in wartime hierarchical controls, cost estimates must be highly subjective and extremely crude.

INADEQUATE INFORMATION ON CONSUMER PREFERENCES. Assuming central government wishes to choose and allocate so that citizens get what they want out of their scarce resources, it will lack information about citizens' preferences. Everyone wants food, shelter, and clothing; but the variety of each of these produced in Western economies is almost beyond the capacity of central decision makers to grasp. In a price system, consumers can register their preferences every time they make a purchase, but in central control there is no such simple solution. Direct voting on individual commodities and services is out of the question—who would like to face a ballot as long as a Sears, Roebuck catalogue? And in any case, consumers do not and cannot work out details of their possible needs as far ahead as an election period. Ordinarily the only solution open to central control is that leadership makes the choice. Aided by sampling of consumer preferences through questionnaires and interviews, leaders can hope to approximate consumer preferences.

In such a solution are two great difficulties. First, consumers themselves do not know their preferences for many commodities until a particular need arises of the kind that in a price system sends them off to a shop. Second, consumers cannot express their preferences, nor can leaders on their behalf, without knowing their costs; hence, information on consumer preferences will always be defective if cost information is defective. Of course arbitrary costs estimates can be given to the consumer to enable him to respond to a questionnaire. He can be told, for example, that a refrigerator will cost only one-third as much as an automobile. He will then choose, but he will choose among alternatives that do not actually exist. For the central authority cannot in fact afford to offer one automobile or three electric refrigerators as alternatives. The two alternatives demand quite unequal amounts of resources. As we have shown, without a quantification of marginal costs, the central authority does not know whether an automobile costs as much as three, four, five, or six refrigerators.

FAILURE OF THE OVERVIEW. Traditionally it has been argued that a major virtue of hierarchy and polyarchy is that they permit a comprehensive central examination of the economizing process as a whole so that its various parts may be coördinated. In actual fact, they do not work that way. Even within one sector of the economy, they are forced to operate through a crude kind of marginalism— the very antithesis of planning through the omniscient overview.

An excellent illustrative study of this difficulty of central control is Ely Devons' account of his experiences as coördinator of British aircraft production in the Second World War. Those in control of aircraft production planning in Britain gradually abandoned hope for central comprehension of the process in favor of marginal adjustments which could be grasped.

First, at the level of central allocation of resources:

It would have been quite impossible for the central allocating authorities to have considered *de novo* the problem of the allocation of resources between M.A.P. [Ministry of Aircraft Production], the Services and other uses. At most they could deal with the effects of a relatively small change as compared with the then existing or expected situation. Even with such changes, the central allocating authorities could not consider the use of all resources at once, interrelated though they were. Separate committees dealt with man-power, raw materials, factory building, etc. . . . No committee ever considered whether the allocation of resources in total to each use was correct, but took the existing plans of individual departments . . . as given, and then tried to reach agreement on which departments should bear the deficit in supplies which was expected in some forthcoming period.[9]

Second, the Services could not calculate their requirements according to a central plan but instead called for marginal adjustments in production in the direction thought desirable.

Third, the Ministry of Aircraft Production "could calculate accurately its requirements of resources for aircraft production only when small changes in the existing level of output were involved. Attempts were often made to deal with large changes but the resulting calculations were open to a very wide margin of error."[10]

Similar failures of the overview marked hierarchy in World War II in the United States. As we shall show later, the appointment of production czars to expedite critical production with little

[9] Ely Devons, *Planning in Practice,* The University Press, Cambridge, England, 1950, pp. 19–20.
[10] *Ibid.,* p. 19.

regard to central plans[11] and the concentration of calculation on aluminum, copper, and steel in the Controlled Materials Plan represent attempts to substitute a workable partial view of the choice-allocation processes for an overview.[12]

PROBLEMS OF CONTROL

Suppose that in central control, costs and consumer preferences are known, an overview is possible, and occupational preferences can be weighted into costs. There would yet remain the very practical task of assigning particular inputs to particular enterprises for the production of particular outputs. Although information on preferences and costs would be sufficient to match inputs and outputs, information itself does not constitute a method of control, which is what would be required next.

Now we do not say that in hierarchy delegation and decentralization cannot somehow assign all the inputs to their correct outputs. But clearly hierarchy's general shortcomings will be much in evidence, for allocation places an enormous burden on the central bureaucracy of government. By contrast, the price system offers at this point a highly specialized set of control techniques with heavy reliance on spontaneous cues, rewards, and penalties to induce holders of resources to move to the desired allocations.

CENTRALIZATION AND DECENTRALIZATION. Although it has been discussed before,[13] the inevitable struggle between centralization and decentralization becomes a major difficulty in politico-economic control when hierarchy is used for allocation.

Devons writes of his experience in aircraft planning:

Every attempt at planning reveals those two problems, first the need to split up the field to be covered so that each administrative unit can deal efficiently with its own sector; and second, the need to secure that the actions of these separate units all fit into the general plan. But

[11] We recognize that, because bottleneck planning arises out of the failure of the overview, it often appears to be an attempt to achieve coördination by confusing coördination further. The device of the production czar, for example, posed serious problems for other wartime agencies because of the czar's autonomy. Cf. H. M. Somers, *op. cit.*, pp. 27–28.

[12] See also the summary statement of difficulties, largely those of a faulty overview, in the War Production Board history: U.S. Civilian Production Administration, *op. cit.*, pp. 982–986.

[13] Chapters 8 and 9.

the implementation of those principles always leads to a conflict. For the first requires delegation and devolution, so that plans can be manageable and realistic; and the second requires centralization, so that plans can be co-ordinated.

This conflict between devolution and centralization appeared at every stage in the administrative hierarchy. At each level the co-ordinators regarded the plans of the individual sectors as futile and wasteful, because they took no account of what was happening elsewhere; and those in charge of individual sectors regarded the plans of the co-ordinators as theoretical, academic, and unrelated to the real facts of the situation.[14]

And this problem ran through every level of the planning process from top to bottom.

On the highest level there was a conflict between the central co-ordinators in the Cabinet Office and Ministry of Production and the planners in the individual departments. The supreme co-ordinators struggled for more centralization, the planners in each department for more to be left to their discretion. But inside each department, the planners, who argued for delegation when dealing with the central organs of Government, argued for centralization of decisions inside their own departments. And they, in turn, were in conflict with the individual production divisions in each department, who regarded the work of the central planners in their own departments as unrealistic. The tables were turned again in the relations between the individual production divisions and the firms. For to the firms the officials of M.A.P., even at the production level, were co-ordinators who knew little of what was really happening inside the factories. And no doubt the same conflict was repeated at various levels inside the individual firm and factory organization.[15]

This is simply a candid and penetrating statement of some of the essential characteristics of hierarchical control. It is not a polemic from the pen of someone who wishes to show the impossibility of hierarchical planning. As a matter of fact, Devons does not believe that any system other than a hierarchical one could have been used to supervise the manufacture of aircraft during the war, nor does he believe that at the time any basic structural or procedural improvements could have raised the level of the ministry's performance substantially above what it was. But even where hier-

[14] Ely Devons, *op. cit.*, p. 14.
[15] *Ibid.*, p. 14.

archy is essential, it is burdened with the conflict between centralization and decentralization.[16]

How does the price system avoid this conflict? The simplest answer is that there are no central decisions ordinarily to be taken in it, hence no conflict between them and the decentralized decisions of business firms, consumers, factory owners, and workers. To understand just how a price system avoids the necessity of central coördinating decisions is, of course, to understand the whole complicated pattern of organization by price; but one can approach the kernel of the matter by noting again the importance of the margin.

At any given time in a price system, the major decisions regarding aggregates of production of different kinds of goods and services have already been made. At any given time, therefore, the only relevant decisions in a field structure are those pertaining to margins which must be adjusted. But decisions for a marginal increase or decrease in production of a commodity require no central decision, or even any comprehensive survey of the allocation of resources. All that is required is that some cue inform producers that consumers want somewhat more or less of a commodity and that some incentive is offered to producers to induce them to respond. Prices, inventories, profits, and losses all can vary to provide both cue and incentive.

To be sure, in unusual cases in which extremely large aggregates must be reconsidered, as, say, at the outbreak of a war, the price system is called to make adjustments much greater than those which can be described as marginal. But then, of course, the price system cannot perform well, and typically central control takes over. The deficiency of hierarchical organization in this respect is simply that it operates under the limitations of conflict between centralization and decentralization in the many and more typical cases aside from war when the mechanism for marginal adjustments of the spontaneous field structure can and does work without such a conflict.

Aside from war and other emergencies requiring sudden large

---

[16] Michael Polanyi has constructed an ingenious demonstration that, because of limitations on the span of calculation and control, hierarchical controls run into almost impossible difficulties. "The number of relations requiring adjustment per unit of time for the functioning of an economic system of n productive units is n-times greater than can be adjusted by subordinating the units to a central authority." Michael Polanyi, *The Logic of Liberty*, University of Chicago Press, Chicago, 1951, chap. 8. But, because spontaneous and hierarchical controls are actually more complicated than in his model, his inferences about the real world are invalid.

changes, the price system offers a workable method of getting around the disabilities imposed on economic organization by the conflict. And, on the other hand, hierarchical coördination cannot be adjusted, as the German experience illustrates, to a marginal calculation which avoids aggregative decisions because, in the absence of a price system, objective and fairly accurate measures of marginal values are impossible.

CONFUSION OF FACT AND GOAL. Another characteristic difficulty in central control is illustrated in British aircraft production. Quotas for aircraft factories had to be accurate if the figures in them were to be used—as they had to be—in calculating output and requirements for overall coördination. But at the same time, the quota could not help but constitute a goal for the factory. This mixture of statistic as fact and statistic as goal gave rise to insoluble problems.

The use of statistics as goals or targets had the advantage of stirring the firms to greater accomplishment than would a quota based on an expectation of what they would produce, and it also served to inflate the figures on expected aircraft production so as to "justify" the inflated estimates of requirements which the ministry believed it was necessary to turn in to the central allocating authorities in order to get enough of their resource needs satisfied.

The case for "realistic" statistics was in the demonstrated waste of target planning. Each production director soon discovered that target programs were never accomplished in fact, and he would then have to decide for himself what production in his jurisdiction was necessary to fit into the production program that would actually be realized. Since he had little information on other requirements and programs, he had to proceed on guesswork and rumors. "At the worst, this resulted in each production director treating the official aircraft programme as a worthless scrap of paper. . . ."[17] He became his own central planner.

This can be well illustrated from the state of the Stirling and Lancaster programmes in the summer of 1942. For some time the programmes for firms producing Stirlings had been drawn up on a basis which allowed for a very generous carrot element, and it had become obvious to all concerned that the firms would fail to achieve their programmes by a wide margin. Directors in charge of component produc-

[17] Ely Devons, op. cit., p. 30.

tion for the Stirling were, in consequence, placed in a serious dilemma. For either they adhered scrupulously to the printed aircraft programme (which they were continuously being urged to do), or they made their own decisions as to the correct Stirling programme. Some followed the former course; and large quantities of unwanted Stirling components were produced at the expense of components urgently needed for other aircraft. Other directors made guesses as to the probable Stirling output; some of these guesses were too high, some too low. The result was that there were as many different Stirling aircraft programmes being used for planning component production as there were production directors. And the rot spread quickly; for once the idea gained currency that the aircraft programme need not be adhered to for one aircraft, nobody worked to the aircraft programme at all.[18]

On the other hand, a major argument against realistic planning was that it would make "the programme itself the bottleneck in expanding aircraft output." If planning were realistic, with figures based on reasonable expectations of firms' production, it would underestimate what an efficient firm could achieve and forgo the possibility of taking advantage of improved methods which appeared irregularly from time to time. Moreover, many firms would always fall below their quotas; and, if quotas were adjusted in each case to their past performance, their new performance would again fall below quota, at least until the quota was so low that it could be easily reached by the firm, in which case it was, of course, too low.

This was a conflict between two principles which never was satisfactorily solved and never could be, either by the publication of two sets of figures, which the impossibility of secrecy made impractical, or by any other device. It remains as an inevitable difficulty of hierarchical production planning. Yet it is a difficulty which price system coördination does not suffer from, since there are no targets in a price system. The crude cues and goals embodied in quotas are unnecessary.

AN ILLUSTRATIVE EXAMPLE. The difference between price system and central controls is illustrated in an incident from the control of shipping in World War II. In 1944, in a memorandum to James F. Byrnes as head of the Office of War Mobilization and Reconversion, the President expressed concern over the rate of

[18] *Ibid.*, p. 31.

ship construction. Subsequent investigation revealed that in large part the shortage of shipping was derived from methods of utilizing existing ships. After learning that large numbers of loaded ships were being held up in ports for weeks because of inadequate attention to unloading, Byrnes reported to the President that "too many ships are being used as warehouses."[19]

Now without suggesting that in these particular circumstances price system controls could have been used, the example can make clear the difference between price system and hierarchical controls. In a price system, the cost of holding a ship idle can be compared with the cost of quicker unloading, and these in turn can be compared with the cost of new ship construction. Moreover, the cost of holding ships idle will induce shippers to escape the cost by rapid unloading, unless the cost of rapid unloading is still higher than the cost of holding the ship idle. Furthermore, costs will induce shipping companies to build more ships when new construction is more economical than high-cost efforts to obtain fuller utilization of existing capacity. In hierarchy, however, a special investigation is required and specific instructions have to be issued. In this case, General Somervell informed the Commanding General, European Theater of Operations: "There is no alternative but to deny your request for more ships in excess of your capacity to unload them until you have restored to useful service a portion of those now immobilized."[20]

Notice the kind of instruction that must be given in cases like this: the military is required to restore "a portion" of the idle ships to useful service. How many? What is a reasonable number of ships to have immobilized at any one time? The answer is that more rapid unloading should proceed to the point where the marginal cost of shipping plus more rapid unloading are as high as the marginal cost of shipping plus new construction. Price system controls apply rewards and deprivations to that end; hierarchical prescriptions can only suggest the general direction of the appropriate alteration in policy. And sometimes not even that; perhaps it would have been better after all to build more ships than to add to the burdens of overseas military commanders. In the absence of control through cost, no one can say.

[19] H. M. Somers, *op. cit.*, pp. 134–135.
[20] *Ibid.*, p. 135.

III. Shortcomings of the Price System for Choice and Allocation

In certain circumstances the choice between central controls and price system is simplified by the demonstrable incapacity of the price system to deal with some kinds of choice and allocation problems. To identify these choice-allocation situations is to take a second step toward understanding the functions appropriate to price system and central controls. Because most people are familiar with them, the areas in which an unmodified price system cannot successfully operate can easily be identified. We shall, however, try to list them more precisely than is possible when they are described, as is frequently the case, with such terms as "collective needs" and "social costs." Because the price system is a highly differentiated mechanism, its shortcomings might be expected to be very specific. This, indeed, is the case.

HIGH COST OF A SHARABLE GOOD TO ANY ONE INDIVIDUAL IN THE MARKET

Individual market choices are often superseded because of the high cost to any one individual of a commodity or service, the use of which can be shared. High cost is, in fact, one reason for collectivizing the choice of national defense; left to their own resources, not many individuals could provide the materials and manpower necessary to defend themselves from an unfriendly foreign power. Whether individuals desire defense each for his own person or for other individuals in the national group so that they may control a common government and enjoy a common culture, high cost to individuals makes choice through the price system wholly ineffective.

To take another example, fortunate individuals might buy education for their children on the market, but the cost of buying literacy for a whole population would be prohibitive to any individual. Similarly, one is prevented by high costs from handling problems of sanitation and disease beyond one's own household or neighborhood, or from building highways or establishing a police force and a judiciary. Another example is the use of agricultural subsidies in the Scandinavian countries to provide for minimum domestic agricultural production to prevent starvation in case of war.[21]

When a sharable commodity or service is beyond the reach of any individual acting through the market or attainable only with great sacrifice of alternative goods and services, a number of alternatives are open to him. Sometimes he can purchase the good jointly with a few other people. But for a number of reasons voluntary arrangements for joint purchase may be deficient. Unless the group includes the whole community or nation, the cost may still be prohibitive. Or, because of the "free rider" problem, the group may be unable to finance the purchase unless compulsory payments are exacted from its members. Then, too, where agreement on the course of action approaches unanimity, the administrative convenience of delegating the choice to a government agency may be preferred by consumers to the labor of maintaining their own voluntary groups. Hence, where cost is high either subsidy or outright choice through central government is often necessary.

When the choice is collectivized, the price system can still be employed both to calculate costs and to allocate resources in response to the choice centrally made. But the price system no longer offers every individual consumer a price, hence a cost, with which he can compare alternative values at the margin. Even if he votes for highways, schools, or aircraft carriers, he cannot balance margins quite as he could on the market; when the choice is delegated to a legislature or bureaucracy, the process of rational calculation is even further removed from that of market choice. These propositions do not mean that collective choice is necessarily less rational;[22] they simply describe the manner in which the price system is displaced.

INADEQUACY OF PRICE SYSTEM REWARDS

The rewards of the price system may be inadequate to achieve a desired response or to achieve it quickly enough. British or American armed services in the Second World War could not have been recruited through such rewards. To recruit the millions of men in the services through price system techniques, wage payments totaling more than the national incomes of the two economies would have been required.

[21] Henning Friis (ed.), *Scandinavia Between East and West*, Cornell University Press, Ithaca, 1950, pp. 93–94.
[22] The rationality of collective choice is appraised in the immediately following chapter.

EFFECTS OF REWARDS ON DISTRIBUTION OF CLAIMS

More frequently, price system rewards are potentially adequate but cannot be used because of their effects on the distribution of income. The conflict between the use of price system rewards and the attainment of a preferred distribution of incomes is deep. Despite a sentimental attachment to his property, an old settler whose homestead blocks the right of way for a new highway can presumably be induced to move if he is promised half the wealth of the world or more; but he is less likely to be offered riches than to be moderately paid and then evicted through the hierarchical powers of government. The United States might have recruited its German occupation forces by handsome wage offers; but, again, consequent income gains to soldiers and income losses to civilians appear—at least to civilian policy makers—less desirable than the use of conscription for recruitment. It is also possible that sufficient money rewards for some kinds of risky investment are in conflict with a desirable distribution of income.

ADVERSE EFFECTS ON CHOICE AND ALLOCATION OF THE DISTRIBUTION OF CLAIMS

Choice and allocation in a price system respond to a pattern of distribution of claims. Allocation to low-income groups of some particular goods and services like education and medical care may not be regarded as satisfactory. This being so, either money income must be redistributed or these goods must be centrally allocated. Central allocation may proceed either through subsidization, which actually combines collective and market choice, or through outright collective allocations, as, for example, in direct relief programs and public education.

Even with an "ideal" distribution of money income, the allocation to the lowest-income groups of a number of goods such as education, medical care, housing, occupational training and retraining, recreation, transportation, fire protection, food, and clothing will often be regarded as unsatisfactory. All Western societies employ a common variety of techniques to collectivize to a degree the allocation of these goods. A wide agreement is thus implied that market choice with existing distribution of money income is frequently unsatisfactory and that the remedy cannot always be redistribution of money income. Moreover, no redistribution of cash income can avoid the necessity for collective allocation to meet unpredictable needs such as medical care for prolonged illness. Although insurance is often possible, family income cannot be tailored to cope with all important uncertainties.

The distribution of money income may also create undesirable inequalities in function and status which only central allocation can correct. In the American Civil War, conscripts were permitted to hire substitutes and thereby free themselves from military service. Public policy has since been more careful to avoid concentrating the hardships of military service on the low-income groups. In many societies it is now a principle that manpower for war be recruited hierarchically. Western societies have also decided that, regardless of the provocation of poverty, no man can sell himself into slavery. As in the case of military conscription, there are several reasons for this principle, but among them is the desire to forestall certain "free" market choices which, under the pressure of immediate circumstances, sometimes appear rational to members of low-income groups. In Western societies many people wish to guarantee to everyone not only a minimum allocation of certain goods but also a minimum bill of rights, duties, and privileges.

THIRD-PARTY DAMAGES IN PARTICULAR TRANS-ACTIONS

A long-recognized limitation on individual market choice lies in the possible adverse consequences of a transaction for persons other than the buyer and seller, who alone can protect their own interests. Traditional examples are deforestation and soil erosion, smoke and other pollution of the air, destruction of recreational areas by factory waste products discharged into waterways, unsightly back yards, and various nuisances in residential areas. These evils have stimulated the invention of a host of collective controls such as smoke-control ordinances, zoning, neighborhood land-use agreements, sanitation regulations, and reforestation.

Almost everyone agrees that where the values of a large number of people are involved in a transaction, the control over choice and allocation cannot be left wholly to buyer and seller. But quite commonly market choices are also displaced where no more than one or two persons are harmed by a transaction if the damage is substantial. Sometimes, for example, zoning is used to forbid commercial construction simply to protect a single residence.

In any transaction unfavorable third-party effects can be

identified; but it is probably not commonly recognized how seriously these effects qualify the case for market choice. No simple formula can determine when a third-party effect warrants modifying market choice through hierarchy; ultimately it is a matter of one's values. But from the conflict between market choice and the protection of third-party interests, a whole spectrum of inferences can be drawn as to the extent to which central choice and allocation should replace the market. One can see the range of possible adverse consequences of a transaction in the kind of costs that are incurred by third parties.[23]

INDIVIDUAL MARKET COSTS. The discharge of smoke into the air from a factory may impose house-cleaning and clothes-cleaning costs on people who work or live in the area. Or it may reduce property values near the factory. This is a commonly recognized and clear-cut case of damages to third parties.

SHARED MARKET COSTS. Deforestation may reduce the value of a collectively owned recreational area. Moreover, when the community undertakes a program for control of third-party damages, as in the case of smoke, fire, traffic, or water-pollution control, individual market values may be protected but individuals collectively bear the loss through taxes to support the control measures.

NON-MARKET COSTS, BOTH INDIVIDUAL AND SHARED. Third-party damages may be severe even when no market value is affected and no market costs are incurred for protection or repairs. The amenities of life may be adversely affected by noise, neighbors, or congestion. Although no particular asset, individual or collective, is reduced in market value, there can be wide agreement on the fact of a loss for any individual who dislikes noise, neighbors, and congestion. These damages are like the others already mentioned, except that they do not actually appear as market costs. The extent of these damages could, of course, be stated in terms of the cost of repairing them. But the fact that the damages go unrepaired indicates that the damages are not so great a cost as the cost of repairs. Especially important examples of third-party damages of this kind are those arising from individual saving decisions, for they have great

[23] For an attempt to measure the extent of these losses, see K. William Kapp, *The Social Costs of Private Enterprise*, Harvard University Press, Cambridge, 1950, which, however, includes other social costs than third-party effects.

consequences both for economic stability and for the rate of economic growth.[24]

THE NON-MARKET COST OF THE PATTERN OF CHOICE ITSELF. A common but little discussed third-party effect is what one person loses when another person buys, sells, or consumes in a way that is offensive to him. Temperance people may suffer a loss from the consumption of alcohol by individuals they never see. The rich are often offended by the spending habits of the anonymous poor. Almost everyone attaches some importance to how other people spend their money and hence may feel some loss when they do not spend as one wishes. Or one may suffer when his friends spend because he cannot keep up with them.

Although losses of this kind may be quite as great as other third-party damages, they are not often thought sufficient justification for displacing market choice. Instead, by manipulation and spontaneous control, individuals seeks to control the market choices of others. The practical significance of this kind of third-party effect is that it shows that there are not merely a limited number of fairly clear third-party damages for which the inadequacy of market choice can be conceded; instead, third-party effects are universal. Hence the case for market choice must be carefully qualified.

THE NON-MARKET COST OF IRRESPONSIVE CONTROL. An especially important type of non-market loss is that suffered by many members of a community when an individual is permitted to buy police protection for himself or the services of the judiciary or the military. Where third-party effects are undesirable kinds of control, market choice must be superseded. A good deal of bribery and corruption in politics is nothing more than an attempt to buy on the market the services of judges, administrators, and legislators. Bribery and corruption are a black market for these services; they are an attempt to bring back on the market services for which a group has attempted to establish collective choice.

All these third-party damages from particular transactions are sometimes described as social costs. But the term "social cost" is

[24] There are, of course, still other reasons for deficiencies in individual market choices on savings. See, for example, Abram Bergson, "Socialist Economics," in Howard S. Ellis (ed.), *A Survey of Contemporary Economics*, published for the American Economic Association by The Blakiston Co., Philadelphia, 1949, pp. 414–415.

ambiguous; often it embraces all inadequacies of the price system. For example, unemployment is often referred to as a social cost simply because it is regarded as a social evil, although not necessarily attributable to a particular transaction. Third-party effects are also sometimes included in the concept of external gains and losses in consumption. But the losses discussed here include those growing out of consumption and business expenditures alike. Third-party damages also arise from occupational choices, as when wage earners choose their occupations and conditions of work solely in response to market controls.

OBJECTIONS TO PRICE SYSTEM AGENDAS

In some circumstances where none of the foregoing shortcomings of the price system are present, people may nevertheless object to facing price system agendas. Even if they can successfully give effect to their choices through the market, they may not wish to be put in a position in which they must exercise market choice. The market-choice mechanism itself is for some reason objectionable.

There are several possible explanations for their immediate preference for an alternative to market choice. In the first place, most people do not always like to act economically toward members of their family and their friends. Individuals like to perform services for each other without a market calculation of the values of the exchanged favors. Secondly, they often wish to delegate choice to someone more competent. Quite possibly most parents welcome a governmental decision on when and how children should be occupied in school. And they welcome a degree of hierarchical control over the sale of pharmaceuticals and certain other commodities for fear of their own ignorance.

Thirdly, individuals sometimes wish to escape market choice simply because it is time-consuming and they believe choice can better be delegated to hierarchy. Again, public education may be an illustration. Finally, individuals sometimes prefer to delegate choice and allocation to a central hierarchy so that temptation is put out of reach. The market sometimes tempts individuals to make choices whose immediate appeal overcomes their better judgment. They prefer, therefore, to be compelled, say, to meet certain minimum standards in building construction rather than take advantage of the immediate opportunities to skimp and cut costs that the price system offers.

INCOMPETENCE IN INDIVIDUAL MARKET CHOICE AND ALLOCATION

But whether one prefers to delegate choice or to choose on the market, it is true that, just as a river cannot rise above its source, the level of rationality in market choice and allocation can be no higher than that of the knowledge and intelligence of individuals in the market. True enough, polyarchy and hierarchy suffer the same disability; but it is important to recognize that this is a disability from which the price system is not free. Price system choice and allocation may operate at an extremely low level of rationality. If this appears too obvious a point to deserve mention, economists at least will recognize how frequently the possibility allegedly inherent in market choice for each chooser to balance his margins, to compare gains and losses for himself, has seemed to imply that market choice is more rational than hierarchical choice. We shall discuss this further in the next chapter.

IMPERFECTIONS IN CONTROL OF ENTREPRENEURS

All the above inadequacies of the price system with respect to choice and allocation will be found even in an "ideal" price system. But no real-world price system will be "ideal." A remaining shortcoming of all real-world price systems is that control over the entrepreneur will always be imperfect. Again, although imperfections in control mark all the four central processes, imperfections in price system control should not be minimized. In a particular circumstance they may be decisive in the choice among alternative techniques.

INSTABILITY

As a shortcoming of the price system, instability is discussed in a later chapter. But it is worth noting that instability sharply reduces the effectiveness of a price system for choice and allocation. In depression, price system cost calculations are invalid; yet they continue to serve a part of a cue and incentive system that keeps resources out of the market. With fourteen million unemployed in 1933, Americans could not pay the money "costs" of putting the unemployed to work. In inflation, as will be seen, price system allocation of resources may be deficient on several counts. Restrictions on the use of the price system in international trade since World War II are in large part due to its defects in time of inflation.

OTHER SHORTCOMINGS OF THE PRICE SYSTEM

Price systems suffer from still other shortcomings. It ought to be remembered, however, that this chapter deals only with their shortcomings in the choice-allocation processes. Moreover, it identifies the inherent shortcomings of price systems and not merely weaknesses the inevitability of which is problematical. Even within these limits the shortcomings are impressive. The price system is in some ways like a highly specialized tool or machine. Where it can be used, it permits rapid and precise work. But, like all specialized instruments, its application is limited; and, as with a specialized tool, products themselves sometimes must be altered to fit it.

IV. Combination of Price System with Central Control Techniques

RANGE OF VARIATION

So far we have considered price system and central control techniques for choice and allocation as though they were opposite poles on a continuum. But neither kind of technique is ever found in pure form. A third step toward understanding the appropriate functions for each can be taken by considering some of the various forms which these techniques take. The range of possible uses to which these techniques can be put covers a wider array of alternatives than is often believed. Almost everyone realizes that, beginning at the price system pole of a continuum, various hierarchical or polyarchial modifications such as subsidies, licenses, free services, and price controls are often desirable; but the possibilities of modifying polyarchy and hierarchy with price system techniques at the other end of the continuum are less familiar.

We shall not attempt to be comprehensive at this point; our primary purpose is to uncover a few often neglected possibilities for economizing with a minimum of price system. The particular purposes that can best be served by these possible combinations of central control and price system are not commonly those consistent with our values; nevertheless, understanding them is a prerequisite to good judgment on the appropriateness under different circumstances of price system and central control.

In a price system, prices are used as cues, as measures, and as rewards and penalties. More specifically, they are used to present cost information to choosers; express or register choices, whether of consumers, entrepreneurs, or producers; signal and motivate responses of resource holders; distribute income shares; facilitate in several ways the savings-investment process; ration scarce stocks of goods; distribute surpluses; register scores or measure certain kinds of accomplishments, as in profit and salary rates before taxes; provide a measure of "technical" efficiency; and permit comparison of costs among departments or enterprises. Conversely, near the hierarchy end of the continuum, prices may be used for only one or two of these many purposes.

A HYPOTHETICAL ECONOMY

As a third step, therefore, in the effort to understand the appropriate functions of price system and central controls, the example of a hypothetical economy of a particular type can be used. The minimum functions prices might perform can be seen in an examination of how an economy might rationally be organized in circumstances where the economizing function is simplified by relatively little regard for preferences of the masses of citizens and by an emphasis on the development of productive capacity rather than on the production of a wide variety of commodities and services. The USSR is such an economy; but how closely, if at all, its politico-economic processes follow the possibilities we outline we do not know, except that there is apparently some similarity.[25] If the discussion of a hypothetical economy appears to approach the main issues in the choice between price system and central controls with puzzling indirection, it is only because the complexities of the issues demand an incremental approach.

CHOICE. If we begin with the assumption that economic development is to conform to the wishes of leadership and not to those of the citizenry except as leadership decides, and if we further assume that leadership is more interested in industrialization or military

[25] Because information is limited, opinions vary on the degree to which Soviet prices represent rationally calculated costs. Cf., for example, Naum Jasny, *Soviet Prices of Producers' Goods*, Stanford University Press, Stanford, 1952; Abram Bergson, *Structure of Soviet Wages*, Harvard University Press, Cambridge, 1944; Harry Schwartz, *Russia's Soviet Economy*, Prentice-Hall, New York, 1950; M. C. Kaser, "Soviet Planning and the Price Mechanism," *Economic Journal*, March, 1950, pp. 81–91; "Some Recent Developments in Soviet Economic Thought: Economic Choice Between Technological Alternatives," *Soviet Studies*, October, 1949, pp. 119–127.

preparedness than in gratifying consumer desires, it follows that leadership cannot rationally allow consumer free choice to control production. At once the price system loses one of its major functions.

Of course, consumer free choice can still serve several purposes, if leaders wish. If leadership wishes to be guided to a degree by consumers' preferences in deciding what consumer goods will be made from that part of productive capacity assigned to consumer good production, leadership will presumably distribute each consumer good through a market for a price. Leaders can then infer from inventories and sales at various prices a pattern of consumer preferences. They will be careful to use this information only as raw data for the development of their own output goals and will not permit consumer choice to call directly for responses in production as in a price system. Aside from using consumer prices as information on what might be produced, distribution of consumer goods at prices in markets also serves the leaders' purposes by making hierarchical rationing of each commodity unnecessary, yet limiting the total consumption of each commodity. Distribution through prices can also be used to permit differences in consumer tastes to have some influence on the distribution of goods among consumers.

The irrationality of consumer sovereignty through consumer free choice is clear enough under the assumptions stated. But some critics of central control are quick to point out that, in the absence of a registration of preferences such as is accomplished through market prices emerging from free choice, production goals are indeterminate or arbitrary. That is to say, there will be no test by which leaders' choices may be shown to be correct or mistaken.

An unhappy kind of confusion runs through this criticism. The decisions of consumers in a price system are also indeterminate or arbitrary in the sense that there is no test by which they may be shown to be correct or mistaken. All that can be said about the correctness of consumers' choices is that, if consumers think themselves to be in error, they are free to alter their choices (so also is leadership). In appraising the correctness of their own choices, they may be ignorant, misinformed on particular points, uncritical, or emotionally irrational. Once a set of market prices reflects the choices made by individuals, we can then say that production goals can be checked against the responses called for by the set of prices. But the set of prices may be a product of the same kind of foolishness, ignorance, and stupidity that may afflict leadership when it sets production goals.

Hierarchy of the type we are discussing does not substitute something arbitrary or even subjective for something demonstrably right or wrong and in any case objective. Instead it begins, as does the price system, with arbitrary and subjective choices which may be wise or foolish. But it then can dispense with the necessity of translating these preferences into a set of prices indicating what responses are demanded.

To be quite specific, one reason it can pass over this process is that leadership is not interested in communication from masses of consumers to those actively in charge of production; it wishes communication only within leadership. The other reason is that, in the absence of competing leaders, all striving through price offers to win their preferred responses from the productive enterprises, there is no need for leadership to communicate its own preferences to enterprises through prices. On the basis of cost information available to it, leadership can much more simply and directly place its orders in physical terms.

If it is still alleged that central control is less rational than consumer free choice, the allegation can only mean that no leadership is competent to work out production goals for an economy. To this it can only be replied that, if the preferences of leadership are to be satisfied, no other group is more rational and certainly consumers are not. In an economy like the Soviet, where development goals are less complex than in a high standard of living economy with great scope for the expression of different goals by millions of different people, it is not at all impossible that choice can be made (assuming only adequate cost information, which we shall discuss below) with a high degree of rationality.

COST CALCULATIONS FOR LABOR.   Assume that in this hypothetical economy leadership has found it advisable to use wage differentials as well as command both as a control over worker productivity and as a method of allocating labor from one area or occupation to another. It does not follow that these differential wage rates should be taken to represent the cost of labor in different occupations and areas as they would in a price system. Leadership has a choice between calculating labor costs as though the labor supply were homogeneous and calculating differential labor costs for different occupations.

The latter alternative is ordinarily essential in Western economies; its merit is that labor costs so calculated take account of differences in scarcity of different kinds of labor. Labor costs thus show that the alternatives forgone in using labor depend upon the kind of labor used. But an objection to using differential costs based on wage differentials is that the wage differentials are largely payments to overcome a worker's personal preference for an alternative workplace or occupation, and personal preferences are not relevant to an appraisal of the values forgone to leadership in using labor in any particular place or way. These wage differentials misstate costs to leadership.

It may be asked, however, whether leadership does not in fact have to pay these differential rates to control the allocation of labor. If so, are these payments not costs that ought to be taken into account by leadership? The answer is that these differentials are disbursements that have to be matched by consumer goods production or taxed away again so that they are never spent; but, because in neither case do they necessarily require leadership to allocate more resources to consumer goods production than otherwise or in any other way to sacrifice an alternative, they do not represent costs.

It will therefore sometimes be rational to discard actual wage payments as evidence of cost and attempt to price labor so as to measure scarcity costs exclusive of worker preferences. This would require, however, subjective estimates of cost because market tests of scarcity do not distinguish between scarcity due, say, to a shortage of trained workers and that due to preferences of workers to work elsewhere. A still better alternative, therefore, might be to recognize the possibility, through subsidized or forced mobility, as well as through education, occupational training, and adult retraining, of reducing the heterogeneity of the labor force to the point at which a standard wage cost for all workers would no more misrepresent wage costs than would an attempt to vary rates according to subjective and easily mistaken estimates of scarcity.

The possibilities of doing this in an economy of little personal liberty are rather good. It is not by any means necessary to make the population homogeneous with regard to skills. All that is required is that particularly scarce skills be made more plentiful relative to the demands for them so that, no matter how great the remaining heterogeneity of the labor force with resp ct to skills and locations, the pattern of heterogeneity matches the ieterogeneity of the demands for labor. And this matching is pr. imably more easily accomplished in a relatively backward econ ·ι.y in which industrialization and mechanization have not created quite the overwhelming need for semiskilled, skilled, clerical, and professional workers that is characteristic of the most advanced Western economies.

To be sure, this scheme for a flat wage cost is not well designed to take account of short-run scarcities and the alternatives that are forgone in using scarce labor before a greater supply of it can be trained or moved in. But the force of this objection is somewhat reduced when leadership is primarily concerned with relatively long-run objectives and therefore with costs useful for calculation of production goals for some years ahead. The costs most relevant to choices that will remain somewhat stable over a period of years are less the immediate alternatives forgone than those to be forgone over a longer period.

CALCULATION OF NATURAL RESOURCES COSTS. Resource cost calculations depend directly on labor costs. Taking any arbitrary standard price of labor as the basis of cost calculations, we can see that the cost of any natural resource in this hypothetical economy would be based on the labor costs of extracting it. But a rational use of a resource would ordinarily seem to require that an additional element in resource price cover what might be called the scarcity value of the resource itself, aside from its extractive costs. If it is a scarce resource, it cannot be used for every purpose. If the resource is to be rationed out to its most highly valued employment, a high enough price, so it would seem, will deter leadership from committing it to an impossibly large number of uses.

What is an impossibly large number of uses? It depends upon subjective judgment concerning a desirable or tolerable rate of depletion of the natural resource. Because no one can read the future with any confidence, any one of a number of arbitrary prices can be defended as no more demonstrably incorrect than any other. The pricing problem is thus again somewhat simpler than might be expected. In economic theory, a resource price is correct if it clears the market between private-owner sellers and buyers of natural resources. But it is then correct only in a formal sense. It is not correct if the estimates of rates of depletion of buyers and sellers turn out to be incorrect. Hence the possible errors in the arbitrary resource prices of the hypothetical economy are not necessarily more serious than the errors, say, in competitive pricing.

CALCULATION OF COSTS OF INTERMEDIATE GOODS. The calculation of costs of goods made with labor and natural resources and to be used up in the productive process is not difficult. Leadership need only add the labor and natural resource costs together. Again, short-run scarcities of intermediate goods are not adequately reflected in costs so derived, but, again, the force of the objection is somewhat diminished in an economy concentrating on long-run plans for development.

CALCULATION OF TOTAL COST OF GOODS. For the total cost calculations that leadership needs for rational choice, all that remains to be done is to add labor costs and natural resource costs to the costs of intermediate goods consumed in the productive process. For a great many commodities, adequate cost calculations will turn out to be surprisingly simple, for natural resource costs, aside from extractive labor costs, will be trivial. Moreover, in any calculations of labor input requirements for a commodity, a degree of error is inevitable; hence for many commodities the scarcity cost of natural resources will be much less than the variation of labor cost due to error. For these many commodities, therefore, the scarcity cost of natural resources can be ignored, and cost can be calculated by adding to direct labor costs both the extractive labor costs of resources and the costs of intermediate goods.

But if for these intermediate goods resource scarcity costs are likewise unimportant, a reasonably good estimate of costs can be derived purely from labor costs, both direct and indirect. Finally, because labor costs do not differ for different kinds of labor, cost can simply be stated in terms, say, of man-hours of labor. Production can then be planned and allocated without the use of any money costs at all. Money and prices can be dispensed with for choice and allocation.

CAPITAL COSTS. But we have left out of the picture so far the cost of using capital funds. Capital requirements need not be added into costs. It is possible for leadership to make its choices of production goals on the basis of two primary considerations—the number is not beyond the power of human comprehension. The first basis is the cost of each alternative built up in the manner just described; the second is capital funds required for each alternative. It would, of course, be impossible for individual consumers acting separately in a price system to make their choices on the double basis of money costs to them as consumers and in addition drains on the community's supply of capital funds; but it is not at all impossible for a central leadership to do so. Unless all consumers acting separately are required to forgo an alternative when they use capital, their total demands for capital will outstrip its supply. Hence a price must be put on it. But leadership will only cheat *itself* by excessive demands on capital; hence it is motivated to restrict its demands, whether capital is priced or not.

It may be objected that the individual enterprise management may be wasteful of capital if it is not included in its costs, but this is not inevitable or even probable. Every participant in the cost-estimating and choice-making process understands that two criteria are used: cost and drains on available capital. It would be important for an enterprise management seeking permission for expansion to promise not only low costs but also a minimum need for capital funds.

It may yet be objected that the relative importance of cost reduction as against reduction of drains on capital supply could not be objectively stated, as in a price system where capital requirements appear in costs. This objection can be granted; a dual restraint is less rational than a single. But, again, in a centrally directed hierarchy, little might be gained by reducing the two criteria to one. In the first place, leadership's sense of the relative importance of reducing cost or economizing on capital could be communicated to enterprises —even in considerable subtlety. Secondly, the availability of capital in a rapidly developing economy is not necessarily stable; and there is consequently much to be said for making preliminary choices on the basis of costs. Subsequently these choices can be modified to take account of capital needs, or—and this is important—the capital supply can be adjusted within limits to fit the preliminary choices.

Something of this same process of choice by a double criterion goes on in Western economies among private businesses. Businessmen plan expansion of various lines of production not only according to their cost estimates, including interest charges, but also according to the availability of funds. They must plan thus because the interest rate does not in fact clear the market in Western economies so as to eliminate the second consideration. Lending institutions ration funds on the basis of risk, as well as through the interest rate.[26]

THE CONTROL OF PRODUCTION. Once leadership makes its decisions on the basis of costs and capital needs, it can direct production through hierarchy rather than price system. Although it may wish to do so, it need not depend on profits or bonuses to motivate managers to respond to the orders placed with the enterprises.

It will often be rational for leadership to ask management to respond to hierarchical directives rather than cost-price relationships where the two cues conflict. Suppose, for example, that a decision on desired output for a particular kind of steel is made on the basis of estimated costs. As production gets under way on the new orders, it turns out that costs were underestimated. Pending a reconsideration of the original decision on the steel quota, it will be more rational to continue production in many circumstances as close to quota as possible, regardless of costs, than to attempt an alteration of quota at the enterprise level. Especially if the central plans have anticipated miscalculations of cost and have allowed for a margin of uncommitted resources to meet shortages, it will be preferable to disregard the price-cost cue and hold fast to the hierarchically determined quota.

PRICES ON CONSUMER GOODS. Prices on consumer goods may be quite arbitrarily determined without regard to the prices used for cost calculations in production decisions. Think of leadership as the purchaser of all goods produced in the economy. Having possession of the goods, leadership can then sell them to individual consumers at any prices it wishes, the only requirement being that prices are consistent with wage and other income disbursements to consumers so that the goods will actually be purchased. This requirement of consistency between consumer goods prices and income share disbursements does not mean that these prices are related to those used for cost calculations, because, as has been explained, income disbursements need not be related to costs.

[26] Henry C. Wallich, "Changing Significance of the Interest Rate," *American Economic Review*, December, 1946, p. 765.

LIMITED NEED FOR PRICE SYSTEM

Let us draw some inferences from the abstractions of the hypothetical economy. It is clear that the hypothetical economy has minimized the need for a price system in two ways: substitution of leadership's goals for consumer goals, and long-run development of productive capacity instead of production of a multiplicity of consumer goods. Surprisingly, such a simplified economizing process does not necessarily sacrifice occupational free choice. Assume that a distribution of skills to different jobs and areas corresponds closely enough to leadership's preferences to make conscription of labor unnecessary. Assume further that leadership is little concerned with the distribution of the national income and is therefore willing to pay workers whatever amounts are required to induce their movement from one job to another. It then follows that occupational free choice can be maintained.

What has been said should make clear how little dependent upon the price system the choice and allocation processes are in certain circumstances. Conceding the high practical value we attach to the price system, we must also concede that sometimes much of it may be dispensed with. To be sure, the particular circumstances in which it may be largely dispensed with are those in which consumer control of production is surrendered, and this is a high-ranking value. Yet the demonstration is useful both in clarifying the extent to which the usefulness of the price system is dependent upon particular goals and more generally in guarding against extravagant claims for it. It is always difficult to avoid either under- or overrating the price system.

V. Price System and Central Controls in Mobilization and War

Ordinarily the values postulated in Chapter 2 cannot be approximated by techniques approaching those of the hypothetical economy just discussed. But they can be in time of rapid mobilization or war, and we can profitably explore the choice-allocation processes in war as a fourth step in the attempt to understand the appropriate functions of price system and central controls. The inquiry is given added point by the many illustrations of imperfections in central controls we have drawn from wartime central controls. If central controls reveal these inadequacies, why are they nevertheless so heavily relied upon in mobilization and war?

The first displacement of the price system in war is, of course, the necessary substitution of collective for individual market choice for a large part of the national income. Implements of war cannot be left to free consumer choice. This displacement poses two immediate questions, one pertaining to military procurement, the other to the civilian economy. Why does leadership rely so heavily on allocations, priorities, and conscription for procurement instead of leaning more heavily on the market—simply making a money offer for what it needs? And for the civilian economy, why does leadership turn to hierarchical devices such as price control rather than holding prices down by limiting consumer spending so that the price system can function? For these two questions there are a number of answers.

It should be noted, however, that hierarchical and polyarchal controls by no means replace price system controls; instead they supplement them. In the United States in World War II the military services were granted five sets of specific hierarchical controls for procurement: to requisition personal property, to issue orders to produce, to set price, to audit records and compel the submission of information, and to issue allocations and priorities.[27] The first four of these were only occasionally used; orders to produce, for example, were issued only twenty-five times up to March, 1945.[28] And even the wider use of priorities and allocations never wholly displaced price system cues and incentives to allocation.

PROBLEMS OF DISTRIBUTION IN WAR

It has already been observed that, because differences in income should not decide who must bear the hardships of military service, governments do not bid on the market for an army but instead conscript it. One might argue that low-paid wage earners should rejoice in the prospects of high wages offered by a leadership bent on recruiting through the price system. But most people hesitate to play upon deficiencies in income to tempt men to take upon themselves war's risks of injury and death. Similarly, it is thought more equitable to distribute many other lesser sacrifices of war not according to money income. For example, when meat or clothing

[27] John P. Miller, *Pricing of Military Procurements*, Yale University Press, New Haven, 1949, p. 103.
[28] *Ibid.*, p. 104.

become relatively more scarce in war, distribution of the reduced supplies according to money income may make it extremely difficult for low income groups to obtain any of the scarce goods. A dstribution of claims tolerable in peace is not tolerable in war or rapid mobilization. For reasons given earlier,[29] reduction of inequalities in money income cannot wholly meet these strains on distribution; and rationing becomes necessary.

Just as the price system in war is not an equitable device for distributing burdens between rich and poor, neither is it satisfactory for distributing resources between private and public uses. It is possible for government to take either too much or too little. In the case of medical services, for example, governments may hire away from civilian practice so many doctors, nurses, and technicians as to endanger the public health. Not even the urgency of military needs justifies crippling the civilian economy on which the armed services rest. Yet for other commodities and services, the price that some few consumers are willing to pay rather than permit government to outbid them may be so great as to force price to a ridiculously high level. A central survey of resources and requirements and a centrally administered allocation between private and public uses are required to avoid competition between the two sectors.

It might be asked: Why not also in peacetime? In peacetime a government does not ordinarily outbid individual consumers because the budget sets limits on what government can spend. In war or mobilization, on the other hand, the pressure to spend, arm, and fight overrides the ordinary limits on government spending. Modern war makes tremendous demands on the economy. By late 1944, 60 percent of all manufactured output in the United States was for the armed services, and about one-third of manufacturing was for munitions. At the same time, more than 55 percent of those employed in manufacturing, mining, and construction were producing for the armed services.[30] Then, too, supplies are adjusted to ordinary peacetime demands; and it is only in war or other emergency that new demands for particular goods grow so large as to threaten to deprive one sector of the economy of its requirements. The difficulty of arriving at a wise decision on the distribution of production between civilian and military is illustrated in the history of the

---

[29] See the discussion of income distribution in Chapter 5.

[30] U.S. War Production Board, *American Industry in War and Transition, 1940–1950*, Part II (WPB Document No. 27), U.S. Government Printing Office, Washington, 1945.

struggles between the Joint Chiefs of Staff and the Office of War Mobilization.[31]

PRODUCER AND CONSUMER PREFERENCES

A further deficiency of the price system in war is one of its great merits in peace. A price system offers a method of reconciling people's demands as consumers for a particular pattern of production with people's desires as workers and other producers to choose their own occupations. Where consumer demands call, say, for 2 percent of the nation's manpower to be engaged in structural steel work while workers' preferences direct only 1 percent of them to the trade, the adjustment of prices, costs, and wage rates in the industry can eventually accomplish an increase in price, thus reducing consumer demands, and an increase in wages, thus increasing the attractiveness of the trade. The adjustment is from both sides; it cannot be said either that workers have to comply with consumers' wishes or the opposite.

Now while this is desirable in peace, in time of war most people wish to assert the power of the government as a consumer at the expense of producer preferences. Where to work, how many hours to work, how to use plant and equipment—all these choices become "semi-luxuries" in wartime. Hence, even if policy does not usually go so far as to conscript civilian labor, it commonly turns away from price system to hierarchy. For example, in the United States in World War II the allocation of labor was hierarchically controlled by such devices as subsidized transportation, prohibitions on hiring some types of labor except on referral from the United States Employment Service, and restriction of movement of workers from one area to another in certain circumstances except on referral from the Employment Service.[32]

THE PROBLEM OF INFLATION

Many other deficiencies of price system in wartime are bound up with the possibilities and consequences of inflation. Suppose, all the above objections aside, that the government decides to mobilize resources by bidding for them on the market. It would not be long before the consequences of this decision became apparent in infla-

[31] H. M. Somers, *op. cit.*, chap. 4.
[32] Seymour E. Harris, *Price and Related Controls in the United States*, Mc-Graw-Hill Book Co., New York, 1945, pp. 288–289.

tion and in the consequences of inflation for the distribution of real income.

Prices would be expected to rise sharply—in some cases to nonsensically high levels—on those goods and services bought by government, with the result, first, that their sellers would reap unexpectedly large incomes. In its most spectacular form, this is the problem of the profiteer. In Great Britain in World War II "from the natural repugnance that war should bring windfall gains and from the bitter memories of 1914–1920 there had developed an obsession about profiteering";[33] the same was true of other countries as well.

Secondly, persons whose manner of living made them relatively more dependent on commodities whose prices rose most sharply would find their real incomes badly cut while those who had been spending heavily on other commodities would be less hard hit. Thirdly, previously existing inequalities in income would be much exaggerated in real terms. If government drives up the price of meat, high-income families will still be able to buy at least small quantities, but low-income families will find meat beyond their budgets. Or the inflation, offset for many people by their higher earnings, falls as a burden on large families, workers in badly paid industries, and persons dependent upon social security and other fixed incomes.[34]

One might ask if it is not possible to forestall such an inflation, through either taxes or borrowing, by reducing the spendable income of individuals in order to offset the increased expenditure of government. Even if private expenditure could be so reduced, government spending would still raise prices on particular commodities and services with the results for income distribution just mentioned. Because the needs of the military are different from the needs of the civilian population, new scarcities would exist that did not exist before; and prices would be much altered.

Actually, it appears to be impossible to reduce private spending by an amount sufficient to offset increased government spending; inflationary pressures are therefore worse than might first appear. An income tax heavy enough to accomplish great reductions in the spending of high-income families must take more than 100

[33] W. K. Hancock and M. M. Gowing, *British War Economy*, His Majesty's Stationery Office, London, 1949, p. 157.
[34] *Ibid.*, p. 169.

percent of their incomes, since they can spend out of their past savings; but the incentive effects of taxes even well short of 100 percent may be so serious for production that they cannot be attempted. Moreover, income taxes sufficiently heavy to destroy a great fraction of consumer spending would be ruinous to families whose financial commitments had been made on the assumption of no great changes in taxation.

Some of the adverse consequences of taxation can be avoided by the use of spendings or sales taxes and by allowing tax deductions or moratoria to take account of differences in individual and family circumstances. Yet, as taxes become heavier, the consequences of their imperfect adjustment to particular circumstances become increasingly serious. Lastly, heavy taxes often run the danger of undermining worker morale and become a threat to industrial peace which governments cannot afford to risk.

In Britain, for example, in World War II: "Indirect taxation could not be increased to levels sufficiently penal without falling heavily on semi-necessities, and this would be socially inexpedient. If direct taxation were raised beyond a certain point, people with heavy standing obligations—such as rents, insurance, school fees, or contributions to cultural enterprises—would supplement their income by selling capital assets. Moreover, even in wartime, such taxation might reduce the will to work. Succeeding wartime budgets did not in fact attempt to raise income tax above the 1941 level."[35]

Within limits, government borrowing can come to the aid of taxation, but it cannot forestall inflation in the kind of war waged by nations today. Although compulsory borrowing through war bonds can greatly increase private saving, when borrowing becomes compulsory it runs into much the same limits as does taxation.

Inflation being inevitable, hierarchical controls in the form of price ceilings, rationing, allocations, and priorities will supplement or supplant the price system in some of its functions or in certain sectors of the economy. The effects of wartime inflation on income distribution are in themselves sufficient to call for these controls, but other consequences of inflation, such as its effects on the allocation of resources, will likewise make the controls desirable.

[35] *Ibid.*, p. 328; cf. Tibor Scitovsky, Edward Shaw, and Lorie Tarshis, *Mobilizing Resources for War*, McGraw-Hill Book Co., 1951, chap. 1.

SIZE OF ADJUSTMENTS CALLED FOR

Still another group of deficiencies in the price system organization centers on the size and character of adjustments called for by
large-scale war. The price system is a mechanism for making marginal adjustments. Its cues, rewards, and penalties are sufficient to
induce a reallocation of manpower or resources where they are
strong enough to move a marginal group of workers or resources,
for such a movement is ordinarily all that is required. It has not been
demonstrated in these chapters, however, nor can it be very convincingly argued, that price system cues and rewards can signal
and provide incentive for transfers so large as to require more than
a margin of resources to move.

War calls for large changes at a time when the cues and rewards of the price system are weakened by heavy taxation.[36] In
addition, the changes called for are frequently only temporary and
sometimes heavy with risk. In the ordinary expectation of profits
in a price system, a business will be reluctant to build a new plant
only to find excess capacity on its hands a few years later. Nor will
it be induced to build a new plant in an area immediately subject,
say, to heavy bombing. Under the circumstances, the cues and penalties available to hierarchical coördination becomes necessary to
supplement those of the market.

The extent to which price system cues and incentives fall short
in time of war, when the size of the investment required and the
risks of plant expansion are large, is indicated by the amount of government investment in plant and equipment during World War II.
The United States government invested $15 billion in plant and
equipment. Allowing for the specialized nature of much of the
equipment and the high costs at which it was built, this investment
accounted for something approximating 15 percent of postwar
plant capacity in manufacturing. Ninety-nine percent of American
capacity for explosives, assembling of munitions, and shell loading;
90 percent of capacity in aircraft and ships; and large fractions of
capacity in chemicals, rubber, petroleum, coal, metal products, machine tools, machinery, and electrical equipment were government
owned at the end of the war.[37]

---

[36] And, if taxes are heavy enough to restrain inflation without hierarchical controls, price system cues and rewards are further weakened.
[37] A. D. H. Kaplan, *The Liquidation of War Production*, McGraw-Hill Book
Co., New York, 1944, chap. 4.

REDUCED IMPORTANCE OF PRICES

One of the most serious objections to price control and hierarchical allocations is that prices no longer serve as measures of costs when they are not free to clear markets and reflect relative scarcities. In wartime this objection is somewhat less serious than it superficially appears to be. Where the alternative to price control, rationing, and allocations is a rise in prices, powerful incentives operate to hold resources off the market in anticipation of price increases. To a degree, therefore, government has a choice of misallocating some of its resources through faulty costing or encouraging them to be hoarded. Misallocation may be the lesser of the two evils.

Furthermore, even if costs continue to be measured by prices, in time of war or heavy mobilization prices may be very poor indicators of alternatives. In the first place, they include, among alternative values forgone, occupational and other preferences of individual workers; and we have seen that these preferences, although they affect wage rates and money costs, are not alternative values forgone by leadership expressing widespread agreements on values activated by war. For a society wishing to value such preferences much more lightly than in peacetime, the inclusion of these preferences in measures of cost is quite misleading. Secondly, the timing of procurement becomes so important that customary measures of cost are again misleading.[38] Costs may be less important than estimated date of delivery in influencing choice. In different words, the only relevant costs are the costs of obtaining the commodity at a particular time, and prices do not always measure these.

Thirdly, choices cannot be made on the basis of customary cost or price estimates because location becomes a critical variable in wartime. Location is important for strategic reasons, of course; beyond that, in the haste of wartime production it is necessary to bring production to the labor supply rather than schedule production in low-cost firms in the hope that an adequate labor supply can be found.

The consequence of these imperfections in market price as a guide to cost is that, even if market price could by some magic continue to serve up the same kind of cost estimates as in peacetime, those in control of war production could hardly rely on these estimates and would in any case have to make their own cost estimates.

[38] For some comments on this in the British experience in World War II, see E. A. G. Robinson in D. N. Chester (ed.), *Lessons of the British War Economy*, The University Press, Cambridge, 1951, p. 53.

Their own estimates might regard market prices as relevant if not sufficient for a correct appraisal of alternatives. But measures of cost in physical terms would be unavoidable and presumably the "bottleneck principle" would properly become the major focus of their attention.

The experience of many economies in war appears to confirm the importance of the "bottleneck principle." ". . . The golden rule of all planning is that it must be done in terms of the scarcest of the resources."[39] The difficulties of planning by bottlenecks vary from one situation to another, but it is in any case the key to wartime planning. Although the appearance of a bottleneck is evidence of previous error in planning, bottlenecks not only serve to signal the need for a correction but become the basis for planning ahead. The reason for this is the inevitable failure of the overview and the consequent necessity for a crude marginalism. The bottleneck reveals the critical margin at any time.[40]

In the United States, "throughout World War II we initiated priority, allocation, or programming to deal only with the items in tightest supply. Determinations of shortage were translated into administrative action only when critical needs were not being met."[41] And the Controlled Materials Plan, which organized allocation around steel, copper, and aluminum, achieved its success partly because it focused administrative action on these three bottleneck items.[42] The appointment of production czars for particular commodities, like rubber, or of individuals charged with a responsibility to achieve a particular goal in disregard of overriding directives, as in Nelson's appointment of L. R. Boulware to deal with the escort vessel program, is a further example of the bottleneck principle in planning.[43]

For some years in the Second World War a relatively adequate supply of manpower in the United States made it possible for production authorities to plan in terms of bottlenecks appearing in steel and in particular materials. All of these could be allocated much

---

[39] *Ibid.*, p. 57.

[40] See Ely Devons, *op. cit.;* cf. also the earlier discussion in this chapter of the failure of the overview.

[41] David Novick, Melven Anshen, and W. C. Truppner, *op. cit.*, pp. 386–387.

[42] For a description of the operation of the plan, see *ibid.*, chap. 8.

[43] Cf. Luther Gulick, *op. cit.*, pp. 100–101. We recognize that there is disagreement on the success of the production czar device and the Controlled Materials Plan. See, for example, H. M. Somers, *op. cit.*, pp. 27–28; and David Novick, Melven Anshen, and W. C. Truppner, *op. cit.*, chap. 8.

more simply than labor, and all could be more easily quantified than the diverse resources called labor. In Britain, on the other hand, a manpower shortage called for planning in terms of labor resources, which are both somewhat immobile and heterogeneous. In addition, British planning had to take account of specific scarcities in particular sectors of the economy—sometimes shipping space, sometimes a critical raw material, sometimes a specialized skill. Britain's bottlenecks were more difficult to deal with, but the allocation process was much the same in both countries.

DUAL PRICES

A final difficulty with the price system in wartime remains. Assume that government procurement is accomplished with hierarchical controls. But assume further that taxation is sufficient to restrain inflation in the civilian sector of the economy. Why is it not then possible to operate a price system in the civilian sector?

Several difficulties would arise from the consequent use of a dual set of prices, one controlled by hierarchical techniques, the other controlled by the cues and incentives of the price system. Taxes heavy enough to control the general level of prices are not sufficient to hold down the prices of particular commodities and services the supplies of which have been very sharply reduced. If their prices rise, sellers receive windfall gains and buyers suffer windfall losses. The consequences for real-income distribution may be serious, especially if many of the buyers of the particular commodities are members of low-income groups.

Another difficulty in dual prices is income inequities between wage earners and resource owners in the civilian sector, on the one hand, and those in the government sector, on the other; they will not receive the same wages and prices for their services. Still other problems arise from conflicts in incentives as a result of these income inequities; it may become difficult to enforce hierarchical controls over some resources if the civilian sector offers high returns to them. For some resources the civilian sector will play the role of a black market in obstructing hierarchical controls.

WARTIME AND PEACETIME ECONOMIZING

What has been said about choice and allocation in wartime confirms the shortcomings of the price system discussed earlier in the chapter. Wartime economizing serves as a case study of the deficiencies of the price system; and in particular it stresses the limitations imposed upon the use of the price system by price system repercussions on the distribution of income. It is a case study significant for peacetime economizing because the circumstances that displace the price system in war always are present in particular sectors of the peacetime economy, as our earlier list of shortcomings of the price system reveals.

Wartime economizing should not, however, encourage facile generalization about the possibilities of dispensing with the price system in peace. For, to repeat a point made often, it is above all the subordination of consumer sovereignty to control by leadership that permits the displacement of the price system. This subordination is more limited in peace than in war.

On the other hand, it is only fair to say that, where the price system gives way to central control in peacetime, the level of performance of central controls might be expected to be higher than in war. The substitution of central control in peacetime is marginal rather than comprehensive. Then, too, peacetime central controls need not operate with such speed as in war, nor need they cope with sudden changes in demand put upon resources or with sudden and substantial destruction of assets. In the immediately following chapter we come to grips with many of the problems of central control and price system as they are typically combined in peacetime choice and allocation processes.

15

Price System, Hierarchy, and Polyarchy for Choice and Allocation (Continued)

The preceding chapter investigated the limitations of central and price system controls over choice and allocation, first considering them both as limiting cases on a continuum. It also examined both the range of variation in use of price system and central control techniques and the functional relationship between the use of these techniques and particular social goals. Finally, it analyzed wartime choice and allocation processes as a case study of the shortcomings of the price system.

We now need to turn to two groups of issues: those pertaining to the relative rationality in Western economies of collective and market choice and those pertaining to the relative effectiveness of allocations through government prescription and through market manipulation.

These are important issues because policy does not usually choose between price system and central control, but between different combinations of them. The possibilities of collective choice in an economy largely dependent on a price system raise very practical problems of policy in Western economies. So also does the choice in particular situations between allocation through the controls of the price system and allocation by hierarchical prescription.

I. The Relative Rationality of Collective and Market Choice

In the economizing process, choice is not simply a process by which individuals choose what they want. For the wants of different people are inconsistent with one another—even to the point at which social stability is weakened by the attempts of different people to give effect to their conflicting choices. The social process of choice must, therefore, somehow achieve a reconciliation of inconsistencies. The chapter on rationality outlined some methods of reconciling choices so that some consistent set of choices is agreed upon as controlling: voting, individual market choice, delegation, and autonomy. These are the fundamental goal-scheduling devices. Within this perspective we now wish, as a fifth step in the appraisal of price system and central controls, to examine the merits of market choice as against the polyarchal device of voting and the hierarchical device of delegation.

In economizing, both voting and delegation to leaders would be extraordinarily difficult if completely divorced from the price system. But they are not wholly divorced, for costs are usually stated in prices no matter what the mechanism of choice. In most Western economies, collective choice is facilitated by the quantification of costs through the effects of the market choices that have not been collectivized. Hence, in Western economies collective choice can operate more rationally than in a more extreme form of central control without any dependence on the price system.

In many situations market choice, on the one hand, and voting and delegation, on the other, are not in fact alternatives. One cannot choose national defense or police protection through individual market choice. Yet for some commodities and services the choice is not only open but currently debated. For medical care, housing, and education, and to a degree for food and clothing, there is disagreement on the appropriateness of collective choice and individual market choice. Almost inevitably, income redistribution programs raise the issue, because income distribution can be altered either through outright transfers of money from one income recipient to another or through a collective decision on housing, education, medical care, or food and clothing. The importance of the issue is indicated by the present scope of collective choice; in Great Britain collective choice through national and local governments has been estimated to account for about 40 percent of the national income.[1]

MARKET CHOICE AND VOTING

We shall first consider voting in comparison with market choice.

ADVERTISING. Some of the stanchest friends of the price system are hesitant to defend the rationality of consumer choice on the

[1] Barbara Lewis and R. H. B. Condie, "The British Social Security Program," *The Journal of Politics*, May, 1950, p. 342.

market against the charge of its corruption by sellers, primarily through advertising. Moreover, advertising contravenes one of the conditions—that consumer choices be autonomous—from which economic theory argues that a price system approximates an optimum allocation of resources. We may as well begin here to try to unravel the tangled threads of fact and fancy on consumer rationality.

Advertising often misinforms, confuses judgment, and debases taste; in all this, it obstructs rationality. But in so doing, it is less distinctive than immediately appears. For advertising is a method of control by leaders over non-leaders, and when have leaders not been guilty of these sins? As an operating organization the price system can no more dispense with leadership than can polyarchy or hierarchy. Liberal economic theory like liberal political theory has tended to gloss over this fact; leaders in a competitive system as in government are assumed to be rather passive agents of consumers or citizens. Nothing, of course, could be a more mistaken emphasis. Leaders have goals of their own. Leadership gives them opportunities to acquire additional status, wealth, security, power; and these in turn, as Marx correctly saw, help them to influence communications, education, politics, religion—indeed, the whole process of social indoctrination. Thus they influence the creation of wants, preferences, and norms. The evils of advertising are great; but because they are not peculiar to market choice, they are not a very useful criterion for deciding whether market choice is or is not less rational than voting.

A comparison of advertising with partisan political campaigning is not beside the point. An elaborate comparative study of the two would be well worth undertaking even if it could not establish which of the two least obstructs rational choice. There is hardly any charge that can be brought against advertising that is not valid also as a criticism of campaigning for votes. The advertiser often wins customers by appealing to their prejudices or fears for social acceptance. So also does the candidate for office win votes. The advertiser does not seek to give information; he wants to implant beliefs whether they are true or false. Again, the same can be said for the political leader. The advertiser appeals to the lowest common denominator, but no more so than does the politician. Advertising is costly; so is campaigning. And if advertisers manipulate people with singing commercials, politicians do it with hillbilly bands.

As we have said, advertising, like political campaigning, represents an attempt by leaders to manipulate non-leaders. Reprehensible as this manipulation often is, in both advertising and politics it also serves several purposes widely regarded as desirable. Leadership is a major source of information; competing leadership, a source of criticism. Consumers and voters would be in desperate straits if they had no other information than sellers and politicians gave them. But this is not to say that the contribution of sellers and politicians is negligible.

In voting, the virtues of political campaigning are taken for granted; almost everyone believes that competition among ideas is necessary to rational choice at the polls. The kind of competition generally regarded as desirable is one relatively unregulated, not supervised by a board of censors. The voter is expected to take it upon himself to sift out the good ideas from the bad, the facts from the falsehoods, and the responsible politician from the demagogue. In assuming this responsibility, he runs a great risk because he often cannot or does not wish to distinguish truth from falsehood. Yet he cannot dispense with what he learns from political leadership. In the market, the merits of a free competition among ideas are less well understood; but for all the cupidity of sellers, they, too, inform and criticize; and the consumer would choose even more blindly without them.

No doubt the competition of ideas in the markets of the price system has exhausted the possibilities of informing consumers on the merits and defects of potatoes. With a high and rising standard of living, however, consumers need information on what they may expect from different refrigerators, automobiles, radios, lawn mowers, bicycles, houses, rents, vacations, hair curlers, hats, cigarettes, movies, and liquors. The information they receive will be heavily interlarded with misinformation, just as when they are told by their political leaders that grass will grow in the streets if the opposition comes to power. Still, consumers are much dependent on it; they rely on it to learn of new alternatives open to them as well as to sharpen their discrimination.

There appear to be immense possibilities for raising the level of rationality in consumer choice through consumer research and regulation of advertising practices, but clearly the same kinds of possibilities are open for improving voter rationality through research and regulation of campaign practices. This is by no means the best of all possible worlds. The point is only that the deficiencies in consumer rationality are matched by similar irrationalities in voting. They both originate in the desire of leadership to control non-leaders.

Are there no differences between advertising and campaigning? Obviously there are many. For example, overt criticism of the opposition is developed to a high art in politics; but government regulation and business ethics combine to minimize it in advertising. One result is that many consumers guard against falsehood in advertising by assuming that everything the advertiser says is false unless some quite independent evidence confirms him. Because many people do not believe what advertisements tell them (even if they do what advertisements tell them to do) and because hundreds of competing claims serve to throw light on one another even if they do not explicitly challenge each other, advertising may be no more successful than campaigning in representing falsehood as fact.

Other differences between politics and selling may be cited. The differences suggest that advertising is often more audacious in what it attempts. In this respect it ranges over greater extremes than does political debate. Rarely do candidates for office rest their whole campaigns on appeals comparable, say, to those used in cigarette advertising—on simple, dogged repetition of almost meaningless but suggestive slogans. On the other hand, candidates are rarely so purely informative as are the great majority of the advertisements in, say, the Sunday edition of the New York *Times*. Without a comprehensive study of the differences between campaigning and advertising, it would be foolhardy to conclude that one exceeded the other in its contribution either to rationality or to confusion.

One further observation is relevant. The goals achieved by a given action may be ranked high or low on the preference scale of the individuals concerned. A social process may be highly efficient in achieving low-ranked goals and extremely inefficient in achieving highly ranked goals. In this respect, neither voting and reciprocity, nor delegation and hierarchy, nor market choices and price system have any particular claims to superiority. All often manage to be highly efficient at a low level of goal achievement, because of inadequate discussion and insight into wants, faulty communication, lack of responsiveness, or demagoguery and misrepresentation. An element of coercive delegation is possible both in the price system and in polyarchy. In both, the elites may keep effective protest and discontent down to a manageable level by satisfying low-ranked goals without ever finding it necessary or profitable to concentrate on highly ranked ones. Advertising, slogans, manipulation of unconscious erotic and infantile wants, and other forms of propaganda may divert people from awareness of, or attempts to achieve, their higher preferences in order to concentrate on their subordinate ones.

To decide when this takes place is, as a practical matter, extremely difficult. How can one know whether people are concentrating on their low preferences when they cannot articulate, or may even be unconscious of, their more highly ranked ones? Are people who buy television sets, chromium-trimmed automobiles, and corrupt politicians instead of slum clearance and education misled as to their goals or merely expressing highly ranked goals that sensitive observers find repellent? European observers are frequently fooled by their observations of the United States because they cannot grasp the fact that this country is a genuinely mass society such as in all probability has never existed elsewhere on such a vast scale. Leadership here is much more responsive to popular taste than elsewhere. Paradoxically, the European often tends to explain this fact by turning it upside down: if the "masses" express bad taste, it is because they are manipulated and exploited by their leaders, the "capitalists."[2] Yet the facts are perhaps more convincingly explained by saying that American consumers are getting about what they want, and not what an educated European thinks they ought to want—and, under some circumstances, might in the name of freedom compel them to take.[3]

KNOWLEDGE OF COSTS.   Once over the hurdle of seller influence on the buyer, some economists have built up a rather impressive demonstration that consumer market choice is less irrational than voting. It is worth while to examine their line of argument, for not all economists agree on it, and we can organize our discussion around it.[4]

[2] Cf. Mary McCarthy, "Mlle. Gulliver en Amerique," *The Reporter*, January 22, 1952, pp. 34–37.
[3] For an interesting attempt to judge consumer rationality, taking recommendations of Consumer's Union as a working test of correct choice, see Alfred R. Oxenfeldt, "Consumer Knowledge: Its Measurement and Extent," *Review of Economics and Statistics*, November, 1950, pp. 300–314.
[4] For an example of the kind of demonstration to be found in the literature of economics, see Alfred C. Neal, "The 'Planning Approach' in Public Economy," *Quarterly Journal of Economics*, February, 1940, pp. 246–254.

A principal virtue of market choice, it is argued, is that the chooser knows the costs of any selection among alternatives. On the other hand, the voter often chooses without knowing costs. He is frequently ignorant of the total cost of what he votes for; in any case, he will only rarely know what his share is of the cost incurred collectively, because he cannot ordinarily calculate what the effect of any particular collective expenditure is on his own tax bill. Consequently, only the consumer balances margins—compares value received at the margin with value forgone at the margin.

Having argued in the chapter on economizing that quantification of costs and balancing margins is an enormous aid to rationality, we can hardly deny the strength of this argument. Individual market choice is indeed superior to collective choice in this respect. Still, the argument hardly touches the important practical issue—whether, in the kinds of cases in which choice is commonly collectivized in Western economies, there is some loss of rationality. Is collective choice for national defense, highways, medical care, housing, education, and sanitation less rational than if these choices had not been collectivized?

If the issue is posed this way, the answer is fairly clear. These choices are collectivized because of particular shortcomings in the price system that make it an inappropriate mechanism for choice or allocation. These choices are collectivized because of the third-party costs of individual market choice, because of imperfections in market choice due to income inequality, because of the effects of market choice on the distribution of income, status, and privilege, or because these sharable goods and services are costly beyond the capacity of individuals to purchase. Hence, other things being equal, market choice in these cases is more irrational than voting because it misrepresents costs to individual buyers and prevents their balancing their margins of value received and value forgone.

Sometimes the superiority of market choice is put in a slightly different way. It is argued on the ground that the consumer can make his choice effective only by meeting its costs at the time of choice. He chooses by making a payment; hence, his preferences are tested by an actual choice situation. Conversely, the voter can express an irresponsible preference because he can choose now and pay later. But this argument is also deficient. If choice is commonly collectivized because for particular goods and services the market misstates costs, voting is all the more rational for being able to escape the market's necessarily erroneous estimate of value received and value forgone at the margin.

Sometimes the issue is simply this: *The market can quantify, but only by quantifying innaccurately. A more correct measure of costs must necessarily be non-quantitative.*

It is also sometimes argued as a virtue of individual market choice that the individual market chooser needs to know less and actually can know more about his alternatives than does the voter. To begin with, the argument runs, the consumer need only know what the consequences of his choices are for himself and his family. His choice will be rational to the degree to which he can judge a purchase in these limited terms; voting, on the other hand, requires a knowledge of public affairs, specifically of the broad consequences for the society if one's own views prevail. If this argument is correctly stated, however, it turns out to mean something quite different from what it seems to imply.

For again, when, say, third-party effects of a consumer's choice are significant, it is not true that the consumer need only know the consequences of his decision for himself and his family in order for his choice to be rational. He must know the consequences for the third to the nth parties. Rational consumer choice can escape the need to consider broad consequences only if it is limited to choices in which there are none.

Consumer choice, it is also sometimes declared, deals in alternatives which call for small alterations in production while collective choice is followed by much larger alterations. Consequently consumer choice is more rational. This statement is true enough, but quite misleading. A better one is this: Where consumer choice is not irrational because of third-party effects or because of high costs of choice to a single consumer, it sometimes permits the achievement of a high degree of rationality by breaking down major alternatives into a large number of alternatives each posed to a single chooser; but, where alternatives cannot be broken down, the increment of change can often be more rationally appraised through voting. Thus, a major choice as between two steel capacities in an economy can be successfully reduced to individual consumer choices on the market in what are sometimes called normal circumstances. But voting (or, as we shall see, delegation) may be more rational if the issue is, as in economic mobilization, a rapid and large adjustment in steel capacity.

KNOWLEDGE OTHER THAN OF COSTS. Aside from relevant cost information, it is sometimes alleged that consumers are better informed as choosers than are voters. The allegation is ambiguous. Again, consumers choosing on the market are commonly quite ignorant of third-party damages; and even if not, their knowledge does not always influence their choice. But perhaps such an allegation is meant to suggest that information is more easily to be found on market choices or that the level of discussion of alternatives is higher. Here it can only be said, as with advertising, that systematic research can perhaps uncover differences worth generalizing about; but differences are not obvious.

To be sure, a choice between two kinds of bicycles calls for fairly concrete and easily understood facts while a choice between one Presidential candidate and another or between slum clearance and street improvements ideally requires facts not available at all. But again, this distinction confuses the relative difficulty of two quite different kinds of choice situations with the relative merits of two different techniques for scheduling goals. As long as many difficult choices must be made collectively because of the deficiencies of market choice, it will always appear superficially that rationality can be carried to a higher level through market choice. As for level of discussion, discussion accomplishes a vigorous exchange of information and misinformation both in market choice and in voting. Voting, of course, compels the participants in the discussion to consider the broadest implications of alternatives, which means that it has the merit, not only of taking known third-party effects into account but of exploring possible but yet unknown costs and returns.

Perhaps what some people mean when they say that collective choice is less rational than market choice is that collective choice is less rational when choice has to be collectivized than market choice is rational when market choice can be employed. This is much like saying that a pig is fatter than a giraffe is tall. Yet there may be an issue hidden here. Let us grant that collective choice is more rational than market choice when the shortcomings of the price system make market choice inappropriate. Let us also grant that market choice is more rational where these shortcomings are absent. Is it possible to go any further?

It would be surprising if individual mental processes became somehow clogged or crippled simply because they were faced with a vote instead of a purchase. No; if there are any differences, they are to be found in circumstances external to the individual. Again, costs appear to be the main issue. It is easy to compare the irrationality of collective choices as they are commonly made with the superior rationality with which they might be made if every voter had reasonably accurate cost estimates such as might easily be given to him by political leadership. The contrast between what the voter knows about costs and what he might know is striking; but where market choice is wholly appropriate, there is no great discrepancy.

But if this can be charged up as a source of irrationality in collective choice, market choice almost always suffers from a serious deficiency from which collective choice is free. The whole process of choosing has itself an influence on one's identifications, therefore on the self, and therefore on the goals one seeks to maximize. On the whole, the process of making market choices tends to narrow one's identifications to the individual or, at the most, to the family. The process of voting, on the other hand, with all that it presupposes in the way of discussion and techniques of reciprocity, tends to broaden one's identifications beyond the individual and the family. If the individual can balance his margins more precisely in market choices than in voting, it is in part only because the self whose goals he is concerned with tends to be narrower in market choices than in voting. The whole problem of solidarity and consensus is largely by-passed by market choices; and indeed, economists have, by and large, neglected these questions. Yet a system that stimulates the narrowest of individual identifications rather than a broader sense of social solidarity does not necessarily produce rational choices even if it provides better opportunities for balancing margins.

THE PARADOX OF VOTING.   The paradox of voting, as it has been called, is a minor difficulty in voting that people with a mathematical turn of mind enjoy toying with. One author has put the paradox this way:

Let A, B, and C be the three alternatives, and 1, 2, and 3 the three individuals. Suppose individual 1 prefers A to B and B to C (and therefore A to C), individual 2 prefers B to C and C to A (and therefore B to A), and individual 3 prefers C to A and A to B (and therefore C to B). Then a majority prefer A to B, and a majority prefer B to C. We may therefore say that the community prefers A to B and B to C. If the community is to be regarded as behaving rationally, we are forced to say that *A* is preferred to *C*. But in fact a majority of the community prefer *C* to *A*.[5]

It follows, the argument runs, that in such situations majority rule by voting is deficient for making rational decisions.

No doubt there are some logical difficulties in making rational calculations through voting and majority rule, but the paradox of voting hardly goes to the heart of the matter. The paradox, as stated, is itself subject to important qualifications. First, we are not "forced" to say that *A* is preferred to *C* unless we first postulate a "community" preference that is different from the preferences of the people in it. We are no more "forced" to say that the "community" prefers *A* to *C* than we are "forced" to say it prefers *C* to *A*, or *B* to *C*. Two people prefer *A* to *B;* two (a different pair) prefer *B* to *C;* and two (still a third pair) prefer *C* to *A;* conversely two people would vote against *A* as the *most* desirable alternative, another pair would vote against *B* as the *most* desirable alternative, and a third pair would vote against *C* as the *most* desirable alternative. In this situation one can only say that the majority is not agreed on the most desirable alternative; nor is any one choice more rational than the others. There is no "community" preference.

Second, the paradox is not an empirical observation of a common difficulty in polyarchies. The difficulty may or may not exist as an empirical fact. And, in fact, if the disagreement indicated were commonplace, polyarchies could not exist. One reason that it is not an important and common difficulty is that the paradox leaves out an implied value that does influence choices. Why do these three people wish to determine their policy by majority rule in the first place? It must be that the majority process itself has some value for these people. But if that is so, then an additional set of alternatives has to be added: namely, that 1, or 2, or 3, or all of them prefer *some* agreement (and maintenance of the majority rule process) to *no* agreement. In a word, what are the consequences of not coming to an agreement? If these people regard the consequences of disagreement as adverse—and if they did not they would not have employed majority rule in the first place—it would be quite rational for them to compromise. All may agree, for example, that it is better to settle on alternative *A* than to disrupt the community.

The paradox also assumes a prior knowledge of one's order of

[5] Kenneth J. Arrow, *Social Choice and Individual Values*, John Wiley and Sons, New York, 1951, p. 3.

preferences and complete rigidity in choices. If this were so, then majority rule (and polyarchy) would probably provoke civil war and political dissolution much more often than they do. Many people discover their preference in the process of deciding; and one of the factors that influences their preferences is what other people seem to want.

FREEDOM IN VOTING AND MARKET CHOICE. The issue of compulsion versus freedom in voting is sometimes raised either (1) to demonstrate directly the superiority of market choice or (2) to argue that only free choice can be rational. The position often taken is that market choice is free choice—each individual chooses as he wishes and there are no outvoted minorities—but voting compels those outvoted to make an expenditure against their wills. We cannot do much more with this argument than refer to our discussions in earlier chapters on freedom and on its relation to the four alternative control devices. There we observed that hierarchy was uncritically and mistakenly often identified with compulsion and spontaneous control with freedom. The freedom of the parent of school children is often but not necessarily more infringed on by his being outvoted on a new school for his community than by the influences through which he is reluctantly led to dress his children as well as their schoolmates are dressed or to provide them with television because "all the others have it."

For many purposes one can, of course, distinguish governmental infringements on freedom from those of spontaneous control, but one should not fall into the trap of calling only one of them compulsion or of assuming one to be more dangerous or less happy than the other as a general rule. Beyond this general caution, three more particular considerations point up the compulsion that is disguised in "free" consumer choice.

First, as has already been observed, differences in income shares produce great consequences for consumption, status, and control; freedom is therefore sometimes inconsistent with market choices that reflect inequalities in income. Second, market choices coerce third parties. This proposition simply puts all we have been saying about third-party effects into terms of control rather than terms of consumption and market value. Where third parties are coerced—where, for example, they are compelled to pay for and undertake

smoke control, move away, or accept a reduction in their assets—
they may feel free only if they can supplant consumer choice with
voting and hence express their third-party interests. Third, choosers
are not free in the market if high costs prohibit a choice that could
be made available to them by sharing the commodity through collective choice.

The particular relationship between consumer *freedom* and *rational calculation* is explained in this way: If each consumer is free
to choose as he pleases and if he knows the values to be received at
the margin in any choice, as well as the values to be forgone, he will
maximize his welfare. Freedom is thus necessary to rationality.
Given a number of assumptions, such a statement can be made
formally correct, but it says almost nothing about the relative rationality of voting and market choice. What it commonly means is
that, assuming rational behavior—defined as choosing more value
rather than less an individual faced with choices which he is free
to make will choose those alternatives which he prefers. Thus the
statement is used simply to define rationality. Although this tau-
tological statement can be put to very good use in theoretical analysis, it is not informative in our present context.

In comparing freedom in voting and market choice one must
recognize that the two techniques present to the chooser different
sets of alternatives. Before it can be said that his choice is free, it
must be asked whether the kinds of alternatives are frustrating or
satisfying. In many cases, for reasons just given, choice to a consumer presents alternatives all of which are frustrating, as when his
income is extremely low. In some circumstances, therefore, the concept of a freely choosing consumer is a contradiction within itself.
But that difficulty aside, it is still not necessarily true that a freely
choosing consumer will maximize his welfare through market
choices. Whether he does or not will depend upon the size of his
income in relation to standards of living and expenditure set by
other market choosers, as seen in the earlier discussion of income distribution. And these difficulties aside, whether he maximizes his welfare depends upon his knowledge and motives, which are not necessarily superior in market choice. Finally, these difficulties also aside,
a further demonstration is required to show that, even if he maximizes his welfare in terms of choices fairly immediate to him, market choice is a rational goal-scheduling device. Such a demonstra-

tion must assume away such deficiencies of market choice as third-party effects and prohibitive costs of sharable goods.

PERSPECTIVE ON VOTING AND MARKET CHOICE. From the foregoing discussion of market choice and voting, it ought to be perfectly clear that market choice is deficient in a large number of circumstances and that many of the claims made for it have not been properly qualified. In appraisals such as this, it is inevitably difficult to maintain perspective; but what is important to see is the inadequacy of market choice in particular circumstances without at the same time losing sight of the great merits of market choice where such difficulties as third-party effects are minor. For where they are minor or absent, market choice affords a rather precise method of goal scheduling in which a high degree of coördination of individual choices emerges from a spontaneous field.

DELEGATED CHOICE

To simplify the discussion, we have to this point taken voting to be the alternative to market choice. But in fact, delegation of choice to leadership is often a more rational alternative than voting, and in the real world voting almost always is accompanied by some delegation. All the objections raised against market choice, however, are as relevant to the case for goal scheduling through leadership as to the case for voting; consequently we need only extend the discussion a little further to take account of some particular issues pertaining to delegation.

The most common objection to delegation, the validity of which must be granted, is that it puts choice into the hands of persons who are not choosing only for themselves, as in both market choice and voting, and who at the same time lack criteria for choice on behalf of others. They will find it difficult to decide the relative worth to non-leaders, for whom they choose, of a hospital in one city, a school in another, housing or medical care for the low-income groups, or better clothing as against better furniture.

Why, then, do choosers delegate their choices? Sometimes voters will wisely delegate choice to leaders simply to save themselves time and trouble, or because they do not wish to bear responsibility. Choice is also delegated because leaders are expected to be or to become more competent choosers than non-leaders. An extreme case of this is the delegation of some kinds of choice to military leaders on the reasonable assumption that they know what commodities and services are required for waging war. One may also delegate choice with respect to educational services to school boards, preventive medical services to experts in that field, housing to housing administrators. It is not necessarily true in any of these fields that delegated choice is less rationally made than market choice. And where consumer choice is different from leadership's choice, consumers may delegate in the hope of raising their level of tastes, as is possibly the case in education and in municipal administration of artistic and cultural services.

Given the deficiencies in market choice which call for collective choices, given the complexity of the choices to be made, and given the time, energy, and competence required to make them, voters will often prefer to delegate their choices and will find their choices more rationally made as a consequence. Even for relatively simple choices, say, with respect to land use in American towns, voters cannot ordinarily cope with the choices to be made and must turn the responsibility for zoning over to leadership. And leadership may make its choices quite irrationally before voters will correctly decide that they could do better directly through either market choice or voting.

Again, some people will be tempted to speculate whether a pig is fatter than a giraffe is tall, asking themselves whether hierarchical leaders far removed from the masses of people for whom they act can choose as rationally as individuals can choose for themselves. But this approach avoids the meaningful issue. Given the shortcomings of market choice and the impossibility of voting on many kinds of questions, the choices of very foolish leaders will often be much more rational than the badly calculated choices of individuals in the market. On most school expenditures, for example, market choice and voting are out of the question. *Where the price system is an inappropriate mechanism, market choices are certain to be irrational; but delegation either may or may not be.*

II. Hierarchical and Price System Allocations

A final issue concerning the appropriate functions of price system and central controls is posed by the alternatives: price system allocation and hierarchical allocation. The question of which is more appropriate arises in connection with both collective or central choice and market choice. We shall examine the alternatives as a sixth step in appraising price system, polyarchy, and hierarchy.

TWO METHODS OF ALLOCATION

FOR CENTRAL CHOICE.   Like the price system, a central control system is actually decentralized, though to lesser degree and in a very different way. Decentralization is accomplished by delegating authority to members of a hierarchy at descending levels. Central control is thus marked by long chains of control; the specialized instrument of central control is a bureaucracy.

It is convenient, however, to distinguish between (1) hierarchy in its most bureaucratic form, with chains of control reaching down through prescription to the individual citizen in economic life, and (2) hierarchy in a mixed form, in which a lower level of the bureaucracy controls citizens in the economic process not through prescription but through price system controls.

What has come to be called "physical" planning is predominantly of the first type. The name is a misnomer. "Physical" planning is no more "physical" than any other type of planning (whatever that word, in this connection, can possibly mean). "Physical" planning is an attempt to substitute for the cues of the market a different set of cues emanating from superiors and accompanied by the expectation of punishment for disobedience.

The second type employs price system controls for allocation but does not subordinate control to consumer free choice or necessarily use prices to achieve an accurate measure of costs. It is distinguished from the first type in that it does not prescribe responses. Hierarchical control over allocation directs investment, for example, by a specific instruction to a particular potential investor, whether private businessman or public servant. In price system control, the controllers determine investment by manipulating the costs or returns on investment.

In both cases a hierarchy is required; but in the second case the bureaucracy does not go so far as to issue an order to the investor, interpret it for him, send out agents to enforce observance, and prosecute violators. Gain and loss on the market are counted on to guarantee the desired response. If the desired response is not forthcoming, a further manipulation of price or cost is called for; but even here the bureaucracy does not have to enter into the complications of instructions to or negotations with each potential investor. Price system allocation thus calls for fewer central decisions, a less complicated hierarchy, and a smaller bureaucracy.

FOR MARKET CHOICE.   Similarly for individual market choice, allocations may be through hierarchical controls or price system. In this case, of course, the use of hierarchical controls achieves a mixture of price system and hierarchy, whereas, for collective choice, it is the use of price system allocations that achieves a mixture of controls.

Although the use of price system allocations with collective choice is common, the use of hierarchical allocations with market choice is not. Yet the combination is employed in critical allocations, as illustrated in the coördination of British transport by hierarchical, as well as price system, allocations. The combination should be distinguished, however, from hierarchical allocations designed, not to control resources in response to market choice, but to substitute collective choice for market choice. Many of the hierarchical controls over British transport are of this second type. So also are controls over the allocation of industry and over capital investment programs. These are designed to modify market choices in the interest of collectively chosen goals and are not simply devices to improve the response of resources to market signals.

Although hierarchical allocations play only a small role in the United States at present, other Western economies are more heavily dependent on them. In Great Britain, for example, hierarchical allocations are effected through many governmental techniques, such as power to buy and sell scarce materials for British industry in order to accomplish allocation where British industries cannot assure themselves of adequate supplies through the market, through ship licensing as a control over ship movements, through foreign exchange controls, through power to determine allocation of a firm's output between domestic and foreign markets, and through licensing of construction, licensing of imports and allocation of imports to British industry, and controls over location of industry.

THEIR RELATIVE MERITS

The choice between hierarchical allocation and price system allocation is concretely posed in such questions as: To wage war, or build highways, shall labor be conscripted or hired? Shall the responses of British road and rail haulage services to the market demands for them be coördinated by central directives or by the market? Shall textile imports respond to market bids or be allocated by licenses?

THE MAJOR REASON FOR PRICE SYSTEM ALLOCATIONS. The core of the case for price-induced allocations is, of course, that they are an essential part of an elaborate price system process through which costs can be represented in prices and in which costs take account of occupational and other producer preferences. This has been explained in earlier chapters; all we need say here is that without market bids for resources the quantitative measurement of the alternative values become impossible. In short, if somewhat crudely, the performance of the price system as a whole is immediately dependent upon bidding for resources through the market.

MERITS OF HIERARCHICAL ALLOCATIONS. But a first great virtue of mandatory, hierarchical allocations is that they can sometimes accomplish a large movement of resources more rapidly than can the cues and incentives of the price system. This fact is illustrated in wartime economizing but an illustration can also be taken from investment controls in Great Britain since the Second World War, where hierarchical allocations of capital to housing and hierarchical regulation of the location of industry have probably achieved a more immediate response than would have been possible had the British government worked solely through money cues and incentives. Speed in reconstruction comes to be highly prized in a country like Britain where World War II reduced national wealth roughly by one-fourth.[6] Even if mandatory controls such as these eventually falsify prices as a measure of costs, the consequent misallocation of resources may be a less serious evil than a slower allocation through price system cues and incentives. The alternatives simply pose a choice between two kinds of misallocation.

Second, it follows from the shortcomings of the price system that the primary objection to hierarchical allocations—that they falsify cost calculations—is not always true. For costs may already be falsified for any of the reasons discussed earlier. If they are inaccurately stated in prices, allocations through money cues and re-

[6] The estimate is from W. K. Hancock and M. M. Gowing, *British War Economy*, His Majesty's Stationery Office, London, 1949, p. 551.

wards may result in serious misallocations which hierarchical allocations might be able to avoid. Inaccuracies in cost calculation may mislead both market and collective choice, it has already been explained; the point here is that market cues and incentives for allocation must accept market costs as influences on responses of those holding resources, while, on the other hand, hierarchical allocations need not. To induce a response, say, from a businessman, money rewards must cover his money costs, whether these are correct costs or not. Hierarchical allocations can simply disregard inaccurate money costs, alter them by fiat, or cover them by expenditures which are not permitted to influence the actual allocation.

Third, the effects of income distribution complicate allocations just as they complicate choice. Hierarchical allocations are necessary when it is not thought desirable to allow income differences to influence responses, a possibility discussed with reference to wartime controls. Fourth, hierarchical allocations may be desirable to avoid windfall gains in income shares for holders of resources whose responses can be induced only by very large monetary incentives. Taken together, these last two considerations give hierarchical allocations a larger role to play in time of inflation than otherwise, for in inflation falsification of costs and adverse income consequences of price incentives may be serious.

Fifth, where inflation arises in a price system, a compelling reason for hierarchical controls is to keep prices from rising further in response to market bids for resources. In this circumstance hierarchical allocations play the same role as rationing of consumer goods. Mandatory import controls and quotas for domestic allocation in Britain and Scandinavia since World War II thus have as one of their purposes the control of prices on import resources from abroad.[7]

Sixth, price system cues and incentives may be too weak to induce the allocations desired. The most dramatic example of the failure of price system allocations when risks are large and required investment is heavy is in the production of atomic energy. Almost all the great investment in capacity and equipment has been hierarchically allocated through government-owned plants leased to

[7] Petter Jakob Bjerve, "Government Economic Planning and Control," chap. 3 in Henning Friis, *Scandinavia Between East and West*, Cornell University Press, Ithaca, 1950, pp. 49–112; Sir Henry Clay, "Planning and the Market Economy: Recent British Experience," *American Economic Review*, Papers and Proceedings, May, 1950, pp. 1–10.

private operators. It has also been shown in the preceding chapter that allocations of new investment in World War II were predominatly hierarchical because of the inadequacy of price system incentives.

SHORTCOMINGS OF HIERARCHICAL ALLOCATIONS. On the other hand, an effective method for enforcing hierarchical allocations is often lacking. At the outbreak of World War II, for example, the British government's policy to increase agricultural output could best be implemented by covering farmers' increased costs and allowing them an increase in their incomes.[8] In this case outright production orders and requisitions would have been difficult to enforce. To be sure, price and income offers may be quite ineffective, because sellers anticipate higher prices, or they may be effective only at "profiteering" prices.[9]

Moreover, because of its emphasis on command, hierarchical allocations often run into difficulties by imposing a prescribed penalty on an act that is rewarded at the same time by the price system, even if only through a black-market price system. Although no control system can completely escape the competition of conflicting controls, market manipulation can often ease the enforcement problem. Governments that wish to encourage school attendance of children short-cut many of the enforcement problems by making attendance inexpensive, as most governments do. Likewise, it is often easier to control the volume of imports by adding to their costs through taxes than by prohibiting otherwise attractive imports.

Enforcement problems for mandatory allocations often become those of suppressing a black market. One of the most delicate questions is, paradoxically, the degree to which the black market need be suppressed in the interest of making the mandatory allocations effective. As it has been observed for the German Nazi economy[10] and as is increasingly suspected to be the case for

[8] W. K. Hancock and M. M. Gowing, op. cit., p. 159.

[9] "When the War Office went into the market to buy sacks, it met with an unsatisfactory response. . . . In March 1915, it received a swarm of unsatisfactory offers, together with one large offer from a speculator who hoped to corner the whole supply of sacks and make a 100 percent profit. . . . This impudent action stung the War Office. . . . It sent officials to Liverpool to requisition the stocks of the sack merchants there. . . ." Ibid., p. 15.

[10] Walter Eucken, "On the Theory of the Centrally Administered Economy," Economica, May, 1948, pp. 98 ff.

the Soviet economy as well, black markets may be indispensable to mandatory allocations—or, to put it another way, mandatory allocations without the supplement of a black market can rarely succeed. Allocations are often neither detailed nor flexible enough to take account of changing needs for innumerable materials used in production; either the enterprise enters the black market or it fails to meet its quota.

OTHER DIFFERENCES BETWEEN HIERARCHICAL AND PRICE SYSTEM ALLOCATIONS. Where, as is sometimes the case, price system allocations are referred to as "framework" planning in contrast to "physical" or "direct" control, the implication inevitably creeps in that they permit more freedom than the latter. In view of what has already been said about the relationships between command, manipulation of field, and freedom, this conclusion is hasty. True enough, market manipulation avoids the frustrations of command and both the annoyances and the invasions of privacy required to enforce commands. Nevertheless, it can compel people to do what otherwise they would not choose to do. And its impersonality is often a source of annoyance or despair; for individuals are sometimes more bitterly frustrated by a high price, which does not enable them to identify the culprit, than by a command, whose source can often be identified. It is also true that a central authority can drive a man to bankruptcy by raising his costs and yet escape the responsibility that would attend the imposition of an equivalent penalty, say, through command.

Price system allocations are ideally suited to control when leadership is indifferent as to who responds but wishes only to achieve a response from some proportion of non-leaders—for example, in control over the total volume of investment spending. Here the purpose of control may be to reduce spending by, say, 20 percent. Simply by raising the costs or lowering the returns on investment expenditure, leadership can escape the responsibility for deciding who in particular must curtail his expenditures. If the response is too great or small, subsequent adjustments in costs or returns can increase or reduce spending by the desired amount. This advantage also has its drawbacks, we have seen, for control over different persons will vary according to their incomes, market positions, or assets; and this variation cannot always be tolerated.

Another difference between hierarchical and price system

allocations is that the latter, like the price system generally, neither depends upon nor necessarily encourages a high degree of individual identification with the social group as a whole. The individual simply responds in view of his self-interest rather narrowly conceived. Hierarchical control, on the contrary, often cannot be enforced unless individuals feel a moral obligation to accept the rules of the society in which they live. And the promulgation of new rules is often accompanied by an attempt by leadership to strengthen the obligation.

Let us not exaggerate the differences; the two methods of allocation have much in common. Within the bureaucracy administering hierarchical controls or manipulating the market, internal controls connecting the upper with the lower levels of the bureaucracy lean heavily, of course, on both command and manipulation of field, as well as on the inevitable spontaneous controls that no system wholly dispenses with. And reciprocal control exists between hierarchical superiors and subordinates, as well as between the controlled citizens and members of the hierarchy. And finally, as was explained in the chapters on bargaining, leaders of various groups will bargain with leaders in the hierarchy.[11]

III. Improvements in the Choice-Allocation Processes

The prerequisite of rational choice and allocation is not simply that price system techniques be used in their most effective sectors of the economy and hierarchical or polyarchal techniques in theirs but also that policy should exploit the possibilities of raising the effectiveness of each. Now although we do not wish to prescribe policy in each of the many fields in which the choice-allocation processes may be improved, it may be desirable to suggest briefly the kinds of possibilities that are in fact open. This is the seventh and last step in our appraisal of price system and central controls for choice and allocation.

IMPROVEMENTS IN PRICE SYSTEM CHOICE AND ALLOCATION

Many of the shortcomings of price system choice-allocation processes are remediable with little—sometimes no—modification

[11] For an excellent illustrative discussion of collective and market choices and price system and hierarchical allocations in the particular circumstances of postwar reconstruction in Scandinavia, see Petter Jakob Bjerve, *op. cit.*

of the price system. The level of knowledge and judgment brought to bear on market choices can be raised enormously through systematic consumer education and research; these are possibilities still largely unexploited.

Relatively small sums for research into the technical qualities of common consumer goods would accomplish much, and it seems hardly possible that the expenditure of government funds for such purposes would add so much to the complications of polyarchy and hierarchy as to throw doubt on the wisdom of such programs. The adoption of standard grades for some commodities, either voluntarily through industry organization or through law, would appear to offer the same gains at the same small cost. Restriction of advertising has often been proposed to cope with the irrationality of consumer choice, but, because advertising is both misleading and informative, a policy for its regulation is not easily to be found. It may, however, be worth looking for.

In addition, costing in a competitive price system can be much improved with beneficial results for choice and resource allocation. Cost accounting hardly exists in thousands of small firms, and in the best of firms accounting practices are not fixed but are in fact continually improving. Unionism affords a possibility of improvements in the costing of labor in different markets and of different skills, although whether this potential can be realized depends upon variables we have not yet examined. Where monopolistic cost-price calculations and policies arise from the businessman's desire to protect himself from insecurity, stabilization may lead to substantial improvements in costing and resource allocation. The grotesque miscalculations of cost characteristic of periods of unemployment need not be taken as inevitable.

Recent research into the relationship of market structures and price policies holds out some hope that small doses of hierarchical controls over market structures may be used to improve price policies. They are tied up, of course, with the problem of narrowing the discretion of sellers.

Even in fields where inadequacies of the competitive price system seem to call for increasing use of collective rather than individual market choice, there are undeveloped possibilities of improving individual choice rather than supplanting it with collective. Inequalities of income and not inadequacies in the price mechanism are often at the root of what appear to be imperfections in individual choice. It is a matter of debate, for example, whether deficiencies in medical care in the United States are due to irrationality and other defects in individual market choice which call for its replacement by collective choice or instead to inequality of income, which may be remedied more simply than by abandoning individual choice through a price system. (Of course, to a large extent, medical care is simply a problem of risk and insurance.)

IMPROVEMENTS IN CENTRAL CHOICE AND ALLOCATION

The prerequisites of more rational collective choice begin with the prerequisites of improving hierarchy and polyarchy generally, as discussed in the chapters on hierarchy and polyarchy, since collective choice will ordinarily be initiated through polyarchy and delegated to members of a hierarchy. But we need not review the discussion of those chapters, except to suggest once more that the greatest single aid to rationality in collective choice and allocation is probably to be had by coördination of political leadership through unified political parties.

More particularly, govermental budgeting can be much improved. Expenditure and revenue decisions are often poorly coordinated, so that choices are made without attention to costs. What is perhaps worse, public spending often proceeds as though it were not a fact that wants or needs for public services were a function of their costs.[12] Procedural and organization reforms capable of making headway against these difficulties are not hard to find.[13]

One objective should be to make cost information available in a variety of ways so that costs of different collective expenditures can be compared. Several alternative federal budgets in the United States, for example, could be used to facilitate cost comparisons. Some types of veterans' expenditures might be classified in one budget as military, in another as social security, in still another as educational. It ought also be possible to see veterans' expenditures in terms of per capita disbursements to veterans as well as per capita expenses per taxpayer. Even if many of these estimates are rough, rationality should be much improved by increasing the number of

[12] See Herbert A. Simon, Donald W. Smithburg, and Victor A. Thompson, *Public Administration*, Alfred A. Knopf, New York, 1950, p. 509.
[13] See Arthur Smithies, "Federal Budgeting and Fiscal Policy," in Howard Ellis (ed.), *Survey of Contemporary Economics*, published for the American Economic Association by The Blakiston Company, 1948, pp. 174–209.

margins at which value received and value forgone may be compared.

A second possibility is to sell some government services now distributed free. The recent revival of interest in toll highways in the United States reflects new possibilities for matching gains and losses for particular expenditures. These possibilities are much improved in high standard of living economies with much redistribution of income, for a major objection to putting government services on a fee basis has traditionally been the regressive character of the levy.

Still other possibilities might be named, but we wish only to suggest the potential improvement in rationality that might reasonably be expected. Because new techniques of control are constantly being invented, we should not judge the possibilities either of price system or of hierarchy in terms of their present performance.[14]

For any large-scale departures from the price system in the direction of hierarchical allocation of resources, as in heavy mobilization and war, the primary requirement of rationality appears to be, as we have said before, allocation planning in terms of bottlenecks. Bottlenecks planning is a form of incrementalism, which is, we have often emphasized, a fundamental pillar both of calculation and of control. A comprehensive overview of resource allocation in time of major reliance on mandatory allocation calls for the comprehension of more variables than man can grasp at one time. The incremental principle, in the particular form of bottleneck allocation, is modest enough to achieve sometimes a satisfactory degree of rational control.

Finally, it may not be widely recognized how much collective choice and allocation may be improved simply by making information more accessible and systematizing it for particular purposes. Commenting on British wartime planning, E. A. G. Robinson wrote: "Certainly we started in a state of almost complete statistical nakedness. . . ."[15] British and American planning in wartime only

[14] On the extent to which federal budgeting practices have improved in recent years, see *ibid.*, pp. 179–182. For an account of past and proposed improvements in British budgetary practices, see Basil Chubb, *The Control of Public Expenditures*, Oxford University Press, New York, 1952.

[15] In D. N. Chester (ed.), *Lessons of the British War Economy*, The University Press, Cambridge, 1951, p. 43. And as for the United States: "In early 1940 a tremendous mass of information was available in Washington pertaining to the operation of the industrial system. The data, however, could not be coordinated nor organized to present a comprehensive statement of resources. Data on potential war

rarely made use of precise calculations of input-output coefficients,[16] although since the war some substantial strides have been made toward facilitating such computations and using them in the decision-making process.[17]

For many Western economies the situation today is no better than in Britain and the United States ten years ago. The Marshall Plan was an important factor in influencing national governments to collect basic data on their own resources and needs, and national income accounting has made it possible for these government agents to systematize their data so that they could be brought to bear on decisions. Still, much is to be done; it is probably fair to say that the collection and organization of statistical data for collective choice-allocation processes is only beginning.

---

demands were for all practical purposes non-existent. . . . Experience of the WPB shows that it never fully recovered from these early statistical deficiencies. . . . We were as ill prepared to create and use the proper techniques for collective information as we were to wage modern war. . . ." David Novick and George A. Steiner, "The War Production Board's Statistical Reporting Experience," Parts V and VI, *Journal of the American Statistical Association*, September, 1949, pp. 441–442.

[16] E. A. G. Robinson, in D. N. Chester (ed.), *op. cit.*, p. 46.

[17] See T. C. Koopmans, *Activity Analysis of Production and Allocation* (Cowles Commission Monograph 13), John Wiley and Sons, New York, 1951.

16.

Price System, Hierarchy, and Polyarchy for Other Economizing Processes

The two preceding chapters have examined the functions of central and price system controls with respect to the choice and allocation processes. This chapter continues the examination of these alternative controls with respect to processes for distribution, stabilization, resource development, and high resource output. The distribution process poses the fewest problems; because the problems are widely understood, we shall deal with them quite briefly.

I. Techniques for Distribution of Claims

COMMON TECHNIQUES

Money income is first distributed largely through market payments. But this distribution is subsequently much altered by government transfer payments. Taxation reduces personal disposable money incomes; and pensions, relief payments, unemployment compensation, and the like increase them. Although the net effect of these changes has not been very precisely measured,[1] their effect is to shift the distribution of money income toward equality. As for real income, its distribution depends upon the distribution of money income as modified by transfer payments; upon free and subsidized government services, like education, housing, and medical care; and, finally, upon the choice-allocation processes. The effect of government services is, again, to shift distribution toward more equality.

These techniques of distribution operate largely to distribute claims and real incomes among families; within families the distribution of claims and of real income is accomplished in ways too familiar to be worth detailing. Finally, both between and within families, claims and real income are again redistributed through gifts, as well as through default of debts, theft, and gambling.

[1] Cf. Chapter 5.

All this is familiar, and these alternative processes pose only a few questions of policy at the level of the present discussion. Price system distribution produces inequality of income widely regarded as intolerable; hence hierarchical controls over distribution such as transfer payments and free government services are everywhere accepted as necessary. Clearly, too, they are necessary to achieve the goals in distribution discussed in Chapter 5. At the same time, because occupational free choice is a high-ranking value in Western society, very few people today propose to "eliminate the wages system." And, aside from the merits of occupational free choice, given other values postulated in this book, resource allocation through a price system requires the calculation of resource costs through differential market payments to them.

PRINCIPAL ISSUES

The principal issues posed by alternative techniques for distribution are these: Is the incremental movement toward more equalization that is widely held to be desirable[2] more rationally accomplished by hierarchical devices like taxation, transfer payments, and subsidized government services or by alterations in market distribution? And, if by alterations in market distribution, is it more rationally accomplished by altering earning capacities or simply by changing the price of labor and other resources through hierarchical prescription?

HIERARCHICAL DETERMINATION OF RESOURCE PRICES AND WAGE RATES. Taking the second question first, we find that one major objection to changing wage rates or prices on other resources simply by hierarchical prescription is that such a procedure falsifies resource prices as measures of cost. In real-world situations, costs may for other reasons already be so falsified that this objection loses much of its force. Nevertheless, it can hardly be dismissed; and if costs are not otherwise falsified or can be corrected, it becomes a powerful objection to outright wage or price pegging. A further objection to outright alteration in resource prices without regard to productivity is that stabilization may be threatened. Either unemployment or inflation is a possible consequence, the latter more probably. In the light of these very serious objections to altering prices and wages, this technique for redistribution of claims is ap-

[2] We also regard it as desirable; cf. Chapter 5.

propriate only when its limitations are offset by marked advantages over other techniques.

Two such advantages must be conceded. First, as an alternative to transfer payments and subsidized services, in circumstances where alteration of earning capacity is too slow or uncertain, it avoids the possible adverse incentive effects of the taxes necessary to support government transfer payments and subsidies. Second, given certain widely held values in Western culture, income recipients may have a strong preference—it does not matter whether it is rational or not—for receiving income shares in market payments rather than in government checks or services.[3]

CHANGES IN PRODUCTIVITY.   But changes in market payments brought about by changes in earning capacities are subject to none of the objections brought against outright hierarchical alterations that are not matched by changes in productivity. Nor are they subject to the limitations imposed on transfer payments and government services by the possible disincentive effects of taxation. They are, however, slow-working changes. Furthermore, not all individuals whose incomes are inadequate are capable of increasing their earning capacities; consider especially the disabled and the aged.

Looking ahead one or more generations, it is on balance probable that the smoothest road to more equalization is through aids to education, occupational and professional training, mobility, and health, all of which have the effect of equalizing earning opportunities.

TRANSFER PAYMENTS AND GOVERNMENT SERVICES.   This last conclusion leads to a second conclusion: the most effective short-run methods for equalization are tax reform, transfer payments, and subsidized government services. For despite their possible effects on incentives,[4] they accomplish three things. First, they act immediately on the distribution of real income and do not defer

---

[3] The principal example of redistributing income by pegging prices is in agriculture. Aside from the adverse effects of price supports on the rest of the economy, price supports have apparently given the greatest income gains to high- rather than low-income farmers. It has been estimated that, under present price programs, if farm income were increased by one billion dollars, fewer than 25 percent of the farmers would receive 75 percent of the total. D. Gale Johnson, *Trade and Agriculture,* John Wiley and Sons, New York, 1950, p. 90. Yet given the alternatives, it is not entirely clear that price supports are unwise.

[4] As Chapter 5 suggested, these should not be exaggerated.

the achievement of a preferred distribution entirely to a future far removed. Second, they alone can be directed with precision to meet the income needs of particular groups, like the aged and the disabled. Third, and in the long run most important, they are the methods by which education, occupational training, health, and mobility can be made available now so that the advantages of these aids to earning capacity can be enjoyed later. The greatest question concerning methods of distribution is how far taxation and transfer payments should be carried, a question answerable only by reference to the limits of equalization discussed in Chapter 5.

DISTRIBUTION OF WEALTH. If market distribution is to be made more equal, earnings from all resources should be equalized; this statement reveals the critical importance of redistribution of wealth as a lever on market distribution. Property is a source of inequality, as was observed in Chapter 5, not only because as a source of income it is unequally held but also because it greatly affects the distribution of opportunities open to each successive generation.

One of the most striking recent evidences of the critical role of the distribution of wealth in controlling the distribution of income is in a theme running through the *New Fabian Essays*, a collection of papers in which a group of prominent British socialists have attempted to rethink the socialist position now that the older socialist goals have been won. Conceding that public ownership of industry has been a disappointment to many socialists, and finding that alternative politico-economic techniques are better adapted to achieve the goals once thought attainable only through public ownership, these thoughtful essayists still find—or find again—in the private corporation a major obstacle to the degree of income equality they seek.

OTHER METHODS. Some income problems can best be attacked through still different techniques. For example, inadequate medical care may stem not from any genuine inadequacy of income or scarcity of service but instead from a family's desire to spend its money income on other services. In such a case, what appears superficially to be an income problem may be more successfully attacked through education in consumption, through compulsory consumption of medical services, or through a subsidy supported by its own recipients. The price policies of business firms can also be used within limits as a substitute for redistribution. Price policies in firms producing a variety of products or styles probably achieve a substantial equalization of income by covering a disproportionate share of costs from the higher-priced items sold to higher-income groups.

For status, cultural and social opportunities, and other problems centering on the relationship between inequalities in income and desirable development of human personality—these being the problems with which policy can least competently cope through redistribution—alternative avenues of reform are possible. A minimum common educational background, for example, would presumably do much to minimize those differences, as in speech, manners, and outlook, which in later life make strangers out of friends and form class lines. Or, alternatively, education might stir pride in cultural differences. However, these objectives are not always within the reach of government policy. Status changes, class lines are drawn and redrawn, sharpened or blurred; and one can observe in these alterations some substantial gains, as well as losses. A nation cannot, however, legislate class lines, nor can it always regulate specific institutions and movements.

In an earlier chapter low income was shown to be primarily attributable to old age, broken homes, color, educational deficiencies, and lack of occupational skill. So far as low income is a problem of age, amelioration cannot proceed through improving earning capacities, instead it must work through old-age pensions and medical care. So far as it is a problem of broken homes, in which widowed mothers are not free to enter the labor market, improvement requires improved opportunities for employment for women, especially part-time work, but also adequate survivor's insurance, benefits for dependent children, day nurseries, school lunches, and other techniques aimed at the very particular problems of the widowed mother. So far as it is a problem of color, redistributive schemes can do far less than a wide variety of reforms in government and in individual attitudes and action to remove barriers to economic improvement for members of minority groups. And for lack of education and lack of occupational skill the solution is to be found both in removing economic barriers to education and training and in removing, as in the case of minority groups, certain social barriers to improvement in economic position.[5]

[5] For a discussion of other techniques to assist these particular low-income groups, see the testimony of Dewey Anderson, U.S. Congress, Joint Committee on the Economic Report, *Hearings*, Subcommittee on Low-Income Families, December 12–20, 1950 (81st Congress, 1st Session), U.S. Government Printing Office, Washington, 1950, pp. 485–511.

COLLECTIVE BARGAINING.   Although collective bargaining as a distributive technique logically belongs to the following chapter, we can take brief note here of its limitations. Although highly touted in some circles, redistribution through collective bargaining is a dubious technique. In the first place, those who have examined statistics on wage movements cannot agree on whether, up to this date, unions have had any significant effect on wage rates.[6] Secondly, unionism at best appears to have a somewhat capricious effect on income shares. To be sure, union policy whittles away at many apparently unjustified and accidental inequities in the wage structure within plants and industries. On the other hand, it has most successfully raised wages, it would appear, among the better-paid earners. Collective bargaining in the United States, for example, began among the "aristocracy of labor" and only slowly spread to the unskilled.

In any case, because of their effects on bargaining power, differences between labor markets and between product markets that have nothing to do with the relative desirability of increases in income in one market or another become controlling factors in income distribution. And lastly, unless wage rates match productivity, collective bargaining suffers from the same disability as does hierarchical alteration of wages and resource prizes; it falsifies wage costs.

II. Techniques for Stabilization

As the term is often used, stability is almost synonymous with organization or with coördination. But it will be remembered that in this book stability refers to an adjustment between the total claims made upon resources and the resources available. Stabilization processes are, therefore, those which guard against an excess of claims, a shortage of claims, and erratic or cyclical maladjustments in either direction.

What are the functions of price system, polyarchy, and hierarchy in achieving stability?

[6] See, for example, Milton Friedman, "Some Comments on the Significance of the Labor Unions for Economic Policy," in David McCord Wright (ed.), *The Impact of the Union,* Harcourt, Brace and Co., New York, 1951, pp. 204–234; Paul H. Douglas, *Real Wages in the United States, 1890–1926,* Houghton Mifflin Co., Boston, 1930; Arthur M. Ross, "The Influence of Unionism upon Earnings," *Quarterly Journal of Economics,* February, 1948, pp. 263–286; Harold M. Levinson, *Unionism, Wage Trends, and Income Distribution, 1914–1947* (Michigan Business Series), University of Michigan Press, Ann Arbor, 1951.

THE PROBLEM: INFLATION AND DEFLATION

CONSEQUENCES OF INSTABILITY. Where, in the absence of a price system, a central plan demands less from resources than they can provide, a consequent waste of resources is obvious. If more is demanded than can be supplied, one unhappy result is unpredictability in results. The plans being impossible, they cannot be fulfilled; and it will not be possible to know which part of the plan will be carried through and which not. Given the impossibility of fulfilling the central plan, another consequence is that individuals and groups within the economy will make their own plans to fit their own goals. Those individuals who have immediate control over resources will be strategically placed to achieve their own goals; others will not.

In the consequent discrepancy between prescribed and operating organization, the distribution of real income may shift markedly toward individuals strategically placed with respect to control over resources. A still further consequence is that, if the central planners attempt to make the best of the situation by replanning the distribution of certain critical goods, their efforts will require a greater detail of hierarchical control over economic activity than had at first been contemplated.

But for reasons presently to be explained the problem of instability is primarily a problem of price systems or of economies in which price systems play a large, even if not dominant, role. For the tendencies to over- or undershoot the mark are stronger in a price system than in hierarchy.

Because claims are made effective through spending money, overshooting the mark takes the form of too much spending. As in hierarchy, unpredictability is one undesirable consequence. Where spending runs to excess, buyers may find supplies *unpredictably* exhausted; or, to the extent that many prices rise, consumers find their real income unpredictably reduced by the reduced purchasing power of their money incomes. Where claims run beyond available supplies, some individuals must be thwarted in their attempts to make their claims on resources effective, and it cannot always be predicted on whom the frustrations will fall.

Again, a second consequence of overshooting is that resources will be allocated by mechanisms that produce *predictably* undesirable results. As everyone knows, resources will be allocated through the influence of personal friendship with a supplier, through black markets, and through intimidation, as well as through higher prices. Each of these methods distributes real income in a pattern different from that which would have prevailed in the absence of the inflation. Although the new distribution might conceivably be an improvement over the old—even a black market may serve a useful purpose in this respect—ordinarily the new pattern is not desirable, for real income is shifted toward individuals with immediate control over resources—toward those in positions of power who have favors to grant and toward high-income recipients. The effect is to aggravate inequality of real income, control, and status. And real income is also arbitrarily shifted both from those with fixed money incomes to those whose money incomes rise with prices and from creditors to debtors.

Because there are strong cumulative tendencies in inflation in a price system, all the above problems are easily aggravated. Moreover, if hierarchical devices are employed to stop the inflation or to control some of its consequences for distribution of real income, control, and status, a further consequence is that hierarchy itself produces new problems. Price controls, rationing, central allocations, import-export controls, and the like may be preferable to black markets. But they result in prices which misstate costs, often drive resources into lightly controlled sectors of the economy in which luxuries are produced, and undermine motives to entrepreneurial efficiency.[7] Considering all the shortcomings of hierarchy, the fact that a going inflation often leads to its substitution for the price system is enough to show the adverse consequences of inflation.

At the other extreme, *under*shooting the demands made upon resources in a price system means waste of resources and sets in motion cumulative tendencies to further reductions in spending. But these are not always the major evils of deflation. The problem of unemployment is not simply a problem of lost commodities and services; in particular, unemployment of labor in a price system is a catastrophe on many counts. It takes away the income of the unemployed, plagues them with insecurity, undermines their social status, and may even go far enough, as in the United States in the 1930's, to foster proposals to disfranchise them and in other more subtle

---

[7] See Sir Henry Clay, "Planning and Market Economy: Recent British Experience," *American Economic Review*, May, 1950, pp. 1–10; see also Erik Lindahl, "Swedish Experiences in Economic Planning," *American Economic Review*, May, 1950, pp. 11–20.

ways to create a second-class citizenship for them. This sequence
of events is inevitable when claims to status and respect are tied
closely to income, income to productivity in the market, and productivity, of course, to the job.

One of the curious consequences of unemployment in a price
system is the way in which it falsifies prices as measures of costs.
If resources are otherwise unemployed, their use is not at the cost of
a forgone alternative; yet money costs will not fall to zero for these
resources and will continue to be a barrier to their employment.
Of course, once a decision is reached, say, by a public authority, to
employ the idle resources, then the cost of employing them in any
one use becomes the alternative use forgone; but even at this point
money costs do not correctly represent these alternatives in periods
of unemployment.

TENDENCIES TOWARD INSTABILITY IN PRICE SYSTEMS. In
a centrally controlled economy, mismatching of claims and available supplies is possible for a number of reasons. Estimates of supplies may go astray on calculations of output per worker, rate of
technological improvement, gains from planned improvements in
coördination among plants in an industry or among related industries. And estimates of demands may go astray, for example, on
simple but inevitable miscalculations of weather and coal requirements. In a price system, these central miscalculations are avoided,
but mismatching occurs for several other reasons.

The causes of mismatching are well known. In the first place,
people do not spend all their money incomes. Second, although
through savings they make their unspent incomes available to businessmen for business investment spending, businessmen do not always wish to spend. Third, no one-to-one relation ties intended savings to borrowing in any case; banks and other lenders can make
available to borrowers either greater or smaller funds than have
been made available to banks by depositors. The volume of bank
credit creation is, of course, highly variable.

For still other reasons, spending bears only a loose relationship
to income. Spending can be enlarged in anticipation of receiving income or decreased in fear of income loss. All the specific institutional arrangements through which spending is planned and accomplished, such as banking, circulation of checks, savings accounts,
and credit practices of sellers, influence the relation of spending to

income. Even quite specific practices such as those governing the frequency of wage payments will affect the volume of spending from a given income. Finally, spending will be heavily influenced by government transfers of income from taxpayers to recipients, say, of unemployment insurance, by tax policies, and by government expenditures in general.

In brief, for controlling aggregate spending the price system lacks spontaneous cues and incentives similar to those which effect a systematic control over the choice-allocation processes. Given a level of spending everywhere agreed to be disastrously low, each individual in a price system is nevertheless often cued and rewarded to hold his own spending to a minimum.

PREREQUISITE CONTROLS

COMMAND AND MANIPULATION OF FIELD. Because the spontaneous controls of the price system are inadequate for stabilization and because the problem is one of coördinating aggregate spending and available resources, unilateral control is required. One possibility is manipulation of the fields of consumers and businessmen. Through taxation and subsidies, individual incomes can be altered to induce changes in spending; and government purchases can stimulate both business spending and the spending of individuals whose incomes are enlarged as a consequence. Changes in the terms of credit and in the rate of interest are still other examples of control through manipulation of field.

The other possibility is command. Outright prohibitions can be levied on certain kinds of transactions, as illustrated by regulation of installment buying. Departments of government can simply be ordered to increase or decrease their spending, and new governmental functions can be taken on, as old ones abandoned. Government spending is, of course, a command technique when it accomplishes a change in spending by prescription and a technique for manipulation of field where it has secondary consequences for the spending of private individuals. It is usually both at the same time.[8]

Manipulation of field through manipulation of the market is

[8] Although economists are not entirely agreed on which of the large variety of central controls are most appropriate, there is agreement that central stabilization controls of some sort are required, if only—to illustrate the minimum use of them— to maintain monetary stability by relatively simple policy rules. Cf. the discussion on stabilization policy by six economists in *American Economic Review*, Papers and Proceedings, May, 1951, pp. 181–200.

excellently suited to stabilization, although we do not mean to deny a large place to command. Stabilization requires that someone's spending be increased or decreased, but for stabilization it does not matter whose. Market manipulation that seeks to curtail investment spending by reducing the stimulus of government spending can be carried to the point at which it accomplishes its purpose without ever specifying who must respond and without enforcing obedience on any particular individuals. In circumstances in which the choice will appear to him to be a real one, each individual decides whether he will respond or not. While control is achieved, it often rests lightly on the controlled.

CONTROLS FOR A HIGH-COST INFLATION.   One kind of inflation cannot be controlled by market manipulation as a method of manipulating fields. This is an inflation in which prices are pushed up from below by higher costs rather than pulled up from above by excessive spending. Possibly the greatest threat of this kind of inflation is to be expected from collective bargaining. Pushing up costs need not produce inflation, of course; it may only cause unemployment. But because most Western societies prefer inflation to unemployment, their governments can be expected to convert unemployment into inflation by increasing spending sufficiently to cover the high costs. In this eventuality, they cannot then turn around and use their ordinary anti-inflation weapons to reduce spending again.

The solution to a high-cost inflation requires that those who can control costs be restrained before they raise costs or that command controls be imposed on prices and wage rates. For reasons that will become increasingly clear in the following chapter on bargaining, in neither of these alternative prerequisites can we currently place much confidence. It is quite possible that a solution can be found only in subtle changes in the roles played by businessmen and trade union leaders; the problem may in fact be a classical case of the impossibility of controlling particular acts in the absence of appropriate roles. Because a high-cost inflation is a product of the functioning of major bargaining groups, we shall postpone further consideration of it until the following chapter.

AGENDA, ROLE, AND PERSONALITY.   What has been said is enough to show that instability is an especially serious problem in price system agendas and that the first prerequisite of stabilization is an agenda in which a central authority exercises controls over the particular acts of all spenders in the economy. How important, then, are role and personality?

Until the late thirties, instability was most commonly regarded as a problem of cyclical fluctuations in spending. This being so, stabilization appeared to require government control of particular acts through market manipulation rather than alterations in role or personality. Accordingly, proposals were made for regulation of bank lending activities, for tax adjustment, and for variations in government spending in order to induce individuals to spend more or less at particular times. By 1938, however, some economists in the United States, and to a lesser degree abroad, were less concerned with cyclical fluctuations than with tendencies to chronic unemployment.[9]

Although techniques for control of spending in particular places and at particular times were appropriate to the new problem, these economists now felt less confident of their adequacy and were troubled by the possibility that the entrepreneurial role had changed in such a way as to make high levels of employment difficult except by means of permanent reliance on heavy government spending. Schumpeter's *Capitalism, Socialism and Democracy*,[10] for example, spelled out plausible hypotheses explaining subtle changes in the role of the businessman.

Today, the view has again changed. Generalizing from the years since 1945, some economists believe that for some time to come instability will typically take the form of chronic tendencies toward inflation.[11]

First, government expenditures are high because of the present scale of mobilization for defense, a scale that may become larger in the decades to come. Second, because the military is less disposed to haggle over price or refuse to buy at an unduly high price and because its purchases are often concentrated on particular scarce commodities and resources, military procurement results in more inflationary pressure than would the same volume of spending by

[9] Alvin A. Hansen, "Progress and Declining Population," *American Economic Review*, March, 1939, pp. 1–16.

[10] Joseph A. Schumpeter, *Capitalism, Socialism and Democracy* (2nd ed.), Harper & Brothers, New York, 1947, Part II.

[11] Albert G. Hart, *Money, Debt and Economic Activity*, Prentice-Hall, New York, 1948, chap. 19; Joseph A. Schumpeter, "The March into Socialism," *American Economic Review*, May, 1950, pp. 446–456; John K. Galbraith, *American Capitalism: The Concept of Countervailing Power*, Houghton Mifflin Co., Boston, 1952.

civilian agencies or nongovernmental spenders.[12] Third, both re-construction and development spending is heavy in Europe and in underdeveloped countries. Fourth, many Western governments are politically committed to high levels of employment. Fearful that a too rigorous control of inflation may produce depression, they find themselves resigned to permitting an upward drift of prices. Fifth, as noted before, collective bargaining may produce inflationary wage costs. Sixth, the political success with which each pressure group can maintain its own position by winning gains to match price increases constitutes a cumulative inflationary force; in one form, this is the familiar problem of the wage-price spiral.

Lastly, government welfare and security expenditures are high in a postwar world in which whole populations seem to have revised their income and security demands upward. The emergence of these new demands in Great Britain has been vividly pictured:

By the end of the Second World War the Government had as-sumed and developed a measure of direct concern for the health and well-being of the population which, by contrast with the role of Gov-ernment in the nineteen-thirties, was little short of remarkable. It was increasingly regarded as a proper function or even obligation of Gov-ernment to ward off distress among not only the poor but almost all classes of society. New obligations were shouldered, higher standards were set. The community relinquished, for instance, a ten-year-old practice of not providing cheap school meals unless children were first proved to be both "necessitous" and "undernourished." Developments in the scope and character of the welfare services did not happen in any planned sequence; nor were they always a matter of deliberate intent. Some were pressed forward because of the needs of the war machine for more men and more work. Some took place almost by ac-cident. Some were the result of a recognition of needs hitherto hidden by ignorance of social conditions. Some came about because war "ex-posed weaknesses ruthlessly and brutally . . . which called for revo-lutionary changes in the economic and social life of the country."

If dangers were to be shared, then resources should also be shared. Dunkirk was an important event in the war-time history of the social services. *The Times*, a few weeks after the evacuation, gave expression to these views. "If we speak of democracy, we do not mean a democ-racy which maintains the right to vote but forgets the right to work

[12] Tibor Scitovsky, Edward Shaw, and Lorie Tarshis, *Mobilizing Resources for War*, McGraw-Hill Book Co., New York, 1951, pp. 130–131. For an analysis of the effects of military procurement on prices, see John Perry Miller, *Pricing of Military Procurements*, Yale University Press, New Haven, 1949.

and the right to live. If we speak of equality, we do not mean a political equality nullified by social and economic privilege."[13]

Possibly instability will soon show a still different face. It may be that mobilization for defense is by itself sufficient to explain what appears to be a new chronic inflation; if defense expenditures were greatly reduced, perhaps inflation would be regarded as improbable. Even with continued mobilization expenditures, inflation is not demonstrably inevitable. The course of prices in the United States since 1951, for example, is not so consistently inflationary as to prove the inevitability of inflation.

Yet the magnitude and persistence of the problem is revealed in the extent to which planning since 1945 has come to be identified with controlling inflation. Much of the economic activity of central governments since the end of World War II has been a laborious and costly effort to remedy the evils of demanding more from resources than they can provide. One can observe, for example, how little Britain's annual "economic plan," the Economic Survey, attempts to lay out actual prescriptions for economic development during the year and how much of the survey is concerned with estimating the requirements of stabilization.[14] Or consider the persistent inflationary difficulties of French reconstruction after World War II.[15]

Even if it should not be chronic, the new problem of inflation throws into focus the importance of control through role and personality even more than did the unemployment of the thirties. Its control requires, to be sure, the same battery of techniques for control of spending as have generally been required for stabilization. And, it may be added, the development of improved economic statistics and of national income accounting in recent years has put into the hands of governments useful new tools for rational calculation of the volume of spending appropriate to available resources. But what specific controls over particular acts can be employed to

[13] Quoted, with many deletions not indicated, from Richard M. Titmuss, *Problems of Social Policy*, His Majesty's Stationery Office, London, 1950, pp. 506–508. For still other factors which have been mentioned as stimulating chronic inflation, see "Agenda for the Age of Inflation—I," *The Economist*, August 18, 1951, pp. 382–384.

[14] See, for example, *Great Britain, Economic Survey for 1951*, Cmnd. 8195, His Majesty's Stationery Office, London, 1951. The content and use of the Economic Survey are described in Ben W. Lewis, *British Planning and Nationalization*, The Twentieth Century Fund, New York, 1952, chap. 1.

[15] R. V. Rosa, "The Problem of French Recovery," *Economic Journal*, June, 1949, pp. 154–170.

induce citizens to pay higher taxes without turning their Congressmen out of office? Or to induce Congressmen to run the risk of losing office by raising taxes? Or to induce trade union leaders and businessmen to negotiate wage rates that do not threaten inflation? Or to restrain farmers and their spokesmen from pressing for protection of their incomes at the cost of inflation? The prerequisites of stabilization in a price system rest on subtle characteristics of personality and role; and one of the great unknowns in economic policy in every Western society is whether personality and role are consistent with an acceptable degree of stabilization.

It may turn out that the possibilities for stabilization in a price system hinge on one of the causes of the new inflation: government commitments to full employment. If an agreement among the politically active calls for extremely high levels of employment, their goal may not be purchasable except through inflation or a wide use of hierarchical controls over prices and wages. This possibility has already become a major issue in stabilization planning.[16] It again highlights the dependence of stabilization upon intangibles, specifically upon social goals, which are in turn dependent upon role and personality.

To the extent that stabilization in a price system requires alterations in role and personality, we do not propose that governments should use hierarchical techniques to alter them. Instead—and this is our final conclusion—the prerequisite to stabilization is continued experience with instability until its consequences for individuals so change their fields as to produce requisite changes in their roles and personalities, hence in their particular acts. For leaders and non-leaders alike this it what stabilization requires.

III. High Resource Output and Resource Development

For the processes of high resource output and resource development, what are the relative merits of price system and central controls?

[16] See United Nations, Department of Economic Affairs, *National and International Measures for Full Employment. Report by a Group of Experts Appointed by the Secretary General*, United Nations, Lake Success, N.Y., December, 1949; Jacob Viner, "Full Employment at Whatever Cost," *Quarterly Journal of Economics*, August, 1950, pp. 385–407; Arthur Smithies, "Full Employment at Whatever Cost: Comment," *Quarterly Journal of Economics*, November, 1950, pp. 642–647.

The earlier discussion of incentives to diligence, innovation, and investment has already made clear the scantiness of knowledge on the prerequisites for the two processes. Everyone knows that resources may be developed and their outputs increased through the savings-investment process; through invention and innovation of tools, machines, and methods; and by the development of human capacities. Beyond this, it is difficult to go.[17]

Because the price system contains the possibility of objective measures of internal efficiency of the enterprise and makes survival of the enterprise contingent upon its performance, it is sometimes taken for granted that the price system is ordinarily the most appropriate control mechanism for high resource output and resource development. Actually, its merits are not so easily demonstrated, and it suffers from serious disabilities.

One of the great contributions of the price system to economizing is that it makes possible manageable agendas. But, although the agendas relevant to choice and allocation are much simplified in a price system, simplification of agendas does not necessarily encourage more vigorous pursuit of resource development and high resource output. If steel is to be allocated to its most preferred uses, it is clear that the problem of where it should go is simplified by an agenda that reduces the necessary decisions to simple decisions to buy and sell. But if the supply of resources is to be enlarged or their output increased by vigorous pursuit of training, invention, innovation, and good work habits, price system agendas do not significantly alter the kinds of decisions that must be made.

Simply because development depends upon allocation, the price system does, of course, make one great contribution to resource development in providing an allocation mechanism; but we wish to go beyond that. Going beyond, what is required is the kind of per-

[17] As observed before, economics has only recently been giving resource growth the attention that potential improvements in these processes appear to warrant. And even today, processes for increasing output of existing resources are somewhat neglected in economic theory.

For summaries of existing theories of economic growth, see James S. Duesenberry, "Some Aspects of the Theory of Economic Development," *Explorations in Entrepreneurial History*, December 15, 1950, pp. 63–102, and Joseph J. Spengler, "Theories of Socio-Economic Growth," in Universities-National Bureau Committee on Economic Research, *Problems in the Study of Economic Growth*, National Bureau of Economic Research, New York, 1949. See also Joseph Schumpeter, *The Theory of Economic Development*, Harvard University Press, Cambridge, 1936; W. W. Rostow, *The Process of Economic Growth*, W. W. Norton and Co., New York, 1952; and P. N. Rosenstein-Rodan, "Problems of Industrialization of Eastern and South-eastern Europe," *Economic Journal*, June-September, 1943, pp. 202 ff.

sonality and the kind of role playing that stimulates good work habits, experiment, innovation, and, within limits, taking large chances. To a degree this is confirmed by a common impression that differences among countries in output per worker, in the efficiency of managerial practices, in the rate of innovation, and in the pace of economic life generally are more a function of cultural differences than of particular controls.[18] It is, of course, possible that particular controls and institutions can be manipulated to encourage creative, imaginative personalities and roles; but existing knowledge is insufficient to hold out much assurance of success. The choice between price system and central control in a modern industrial society that is highly bureaucratized in any case is not necessarily a significant choice in this particular respect.

An understanding of the prerequisites is also difficult because goals for resource output and development are not easily defined. Everyone agrees that the processes can be overdone as well as underdone. For, although rational economizing calls for high output and resource development, it does not call for maximum output from resources or for the maximum rate of growth possible. It is not desirable that people should discharge all their energies into their jobs, leaving nothing for their leisure time. A preoccupation with gainful employment is not without dangers to one's roles as citizen, friend, and neighbor. And as for growth, where future gains are often at the price of immediate satisfactions, no formula is available to say when the future gain is worth the present loss; it is a matter of subjective preference.

COST REDUCTION IN AGENCY AND ENTERPRISE

Let us, however, examine the issues to the extent that knowledge permits. We can best approach them by taking the business enterprise and the centrally controlled agency as units, for the processes for achieving a high rate of development and those for encouraging high output are both largely anchored to the incentives that induce participants in the work of agencies and enterprises to reduce costs. (As a matter of fact, it is not always possible to separate the two kinds of process, as when a businessman installs machinery to increase output per worker.) We can then approach re-

---

[18] John E. Sawyer, "Social Structure and Economic Progress: General Propositions and Some French Examples," *American Economic Review*, Papers and Proceedings, May, 1951, pp. 321–329.

source output and development through a study of cost reduction in two different kinds of organization.[19]

AGENCY AND ENTERPRISE DISTINGUISHED. The two kinds of organization that need to be distinguished are those controlled by a price system and those controlled by polyarchy or hierarchy. For simplicity, we shall limit the term "enterprise" to organizations controlled by a price system and the term "agency" to organizations centrally controlled. It is tempting to simplify terminology by calling the one a business organization and the other a government organization. But this would lead to egregious error because government organizations may be government departments, bureaus, or agencies—all controlled centrally—or business enterprises—largely controlled by the price system.

Many organizations are, of course, part enterprise, part agency; they are controlled in part by the price system and in part by hierarchy and polyarchy. The British nationalized industries are an illustration, as are also the Tennessee Valley Authority, the United States Post Office, and—for that matter—any "private" business enterprise subject to central controls. But, for simplicity, we shall discuss the two types of organization as though they were not mixed.

SIMILARITIES BETWEEN AGENCY AND ENTERPRISE. In appraising the differences between agencies and enterprises, we must not overlook their similarities. First, despite the differences in control over what and how they produce, both kinds of organization recruit labor and other resources in a price system. Second, cost reduction depends on the performance of managers and subordinate employees alike in the organization. Moreover, a critical variable is the ability of management to affect the motives and performance of the subordinates. Third, both kinds of organization can be either large or small. To be sure, the price system permits a greater degree

[19] Cost reduction is a product of the speed and precision of every decision and act of every member of an organization. Many decisions with respect to resource output and growth are also decisions on resource allocation. In actual fact, therefore, allocation processes, at least as seen from within an enterprise, are a part of the processes by which high resource output and growth are achieved. We recognize this relationship and know that the written word can never take account of all the complexities of the world it seeks to describe. Having already separately discussed allocation processes, we must proceed to examine cost reduction processes to throw light on resource output and development without simply repeating what has already been said on allocation.

of decentralization in the economizing process than does hierarchy or polyarchy; nevertheless, an enterprise can be extremely large and highly centralized. Fourth, it follows that both types of organization are typically organized internally as hierarchies. Even more specifically, both are operated by bureaucracies. Fifth, the primary monetary incentive to management is salary instead of profits.

This fifth point is crucial to an understanding of similarities between organizations controlled by a price system and organizations controlled centrally through hierarchy or polyarchy. In small businesses, of course, profits cue and reward businessmen in much the same fashion as was described by Adam Smith. In modern corporate business, however, profits and dividends on stock in the company are minor sources of management income.[20] Not that profits are not still a cue and a reward, but the social mechanism by which they become so is more complicated than it once was.

The cues of the price system are immediate cues to the small proprietor because business profits and losses are almost indistinguishable from personal gains and losses. But in a large corporation, as we have said before, members of the hierarchy must be instructed or otherwise brought to treat corporate profits and losses as though they were personal gains and losses—that is, to seek one and avoid the other. Or, where the growth of the business or its good reputation seems more desirable a pursuit than profits, members of the corporate bureaucracy must be brought to recognize these goals. A complicated internal hierarchy must somehow produce a pattern of incentives to substitute for personal profit and loss.

In short, in large corporations the cues of the price system are not directly communicated to anyone within the internal hierarchy; and the internal hierarchy must provide a communications system to bring the market cues to bear on its particular members. Similarly, the rewards and penalties of the price system are not visited directly upon any decision maker within the hierarchy; the hierarchy must devise supplementary methods for transforming corporate profits and losses, or gains in position or reputation, into rewards and penalties for its members.

A sixth similarity between agencies and enterprises is that basically the same controls producing identification of the member

[20] See Robert A. Gordon, *Business Leadership in the Large Corporation*, The Brookings Institution, Washington, 1945, Part III.

with the organization and loyalty to it are to be found in both. Hence, in centrally controlled agencies there will be executives quite as eager, ambitious, keen, and devoted as in enterprises. Perhaps more exhaustive research than has so far been undertaken will disclose differences not now recognized. But, folklore to the contrary, we find no evidence that one or the other of these two types of organization is generally superior; in this respect, executives of the Department of Agriculture are indistinguishable from executives of American Telephone and Telegraph.

Seventh and last, competition is a major source of motivation in both types of organization. To be sure, one may speak of some types of enterprises as competitive, whereas one does not describe an agency by the term. But this is to use competition in its rather narrow technical sense taken from economic theory. Competition as rivalry, on the other hand, is universal; it plays no smaller role in agencies than in enterprises. In both organizations prestige, promotion, increased salaries—almost every reward that can be won within the organization—are dependent upon one's competitive performance.

STRONGER INCENTIVES TO COST REDUCTION IN ENTERPRISES

The similarities between agencies and enterprises suggest caution in generalizing about differences in incentives to cost reduction in the two kinds of organization. Nevertheless several reasons can be cited for believing that incentives to cost reduction are stronger in enterprises.

In the first place, of course, agencies often suffer more from the disabilities of hierarchy and bureaucracy discussed in Chapters 8 and 9 than do enterprises. Red tape, passing the buck, rigidity, and timidity obstruct a vigorous pursuit of cost reduction. Of course, large enterprises are also bureaucracies marked by these same deficiencies; the difference is that the external controls over an enterprise are not hierarchically or bureaucratically administered, while those over agencies often are. Hence although top management in an enterprise stands at the head of a bureaucracy, it displays fewer of the pathological traits of bureaucracy than does top management of an agency, which often looks up to a bureaucracy as well as down to one.

But beyond the discussion of the earlier chapters, more specific reasons can be given for the superior strength of incentives to cost reduction in enterprises.

CONTINGENT APPROPRIATIONS.   Consider a typical agency. Its function is prescribed by a legislature or other official superior. On an estimate of its resource needs, various factors of production are assigned to it, or it may be allocated a fund which it may spend on necessary labor, materials, and other factors. How are the required resources or funds to be estimated? A common method is for the superior organization to examine the subordinate agency's budget for the operating period just ending. The superior will make a new allocation after asking whether the old allocation was excessive or inadequate, whether any changes of function call for an adjustment in requirements, whether any economies can be achieved in labor or material requirements, and so forth. In order to protect its budget, the management of the subordinate agency will therefore be careful to use up its past appropriation; and in reporting to its superior, it will emphasize the many burdens the agency carries.

Moreover, the agency will ordinarily know that economies in operation will not be taken by the superior to justify a larger appropriation for the future but will instead reduce the new appropriation. To the members of an agency—who know that if the cost of a commodity falls, consumers may spend more money on it than before—the more or less inevitable tendency to cut appropriations when the agency admits to having reduced its costs will seem irrational and in any case will threaten their security. Hence the agency's desire to prove itself efficient will often be at war with its desire to protect its appropriation.

Again, Devons' account of the difficulties on this score in the British Ministry of Aircraft Production is illustrative. It fell upon him as coördinator in the ministry to determine what the alternative production possibilities were. Among the many obstacles to his getting the facts was the difficulty of obtaining information from members of his own organization. Suspicious of the power of the central authorities in the ministry, the production directorates were reluctant to reveal information. Sometimes also they wished to conceal the facts because they were falling short of expectation, or perhaps because they were demanding more resources than their production schedule would seem to warrant to any observer outside the directorate itself. How serious the "simple" problem of getting the facts straight could be is indicated.

In order to get the information they needed, the planning directorate used two main lines of attack. Firstly, they engaged in the most subtle forms of spying they could contrive. . . . The other main line of attack was to discover officials, either at M.A.P., the firms, or the Air Ministry, who attached greater importance to the achievement of maximum aircraft output than to the prestige of their own directorate, cultivate their acquaintance or even friendship where this was possible, and use them as the main instruments of coordination. . . .[21]

Another difficulty arises in prescribing what is to be achieved with an appropriation. Again, the ministry's difficulties are illustrative; it failed to find a satisfactory goal system. For resource output as well as for allocation—the two are often inseparable—neither "realistic" budgeting nor "target" budgeting is satisfactory. An appropriation based on a realistic appraisal of what may be expected from an organization substantially weakens its incentives to increase its input-output ratio. Yet, as we saw, target budgets are unsatisfactory because they are known to be unattainable and hence result in a failure of coördination.

Even if some agencies minimize all these difficulties, one can imagine a more desirable arrangement in which appropriations are more immediately contingent upon output and in which each contemplated change in appropriations to an agency is tested against a contemplated increase in the agency's production. One can also imagine an arrangement through which savings from cost reduction might make it possible, without consultation with the superior, for the subordinate agency to increase its production, thus producing a powerful incentive to cost reduction. Such arrangements as these would eliminate the problem of concealing information and of wasteful spending to use up past appropriations. In the simplest terms, they would provide agencies with resources immediately and directly contingent upon performance of services.

The price system contains, of course, just such an appropriations mechanism simply because the enterprise obtains its "appropriation" by selling its services for a price. Its contingent appropriations mechanism is the primary source of the incentives in

[21] Ely Devons, *Planning in Practice*, The University Press, Cambridge, England, 1950, p. 183.

enterprises to minimize costs. It is a mechanism to be found in all variants of the price system.

To be sure, in certain circumstances enterprise management can obtain funds by restricting output rather than by producing. The effectiveness of the contingent appropriations mechanism therefore depends on how effectively the enterprise is controlled by the primary and supplementary controls discussed earlier.[22] (Incidentally, it ought to be noted that the contingent appropriations mechanism does not depend solely on market competition because there are still other forms of supplementary control. Cost cutting in enterprises cannot simply be attributed, as it so often is, to competition.)

ORGANIZATION GOALS. Derived from this major difference between enterprises and agencies are a number of other differences, some of them reinforced by still other influences. For one thing, it appears that managers of agencies do not necessarily fix upon cost reduction as an organizational goal, as do enterprise managers. The agency's goal is often simply to attain a particular objective; the enterprise's goal is always to attain a particular objective with a favorable input-output ratio. The agency may only seek to produce a service; the enterprise seeks to produce a service cheaply. To enterprise managers the low cost at which they produce can represent an even more exciting achievement than the product itself. True enough, agency management will ordinarily feel some interest in producing cheaply, but its appropriations are not closely enough tied to its achievements in cost reduction to give it the enterprise's powerful motive to reduce costs. Hence it will not ordinarily be possible for the members of the hierarchy to fasten on cost reduction as a—perhaps the—major organizational goal.

Another reason for the importance of cost reduction as an organizational goal is that enterprises often have an identifiable, countable product for which a unit cost can be calculated, and agencies frequently do not. But this is because enterprises can operate only where there is such a product; and we should not therefore attribute a merit to the price system where actually a limitation is revealed. Still another reason is that, while the relation between available funds and amount of production in an agency is prescribed by a superior, management of enterprises can thrive on the responsi-

[22] Chapter 6.

bility and challenge stimulated by its own control over receipts and production plans.

STATUS AND PRESTIGE. When cost reduction is conceived of as a major organizational goal, it is not long until favored status and prestige are accorded the cost cutter by others in or outside the enterprise. This development intensifies the importance of cost reduction and, incidentally, helps explain why those from managerial roles in enterprises may occasionally continue to be cost cutters when they transfer to agencies where the customary managers are less concerned with costs. This tendency is illustrated by the caution with which some businessmen brought into the United States government's stockpiling program at the outset of the Second World War bought raw materials, whose inflated prices cued habitual responses—in this particular case, the wrong ones.

MULTIPLICITY AND DIVERSITY OF OBJECTIVES. Another explanation for the emphasis on cost cutting in an enterprise is that its objectives are customarily few and similar. On the other hand, any one agency organization may be saddled with a variety of diverse functions, as in the case of the United States Post Office, which must, among other duties, deliver the mail, prohibit the mailing of obscene and other illegal documents, provide rewards for loyal party members, keep custody over small savings, and sell bonds. Although all of these are functions well worth performing, the multiplicity and diversity of function make it difficult to measure costs, desirable sometimes to hide costs, and in any case wise to play down the importance of costs.

UNCOÖRDINATED REVENUE AND EXPENDITURE DECISIONS. A secondary and remediable yet nevertheless serious obstacle to the development of incentives to cost reduction in agencies lies in the fact that one superior may prescribe functions and expenditures while another appropriates resources or funds. Even worse, in the United States it is not uncommon for a body of lawmakers to vote functions upon an agency to satisfy the voters and then frustrate its work by failing to appropriate adequate funds. Knowing that functions and resources may be quite unrelated, managements of agencies can hardly be expected to take the same attitude toward costs as managers of business enterprises, where this kind of discrepancy cannot arise unless the enterprise is disbanding.

"AUTOMATICITY" OF PRICE SYSTEM PENALTIES AND RE-
WARDS.   As in the choice-allocation processes, the spontaneous rewards and penalties of the price system are brought to bear on cost
reduction whether anyone plans it that way or not. But it is beyond
the energies of Congressional committees or other superiors to examine every disbursement of subordinate agencies to determine
whether costs are at a reasonable minimum. Although sampling is a
necessary aid, it is imperfect. Extremely large disbursements can be
made without any check at all until too late, as in the Hanford
"overrun" where $16.5 million was spent, as compared to an original
estimate of $6.2 million, before the deficit apparently came to the
attention of any superior with power to act.[23]

Even if this is an extreme case, understandable as the product of
urgency, secrecy, and innovation, less sensational examples are
plentiful. They do not imply that hierarchical supervision is always
unsatisfactory; they simply point up the fact that a check on costs
becomes a burden on some part of the hierarchy, while in a price
system much of the task is accomplished as a by-product of consumers' purchases.

CONTROL BY PRODUCT OR BY PROCEDURE.   A further difference in attitudes toward cost reduction arises from the freedom allowed to enterprise management to experiment with new processes
and devices. The test of their success is what they achieve, not how
they do it. In agencies, on the other hand, because objective tests of
efficiency by product or service are lacking, supervisors must fall
back on testing efficiency by the means used to perform the functions of the agency. Hence the superior needs to know as much
about techniques as the management of the subordinate agency itself, which is ordinarily not possible; or old and known methods are
held to because the test cannot be applied to managers who innovate
freely.

This is, however, a distinction in favor of enterprises that must
not be pushed too far. For often the only adequate check on efficiency is through supervision of means, as when quality of work is
extremely important. Indeed, product and means sometimes cannot
be very sharply separated—medical services are an example. Where
means are important, the price system is deficient. To supervise the
means, hierarchy must sometimes displace it.

[23] See U.S. Congress, Joint Committee on Atomic Energy, *Investigation into
the United States Atomic Energy Project: Hearings* (81st Congress 1st Session),
May 26–July 11, 1949, 22 vols., pp. 329 ff.

SHIFTING VERSUS REDUCING COSTS. Agencies offer their managements a choice when costs are so high as to interfere with the
accomplishment of a desired objective. Management may attempt to
reduce costs by more efficient methods, or it may seek to shift costs
to another part of the hierarchy. Thus the managers of western
reclamation projects have sought—and successfully—to escape interest costs on investments in irrigation projects. In a price system,
however, every tub must stand on its own bottom. This is something
of an overstatement of an important difference between agency and
enterprise; enterprises sometimes receive governmental subsidies,
and agencies can be made to stand on their own feet. Notwithstanding, it is much more difficult for relatively autonomous enterprises to shift costs elsewhere; conversely, management of agencies
may be greatly rewarded for creating a false impression of efficiency
by shifting costs.[24]

GROWING POINTS. Finally, market enterprises may be superior
with respect to cost reduction because the points at which costs are
reduced become the growing points of the economy. That is to say,
cost reduction in any enterprise immediately puts that enterprise in
a favorable position to expand its operations, at the same time providing incentives to management to take advantage of the possibility. In agencies, cost reductions may pass unnoticed and, if noted,
may not induce the superior to prescribe an expansion of services.
In some circumstances a preverse tendency may appear to pour
more resources into the least efficient agencies, for these will appear
to need more generous appropriations if their work is to be carried
out.

DEFICIENCIES IN COST REDUCTION IN ENTERPRISES

Despite the superiority of enterprises on all the above counts,
cost reduction in enterprises is on some other accounts questionable
or deficient.

INCENTIVES TO WORKER PRODUCTIVITY. One possibility is
that the incentives toward cost reduction on the part of subordinates
in the enterprise may be weak. Output restriction among wage earn-

[24] Of course, as we have already said, enterprises are often inefficient because
they shift costs through third-party damages. Agencies, particularly government
ones, may often be more sensitive to third-party damages.

ers, whether unorganized or organized, is a universal phenomenon. Estimates of potentially achievable gains run very high.[25] Just what is assumed in these estimates is not ordinarily clear, but the unanimity of observers on the belief that gains of 25 to 50 percent are possible should open anyone's eyes to the possibility that motives to cost reduction in enterprises are far from some kind of practical ideal. However, the same kind of potential for increase in productivity is also to be found in agencies. Hence, one cannot immediately generalize from the inadequacies found in enterprises to the superiority of agencies. Yet the great gap between achievement and potential raises some questions.

Are the insecurities of the price system a source of work restriction more damaging to efficiency than restrictive practices in agencies? Are the tensions which have grown up in enterprises between employer and employee, between owner and nonowner, between capitalist and worker, more damaging to cost reduction than comparable tensions between superior and subordinate, employer and employee, in agencies? The surprising fact is that, for all the many studies of these insecurities and tensions, as well as of their effects on output, we have little that permits comparison. Enterprise and agency may or may not be quite different in these respects; and differences between price mechanisms themselves   between private and public enterprise, for example—and between different kinds of hierarchy may be even more consequential for worker output.

RISKS OF INNOVATION.   It is uncritically accepted in some circles that the manager of an enterprise will take risks where an agency manager will not; the one is complimented by being called an enterpriser, the other damned as a bureaucrat. Nevertheless, as in atomic energy development, the costs and risks of innovation are sometimes so great that the incentives of a price system are inadequate to induce a desired response. A different set of incentives is required, one offering a more secure reward and some protection against too severe a penalty. Thus, in the United States, governments spend more money on research than do business enterprises and universities combined, and government plays a leading role as innovator in such differing sectors of the economy as agriculture and atomic energy. Since World War II the federal government has become the major

[25] See R. P. Lynton, *Incentives and Management in British Industry*, Routledge and Kegan Paul, Ltd., London, 1949.

support of technical research and development expenditure, even excluding expenditures on atomic energy.[26]

SHIFTING THE COSTS OF INNOVATION. A final and critically significant difference between enterprises and agencies is the greater ease with which management in enterprises can escape the social costs imposed on third parties by cost reduction. As everyone knows, change is disruptive; it works severe hardships on persons whose status or function is reduced, whose neighborhoods are destroyed, or whose roots in the community are torn up when they must move elsewhere to seek a new home or job. Because agencies are coördinated by superiors who are responsible for what their subordinates do, it is often difficult for agencies to innovate in disregard of the consequences for displaced persons. In a price system, however, it is easy for an enterprise to displace its workers, destroy a neighborhood, even undermine the livelihood of a town, because controls over management simply call for a product at low cost and raise few questions about means.

Thus third-party effects of innovation influence agency decisions much more than they do the decisions of enterprises, where those injured cannot control the decision. This is both a major source of irrationality in the price system and a major encouragement to innovation.

Curiously, this kind of irrational innovation is much admired, and fears are often expressed that agencies will be inevitably hampered in innovation by the interests of persons fearing displacement. Such an attitude reflects an irrational preoccupation with the virtues of change. Yet one may regret the irrationality of change in the price system and still fear for innovation in agencies. For one may fear the irrationality of policy guided by small groups adversely affected by change who capitalize on the political indifference of the large masses who stand to gain.

PREREQUISITES OF HIGH RESOURCE OUTPUT AND DEVELOPMENT

What then are the prerequisites of high resource output and development?

---

[26] President's Scientific Research Board, *Science and Public Policy*, U.S. Government Printing Office, Washington, 1947, vol. 1, p. 12. Before World War II, industry accounted for roughly two-thirds of the total.

AGENCY AND ENTERPRISE AS ALTERNATIVES. Ordinarily a concern for high resource output will not initiate the displacement of hierarchy by price system or vice versa. But resource output may quite rationally be a marginal consideration—hence a decisive one —where the superiority of one technique over another is not clearly established by other criteria, such as distribution, choice, or allocation. One is hard pressed to find instances where agencies have replaced enterprises primarily to increase resource output; on the other hand, decisions to regulate railroad consolidation in the United States, to bolster agricultural prices, to develop atomic energy through government research, to license imports, or to provide free medical care were presumably not made without some attention to resource output. Resource output may also have been a decisive consideration in controlling the limits to which some of these programs have been carried.

Resource output is a marginal consideration for at least two reasons. The first is that the choice between price system and central controls is often largely dictated by the inability of price system or central controls to handle a choice-allocation problem at all, as in national defense, which obviously calls for hierarchy quite without regard to a large range of possible consequences for resource output. The second is that the knowledge of factors governing resource output is not developed to a point at which resource output can become decisive. In view of the importance of high resource output as against further refinements in choice and allocation, a decision to nationalize or denationalize British steel may eventually turn out to have been correct or incorrect largely because of effects on resource output. But for the present, the state of knowledge does not permit prediction of the consequences.

SPECIALIZED CENTRAL CONTROLS FOR RESOURCE OUTPUT AND DEVELOPMENT. Clearly, however, a concern for cost reduction will often call for supplementary hierarchical and polyarchal devices to improve the output, quality, or quantity of resources available to both agency and enterprise. Some idea of the dependence of reconstruction and development on hierarchical techniques can be had simply from a listing of agencies in which the United States alone or coöperatively with other nations attempts to encourage overseas development and reconstruction. The list is impressive: Mutual Security Administration, Department of

State Technical Assistance Program, U.N. Economic and Social Council (technical assistance and other aids), International Bank for Reconstruction and Development, International Monetary Fund, World Health Organization, Food and Agriculture Organization, United Nations Educational, Scientific, and Cultural Organization (including projects like its Haitian Valley development work), Department of Agriculture, Export-Import Bank, Department of Commerce, Department of the Interior (for U.S. dependencies), Tariff Commission (market surveys), Department of Defense (offshore purchases), and Federal Reserve Board and Banks (technical assistance on finance). Even this long list is not complete.

Recently several developments have emphasized the dependence of growth on central controls. The first is the growing importance of collective choice, as in housing and urban redevelopment, choices that are often dependent upon investments which enterprises cannot or will not make. A second is that aspirations are running beyond the capacity of price system techniques. The American two-billion-dollar investment in the atomic bomb is an example of a gamble that a few years earlier would have been out of the question, even for government. Western reclamation projects in the United States now envision what would earlier have been dismissed as heroic but foolish plans to use the water resources of Oregon to bring irrigation to the arid Southwest.[27] In projects such as these, third-party effects are enormous.[28] Moreover, uncertainties in cost calculation and in returns also call for hierarchy. Third, defense needs require resource development not profitable in a price system.[29] Fourth, the development of backward areas involves risks and costs that price system incentives only very slowly overcome. Fifth, human capacity is increasingly recognized to be the resource capable of the greatest development; but education and specialized training are not produced in sufficient quantity by enterprise in a price system.

IMPROVEMENTS IN AGENCY AND ENTERPRISE. Although we have been occupied with distinguishing between the capacities of

[27] *Time*, July 30, 1951, pp. 48–51.

[28] For examples of the third-party effects of development programs, see H. W. Singer's "vicious circles" in his "Economic Progress in Underdeveloped Countries," *Social Research*, March, 1949, pp. 1–11.

[29] See the report of the President's Materials Policy Commission, *Resources for Freedom*, U.S. Government Printing Office, Washington, June, 1952, 5 vols.

price system and hierarchy for resource output and growth, each can be improved in several ways. For enterprises, the major prerequisite of improvement appears to be the reduction of risks which deter venturesome investment; to this goal both economic and political stability can contribute greatly, although a host of other specific devices have also been proposed. For agencies, a number of possibilities deserve mention.

One prerequisite for stronger motives to cost reduction in agencies is a change in public attitudes toward failure. Although many people bear the costs of unsuccessful business ventures into new methods and products, on the whole it is not a source of public complaint against a market enterprise that it has met with a costly failure. In agencies, on the contrary, costly failure is commonly scandalous; hence every innovator can look forward to the possibility of a Congressional inquiry. But innovations are not innovations if they always succeed.

Thus a prerequisite of innovation is the acceptance of a counterpart in hierarchy of a healthy failure rate in the price system, where, as in the United States, in any one year from 5 to 20 percent of businesses will be discontinued (some, however, for reasons other than unprofitability).[30] This is not a pious hope; the Hanford "overrun" of over 10 million dollars provoked no storm of disapproval, and it is not unreasonable to expect that the virtue of failure will come to be recognized in fields where the urgency of experiment is less than in atomic energy.

Professionalization of, and specialization in, cost reduction has already been recognized as a further prerequisite in hierarchy; hence such agencies as the Budget Bureau and General Accounting Office. Still other techniques may be attempted. The Atomic Energy Commission's contract system is apparently successful in combining agency responsibility for *output* with specialization of the contracting enterprises in *techniques* for efficient production. To be sure, the two groups and the two kinds of function are not wholly separated.

A further prerequisite is a miscellany of administrative reforms to stress function rather than means employed, to encourage measurement of results in terms of cost, to prevent shifting of costs, and

[30] Alfred R. Oxenfeldt, *Industrial Pricing and Market Practices*, Prentice-Hall, New York, 1951, pp. 10–11.

to coördinate revenue and expenditure decisions. Nor are any of these reforms pious hopes either; they are in progress.[31]

Finally, a number of possible techniques need to be brought to bear on undermining resistance to change where the change is desirable. For this purpose, policy has not adequately explored the possibility of reducing the hardship of change by compensating those injured, by controlling the rate of change, perhaps even by speeding change so that its transitional effects are not prolonged. The level at which policy now operates is illustrated by provisions for compensation to railroad employees who are displaced by consolidation of facilities. Because the costs of compensation fall on the railroads themselves, they serve not to compensate those injured but to make cost reduction through consolidation itself so costly as to be prohibitive.

Party unity, the merits of which we have argued on other grounds as well, would also help overcome resistance to change, because it would reduce the political strength of particular pressure groups who act at the expense of the "majority." It might also even be desirable to increase the autonomy of particular agencies to allow them some of the same irresponsibility that enterprises enjoy in initiating changes with third-party consequences. This is in effect a proposal to make hierarchy irrational where the price system is irrational; its merits hinge on the possibility that minority groups will otherwise irrationally restrain innovation.

Quite possibly, the greatest contribution still to be made to cost reduction will be derived from some method of raising the level of performance of subordinate workers in agencies and enterprises alike. The possibility of unleashing the energies of employees in all kinds of organizations is well on its way to becoming one of the most exciting possibilities of our times. The day was when socialization of industry held out this promise to many reformers; but these hopes have largely vanished. From what meager evidence exists, it appears that this potential is not to be freed by any simple formula; if it is to be had at all, its achievement will almost certainly be the product of countless minor adjustments in social organization. For the development of this potential, the choice between hierarchy and price system may be largely irrelevant. As we shall presently see, bargaining may offer more hope than either.

[31] See, for example, Clarence E. Ridley and Herbert A. Simon, *Measuring Municipal Activities,* International City Managers' Association, Chicago, 1943.

IV. Some Concluding Observations on Price System and Central Controls

It may be wondered why we have not considered monopoly and other general forms of unresponsiveness in a price system to constitute a plausible case for supplementing or supplanting price system with hierarchy. The answer to this is twofold: In the first place, we have been attempting to identify particular failures in the control process, as, for example, the incapacity of controls in the price system to protect third parties, their failure to insure a satisfactory degree of stability, their disregard of claims not enforced by spendable income.

Second, so far as there is a kind of general residual problem of unresponsiveness because price system controls over the entrepreneur are never perfect, the substitution of hierarchy for price system is not an appropriate solution. For where competitive or bargaining controls in the price system are inadequate, hierarchical supplementary controls in a price system are alternatives. If these controls over the entrepreneur within the price system prove to be inadequate, they can hardly be adequate outside the price system and as an alternative to it, except, of course, to deal with the very particular problems discussed in this and the preceding chapters. In situations in which market controls are objectionable only because they are insufficiently binding upon the entrepreneur, hierarchy without market controls will prove less satisfactory than hierarchy with market controls.

It will also be noticed that the appraisal of price system and central control has not been cast in terms of freedom and coercion. The kinds of alternatives appraised are all consistent with the values postulated in Chapter 2 and hence do not pose this issue. Essentially, the position developed is that price system, hierarchy, and polyarchy are all forms of control. It is obviously not true, as extremists sometimes put it, that the price system is a form of freedom, and hierarchy and polyarchy forms of control. Each form of control considered has its characteristic frustrations.[32]

[32] Cf. Chapter 4.

17.

*Bargaining as a
Politico-
Economic Technique*

A politico-economic system organized exclusively by bargaining is not so easily imagined as one organized exclusively by a price system or central controls. As a concept, a bargaining system lacks clarity. Lacking confidence in bargaining in a central role, the advocates of bargaining techniques have for the most part offered them as modifications of central and price system controls. Nevertheless, a group of techniques for politico-economic organization including collective bargaining, worker participation in managerial decisions, and informal or formal national bargaining among leaders of business, labor, and agriculture all reflect a common nuclear belief in the organizing potential of bargaining in politico-economic life.

Bargaining, it will be remembered, is a form of reciprocal control among leaders. Hence bargaining commonly means reciprocity among representatives of hierarchies, and in the bargaining techniques just mentioned the number of subordinates in each hierarchy is extremely large. Bargaining is therefore not the clean-cut alternative to hierarchy that it is sometimes thought to be; it may in fact avoid few of the evils of hierarchy, at the same time aggravating problems of coördination. On the other hand, bargaining is increasingly turned to as the only practicable alternative to the monolithic state.

Because bargaining lacks a widely accepted theoretical rationale,[1] it is often proposed only as the least of alternative evils; and its merits are linked closely to its expediency. Hence in some circles its advocacy has come to be mark of the "realist," of hard-headedness and political sophistication. Bargaining is also in good repute because the higgling and bargaining of the market place seem to link the term with the "free enterprise" system. But bargaining may in

---

[1] Except as a supplementary control in a price system, as found in the theory of duopoly, oligopoly, and bilateral monopoly.

fact constitute a radical modification of or alternative to the "free enterprise" system.

To be sure, some kinds of bargaining are methods of enforcing competitive controls in the price system. And others constitute a noncompetitive device for control through bilateral or reciprocal monopoly within a price system. These two possibilities, discussed in an earlier chapter, tend to disguise the fact that still other kinds of bargaining are controls that substantially modify the effectiveness of consumer free choice and the other essential processes of a price system. Indeed, many proposals for bargaining envisage the displacement of the price system; even modest proposals for "bringing business, labor, and agriculture together" would unwittingly transfer functions from the market to the White House. Like hierarchy, bargaining is clearly an alternative to a price system; and it is as an alternative that we shall appraise it in this chapter.

The general characteristics of bargaining have been discussed in earlier chapters. Moreover, because bargaining is a method of coordinating hierarchies, many of its general characteristics are those of hierarchy, which has also been discussed at great length both as a general process and as a technique for economizing. To push on toward a better understanding of bargaining, we shall now appraise several of its particular techniques in terms of the goals sought by their use.

I. The Control of Industry

Worker control of industry is one common form of bargaining. Worker participation in the decisions of the plant, firm, or industry already takes place through collective bargaining, particularly in the United States.[2] But there are also numerous proposed or existing techniques for increasing the degree of reciprocity between workers and employers beyond what is supposedly achievable by collective bargaining.[3]

[2] Cf. Neil W. Chamberlain, *The Union Challenge to Management Control*, Harper & Brothers, New York, 1948.

[3] Cf. International Labor Office, *Cooperation in Industry*, Geneva, 1951. International Labor Office, *Labor-Management Cooperation in France*, Geneva, 1950. Quentin Lauer, S.J., "Co-Management in Germany," *Social Order*, January, 1951, pp. 11–22. Leo C. Brown, S.J., "Labor-Management Cooperation, a Progress-Survey of European Developments," *Social Order*, May, 1951, pp. 211–223. Bruno Broecker, *Wirtschaftliche Mitbestimmung der Betriebsräte? Eine Frage aus dem Bereich der Wirtschaftsdemokratie*, C. E. Poeschel Verlag, Stuttgart, 1948; cf. particularly the collation of Weimar law, Control Council decrees, and constitutional articles of

PROPOSALS FOR WORKER CONTROL

Demands for reforming the structure of industry in order to give workers some form of participation in decisions is as old as industrialism itself.

One of the recurring goals of socialists for over a century has been "economic democracy, self-government in industry." Ever since Leo XIII wrote *Rerum Novarum* in 1891, and particularly since Pius XI published *Quadragesimo Anno*, left-wing Catholics have strongly supported such a reform of the enterprise. Even conserative American trade union leaders have sometimes advocated worker participation. During the First World War the railway brotherhoods sponsored the Plumb Plan calling for government ownership of the railroads and their operation by a fifteen-man board, five of whom were to be elected by the railroad employees.

And in 1940 Philip Murray of the CIO submitted to the President an Industry Council Plan that carried the unanimous endorsement of the CIO executive board. It called upon the President to establish an Industry Council in each "basic defense industry," composed of equal representation from management and labor in the industry, with a government representative as chairman. The Industry Councils, armed with the necessary legal powers, would "coordinate the production facilities" of their industries, allocate raw materials, contracts, and plant facilities, adjust the labor supply, and "engage in active planning."

DISILLUSIONMENT

On the whole, socialist governments and nationalization seem to have disappointed whatever hopes existed among their followers for a rapid "democratization of industry" through worker participation. Workers in nationalized industries soon found that they faced the same old hierarchical structure, the same old gap in power

the various *Laender*, pp. 65 ff. Harold Rasch, *Grundfragen der Wirtschaftsverfassung*, Helmut Küpper Verlag, Godesberg, 1948. William Heston McPherson, *Works Councils Under the German Republic*, University of Chicago Libraries, Chicago, 1939. Pierre Lassègue, *La Reforme de l'entreprise*, Librairie du Recueil Sirey, Paris, 1948. Val R. Lorwin, "The Struggle for Control of the French Trade-Union Movement, 1945–1949," chap. 12 in E. M. Earle (ed.), *Modern France, Problems of the Third and Fourth Republics*, Princeton University Press, Princeton, 1951. Margaret Cole, *Miners and the Board*, Fabian Publications, London, 1949. G. D. H. Cole, *National Coal Board*, Fabian Publications and Victor Gollancz, London, 1948. Acton Society Trust, *The Future of the Unions*, London, 1941. Acton Society Trust, *The Men on the Boards*, London, 1941. Clinton S. Golden and Harold J. Ruttenberg, *The Dynamics of Industrial Democracy*, Harper & Brothers, New York, 1942, Appendix 1.

between boss and worker, sometimes even the same old faces. Government bureaucrats replaced nongovernment bureaucrats; so far as power relations within the plant or industry were concerned that was about the full extent of the change. After debating the question of workers' control at every annual convention for years, and long after worker representation on boards of management of nationalized industries had become settled policy for the future, when the Labor party came to power in 1945 it immediately scuttled the idea of workers' representation in the nationalized industries.[4] Six years later G. D. H. Cole argued that so far English socialism had failed, partly because it had neglected to democratize industry and therefore had not accomplished any real revolution in power relations in English society.[5]

RECENT GERMAN PROPOSALS

On the Continent after World War II, however, arrangements for works councils were won in one country after another by collective bargaining, constitutional provision, or statute. The most radical demands came out of the historic center of the socialist movement: Germany. *Mitbestimmungsrecht* became a fundamental tenet of the trade union movement and the Socialist party— a tenet shared, moreover, by wide circles of the Christian Democratic Union. Co-management replaced nationalization as the central core of socialism and political trade unionism in Germany. Most of the constitutions of the *Laender* in western Germany written after the war contained provisions permitting co-management. Finally in 1951, after lengthy and partly fruitless negotiation between employers and employees, extensive discussion in German press and periodicals, numerous alternative proposals from all sides, a strike threat in the Ruhr, and dire warnings from the American National Association of Manufacturers, the Bonn government passed legislation providing for co-management in coal, iron, and steel industries.[6] The results are still indeterminate; but it is at least possible that, in its redistribution of power, status, and respect, this will prove to

[4] Robert A. Dahl, "Workers' Control of Industry and the British Labor Party," *American Political Science Review*, October, 1947, pp. 875–900.
[5] G. D. H. Cole, "Shall Socialism Fail?" *The New Statesman and Nation*, May 5, 1951, pp. 496 ff.
[6] Later legislation covered other industries in a way highly unsatisfactory to trade unions and socialist movements.

have been one of the most far-reaching steps any Western government has taken since the war.

As with so many other questions, it is difficult to appraise the appropriate role of co-management devices in general. For the important questions are the detailed ones: What powers are to be shared? How big is the unit to be covered? How is co-management to be prescribed? What method is to be used for selecting workers' and other representatives? The combinations and permutations are very great, and often one cannot generalize from one specific proposal to another.

Then, too, evidence on which to base a sound judgment is not yet available. The German experiment is still in its infancy. Because of its potential importance it should command detailed study by observers elsewhere in the West; for conceivably it may prove to be an extraordinarily vital technique for securing a wider sharing of power, respect, and status. But it is too early to say.

AN APPRAISAL

Meanwhile, it is possible to set forth some general propositions.

INADEQUATE CONTROL OVER CO-MANAGERS. *Co-management does not by itself protect the rest of the community against exploitation by the co-managers. Yet it is possible that arrangements can be worked out that would protect the community at least as well as any practical alternatives.*

Reciprocity within plant or industry does not necessarily mean an increase in the responsiveness of industrial policy makers to the larger society. Indeed, some arrangements for internal reciprocity may conceivably create significant opportunities for collusive exploitation by a plant or industry of the rest of the community. For they may simply increase the ease with which representatives of workers and private or government owners can push up wages and prices, restrict production, or prevent modernization, technological advance, consolidation, and shifts in the location of plant—all at the cost of others.

More than anything else it was this consideration that influenced the leaders of the British Labor party to abandon workers' control when they assumed office in 1945. They could not readily reconcile the constitutional and doctrinal legitimacy of the control wielded by the cabinet and parliamentary majority in the name of the whole electorate with any scheme that devolved large chunks of policy making to boards that might not be responsive to the cabinet. Where the opposite choice is made, as in Germany, what will prevent mine workers, for example, from enhancing their position at the expense of coal consumers?

Still, the capacity of workers to exploit the rest of the community is certain to exist (as we shall see in a moment) wherever workers are strongly organized and collective bargaining is accepted. It is at least possible that only co-management is capable of altering the structure of control without destruction of minimum agreement and without resort to government sanctions operable in the long run only by totalitarian leaders. Because of the greater knowledge by workers' leaders of production, costs, and prices in the industry, and because management could no longer be so easily regarded as a private group without "public" responsibilities, co-management might have a sobering effect that can never be achieved through collective bargaining between two rather hostile partners.

But if forecasting is difficult, a general principle is plain enough. Given the values of Chapter 2, workers and their leaders can be permitted to share control only if it is expected that their decisions will produce results roughly within the dominant preferences of the greater number. Wherever "economic democracy" or industrial self-government fails to do so, it is difficult to discern grounds on which it can be justified.

It is not enough to argue that control by workers is at least as justifiable as control by managers or representatives of private owners. If control by private managers and owners is undesirable, in the sense that it does not produce results roughly within the dominant preferences of the greater number, then the problem of reform is one of technical analysis that cannot be solved by any simple formula. The possible combinations of control over management are numerous; there do not seem to be any a priori grounds for preferring one organizational form to another or for prescribing any single solution for every enterprise.

In situations where workers' representation results in exploiting the rest of the community, roughly four solutions are possible. One is, of course, government hierarchy. The boards may consist exclusively of government appointees prescriptively responsive to top political leaders. But the whole idea of co-management and bargaining is thereby abandoned.

A second alternative solution is to insure that workers' representatives are a minority on boards where the majority consists of representatives presumably more responsive to the preferences of the greater number. In Germany, employers, although willing to grant workers 30 percent of the representatives on the *Aufsichtsräte*, were not prepared to concede them 50 percent. This solution had been adopted once before in Germany, during the Weimar period; under the Works Councils Act of 1920, the works councils had the right to elect one or, in most cases, two representatives to membership on the board of directors (*Aufsichtsrat*). The results were by no means dramatic; employers were easily able to circumvent the minority of workers' delegates on the boards, if need be by having a prior private caucus at which all the important or confidential decisions were made.[7] When workers' delegates are a minority, therefore, they turn out to be little more than advisers to the board, able to acquire information, consult, discuss, propose, and warn, but unable to block the action of a determined board.

For this reason it has often been suggested that advisory councils are a better alternative than minority representation. Yet advisory boards are in many ways even less satisfactory. In part, to be sure, the difference lies only in semantics. But there are also certain practical disadvantages of an "advisory" council as compared with "membership" on a board, particularly of a government board where the tricks used by German employers would scarcely be tolerated. For the difficulty of an advisory council, as the British have learned in their consumers' advisory boards and workers' industry councils, is that it is too remote from decisions.

A third possibility lies in introducing consumer representatives to offset "labor" and "management" or "owners." But the difficulties in such a proposal are numerous. In a country like the United States, where a consumer movement is lacking, consumers' representatives would have to be selected by the government; in effect they would simply increase the government's representation, adding nothing to the solution just discussed. In any case, the word "consumers" covers a vague territory; what consumers should be included? Then too, if consumers were a minority, they could scarcely stop a labor-management alliance to raise prices, restrict production, limit innovation, and so on. If they were a majority, they should hardly be permitted to represent narrow consumer in-

[7] William H. McPherson, *op. cit.*, p. 11.

terests, and the mythical distinction between "government" and "consumer" representation ought to be abolished; they should simply be government agents.

A fourth alternative is minority, equal, or majority representation of workers within a rigorously prescribed price system enforced by government hierarchy. Like the first alternative, this would rip the heart out of co-management as a device for bargaining.

A NEW ELITE. *Control, status, and respect will be transferred to a new elite of workers' leaders rather than redistributed to workers themselves. However, even this might be an important gain.*

Co-management or workers' management is often represented as promising vast redistribution of control, status, and respect from "capitalists" or "management" to ordinary workers. Yet it would be illusory to overestimate the extent of any possible shift in control, status, and respect within the modern industrial enterprise. Advocates of "industrial democracy" have probably underestimated the extent to which the subordination in the control and status of the ordinary worker within a large enterprise is dictated by the very structure of a large-scale mechanized industrial operation. In gigantic organizations gradations of control are necessary to keep the enterprise coordinated; a large element of hierarchy is inherent. Socialists in office have been no more able to exorcise this devil than have "progressive" private managers. Yet gradations of control almost inevitably involve some gradations of income, status, and respect within the enterprise—however much one may imagine ideal arrangements for allocating one without the others.

Moreover, it is far from certain that many workers in any country genuinely want to assume the load of obligations necessary to effective "democratization" of an enterprise. Even where leadership groups actively espouse the cause of co-management, as in Germany, there is little evidence that the goal is ranked very highly by ordinary workers: high enough, that is, to induce, them to take an active role in plant politics. To be sure, this is no decisive reason for abandoning the idea, for in so far as workers are uninterested in co-management, this attitude may be due simply to their not fully understanding the instrumental goals necessary to their own desires for respect, status, subjective equality, and security. As in other areas of political life, it might be argued, the problem is to help workers clarify their own thinking and if necessary help them re-shape their attitudes about power.

To shift power, status, and respect from management to an elite of workers' leaders is a long way from achieving the utopia of industrial democracy. For most workers, co-management might mean little more than an annual casting of ballots. Yet that periodic electioneering would keep workers' delegates somewhat responsive to a large section of workers in their plant or industry can scarcely be doubted. Moreover, by greater identification with the new co-managers, the workers' respect and status might well be elevated. Even more important in the long run, the legitimacy of managerial decisions might be strengthened.

LEGITIMACY OF CONTROL. *Indeed, the main motivation behind the quest for some form of workers' participation may be striving for control relationships that will legitimize the role of management. So long as the legitimacy of managerial control is in doubt, not only is coöperation inhibited but workers cannot accede to the control of management without damaging their own sense of respect. In a culture like that of the United States, where the goal of reciprocal control is highly valued, there is bound to be a deep-seated conflict between the control of "private" management and the ordinary citizen's conception of legitimate control.*

According to the prevailing ideology of Jeffersonian and Jacksonian democracy, any large constellation of control was always dangerous. If, as in the case of government, great control was sometimes necessary, it could be legitimized in only one way: by what we call polyarchy. Yet dating back to the Constitutional Convention and indeed running through the whole of American history was a conflicting tradition that justified great control by claims of wealth, class, status, or property. The first view runs right through Jefferson's Democratic-Republicans, Jackson's Democrats and Free Soil to the Populists, Wilson's New Freedom and the New Deal. The second view may be seen in the Federalists, the Whigs, the post-Civil War Republicans.

The rapid rise of the giant corporation after 1850, and especially after what the Beards called the "Second American Revolution," was a smashing offensive against the prevailing credo that great control could only be legitimized through the processes of polyarchy. (In turn, Populism, the New Freedom, the New Deal were powerful counterattacks in national politics.) The giant corporation concentrated control where polyarchy did not legitimize it. Today one American writer has gone so far as to describe the large corporation—"big business"—as the representative institution of American society.[8] This description may be true. Yet from the Jeffersonian point of view the power of corporate managers and owners remains illegitimate, for it is not arrived at through the process of polyarchy that alone can give it the stamp of legitimacy.

Opinion polls over more than a decade provide a strikingly consistent profile of American views about corporate power. An overwhelming percentage of Americans are against government ownership of "big business" or "basic industries."[9] Most people in the United States think the good things about "big business" outweigh the bad.[10] Nevertheless, one of the "bad" things about big business is its power. Most Americans feel that big business is too powerful; they are worried much more about the power of businessmen than about the power of government.[11] Not that they think business has become more powerful than government; indeed, most people believe the national government (though not state government) is still more powerful than big business.[12] But evidently the great power of government is relatively legitimate because it is arrived at through the process of polyarchy, whereas after more than a century of Federalist, Whig, and conservative Republican arguments, a sizable number of Americans still regard great power wielded other than by government as undesirable.

[8] Peter F. Drucker, *The Concept of the Corporation*, The John Day Co., New York, 1946.

[9] In 1938, 70 percent opposed government's owning and operating railroads; see American Institute of Public Opinion poll reported in *Public Opinion Quarterly*, School of Public Affairs, Princeton University Press, Princton, vol. 2, p. 386. In 1941, 81 percent preferred the present business management of their concern to government operation; see AIPO poll, May 20, 1941. In 1948 only 5 percent wanted government ownership and operation of auto companies, 6 percent of savings banks; see Fortune Poll, November, 1948, reported in *Public Opinion Quarterly*, vol. 12, p. 760. In 1948, 75 percent wanted to continue private ownership of the basic industries; see Fortune Poll, December, 1948, reported in *Public Opinion Quarterly*, vol. 13, p. 163.

[10] Survey Research Center of Institute for Social Research, *Big Business from the Viewpoint of the Public*, University of Michigan, Ann Arbor, 1951, Table 5, p. 18.

[11] *Ibid.*, p. 27; Table 10, p. 26; Table 82, p. 109. And cf. AIPO poll, May 6, 1941, comparing power of government in Washington with "rich men and large corporation and labor leaders." Cf. also Fortune Poll on centralization in Washington, *Fortune*, November, 1948, p. 37.

[12] Survey Research Center of Institute for Social Research, *op. cit.*, Table 5, p. 18.

In so far as liberal doctrine has dealt with the problem of the legitimacy of big business power at all, it has fallen back on two tactics. One is "natural rights": the attempt to drape the mantle of "natural rights to private property" over the giant corporation. But the concept of a natural right to property when applied to the giant corporation is little short of facetious.

The second line of defense is to describe the power of businessmen as not willful and arbitrary but strictly controlled by the price system. Nineteenth-century economic theory treated the entrepreneur as little more than a passive agent of the price system; over against this, Marx and other socialists tried to undermine the legitimacy of the entrepreneur's power by arguing that his position in the enterprise gave him wealth, status, and power with which he could dominate and exploit the whole society. Both positions appear to overstate the case.

The price system as it operates in the real world, we have argued in an earlier chapter, does in practice control business management. If the question is reëxamined without ideological blinders it will be seen that even the advent of the giant corporation has not eliminated or perhaps even significantly reduced the effectiveness of control over business.[13] It is easy to exaggerate the willful and arbitrary character of managerial power, easy to underestimate the degree to which a price system even in the conditions of the real world subjects managers to effective control.

Yet it must also be admitted that business leaders are far from the passive agents of consumers envisioned by classical economic theory. For they have very considerable areas of discretion. Investment policy, labor relations, advertising, relations with the local community, recruitment, location of plants, vacations, health, safety, shutdowns, transfers, political subsidies, propaganda, treatment of minorities, plant design and layout—on these and a host of other decisions management has very great though by no means unlimited discretion. These are all questions of great import to the rest of society; and no price system is adequate to indicate community preferences on such matters.

Thus in a society where the goal of democracy and the techniques of polyarchy are powerfully indoctrinated, "private" management faces an irresolvable dilemma. Management cannot logically justify its control except by showing that it is an agent of the

[13] Cf. Chapter 7.

society; yet if it is an agent of the society, management can scarcely justify its untrammeled discretion over decisions of such high value to the rest of society as those cited above. Co-management is one effort to convey legitimacy to discretionary decisions that cannot be adequately influenced through the price system.

Yet even this reform might prove inadequate; for as we have already shown, once the question of legitimacy is raised, it is difficult to justify the control of any particular minority organization over managerial decisions of giant corporations. Possibly the only workable solution for the long run is the professionalization of management, minority worker representation on the boards of directors, and majority representation secured either by direct government appointment or by giving the government the power to veto directorships.[14] There are obviously many difficulties in any such solution. Although these are thorny problems, if the management of the big corporation is to enjoy legitimacy in American society, they may someday have to be solved.

SIMILARITIES TO COLLECTIVE BARGAINING. *The central problems raised by co-management are similar to those raised by collective bargaining.*

To argue that participation of workers in management would automatically open the door to unlimited wage and price rises, restrictions on production, and declining incentives to economize is to overlook the enormous control over these decisions already possessed by trade unions. To shift the point at which workers exert their power from the collective bargaining conference to the directors' table is less significant than might at first sight appear. The difference between the power to influence management possessed by leaders of highly organized workers as compared with unorganized workers is enormous; the development of a highly organized, national trade union movement represents a revolutionary shift in power in comparison with which co-management may prove to be marginal indeed. In the United States and Great Britain the decisive change has already been made; what workers might get from co-management to some extent they can already achieve, and are achieving, by collective bargaining.[15]

[14] Robert A. Gordon, *Business Leadership in the Large Corporation*, The Brookings Institution, Washington, 1945, chap. 14.
[15] Cf. Neil Chamberlain, *op. cit.*

Let us therefore now turn our attention to collective bargaining as a second kind of bargaining technique.

II. Collective Bargaining

To a great extent American workers achieve through collective bargaining what French and German trade unionists seek to achieve through government action. Conversely, the unwillingness or inability of European trade unionists to obtain certain goals won in the United States through collective bargaining induces them to favor government prescription. In France, neither employers nor trade unions have ever learned to bargain collectively.[16] Indeed, since 1939, wages have been set by government decree. And in Germany since the war, a desire for price stability plus a powerful fear of price inflation have both inhibited collective bargaining. On the other hand, in the Scandinavian countries, where collective bargaining is habitual, works councils and similar arrangements have been mostly the product of collective agreement, not legislation.

It would be frivolous to consider whether trade unions might be eliminated in Western societies in order to avoid the problems they create. In Western polyarchies there is no acceptable alternative to powerful trade unions. Moreover, value questions to one side, no political alliance in a polyarchy is likely even to attempt the destruction of trade unionism. Liberal and labor governments would not destroy the trade union movement if they could; conservative governments could not do so without losing votes and wrecking agreement, both of which they must prize if they are committed to polyarchy.

The trade unions are an enclave of power within modern democratic societies, a component in a social confederacy that cannot be restrained too much without flying apart. The trade union movement can therefore successfully demand and secure the opportunity to bargain even with the government itself. Representatives of no parliamentary majority can exercise "the last say" over questions in which trade unions are vitally concerned; the "last say" on such questions lies to some extent with the trade unionists; and the elected spokesmen for the greater number must always be prepared to bargain with the trade unions or face a prospect of violence, chaos, and repression such as no intelligent believer in polyarchy can regard as a preferable alternative to bargaining.

[16] See V. R. Lorwin, *op. cit.*, p. 213.

MAJOR ISSUES

Reciprocity in the form of collective bargaining raises at least three basic issues of public policy: (1) the problem of the economical use of labor resources—restrictions on output, labor mobility, recruitment, training, and so on; (2) the problem of work stoppages which interrupt production essential to acceptable levels of welfare; (3) the problem of unionism's impact on the price system—that is, the possibility that union demands for wages and related items such as shorter hours, pensions, and vacations with pay will raise labor costs to a point where economic stability and coordination through the price system are threatened.

The first is a problem that does not appear to raise any basic questions as to alternative forms of economic organization. To the extent that the problem is solvable, it requires a careful inspection of particular techniques—much as does the problem of industrial monopoly. Such a solution calls for specific detailed policies that we do not feel it necessary to discuss in this book. This is not to say that policy makers should be indifferent to the problem, only that it is at a level of detailed analysis we cannot undertake here.

STRIKES

The second problem—interruption of "essential" production —raises more fundamental issues because it goes to the heart of the collective bargaining process itself. For the strike is such an essential technique of collective bargaining that it cannot be eliminated without eliminating collective bargaining itself. Collective bargaining is a form of reciprocal control which workers and their leaders have developed with the passive or active consent of the dominant decision makers in Western societies. They have developed it as an alternative to the combination of hierarchical control by the employer and spontaneous field control exerted through the price system, a combination they felt intolerable. The main techniques by which workers' organizations enforce bargaining as a substitute is the strike, a device through which workers' organizations can influence the behavior of employers. In short, the strike is a fundamental technique of control requisite to bargaining. It does not represent an abnormality or breakdown in collective bargaining any more than the practice of voting unpopular officials out of office is an abnormality or breakdown in the reciprocal arrangements customary in polyarchies.

The strike weapon is effective in influencing the employers' behavior primarily because it interrupts production. Yet to interrupt production sometimes so vitally damages the goal achievement of other people in the community—third parties who are neither strikers nor struck employers—that measures have been taken to prevent or prohibit strikes. As union organization and the strike weapon developed, types of employment were picked out pragmatically and sometimes irrationally where community sentiment or government controls were mobilized to inhibit strikes: in the military, police, hospitals, many kinds of government employment, and often in public utilities. Yet as the power, size, and solidarity of trade unions have grown, it has become more and more difficult to distinguish between these reserved occupations and many in which strikes have traditionally been tolerated. For in a highly industrialized and interdependent society, damaging effects on the goal achievement of third parties are possible in one industry after another: transportation, communication, coal, steel, aircraft, munitions, and military supplies, to name a few. In periods of partial or full mobilization, almost no industry is entirely excluded.

None of the ways by which interruptions to "essential" production might be inhibited promises security.

LOCAL BARGAINING.   Sometimes it is proposed that collective bargaining, and perhaps union organization, should be restricted to one firm or plant. It is difficult to regard such a program as other than utopian. Indeed, the proposal enormously exaggerates the power of law and prescription to restrain the behavior of great numbers of people compactly organized in pursuit of goals they value highly. The fact is, trade unionists could not be effectively barred from acting on an interfirm basis with any action short of stamping out the trade union movement itself; the administrative difficulties in preventing trade unions from acting in concert in two or more plants or firms seem insurmountable. No likely combination of political leadership can be imagined that would pass such a law in any Western polyarchy, let alone attempt to enforce it.[17]

WITHERING AWAY OF THE STRIKE.   A quite different but more probable development is that collective bargaining will tend to take

[17] For a discussion of the problems of local bargaining, see Neil W. Chamberlain, *Collective Bargaining*, McGraw-Hill Book Co., New York, 1951, chap. 8.

place without the actual occurrence of a strike. That is to say, the *threat* of a strike might replace the strike itself as the central technique of control. After all, most collective bargaining does proceed without the actual execution of the strike threat. Wherever employers through long experience with collective bargaining accept the legitimacy of unions and understand their power, the threat of a strike may be sufficient to induce collective bargaining. Or where the threat of nationalization hangs heavy over the head of industries that are unable to deal peacefully with their workers, collective bargaining may proceed without strikes.

Yet it is clear that this solution will only work where there is some possibility of strikes; confidence that they will not occur can therefore never be unlimited. Moreover, it must be admitted that neither Great Britain nor the United States has yet arrived at this stage, nor can one be sure that either society ever will. The withering away of the strike may proceed about as slowly as the withering away of the state.

Two more aspects of this solution are important. First, this is not a solution that can be achieved simply by legislation; if it occurs at all, it will be an unlegislated product of social growth and experience. Second, if the strike withers away, it may be because collective bargaining has degenerated. Collusion may take its place. Or management may surrender to unions. Or union leaders may accommodate themselves to management. Each of these alternatives would solve the problem of maintaining production by creating another of equal magnitude. Either workers would lose their control or the third problem cited above would loom up as the central issue: reconciling trade union control with economic stability and the price system.

HIERARCHY IN BARGAINING. Another development already taking place is three-way bargaining, with government officials as the third element. Government officials can manipulate public opinion, employ the threat of legislation, or exercise emergency powers. Three-way collective bargaining is hardly more likely than two-way bargaining to prevent an interruption of essential production. The more common tripartite bargaining becomes and the more the mythology of government supremacy is worn away by the hard fact of union power, the less influence government is likely to exert. Of course, government can often avoid a stoppage by granting concessions to the union, but this policy soon poses the third problem again: the effect of union demands on stability and the price system.

Yet the inability of government to inhibit strikes in essential industries is bound to generate another development: an increase in the control of government officials until bargaining recedes before the hierarchical controls of government. In 1946 President Truman broke a railroad strike with a threat of drafting railroad workers into the army—an emergency proposal of such violence that it alienated even conservatives like Senator Taft. Subsequently the injunction, once a weapon of employers against unionists and therefore once outlawed in order to tip the balance more evenly toward unionists, was restored by the Taft-Hartley Act as a weapon of government officials against strikes which, in the judgment of the President, threaten national safety. Employers unable to prevent the strike threat from being executed have found their firms taken over by the government as an emergency action.

What is perhaps even more important, with controls like these in the background and the prospect of further legislation if public opinion is outraged, government officials can exert greater influence in the bargaining process. Thus the pattern that emerges is a pragmatic combination of three-way bargaining and government hierarchy. The change is by no means as spectacular as it seems at first blush. Even in the absence of government intervention, collective bargaining between employers and trade unions has become more and more a matter of negotiation among relatively few giant hierarchical organizations.

No doubt this has proceeded furthest in Sweden, where the labor market is governed by collective contracts, mostly nationwide and entered upon under the auspices of the central employer and employee organizations.[18] But even in the United States, in less than a generation a fundamental change has taken place. To a great extent union locals simply follow the wage policies of the national unions. To some extent the national (or "international") unions even follow general policies of the parent organizations, the AFL or CIO. A more significant centralization of influence results from the development of pace setters, the key unions and key employers in key industries, whose agreements constitute key bargains fol-

---

[18] Gunnar Heckscher, "Pluralist Democracy, The Swedish Experience," *Social Research*, December, 1948, p. 426.

lowed to varying degrees by many other employers and unions.[19] Thus it becomes more and more important for government officials to have sufficient control to influence these key bargains during the course of tripartite negotiations.

The present combination of centralized bargaining plus government hierarchy may be only a transitional stage to even less bargaining and more government hierarchy. Because industrialization and interdependence are not likely to decrease, whereas the understanding of their consequences probably will increase, it is all but inevitable that techniques like the injunction now widely regarded as having an emergency character will become customary. The terminus may be some form of compulsory adjudication.

COMPULSORY ARBITRATION. Compulsory arbitration is possible as a limiting case of tripartite bargaining. Like law enforcement in general, compulsory adjudication or similar government action cannot develop much faster than the agreement in favor of it.[20] In Western societies legal sanctions are a form of marginal control that are effective only when they are simply a slight increment of influence in behalf of norms for which widespread agreement already exists. When this is not the case, the norms will be flouted. The alternatives then are either to repeal the prescribed but inoperable rule, as with Prohibition; or to let it remain prescribed but inoperable (with the danger that this discrepancy will be generalized to other laws); or to mobilize a sizable increase of control in the hands of government officials charged with enforcing the law.

Obviously the last is difficult in polyarchies; for if the norm is not supported by widespread consensus, political competition is unlikely to result in political leaders capable of mobilizing power in behalf of the unpopular norm. However, in a case like that of a strike interrupting essential production, one additional possibility is that the community will become polarized. Few people will remain indifferent, and government officials reflecting the opinions of a majority of the politically active may be granted enormous prescribed control to deal with strikers. This situation would be far different from the breakdown of law enforcement under Prohibition; for it might create a level of active or suppressed violence that would undermine the conditions of polyarchy.

What has just been said points back to a principle enunciated earlier. Bargaining and other techniques of reciprocity among intermediate groups are neither justifiable nor likely to be tolerated without limit unless the bargaining process produces results that roughly accord with the preferences of the greater number among the politically active. When they fail to do so, and where spontaneous field controls will not work, government hierarchy is the only alternative compatible with polyarchy. Yet it has just been shown that this alternative applied against powerful trade unions may either be futile or else threaten the very conditions of polyarchy. Thus polyarchies face a terrifying dilemma that in the last analysis can only be resolved by the original partners to the collective bargaining process.

NEW IDENTIFICATIONS.   Is it, then, possible that employers and trade unions will develop sufficient identification, widespread loyalties, ties with the rest of the community, and norms of coöperation and restraint so that the dilemma need never be faced? The experience of Sweden suggests that this eventuality may be possible. Paradoxically, this solution may only occur when trade unions and employers are so powerfully organized into hierarchical combines that a cessation of bargaining and resort to the strike would clearly produce widespread destruction of goals highly ranked throughout the society. In other words, only when trade unions and employers obviously *can* destroy will they be powerfully impelled not to do so.

Meanwhile it seems reasonably evident that the search for assurance against the interruption of essential production is a chimera. The possibility of strikes seriously imperiling important goals can be reduced; but short of the Draconian measures possible only in a totalitarian society it can hardly be eliminated. Whether any of the measures just discussed will keep strikes to a tolerable level is indeterminate. For this is a matter not merely of limiting the interruption of production regarded as vital but—and in some ways this is even more important—of preventing anxieties, even if irrational ones, from arising in the presence of a strike threat and being mobilized in behalf of measures that would enhance government hierarchy at the expense of minimum agreement. No one can now say what outcome is most likely. Within a generation the answer will no doubt have been given.

STABILITY OF THE PRICE SYSTEM

The third problem posed by collective bargaining is that it might seriously obstruct the price system.

Collective bargaining is an alternative both to government hierarchy and to the price system.[21] This statement does not mean that a nation with a fairly effective price system cannot employ collective bargaining; it only means that collective bargaining limits or excludes the operation of the price system with respect to decisions covered by collective bargaining. The more decisions covered by collective bargaining, the fewer will be made through the price system.

The question is: Does collective bargaining go too far (by some standard) in displacing the price system? If trade unions largely displaced the price system as a coördinating device, effective economizing would prove impossible. This, it should be kept in mind, is but a possibility. No one can say with certainty that trade unions will inevitably make impossible any significant use of the price system. But it cannot be gainsaid that there is widespread concern with their consequences.[22] Another generation of experience with this problem, as with the preceding one, will probably provide the answer. Meanwhile, let us examine briefly the shape of the problem.[23]

CONSEQUENCES FOR THE PRICE SYSTEM. Some of possible results of a successful pursuit of wage increases by powerful unions are these:

[21] Collective bargaining is also an example of noncompetitive bargaining as a supplementary control in a price system: but union power, we are arguing, goes beyond that to become an alternative to price system control. Cf. Chapter 6.

[22] David McCord Wright (ed.), *The Impact of the Union*, Harcourt, Brace and Co., New York, 1951; Melvin W. Reder, "Theoretical Problems of a National Wage-Price Policy," *Canadian Journal of Economics and Political Science*, February, 1948, pp. 46–61; Henry C. Simons, "Some Reflections on Syndicalism," *Journal of Political Economy*, March, 1944, pp. 1–25; Fritz Machlup, "Monopolistic Wage Determination as a Part of the General Problem of Monopoly," in Economic Institute Proceedings, *Wage Determination and the Economics of Liberalism*, Chamber of Commerce of the United States, Washington, 1947, pp. 61 ff.; see also the article by Jacob Viner in *ibid*.

[23] For a fuller discussion, see Charles E. Lindblom, *Unions and Capitalism*, Yale University Press, New Haven, 1949.

1. At full employment, increases in costs resulting from wage gains may stimulate inflationary price increases.

2. High labor costs may produce unemployment. Trade unionists may price their members out of the market, as the building trades are sometimes alleged to have done in the late thirties. Or high labor costs may raise prices in one industry and produce unemployment in another industry consuming its product but more sensitive to price increases. Or decreased sales in one industry because of price rises may curtail employment in industries selling to it.

3. Government fiscal and monetary measures to increase spending and eliminate unemployment induced by high wages may be inflationary. That is, the expenditure necessary to stimulate employment for the unemployed may have to be so great as to induce price rises generally. Faced with this prospect, government policies may vacillate between inflation and unemployment.

4. If wage increases result in inflation, inflation may result in a vast displacement of the price system by hierarchical controls. The habitual response of Western governments to inflation is hierarchical controls, a lesson learned in two world wars. Price controls, rationing, priorities and allocations, import and export controls—these displace the price system when governments act against inflation. Even in the absence of cold war, these could become permanent features of Western societies if trade unions induce inflation through wage demands.

ARE THESE CONSEQUENCES INEVITABLE? Whether these consequences will come about depends upon answers to two controversial questions: first, whether the trade union movement in, say, the United States has enough control to bring about these results; second, even if it has enough control, whether the decision makers in the trade union movement would use their control to produce these results.

As to the first question, we can add little to the preceding discussion about strikes in essential industries. To say that trade unions have enough control is to say that neither employers nor government can inhibit strikes except by agreeing to raise wages or some equivalent action. Under conditions close to full employment, and assuredly under any conditions already bordering on inflation, employers are much less likely to offer strong resistance to union demands. Price increases can easily be passed along. And the marginal controls usually wielded by the government are likely to be inadequate when the two other bargaining partners tacitly agree. If it is not certain that unions have the necessary control, neither is it certain that they do not. An appraisal of collective bargaining must take account of both possibilities.

Assuming for the purposes of analysis that trade unions do have enough control over wages to induce inflation, or unemployment, or substantial growth of government hierarchy, or all three, will they use their control even if it does produce these results? An answer to this second question depends upon two factors: the goals of those who make decisions in trade unions and the rationality of their calculations. Their goals may not include inflation, unemployment, and government hierarchical controls over wages, but they might nevertheless make irrational calculations that would produce these results; conversely, the goals of the dominant decision makers might include these results, but their irrational calculations could prevent them from taking the necessary steps to achieve these goals.

As to union goals, it would be tempting to reject out of hand the preposterous notion that any trade unionists would ever want inflation, unemployment, and government hierarchical controls over wages. Few trade unionists would say so. Yet it is possible that some unionists, and perhaps enough unionists to bring inflation about, might gain at the expense of others by some degree of inflation caused by wage rises. Even wage increases that produce unemployment could directly favor those who were most influential in union decisions. As to the growth of government hierarchy, trade unionists are divided in their attitudes about government control over wages. The old hostility of AFL leaders to government intervention in collective bargaining has significantly declined as trade unionists have learned that a sympathetic government might provide a better decision than a hostile employer. An ideological change may also be taking place reflecting the underlying doubt of many people about the legitimacy of managerial decisions. For all these reasons the possibility that trade unionists might pursue wage-raising policies even if they knew these would produce inflation, unemployment, or government intervention, or all of these, cannot be ruled out.

On these points, however, empirical evidence is inadequate, vague, and contradictory. Having twice within their memory experienced severe inflation, German trade unionists after World War II exercised astonishing restraint in limiting their wage demands. In Sweden, dominant trade union opinion seems increasingly to regard distribution of income as properly a matter for electorate and government to decide, not workers and trade unions; wage demands therefore increasingly tend to follow trends in productivity. In Great Britain under the Labor government, trade union leaders entered into a voluntary wage freeze that held remarkably well for five years.

Moreover, the very uncertainty as to where unemployment and inflation may strike can be inhibiting. It would be different, perhaps, if every trade unionist could rationally calculate his gains and losses from inflation or unemployment and adjust his actions accordingly; we would then have the true economic man in trade union politics. But this calculation is often impossible. He cannot always be sure that *if* inflation results he will come out ahead, or that *if* unemployment ensues he will be the gainer. Then, too, he is unavoidably a social animal; he identifies with a variety of groups some of whose members will be adversely affected even if his own individual fortunes prosper. His son, brother-in-law, friend, cousin, fellow trade union member, coreligionist, neighbor, or member of the local lodge of the Fraternal Order of Eagles may all suffer. If their hardship is produced by the action of his union, then the tensions, implied or overt criticism, hostility, loss of friendship, respect, and sympathy, guilt, or embarrassment will contrive to inhibit such action in the future.

Where trade union leaders are active members of a political party or a coalition intent on getting or staying in office, they are further restrained by the fear of alienating potential voters. Indeed, as in Great Britain, trade union leaders may be so concerned about the electoral fate of their party as to endanger their own trade union following by excessive loyalty to the party's policy of wage restraints.

Workers and their leaders may also find alternative methods for increasing their welfare that diminish the pressure on wages. Social security through government is to some extent an alternative to security through wage demands and related goals of collective bargaining. Income redistribution, medical care, public housing, government scholarships, and the like are partly alternatives to achieving comparable goals through wage increases.

The problem of goals boils down to the question whether a sufficient number of influential trade union members would really regard themselves as benefiting by wage rises even at the cost of inflation, unemployment, or government intervention. Evidence from postwar experience is inconclusive because one cannot be sure either as to the actual alternatives available to workers or as to their comprehension of whatever alternatives there were. Inference from public opinion polls or one's own reactions is dangerous. It is reasonable to suppose that the more widespread the unemployment, the more galloping the inflation, or the more powerful the resulting government inhibitions on wages, the more undesirable these consequences of wage raising would become to trade unions themselves. Surely at some point few trade unionists, if they understood the alternatives, would rationally prefer wage rises and inflation to wage stability or productivity increases and general economic stability. But it is impossible to forecast where this point would be; presumably it varies from one time to another, one trade union to another, and pretty clearly from one country to another.

If we assume that workers would not choose these consequences if they understood the alternatives, the problem is then mainly one of rational calculations. The extent to which workers are in a position to make rational choices between excessive wage rises and a stable price system depends on a growth in general economic literacy. This is not so discouraging a prospect as it may sound. Increasing government intervention in labor disputes; closer contacts between trade union leaders and government officials; widespread fears of inflation and unemployment; the painful experiences of widespread inflation and unemployment; development of expert trade union and government bureaucracies in close communication with one another—all these make the consequences of trade union choices more evident to trade union members than was conceivable even a generation ago.

But as in the case of strikes, quite possibly the main prerequisite for heightened rationality is the development of comprehensive and hierarchical trade union organization. For at the point where, as in Sweden, a decision by centralized trade union leaders to demand higher wages is expected to influence the entire trade union movement throughout the length and breadth of the country, and so the entire national economy, the results of collective bargaining can no longer be easily concealed from even the dullest member. Whether such a solution is an altogether happy one is an open question; yet it may be the only one open in modern industrial societies.

UNIONS AND SMALL-GROUP VALUES

The major objection to solving the strike problem or protecting the price system by encouraging new and broader identification is that the union is an important form of small-group life and consequently its small-group identification should be safeguarded.

Frank C. Tannenbaum has argued eloquently from the history of guilds and villages throughout the world that "men, when grouped together physically in their labor, tend to become a community"; that the industrial revolution and nineteenth-century individualism ruthlessly destroyed this age-old, world-wide type of community; that the modern trade union is the successor to the medieval guild, manorial court, and village as a true "society"; and that "the trade-union is our modern 'society,' the only true society that industrialism has fostered. As a true society it is concerned with the whole man, and embodies the possibilities of both the freedom and the security essential to human dignity."[24] It follows that community life should be organized around the trade union; that trade unions should become the "estates" of modern society; and that neither government nor stockholders but the trade unions should gradually take over a large share of ownership in their industries.[25]

Much of what Tannenbaum argues is no doubt true. But can the trade union really fulfill the functions of small groups? If it cannot, then one can hardly agree that it is a complete society, or an adequate successor to the small-group life found in the guild, manor, and rural village. Surely no institution can claim to be the one around which the rest of society should be organized if it is incapable of executing the basic functions of small groups.

Very few people will today deny that trade unions are enormously important organizations for achieving many highly ranked *instrumental* goals. But these are goals that trade unions can achieve not as small groups but only as rather large groups. To be sure, membership in a trade union local offers some opportunities for friendship, status, respect, and affection. Yet compared with the workplace and the neighborhood, trade union contacts are sporadic

[24] Frank Tannenbaum, *A Philosophy of Labor*, Alfred A. Knopf, New York, 1951, pp. 25, 31, 59, 198.
[25] *Ibid.*, chaps. 9, 10, 11.

and intermittent except for a small group of enthusiasts and functionaries. The modern trade union is *not* the full successor to the manor, guild, and village, precisely because social life has been splintered into fragments. Where the manor encompassed almost the whole of one's life in rural areas and where guild, workplace, market, neighbors, and family were an integrated social unit in the towns, the trade union is only one small fragment of the worker's life. Nor can it ever be anything more unless the trade union is integrated into neighborhood and workplace to a degree that is almost inconceivable with modern industry.

The trade union suffers from further weaknesses as a small group. As an organization for social indoctrination and control it is weak because its goals are limited, its contacts are intermittent, and, most important of all, it has only indirect influence on children. No social organization that does not include children can ever be wholly effective as an agent for social indoctrination and control.

Finally, given the organization of modern industry, the trade union has inevitable tendencies to giantism. Like the coöps, the more successful trade unions become in their avowed goals, the larger they must be and the less like small groups. As a number of observers have pointed out, the iron law of bureaucracy operates in trade unions too.[26] Even union locals are often great leviathans with thousands of members who meet sporadically as a mass and have little other contact; it would be foolish to hope that the River Rouge local of the United Automobile Workers, for example, could perform the functions of a small group, however valuable it may be as an intermediate group. Perhaps because the growth of great control in the hands of union leaders is so recent as compared with corporate control, and still subject to such extensive propaganda attacks, the control of union leaders is even more disturbing to most Americans than is the control of corporate management and ownership, as polls taken ten years apart have shown. In 1941, 75 percent of a sample poll thought too much power was in the hands of labor leaders as compared with 59 percent who thought a few rich men and large corporations had too much power.[27] In 1950, although

[26] Joseph Goldstein, *The Government of British Trade Unions: A Study of Apathy and the Democratic Process in the Transport and General Workers Union*, Allen and Unwin, London, 1952; Bernard Barber, "Participation and Mass Apathy Associations," in A. W. Gouldner (ed.), *Studies in Leadership: Leadership and Democratic Action*, Harper & Brothers, New York, 1950, pp. 477 ff.
[27] American Institute of Public Opinion poll, May 6, 1941.

respondents were worried about the power position of big business, they seemed to be even more worried about labor unions.[28] Despite their importance, then, trade unions do not seem to promise by themselves a social structure based on legitimacy within which small-group functions can be satisfactorily carried on.

III. National Bargaining

The growth of gigantic organizations like trade unions, corporations, and farmers' associations has, as we have seen, led to serious difficulties of legitimizing their control within a polyarchal order. There is a flat contradiction between the concept of a "sovereign people" and the plain fact of pluralistic social organization. For often enough there is no "sovereign people." Many decisions are made by a loose confederacy of giant organizations each with great control over the others. Under these conditions decisions can be arrived at only through horse trading, bargaining, the negotiation of treaties. Stripped of its glamour, shorn of its magical legalistic incantations, government very often turns out to be simply one of the bargainers. However undignified it may seem to the disciple of Bodin, government must engage in horse trading with corporations, trade unions, farm organizations, and other groups with control in the society.

More specifically, people called government officials often lack sufficient rewards and penalties to enforce decisions by unilateral, hierarchical means: from time to time they must sit down with trade union officials, business officials, farm organization officials and negotiate unstable peace treaties—or, better, temporary armistices. None of the treaty negotiators really wants war; none, including government, has enough power by itself to enforce peace; each must bargain with the others. Government officials do not represent a "sovereign people"; they represent some people who cannot always enforce their goals on other people in the society. The attempt to do so might result in shattering violence, civil war, and even defeat. Sometimes the sovereign people is neither sovereign nor a people.

How can these bargaining controls be legitimized? In the United States a style of thought that we call "national bargaining"

---

[28] Survey Research Center of Institute for Social Research, *op. cit.*, Tables 81, 82.

has grown up in recent years in part, at least, to rationalize the plain social facts of life. A style of thought rather than a carefully articulated theory, it is nowhere clearly set forth. It is fugitive and ambiguous.[29] Terms are often imprecise and undefined. Frequently its advocates deliberately eschew theoretical formulation of their assumptions. In some respects the rejection of formal theory may render the inarticulated theory more influential than it would otherwise be. The crude and untheoretical pragmatism of the thought style may often influence policy without any policy maker's being aware of it. These characteristics also make it difficult to discuss, because any particular proposition that is shown to be untenable can be withdrawn and a more acceptable one substituted without in any way bringing about a modification of the implied theory as a whole.

THE POSTULATES OF NATIONAL BARGAINING

Despite these difficulties, perhaps a fair summary would run something like this: A basic postulate is that gigantic groups, or interests, or social organizations are, for reasons indicated in the preceding parts of this chapter, here to stay. The main groups or interests are usually defined as business, labor, and agriculture, or, as Nourse has classified them, "workers, capitalists, and managers, with the farmer standing as a special type of worker-manager." "Corporations, unions, and political parties are organized pressure groups . . . ," wrote J. R. Commons. "The economic pressure groups really become an occupational parliament of the American people, more truly representative than the Congress elected by territorial divisions."[30]

[29] Perhaps the most coherent statement of the theoretical assumptions will be found in E. G. Nourse, "Collective Bargaining and the Common Interest," *American Economic Review*, March, 1943, pp. 1 ff. The viewpoint also has shown up in the Council of Economic Advisors; cf. *Business and Government, Fourth Annual Report to the President* by the Council of Economic Advisors, U.S. Government Printing Office, Washington, December, 1949. Traces of the thought style may be detected in the writings of J. M. Clark, especially in *Alternative to Serfdom*, Alfred A. Knopf, New York, 1948, and in his *Guideposts in Time of Change*, Harper & Brothers, New York, 1949. Cf. also Clark Kerr, "Labor Markets: Their Character and Consequences," *American Economic Review*, May, 1950, pp. 278 ff. See also Kung Chuan Hsiao, *Political Pluralism, A Study in Contemporary Political Theory*, Harcourt, Brace and Co., New York, 1927, and Alfred de Grazia, *Public and Republic, Political Representation in America*, Alfred A. Knopf, New York, 1951.

[30] John R. Commons, *Economics of Collective Action*, The Macmillan Company, New York, 1950, p. 33.

Consumers are sometimes included as a fourth interest, but
their obvious lack of organization is an embarrassment; and they
may be ignored or excluded by what appears to be, not a theoretically consistent statement, but merely a dubious rationalization of
the fact. In a series of declaratory propositions, Nourse argues:

> . . . Adjustments economically sound for workers, managers, and
> capitalists in the broad view and in the long run must take account of
> the interest of the consumer. Furthermore, that interest is constantly
> and effectively registered by consumers through their market behavior,
> and this can be interpreted and generalized with greater technical com-
> petence through the machinery of collective bargaining than it can be
> expressed by the group representatives of consumers sitting in on bar-
> gaining conferences. The situation, however, is distinctly different if
> consumers are organized in a responsible consumers' co-operative for
> negotiating prices at which they will buy stated quantities of specified
> articles.[31]

In practice, categories like "workers," "capitalists," and "farmers" turn out to mean specific organizations. Business means the
National Association of Manufacturers and the Chamber of Commerce; labor means the AFL, CIO, and the brotherhoods; farmers
means the Farm Bureau, Grange, and Farmers' Union. Even more
precisely, it is, of course, the leaders of these organizations who
must be spokesmen and negotiators for the "interest" when bargaining begins.

THE "CONSERVATIVE" AND "PROGRESSIVE" VIEWS. Two
different views or emphases about national bargaining may be distinguished, the one "conservative," the other "progressive." In the
conservative view represented by Nourse, national bargaining is
seen as an alternative to government hierarchy. Nourse argues that
"government determination of economic issues" suffers from three
inherent weaknesses: it cannot discover the "common interest" as
well as can the parties to a dispute; "it lacks the necessary intimacy
and flexibility to apply generalized formulas to the particularized
situations which make the real body of business life"; and "it does
not link responsibility and reward."[32]

All this may be true; the difficulty, however is that interest
organizations, even if reformed along the lines optimistically ad-

[31] E. G. Nourse, *op. cit.*, p. 18 n.
[32] *Ibid.*, pp. 9–11.

vocated by Nourse, are subject to the same weaknesses. As we have already shown, there is no guarantee that bargaining among organizations will necessarily produce results that accord with the highly ranked preferences of the greater number; gigantic bargaining organizations can be as much out of touch with "particularized situations" as the government, and their members have less well-organized channels of protest and demand than citizens do; finally, bargaining decisions do not necessarily link responsibility and reward—indeed, they may simply push off the costs to those who are not represented, particularly when, as under Nourse's proposals, consumers are "represented" only through the bargaining of workers, capitalists, and managers.

Because of these difficulties, the "progressive" view emphasizes that government officials may have to participate in the bargaining process to represent "the public interest." ("The public interest" is usually left totally undefined. Rarely can it be read to mean the preferences of the greater number. Often enough a precise examination would show that it can mean nothing more than whatever happens to be the speaker's own view as to a desirable public policy.) Ambiguity becomes even more profound from here on, but probably most "progressive" advocates would agree on these propositions: The government should avoid "coercion" as much as possible; that is to say, it should eschew command. Nevertheless, the possibility that government may employ command gives government officials power to influence the bargaining process in a direction favorable to "the public interest." Other motivations favorable to a settlement in "the public interest" are the possibilities of hostile public opinion, which in turn may generate government hierarchical controls; damage to the groups' long-run preferences for stability and productivity; and a rather broad identification with people and groups outside the organization itself, hence a more inclusive set of goals than is commonly assumed to exist among interest groups.

The government thus plays in the bargaining process a balance-of-power role, not unlike that of Great Britain in European politics during the nineteenth century.[33] It is therefore important that government officials intervene only in critical, strategic, or key situations. And all this means that intervention by government officials must be carried on with little restrictive legislation, wide discretion, limited reporting or responsiveness to Congress, close

[33] J. M. Clark, *Alternative to Serfdom*, p. 129.

liaison with the White House, and opportunities for secrecy and dispatch not open to the more routine government agency.

AN APPRAISAL

What may be said about these somewhat elusive ideas? That they contain a core of truth and common sense is no more to be denied than that they contain much that is woolly and confused. The references to the obvious facts of modern social life are true; the inferences from these are confused.

Intervention of government in key labor disputes is undoubtedly necessary. Reliance on governmental command controls may undermine collective bargaining or polyarchal consensus. Tripartite boards seem to have worked relatively well both in World War II and in the Korean war. Participation of trade union representatives may help to convey status and respect to workers. Trade unions and employers undoubtedly share some common values that can be activated by other participants. National bargaining may produce self-restraint because the consequences of failure are so visible. All these and many other possible gains of national bargaining may be conceded without establishing that national bargaining will solve the crucial problems of modern bargaining.

Now it may be argued that theory is inherently so rigid and abstracted from reality that pragmatism bordering on opportunism is actually a more subtle, sophisticated, and realistic approach than anyone with a liking for theoretical precision is likely to comprehend or admit. Certainly there is a measure of truth in this assertion. Wherever concrete policy choices must be made, articulated and formal theory tends to be inadequate. The best administrator is not often a good theorist, and vice versa. Balancing marginal effects on a number of goals, timing, judgment of factors imprecisely known, taking calculated risks—all seem to require a temperament and style of thought not necessarily, perhaps only rarely, congenial to theory.

But if the theorist grants the administrator this much, administrative intuitionism cloaked in theory must expect to meet certain minimum standards of consistency, precision, and verifiability—unless administration, like dialectical materialism, is to be considered a mystery impenetrable to laymen and capable of harboring inner contradictions because it embodies a higher logic known only to the high priests of the administrative temple. If it goes far enough to reject theoretical precision and testability, it assumes that any proposition is as valid as any other proposition or, alternatively, that the test of a correct proposition is who says it. To some extent the national bargaining style of thought, particularly its "progressive" version, leaves the field wide open for the operator whose creed is: "I may not be able to tell you what I am doing and why, but if you will only leave everything to me I'll see that it comes out all right."

There are many inadequacies in the theory or style of thought we have outlined; let us briefly summarize a few main points.

NOT AN ALTERNATIVE TO GOVERNMENT HIERARCHY. There is no reason to suppose that national bargaining is an efficient alternative to government hierarchy. At best it can only be a useful supplement. For one thing, national bargaining probably cannot achieve some of the results suggested for it. It is highly doubtful, for example, that bargaining alone will stabilize the economy, although it may be a helpful adjunct. There are many other important activities that cannot be coördinated by national bargaining and for which hierarchy is required: income distribution, slum clearance, public housing, social security, and medical care, to cite some important examples. In addition, there is no guarantee that bargaining among nongovernmental groups will produce decisions that even crudely accord with the preferences of the greater number; to secure these, the government hierarchy must, at the very minimum, intervene in the bargaining process.

NOT AN ALTERNATIVE TO NONGOVERNMENTAL HIERARCHY. Nor is national bargaining an alternative to nongovernmental hierarchical coördination. It is true that national bargaining among nongovernmental groups may reduce the need for government hierarchy; this is probably what advocates have in mind when they speak of national bargaining as an alternative to government economic planning. Yet as we have seen, in so far as government must intervene in the bargaining process it will have to develop some hierarchical controls if it is to have any real influence on the bargain.

But even more important is the overestimation of the extent to which national bargaining reduces nongovernmental hierarchical controls. In order for national bargaining to work as it does, say, in Sweden, leaders of the organizations involved must have considerable hierarchical power; national bargaining is effective because it takes place among gigantic hierarchical organizations; decisions by the leaders are unfailingly complied with by their subordinates; unions and employers throughout the country fall into line. National bargaining is not so much an alternative to hierarchy as a coordinating device as it is an alternative to the price system. But in supplanting the price system, national bargaining may increase, rather than decrease, the need for hierarchical controls. For government and nongovernment hierarchy then becomes necessary to insure the coördination no longer achieved through the price system.

ENCOURAGEMENT TO HIERARCHY. The last point suggests that the advocates of national bargaining may be thinking in terms of static arrangements rather than a dynamic society. National bargaining is not simply a mechanical outcome of national hierarchical organizations with great control; the practice, habits, and encouragement of national bargaining may also stimulate a social environment favorable to it. One consequence of national bargaining may there-' fore be the growth of hierarchy. For if national bargaining must be made to work, the less unilaterally controlled an organization is, the less suitable it is for negotiating agreements binding on its "members." In armistice negotiations its generals would be unable to speak for their polyglot armies. Either national bargaining would have to be abandoned or national policy would have to favor the growth of hierarchical control.

CONSEQUENCES FOR POLITICAL EQUALITY. As a substitute for or supplement to polyarchy, the central problem of national bargaining is to insure that the armistice agreements signed by the negotiators fall within the high-ranking preferences of the greater number of citizens. Advocates of national bargaining have never come to grips with this problem. Sometimes they have confused the whole issue by introducing a conception of "equality" or "balance" among organizations. What "equality" or "balance" consists of is never made clear. But even if it were, on what grounds can one argue that any two or more giant organizations should be "equal"? Such a concept has nothing to do with political equality or subjective equality among people; it is a crude anthropomorphism.

To borrow a phrase of Koestler's, this major error might be called the fallacy of *the false equation:* that the arguments for political and subjective equality among individuals can be transferred to groups. But, of course, this is absurd. Indeed, the two are mutually contradictory. For political and subjective equality among individuals again and again runs flatly counter to equality of control among groups; for example, given the first goal, a group of ten million workers should be able to outvote a group of one thousand employers, but given the second goal, any group, no matter what its size, should have the same power as any other group.

How far can the absurdity go? Should the "rich" have equal bargaining power with the "poor"—even if the rich are 1 percent of the population and the poor are 20 percent (John Adams thought so; but even in 1787 it was impolitic to insist on the point at the Constitutional Convention). Should both be equal in power to the "middle class," even though the latter comprise, say, nearly 80 percent of the population? The fact is, the idea of some kind of equality or balance among groups appears to be a reversion to medieval ideas growing out of the existence of somewhat permanent, fixed, identifiable interests (*Stände* or *estates*) such as nobility, clergy, and commoners. The democratic revolutionaries of the eighteenth century recognized the fundamental incompatibility between control based upon some kind of constitutionally prescribed balance among interests or *estates*, irrespective of numbers, and equality based upon a recognition of the natural right of each individual to equal control, participation, and dignity. In 1789 the change was symbolized in France (nor was it merely symbolic) when the revolutionary Third Estate first demanded that instead of sitting separately, as in the Estates-General, the three estates should sit together, and then in the last week of June forced the other two to join them—no longer in an Estates-General but in a National Assembly.

Recognizing all this, advocates of national bargaining, when they become aware of the consequences of their position, give up "equality"—perhaps this is why the vaguer term "balance" so often creeps into their discussions.

On one page Nourse writes, "There must be functional equality among the parties." What "functional equality" might be is never made clear, except that it is good. Three pages later, however, he tells us that "We need to get beyond such crude concepts as that sometimes voiced in the claim that labor should have a voice 'equal' to that of capital in management. The attempt to define equality for noncomparables must give place to the search for a workable pattern of bargaining relationships by the parties whose roles are widely different but mutually indispensable."[34] Evidently "functional equality" means that all parties should be equal, but—as on George Orwell's *Animal Farm*—some should be more equal than others.

One cannot help feeling that the key words of the national bargainers, however sincerely they may be employed, possess all the characteristics of symbols used purely for manipulative purposes: they arouse positive emotional responses and are vague enough to be filled in at the discretion of the user. To oppose "equality" is to favor "inequality"; to oppose balance is to prefer "imbalance." Few people in the United States would have the temerity to advocate inequality and imbalance, even though they might mean by these words precisely what the advocates of national bargaining mean by equality and balance.

One can never be sure whether "balance" means the existing relations between organizations or some desired new position. "Balance" can be a subtle disguise for the *status quo;* existing elites in business, farm organizations, and trade unions acquire a vested interest in balance, because presumably any disturbance to their positions is a sign of imbalance.

Nor do we resolve our difficulties by postulating that the organizations involved should be "democratized." For example, Nourse tells us that one of the conditions to be met "if collective bargaining between or among functional interest groups is to realize its potentialities as the mechanism best suited to advance the distinctive ends of economic life" is "democratic representation of individuals in local groups and of local units in overhead organizations."[35] For one thing this is at best only a distant and at present unrealized goal; shall we then postpone national bargaining until this goal is achieved? In many ways, too, it is an unrealistic, even utopian goal. The conditions of hierarchy are omnipresent; political equality is a rare plant requiring careful cultivation and a most favorable climate.

How, for example, can one democratize the large corporation? Most national trade union leaders are infinitely more responsive to rank and file than boards of directors are to stockholders; but even in trade unions, to be in office and therefore in a position to manipulate the wealth, status, and power of office makes it difficult for op-

[34] E. G. Nourse, *op. cit.,* pp. 11, 14.
[35] *Ibid.,* p. 11.

position to arise and express itself. The habits, organizations, and legal protections for intra-organization democracy are much weaker than in governmental politics. Nor is there for nongovernment organizations anything like the amount of press and radio coverage, investigation, outside criticism, and public attention that exists for government.

In some ways the idea of national bargaining—particularly in its conservative version—is an extension from individuals to groups of the nineteenth-century liberal conception of politics: government is still only to play the role of night watchman. Yet in one way it is a betrayal of a basic core of liberal thought—the idea of political equality. It is one thing to recognize that in plain fact the greater number cannot always rule; that faced with the power of gigantic social organizations of enormous control, their representatives in government must sometimes bargain, concede, compromise, and appease in order to avoid the destruction of minimum consensus, severe repression, bloodshed, violence, and perhaps even civil war. But it is quite another to turn this social fact into a prescription of the desirable, and to argue in effect that politicians should not even attempt to exercise "the last say," but should turn that power over to national organizations bargaining among themselves. For if the goal, and the machinery for approximating political equality, majority rule, and polyarchy are abandoned, then it is difficult to find any criteria within the Western tradition to justify one bargain as against another.

NATIONAL BARGAINING AND DEMOCRACY

The advocates of national bargaining, like other groupists, call attention to certain vital facts of life. It is not so much their descriptions as their prescriptions that one finds it necessary to contest here. In rejecting some of their prescriptions, we must be careful not to ignore the important core of solid worth in their thought. Democracy as the early ideologues sometimes envisioned it does not and probably will not exist in the nation-state. Individuals participate in, identify with, and are loyal to many organizations other than the nation-state.

A vast number of decisions, many of them highly important, are made in these organizations. They therefore serve to decentralize, fractionalize, and organize the control that otherwise either must remain unused for achieving goals desired by many people or must accrue to government officials. The existence of numerous, often powerful, sometimes gigantic social organizations is thus an alternative to frustrations in one's capacity for action, or to loss of freedom from the innumerable frustrations created by a gigantic leviathan state.

But in many cases, decisions made by social organizations affect other people outside the organization. Some of these others who are affected are also organized; in such situations, decisions acceptable to all those who are significantly affected may often be achieved by bargaining between or among the leaders of the organizations. But some of the others who are affected have no powerful organization except government; their organizations are political parties, pressure groups, legislatures, executives, government bureaucracies. Hence government must be able to enter the bargaining arena and bargain for the goals of such people. In still other cases, the results of unlimited bargaining might be to impose on the greater number the goals of a powerful minority. Here the government must have enough control to enter into the bargain, to set it aside, if necessary even to determine the decision. Anything less is an abdication of the democratic goal.

POSTSCRIPT

18.

Postscript

An oversimplified but useful description of intellectual history might find in modern man's attempt to control his environment three great tidal movements. The Renaissance was the first, when Western man rediscovered an old faith in his capacity for controlling his environment through observation and reason. Liberalism was the second; it embraced twin goals: rational control over governments through democracy and rational control over "economic" affairs through capitalism. Democratic socialism was the third; it held that man's rational control over both government and "economic" affairs could be vastly strengthened by governmentalizing economic affairs. In all three cases the tide has risen high and then receded.

Although these fluctuations in ideas, faiths, and social policies are far too complex for easy generalization, three points seem to us significant: classic liberalism and classic socialism suffered from rather similar limitations, but these deficiencies never reached to the core that is identical in both, and the core is still the grand strategy of rational democratic social reform.

Classic liberalism and classic socialism[1] both underestimated the extent to which an industrial society requires the use of hierarchy. Here partisan explanation has come full circle: at one time liberals all but explained the hierarchical controls of business leaders right out of existence; socialists in turn wrongfully ascribed hierarchy to capitalism; now antisocialists incorrectly attribute the prevalence of hierarchy in modern life to the progress of socialism and the welfare state. Jefferson was one liberal democrat who knew better, knew that an industrial society would generate hierarchical controls.

[1] In speaking of classic liberals (Smith, the later Bentham, Ricardo, the Mills, for example) and classic socialists (Marx, Engels, Kautsky, Bernstein, Jaurès, the Webbs, for example) we are deliberately oversimplifying and condensing some dominant trends of thought at the risk of injustice to the subtlety, sophistication, and realism of their thinking. Thus Eduard Bernstein was as intelligently critical of many important socialist blind spots as any nonsocialist; and, as is well known, between the first and third editions of his *Principles of Political Economy* J. S. Mill began to question the classical liberal formulation on private property.

511

Both groups also claimed too much for the competitive price system. The classic liberals vastly exaggerated the extent to which economic life could be coördinated through the competitive price system. Innumerable inadequacies mark the price system in the real world. These inadequacies are felt by unemployed workers, impoverished families, the aged poor, the sick and disabled. They are revealed in vast inequalities of education, income, status, control, opportunity—in a word, in unequal freedom.

These evils were of course articulated by socialist intellectuals like Marx, Engels, the Webbs, Shaw, Kautsky, Rosa Luxemburg, and Blum. Yet these socialists failed to distinguish the weaknesses inherent in the competitive price system from those produced by a whole variety of particular social policies. Hence in their own way they likewise overestimated the effects of the competitive price system.

Both groups, too, seem to have underestimated the function of private property in one direction and overestimated it in another. "Private property" is a shorthand term for a bundle of legal claims and privileges. In their preoccupation with the distribution of income and wealth, socialists neglected the functional importance of these legal claims and privileges. By transferring ownership of great accumulations of industrial assets from private to public hands, they sought to strike at income inequality. What they forgot was that private property is more than claims to the income from assets; it is also a system of rules concerning the use of the assets. And on these rules is built a system of cues and incentives which, despite its many imperfections, helps to coördinate economic activity.

Not realizing that they were in fact proposing to destroy an elaborate control mechanism, socialists sometimes offered nothing in its place, except another method of distributing income. They had not advanced much beyond Proudhon's "Property is theft." More often, of course, they had some proposal for control, but they slighted the problem and disposed of it with naïve solutions.

Not surprisingly, the friends of private enterprise often fell into the same error of underestimating the role of property. Many were incapable of defending private property except by identifying property with wealth and income. They fought on the side of private property only because they preferred the distribution of income that private property accomplished. To the other social functions of private property they were often as blind as the socialists. What is worse, they undermined their defenses by converting complicated questions pertaining to private property into simple moral questions of inequality in income and wealth. Yet with the decline of natural rights doctrines or, as in the case of *Rerum Novarum*, their conversion into an attack on laissez-faire liberalism, moral arguments against large-scale private property became increasingly persuasive, and in the end the private enterprisers were forced to concede more than if they had staked their case on a factual and analytical examination of the coördinating function of private property.

The socialists often overestimated the role of property when they held it responsible for evils that do not disappear with the advent of public ownership. These socialists understood that the rules of private property accomplished much more than the distribution of income; they saw property as power, as a system of control through which the competitive price mechanism operated. They correctly perceived that by-product rewards and penalties accomplished an allocation of assets. But when they went on to protest against the discipline imposed by owners over workers, against inequality in control and status, and against the harshness of industrial life under private enterprise, they often confused the results of private property with the results of large-scale organization, specialization of function, delegation, and strong impersonal discipline. The parallel confusion of the liberals was their exaggeration of the gains of modern industrial production that could be attributed to private property in business enterprise.

To the confusion of both socialists and liberals, property as a social institution has turned out to be indestructible. That is to say, many of the rules subsumed under private property were necessary to achieve goals the socialists themselves espoused. If in an assault on private property these rules were to be abolished even in one industry, very much the same ones under some other name had to be made effective to take their place. Hence, in this final period of disillusionment some socialists came to accept a new doctrine of socialization: that managers of government-owned enterprises must be relatively free from parliamentary control and must carry on—within very broad prescriptions—much as if they were private enterprisers.

These limitations brought both classic liberalism and socialism to dead ends. If in the United States it appears superficially that socialism is dead but liberalism survives, the opposite appears to be the case in much of Europe. Actually both movements have been discredited by their limitations. And even where liberalism survives, the liberal's earlier exuberance and optimism have often turned—with those who hold the classic doctrines intact—into a bitterly pessimistic denial that man can progress much beyond the limits of nineteenth-century "capitalism." As a doctrine of faith in man's capacity to exert rational control over his environment, classic liberalism was displaced years ago by socialism—this even among American intellectuals who were rarely converts but were in fact socialist sympathizers.

Why classic liberalism as a faith came to a dead end first is a long story. No doubt its defeat by socialism was aided by the fact that the undoubted hardships of "capitalism" were known and those of the promised "socialism" were not. In any case, it was only for a time that socialists became the new apostles of hope for rational social action and control at a time when the liberals had lost heart. Then socialism too came to a dead end.

The suddenness of socialism's decline is easily missed. It was only a few years ago that a socialist party came to power in Britain at the close of World War II. It was a party for the most part confident of traditional socialist remedies—primarily government ownership of industry—as a cure for Britain's problems. In less than five years the mood of the party was drastically changed, and many of its leaders were subordinating distinctively socialist remedies like nationalization to miscellaneous programs like credit control, social security, capital development, and town planning which are the common property of all British parties.

The change was not limited to one country. In 1951 delegates from the democratic socialist parties of the various nations met in Frankfurt am Main to create a new socialist international. In their Declaration of Aims and Tasks, which redrew the blueprints for socialist society, their disillusionment with the socialization of industry found its expression in the statement: "Socialist planning does not presuppose the public ownership of all the means of production." Their disillusionment had many sources but perhaps none more important than the British experience with nationalization in the five preceding years.

This was indeed an abrupt end to a long road. For public enterprise had long been a central article of faith in many socialist creeds, the Great Divide separating the socialist from the reformer, progressive, or liberal. It was the issue on which the socialist himself drew the distinction between creating a new economic order and patching up the old.

To perceive the core of thought common to the Renaissance, liberalism, and socialism alike, it is necessary to understand, however, that the socialist movement came to a dead end not solely because of its failures but in very large part because of its successes. On several major points the socialists were largely correct.

More than anything else, their case for public ownership was a case against the price system—in a period when exaggerated claims were made for it. The socialists were among the first to grasp the range of problems and circumstances for which the price system is an inappropriate social mechanism; many, for example, were deeply stirred by the inequality of market distribution of income and by the price system's neglect of community needs at a time when Social Darwinism rationalized these now admitted shortcomings of the price system.

Secondly, they fixed upon legitimacy of control as a central issue in social life. They perceived a parallelism between the legitimization of control in government by polyarchy and its desirable legitimization in enterprise through some comparable process. Thirdly, in later years they perceived the inadequacies of competitive controls in a price system and the necessity for supplementary hierarchical controls if the price system was to be maintained. Although still other accomplishments can be named, this is enough to demonstrate the insights of the socialists.

Of these great issues, is there not now wide agreement that the socialists were largely correct? On income distribution and collective needs, for example, both informed opinion and public policy in the Western economies are now closer to the Fabians than to Gladstone and his Liberals, closer perhaps to Marx than to Herbert Spencer. Or, on illegitimate control, one may cite legislation on labor, securities and exchanges, monopoly and trade practices, income and inheritance, land use, location of industry, food and drug processing, and corrupt political practices to demonstrate that today almost everyone agrees that many controls once exercised by businessmen cannot be left in their hands. Here, the present generation is closer in its thinking to Jean Jaurès, Eugene Debs, and Kier Hardie than to the Schneiders, Commodore Vanderbilt ("The public be damned!"), and—to take less extreme examples—Stanley Baldwin and Calvin Coolidge.

Almost everyone has become a socialist, and major socialist

criticisms of the economic order have been accepted and acted upon. As a distinctive body of thought and as a radical political movement, socialism has failed to maintain its character because it and other movements have largely converged.

The Central Core

What then is left of the grand strategy, sketched out by the Renaissance, by liberalism, and by socialism, of man's rational calculation and control over his environment? Is this strategy a dead end too, either because of its failure or because of its successes? To ask this is to ask what the central core of beliefs underlying these movements is.

The central core seems to us to be a threefold belief in the desirability of extending freedom as far as it is possible to do so, in accepting the equal value of each individual in his claim to freedom, and in the possibility of achieving progress in extending freedom and equality through man's capacity for rational calculation and control.

The very strength of such a threefold belief has also been its weakness. For the belief always leaves the question of means open-ended, potentially a matter for reëxamination with each change in social technique. Yet because the core of belief is abstract, those who subscribe to it are tempted to fix on some particular means.

As with classic liberalism and socialism, this confusion of the core belief and particular means has become characteristic of the new liberalism. Particularly in the United States, neoliberalism often is characterized by an almost doctrinaire fixation on certain means— particularly those legitimized during the critical years of the New Deal, such as unquestioned support for trade unions, a strong preference for action by national government as against state and local units, and support for a more powerful executive and bureaucracy as against Congressional "interference." How tempting it is to let an affection for particular means block comprehension of the ends specified in the Renaissance-liberal-socialist core of values is at least suggested by the ease with which many neoliberal and socialist intellectuals became captivated by communism—which used many socialist means like government ownership to achieve ends entirely alien to the Renaissance-liberal-socialist tradition.

A central assumption of this book is that, despite all that has happened, the central core of belief is still viable; we believe that the examination of alternatives set forth in preceding chapters affirms that view.

Three particular points flow from that affirmation. First, as we have already said numerous times, a faith in grand alternatives is, in one sense, obsolete. Socialism and capitalism, planning and non-planning, welfare state and laissez faire—these are not the alternatives open to Western societies. In another sense, however, what we have defined as the Renaissance-liberal-socialist tradition is itself a grand alternative to certain rivals. One alternative, of course, is totalitarianism, which explicitly or implicitly—depending on its form—rejects the central core of values we have postulated. Another is to reject industrialism and its fruits in order to avoid its evils. The consequences of the first are now so well known and those of the second so poorly known that we reject them as alternatives.

Yet—and this is the second point—it cannot be gainsaid that to affirm the values of expanding freedom, equality, and rational social action is a kind of act of faith. Not only are we—and, as we believe, others—unable to demonstrate the "ultimate rightness" of these values, but we cannot even demonstrate conclusively that the characteristics of man and social organization make these values attainable enough to serve as relevant social goals. Nevertheless, if in the last analysis the affirmation of these values is an act of faith, the argument of the preceding chapters shows, we believe, that it is not a mere act of faith; for a systematic examination of basic social processes lends powerful support to the belief that the core values are attainable to a highly significant degree in Western societies.

Thirdly, it follows that the viable element in the belief is less a commitment to particular means than to the general processes of rational calculation and control, which require a vast variety of particular and changing techniques. Not, of course, that means can ever be safely neglected; on the contrary, rational calculation and control require minute, systematic, and scientific examination of means. But with the accumulation of knowledge and experience, one must sensibly expect that the progressive means of one generation will become, at least in part, the obstacles to rational calculation and control by the next.

Because means must be regarded simultaneously as crucial and yet constantly open to change, incrementalism is indispensable to rational calculation and control. And, significantly, just as a commitment to the central core of values logically produces a commitment to incrementalism, a commitment both to the central core and to incrementalism has, in the long pull, created basic agreement on means among the warring factions that grew out of the Renaissance tradition. Thus socialists who firmly held to the central core—Attlee and Blum, for example—finally became incrementalists despite a formal loyalty to a grand alternative. Incremental changes in turn converted the means of classic liberalism into those of neoliberalism, and the means of neoliberalism have converged with those of the socialists. Hence the central core has outlasted the particular techniques that were the fad of a generation or even a century.

New Directions

Yet if there is now a considerable degree of actual and potential agreement on means among those who are committed to the core values, does this agreement necessarily hold great promise for the future of those values? Aside from obstacles to fulfilling the agreement of the kind reviewed in this book, does the agreement cover only unimportant means?

It might well be argued that concern with social processes such as price system, hierarchy, polyarchy, and bargaining is concentration on the wrong means. For these are, after all, instrumental techniques that, however vital they may be, are somewhat remote from the immediate sources of prime goal attainment. One's freedom finally depends upon attaining important prime goals such as dignity, respect, love, affection, solidarity, friendship. To the extent that individuals lack these, they cannot be free.

Most assuredly there is a profound danger of drifting far away from the prime goals that are important to freedom. One vast current of modern thought pushes relentlessly away from concern with prime goals. Examine, for instance, these two quotations:

In modern society democracy demands that the family institution be protected . . . [because] . . . a happy home life will stimulate the worker's enthusiasm in constructive work.[2]

We control a man's environment in business and lose it entirely when he crosses the threshold of his home. Management, therefore, has a challenge and an obligation to deliberately plan and create a favor-

[2] Quoted in J. M. H. Lindbeck, "Communist Policy and the Chinese Family," *Far Eastern Survey*, July 25, 1951, p. 140.

able, constructive attitude on the part of the wife that will liberate her husband's total energies for the job.[3]

The first are the words of a Chinese communist leader; the second, of an American business executive. Both fit the spirit of the Leningrad statue erected to the memory of a small child who betrayed his parents. What is even more ominous, in their incredible perversion of values they capture much of the spirit even of many modern liberals and socialists.

One common way of putting the case against a concern with means of the kind discussed in this book is to say, as is often said about liberalism and socialism, that the problem is not to change man's environment but to change the "nature of man." Yet surely this is a false antithesis. For as we have seen, to control man—hence to change his "nature"—one must act on his field. A basic way of acting on man's field is to manipulate his environment of information, rewards, and penalties. Hence one cannot change "the nature of man" without first acting on his environment, at least in this specific sense.

But a more relevant way to put the case is to say that both liberals and socialists have concentrated on certain limited aspects of man's environment and excluded others equally or more important to his prime goals. In rebuttal, we can only say, first, that a solution to problems of poverty, economic insecurity, maldistribution of income, hierarchical controls, governmental techniques, etc., appears to us to be a necessary condition for raising the level of prime goal attainment, even if it is not a sufficient condition; and second, that the particular way in which these problems are solved has a very close bearing on the level of prime goal attainment.

Yet is there not some validity to the charge? We think there is. And to those committed to the central core, one task of the future is to discover and perfect those means that bear more directly on the level of prime goal attainment. Several directions of future reform suggest themselves; here we can do no more than to sketch them briefly.

SMALL GROUPS

One highly important source of prime goal satisfaction is the small groups within which men must live with their fellows. To be

[3] W. H. Whyte, Jr., "The Wives of Management," *Fortune*, October, 1951, p. 86.

sure, in some quarters small groups are over-romanticized. As one writer has said, "A group is neither good nor intrinsically cooperative simply because there are few people in it."[4] Nevertheless, under the most favorable conditions small groups can do some things better than any large group can under the most favorable conditions.[5]

In so far as it is attainable at all, for most people much of "the good life" is found in small groups. Family life, the rearing of children, love, friendship, respect, kindness, pity, neighborliness, charity: these are hardly possible except in small groups. If one could somehow destroy the large groups and leave these things standing, the loss of the large would be quite bearable. But if one maintained the large groups and destroyed these values, the impoverishment and barrenness of living would be incalculable. For to most people the meaningful center of life is made up of the small groups of which they are a part, into which they are born or are accepted, among which they grow and live, marry, beget children who beget grandchildren, acquire friends, eat, talk, share in ceremonials, celebrate the newborn, and mourn the dead.

The nation-state can only provide the framework within which "the good life" is possible; it cannot fulfill the functions of the small groups that must make up the immediate environment of good living. To the extent that it attempts to do so, the nation-state must provide either an impoverished substitute for, or a grotesque perversion of, small-group functions. For it is on small groups that most people must rely for love, affection, friendship, "the sense of belonging," and respect. Small groups carry on the main burden, too, of indoctrination and habituation in identifications and norms, transmitting the habits and attitudes appropriate to polyarchy, creating the kinds of character or personality desired in a society, and exerting control through spontaneous and manipulated field controls.

A number of distinguished writers have tried to suggest means for enriching small-group life—for example, Mary Parker Follette,[6]

[4] Charlotte Luetkens, "The Myth of the Small Group," *Synopsis, Festgabe fur Alfred Weber*, Verlag Lambert Schneider, Heidelberg, 1948.

[5] The important writings on small groups have been summarized by Edward Shils, "The Primary Group," in D. Lerner and H. D. Lasswell, *The Policy Sciences*, Stanford University Press, Stanford, 1951.

[6] *The New State, Group Organization the Solution of Popular Government*, Longmans, Green and Co., New York, 1918.

G. D. H. Cole,[7] Lewis Mumford,[8] and Baker Brownell;[9] but the rising tide of centralization of the past half-century has swept by them. Thus the Greenbelt experiments of the New Deal are all but forgotten and the Town and Country Planning of the British Labor party was among the first of its programs to feel the ax. (Significantly, the major casualty preceding it was the abandonment of workers' control as a technique.)

Yet it seems altogether possible to us that the next half-century could produce a tremendous increase in small-group amenities, life, vigor, and autonomy. We have not regarded it as a part of our purpose in this book to explore the techniques by which this might be attained. But we would be failing in our purpose if we did not emphasize that every present and proposed use of price system, hierarchy, polyarchy, and bargaining should be carefully examined and reëxamined to determine its costs and benefits to small-group life. For those in search of adventure and revolution within the framework of the Renaissance-liberal-socialist core of values, perhaps no route offers such exciting possibilities.

THE PLANNING OF PERSONALITIES

Even the creation of a healthy small-group life is a roundabout route to prime goal attainment, and hence to freedom. Why not act directly on the individual's personality? Is not the most promising technique for increasing prime goal attainment to develop personalities capable of joy, love, friendship, spontaneity, kindness, respect, and dignity?

Concern with influencing individual personalities by social action is a very old matter. Plato, of course, put the shaping of personalities at the very center of his proposed society; Aristotle, although more moderate, was scarcely less preoccupied with the problem. Almost two thousand years later, Machiavelli (in the *Discourses*), and subsequently Rousseau emphasized equally strongly the need to shape the personalities of citizens to fit them to their civic rights and obligations, particularly in republics. A plausible case could be made that Machiavelli was driven to the prescriptions of *The Prince* only because he concluded that rational social action to change men's personalities to fit them to a republic,

[7] *Local and Regional Government*, Cassell, London, 1947.
[8] *The Culture of Cities*, Harcourt, Brace and Co., New York, 1938.
[9] *The Human Community*, Harper & Brothers, New York, 1950.

as he outlined in the *Discourses,* had become impossible in the Italy he knew.

Yet in the liberal interlude this age-old problem was sometimes slighted. It was recognized that the general framework of society and its techniques might have an influence on character or personality; thus the preoccupation with education and Jefferson's concern with maintaining an agrarian environment to nurture a democratic personality. But this approach—like the focus of this book—represented a concern with techniques somewhat remote from actions designed to exert direct and immediate control over the development of human personalities.

By concerning themselves with the general framework of society rather than direct control over personalities, liberals solved a psychological problem and appeared to believe they were solving a moral one. The psychological problems rise out of the dread responsibility of deciding what type of human being is to be fashioned, a responsibility so overwhelming that men have usually prefered to delegate the decision to a Prometheus or an omnipotent Creator. There is a frightening arrogance in the thought that human beings should decide in whose image other human beings should be created.

The psychological problem aside, it might be said that the moral problem was solved by avoiding direct action in shaping human personalities, in order to follow the categorical imperative of Kant according to which men are to be treated as ends and not means. Yet this is to avoid the problem rather than to solve it. First, one is faced by the plain fact that the human being is highly plastic material. Hence whether men take social actions consciously and purposefully or not, their social processes do in fact help to mold personalities. Second, the moral distinction between controlling the broad framework and direct control is very shaky. To support, say, a "progressive" system of education or, like Jefferson, a high degree of social decentralization because of their allegedly desirable effects for human personality is to commit oneself to a decision that some types of personality should be fostered and not others.

Third, to act directly on the human personality is not necessarily to treat man as a "means," in Kant's sense, if one is concerned with maximizing the capacity of that human personality for freedom. One treats man as a "means" in Kant's sense only if he is looked upon exclusively as an instrument to one's own goals. But as everyone knows, many individuals are unable to achieve high-ranking prime goals such as love, affection, friendship, joy, and enthusiasm, because of personality difficulties. To desire their freedom is scarcely to treat them as "means."

Finally, to the extent that one believes that some norms, attitudes, and social processes foster widespread opportunities for freedom and others do not, one is logically committed to favoring the kinds of personalities predisposed to the norms, attitudes, and social processes that one desires. It now appears to be fairly well established that some personality types are predisposed to anti-Semitism, ethnocentrism, and authoritarianism.[10] Karl Mannheim,[11] Harold Lasswell,[12] and others have also depicted the broad requirements of a personality predisposed to the processes of polyarchy and the goals of democracy. No more than totalitarians can democrats shrink from the prospect of social action directly to foster desired personality types in their society.

Yet the question remains: What kind (or, more likely, kinds) of human beings do we want? This is an ethical question, a profound one.[13] We pose it here, without answering it directly. Yet rational social action presupposes an answer.

The technical problem is this: Through what social processes should action take place? Clearly the answer to this question is dependent upon the answer to the preceding question: What kind of human being is wanted? Without having an answer to this prior question, we can only suggest some general approaches to the dependent one.

First, a great deal more needs to be known about the conse-

[10] T. W. Adorno and others, *The Authoritarian Personality*, Harper & Brothers, 1950.

[11] *Freedom, Power, and Democratic Planning*, Oxford University Press, New York, 1950.

[12] "Democratic Character," in *Political Writings of Harold D. Lasswell*, Free Press, Glencoe, Ill., 1951.

[13] The difficulties of securing agreement on an answer are suggested by the following:

"AMSTERDAM, the Netherlands, Aug. 24—Humanists and ethical culture leaders from ten countries, meeting in their first international congress, have found that their three days of discussion so far have produced more questions than answers.

"Summing up the intensive deliberations on the 'humanization of man in society,' which took place in six sections and in the plenary session, Dr. Horace Freiss, Columbia University Professor of Philosophy, reported that it had been impossible to agree on an 'ideal human type.'" The New York *Times*, Aug. 25, 1952, p. 4.

quences of existing social processes for personalities. Although much speculation, insight, and hypothesis exist, there does not appear to be much firmly grounded knowledge. Is it really true that a competitive price system creates a "competitive" personality, or is this an error stemming from superficial relation between two verbally similar but actually dissimilar phenomena? Or does a competitive price system actually create a conformist, coöperative, other-directed individual? What are the consequences of big business? Of growing hierarchy in business, government, trade unions, churches, universities? If one thinks in realistic alternatives, are the consequences of a competitive or bargaining price system for the personalities of participants less, or more, desirable than the substitution of hierarchy, political bargaining, or collective bargaining?

Conceivably, if answers to these questions were known they would indicate gains and costs of alternative politico-economic techniques far more important than any we have emphasized in this book. But our impression is that, so far, specialization of skills has meant that those most qualified to examine personalities have possessed only limited understanding of the politico-economic techniques they thought they were appraising.[14]

Second, therefore, here is a situation in which incrementalism is necessary and the holistic utopianism of a Plato is highly dangerous. In fact, of course—and this is the third point—a very considerable amount of incremental social action to affect personalities actually takes place in American and other Western societies. Much of the reform of educational curricula and extracurricular activities in the United States, for example, is explicitly or implicitly intended to stimulate the development of certain personality types regarded as desirable by the politically active.

Fourth, just as most of the social action explicitly designed to affect personalities now takes place in the United States in small groups, so should this feature of our society be strengthened by incremental action. For the central problem of affecting personalities is not merely what to do but—this may be even more crucial—what to avoid doing. The great danger of concentrating on the deliberate and purposive affecting of personalities is the opportunities it creates

[14] The usefulness of insightful works like Karen Horney's *The Neurotic Personality of Our Time* (W. W. Norton and Co., New York, 1937) and Erich Fromm's *Escape from Freedom* (Farrar and Rinehart, New York, 1941) seems to us to have been considerably reduced by this difficulty.

for manipulation by leaders.[15] The "New" Soviet Man may well be a case in point.[16]

What are the major protections against manipulation—using a human personality exclusively as a "means" to one's own goals rather than as a being whose own freedom is to be maximized? No protections are ironclad, but certain ones, if not necessarily sufficient, appear to be necessary. One basic protection, of course, is polyarchy itself. Another is a widespread tolerance of a diversity of personality types combined with social processes for guiding each into roles that fulfill the demands of the particular personality without significantly impairing the highly ranked goals of others. No doubt a third is a widely held norm that prevents governments from acting in this area except when there is agreement approaching unanimity among the politically active.

Within this context, two kinds of relationship help to define the social organizations most suitable for purposive action on personalities. One is the relationship of *love, affection, or friendship.* Malinowski found, for example, that "systematic or tyrannical abuse of authority is not to be found under primitive conditions"—one reason being the ties of love, kinship, friendship, and respect characteristic of many of these societies.[17] Another and closely related condition is the existence of *face-to-face relations*, in which the individual is more easily seen as a human being on whom the consequences of an action can be observed and less easily transformed into an abstract object. One is reminded of the Chaplain in *Saint Joan:* "I let them do it. If I had known, I would have torn her from their hands. You don't know: you haven't seen: it is so easy to talk when you don't know. You madden yourself with words: you damn yourself because it feels grand to throw oil on the flaming hell of your own temper. But when it is brought home to you; when you see the thing you have done; when it is blinding your eyes, stifling

[15] Cf. T. W. Adorno, "Democratic Leadership and Mass Manipulation," in A. W. Gouldner (ed.), *Studies in Leadership: Leadership and Democratic Action*, Harper & Brothers, New York, 1950, pp. 418 ff., esp. p. 429, and Leonard Doob, "Propagandists vs. Propagandees," *ibid.*, pp. 439 ff.

[16] Evidence here is, of course fugitive. Cf. however the descriptions of Georges Glaser in his autobiographical novel, *Secret et Violence* (translated from the German by Lucienne Foucrault), Éditions Corréa et Cie., Paris, 1951, pp. 315 ff.; George Fischer, "Der Fall Wlassow," *Der Monat*, June, 1951; Czeslaw Milosz, "Murti-Bing," *The Twentieth Century*, July, 1951, pp. 9–23.

[17] Bronislaw Malinowski, *Freedom and Civilization*, Roy Publishers, New York, 1944, pp. 118–119, 121, 266–267.

your nostrils, tearing your heart, then—then—O God, take away this sight from me!'"

Moreover, these two relationships would appear to be the technically most suitable conditions for acting effectively on personalities, for in these two relationships the most highly ranked rewards and deprivations are typically brought to bear on behavior. What this fact points to, of course, is the importance of the small group, employing spontaneous and manipulated field controls, as the basic, least dangerous, and perhaps most efficient unit for affecting personalities.

In all events, one thing is clear. Rational social action through large-scale processes of hierarchy, polyarchy, bargaining, and price system (what is sometimes called national economic planning) can at best provide only a framework within which the good life is attainable. Maximum attainment of the important prime goals, such as love, affection, friendship, respect, dignity, and solidarity, requires integrated personalities capable of expressing and receiving these responses, and vigorous small-group life capable of stimulating them.

Painfully little is now known about the requirements of rational social action in such critical matters as these; yet the potential gains of rational social action in this critical matter of achieving prime goals may well dwarf anything that is attainable by action through the larger politico-economic processes discussed in this book. Thus, the new and potential agreement we have spoken of in this and the first chapter, and demonstrated throughout the book, marks an important and yet only preliminary victory in Western man's struggle to achieve through rational calculation and control the core values described with the well-worn words "freedom," "equality," and "progress."

INDEX

Socialization, 470, 513
and mandatory price mechanism, 187 ff.
   See also Government, ownership; Nationalization
Socialized medicine, 11
Social organization, 33
and social indoctrination, 34
Social pluralism, 319, 355
and agreement, 302
and bargaining, 324
and communication, 305
and hierarchical organizations, 306
and mass democracy, 306 ff.
and plural membership, 305
and political bargaining, 326
and polyarchy, 302
and Rousseau, 303
and social organizations, 303
and tyranny, 306
Social sciences, 18, 22, 27
Social security, 15, 136, 358, 514
and collective bargaining, 494
Social techniques, 49
Society of Friends, 90
Sociology, 43
Socio-political processes, 22 f., 172
agenda, 371
incentives, 371
role, 371
techniques common to, 370 f.
Solicitor's Office, 74
Solidarity, 50, 102, 108, 268, 360, 518
Solow, Herbert, 80 n.
Somers, Herman M., 361 n., 363 n., 376 n., 379 n., 384 n., 405 n., 410 n.
Somervell, General Brehon, 384
South Carolina declaration of secession, 238
Southern Democrats, *see* Democrats
Southern United States, 279, 297, 332
and white supremacy, 295
Sovereign, 498
Soviet Union, *see* Union of Soviet Socialist Republics
Spain, 278
Specialization, 78, 242, 245, 249, 252, 306, 524
in bureaucracies, 235 f.
Spencer, Herbert, 515
Spending, 13, 433, 452
and stability, 447 ff.
Spengler, J. J., 149 n., 454 n.
Spontaneity, 40, 448, 521
Spontaneous choices, 125
Spontaneous field control, 99–104, 107, 118, 125, 237, 242, 434, 485, 490, 520

Spontaneous field control—(*Continued*)
and competition, 194 ff.
definition, 100
and free choice, 103
and freedom, 118
"invisible hand," 195 ff.
and learning, 103
and manipulated field control, 175, 526
and monopoly, 194 ff.
paradoxes, 100
and planning, 101
and price system, 175, 177 f., 182, 183, 186, 194 ff.
and reciprocity, 104
and subjective equality, 104, 123
systems, 267
and tyranny, 118
and ubiquity, 102
Stability, 13, 129 f., 131, 132, 299, 339, 358, 439
and allocation, 445 ff.
and central control, 444–453
and collective bargaining, 449, 485 ff., 487 f., 491 ff.
and command, 448 f.
costs, 447
and distribution, 440, 446
and hierarchy, 444–453
and high-cost inflation, 449
and manipulation of field, 448 f.
and national bargaining, 503
political, 339
and polyarchy, 444–453
and price system, 444–453
and price system for choice and allocation, 392
and primary control, 178
and spending, 447 ff.
techniques for, 444–453
   See also Full employment
von Stackelberg, Heinrich, 202
Stakhanovism, 108
Stalinists, 171
Standard costs, 198
Standards of living, 132
State Department, 344, 363
States rights, 360
Statistics, 437, 438, 438 n., 452
Status, 50, 105, 138, 145, 250, 251, 254, 256, 280, 281, 304, 315, 326, 331, 342, 356, 360, 364, 443, 475, 480, 502, 513
agency and enterprise, 462
and bureaucracy, 243
and distribution, 138, 150 f.
groups, 15
and worker control, 479 f.